MACROECONOMICS

Theory and Policy,

3rd Edition

by B. Modjtahedi

University of California, Davis

cognella
San Diego, CA

First published in the United States of America in 2011 by Cognella, a division of University Readers, Inc.

15 14 13 12 11 1 2 3 4 5

Printed in the United States of America

ISBN: 978-1-60927-010-0

cognella™

www.cognella.com 800.200.3908

CONTENTS

PREFACE

THIS BOOK WAS written for students taking an economics course for the first time. In writing this text, I had in mind not only the traditional full-time student, but also a large number of professionals pursuing degrees in economics, finance, or related fields. This book has grown out of a decade's worth of lectures I have given, both at the University of California–Davis and other universities.

Around the turn of the 20th century, British economist Alfred Marshall defined economics as the study of human beings in their ordinary business of life. Economics—especially microeconomics—studies the economic decisions made by people in their everyday lives. You have made a decision to go to college, to buy this book, and to read it. I have made a decision to write this book so that you buy and read it. For us, the definition conveys two messages: In the first place, economics should not be a very difficult topic to study. Second, the issues discussed in economics texts and classes should be relevant to our lives.

In keeping with the spirit of Marshall's definition, I have tried to explain everything using simple language, without sacrificing rigor. Both microeconomic and macroeconomic portions of the text pursue an overarching objective of achieving a desired or optimal economic outcome. In the macro portion, this is full employment, price stability, and long-term growth. In the micro section, it is economic efficiency. I have tried to keep tight transitions from one chapter to the next. Every chapter explains what we have learned, what we don't know yet, and what we will learn in the upcoming chapter.

Students learn from repetition and continuity. I have applied this concept in the book to every extent possible. In each chapter, I repeat the background materials necessary to understand the discussions in the chapter. At the end of the chapter, I also provide a summary of the main points covered in that chapter. Continuity derives from pursuing the goals of full employment and price stability, and the role of economic policy throughout the book. Unlike many other texts, I define the concepts of potential output, natural unemployment rate, inflation, and economic growth early on, so students know from the beginning what the overall goal is.

This is both an analysis- and policy-oriented book. From the beginning, it emphasizes the need for models in order to analyze the real-world economic problems. The text develops the basic macroeconomic model step by step, using real-life examples. The main objective of the book is to teach students how to conduct macroeconomic analysis, rather than bombarding them with massive amounts of disparate facts and figures. However, in nearly every chapter, I present the empirical evidence to support the particular model or theory.

The microeconomic foundation is covered in Chapters 1 through 4. The core closed-economy macroeconomic portion of the text consists of Chapters 5 through 19. Chapter 5 defines the concept of gross domestic product (GDP). The definition of

GDP in this book is somewhat different from those presented in other textbooks—and I believe, more accurate. Interestingly enough, this accuracy makes the concept more, rather than less, intuitive and understandable. Like most other chapters, I have written this particular chapter in such a way as to provide instructors with a degree of flexibility on how to cover it. Some may confine the coverage to the basic definitions, and move on to the remaining chapters. Others may cover the whole chapter.

Chapter 6 defines the basic macroeconomic concepts of inflation, unemployment, and growth. This chapter lays down the main reasons why macroeconomists concentrate on the study of these concepts. They discuss the costs and benefits of these phenomena, using simple examples.

The remaining chapters develop the basic short-run and long-run models in a step-by-step manner. Interaction between theory and empirical evidence is at the heart of the exposition of macroeconomics in this book. For example, I provide data on the relationships between money supply growth rates, inflation rates, and GDP growth rates to build students' confidence in the models presented.

Chapter 16 is about economic growth. The fact that this topic is covered in a later chapter rather than an early one does not mean it is less important than the other chapters. This is only for pedagogical reasons. I think this particular sequence results in a better flow of the materials. Other instructors, on the other hand, may want to cover this chapter early on. This chapter has been written in such a way that it can be covered before Chapter 7. The other chapter that can be used earlier is Chapter 20, which is about fiscal policy. Chapter 11 summarizes the debate on the demand management policies.

Following are some distinctive features of this textbook:

- GDP is defined as the market value of *all* the goods and services produced, rather than the *final* goods. This makes the definition more accurate and intuitive. The relation to the concept of final goods is also described. (Chapter 5)
- The concepts of growth, inflation, and unemployment are defined early. Chapter 6 also defines potential GDP and the natural rate of unemployment. The early introduction of these concepts facilitates the discussion on short run versus long run, as well as the reasons for undertaking demand management policies.
- The book makes it clear at the very outset in Chapter 7 that the government cannot just increase spending (G), without any consideration of how to finance it. The government can do this either by raising an equal amount of taxes, borrowing, or printing money. The implications of each financing method are fully discussed in the remaining chapters.
- In view of the topic emerging during the recession of 2007–2008, a discussion of the liquidity trap—and how the economy can fall into it—is presented in Chapter 9.
- Credit risk is another issue that came out in the 2007–2008 financial crisis. Chapter 10 provides a short discussion on this issue.
- Chapter 10 also provides a full discussion of financial crowding. It shows how in the classical model of saving and investment, "everything crowds out everything else." It then provides a discussion of government budget deficits in this environment. I don't know of any textbook that provides such a detailed discussion of this topic. One surprising result is that even a balanced-budget increase in spending could crowd out private spending.
- The Phillips Curve is presented as a model of inflation and unemployment, rather than just as a menu of choices faced by policy makers. The rate of growth of the money supply is added to the graph, to indicate the long-run tendency of the inflation rate. (Chapter 15)
- A chapter is added in this edition that summarizes the debate on demand management policies. (Chapter 21)
- The mathematics background for this book is minimal. Nevertheless, a section in Chapter 1 covers the entire math students need to know to follow the materials in the text.

Several individuals read and made valuable comments on different chapters of the microeconomics and macroeconomics texts. In particular, I would like to thank Kevin Hoover, Esen Onur, Nahid Movassagh, Bob Modjtahedi, and Kate Griaznova for taking the time to read and provide feedback on several chapters of the microeconomics and macroeconomics portions of the text. Special thanks are due to Theodore J. McCarthy, who edited the entire manuscripts for both the micro and macro portions. He provided numerous insightful comments that significantly improved the exposition of the materials in several places. I am also grateful to Fayha Lakhani, who patiently and competently compiled the index, glossary, and the table of contents for the earlier editions of both the macro and micro portions of the text.

I would additionally like to thank Jessica Knott, the senior project editor at Cognella Publishing, for her excellent editorial feedback as well as design suggestions. Her efforts have been invaluable and are sincerely appreciated. I would also like to thank the staff of the University Readers/Cognella, especially Melissa Accornero, for their encouragement and support.

Last, but not least, I would like to thank my many past students at UC Davis and elsewhere, for their comments and questions on the previous editions of the text. In fact, it was mostly my students who encouraged me to convert my lecture notes into a textbook. I am very grateful to them all.

B. Modjtahedi

University of California–Davis
Davis, California November 2010

CHAPTER 1

What Do Economists Do? We Model for Food

INTRODUCTION

SCARCITY
The idea that human material wants are unlimited in relation to the available resources in the economy.

Alfred Marshall, a British economist, defined economics as "the study of mankind in his ordinary business of life." You can study "mankind" with respect to many different attributes. Economics generally analyzes the behavior of people and institutions that arise because of *scarcity*. Scarcity means that human wants are unlimited in relation to the available resources in the economy. Unlimited wants means that people in general prefer to have more of everything. They want to be able to buy more food, more appliances, better homes, better cars, and so on. Resources are the things we use to produce goods and services. They are also called *production inputs* or *factors of production*. Economists distinguish three types of resources:

ALFRED MARSHALL

FACTORS OF PRODUCTION
Resources that are used to produce goods and services: labor, land, and capital. Identical to production inputs.

1. Land. Land consists of all the resources given to us by nature. Perhaps *natural resource* would be a better term for this production factor. Land includes land itself that is used in agriculture—as well as forests, underground resources, minerals, and underwater resources. If we stretch the definition a bit, we can also include such things as solar energy or wind power to produce electricity in this category. At any given point in time, these are limited in supply. In the long run, we might be able to increase their supply somewhat using more efficient cultivation techniques, better fertilizers, new discoveries, and so on. In this book we will generally assume that the amount of land is constant and we will ignore it. This is to keep our stories simple without affecting any of our conclusions.
2. Labor. Labor is human effort. It is measured by the "person-hour." If we have one worker working 10 hours and another working 5 hours, then the total is 15 person-hours. This resource is limited for two reasons:

   - There are a limited number of people in any society over a given period of time.

PRIVATE CAPITAL
Capital goods owned by private citizens.

PUBLIC CAPITAL
Capital goods owned collectively by the public.

HUMAN CAPITAL
All the knowledge, skills, and expertise acquired and possessed by an individual.

- Each person has a limited number of hours available to him or her during that time period.

3. Capital. By capital we mean all *produced means of production.* There are goods that human beings produce in order to use them to produce other goods. They include *private capital* owned by private citizens, such as trucks, tractors, and manufacturing plants, as well as *public capital*, owned collectively by the public, such as roads, bridges, or national parks. Another capital category is the *human capital*. By this term economists mean all the knowledge, skills, and expertise acquired and possessed by an individual. This fits the definition of capital because an individual acquires it through education or learning by doing.

A worker installs a seat into a Ford F-150 at an assembly plant in Missouri.

Scarcity means that with the available resources, we cannot satisfy the collective wants of all the members of a society. In other words, if we asked all members of society how much of each goods and service they would like to have if money were no object, we would realize that we do not have enough resources to produce all those things. We will analyze the question of scarcity more fully in the next chapter.

Scarcity implies that every society has to answer three questions. These are called the "what," "how," and "for whom" questions.

1. What goods and services should the society produce? Should we produce more consumer goods such as food and clothing, or more capital goods such as trucks, tractors, and computers? Should we produce more civilian goods, or more military goods?
2. How should these goods and services be produced? There are generally different ways of producing the same goods. We can produce cars, either by using a lot of labor and not much capital equipment, or by a lot of robotics and not much labor. We can produce agricultural products by using a lot of land, but without any fertilizers and pesticides, or with less land, and a lot of fertilizers and pesticides. We can produce electricity using fossil fuel such as oil and natural gas, or using renewable sources such as wind, water, or solar energy.
3. For whom should we produce these goods and services? This question is about the distribution of income in the society. Should the distribution be nearly equal so that all members of the society can buy the same amounts of the goods and services produced, or should we allow some inequality in the distribution of income? How much inequality is tolerable?

Every society, whether small or large, primitive or modern, capitalistic or socialistic, must answer these questions. In a small traditional village, the elderly might decide on these questions. In a free market capitalist system, these questions are answered mostly by the private sector of the economy, but governments heavily influence the choices made by the public. In socialist economies, a central planning bureau generally makes all the decisions.

MICROECONOMICS

Economics is broadly divided into two fields: microeconomics and macroeconomics.

> *Microeconomics studies the decisions made by one decision-making unit and economic conditions prevailing in one particular market or industry.*

A *decision-making unit*, or a decision maker for short, can be an individual or a firm. A *firm* is any entity that demands the services of production factors such as land, labor, and capital. It supplies output to consumers to make money. In economics, that money is called *profit*. Profit is the excess of what firms receive from the sale of their products to consumers over their production costs. Production costs are what they pay to production factors they use. We will assume that firms decide how much of each production factor to hire and how much goods and services to produce in order to maximize their profits.

A *market* is any institution that brings buyers and sellers of a goods or service together. The market could be small—like the garage sale market in a small town—or big, like the currency markets in which world currencies are traded. It could be in a physical location, like weekend farmers' markets, or it could be interconnections of computers, such as some financial markets. An *industry* is a collection of firms that produce identical or nearly identical products. Examples are the textile industry and the automobile industry.

Economists assume that a decision maker makes an economic decision or takes an action to *maximize satisfaction*. Generally, that action or decision is either to *buy* something or to *sell* something. Satisfaction could be either in monetary or subjective terms. The owners of business firms would measure satisfaction in terms of their profits. The higher the profits, the more satisfied they are. Consumers' satisfaction, on the other hand, could be subjective—the "happiness" they would derive from consuming goods and services. Meet a few decision makers you will encounter frequently in this book:

As a **consumer**, you decide how much of a particular good to buy on the basis of the price of that good, the prices of related goods, and the level of your income. For example, in buying a car, you will consider its price, compare it to the prices of other cars, have one eye on the price of gasoline, and be mindful of your budget. Where did you get the money to pay for the car?

As a **worker,** you decide how much labor service to supply to business firms, given the wage rate and goods prices. The *wage rate* is the income you earn per unit of time, say per hour or per year, for your labor services. You would be mindful of the prices of goods and services, because ultimately you are working in order to make money to be able to buy goods and services. Therefore, it is always the relationship between the wages you earn and the prices of the goods and services you buy that is important for your decision. For example, if prices increase from one year to the next, you would want to earn a higher wage rate for the amount of work you are performing.

For a lot of people, labor is not the only source of income. They also make money from assets they own. An *asset* is anything that has value because it is expected to bring some benefits to its owner in the future. Examples include stocks, bonds, or real estate. The benefits could be monetary or nonmonetary. For example, a rental property brings rental income to its owner, while a home provides shelter service.

Who would hire you and pay you? Business firms would. As an **employer**, a firm decides how much labor to hire, given the price of the product it is producing and the wage rate it has to pay. The employer hires labor to produce and sell its product in the goods market at the market price. The revenue that the additional unit of labor would bring into the company is the benefit of hiring

DECISION-MAKING UNIT
An economic unit such as a consumer, producer, employer, laborer, lender, or borrower that makes a decision with the goal of furthering an economic objective.

FIRM
Any entity that demands the services of factors of production such as land, labor; and supplies output to consumers with the goal of maximizing profits.

PROFIT
The excess of what firms receive from the sale of their products to consumers, over their production costs.

MARKET
An arrangement, institution, or mechanism that brings buyers and sellers of a good or service together.

INDUSTRY
A collection of firms that produces the same or similar products.

WAGE RATE
The income workers earn per unit of time, say per hour or per year, for their labor services.

ASSET
Anything that has value because it will bring some benefits to its owner in the future.

that unit, while the wage that the firm would have to pay for that unit is the cost. Firms, of course, have other expenses as well. They have to pay rent on the land and interest on the money they borrow.

Employers are methodical and cautious when making wage and hiring decisions. What skill sets do you possess to increase your chances of getting hired?

Why would a firm want to hire you? Firms hire workers and use other production factors to produce output and sell it to consumers. As a **producer**, a firm decides how much of a good to produce and sell, given the market price of its product and production costs. Firms use factors of production—land, labor, and capital—to produce output. The production cost is what they would pay to hire or use factors of production. Revenue is what they receive from selling their output.

Often, one person or entity makes more than one decision. In the above examples, the consumer and the worker are generally the same person. They make consumption decisions on the basis of the money they earn from working. Generally, we combine these two decision makers into one unit and call it the **household**. Similarly, the employer and the producer are the same person. An employer hires workers to produce things. We usually combine employers and producers into one decision-making unit called the **firm**.

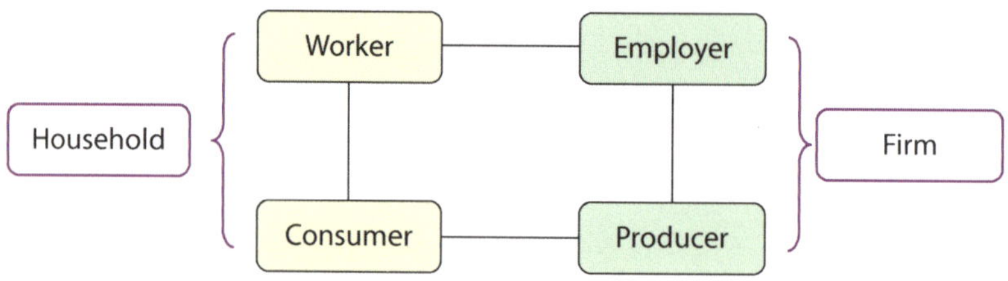

These are, of course, not the only decisions faced by households and firms in a society. People also decide on how much of their money to invest in stocks, bonds, and real estate, and how much to keep in the banks. They also decide how much to lend and borrow. Moreover, the same person sometimes makes all these decisions. For example, the owner of a restaurant employs people to produce and sell meals. He also works in his own restaurant. Finally, with the money he makes from his business, he decides how much to consume, and how much to invest in stocks and bonds.

Microeconomics takes a typical consumer and studies her decision to buy a particular good, such as a car. Then it takes a typical producer and analyzes his decision to produce and sell cars. It finally assumes that there are many such consumers and producers who come together in the market for cars. The collection of all the producers of cars constitutes the car industry. Similarly, microeconomics studies the market for labor by considering the workers who are willing to supply their labor services and the employers who are willing to hire them.

MACROECONOMICS

AGGREGATE LEVEL OF OUTPUT
The sum total of all the goods and services produced in a country.

GENERAL PRICE LEVEL
An index of the average of the prices of all the goods and services produced in the country.

Macroeconomics, on the other hand, analyzes broad economic aggregates. What this means is that macroeconomics studies economy-wide variables. It is not concerned with one particular product, such as bread. It instead looks at the sum total of all the goods and services produced in a country. This is called the *aggregate level of output*. Instead of studying the price of one particular product, macroeconomics analyzes the behavior of the prices of all the goods and services produced in the country. It studies some average of all these prices. This average is called the *general price level*.

Finally, instead of studying just one worker or one employer, macroeconomics studies the *overall employment* in the economy. Overall employment means the total number of people who have jobs.

OVERALL EMPLOYMENT
The total number of people who have jobs

Of course, these are not the only variables we study in macroeconomics. We also analyze the behavior of some other variables, such as aggregate or national consumption, national saving, interest rates, and wage rates. But ultimately, we are interested in these other variables because of their effects on the three major macroeconomic variables—aggregate level of output, the general price level, and overall employment.

Macroeconomics studies the behavior of aggregate economic variables, such as the aggregate level of output, the general price level, and overall employment.

Why do we need two different fields? Macroeconomics and microeconomics are *related* but *different*. They are related, because the total production in the economy of all the goods and services must be just the sum of the products produced by individual producers. Similarly, if the price of every good and service increases by 5%, then the general price level must increase by 5%. The same is true for consumption. We expect that if the consumers' incomes in the society increase with the overall prices remaining the same, each individual consumer will consume more of everything. Thus, the aggregate level of consumption will increase. Or, if the wage rate drops in the society relative to goods prices, then the cost of production for every producer will go down, resulting in more employment and more production.

However, the two fields are also different. Frequently, microeconomic relationships do not carry over to aggregate relationships. There are problems that are aggregate in nature and cannot be analyzed by microeconomic tools. A couple of examples will clarify this:

Example 1

Microeconomics: Suppose you go shopping in the morning to find that the price of corn flakes has gone down by 5%. You will buy more corn flakes for two reasons: First, you will substitute the corn flakes for the other kinds of cereals, because their prices are now relatively higher. This is called the *substitution effect* of a price reduction. Second, since the price of corn flakes has decreased, if you buy the same amount of corn flakes, you will have more money left in your pocket that you can spend on every good, including corn flakes. It is as if your income has increased. This is called the *income effect* of the price reduction.

SUBSTITUTION EFFECT
In the case of consumer behavior: When the price of a good decreases, people substitute the now cheaper good for its substitutes. In the case of labor supply: When real wage decreases, workers substitute leisure for labor, so that the quantity of labor supplied decreases. The substitution effect results in a positive relationship between the real wage and the quantity of labor supplied.

INCOME EFFECT
In the case of a consumer: When the price of a good goes down, it is as if the consumer's income has increased. In the case of a worker: When the wage rate increases, the worker may decide to supply less labor, because now she can earn the same income as before by working fewer hours.

Macroeconomics: What if the price of every good goes down by 5%? Then, unlike the above example, the relative prices will remain the same, and there will be no substitution effect. But will the nation buy more of all the goods because of the income effect? We cannot even answer this question without further information. As you will learn later in this book, if the prices of every good and service go down by 5%, the total income earned by everyone in the economy will also go down by 5%. To illustrate the reason for this, if you pay $100 to buy a textbook, it is expenditure for you, but income for the recipients of that $100. Suppose the bookstore pays $70 of that $100 to buy the textbook from the publisher. This $70 constitutes part of the incomes of the people in the publishing company. The bookstore pays $20 out of that $100 as wages to the workers, rent for the shop, and interest to the bank. These constitute the incomes of the recipients of this $20. Finally, the bookstore owner pockets the remaining $10 as profit. This $10 becomes the owner's income.

You see that if all prices fall by 5%, the total income will also fall by 5%; there will be no income effect from this general fall in prices. The aggregate purchasing power of all the people in the economy will remain the same. It seems that people overall will not increase their purchases of goods and services. However, *this conclusion* may not be correct, either. We will address this question later in the book. The intent of this example was merely to show that we cannot always analyze questions involving overall or aggregate magnitudes using microeconomic tools.

The above example demonstrates what is called the *fallacy of composition*—that is, the fallacy that what is true for one individual in a group may not be true for all the individuals comprising that group. If one bidder at an auction shouts loudly, she will succeed in attracting the attention of the auctioneer, but if every bidder does the same, none will succeed. The following example applies this concept to further demonstrate the distinction between microeconomics and macroeconomics.

FALLACY OF COMPOSITION
The mistkaen belief that what is true for one member of a group is true for all members.

Example 2

If a single wheat farmer produces more wheat in a year, he will make more money. This is because the additional output from one farmer will be too small relative to the whole market to have any effect on the price of wheat. Therefore, the farmer will sell more wheat at the same price, enjoying a greater amount of profit. However, if all the wheat farmers produce more wheat due to, say, better-than-normal weather, then the price of wheat will fall in the market, and they may all suffer a loss.

MACROECONOMIC MARKETS

Interactions among several markets determine the levels of the three macroeconomic variables. These include the *goods and services market*; the *factor market*; the *financial markets*; and the *foreign exchange market*. In macroeconomics, we analyze the four markets in their aggregate forms.

GOODS AND SERVICES MARKET
A market in which business firms produce and supply goods and services to the market, and households, firms, the government, and foreigners buy them.

FACTOR MARKET
The market, such as the labor market, in which firms demand production factors, and households supply these resources to the firms.

FINANCIAL MARKETS
The market in which the deficit group (those who spend more than what they earn) would obtain the needed money from the surplus group directly.

FOREIGN EXCHANGE MARKET
A market in which foreign currencies are traded.

1. Goods and Services Market

In the goods and services market—or just the goods market for short—business firms produce and supply goods and services to the market. Households, firms, the government, and foreigners buy these goods and services. For example, a firm produces bread that is purchased by households, another produces trucks that are purchased by other firms, and still another firm produces computers that are purchased by households, other firms, the government, and foreigners. The buyers' *expenditures* on the goods and services purchased constitute the business firms' *revenues.*

2. Factor Markets

In this market, firms demand production factors that the households supply. Firms pay compensation to the suppliers of these resources in the form of wages, rent, and interest, which form the *incomes* of the households supplying these resources. These factor payments constitute the *production costs* of business firms. Figure 1 shows the flow of funds in the goods and factor markets. Such a diagram is called a *circular flow diagram*. This figure excludes the government to keep things simple. Moreover, since inter-firm transactions cancel each other out, they are not shown in this figure.

CIRCULAR FLOW DIAGRAM
A diagram showing the flow of funds between the goods and factor markets.

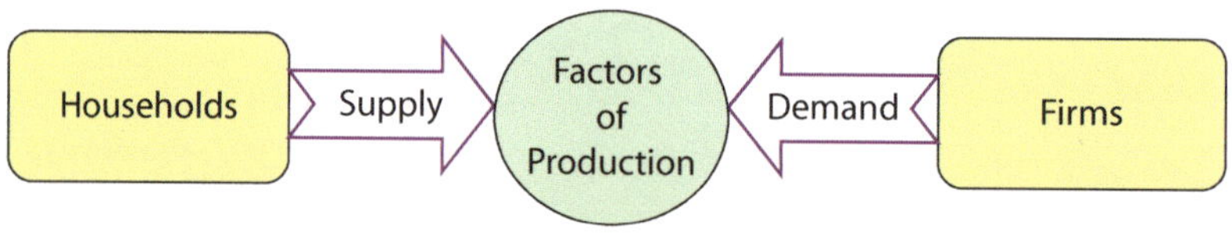

3. Financial Markets

There are people in this world who, believe it or not, earn more than they can spend. These people are called *surplus spending units* or *savers/lenders*. There are other people who spend more than they earn. These are called—you guessed it—*deficit spending units* or *investors/borrowers*. The first group consists mostly of households that save for old age. The second group includes firms that want to invest money on productive assets but don't have a sufficient amount of funds; households who want to buy homes, cars, or appliances, but are short of cash; or the government, which spends more than what it collects in tax revenues. If we could bring these two groups of people together, the surplus group could provide funds to the deficit group, and the national well-being would increase. Firms would be able to buy machines and equipment, households could purchase homes or appliances, and the government would be able to build roads, bridges, and schools. The surplus group would receive some money in the form of interest or dividends as a reward for providing the funds to the deficit group. This would be a win-win situation.

SURPLUS SPENDING UNITS OR SAVERS/LENDERS
People, firms, or governments that earn more than they can spend.

DEFICIT SPENDING UNITS OR INVESTORS/BORROWERS
Households, firms, or governments that spend more than they earn.

Figure 1: The Circular Flow Diagram

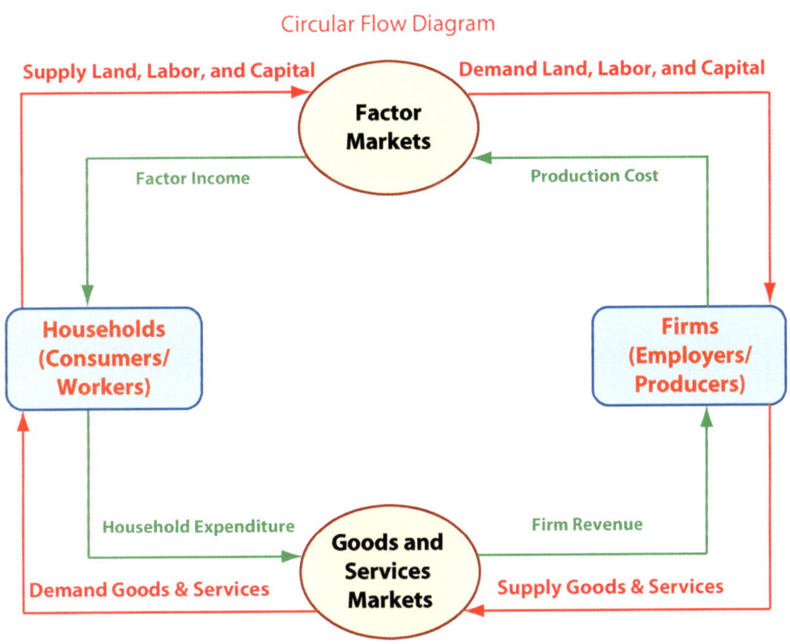

The investors/borrowers would obtain the needed money from the savers/lenders directly in the financial markets, or indirectly through *financial institutions*. If you lend money to your uncle, this would be called *direct finance*. You will be the supplier of the funds in the financial market, and your uncle the demander. Firms raise cash in the financial markets, either through the sale of *bonds* or issuing of *stocks*. Issuing bonds is just borrowing money with interest. For example, a firm writes on a piece of paper called a bond or a *promissory note*, "*I promise to pay to whoever brings this piece of paper to me next year the sum of $110.*" It then sells this piece of paper to you in the financial market for, say, $100. In essence, the firm borrows $100 from you and promises to pay you back the borrowed money after one year, plus $10 of interest. In this example, the interest rate is 10% of

FINANCIAL INSTITUTIONS
Institutions that help channel funds from those who have to those who need. Direct finance Raising cash directly by selling stocks or bonds to investors, bypassing financial institutions such as banks.

BONDS
Also called IOUs. Financial instruments that are issued by an individual, a firm, or a government when borrowing money. They promise to pay predetermined and fixed amounts of money in the future.

STOCKS
Ownership rights in a corporation.

PROMISSORY NOTE
Same as a bond or an IOU.

the borrowed money. The market that brings lenders and borrowers together is called the *loanable funds market.*

LOANABLE FUNDS MARKET *The market in which borrowers borrow money from lenders.*

DIVIDENDS *The profits distributed to shareholders by a corporation.*

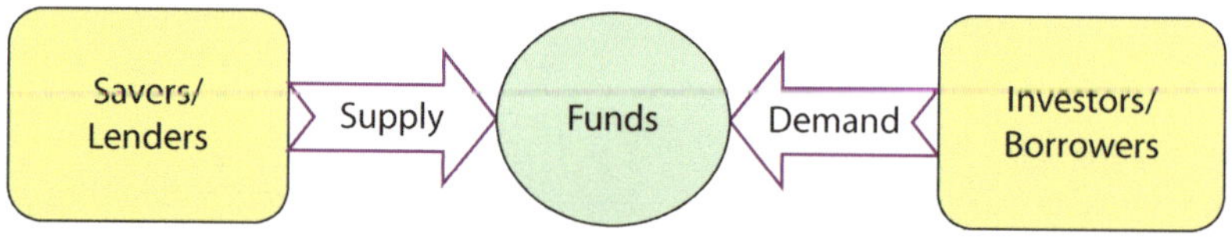

STOCK MARKET *The market in which shares of corporations are traded.*

Issuing stocks means selling part of the corporation to strangers. The strangers are then called the stockholders or shareholders. They share in the profits and assets of the corporation. For instance, suppose that a corporation has issued and sold 100 shares to different people. These 100 shareholders then collectively own the corporation. Each shareholder in this example owns 1% of the corporation; it is, therefore, entitled to 1% of its assets and profits. The profits distributed to these stockholders are called *dividends.* Let's say that if the corporation makes a profit of $100,000 in a year, each shareholder is entitled to $1,000 of that profit. If the corporation decides to distribute the whole profit to the shareholders, then each shareholder will receive $1,000 in dividends. Unlike bonds, the corporation does not have to pay you any dividends in a particular year. It may decide to plow back all the profit into the business and buy some equipment. Or, it may go out of business, in which case you lose your money. The market where corporate stocks are sold is called the *stock market.*

Figure 2: The Financial System

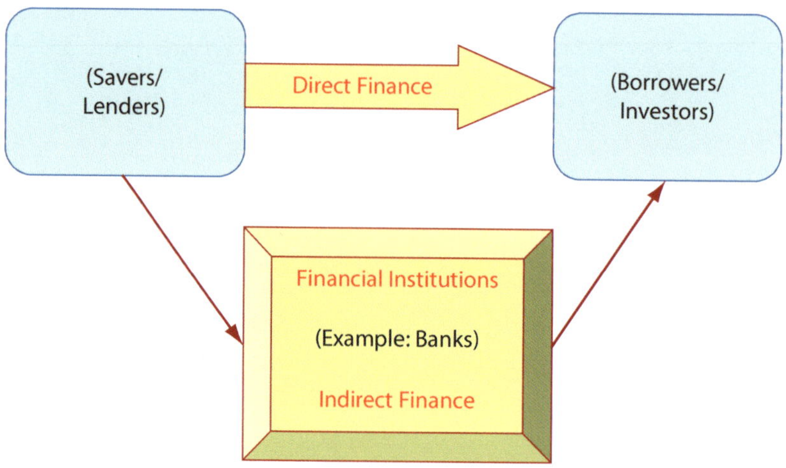

INDIRECT FINANCE *This is when some people deposit their excess money in a financial institution such as a bank, a credit union, or a pension fund. Then, other people who need money borrow it from the financial institution.*

FINANCIAL INTERMEDIARIES/ FINANCIAL INSTITUTIONS *Institutions that help channel funds from those who have to those who need.*

FINANCIAL SYSTEM *The combination of financial markets and financial institutions.*

In the case of *indirect finance,* the people in the surplus group deposit their excess money in a financial institution such as a bank, a credit union, or a pension fund. Then, someone who needs money borrows it from the financial institution. Financial institutions exist to facilitate the channeling of funds from the surplus group to the deficit group. For this reason they are also called *financial intermediaries.* The combination of financial markets and *financial institutions* is called the *financial system.* Figure 2 shows the flow of funds in the financial system.

4. Foreign Exchange Market

Stocks and bonds are not the only assets traded in the financial markets. A very important financial market is the market for foreign currencies. This market is called the foreign exchange market, and it is probably the biggest financial market. Two groups of people participate in this market. Suppose Americans want to buy British goods, services, and assets. The British sellers may not accept U.S. dollars for the items they sell. The American buyers may not have the British pounds to pay the British sellers. The foreign exchange market facilitates such transactions. For example, the American buyers buy the needed British pounds in this market and send it to the British sellers of goods and services. Similarly, the British residents who buy American goods, services, and assets need to take their British pounds to the foreign exchange market, buy U.S. dollars, and send the dollars to American sellers. So in the British pounds market, Americans buy and the British sell British pounds.

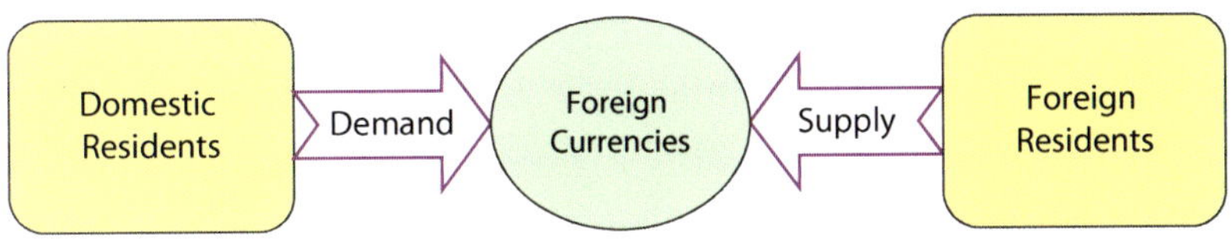

Buyers of foreign goods, services, and assets are not the only people who participate in the foreign exchange markets. Another group of people who heavily use the facilities of the market are speculators. Speculators buy foreign currencies, hoping that their values will increase in the future so they make money out of the price appreciation.

POSITIVE AND NORMATIVE STATEMENTS

Economists distinguish between two types of statements. Some statements are about how things are, or how we think they are. These statements make no value judgment on whether any particular state or outcome is good or bad. Here are some examples:

- The average price of gasoline in the United States is $4 per gallon.
- We are entering a recession, and therefore unemployment could increase.
- OPEC raised the price of oil, so we expect goods prices to rise in the United States.
- If the Fed increases the interest rate, the U.S. inflation rate could go down.
- More that 50 million people in the United States do not have health insurance.

Such statements are called *positive statements*.

Positive does not mean "true." You can affirm or refute a positive statement. In fact, you can use this as a criterion to tell whether a statement is a positive statement. You can say "Yes, that is true"; "No, that is not true"; or "No, I don't think that is true." For example, the last statement about health insurance probably is not true (in 2007). At the time of writing this book, an estimated 47 million Americans did not have health insurance. Nevertheless, the statement is a positive statement.

Normative statements involve norms or judgments. The person making the statement considers the present state of things or the outcome of a decision to be good or bad. Here are some examples:

POSITIVE STATEMENTS
Statements that do not make any value judgments about whether any particular state or outcome is good or bad.

NORMATIVE STATEMENTS
Statements that involve norms or judgments. The person making the statement considers the present state of things or the outcome of a decision to be good or bad.

- *The price of gasoline is too high. (The present state is bad.)*
- *The government should pursue a pro-growth policy in order to increase the rate of growth of output to 3%. (The outcome is good.)*
- *We are entering a recession, and therefore the government should try to keep unemployment from rising. (The outcome is good.)*
- *The current rate of inflation is too high; it is hurting people. (The present state is bad.)*
- *We should try to reduce the inflation rate. (The outcome is good.)*
- *We should not pursue active stabilization policies (The outcome is bad.)*

Note that you cannot affirm or refute the above statements. When someone says, "gasoline prices are too high," you will not be able to affirm or refute that statement, since you don't know how high is "too high." If you say "Yes, I also think gasoline prices are too high," you are not affirming the statement. You are just making another normative statement. In economics, we mostly concentrate on positive questions. For instance, we tell the world that if you try to lower the unemployment rate, you may end up increasing the inflation rate. You cannot lower both in the short run. Then we leave it to others (e.g., politicians and voters) to decide whether they want to reduce inflation or unemployment.

A positive statement by an economist: In the short run, you can either reduce inflation or unemployment, but not both.

A *normative statement* by a policy maker: Current unemployment is a more serious problem. We should reduce unemployment and forget about inflation.

This is not to say that economists do not make *any normative statements. The very fact that economists propose policies to change the course of some events indicates that they regard the status quo as undesirable. As an example, they mostly advocate free trade policies among different countries, since they generally believe that trade restrictions—such as tariffs or quotas—between nations have economically undesirable effects, and that easing of these restrictions will produce better outcomes. However, they are careful to define the meaning of "better outcomes." They may define it as the increased quantities of goods and services consumed by the trading nations, for instance.*

ECONOMIC MODELS

Economists conduct analyses using economic models. It is fair to say that almost anything you will study in economics is in terms of some sort of a model. Economic models are simplified versions of reality that economists develop to analyze and understand the complex economic relationships that exist in the real world. As such, they are approximations to the real world. Decades ago, a famous Cambridge economist named Joan Robinson likened economic models to area or road maps. In the same way that road maps help us organize our *trips*, economic models help us organize our *thoughts*. Suppose, let's say, that you are to attend a conference in a large city like Los Angeles. You arrive in the city Sunday evening, and the next day you decide to find the place where the conference is held. Imagine leaving your hotel without any maps and without asking anyone for directions, and trying to find the place just by trial and error instead. Chances are you will never reach your destination.

Area maps would be useful in these circumstances for one reason: They do not include any unnecessary details, such as all the buildings or the kinds and names of shops in the streets. All you need is a few lines representing the streets connecting your hotel to the conference place, and this is exactly what the map would show you. A map is a simplified version of the reality that is only used to organize a particular kind of a trip. If instead you were going fishing or camping, you would need another kind of map, with other kinds of information on it. The city map would not be helpful in *this* trip. In either case, a one-to-one map—a map the size of the area itself with all the details included—would be as useless as not having the map at all.

Economic models are similar. To understand a particular problem, economists construct a model that *assumes away* (ignores) all the unnecessary details in order to concentrate on the problem at hand. Since the reality is too complex, a very realistic model with a lot of details would be as useless as a one-to-one map. In this sense, all models are unrealistic. However, they are useful, because they only include the details we care about and these details are based on reality. Moreover, like the area maps, we develop and use different models to answer different questions. A model that is useful to answer one question may be totally useless in answering another question.

Los Angeles is a large and congested city. Referencing an area map and planning for traffic are necessary to ensure prompt arrival. Economists prepare models to understand a particular problem similar to the way we use traffic reports and maps to plan travel.

In fact, people use models in their day-to-day lives to make decisions. Suppose a friend of yours is thinking of renting an apartment in your neighborhood. So he comes to you and asks, "What is your average speed on a typical winter day driving home from the school?" Your typical answer would be, "It depends. Under average rain and traffic conditions, I can drive 30 miles per hour." These are the only important factors affecting your driving speed. You ignore other irrelevant details, such as the kind of music you listen to, or whether someone else is in the car with you. You also explain that if either the rain or the traffic conditions turned out better than the average, you could drive faster. However, you do explain that you cannot exceed the legal speed limit of 45 miles per hour. You just answered your friend's question using a model.

Economic models contain two types of magnitudes: *constants* and *variables*. Constants are those magnitudes whose values do not change. In the above example, the speed limit of 45 miles per hour is a constant. We know you will never drive faster than that.[1] Variables are those magnitudes that can take different values: your speed, the amount of rainfall, and the number of cars on the street can change from day to day. In any model, there are two types of variables. *Endogenous variables* are those variables whose values are determined *inside the model* on the basis of the values of the other variables. In other words, these are the variables whose values we don't know, but are interested in knowing. Simply put, these are the unknowns of the problem. In the above example, your friend was interested in knowing your daily average speed. So this was the endogenous variable of the model.

ENDOGENOUS VARIABLES
Variables whose values are determined inside the model on the basis of the values of the other variables.

The other variables are called *exogenous variables*. The values of the exogenous variables are determined *outside the model* by factors other than the endogenous variables, and are therefore known to the analyst. Exogenous variables are the cause and the endogenous variables are the effect. Endogenous means *inside* and exogenous means *outside*. In mathematics, these are called dependent and independent variables, respectively. In the above example, the amount of rainfall and the number of cars on the street are exogenous variables. Their values are determined outside your model by other factors, like climate or the number of residents in the city. They will not

EXOGENOUS VARIABLES
Variables whose values are determined outside the model by factors other than the endogenous variables, and are therefore known to the analyst.

1 We hope!

depend on your driving speed. Your friend was not interested in the values of these variables *per se*. However, their values would affect your driving speed, something your friend was interested in knowing.

Often, we are interested in analyzing the effect of a change in an exogenous variable on the value of the endogenous variable, keeping all the other exogenous variables unchanged. For example, we ask, all else the same, what would happen to your driving speed on a particular winter day if the rainfall was heavier than normal? In this case, "all else the same" means keeping the other exogenous variable—the traffic condition—unchanged at its average level. Economists frequently use the Latin phrase *ceteris paribus* instead of its English equivalent: all else the same.[2]

CETERIS PARIBUS
A Latin phrase meaning all else the same.

Suppose that now your friend asks a second question: "How long does it take you to get home from school on a typical winter day?" Now we have a second endogenous variable—a variable whose value we are interested in. Your friend's second question cannot be answered with the existing set of exogenous variables and relationships. We need new pieces of information to answer this new question. You remember from high school algebra that to solve for two unknowns, we need two independent equations. We are talking about the same thing here.

You would answer, "*The distance from the school to my house is about 10 miles. Therefore, it takes about 20 minutes to get home.*" So you would add the relationship between speed and travel time to your model to answer both questions. Note that the second relation comes with another constant: the fixed distance between your home and the school, which is 10 miles.

In general, the number of relationships must be equal to the number of endogenous variables in order for us to determine the values of the endogenous variables. The appendix to this chapter reviews most of the math, including an algebraic description of economic models that you will need to know to follow the arguments in this book.

MATHEMATICAL APPENDIX

The math prerequisite for this book is minimal. All you need to know is how to manipulate simple algebraic equations and how to work with graphs. This appendix will review most of the math you need know to be able to follow the material in the book. We start with the definition of a function. A *function* is a *rule* that assigns one—and only one—value to a *dependent variable* for each value of an *independent variable*. The independent variable is the cause and the dependent variable the effect. For instance, the profit earned by a company depends on the amount of output it produces, so profit is the dependent variable and the amount of output is the independent variable. You could spend more if you had more money in your pocket, so the level of your spending is the dependent variable, and the amount of cash in your pocket is the independent variable.

DEPENDENT VARIABLE
Variables whose values depend on the values of some other, independent variables.

INDEPENDENT VARIABLE
A variable whose values drive the values of another variable called the depended variable.

A function can be represented in three forms:

- *Tabular form;*
- *Graphical form;*
- *Algebraic form.*

We will mostly use tabular and graphical forms, although occasionally an algebraic form will sneak in. Moreover, since economics mostly deals with positive numbers, we will ignore negative numbers in this appendix. We will generally be interested in three aspects of a function:

2 Just as in medieval times, this is mainly to make us sound sophisticated.

- *Slope;*
- *Curvature;*
- *Shifts.*

Let's start with the slope.

The Slope

The following table shows the *tabular form* of a function. In this function, Y is the dependent variable and X is the independent variable—variations in X are the cause of the variations in Y. First, note that there is only one Y value corresponding to each X value, so this fits the definition of a function. You can see that an increase in X results in an increase in Y. We say that the relationship between X and Y *is positive.*

X	0	1	2	3	4	5
Y	5	7	9	11	13	15

Figure A1 shows the *graphical form* of the above function. The graphical form of this function is a straight line. This is called a *linear function.*

LINEAR FUNCTION
A function whose slope is constant. The graph of such a function is a straight line.

Figure A1: An Upward-Sloping Linear Function

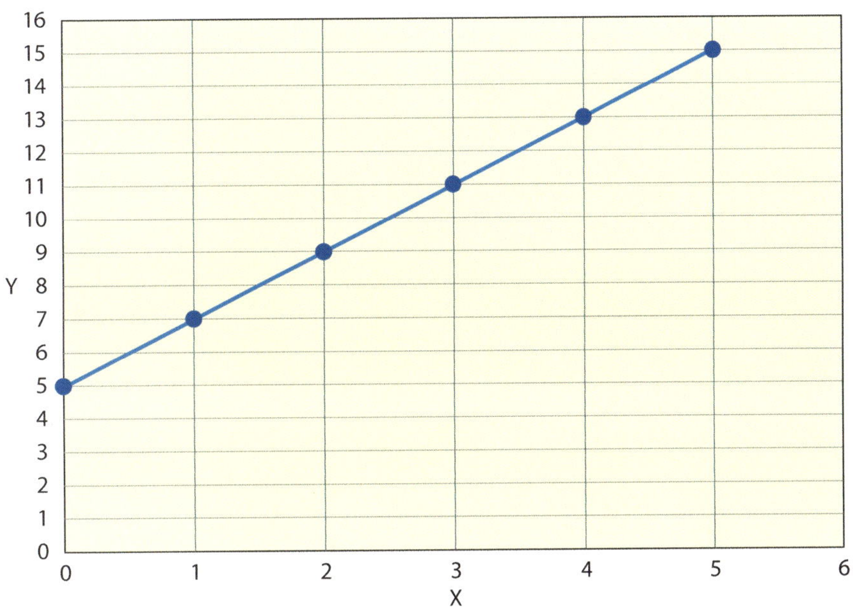

A few features of a linear function should be noted. First, the point where the line crosses the Y-axis is called the *Y-intercept*. In the function above, the *Y-intercept* is 5. Second, the above table and graph show that when X increases by one unit, Y increases by 2 units. Then we say that the *slope* of the function is 2.

Y-INTERCEPT
The point where a function crosses the Y-axis.

SLOPE
The change in a dependent variable for a unit change in an independent variable.

The equation for the slope is:

$$Slope = \Delta Y / \Delta X$$

where ΔY means the change in Y and ΔX means the change in X. In the above function, when X = 1, then Y = 7. If X increases by one unit to X = 2, then Y increases by 2 units to Y = 9. Therefore,

$$\Delta X = 2 - 1 = 1$$
$$\Delta Y = 7 - 5 = 2$$

and

$$\text{Slope} = (9\text{-}7)/(2\text{-}1) = (+2)/(+1) = +2$$

A very important feature of a linear function is that its *slope is constant.* This means two things. First, no matter how much we increase X, the change in Y per unit increase in X will be the same. For example, suppose we increased X by two units from X = 1 to X = 3. We would still get

$$\text{Slope} = (11\text{-}7)/(3\text{-}1) = (+4)/(+2) = +2$$

Therefore, if we increase X by 2 units, Y will increase by 4 units, so that for each one-unit increase in X, Y will increase by 2 units.

The second meaning of the constancy of the slope is that no matter where we start to increase X, the change in Y per unit increase in X will be the same. This is evident from the above table. Let's say, for instance, that we increase X from X = 3 to X = 4. Then

$$\text{Slope} = (13\text{-}11)/(4\text{-}3) = (+2)/(+1) = +2$$

So the slope is the same, 2 units.

Now consider the function presented in the following table:

X	0	1	2	3	4	5
Y	10	8	6	4	2	0

In this case, an increase in X results in a decrease in Y. We say that the relationship between X and Y is *indirect or negative.* Figure A2 shows the graph of this function. The Y-intercept for this function 10 and the X-intercept is 5. The slope of this function is constant at –2. For example, if X increases from X = 0 to X = 1, then Y will decrease from Y = 10 to Y = 8 so that

$$\text{Slope} = (8\text{-}10)/(1\text{-}0) = (\text{-}2)/(+1) = \text{-}2$$

So when the relationship between X and Y is negative, the slope will be a negative number.

To reiterate, what makes a function linear is the constancy of the slope. If the relationship is positive, the line will be upward sloping (you will go up if you draw the line from left to right). If the relationship is negative, the line will be downward sloping (you will go down if you draw the line from left to right). It is important to remember the meaning of slope: Slope answers the following question, *"If we increase X by one unit, by how much will Y change?"*

Figure A2: A Downward-Sloping Linear Function

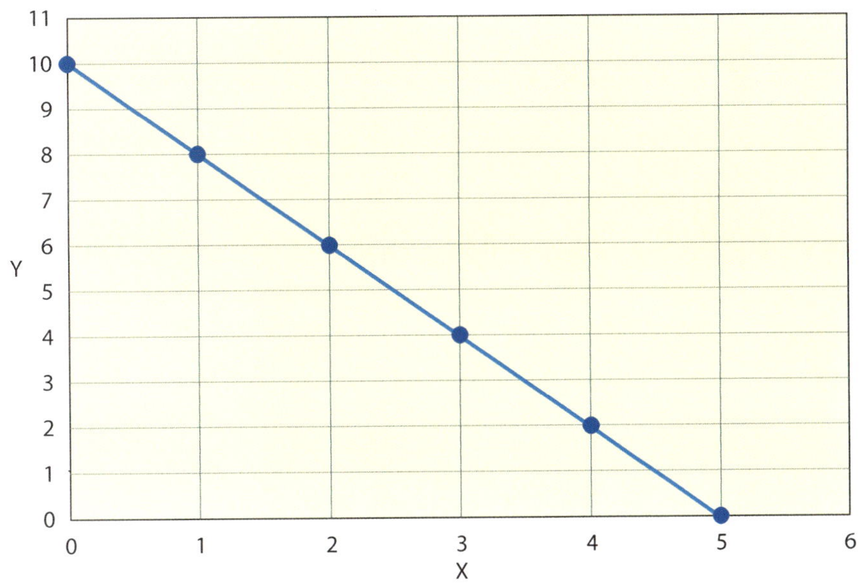

Slopes are important in economics and finance, because they measure the response by a dependent variable to changes in an independent variable. For instance, they provide answers to such questions as: By how much will our company's profit change if we increase production by one unit? What will happen to the government tax revenue if we increase the tax rate by one percent? What will happen to national consumption if we increase national income by one unit?

THE CURVATURE

If the slope of a function is not constant, then the graph of the function will not be a line. Consider the following table. The table below shows that the relationship between X and Y is positive. The slope, however, is not constant. The slope increases with X (as an exercise, calculate the slope at two or three points).

X	0	1	2	3	4	5
Y	1	2	4	7	11	16

Figure A3 shows the graph of this function. This function is *concave from above.*

Figure A3: An Upward-Sloping Function Concave from Above

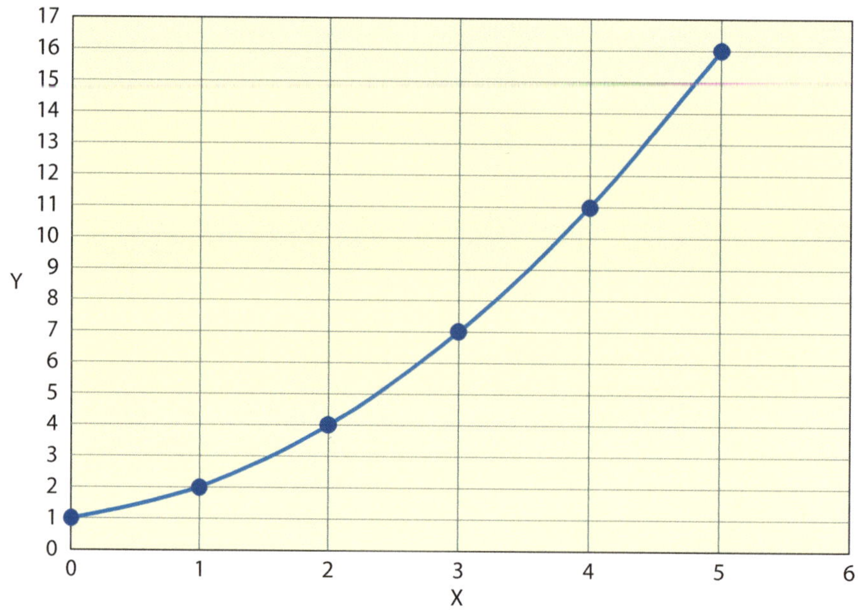

Now consider the function in the following table. Again, the relationship between X and Y is positive, but the slope decreases as X increases (verify this by calculating the slope at a few points).

X	0	1	2	3	4	5
Y	10	16	21	25	28	30

Figure A4 is the graph of this function. This function is *concave from below.* So you see that if a function is upward sloping, its slope is positive. If the slope is constant, the function is linear. If it is not, it can take one of the above two non-linear forms. Curvature indicates whether the function is concave or convex.

Figure A4: An Upward-Sloping Function Concave from Below

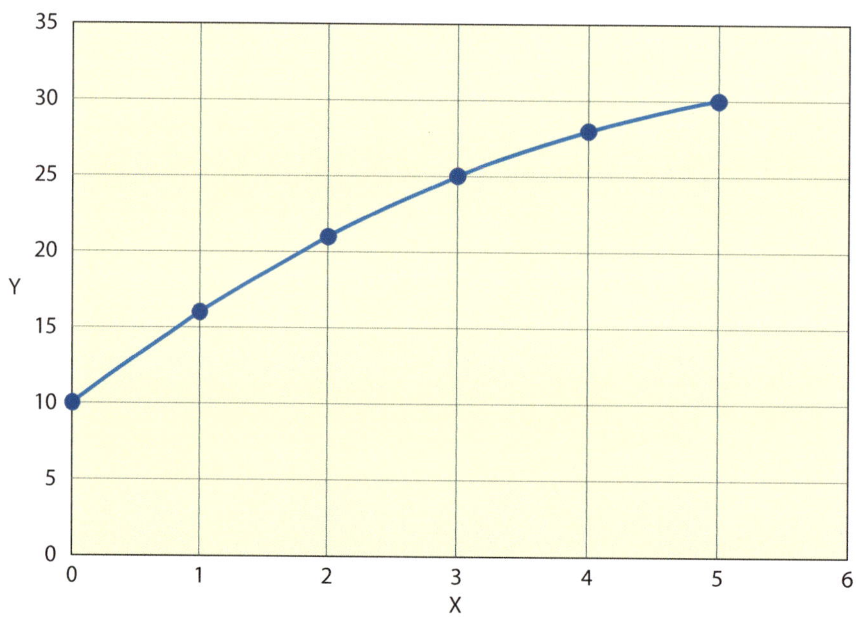

Now consider the following function:

X	0	1	2	3	4	5
Y	35	34	31	25	15	0

Now the relationship between X and Y is negative and the slope is not constant. If X increases from zero to 1, then Y goes down by one unit. So the slope is

Slope= (34-35)/(1-0)= (-1)/(+1)= -1

But if X increases from 4 to 5, then Y goes down from 15 to 0 and the slope is

Slope= (0-15)/(5-4)= (-15)/(+1)= -15

The following is the graph of this function. This function is *concave from the origin.*

Figure A5: A Downward-Sloping Function Concave from Below

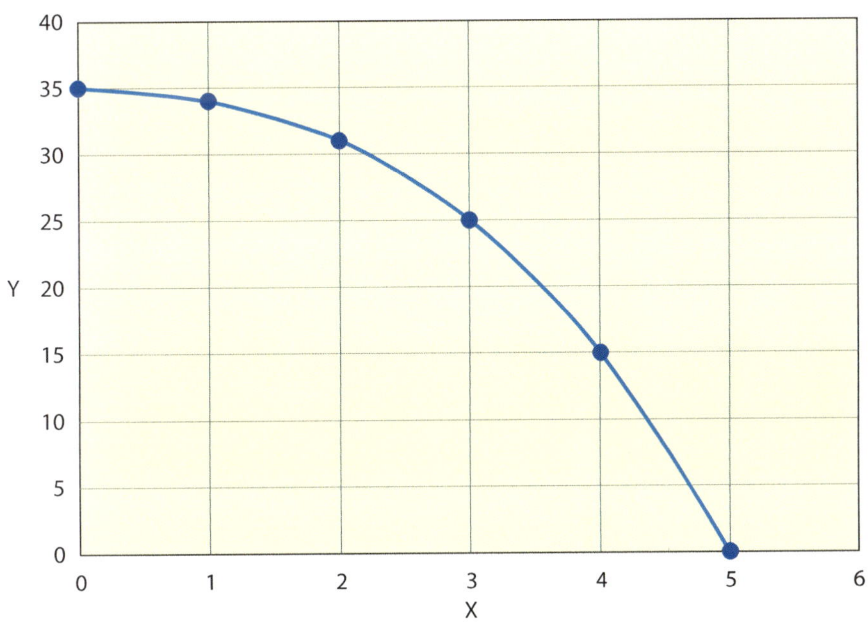

Finally, consider the following function:

X	0	1	2	3	4	5
Y	50	35	25	19	16	15

This function is also downward sloping, but the size of the slope decreases as X increases. Figure 6 is the graph of this function. The function is *concave from above or convex from the origin.*

Figure A6: A Downward-Sloping Function Concave from Above

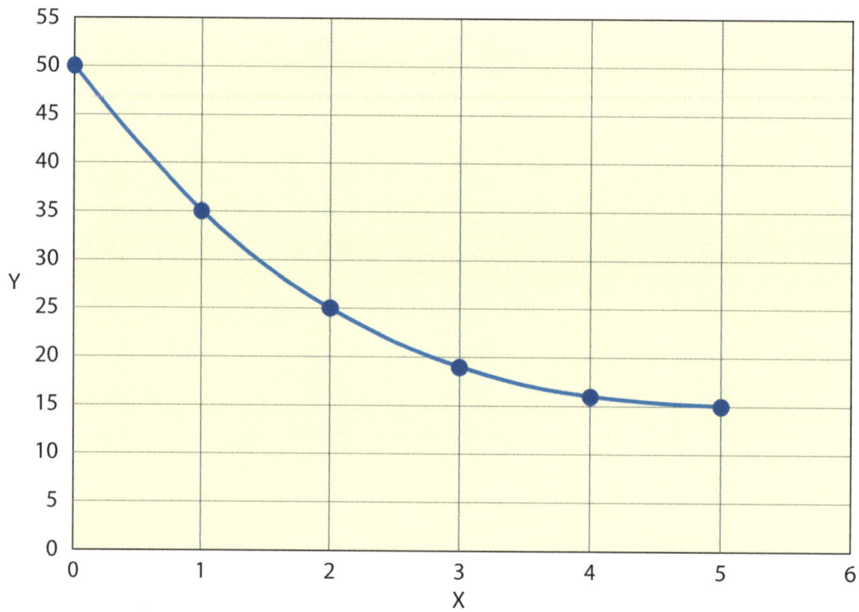

SHIFTS IN THE FUNCTIONS

Many times a dependent variable is a function of more than one independent variable. Suppose the amount of crop production in a region depends on the amount of fertilizer used, as well as inches of rainfall. A household's expenditure on bread depends on the price of bread, as well as household income. Your speed on a highway depends on the weather conditions, as well as the number of other cars on the road.

Suppose Y depends on two independent variables, X and Z, in such a way that for any value of Z, an increase in X will lead to an increase in Y. Similarly, for any value of X, an increase in Z will lead to an increase in Y. For example, assume that for any one-unit increase in Z, Y will increase by 3 units regardless of what X equals to. See the following table:

X	0	1	2	3
Y Before the Increase in Z	3	5	7	9
Y After the Increase in Z	6	8	10	12

What this table says is that, regardless of the value of the Z, a one-unit increase in X will lead to a 2-unit increase in Y. Now if we increase Z, then the value of Y will be higher than before by 3 units at every level of X. Nevertheless, Y still will increase by 2 units with each one-unit increase in X. The following graph shows the function before and after the change in Z. The change in Z causes the function to shift up.

Figure A7: An Upward Shift in the Function

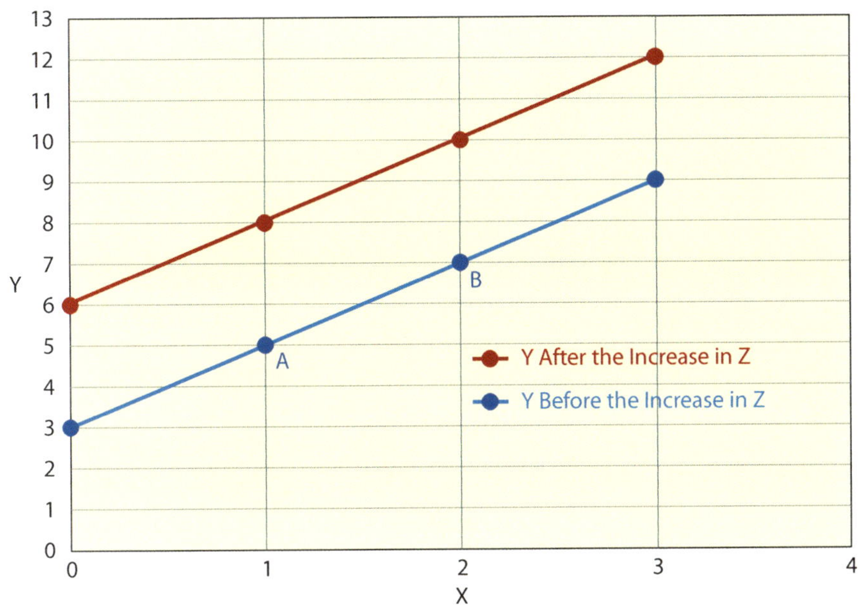

Finally, suppose that, given the value of Z, a one-unit increase in X results in a 2-unit increase in Y. This time, though, an increase in Z results in a 3-unit decrease in Y. See the following table:

X	0	1	2	3
Y Before the Increase in Z	3	5	7	9
Y After the Increase in Z	0	2	4	6

In this case, an increase in Z will result in a downward shift in the function, as in Figure A8.

Figure A8: A Downward Shift in the Function

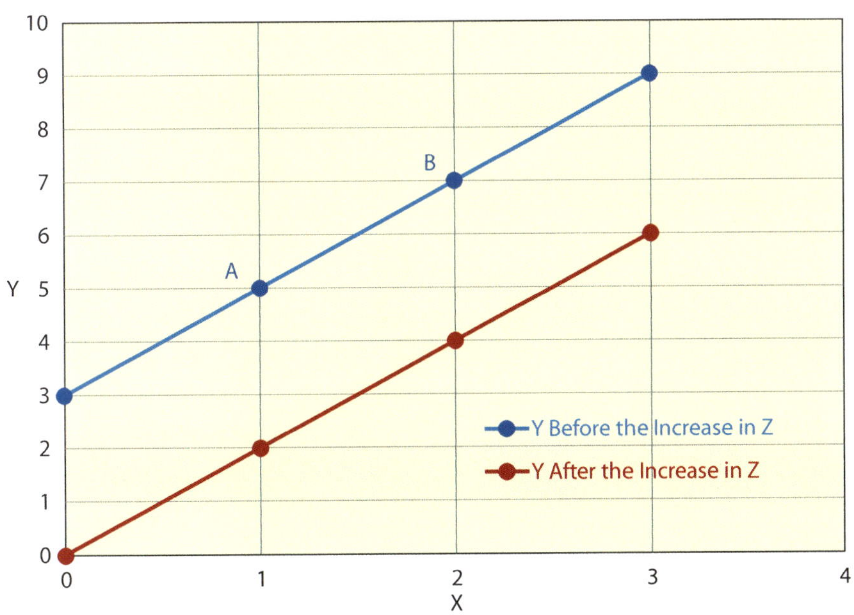

Consider Figures A7 and A8 again. If X increases by one unit from X = 1 to X = 2 while Z is kept constant, then Y will increase from Y = 5 to Y = 7. This will be a movement from point A to point B in both figures. This is called a *movement along the function*. Let's learn the general rule:

> *All else the same, if a variable that is measured along one of the two axes changes, there will be a movement along the function.*

On the other hand, if Z changes, the whole function will shift. This gives us the rule to shift the functions:

> *If a variable that is NOT measured along one of the two axes changes, there will be a shift in the function.*

The direction of the shift in the function would depend on the effect of the variable that is *not* measured on the axes on the dependent variable. In Figure A7, this effect was positive, and so the

TO SUMMARIZE:

1. *Scarcity* means that human wants are unlimited in relation to the available resources in the economy.
2. *Resources* are those things societies use to produce goods and services. They are also called *production inputs* or *factors of production*. They include:
    a. *Land* (natural resources)
    b. *Labor* (human resources)
    c. *Capital* (produced means of production)
3. All societies must answer three economic questions:
    a. *What* goods and services should the society produce?
    b. *How* to produce those goods and services?
    c. *For whom* should we produce these goods and services?
4. *Microeconomics* studies the decisions made by one individual decision making unit and economic conditions prevailing in one particular market or industry.
5. Economists assume that *decision makers* act in their own self interest to maximize their satisfaction. Satisfaction could be in monetary units or could be subjective.
6. Examples of decision-making units are *consumers*, *workers*, *employers*, and *producers*.
7. *Macroeconomics* studies the behavior of aggregate economic variables such as the *aggregate level of output*, the *overall price level*, and *overall employment*.
8. The *substitution effect* of a price change indicates that when the price of a good goes down, people buy more of it because it becomes cheaper relative to its substitutes. Similarly for an increase in price.
9. The *income effect* of a price change indicates that when the price of a good goes down, people will have more money left over if they buy the same amounts of the good. This is like an increase in their incomes. They use this money to buy more of every good and service, including the good in question. Similarly for an increase in price.
10. *Fallacy of composition* is the notion that what is true for one individual is true for the sum of all the individuals.
11. Macroeconomic markets include (a) the *goods and services market*, (b) the *factor market*, (c) the *loanable funds market*, (d) the *stock market*, and (e) *the foreign exchange market*.
12. The *financial system* is the combination of financial markets and financial institutions.
13. *Positive statements* are about how things are, or how we think they are.
14. *Normative statements* involve norms or judgments. They are statements on how things ought to be.

function shifted up. In Figure A8, it was negative, so the function shifted down. These two rules are worth remembering.

EXERCISES

Question 1

The dollar value of all the goods produced by the Chrysler Corporation in a year might well exceed the dollar value of all the goods produced by a small country such as Jordan or Nepal. Still, the analysis of Chrysler Corporation falls in the realm of microeconomics, yet we should use macroeconomic tools to study the economies of Jordan or Nepal. Why?

Question 2

Which of the following statements are positive, and which are normative?

a. An increase in oil prices could cause a recession.
b. Western economies should coordinate their economic policies.
c. The government should pay more attention to the needs of low-income people.
d. The September 11 terrorist attacks did not have much of an impact on the U.S. economy.
e. The government should regulate the stock market.
f. We are growing too slowly; we should speed up to catch up with the rest of the world.
g. I think unemployment is a worse problem than inflation.

EXERCISES FOR MATHEMATICAL APPENDIX

Question 1

Graph the following functions and determine whether they are linear or not:

Function 1

X	0	1	2	3	4	5
Y	8	7	6	5	4	3

Function 2

X	0	1	2	3	4	5
Y	8	9	11	14	18	23

Function 3

X	0	1	2	3	4	5
Y	4	5	6	7	8	9

Function 4

X	0	1	2	3	4	5
Y	30	29	26	21	14	5

Question 2

Consider the functions in Question 1. Suppose that Y is also a function of another variable, Z. A one-unit increase in Z will result in a 2-unit increase in Y, and a one-unit decrease in Z will result in a 2-unit decrease in Y.

a. Given Z, suppose that the value of X increases from 3 to 4. Show this in the graphs. Would this represent a movement along or a shift in the functions?
b. Suppose that Z increases by 3 units. Show this in the graphs. Would this represent a movement along or a shift in the functions?
c. Suppose that Z decreases by 1 unit. Show this in the graphs. Would this represent a movement along or a shift in the functions?

Question 3

Consider the functions in Question 1. Suppose that Y is also a function of another variable, Z. A one-unit increase in Z will result in a 1-unit decrease in Y, and a one-unit decrease in Z will result in a 1-unit increase in Y.

a. Suppose that, given Z, the value of X decreases from 4 to 2. Show this in the graphs. Would this represent a movement along or a shift in the functions?
b. Suppose Z increases by 2 units. Show this in the graphs. Would this represent a movement along or a shift in the functions?
c. Suppose that Z decreases by 4 units. Show this in the graphs. Would this represent a movement along or a shift in the functions?

CHAPTER 2

Private Costs and Benefits: Rational Economic Behavior

INTRODUCTION AND REVIEW

CONSIDER A TYPICAL day in your life. From the time you get up in the morning to the time you go to bed at night, you are affected by a host of government microeconomic policies. Think about the sequence of activities you carry out on a typical day after you wake up; almost all of these activities are affected by some government policy. Here is a partial list:

You go to the bathroom? The Energy Policy Act of 1992 regulates the water flow from the toilet tank. The price of water is regulated by state and city governments. The Americans with Disabilities Act regulates the shapes and sizes of the toilet tanks in the government and commercial buildings.

You wash your hands and take a shower afterwards? The Federal Energy Policy Act of 1992 mandates that "*all faucet fixtures manufactured in the United States restrict maximum water flow at or below 2.5 gallons per minute (gpm) at 80 pounds per square inch (psi) of water pressure or 2.2 gpm at 60 psi.*"

You turn on the heater or the air conditioner and make a little breakfast for yourself? The prices of electricity and natural gas are regulated by state governments. The price of milk is also regulated by most states. The government requires cereal producers to write the ingredient information on the box. The price of bread is affected by all manner of agricultural price support programs and subsidies. The fluoride in your tap water and vitamin D in your milk are your government's doing.

You go out, thinking that you left the government at home? Think again! The government follows you into the street. We have laws about wearing helmets while riding bicycles, buckling seat belts, and using child seats in the cars. The government also mandates automakers to install air bags in the cars. We have traffic laws, and we can only buy unleaded gasoline. The government requires gas stations to post a little friendly notice that the chemicals in that locality may cause birth defects. In some cities, public transportation is subsidized by the government.

You go to school? Public education is free. The government subsidizes tuitions in certain colleges and universities. You can also receive low-interest student loans.

Where do you live? We have rent control in some cities. Some local governments encourage construction of low-cost homes for low-income families. The federal government policy encourages providing low-interest mortgage loans to low-income families. We have truth-in-lending laws. You have to pay property taxes. We have all kinds of don't-bother-your-neighbor city ordinances.

You feel safe at home, somewhat? That is because the government provides national security, as well as law and order. The government also provides private property protection and court systems. We also have fire departments run by city governments.

Why do we have so much government in our lives?

In this book we will try to answer this question. Generally, the government undertakes a policy with the intention of changing the behavior of certain individuals or firms. Therefore, we need to understand why they behave the way they do, and what the implications of their behavior are for the society. We need to construct a framework to analyze and predict people's behavior and the usefulness of government policies. Microeconomics becomes a useful tool in this respect. In the following pages, we will build a simple yet powerful model to explain people's behavior. We will then describe the kinds of behavior that the government intends to modify.

PRIVATE COSTS AND BENEFITS
Costs and benefits incurred or enjoyed by individuals.

SOCIAL COSTS AND BENEFITS
Costs and benefits faced by the society as a whole.

This chapter will describe *private costs and benefits*. These are costs and benefits incurred or enjoyed by individuals. The next chapter will discuss *social costs and benefits*, those faced by the society as a whole. In later chapters we will discuss the relationships between the two.

MICROECONOMICS

MAXIMUM SATISFACTION
Maximum satisfaction is achieved when a decision maker undertakes an activity up to the point where its marginal cost just equals its marginal benefit.

Economics is broadly divided into two fields: microeconomics and macroeconomics. Microeconomics studies the decisions made by one individual decision-making unit and the economic conditions prevailing in one particular market or industry. An industry is a collection of firms that produce the same or similar product. A decision-making unit, or a decision maker for short, can be an individual or a firm. Economists assume that a decision maker makes an economic decision or takes an action to *maximize satisfaction*. Generally, that action or decision is either to *buy* something or to *sell* something. Satisfaction could be either in monetary or subjective terms. The managers of business firms measure satisfaction in terms of their profits. The higher their profits, the more satisfied they are. A consumer's satisfaction, on the other hand, could be subjective—the "happiness" he or she derives from consuming goods and services.

Macroeconomics, on the other hand, studies the behavior of the economy at large—the aggregate economic behavior. For example, it studies questions such as why economies go through cycles of recessions and expansions; why during recessions some workers cannot find jobs; why some economies grow over time, but others remain stagnant; and why the overall level of prices increases over time. Macroeconomics also deals with government policies. In this respect, it tries to answer questions such as whether the government policies are effective in solving the problems of inflation or recession.

This book is about microeconomics, so we will start with a more formal definition of microeconomics:

Microeconomics studies how individuals faced with ***scarcity*** *make* ***choices*** *to achieve* ***maximum satisfaction*** *of material wants.*

The three key terms in this definition—scarcity, choice, and maximum satisfaction—require explanation.

Scarcity

Scarcity means that, while human material wants are unlimited, the resources needed to satisfy them are limited.

a. Unlimited Wants

This means that people prefer more to less. Everyone wants to have such a large amount of goods and services that it is impossible for the society to produce them all with the existing resources.

b. Limited resources

As we saw in Chapter 1, resources are those things used for producing goods and services. They are also called production inputs or factors of production. Resources consist of land, labor, and capital.

Marshall Islands residents awaiting water distribution

Note that scarcity is relative to human wants. In a society where people are vegetarians and do not eat dairy products, there will effectively be an unlimited amount of cows! Cows will not be scarce, because people do not want to consume any product coming from them.

Unlimited wants and limited resources are related to each other in a circular way, and they represent the same concept. Ask everyone in the society what goods and services they would want to have if money were no object. Enter all the responses in your computer and add them up. You will realize that you cannot possibly produce all these goods and services with the existing resources. So by "unlimited," we don't mean "infinity" as in mathematics. Therefore:

- Wants are unlimited in the sense that we cannot satisfy them all with the existing resources.
- Resources are limited in the sense that we don't have enough of them to satisfy all human wants.

Furthermore, scarcity at the national level results in scarcity at the level of individual decision-making units. Since there is only so much land out there, each person can own only a limited amount and many do not own any. The same is true for capital. Although time is not a production factor, it is a constraining factor. We only have 24 hours a day to produce goods and services. This is true for both an individual and the society as a whole.

Choice or Decision

Scarcity necessitates choice. Since we cannot have more of everything, we have to choose. To get more X, we have to give up some Y and Z. We will use the words *choice* and *decision* synonymously. A choice or decision results in the level of some economic activity. For example, a consumer chooses or decides to buy a certain amount of bread; a producer decides to build and sell a certain number of cars; an employer decides to hire a certain number of people; and a worker decides to offer a certain number of hours of labor to business firms. We will use the terms *choice*, *decision*, and *activity* synonymously.

MARGINAL COST
The cost associated with any decision.

MARGINAL BENEFIT
The benefit from any decision.

MARGINAL ANALYSIS
The theory that posits that decisions are made at the margin. Decision makers are assumed to compare the marginal cost and the marginal benefit of taking an action to decide whether to take that action.

The cost associated with any decision is called the *marginal cost* of that decision. Why do we want to make a choice or take an action in the first place? The answer is because it gives us some benefits. Benefits could be subjective, in monetary units, or something else. The benefit from any decision is called the *marginal benefit* of that decision. Analyzing whether an action should be taken by comparing its costs and benefits is called *marginal analysis*.

Marginal Cost

We start with describing how economists define the concept of marginal cost. *All costs arise because of scarcity*. If we want to have more of something, we have to give up some other things. As economists say, "There is no such thing as a free lunch." In economics, *all costs are benefits forgone.*

> *The marginal cost of an activity is the sum of all the benefits forgone because of undertaking that activity.*

OPPORTUNITY COST
The benefit forgone because of a decision.

The benefit forgone because of a decision is also called the *opportunity cost* of that decision. This is because by doing something we give up or lose the opportunity to do something else. Therefore, marginal cost is the same as opportunity cost. Economists have come up with two rules to calculate the marginal cost of a decision or activity.

Rule #1: Include All the Relevant Costs

We should always include the costs arising from a particular decision in our calculation. These are of two kinds:

Explicit Costs: These are out-of-pocket cash outlays. Suppose you decide to buy a cool car for $25,000. This is the explicit marginal cost of the car. It fits the definition of benefits forgone. If you pay $25,000 to buy that car, you will no longer be able to buy other things using that money. With that $25,000 you could have taken a very nice African vacation, bought a yacht, or purchased some stocks and bonds. Be careful! The opportunity cost is not the sum of the values of these alternatives forgone. With that $25,000, you could not have purchased *all* of those things, but only one of them. So what is the opportunity cost of that cool car? It is the value of the *best alternative* forgone. But in this case, all the alternatives foregone are just worth $25,000. Therefore, in the case of explicit costs we don't need to look for all the foregone alternatives and pick the one that is most valuable. The value of all of them will just be equal to the explicit marginal cost. This issue becomes more important in the case of implicit costs.

A Ferrari F430 on the Fiorano Circuit text track.

Implicit Costs: In this case, no cash outlays are incurred, but you still have some forgone benefits. Suppose your favorite rock band is in town. Are you going to attend the concert? It depends on the marginal costs and benefits. The marginal benefit is the joy you get from watching them play. How about the marginal cost? There are two kinds. The explicit marginal cost is the $40 you pay for the ticket, with which you could buy something else. As for the implicit cost, you have to ask yourself what other things you could do during those three hours if you did not go to the concert. You could visit a friend, read a nice book, or paint your room. Again, the opportunity cost is not the *sum* of the values of those three activities forgone. During those three hours, you could only undertake one of those three activities. Which one would you go for? The one you valued most highly, of course. The value of that activity would constitute the implicit marginal cost of going to the concert. Suppose that of the three alternatives, you valued visiting friends most highly. Then the value you place on visiting friends would constitute the implicit marginal cost of going to the concert.

Harvard University (Harvard Union Building)

Note that in the above example the marginal cost is the sum of the $40 explicit cost, and the implicit cost of not being able to visit your friends. This is simply because if you did not attend the concert, you would be able to see your friends *and* have $40 in your pocket.

As another example, going to college involves two kinds of costs. The explicit cost is the tuition you pay the university, rent on the apartment, costs of books, and so on. But there is also an implicit cost. The fact that you have decided to go to college means that you won't be able to have a full-time job. The income forgone from the best job you could have had is part of the opportunity cost. We can generalize:

> *The marginal cost of any activity is the value of the best alternative we have to give up to undertake it. It is the sum of explicit and implicit costs.*

Marginal costs and benefits must be *forward looking*. This is because the costs and benefits occur *after* you make your choice, and as a *result of* your action. This brings us to the second rule.

Rule #2: Exclude All the Irrelevant Costs

These are the costs that are not affected by your decision. They are either sunk or fixed. In either case, they could be explicit or implicit. A rational decision maker should disregard these costs calculating the marginal cost of an activity.

Sunk Costs: These are one-time costs that have occurred in the past and cannot be recovered. They are also called *historic costs*. Suppose that last year when you were moving to your apartment, you paid $200 for a rental truck. That money is gone—it's history! None of the decisions you make today or in the future will change that amount. Therefore, sunk costs should not be taken into account when making decisions. As another example, suppose that last year you spent about 90 hours applying for different universities. During this time you could have done something else. This is an implicit sunk cost. Note that sunk costs refer only to the portions of the historic costs that cannot be recovered. Say that four years ago when you started college, you bought a refrigerator for $3,000. After you graduate, you can sell it for $1,000. Then only $2,000 of that $3,000 is sunk.

HISTORIC COSTS
One-time costs that have occurred in the past and cannot be recovered. Also called sunk costs.

Fixed Costs: Unlike sunk costs, fixed costs are recurrent or ongoing. Nevertheless, they are *not affected by your decision*. You should be careful about this definition. Fixed costs may be quite variable in the big picture; they will just not be affected by your particular decision. Suppose you pay a rent of $800 for your apartment. This can be changed next year by your landlord. However, it will not be affected by your decision to study an extra hour. *With respect to this particular decision*, it is fixed. In other words, even if you do not study an extra hour, you still have to pay the rent. As another instance, in calculating the marginal cost of deciding whether to attend college, you should not include the cost of food; you would eat food even if you did not attend college.[1] These examples indicate an easy way of figuring out if a cost item is fixed or not:

> *A cost is fixed with respect to a particular activity if you would incur it even if you did not undertake that activity.*

The concept of marginal cost has slightly different implications for buyer and sellers of goods and services.

Decision to Buy Something

When the decision is to buy something, the marginal cost is what you *must* give up for it. This is because you do not have that thing, and so you have to sacrifice money or other things to acquire it. That is to say, you *must* pay your tuition and forgo some employment opportunities to go to college. Otherwise, you will not receive that education.

Decision to Sell Something

As in the case of buying something, the marginal or opportunity cost of a decision to sell something is the benefits you forgo for doing so. However, when the decision is to sell something, you already have the good and you don't have to sell it if you don't receive some minimum amount for it. The marginal cost would be that minimum amount of money you are *willing to receive* for that good. Here is why: Suppose the seller of a house requires a minimum of $450,000 for it. The reason for this is that it has cost him that much to build it. It is the sum of explicit and implicit costs. It includes the amount of money he has paid in wages and materials that he could have spent on something else. It also includes opportunity cost of the time and effort expended to build that house.

A home for sale in New Orleans

Consider a similar example. Assume that a used car dealer has paid $8,000 to buy a car from someone. This is the explicit marginal cost of buying the car. However, to buy this car, he has spent some time and effort trying to find different sellers and negotiate prices with them. He could have spent this time and effort on some other activities. Suppose that for him, the value of these forgone alternative activities is $500. Therefore, the marginal cost of buying this used car is $8,500. This $8,500 is the minimum he is willing to accept for the car.

Consider another relatively famous example. Suppose that a scalper finds an unexpired ticket for a game on the sidewalk. Is he going to give it away, simply because he didn't pay anything for it? Of course not! What would be the marginal cost of doing so? It would be the money he *could have received* selling it to the highest bidder. If the first person he met offered him $50 for the ticket, this would constitute the marginal cost of selling it to the second person. If the second person offered him $60 and no one offered higher, *this* would constitute the lowest price he would accept.

As you can see from the examples above, if you sell a product for more than its marginal cost, you will be better off. If you sell for less, you will be worse off. You will remain indifferent if you sell it for an amount equal to marginal cost. So let's remember:

---

1 The above statement was not quite precise. If, without going to college your monthly food expense was $600, but after attending college it increases to $1,000, then only the $600 is a fixed cost. You have to include the additional $400 in the marginal cost. You would not incur this $400 if you did not go to college.

When the decision is to sell something, the marginal cost is the minimum amount of money or something else you are willing to accept for it. You will remain neither better off nor worse off than before if you receive this amount.

Marginal Benefit

We undertake an activity because it gives us some benefits. These benefits could be purely subjective or in monetary terms. If you buy a new car, it will give you a great deal of joy and happiness. This is a subjective marginal benefit. On the other hand, by going to college, you have decided to buy some knowledge for yourself. You expect to derive certain benefits from your decision, some of which are monetary, such as better jobs and higher incomes, and some subjective, such as prestige or a higher social status. When a producer sells a product, it receives money for it. This is a monetary benefit. Marginal benefit is defined somewhat differently for the decisions to buy or sell things.

Decision to Buy Something

Simply stated, the marginal benefit of anything is the value of that thing to you. It is how much that thing is worth to you. Therefore, it is the maximum amount of money or something else you are willing to give up to get it. It is based on a simple idea. Suppose your friend has a winning lottery ticket of $100, but she cannot cash it because she has to take a trip overseas. What is the value of that lottery ticket to you? Ask yourself this question: What is the highest amount of money I am willing to pay to get it? You will, of course, be willing to pay less than $100. If you pay $90, you will end up better off than before by $10. So $90 is not the *value* of the ticket to you. The value of this ticket to you is exactly $100, and that is the most you are willing to pay to get it. If you pay $100 for it, you will come out even. You are not willing to pay more than $100 for it, since if you do, you will end up worse off than before. We can generalize:

When the decision is to buy something, the marginal benefit is the maximum amount of money or something else you are willing and able to give up to get it.[2]

Note two important implications of this definition that will come up later in our discussion of consumer and firm behavior. First, since the marginal benefit of something to you is the *maximum* amount of money or something else you are willing to give up to get it, you will remain indifferent about the exchange if this is the amount that you actually pay. For instance, in the above example, the maximum value of the lottery ticket to you is $100. If you pay $100 and buy it, you will remain no better off or worse off than before. So we also have another equivalent definition of marginal benefit:

When the decision is to buy something, the marginal benefit is the amount of money or something else you are willing and able to give for it and remain indifferent.[3]

---

2 Although you can use things other than money to pay for goods and services, I will generally assume that all payments and receipts are in money.

3 This concept is sometimes called the marginal rate of substitution between money and a particular good, like a can of soda.

The second implication of the above definition is that the decision maker should be *able to pay* for that thing. Economists are interested in the effects of decisions made by people and business firms on the economy. *Willingness* to pay should be backed by the *ability* to pay; otherwise, it just becomes wishful thinking with no real effect on the amounts purchased or produced. Someone might put a very high value on a Hawaiian vacation, but if he does not have enough money to take one, no airline tickets will be purchased, and no hotel rooms will be booked.

Marginal Benefit as Avoided Cost: There is another aspect of marginal benefit that is worth noting. In a lot of cases the marginal benefit of a decision includes the cost that you avoid because of making that decision. The avoided costs could either be explicit or implicit. Implicit costs could include such things as discomfort; inconvenience; embarrassment; fear; risk of injury or death; or the possibility of losing income or wealth. A few examples will make this concept clear. Suppose you want to travel to Los Angeles from Sacramento. You can fly, take a train, or take a bus. If you decide to fly, you would avoid the costs you would incur if you took a bus or a train. As you know, these costs would be the sum of explicit costs (such as ticket prices) and implicit costs (such as long travel time and the discomfort of taking a train or a bus).

In calculating the marginal benefit, we take the avoided cost of the least costly alternative. Suppose, for instance, that the marginal cost of taking a train would be lower than that of taking a bus. Then, the marginal benefit of flying would be the avoided cost of taking a train. Note finally that, if train prices became significantly lower or trains became substantially faster and more comfortable, then the marginal benefit of flying would go down so much that at some point you might decide to take a train instead of flying.

If you think about it, the marginal benefits of certain products or decisions are solely in terms of the costs they help avoid. Think of the marginal benefits associated with installing fire alarms at your home; wearing a seat belt when you drive or a helmet when you ride a bicycle; installing airbags in your cars; or buying fire insurance. In all these cases you take an action to reduce or eliminate the costs of damage to property or loss of life or limb. In all cases, the marginal benefit would be higher the greater the avoided cost. For example, you would be willing to pay a higher insurance premium to insure a more expensive car against theft.

Ultimately note that the concept of marginal benefit as avoided cost is consistent with our overall definition of marginal benefit: as the maximum amount of money or something else you are willing and able to pay for something. Let's say that the sum of explicit and implicit costs of taking a train to Los Angeles from Sacramento is $200. This is the cost you would avoid if you flew. As a result, you would be willing to pay no more than $200 to fly. If the airline ticket price was $200, you would be indifferent between flying and taking a train.

Decision to Sell Something

When the decision is to sell or supply a good or service, the marginal benefit is the amount of something else, such as money, the seller *actually* receives for it. The marginal benefit of selling a hamburger is the money the seller will get for it. Let's remember the general rule:

> *When the decision is to sell something, the marginal benefit is the amount of money or something else you actually receive for it.*

This makes sense, because the seller does not have the power to force the buyer to pay more. All the seller can do is either receive the money offered, or refuse it.

The following table summarizes the four cases:

Decision	Marginal Benefit	Marginal Cost
To Buy Something	Maximum you are willing and able to give up	What you actually have to give up
To Sell Something	What you actually receive	Minimum you are willing to receive

Maximum Satisfaction

Economists assume that decision makers consider the marginal costs and marginal benefits of their decisions before taking any action. They undertake an activity, or increase the level of an existing activity, if the marginal benefit of that activity exceeds its marginal cost. They do not undertake an activity, or reduce the level of an existing activity, if the marginal cost exceeds the marginal benefit. They will not increase or decrease the level of an activity if the marginal cost equals the marginal benefit. This is called *rational economic behavior*.

If marginal benefit > marginal cost,	increase the level of activity
If marginal benefit < marginal cost,	decrease the level of activity
If marginal benefit = marginal cost,	do not change the level of activity (You are at the optimal point.)

So the rule for *maximum satisfaction* is

Marginal benefit (MB) of the decision = Marginal cost (MC) of the decision

MAXIMUM SATISFACTION
Maximum satisfaction is achieved when a decision maker undertakes an activity up to the point where its marginal cost just equals its marginal benefit.

Figure 1 shows the marginal benefit and marginal cost for a hypothetical activity. It assumes that as we increase the level of the activity, its marginal benefit decreases. This does not need to be the case in general. It also assumes that as the level of the activity increases, its marginal cost increases. This does not need to be the case generally either. The graph shows that the first level of the activity will bring a marginal benefit of $9 to the decision maker, while it will cost only $1 to undertake it. The decision maker will therefore undertake that level of activity. Continuing this way, maximum satisfaction will be achieved when the level of the activity is 5, where the marginal benefit of the activity just equals the marginal cost.

Figure 1: Hypothetical Marginal Cost and Marginal Benefit

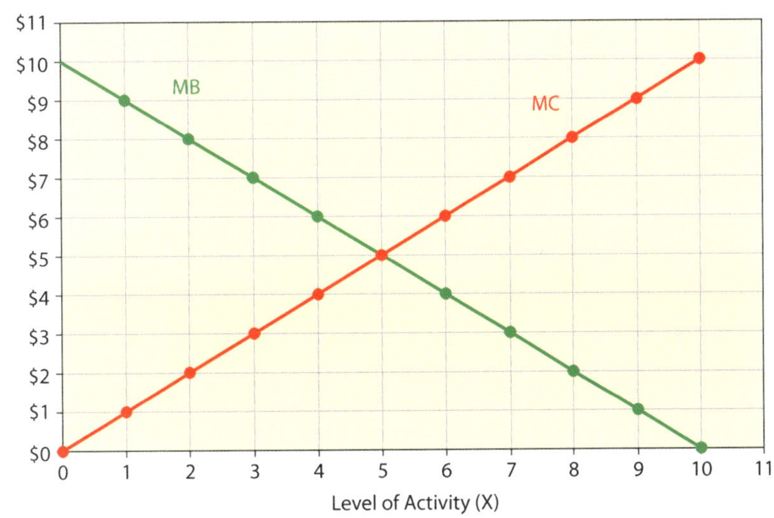

Example 1

Let's decide on the number of hamburgers Harry would eat in a typical week. (See Figure 2.) His first decision of the week is whether to have the first hamburger. For the first hamburger, he is willing to pay a maximum of $7. This is the marginal benefit of the first hamburger. Having had the first one, he must decide on the second one. Now whether to buy the second hamburger becomes his marginal decision. He is only willing to pay $6 for the second burger, and then $5 for the third one. These are the marginal benefits of the second and third hamburgers.

How many would he eat? It depends on the marginal costs. Suppose that the price of a hamburger is $4, and that there are no implicit costs. Then this $4 is the marginal cost of each hamburger. This is what Harry *must* pay for each hamburger. Would Harry take the first one? For the first one he was willing to pay $7, but he has to pay only $4. For this decision, MB > MC and, therefore, he would buy it and become better off. For the second one, he wanted to pay $6, and he has to pay $4. So he would buy it. Continuing this way, he will buy four hamburgers. The fourth hamburger will leave him indifferent. However, he would not buy the fifth one. If he did, he would become worse off. So he will buy four hamburgers per week, as this is where MB = MC.

Figure 2: Hypothetical Marginal Cost and Marginal Benefit

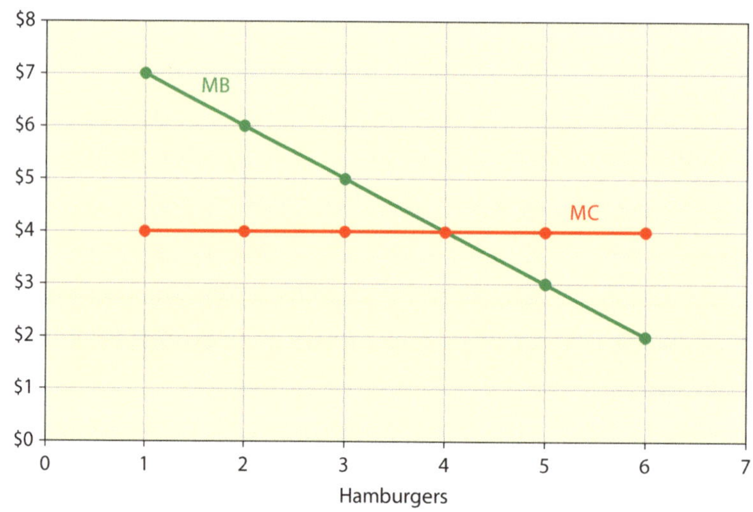

For as long as the price of each hamburger is $4, Harry will keep buying four hamburgers per week. This is the meaning of the expression, "if MB = MC, then the level of activity will remain the same." If next week the price falls to $3, he will increase his hamburger consumption to five. If the price rises to $5, he will reduce his consumption to three hamburgers per week.

Harry should disregard the irrelevant costs. For example, he has spent $2 on gasoline driving to the hamburger place. That money is gone—it is a sunk cost. Or suppose that after every meal he has a chocolate bar worth $1.50. This is a recurrent fixed cost that will not be affected by eating these particular hamburgers. He will incur it anyway, so he should ignore it.

Example 2

You are running a pizza place. (See Figure 3.) How many pizzas will you produce and sell per day? It depends on the marginal benefit and marginal cost of the pizzas produced. Suppose that each pizza sells for $10. This will be the marginal benefit of selling each pizza. The marginal cost of producing the 20th pizza is $4. This is the cost of labor, flour, yeast, electricity, and water that you use to produce that one particular pizza. This is the minimum you would be willing to accept for the 20th pizza. You will produce this pizza since its marginal benefit exceeds its marginal cost. Suppose that the subsequent pizzas cost more to produce. This could be because your workers get tired and become less productive, or perhaps they ask for overtime rates. Suppose the marginal cost of the 50th pizza is $10. Then you will produce 50 pizzas per day.

These marginal costs include both explicit and implicit costs, but exclude the fixed and sunk costs. For example, you don't pay yourself wages. But with your own time spent to produce each pizza, you could have worked somewhere else and received wages. This is a foregone benefit, but not an out-of-pocket cash expense. So it is an implicit cost of production. Or, suppose you bought the oven a couple of years ago. Each time you bake a pizza, you reduce the market value of the oven due to normal wear-and-tear called *depreciation*. This is not an out-of-pocket cash expense either, so it is an implicit cost that should be included in your calculation.

DEPRECIATION
The decrease in the market price or value of any good or asset.

There are also costs that should be disregarded when deciding how many pizzas to produce. The monthly rent on the shop, the interest payments to the bank, and premiums to the insurance company are all recurrent fixed costs that should be ignored. You would pay them no matter how many pizzas you produce. Also, suppose that last year you painted your shop. That cost is sunk and should be ignored.

Figure 3: Hypothetical Marginal Cost and Marginal Benefit

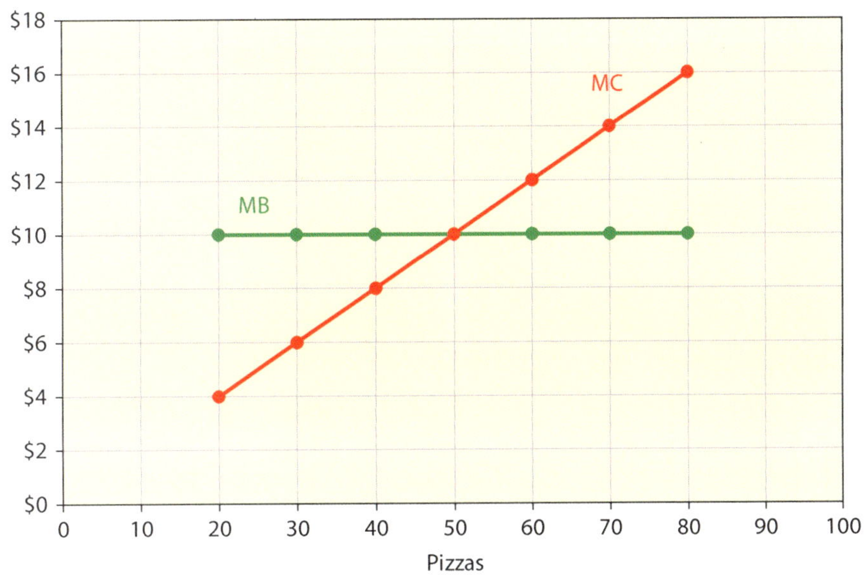

Incentives Matter

People respond to incentives. Your optimal choice will change whenever the MB or MC schedule changes. Suppose, for example, that Harry hears that hamburgers cause heart problems. Then he will be willing to pay less for each hamburger. Let's say that he will be willing to pay $2 less for each hamburger. Then his MB line for hamburgers will shift down from MB_1 to MB_2 (in the top portion of Figure 4), and he will eat only two hamburgers per week. Or, assume that the costs of ingredients to make pizzas increase, so that each pizza costs you an additional $2 to produce. Then your MC line will shift up by $2 from MC_1 to MC_2 and you will reduce your production to 40 units. (See the lower portion of Figure 4.)

Analysis of incentives is an important part of microeconomics. In this chapter, we assumed the person who makes a decision is also the one that incurs the cost and enjoys the benefit of that decision. In the real world, many actors may be involved in or affected by a decision. In such cases, it becomes important to analyze the incentives faced by each. In particular, in any real-world issues we need to answer three questions about a decision:

1. Who makes the decision?
2. Who incurs the cost of the decision?
3. Who benefits from the decision?

Here are a few examples.

Example 1: As an instance close to home, you decide to buy a car. Your parents pay for it, and you enjoy the benefit of using it.
Example 2: Your instructor decides which textbook you should buy. You incur the cost of buying it, and derive the benefit from it.
Example 3: Your doctor decides which medication you should buy. Your insurance company pays for it, and you benefit from it.
Example 4: You decide to beautify your front lawn. You incur the cost, and you and your neighbors enjoy the scene.
Example 5: You decide to drive to work one day. You incur the explicit and implicit cost of driving, such as the cost of gasoline and wear-and-tear of the car. You enjoy the benefit of driving, such as the avoided cost of taking public transportation. However, in the process, you impose some costs on others in the form of greater air pollution or congestion.

As you can imagine, different people involved in a decision face different incentives. You want to buy the fanciest car, while your parents are mindful of the cost. Your instructor wants to adopt a textbook that he or she believes is appropriate for you without much regard for the price, while the price is very important to you. Or, you and your doctor would want the best treatment for you, while the insurance company would want to minimize the cost of the treatment. We will analyze these incentive problems more fully in this book.

GOVERNMENT POLICIES

The government's microeconomic policies are meant to work by changing the incentives faced by certain decision makers. Suppose, for example, that the government thinks that smoking is bad for the society. Thus, through aggressive advertising, it tries to reduce the MB of smoking. Or, it levies a heavy tax on the sale of cigarettes to increase their marginal cost to smokers. The government hopes this will reduce the number of people smoking. Or, suppose that the government thinks that the production of a certain good harms the environment. It then imposes a tax on the production of each unit. This tax shifts up the MC curve for the producers, and they produce less.

> *Government policies affect individuals' behavior by affecting the marginal benefits and marginal costs of their decisions.*

Although there are a lot of policies to change people's behavior, not all of them are justified on economic grounds. Under what circumstances is a government policy to change our behavior justified? Consider the partial list of policies you face on a daily basis mentioned in the opening paragraph. Although they look different and cover quite different areas of economic activity, one common theme is running through them all. In all of those cases, the government is trying to resolve a conflict that the market system is apparently not capable of resolving. That conflict is between *private incentives* of individuals and the *public interest.*

In certain cases, choices made by individuals and firms on the basis of their private marginal costs and benefits may result in outcomes that the society considers less than optimal. In such circumstances, government policy to change the behavior of such individuals *might* be justified. Note that even in these cases, the policy might not be justified if the marginal cost of the policy exceeds its marginal benefit. Here is a concept worth remembering:

Taxes on cigarette sales and production are intended to curb consumption and production.

> *The government's microeconomic policies are justified if private incentives are in conflict with public interest, the market system cannot resolve this conflict, and if the marginal benefit of the policy exceeds its marginal cost.*

Let's go over the partial list of policies again. In all those cases, the conflict between private incentives and public interest can be classified into four categories as follows.

PRIVATE INCENTIVES
Incentives faced by individuals.

PUBLIC INTEREST
Something that is in the interest of the whole society.

Externalities

In some cases, the actions taken by individual decision-making units may either harm or benefit the rest of the society. In these cases, the government wants to reduce the social harm and increase the social benefit arising from these actions. For example, if each individual uses a lot of water, the society as a whole could face water shortages. To reduce the possibility of such an outcome, the government regulates the amount of water flow through toilet tanks, faucets, or showerheads. The same is true about helmet laws, seat belt laws, and air bags. When someone gets injured or dies in a car accident, the whole society suffers. Not only does the society lose a valuable member, it also suffers financial damages, in the form of emergency room expenses and surgeries. The cost of buckling up is much less than the value of all the time spent by doctors, surgeons, and nurses in operating rooms. When an action taken by an individual harms the society, we say that that individual imposes a *negative externality* on the society.

NEGATIVE EXTERNALITY
*A situation in which an action taken by a **decision making unit** harms others, without any compensation.*

A government policy is not justified only when the actions of individuals harm the society. Sometimes we need policies to encourage individuals to increase the level of their activities, since those activities *benefit* the society. This is called *positive externality*. Consider education. If we completely leave the education of children to parents and private schools, some parents may choose not to send their children to school. This is a particularly serious problem in developing countries. By now you know the reasons for the parents' choice. If the marginal cost of sending the children to school outweighs the benefits, some low-income parents may choose not to send their children to school.

POSITIVE EXTERNALITY
An externality situation in which a decision made by a decision maker benefits other people.

The decisions by these parents result in outcomes that the society may regard as undesirable. This is because education not only benefits the person who is educated by improving his or her standard of living, but it also benefits the society at large. For example, the society benefits from a larger pool of scientists, inventors, and discoverers. Therefore, when leaving it all to individuals, the society may not produce a socially desirable number of educated people. We need some government policies that encourage parents to send their kids to school. One such policy is to provide subsidies to schools so they can charge lower tuitions. Another method is for the government to provide free education to its citizens. In either case, the aim of the policy is to reduce the marginal private cost of schooling to parents.

Market Power

Why does the government regulate the prices of water, electricity, and natural gas? It is because these commodities are normally supplied to you by your local utility company. Consumers of electricity, natural gas, or water cannot switch from their local utility company to another one if the local company overcharges them. This problem may be less severe for water, because bottled water has become a fashionable substitute for tap water of late. But still, households use tap water much more than bottled water. Since the consumers are the "captive audience" of the local utility companies, the companies have incentives to charge them very high prices. The conflict between these private incentives of the utilities and the public interest arises in this case, mostly because these goods are necessities. People cannot live without water. Hence, we need government to ensure that the utilities charge "fair prices" to their customers. *Market power* refers to the power of a company to charge high prices to its customers.

Bottled water is a fashionable alternative to tap water. Competition determines the price of bottled water. Through regulation, governments ensure tap water prices are fair.

MARKET POWER
The power to affect market prices. This happens when there are a small number of large sellers or buyers in the market, so that each has some control on the price of the good sold or bought.

Public Goods

The apple that you buy in a grocery store is classified as a *private good*, because if you eat it, someone else cannot eat *that same apple*. There are other kinds of goods that are called *public goods*, because many people can consume them at the same time without reducing their quantities to others. National defense, law and order, or fire protection are some examples. Note that "publicness" is a matter of degree. We all sleep safely at night because the government provides national security, as well as law and order. Everyone enjoys the same amount of national security without depriving the others. We also know that if a fire starts in our house, we can call for help. However, if many houses catch fire at the same time, there may not be enough firefighters to save them all.

PRIVATE GOODS
A private good is a good that is both rivalrous (two people cannot consume the same good), and excludable (the producer can refuse selling it to you—exclude you from buying it—if you do not pay.)

PUBLIC GOODS
A public good is a good that is neither rivalrous (two people can consume the same good, at the same time, and by the same amount), nor excludable (the producer cannot refuse selling it to you—exclude you from buying it—if you do not pay.) The best example of a public good is national defense.

Regardless, public goods create an incentive problem that the market system cannot resolve. Suppose that instead of the government, a private company decides to sell the national security service for a fee. Imagine that! The representatives of Sleep Safe, Inc. would go to Abe's house with their sales pitch: "For a mere $10,000 per year, we promise to shoot down any enemy bomber that enters our air space, so you can sleep safe at night." Then Abe would think to himself, "Why should I pay this company any money? If my neighbor Brad pays that $10,000 and if the company shoots down the enemy's airplanes, then I will be protected all the same." Now, the problem is that Brad is thinking exactly the same thing. Thus, even though national security is in the public interest, the great majority of individuals will try to ride for free. Hence, a free market system cannot provide this vital service.

Asymmetric Information

Frequently, a party to a transaction knows more about the subject of the transaction than the other party. For example, sellers of used cars know more about the cars than the buyers. Buyers of health insurance know more about their health than the insurance companies. Companies that produce drugs or cereals know what goes into those products. It is very difficult, if not impossible, for the average consumer to verify the contents of these goods. The same is true for the octane level of gasoline. This could create an incentive problem. Companies can put cheaper or inappropriate ingredients in the products to increase their profits. This is certainly against public interest. *Asymmetric information* creates another justification for government policy.

ASYMMETRIC INFORMATION
A situation in which a party to a transaction knows more about the subject of the transaction than the other party

A CRUCIAL QUESTION

At this point, we need to address an important question: Is the behavior described above what people *actually* follow, or is it the behavior they *should* follow in order to be rational? The answer to the second question of course is in the affirmative. If you want to be rational, you *should* consider the MC and MB of each decision and settle where MC = MB.

Figure 4: Effects of Incentives

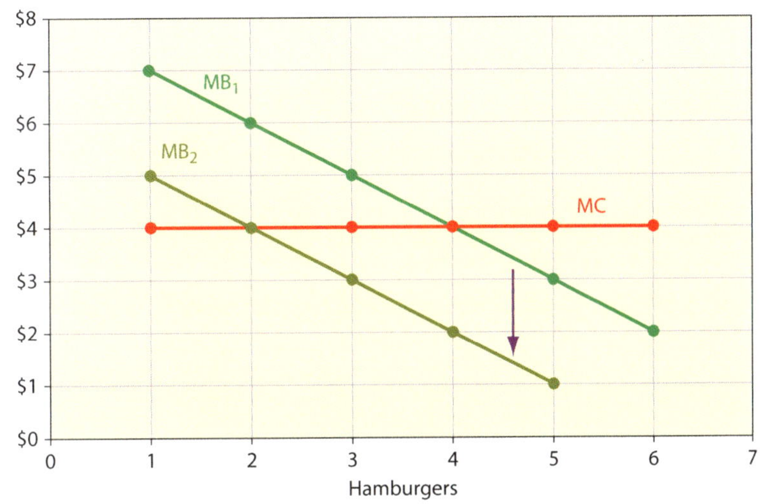

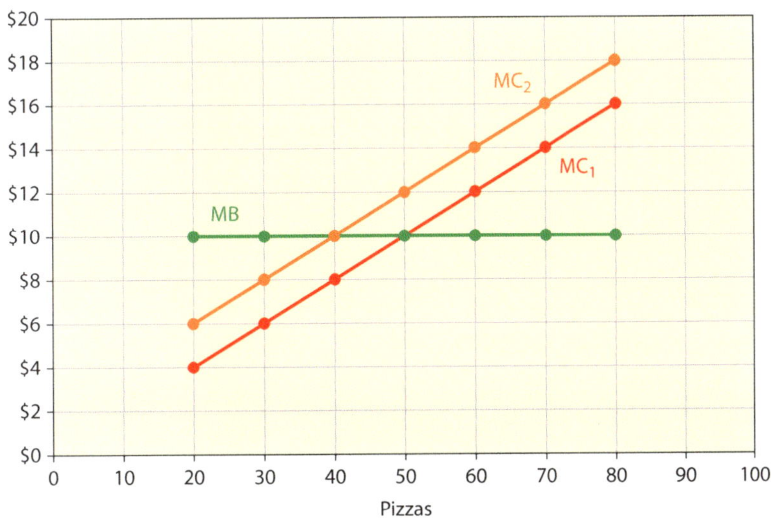

Figure 5: The Effects of Antipollution Policies

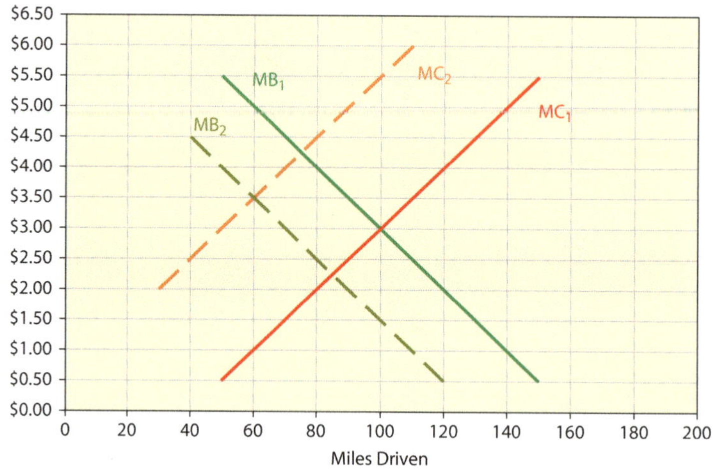

But do people actually follow such a pattern of behavior? The answer is that some people in some cases may behave irrationally. For instance, they may ignore implicit costs or factor sunk costs into their decisions. However, we assume that the society as a whole acts as if its individual members are rational, so we take a typical rational individual from the society and assume that he or she represents the whole society.

Self-Interest and Selfishness

Please note that there is a difference between people acting rationally in their own self-interest and being selfish. Rational economic behavior only means that when you are thinking of taking an action—*any action*—you should compare its marginal cost to its marginal benefit. You should only take the action if its marginal *benefit* is at least as great as its marginal *cost*. Moreover, you should be careful to exclude the sunk and fixed costs from your calculation of the marginal cost—but —include the relevant costs—both explicit and implicit. This has nothing to do with selfishness.

The argument does not imply that people do not pay to charity or help their neighbors fix their fences. What it implies is that in all such activities they compare the marginal costs and benefits to determine the level of the activity. For example, people probably pay to charity or devote their time to charitable activities until the subjective marginal benefit of such activities (for example, feeling good about themselves) exceeds their marginal costs. In fact, this theory can help explain some actual charitable behavior. That is, we would expect higher-income individuals to pay more to charities. The reason is as follows: Assume that two individuals derive the same subjective marginal benefit from giving one dollar to a charitable cause. The marginal or opportunity cost of that one dollar could be much higher for the low-income individual. That one dollar could help pay for some much-needed food or medicine. That single dollar may not be worth as much to a high-income individual who has already purchased most of his or her material needs. As a result, we will expect the higher-income individual to pay more to charities than a lower-income individual.

Scarcity

Unlimited Wants
Limited Resources
- Land
- Labor
- Capital

↓

Choice

Marginal Benefit (MB)
Marginal Cost (MC)
- Includes
  - Explicit Costs
  - Implicit Costs
- Excludes
  - Sunk Costs
  - Fixed Costs

MB > MC Increase the level of activity
MB < MC Decrease the level of activity
MB = MC Maintain the level of activity

↓

Maximum Satisfaction

Optimal decision occurs when MB = MC

Incentives matter:
Any event that changes MB or MC will affect optimal choice

Government policies are hoped to affect people's choices by changing the MB and MC of their decisions

Government policy is justified when there is a conflict between private incentives and public interest

ADDITIONAL EXAMPLES OF MARGINAL COSTS AND BENEFITS

Example 1

Suppose you want to earn a GPA that will make you happy. (Note: We did not say maximize GPA; we want to maximize satisfaction). How many hours per week will you study? Start at the beginning: Should you study the next hour? You will compare the costs and benefits of studying the next hour. Time is a limited resource. As to costs, you may have to keep the lights or the heater on for an extra hour. This will cost you 20 dollars. These are the *explicit* out-of-pocket costs. Other costs arise from the fact that you won't be able to watch TV or go to the movies *in that hour*. These are *implicit* costs. Both kinds of costs are marginal costs and opportunity costs at the same time. The $20 is a part of the marginal cost, because it is the result of the decision to study an extra hour. It is also part of the opportunity cost, because you could have bought something else worth $20 if you had not chosen to study.

There are some costs that are not relevant to your decision. You will not take into account the rent of your room or the insurance premium on your car. Although you are renting the room generally for your education, the amount of the rent will not be affected by that particular decision. Neither will the insurance premium on the car. Suppose you have borrowed some money from the bank to finance your education. Every month you have to pay interest to the bank. The amount of interest paid depends on some benchmark national interest rate, which jumps up and down. So your interest payments are not really fixed *in general* from month to month, but still unrelated to this particular decision. These are all *fixed* costs.

The moving cost that you incurred at the beginning of the year is also irrelevant to your decision. It is *sunk*; you cannot recover it no matter what you do. It is broadly relevant to your education, but not important to the decision at hand.

Suppose that if you study an extra hour, your GPA goes up by a certain amount. The marginal benefit is the pleasure you derive from that extra GPA. This is subjective. You will study that extra hour if you perceive MB≥MC.

Example 2

Suppose you bought a restaurant, perhaps one of two or three in the city. You are open from 11 a.m. to 10 p.m. You are wondering whether to keep the restaurant open for a few additional hours. What if you go until 11 p.m. rather than 10 p.m.? You should compare the costs and benefits related only to *that one additional hour*, nothing else. Let's see what this entails.

We'll start with the *marginal costs*. They could be either explicit or implicit as follows:

- The cost of additional labor, materials, electricity, drinks, and so on. These are the *explicit* costs.
- Perhaps you should be there yourself to oversee the operation. This will involve lost opportunities to do something else. You could have watched professional wrestling on TV, or you could have worked somewhere else and made some money. This is the *implicit* cost. *Whenever a firm uses its own inputs to produce something, it incurs implicit costs.* This is because it could have sold or rented those inputs to someone else and received money for them.

Note that these are all marginal costs, or opportunity costs, and forward looking: all are related to that additional hour. These are the costs relevant to your decision. There are certain costs that will not be affected by your decision to stay open an extra hour. The recurrent ones are the *fixed costs*. They could be either explicit or implicit.

- You are paying interest of $300 per month to the bank for the business loan you took out to buy the oven. *(Explicit cost)*
- You are paying an insurance premium of $200 per month that does not depend on the number of hours of operation. *(Explicit cost)*
- You own the shop. If you had rented it to someone else, you could have made $1500 per month, the going rate in the neighborhood. This is the best you could have done. So this should also count as part of your total cost. In other words, if you do not make at least this much money, you will rent the shop to someone else. *(Implicit cost)*
- None of these will change as a result of operating the store one more hour, so they will not affect your decision. There are other costs that are also irrelevant to your decision: *sunk costs*. They could be either explicit or implicit.
- Two years ago when you were thinking of buying the restaurant, you paid $5,000 to a CPA to figure out the fair market value of the property. That money is gone forever! *(Explicit cost)*
- You spent a lot of time last year researching the cheapest refrigerators and stoves. *(Implicit cost)*

You cannot recover these costs, and they are not recurrent. (The money you have paid to buy the shop and the appliances are sunk, to the extent that you cannot recover the original purchase price. If you paid $5,000 to buy the freezer—and now you cannot sell it for more than $1,000—then the remaining $4,000 is sunk.]

	Marginal Cost	Fixed Cost	Sunk Cost
Explicit	Wages, materials, electricity, etc.	Interest, insurance	CPA fee
Implicit	Own labor	Implicit rent, normal profit	Own search time

Example 3

A lot of electric and natural-gas utilities in the United States provide rebates to their residential customers if they replace their old appliances with new energy-efficient ones. Some utilities may also offer to remove and haul the customers' old refrigerators to make buying a new appliance even more attractive. For example, suppose your electric utility company offers $100 if you buy a new energy-efficient refrigerator. It also offers to remove the old one from your house. This reduces the marginal cost of buying a new appliance. If the price of a new refrigerator is $350, you only pay $250 for it. This reduces your explicit marginal cost. Hauling of your old appliance reduces the implicit "hassle" cost of the decision.

What is the effect of this policy? First let's look at the customer side. The policy is predicated on the assumption that people respond to incentives. It attempts to affect both the marginal cost and marginal benefit of recycling old refrigerators to customers. By reducing the explicit and implicit marginal costs of buying new refrigerators to their residential customers, the company hopes that a large portion of its residential customers will opt for the new appliance. Moreover, since the new refrigerators will use less electricity, they will help reduce the customers' electric bills. Customers will consider these avoided electricity costs as the marginal benefit of the new refrigerators. This will give them further incentives to recycle their old refrigerators.

Now we'll take a look at the company side of the policy. The marginal cost of this policy for the company could be huge. Suppose, for instance, one million customers decide to take advantage of the offer and recycle their appliances. Then the company incurs $50 million in direct rebate expenses and an additional amount in hauling away the customers' old refrigerators and getting rid of them. Suppose this costs the company another $10 million. What is the marginal benefit of this policy to the company? It is the avoided cost of having to spend tens of millions of dollars on capital equipment to produce electricity. Suppose without this policy, the utility had to spend $100 million on new capital. Therefore, it is economically rational to spend $60 million to encourage customers to reduce their electricity consumption, in order to save $100 million on the purchase of new equipment.

TO SUMMARIZE

1. Microeconomics studies how individuals faced with scarcity make decisions to achieve maximum satisfaction.
2. Scarcity is the fact that human material wants are unlimited, while the resources to satisfy them are limited.
3. Scarcity necessitates choice or decision.
4. In making a decision, decision makers consider and compare the costs and benefits arising from that decision.
5. The cost arising from a decision is called the *marginal cost* of that decision. Marginal cost is the same as *opportunity cost*: the value of the best alternative foregone because of a decision.
6. Marginal costs include both explicit and implicit costs.
7. Explicit costs are out of-pocket cash outlays. Implicit costs are benefits foregone without an explicit monetary expenditure.
8. Marginal costs exclude sunk and fixed costs.
9. The benefit arising from a decision is called the marginal benefit of that decision. It is the value of the decision to the decision maker.
10. When the decision is to buy something, the marginal benefit is the maximum amount of money you are willing and able to pay to get it. The marginal cost is the amount you actually have to pay.
11. When the decision is to sell something, the marginal benefit is the amount of money you actually receive for it. The marginal cost is the minimum amount of money you are willing to accept for it.
12. A decision maker will increase the level of an activity if its marginal benefit outweighs its marginal cost. He or she will reduce the level of activity if the marginal cost of the activity exceeds the marginal benefit.
13. A decision maker will neither increase nor decrease the level of an activity if the marginal benefit of the activity just equals its marginal cost. This is the optimal level of the activity, resulting in *maximum satisfaction.*
14. Incentives matter. A change in the level of marginal cost or marginal benefit will cause changes in the level of activity.
15. Government policy may be justified if private incentives of individuals are in conflict with public interest.
16. Government policy affects the private marginal costs and benefits of individuals' decisions.

EXERCISES

In the following exercises, the term *rational* is used in the sense defined in this chapter, i.e., making decisions by comparing marginal benefits to marginal costs and measuring the latter by including explicit and implicit costs and excluding sunk and fixed costs.

Question 1

You have to take a business trip to Los Angeles. Will you fly, or will you take your own car? What factors should you consider in making this decision? Relate your answers to the marginal cost and marginal benefit of this decision.

Question 2

They say it is more expensive for a high-income professional to take a bus than to fly in a long trip. Why do you think this makes sense?

Question 3

Why do people tend to eat more in all-you-can-eat restaurants? Is this rational?

Question 4

Suppose a university representative tells the incoming freshmen "Try to use the gym and other sport facilities as much as you can. Not only can you use them for free, you have already paid for them through your tuition." Is this advice rational?

Question 5

Jennifer owns a hairdresser shop that is open Monday through Saturday. She is renting the space for \$1,000 per month. She also pays \$500 per month for the loan she took out to buy the equipment. Her monthly liability insurance premium is a flat \$250 plus \$100 times the number of days per week the shop is open for business. Two years ago when she was thinking of renting the space, she paid \$1,500 to a CPA to do a cost-benefit study for her. The operating cost (labor, electricity, water, materials) is \$200 per day. On Sundays Jennifer teaches piano to children, making \$200 per day. Jennifer is thinking of opening the store for business on Sundays, in which case she will make \$250 per Sunday. Assume a month has four Sundays in it.

a. With respect to this decision, what is the sunk cost?
b. With respect to this decision, what is the fixed cost?
c. What is the explicit marginal cost of this decision?
d. What is the implicit marginal cost of this decision?
e. What is the marginal benefit of this decision?
f. Should Jennifer open the store for business on Sundays?

Question 6

Governor Schwarzenegger has in mind an energy policy for California that is known as the "33 by 2020 program." This means that by the year 2020, about one third (33%) of all electricity in California should be generated from renewable sources such as wind power, wood, waste, and solar. As an economist working in the state of California, evaluate/criticize this proposal in light of what you have learned in this chapter. (Hint: Think about the MB and MC of the proposal.)

Question 7

President George W. Bush wanted every student in the United States to have access to a high-speed Internet connection. Comment on this policy goal. (Hint: See the previous hint.)

Question 8

We have learned that a government intervention in the marketplace may be justified whenever there is a conflict between private incentives and public interest. In the following situations, identify the conflict that the indicated government policy intends to solve. For the following cases, explain which private party's incentives are in conflict with public interest, and why.

a. Food and Drug Administration approval of the drugs produced by pharmaceutical corporations.
b. Smog check.
c. Seat belt laws.
d. Helmet laws for cyclists.
e. Vitamin D in milk.
f. Free or subsidized education.
g. Fluoride in the drinking water.
h. Generous tax incentives for research and development activities.
i. Providing tax incentives to farmers to induce them to prevent contaminated agricultural water from entering into public waterways.
j. Provision of subsidies and tax incentives for the production of energy from renewable sources (wind, waste, water, solar).

Question 9

Assume that the University of California is planning to construct a new building for the medical school in Sacramento. Among other things, this requires purchasing a large piece of land in Sacramento. Someone suggests that since the university has a large piece of land in Davis already, building the new medical school there would be much cheaper. This would avoid having to buy the Sacramento land. What do you think about this advice? (Hint: Would it be cheaper necessarily to build in Davis if we include the implicit cost of the Davis land?)

Question 10

Identify the sunk, fixed, and marginal costs with respect to the following decision. Be sure to distinguish between explicit and implicit costs. You are thinking of driving to Oakland to visit your uncle this coming Sunday. You purchased your car two years ago for $25,000, but its current market price is only $15,000. Your monthly interest and insurance payments on the car total $2,500. You work for the university bookstore on Saturdays and Sundays, earning $100 per day. The car loses $50 in value for each trip to Oakland. Additionally, you will spend $100 on gas.

Question 11

Identify the sunk, fixed, and marginal costs with respect to the following decision. Be sure to distinguish between explicit and implicit costs. You decide to buy a car. You start looking for good deals in the newspapers, calling different sellers and driving to several dealerships. You spend a lot of time and energy negotiating with the dealers. Finally, you buy a car for $25,000.

Question 12

Identify the sunk, fixed, and marginal costs with respect to the following decision. Be sure to distinguish between explicit and implicit costs. You own and operate an auto repair/lubrication shop. Weekends you spend time with your family. You own the shop, so you do not incur any interest or rent payments. But you have to pay a base premium of $300 per month for liability insurance, plus $20 for each day you open the shop for business. Your daily cost of electricity, labor, and materials is $250. Moreover, the noise and oil spill from your shop annoys the customers of the neighboring businesses. For each day that you are open, other businesses lose a total of $400 in profits.

Question 13

Melissa owns and operates a coffee shop. She hires a worker for $700 per month. Melissa can find a job very easily for $800 per month in a gourmet restaurant. The cost of materials per month is about $500. The monthly rent, insurance, and interest payments amount to $800. These are contractual obligations that may take three to four months to renegotiate. Melissa is currently earning $2,400 in sales revenue. Should she shut down the business?

Question 14

George has nine kids who either work on the farm or help inside the house. Now that we are in the 21st century, he decides to send some of the children to school. The cost of schooling for each child is $2,000 per year. There are no government subsidies in this small agricultural community. The least productive of all the kids is little Liam. His efforts in cleaning the barn and the surrounding area add only $500 per year to the farm income. Next is Megan, with her $750 per year contribution to farm income. However, if Liam goes to school, he could add $3,500 to the family income by being able to read and write the bills, sales orders, lawsuits, and so on. Once there is one literate person in the family, Megan's contribution to family income will only be $3,000 per year if she is educated. The following table shows the figures for every child.

	Contribution of Each Kid to Farm Income	Additional Farm Income if the Kid Goes to School
Liam	$500	$3,500
Megan	$750	$3,000
Peter	$1,000	$2,500
Brian	$1,250	$2,000
Stephan	$1,500	$1,500
Susan	$1,750	$1,000
David	$2,000	$500
Bartholomew	$2,250	$0
Gabriel	$2,500	$0

a. How many kids will George send to school?
b. If the government provides a subsidy of $1,000 per kid, how many kids will George send to school?
c. If the government makes education free, will George send all the kids to school?
a. Why do we have so much illiteracy in third world countries?

b. Would you expect the illiteracy rate to be higher in the agricultural sector compared to the manufacturing sector?

Question 15

Kalvatin just got married and his father gave him a little farm in Nowheria, a developing country. Being poor, the family cannot afford to hire farm workers. Kalvatin and his wife Masmasak work on the farm themselves, and dream of having enough kids of their own to help them on the farm. If the child is a boy, he will work on the farm or tend to the animals; if a girl, she will weave carpets. Children do not come free. They need to be fed and clothed. These costs should not be too high since most of the food and clothing will come from the farm products or domestic activities. Moreover, due to poor health and sanitation conditions in Nowheria, out of every two or three children born, one dies in infancy. This puts another strain on Masmasak's health. However, since the position of women in Nowheria is not high, this is not of great concern to the "family." It is very difficult to put monetary values on costs and benefits in this situation. Therefore, the following table presents some hypothetical numbers.

Kids	Contribution of Each Kid to Farm Income (In Local Currency)	Cost of Each Kid (In Local Currency)
1	150	60
2	140	60
3	130	60
4	120	60
5	110	60
6	100	60
7	90	60
8	80	60
9	70	60
10	60	60
11	50	60

a. How many children will the family plan to have?

b. Some commentators seem to imply that having too many kids by the people of poor third world countries is irrational. "Since they are mostly illiterate, they don't know what they are doing," the commentators say. Are Kalvatin and Masmasak irrational in their decision about the number of kids?

c. Will educating Kalvatin and Masmasak about the world population problem change their decision about the number of children they want to have?

d. Some people tend to believe that overpopulation is the cause of poverty. Do you think overpopulation is the cause of poverty—or is it poverty that is the cause of overpopulation?

e. Some United Nations population experts believe the reason for overpopulation in third world countries is that those people just do not have knowledge of birth control techniques. They travel to such countries and organize seminars to educate the locals about these techniques (apparently these activities have caused riots in some countries.) Will Kalvatin and Masmasak change their decision about the number of kids after attending such seminars?

f. Believe it or not, there are people in some poor third world countries who use a particular population control technique called infanticide—the killing of infants. If the above table showed the data for such a family (our family friends Kalvatin and Masmasak are too humane to even consider such a thing), at what point would they consider such an option? Would the UN efforts mentioned above have any effect on infanticide?

Question 16

Taking the previous question as a hint, why do families in the more advanced capitalist countries have an average of no more than two to three kids?

Question 17

Suppose that several years ago Peter dropped out of elementary school and started to work in his father's hardware store. Because of the increased competition in this industry, Peter is now thinking of going back to adult school, hoping to get a degree and change his career. Going to schools has benefits. Each year of schooling will give Peter some knowledge and skills, enabling him to earn a higher salary. Going to school, however, is costly. The explicit costs include the cost of tuition, books, and transportation. The implicit costs include the salary that he could earn if he worked somewhere instead of going to school. As the number of years of schooling increases, the amount of this lost salary also increases. For example, if he goes on to college after earning his high school diploma, then he will lose an hourly wage that might be slightly above minimum wage. On the other hand, if he continues with his education after receiving his bachelor's degree, the lost wages will be much more substantial.

a. Draw a hypothetical MB and MC graph for Peter with the number of years of schooling on the horizontal axis.
b. Using the above premise as a hint, explain why more people continue with their education after earning their high school diplomas than after receiving their bachelor's degree.
c. Suppose the government provides a better education subsidy so that the tuition fees are substantially reduced. How will this policy affect Peter's decision about the number of years of schooling?

Question 18

Why do more people use public transportation when the price of gasoline increases? Answer this question in terms of marginal cost and benefit of driving. (Hint: Think of marginal benefit as an avoided cost.)

Question 19

In many developing countries, farmers may want to have a lot of children in order to use them on the farm. What do you think would happen to birth rates in these countries if their governments offered farming equipment to these framers at dirt-cheap prices? (Hint: Think of marginal benefit as an avoided cost.)

Question 20

Would more or fewer people install solar panels on their roofs to generate electricity if the price of electricity increases? Why? (Hint: Think of marginal benefit as an avoided cost.)

Question 21

Of all the medical students in the United States, only about 10 percent choose to become primary-care physicians. The great majority choose more lucrative specialties, such as dermatology, ophthalmology, or neurology. By contrast, in some other countries, about 30 percent of medical students become primary-care physicians. Why do you think this is the case? Answer this question by considering the marginal cost of being a primary-care physician. The marginal benefit of becoming a primary-care physician is probably the same in both countries. The explicit marginal cost of going into different specialties could also be the same across countries. Some other implicit marginal costs, such as time and effort spent, should also be the same. For example, in most countries it takes about ten years to become a neurosurgeon. There must be another implicit marginal cost that is causing this problem. To resolve the puzzle, consider this fact: In other countries, the incomes of specialists are about 30 percent higher than those of primary-care physicians. In the United States it is 300 percent higher. How does this fact affect the marginal cost of becoming a primary-care physician?

CHAPTER 3

Social Costs and Benefits: Economic Efficiency

INTRODUCTION AND REVIEW

IN THE LAST chapter, we developed a simple model of rational economic behavior. We observed that the existing resources could not satisfy human material wants. We called this scarcity. Scarcity at the national level results in scarcity at the level of individual decision makers. Each decision maker, be it a consumer or a producer, has access only to a limited amount of land, labor, and capital. Time is also a constraining factor. We assumed that individual decision makers are rational, in the sense that they compare the *marginal private benefit (MB)* of each activity to its *marginal private cost (MC)*. They increase the level of the activity if MB > MC and they reduce it if MB < MC. They leave the level of activity unchanged if MB = MC. This last condition defines the optimal level of the activity, because it results in maximum satisfaction.

MARGINAL PRIVATE BENEFIT
The benefit of a decision that accrues to the decision maker alone.

MARGINAL PRIVATE COST
The cost of a decision that is born by the decision maker alone.

The government enters the picture whenever the activities carried out by decision makers are in conflict with public interest. In other words, the activities carried out by individuals based on their own private marginal costs and benefits yield an outcome that is not optimal from the society's point of view. In this case, government policies to change decision makers' behavior by somehow changing the MB or MC of their activities may be justified. The last chapter concentrated on the first aspect of this issue: namely, the determination of the level of activity chosen by an individual. This chapter will discuss the second aspect, the definition of a socially optimal outcome.

It should be realized that ultimately economics is a social science concerned with people's decisions about production, exchange, and consumption. We analyze individual behavior in order to understand social issues. We like to know the social consequences of the decisions made by millions of individual producers and consumers who use the society's scarce resources to achieve maximum satisfaction of material wants. Since human wants are unlimited—while resources are limited—we like to know how to use these scarce resources in order to maximize the society's well-being. Economics is concerned with just that.

Economics is concerned with how to make the best use of the society's scarce resources to achieve maximum satisfaction of material wants.

Recall from Chapter 1 that all societies must answer three fundamental economic questions of what goods and services to produce, how to produce them, and how to distribute them among members of the society. If you think about it, we cannot answer these questions without having a social objective in mind. That social objective is the maximum satisfaction of material wants for the members of the society. The three questions should be answered with this social objective in mind. How do we guarantee that the kinds and quantities of different goods produced are what people want the most so that they derive maximum satisfaction from them, the production methods used to produce them are the efficient ones, and the distribution of the goods among people is desirable? We will start answering these questions by defining an important concept called *economic efficiency*. To understand this concept, we need to know the definitions of marginal social costs and benefits.

MARGINAL SOCIAL COST AND BENEFIT

MARGINAL SOCIAL COST
The cost of a decision that is born by the whole society.

The definition of *marginal social cost (MSC)* is similar to that of marginal private cost.

The marginal social cost of producing a good or service is the amount of "all the other things" that the society must sacrifice in order to produce this good or service.

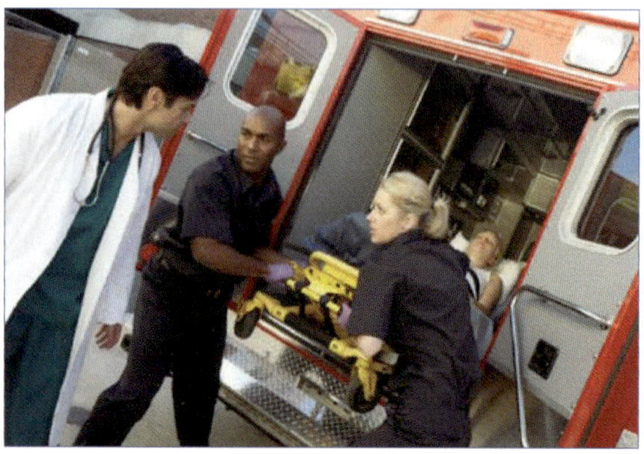

What are the social costs and benefits of building a local hospital?

What are "all the other things?" Suppose we want to build a new hospital in our city. It will take two years, and a lot of land, labor, and capital to build it. During this time period and with all those resources, we could build three modern high schools, four beautiful parks, or two nice highways connecting our downtown to the suburban areas. The marginal social cost of building the hospital is the most highly valued alternative we must give up to be able to build it. We have sufficient number of high schools and parks. The traffic jams in our city, though, drive our citizens crazy. So, for our citizens, the most highly valued alternative would be the construction of the two highways. The forgone highways will be a part of the marginal social cost of building the hospital.

But there is more. People living in the area will experience heavier traffic. The sound of ambulance sirens in the middle of the night will bother the neighbors. Neighbors may be concerned that contaminated materials might be dumped in front of their homes, causing health problems. Residential property values may drop, because of the proximity to the hospital. Recall from Chapter 2 that these problems are called externalities. These costs are also a part of the marginal social cost of building the hospital. The marginal social cost is the cost borne by the society as a whole.

MARGINAL SOCIAL BENEFIT
The benefit of a decision that accrues to the whole society.

The definition of *marginal social benefit (MSB)* is also similar to that of marginal private benefit.

The marginal social benefit of producing a good or service is the maximum amount of "all the other things" that the society is willing and able to sacrifice in order to produce this good or service.

Without this hospital, the patients have to drive to a nearby city for medical treatment. Because of this, many lives could be lost in emergency situations. The marginal benefit of building the hospital is that all these problems will be avoided (recall that avoided cost is a benefit). The citizens are willing to forgo construction of three highways in order to build this hospital. The three highways, then, constitute the marginal social benefit of building the hospital.

Wind farming in Denmark. Wind farming provides renewable electricity but also mars scenery and affects bird migration.

Consider some other examples. The marginal social benefit of building an airport in a city is the cost the passengers would avoid by not having to ride a train or a bus to or from the city. The marginal cost would include the hospitals, schools, parks, or the bridges that the city has to sacrifice, because it does not have enough labor and capital to build them all. However, once the airport is built, the noise will bother the households who live in the vicinity of the airport, and they will experience a reduction in their home values. This cost should also be included in the marginal social cost of building the airport.

As another example, consider building wind farms to produce electricity. Since wind is a clean renewable resource, the marginal social benefit of this project would be the avoided air pollution. The marginal social cost would include all the other goods that the society has to forgo to be able to produce this wind farm. But it will also include the damaged scenery and the loss of life for some animals, such as the birds that get caught in the blades. Externalities are important issues that deserve a chapter of their own. We will talk about them in Chapter 12. Until then, to make our stories simple, we will ignore them.

Recall that, to achieve maximum satisfaction, an individual decision maker will carry out a particular activity until the marginal cost of the last unit of the activity just equals its marginal benefit. Similarly, a society will achieve maximum satisfaction if it produces goods and services up to the point where their marginal social costs just equal their marginal social benefits. Maximum satisfaction for the society as a whole is called *allocative efficiency*, also called *economic efficiency*.

ALLOCATIVE EFFICIENCY/ ECONOMIC EFFICIENCY *Allocating the society's scarce resources to different economic activities in such a way as to produce the kinds and quantities of goods and services that result in maximum satisfaction for the members of the society.*

ECONOMIC EFFICIENCY

A little reflection will convince you that since human wants are unlimited, for the society to achieve maximum satisfaction of material wants given the amounts of scarce resources available, three conditions must be satisfied:

1. **Full employment.** First, we need to have full employment. What is full employment?

    Full employment means there is a job for anyone who is willing and able to work.

    Suppose there are 100 jobs out there and 100 people who are willing and able to work. We call this situation *full employment*. People who are willing and able to work are collectively called the *labor force*. Obviously, unemployment means lost potential output. If we had 110 people willing to have jobs, 10 of them would not find any jobs. These 10 people would be willing to work and produce goods and services. Those goods and services would go toward satisfying some human wants. But since there are no jobs for these people, we lose the goods and services they could have produced.

Properly trained and well-managed employees are a key element to ensuring productive efficiency.

2. **Productive efficiency.** It is not enough to employ everyone in the society who is looking for a job. What if we hire everyone but we mismanage them, or we use the wrong production techniques, or we combine resources in incorrect proportions? In those cases, the resources will not produce their maximum potential. Therefore, it will take more resources than necessary to produce a given amount of output. In some countries you can see a lot of underemployment: people are employed, but not used to their full potential. For example, 50 people produce a good that can be produced by only one person. In that case, those 50 people are not producing the maximum they can. We could take 49 of them to other industries and increase production in those industries, without experiencing any reduction in the quantities of this particular good. Moreover, in this way the particular good can be produced with the least amount of resources: just one person.

   Productive efficiency means that all the resources are fully employed and the employed resources are producing the most they can.

   The flip side of this condition is that if we have productive efficiency, we are using the lowest possible amount of resources to produce a given amount of goods and services. Note that to have productive efficiency, we need to have full employment first. We will not have productive efficiency if we have unemployment, even if the employed resources are producing the most they can.

3. **Allocative efficiency**. Still this is not enough. With productive efficiency, we may not achieve maximum satisfaction of human wants if we don't produce the right kinds of goods and services.

   Allocative efficiency means allocating our scarce resources to different economic activities in such a way as to produce the kinds and quantities of goods and services that result in maximum satisfaction for the members of the society.

   Note that allocative efficiency includes productive efficiency as a prerequisite. In other words, we cannot have allocative efficiency if we don't have productive efficiency. We want to produce the mix of goods and services we want *the most*. Since we always prefer more to less, we cannot possibly prefer a mix of goods that is produced while we have unemployed or mismanaged resources.

You should be aware of the difference between the two concepts of productive and economic efficiencies. Productive efficiency is about *resource use*. It means using the least amount of resources to produce a given level of output, or—essentially the same thing—producing the most amount of output from a given level of resources. Economic efficiency, on the other hand, is about *people's well-being*. Thus, there is more subjectivity in the latter concept. You could be highly productively efficient without being economically efficient.

PRODUCTION POSSIBILITIES FRONTIER

Recall that economic efficiency is achieved when the marginal social cost of producing a good or service just equals its marginal social benefit. Since we are assuming that there are no externalities, the marginal social cost of producing a good or service just equals the amounts of all the other goods and services the society has to sacrifice to produce it. We can describe the marginal social cost of production by a device called the *production possibilities frontier (PPF)*, also called the production possibilities curve. This curve shows the maximum amounts of certain goods a society can produce, given the production levels of some other goods. The whole argument can be demonstrated by assuming that the society produces only two goods. You can think of these two goods as two different *kinds* of goods, such as manufacturing and agricultural goods, wartime and peacetime goods, or consumer and investment goods. We make two assumptions in drawing the PPF. First, we assume that there are fixed amounts of resources available. These include, as you recall, land, labor, and capital. Second, we assume that technology is fixed. Simply stated, *technology* means knowing how to produce things. We are essentially assuming that the time frame is too short to expand the resource base or to learn more or better ways of producing the goods.

PRODUCTION POSSIBILITIES FRONTIER (PPF)
A graph showing the maximum amount of a good or service the society can produce given the production amounts of other goods and services.

TECHNOLOGY
Knowledge of how to produce things.

Consider the following hypothetical data on two goods, which we will call X and Y. Suppose that capital and land used in each industry are specific to that industry, and are immobile between industries. This is not a bad assumption, especially in the short period of time on which we are concentrating. For example, agricultural machines and equipment cannot be used in computer production. Or, a small piece of land that is suitable for a manufacturing plant in a city can hardly be converted into agricultural land. Assume, however, that labor is mobile between the two sectors. Assume further that there are five million workers in the country's labor force. The following table shows the maximum quantities of output that different amounts of labor can produce in the two industries:

Number of Workers (Millions)	Quantity of X	Number of Workers (Millions)	Quantity of Y
0	0	0	0
1	10	1	16
2	20	2	24
3	30	3	28
4	40	4	30
5	50	5	31

From the information above, we can construct the PPF for the country as follows. If the country does not produce any X, all five million workers will be in the Y industry producing 31 units of Y. If the country decides to shift one million workers from the Y industry to the X industry, production of X will increase to 10 units and the production of Y will decrease to 30 units. If we continue shifting labor from the Y industry to the X industry, we can determine all the numbers we need for the PPF, as in the following table.

X	Y
0	31
10	30
20	28
30	24
40	16
50	0

Plotting the above numbers yields the PPF in Figure 1.

Figure 1: Production Possibilities Frontier

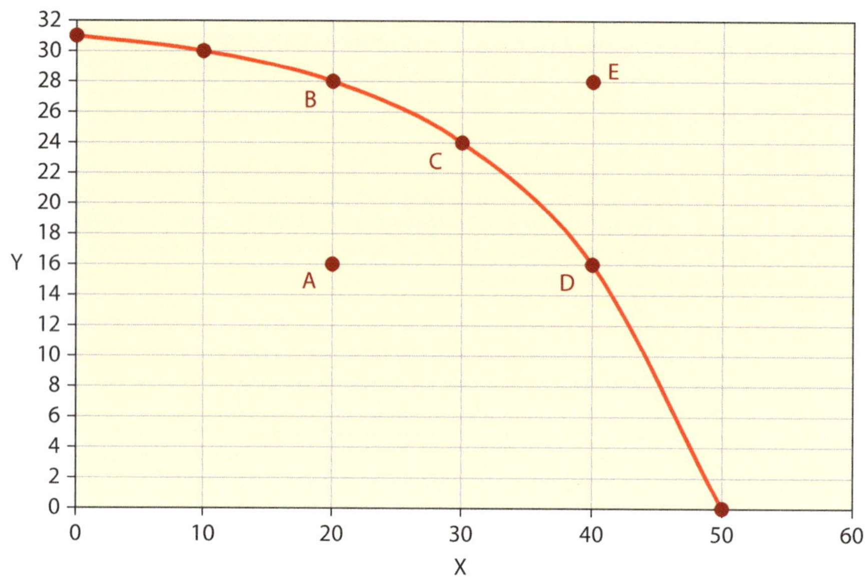

Figure 1 shows that if we produce 31 units of Y, we will not be able to produce any X. At this point, all of the society's resources are fully and efficiently employed in the Y industry. If we decide to produce 10 units of X, we have to shift some of those resources (one million workers in our example) from the Y industry to the X industry. Therefore, the maximum amount of Y that we can produce drops to 30 units. The converse is also true. If we produce 50 units of X, then we cannot produce any Y. If we produce 40 units of X, then the maximum amount of Y that we can produce will be 16 units. *The PPF shows the maximum possible production of Y for any given level of X production, and the maximum possible production of X for any given level of Y production.* Six aspects of this graph should be noted.

First, all the points *inside* the PPF are attainable. An example is point A in Figure 1. However, inside the frontier we do not have productive efficiency. We either have unemployment, or we have full employment but we are mismanaging our resources, or we have unemployment *and* are mismanaging the resources we are using. We are not maximizing Y for a given X, and X for a given Y.

Second, the points *along* the curve are attainable. Examples are points B, C, and D in Figure 1. Along the curve we have productive efficiency. All the resources are employed and used efficiently.

Third, points *outside* the curve are not attainable. An example is point E. We don't have enough resources or know-how to produce the combinations of the two goods outside the frontier, no matter how hard we try. That is why the curve is called a *frontier*.

Fourth, the *slope* of the frontier is negative, due to scarcity. Since we have a limited amount of resources and technology in the short run, and since along the frontier they are all fully and efficiently employed, to produce more of one good we have to reduce production of the other. This is because we have to shift some resources from one industry to the other. For example, to move from point C to point D, we have to sacrifice 8 units of Y to produce 10 additional units of X. The 8 units of Y is *the marginal social cost* of producing the 10 extra units of X due to scarcity.

Economists usually measure marginal cost as the cost *per unit* increase in output. For example, in the above case to increase X by 10 units we have to sacrifice a total of 8 units of Y. Therefore, for each unit of additional X we have to sacrifice 0.80 units of Y. This is obtained by dividing the change in Y by the change in X:

$$\Delta Y/\Delta X = (16-24)/(40-30) = (-8)/(+10) = -0.80$$

We say that the marginal social cost of X in terms of Y is $MSC_X = 0.80$ units of Y per unit of X.

Fifth, the curve is bowed outward, or ***concave*** to the origin, due to the *law of diminishing marginal product of labor*. Look at the tables above. When we hire the first one million workers in the Y industry, they can produce 16 units of Y. The second million workers can increase the production of Y by 8 units, and the third million by 4 units. Each additional unit of labor increases production by less than the previous unit. The reason for this phenomenon is that the additional units of labor get to work with a smaller fraction of the existing capital and land (recall that we assume the amount of land and labor are fixed).

LAW OF DIMINISHING MARGINAL PRODUCT OF LABOR
The same as the law of diminishing returns.

In the X industry, on the other hand, we assume constant marginal product of labor. Each additional unit of labor contributes the same amount to the production as the previous amount. This is not a realistic scenario for most industries. We are making this assumption to show you that we need diminishing returns in only one industry to have a concave PPF.

Now start with X = 0 and Y = 31. If we shift one million workers from the Y industry to the X industry, we will lose 1 unit of Y and gain 10 units of X, so that $MSC_X = 1/10 = 0.10$ units of Y. This is because these one million workers are not very productive in the Y industry, due to too many laborers working there. If we shift another one million workers from Y to X production, we will lose 2 units of Y and gain 10 units of X, resulting in $MSC_X = 2/10 = 0.20$ unit of Y. This means that the MSC_X of producing X increases, and the slope of the PPF becomes steeper as we produce more and more X. Slope should not be confused with curvature. The following table shows the marginal social cost of producing X (MSC_X), in terms of the amounts of Y that need to be sacrificed per unit of X. Even though the production of Y decreases as we increase the production of X, the MSC_X is expressed as a positive number, because the term "cost" will remind us that these are, in fact, sacrifices.

X	Y	MSC_X
0	31	
10	30	0.10
20	28	0.20
30	24	0.40
40	16	0.80
50	0	1.60

Figure 2 shows three graphs of a downward-sloping PPF. In only one case is the MSC_X increasing with the amount of X produced. The middle PPF is linear, indicating a constant MSC_X. The bottom PPF is convex. It shows that as we produce more X, the marginal social cost of producing additional units of X in terms of Y actually decreases. This last case is quite unrealistic.

Sixth, and finally, we have drawn the production possibilities curve assuming a fixed amount of resources and a given technology. If we either have more resources or better technology, the curve will ***shift*** out. We could have more resources if the amount of labor increases through migration or natural birth, or if the amount of capital increases through investment. The physical amount of land is fixed, but its productivity can increase through better cultivation techniques.

Technological progress means that we learn better ways of producing x same goods or producing new goods.

It can occur through research and development, better education, or training.

Figure 3 shows two types of shifts in PPFs. The upper graph shows a shift that is the result of an increase in the amount of resources or a technological progress that affects all industries. Such shifts are called *economic growth*. The lower graph shows a shift in the PPF that is due to technological progress in Y industry that is of no help to the X industry. Suppose, for example, that farmers discover a superior production technique that significantly increases agricultural production with the existing amount of resources. This technological advance has no use in manufacturing. Therefore, if all the resources are transferred to agriculture, more output can be produced in that industry than was possible before this technological progress. This is shown by the increase in the Y-intercept. However, if all the resources are shifted to manufacturing, we can still produce the same amount of output as before, so the X-intercept does not increase.

Figure 2: Concave, Linear, and Convex PPFs

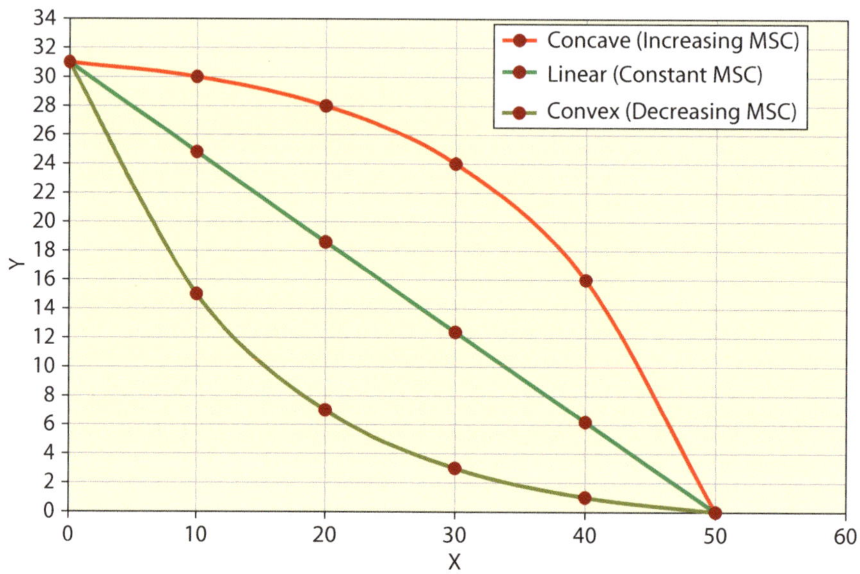

Note that even though the technological progress has taken place in the Y industry, the society can produce more of both goods. The reason for this is quite easy to understand. Now that resources are more productive in Y industry, we can shift some of them to the X industry, thereby producing more of both X and Y. This actually happened in the advanced capitalist countries during the 20th century. As new agricultural machinery and farming equipment were introduced to the agricultural sector, many workers were freed from that sector, and went on to work in manufacturing. As a result, the output of both sectors increased over time. To give you a sense of what was going on, around the beginning of the last century, about 90% of the labor force in the United States was in agriculture. Now, only about 3% of the U.S. labor force works in agriculture, but the amounts of both agricultural and manufacturing production have dramatically increased during this period.

Figure 3: A Shift in PPF Due to Economic Growth

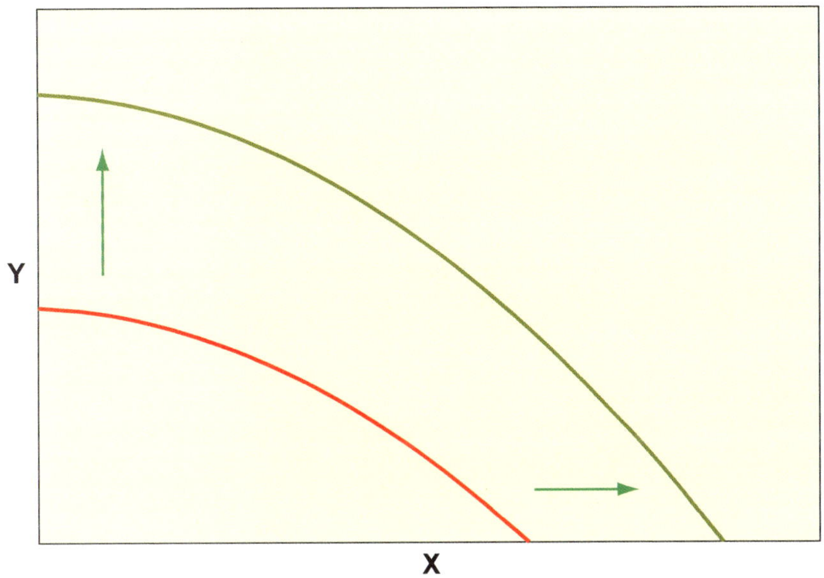

A Shift in PPF Due to Technological Progress in Y Industry

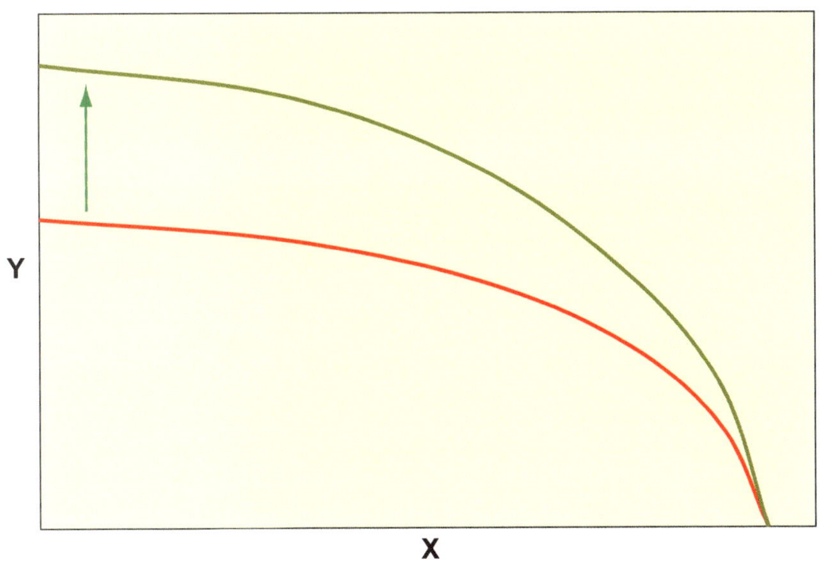

PPF and Economic Efficiency

We are now ready to describe economic efficiency in terms of the PPF. This is pretty straightforward, and we already know most of the story. There are two different ways of showing economic efficiency using a PPF.

Economic Efficiency in terms of MSC and MSB

Take a look at Figure 1 again. At point A, we don't have productive efficiency. We either have unemployment, or we have full employment but are mismanaging our resources, or we have unemployment *and* are mismanaging the resources we are using. If we eliminate productive inefficiency, we can move toward the frontier. At every point along the PPF—such as points B, C, or D—we have productive efficiency. However, not all of them are allocatively efficient. For instance, suppose that of all the points along the PPF, the combination of goods represented by point C results in maximum satisfaction for the society. By definition, then, point C is allocatively efficient.

RECESSION
A fall in the aggregate level of output or real GDP.

A situation depicted by point A can occur in an advanced capitalist economy when the economy is suffering from unemployment. This happens during a *recession*. In fact, a recession is defined as a situation in which part of the resources in the economy is unemployed or underutilized and the amounts of goods and services produced are less than the maximum possible. These episodes, however, are temporary. Recessions do not last forever. Analyses of recessions are the subject of macroeconomics. In microeconomics, on the other hand, we generally assume that the economy is on its PPF.

Assuming that the economy is on the PPF, allocative efficiency can be shown, using the concepts of marginal cost and marginal benefit. Figure 4 shows the MSC_X curve beneath the PPF for the corresponding X values. These numbers correspond to the MSC_X values we derived above.

As you recall, the marginal social benefit of anything is the maximum amount of something else that we are willing and able to give up to get it. Consider some purely hypothetical numbers. Suppose that the society is willing to give up a maximum of 16 units of Y to get the first 10 units of X. So, for each unit of additional X, the society is willing to give up 1.6 units of Y. See the following table. This is the marginal social benefit (MSB) of the first decision. Should we produce the first 10 units of X? Since we are willing to give up 1.60 units of Y, but have to give up only 0.10 units, then we go for it.

Figure 4: Allocative Efficiency

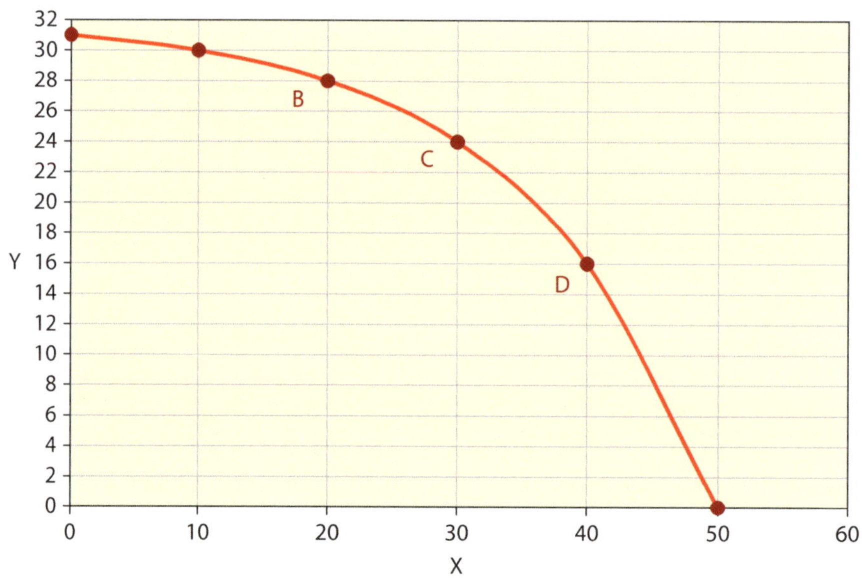

Figure 4: Allocative Efficiency—Continued

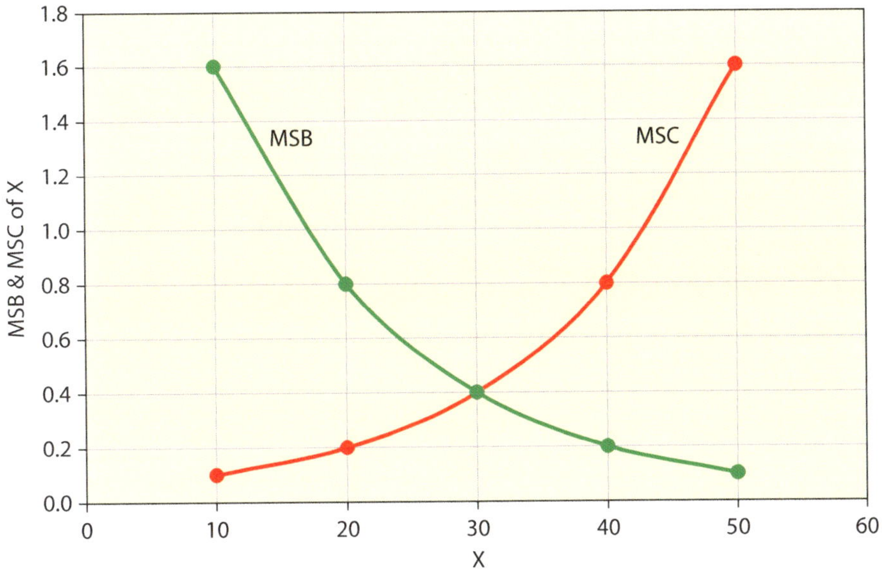

Having produced the first 10 units of X, the decision becomes whether to produce the next 10 units, increasing production to 20 units of X. Suppose the society is willing to sacrifice 0.80 units of Y for each of the next 10 units of X. Then we produce the next 10 units. Continuing this way, the society will achieve maximum satisfaction if it produces 30 units of X and 24 units of Y, where $MSC_X = MSB_X = 0.40$ units of Y per X. Therefore, allocative efficiency will be achieved at point C in Figure 4.

X	Y	MSC_X	MSB_X
0	31		
10	30	0.10	1.60
20	28	0.20	0.80
30	24	0.40	0.40
40	16	0.80	0.20
50	0	1.60	0.10

So in line with our rule for maximum satisfaction, for as long as $MSB_X > MSC_X$ the society's satisfaction will increase if we produce more X. If $MSB_X < MSC_X$, then we should reduce the production of X. If $MSC_X = MSB_X$, then we do not need to change the production since the current mix is allocatively efficient.

Pareto Efficiency

There is another easy criterion that helps us determine if an existing situation is allocatively efficient. It is based on the writings of an Italian economist named Vilfredo Pareto who analyzed these issues in the early 20th century. Since point B is not allocatively efficient, production of the mix of goods represented by that point would not result in maximum satisfaction for the members of the society. Then it must be possible to change the production mix in such a way as to make some people better off, without making anyone else worse off. Put slightly differently: If at the existing production mix it *is* possible to make someone better off—without making anyone else worse off—then the society has not achieved maximum satisfaction and, thus, the production mix is not allocatively efficient.

Furthermore, since point C is allocatively efficient, it must be possible to make some people better off without making anyone else worse off by moving from point B to point C. This would be an improvement in the society's well-being. We call this a *Pareto improvement*. Finally, at point C we have made all these Pareto improvements. Since the production at point C results in maximum satisfaction for the members of the society, we can no longer make any further Pareto improvements once at that point. Allocative efficiency is also called economic efficiency and *Pareto efficiency*. To summarize:

PARETO INEFFICIENCY
When there is room to make some people better off without making anyone else worse off.

PARETO IMPROVEMENT
When, as a result of government policy or a private transaction, some people become better off without anyone else becoming worse off.

PARETO EFFICIENCY
When it is not possible to make some people better off without making anyone else worse off.

1. **Allocative or Pareto inefficiency**: Production of a mix of goods that does not result in maximum satisfaction for the society. By reallocating resources, it is possible to produce a different mix of goods in such a way as to make some people better off, without making anyone else worse off (example: points B and D).
2. **Pareto improvement**: Reallocating resources of the society to produce a different mix of goods in such a way as to make some people better off, without making anyone else worse off (example: moving from point B to point C or from D to C).
3. **Allocative or Pareto efficiency**: A situation in which it is *not* possible to make someone better off without making someone else worse off (point C). This is also called economic efficiency.

As an aside, an economic policy or a program is said to be *Pareto improving* if that policy or program makes some people better off without hurting anybody else. What do we mean by the terms "better off" or "worse off?" Starting with the next chapter, we will analyze this question. We will see that the concept is a bit different for consumers and producers.

Efficiency as the Absence of Waste

We talk about efficiency all the time in our daily lives. We say things like "This office is run very efficiently"; "She is very efficient in organizing her time"; "Government bureaucracy is quite inefficient"; "That is not an efficient way of doing things"; or "We should use electricity more efficiently." What does *efficient* mean in these cases? It simply means the absence of waste.

Efficiency means the absence of waste.

By the same token, if we are inefficient, we are wasting something, somehow, somewhere.

Now let's talk about different concepts of efficiency in this new light. Consider the PPF in Figure 1 again. At point A, we have productive inefficiency. At that point, some productive resources are not being used to their maximum potential—they are being wasted. Under these circumstances, we can produce more X without having to produce fewer Y, or we can produce more Y without having to produce fewer X. If you want to produce more X, just hire some of the unemployed people. Or, if there are no unemployed resources but a lot of mismanagement in the X industry, then manage your resources in X production better. If the mismanagement is in the Y industry, then you can cut the fat there and shift the redundant resources to X production. The point is that you can increase X production without losing any Y, and vice versa.

Now, suppose we are at point B. At point B we are productively efficient—we are not wasting resources. At that point, to produce more Y, we must reduce our X production, and the other way around. However, point B is not allocatively efficient. So we must be wasting something. What are we wasting this time? We are wasting our time and effort in the production of a wrong mix of goods. Because of this, it is possible to make Pareto improvements by redirecting our time and efforts to produce a different mix of goods.

Beggars in Varanasi, India. Is this situation allocatively efficient?

The Two Criteria Compared

The two efficiency criteria are closely related. We can show that if $MSC_X > MSB_X$, then it is possible to make a Pareto improvement if we produce more X, and therefore, the current production mix is not Pareto efficient. To see this point, assume that the society is initially producing 10 units of X. At that point, $MSC_X > MSB_X$; thus, we should be able to make a Pareto improvement by producing more X. Recall that MSB_X is the maximum amount of Y the society is willing and able to pay to get an extra X. So think of MSB_X as the amount of Y that consumers are willing to pay to buy the next unit of X. In our example, they are willing to sacrifice a maximum of 0.80 units of Y to get the next 10 units of X. On the other hand, it takes a sacrifice of 0.20 units of Y on the part of producers to produce the next 10 units. So this is the minimum amount of Y they are willing to accept for those 10 units. Therefore, if the next 10 units of X are produced, their price will be between 0.20 and 0.80 units of Y. Producers will not accept less than 0.20 units, and consumers will not be willing to pay more than 0.80 for those 10 units.

Regardless of where the price falls in that range, one or both groups will become better off without anyone becoming worse off. If the price turns out to be equal to 0.80 units of Y, consumers will remain indifferent, but producers will become better off. If the price equals 0.20 units of Y, consumers will become better off and producers will remain indifferent. If the price falls somewhere in between, both groups will become better off. All three cases will be a Pareto improvement. Therefore, if we were producing 10 units of X, we could make a Pareto improvement by producing the next 10 units. So, the current production mix is not Pareto efficient.

Applying the same reasoning, we can conclude that no Pareto improvements are possible at point C. Therefore point C is allocatively efficient. We see that both criteria give us the same answer.

Economic Efficiency and Income Distribution

You should be aware that all of the efficiency arguments discussed above are predicated on the assumption of a given distribution of income in the society. In other words, given the existing distribution of income among the members of the society, there is a mix of goods and services—the production of which would result in the greatest amount of well-being for the society. You see that efficiency is something desirable in its own right. Even if we have a horrible income distribution, it is still a good idea to change the mix of goods and services we are producing, if doing so makes some people better off without hurting anyone else.

To put it differently, given the existing income distribution, it is always a good idea to increase the size of the social pie. Suppose the distribution of income in a country is unacceptable. Ten percent of the population earns 90 percent of the income, and the remaining 90 percent of the population live in misery. Suppose also that the economy is at point A in Figure 3. If we make efficiency improvements and move to a point like point B, then the amount of all the goods and services produced will increase. Given the same relative income distribution, everyone will receive a greater amount of goods and services.

Another related conclusion we can draw from this discussion is that, although the production of the existing mix of goods and services is allocatively efficient under the current distribution of income, the overall well-being of the society could be greater under a different income distribution. A discussion of income distributions is always rather complicated, for the simple reason that a redistribution of income always benefits those who gain the additional income, but hurts those who lose income. Therefore, strictly speaking, an income distribution generally is not Pareto improving. We need other criteria to judge whether the increase in the well-being of those who gain from redistribution exceeds the decrease in the welfare of those who lose from it. We also need some criteria to aggregate the well-being of different groups of people into an overall social welfare. These are complex issues requiring a lot of value judgments. In this book, we will concentrate on efficiency issues assuming a given distribution of income.

As the above discussion indicates, Pareto efficiency itself is a rather weak condition. For example, suppose in a country one percent of the population receives 99 percent of the income, and the remaining 99 percent of the people are destitute. A very large number of people would consider such a distribution of income unfair. They would certainly agree that some redistribution of income from the rich to the poor would improve the well-being of the society. However, since this redistribution would hurt the rich, it would not pass the Pareto test. Therefore, in this book we will use the Pareto criterion in limited cases, where it provides unambiguous results.

TO SUMMARIZE

1. Economics is concerned with how to make the best use of the society's scarce resources to achieve maximum satisfaction of material wants.
2. All societies must answer three basic economic questions: what goods and how much of each good to produce; how to produce them; and how to distribute them.
3. Full employment means all those who want to work have a job. This is a necessary condition for productive efficiency.
4. Productive efficiency means resources are fully employed and are used to their maximum potential. This is a necessary condition for economic efficiency.
5. Economic, allocative, or Pareto efficiency means production of the types and quantities of goods and services the society wants the most.
6. A production possibilities frontier (PPF) is a table, graph, or formula that shows the maximum amount of a good that can be produced, given the production levels of other goods.
7. A PPF is downward sloping due to scarcity.
8. A PPF is concave to the origin (bowed out) due to decreasing marginal productivity of resources.
9. A PPF can shift out if the quantities of resources increase or industries experience technological progress.
10. Technology is knowledge of how to produce things.
11. The marginal social cost of producing the next unit of a good—X—is the amount of other goods that the society must sacrifice to produce that unit of X.
12. The allocatively efficient quantities of goods and services are those that equalize the marginal social costs and benefits of production.
13. Efficiency means the absence of waste.
14. If the existing mix of goods produced is allocatively inefficient, then the society is wasting time and effort that could be used to improve the well-being of its members by producing the right mix.
15. Pareto improvement means reallocating the society's resources to produce a mix of goods in such a way as to make someone better off, without making someone else worse off.
16. The existing production mix is allocatively efficient if it is not possible to reallocate resources in such a way as to make someone better off, without making someone else worse off.
17. A program or policy is called Pareto improving if, as a result of that program or policy, someone becomes better off without someone else becoming worse off.
18. Efficiency analysis assumes a given income distribution.

EXERCISES

Question 1

A country has a labor force of five million workers. The country is producing two types of goods, X (Xylophones) and Y (Yoyos). The following table shows the maximum amounts of the two goods that can be produced by different numbers of workers in each industry. For example, two million workers can produce 20 units of X or 18 units of Y.

Labor (Millions of Workers)	X	Y
0	0	0
1	10	10
2	20	18
3	30	24
4	40	28
5	50	30

a. Construct and graph the country's production possibilities frontier (PPF).

b. For each level of X, compute the marginal social cost (MSC_X) of producing X in terms of Y. Graph MSC_X against the quantities of X. (Hint: MSC_X is calculated as the negative of the change in Y divided by the change in X.)

c. If the country produced 30 units of X and there were one million workers unemployed, how much Y would it be producing? Show this X-Y combination as a point on the graph.

d. Suppose the country produces X = 20 and Y = 18. Is this combination productively efficient? If not, how many workers are unemployed?

e. The following table shows the marginal social benefit of X in terms of Y:

X	Marginal Social Benefit
0	
10	1.0
20	0.8
30	0.6
40	0.4
50	0.2

Determine the economically efficient quantities of the two goods.

f. As a result of technological progress in the X industry, the workers in that industry can produce four times more than before. Find the new PPF, MSC_X, and the economically efficient quantities.

g. Forget about technological progress. Suppose instead that, as a result of a population increase, the size of the labor force increases by one million workers. If the new laborers work in the X industry, the output of X could increase by 10 units; if they work in the Y industry, the output of Y could increase by 1 unit. Find the new PPF, MSC_X, and the economically efficient quantities.

Question 2

A country has a labor force of five million workers. The country is producing two types of goods, X and Y. The following table shows the maximum amounts of the two goods that can be produced by different numbers of workers in each industry.

Labor (Million Workers)	X	Y
0	0	0
1	10	20
2	20	40
3	30	60
4	40	80
5	50	100

a. Comment on the marginal productivities of workers in the two industries.

b. Construct and graph the country's production possibilities frontier (PPF).

c. For each level of X, compute the marginal social cost (MSC_X) of producing X in terms of Y. Graph MSC_X against the quantities of X.

d. Find the economically efficient quantities of the two goods assuming the following marginal social benefits for X in terms of Y:

e.

X	Marginal Social Benefit
0	
10	4
20	3
30	2
40	1
50	0

Question 3

Suppose that labor is the only scarce resource in a country. Currently, there are 1,000 units of labor available in this country. The country produces two types of goods: military (X) and civilian (Y). Each unit of labor can produce 2 units of X or 10 units of Y.

a. Graph the production possibilities frontier for this country by completing the following table:

X	Y
0	?
500	?
1,250	?
?	2,500
?	1,250
?	0

b. Comment on the shape of the PPF (slope and curvature).

c. If X = 750, what would be the maximum production of Y? How much labor would be used in the X and Y industries? Show this point as point A on your graph.

d. Suppose the country wants to increase its X production by 250 units. What will be the total opportunity cost of doing so? What will be the opportunity cost per unit of additional X produced?

e. Can the country produce X = 1,500 and Y = 3,000? How much labor will be needed in each industry to produce these quantities? Will there be enough labor to produce these quantities, or will there be unemployment? If unemployment, how much will be the lost production in terms of X or Y?

f. Can the country produce X = 1,500 and Y = 2,000? How much labor will be needed in each industry to produce these quantities? Will there be enough labor to produce these quantities, or will there be unemployment? If unemployment, how much will be the lost production in terms of X or Y?

g. Suppose labor supply increases to 1,200 units because of a new immigration policy. Draw the new and old PPFs in the same space. (Assume the productivity of the new workers is the same as that of the old ones.)

h. Suppose that, because of technological progress in the Y industry, labor productivity increases in that industry, so that each unit of labor can now produce 12 units of Y and 2 units of X. Draw the new and old PPFs in the same space (assume labor supply = 1,000).

i. Assume no new immigration policy and no technological progress. Can the country produce X = 1,000 and Y = 6,250? How much additional labor does the country need to produce this combination? Show this graphically.

j. Assume no new immigration policy and no technological progress. Can the country produce X = 1,000 and Y = 6,250? Can it produce this amount if there is a productivity improvement in the X industry? By how much should the labor productivity increase in the X industry alone for the country to be able to produce this combination? Show this graphically.

k. Extra credit: Find the equation of the PPF.

Question 4

Are the amounts of goods and services produced in a recession productively or allocatively efficient? What is the marginal social cost of increasing the production of a good in a recession?

Question 5

Consider the following table that shows production conditions in two industries.

Number of Workers (Millions)	Quantity of X	Number of Workers (Millions)	Quantity of Y
0	0	0	0
1	5	1	10
2	9	2	18
3	12	3	24
4	14	4	28
5	15	5	30

a. Which industry exhibits diminishing returns to labor?

b. Draw the PPF.

c. Find the marginal social cost of X in terms of Y.

d. The following table shows the marginal social benefit of producing X in terms of Y. What is the allocatively efficient mix of production?

X	MSB_X
0	
5	4.0
9	3.0
12	2.0
14	1.0
15	0.5

CHAPTER 4

Supply and Demand

INTRODUCTION AND REVIEW

In the last two chapters, we learned that allocative efficiency means making the best use of resources to produce the kinds and quantities of goods that the society desires the most. This is the point on the PPF at which the marginal social cost of producing an additional unit of a good—in terms of the other good—equals its marginal benefit perceived by the society. At that point, it is not possible to change the production mix to make someone better off, without making someone else worse off. But does the society ever get there? If yes, then how? If not, can we do something about it? *Should* we do something about it? Given that there are millions of producers and millions of consumers who don't even see or know each other, how can the producers in Idaho produce what consumers want in California?

To answer these questions, we begin at the beginning. We take a look at our economy. We see that every year, millions of goods and services are produced and consumed. We ask a simple question: Why do producers make this many cars per year? Why do farmers produce this much rice? Answering such questions will help us understand why producers *actually* produce the amounts they do. But you know by now that what we actually produce may or may not be allocatively efficient. *Actually*, we may produce the wrong mix of goods. We may be at a wrong point on our PPF. After figuring out the question of why producers produce the amounts they do, we will need to go deeper to analyze the question of whether these actual amounts are most desired by the society.

In this chapter we will make two assumptions:

1. There is a large number of small but well-informed buyers and sellers. This assumption will help us avoid the complications that may arise if one or two large producers or consumers have enough power in the marketplace to affect prices. Such power is called market power, the subject of later chapters.

2. The period of time we are dealing with is too short for business firms to be able to change the size and amount of their plants and equipment. This period of time in economics is called the *short run*. Later, we will relax this assumption.

SHORT RUN
the period of time too short for the firms to be able to change the amount of their plants and equipment.

THE MARKET

MARKET
An arrangement, institution, or mechanism that brings buyers and sellers of a good or service together.

In this chapter, we will look at a *market* for a particular good or service. We'll find out why that market actually produces the amount it does, and how it determines the price of that good or service. But first, a definition:

> *A market is an arrangement, institution, or mechanism that brings buyers and sellers of a good or service together.*

Consumers demand and producers supply goods and services. A market could be global and huge, such as the foreign exchange market, in which foreign currencies are traded. It could also be local and small like your local farmers' market. Furthermore, the enormous stock market and the garage sales in your neighborhood are both examples of markets. These are all examples of institutions that bring buyers and sellers together.

On the demand side, we assume there are a large number of small consumers who are contemplating buying a particular good. As rational economic decision makers, they compare the marginal cost and marginal benefit of buying different quantities of the good. On the supply side, a large number of producers compare the marginal cost and marginal benefit of producing different quantities of the good. The two groups "meet" in the marketplace, and transactions take place.

INDIVIDUAL AND MARKET DEMAND FUNCTIONS

The market demand function is a table, curve, or equation showing the quantities of a good that consumers are *willing* and *able* to buy at different prices during a certain period of time.[1] Willingness to buy is related to the level of satisfaction. Given the price, income, and other determinants of demand, a consumer would be willing to buy a quantity that will maximize her satisfaction. Notice also the word *able*. Ability to buy means that consumers' willingness to buy something is backed by money. This is to eliminate wishful thinking and concentrate on the behavior of consumers who have an impact in the market. If someone desires to buy an expensive car but does not have enough money to pay for it, his desire will not have any effect on the price and quantity of that car in the market.

The market demand for a good is the sum of individual consumers' demand for that good. To understand the behavior of the market demand, we consider first a typical consumer's demand for a good. The quantity a consumer is willing and able to buy generally depends on the following factors:

a. Price of the good itself (called own price);
b. Consumer's income;
c. Consumer's tastes;
d. Prices of related goods (called cross prices);

1 Please see the definition of a function in the mathematical appendix.

e. Expected future own price;

f. Other.

LAW OF DEMAND
Keeping all the other determinants of demand constant, as the price of a good increases, consumers will be willing to buy a smaller quantity of the good.

We denote the quantity of the good the consumer is willing and able to buy by q and the price of the good by P. Keeping all the other determinants of demand constant, we assume that as the price of the good increases, the consumer will be willing to buy a smaller quantity of the good. This is called the *law of demand*. If we graph this relationship between P and q, we get the consumer's demand function.

Figure 1 shows the relationship between the price of a brand of breakfast cereal and the quantity demanded by a hypothetical consumer in a month, keeping all other determinants of demand constant. Note that we measure q on the horizontal axis and P on the vertical axis. Figure 1 shows that when the price per unit is $7, our hypothetical consumer is willing and able to buy 2 boxes per month. When the price is $4, she is willing and able to buy 8 boxes per month. We always need to specify a period of time to measure the quantity demanded. Two aspects of this function are important: slope and shifts.

Figure 1: Demand Function of a Hypothetical Consumer

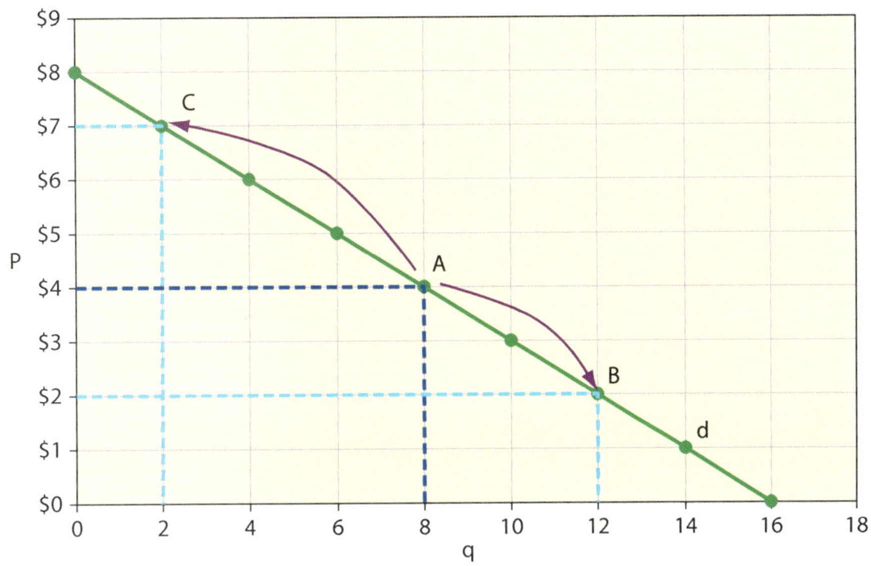

Slope of the Consumer Demand Function:

The slope is negative. The consumer will be willing and able to buy more if the price falls, and vice versa. This is for two reasons: the substitution and income effects. The *substitution effect* is the fact that when the price of a good decreases, people buy the now cheaper good instead of its substitutes. Suppose every month the consumer purchased 8 boxes of the breakfast cereal for $4 each. Now one day when she goes shopping, she realizes that the price of this cereal has gone down to, say, $2 per box. She will say to herself: "Now that this is cheaper, let's buy less oatmeal and donuts and buy more of this cereal."

SUBSTITUTION EFFECT
When the price of a good decreases, people substitute the now cheaper good for its substitutes. Conversely, when the price of a good increases, people substitute the now cheaper substitutes for the good.

The *income effect* refers to the fact that when the price of a good goes down, it is as if the consumer's income has increased. When the price of a box of cereal was $4 per box, the consumer spent a total of $4 × 8 = $32 on that brand of cereal per month. If the price decreases to $2 per box, and she keeps buying buy 8 boxes as before, she will have to spend only $2 × 8 = $16 on this brand per month. She will have $16 left in her purse to spend on all kinds of goods, including this

INCOME EFFECT
When the price of a good decreases, it is as if the consumer's income has increased. Conversely, when the price of a good increases, it is as if the consumer's income has decreased

cereal. In the above example, she spends \$8 of this \$16 on the same brand, so that at the end she spends \$2 × 12 = \$24 on it.

A change in the price of a good would cause a movement along the demand function from one point to another. In the above example, a change in price from \$4 per box to \$2 per box caused a movement from point A to point B. If the price increased from \$4 per box to \$7 per box, then we would move from point A to point C. A change in quantity demanded as a result of a change in price is called just that: a *change in quantity demanded*. This would be a movement along the curve.

CHANGE IN QUANTITY DEMANDED
A movement along the demand curve resulting from a change in price.

Shifts in the Consumer Demand Function

Changes in any of the other determinants of the demand that we kept constant while deriving and drawing it will shift the function. The shift in the whole demand curve is called the *change in demand*. A shift to the right will be an increase in demand; a shift to the left, a decrease in demand. (See Figure 2.)

CHANGE IN DEMAND
A shift in the demand curve.

Consumer Income

The effect of changes in consumer income on the demand for a good depends on whether it is a normal or an inferior good. By definition, a *normal good* is a good that we buy more of if our income increases. Most goods fall in this category, hence why we call them *normal* goods. An *inferior good* is a good that we buy less of if our income rises. This is generally because superior substitutes exist for such goods. This category includes things like second-hand goods, generic drugs, or margarine. The superior substitutes for these goods include new goods, brand-name drugs, and butter.

NORMAL GOOD
A good we buy more of if our income increases. See also inferior good.

INFERIOR GOOD
A good that we buy less of if our income rises.

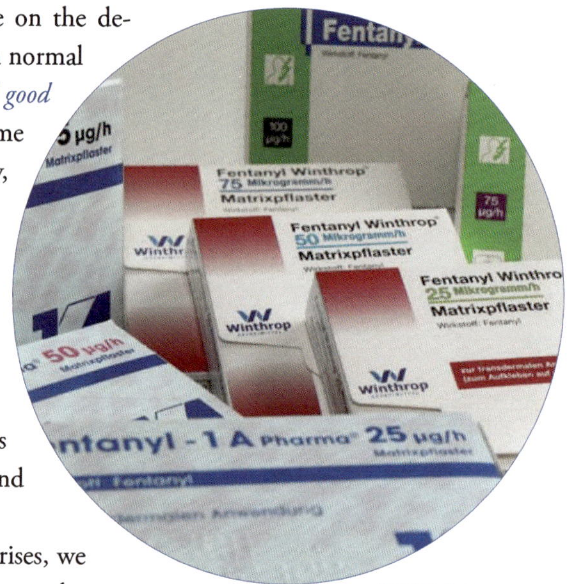

Generic drugs

Consider a normal good. If our income rises, we buy more of it at any given price level. Suppose that our consumer receives a pay raise. As a result, she is willing and able to buy four more boxes of her favorite cereal at any price. Therefore, as shown in Figure 2, her demand function shifts to the right by 4 units. Figure 2 also shows a leftward shift in the consumer's demand function. This can happen if the consumer's income falls and the good is a normal good. It can also happen if her income rises, but the good is an inferior good. For instance, if the consumer's income rises, she may stop going to garage sales.

SUBSTITUTES
Goods such that, if you consumed more of one, you would consume less of the other.

Tastes

Changes in such factors as fashion or health-related concerns will cause the demand for a product to change. The demand function will shift to the right or to the left, depending on the case. For example, if the consumer hears in the news that consumption of this cereal lowers her cholesterol, then she will consume more at any price level. The effect will be a rightward shift in the demand function.

Prices of Related Goods

There are two types of related goods. *Substitutes* are those goods, such that if you consumed more of one, you would consume less of the other. Examples are coffee and tea, Pepsi and Coke, and different brands of corn flakes. If the price of Brand A corn flakes decreases, a consumer will buy more Brand A corn flakes and reduce her demand for Brand B corn flakes. The demand function for Brand B corn flakes will shift to the left. So the relationship between the price of Brand A corn flakes and the quantity demanded of Brand B corn flakes is positive.

Figure 2: Shifts in the Consumer's Demand Function

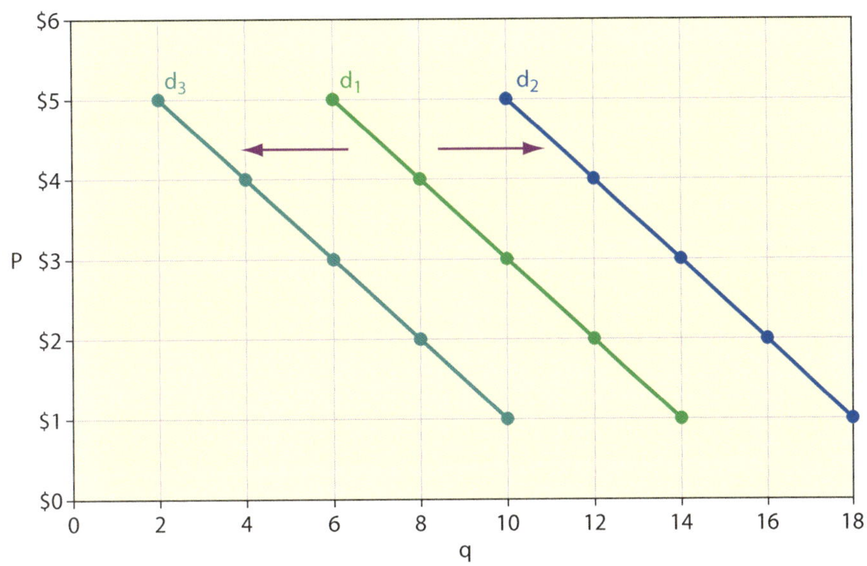

Complements are goods that consumers consume together—when they consume more of one, they will also consume more of the other. Examples are coffee and sugar or corn flakes and milk. If the price of corn flakes decreases, a consumer will buy more corn flakes. As a result, she will buy more milk. So the relationship between the price of corn flakes and the quantity of milk consumed is negative. In this example, when the price of corn flakes goes down, the demand for milk shifts to the right.

COMPLEMENTS
Goods consumers consume together, so when they consume more of one, they will also consume more of the other.

Expected Future Price

Consumers will buy more corn flakes this month if they expect its price to increase next month. The demand function will shift to the right. Note that this result is true only for storable commodities. You are not going to buy more electricity if you expect its price to increase next month, because you cannot store electricity for later use.

Other Factors

There is a host of other factors that affect the demand for a good, but these are mostly product-specific and less general. For example, demand for electricity or natural gas by a household would depend on the above factors, as well as weather conditions, square footage of the house, age of the house, number and kinds of appliances owned by the household, and the number of people living in that house.

MARKET DEMAND FUNCTION

The market demand function is just the sum of individual demand functions at different price levels. For example, suppose there are two consumers in the market. Then at any given price, we add their quantities demanded to get the market demand function. (See Figure 3.) The quantities demanded by the market depend on the same factors that affect individual consumers' demand. However, we will have a larger market demand (shift to the right) if we have a larger number of consumers. So here are the determinants of market demand function. A plus or minus sign indicates whether the relationship between the factor listed and the quantity demanded is positive or negative:

1. Own price of the good (–);
2. Consumers' income
3. Normal goods (+)
4. Inferior goods (–);
5. Tastes (+ or –);
6. Price of related goods (cross prices)
7. Substitutes (+)
8. Complements (–);
9. Expected future price (+);
10. Number of consumers (+);
11. Other (+ or –).

CHANGE IN QUANTITY DEMANDED
A movement along the demand curve resulting from a change in price.

CHANGE IN DEMAND
A shift in the demand curve.

If the amount demanded changes due to a change in the own price, a typical consumer moves on her demand curve from one point to another. So does the market. We call this a movement along the market demand function. As in the case of an individual consumer, we call the resulting change in the amount of demand the *change in quantity demanded*. The whole demand curve shifts when one of the other determinants of demand changes. If the whole demand curve shifts, we call the event a *change in demand*. A shift to the right is called an increase in demand, a shift to the left a decrease in demand. (See Figure 4.)

Figure 3: Deriving the Market Demand Function

Figure 4: Movements Along and Shifts in the Market Demand Function

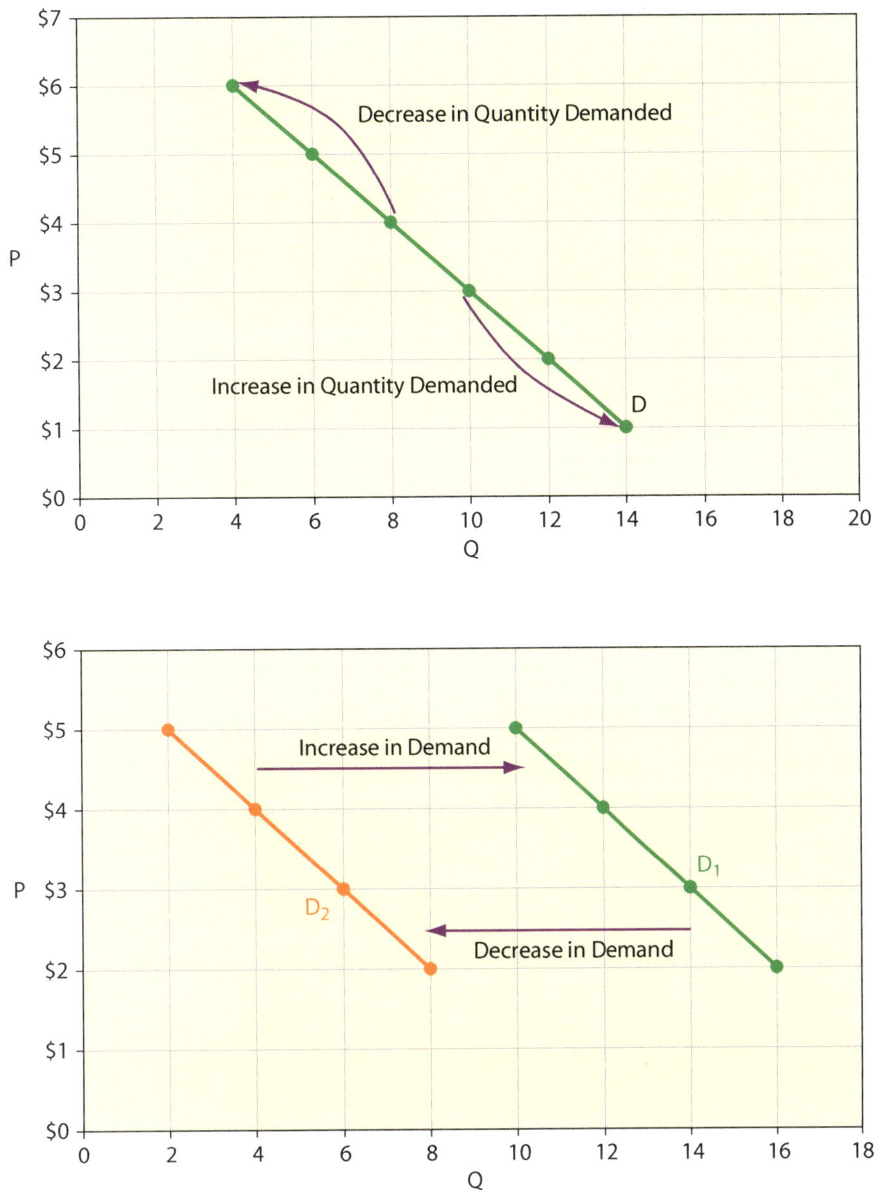

INDIVIDUAL AND MARKET SUPPLY FUNCTIONS

The market supply function is a table, curve, or equation that shows the quantities of a product producers are *willing* and *able* to sell at different price levels during a certain period of time. In the case of production, *willingness to sell* is related to the amount of profits. Profit is the excess of revenues over production costs. Revenue is the money the producer makes from selling the output. Production cost is the sum of payments to production factors the firm uses to produce output. We will assume that the objective of producers is to maximize profits. Therefore, at any given price, a typical producer will be willing to supply an amount of output that maximizes her profit. *Ability to sell* is related to technology and the availability of production factors. The producer should know how to produce the good, and there must be sufficient amounts of land, labor, and capital to produce it.

The market supply function is the sum of individual producers' supply functions. To understand the behavior of the market supply, we consider first a particular producer's supply of a good. The quantities she is willing and able to supply depend on

1. Price of the good (sometimes called own price);
2. Input prices;
3. Technology;
4. Taxes and subsidies;
5. Price of related goods (called cross prices);
6. Expected future price;
7. Other.

LAW OF SUPPLY
Keeping all the other determinants of supply constant, as the price of a good increases, producers will supply a larger quantity to the market.

Let's denote the quantity of the good the producer is willing and able to sell by q and the price of the good by P. Keeping all the other determinants of supply constant, we assume that as the price of a good increases, a typical producer will supply a larger quantity to the market. This is called the *law of supply*. We will provide a more detailed explanation later of the law of supply. If we graph this relationship, we get the producer's supply function.

Figure 5 shows the relationship between the price and quantity of corn flakes supplied by a hypothetical producer, keeping all the other determinants of supply constant. Assume that when the price falls below $1, the producer will not be willing and able to supply any corn flakes. At such low prices, it will not recover its costs. Two aspects of this function are important: slope and shifts.

Slope of the Producer's Supply Function

LAW OF DIMINISHING RETURNS
The idea that, given a fixed amount of capital, the marginal product of labor declines as the firm hires additional labor.

The slope is positive. The producer will be willing and able to supply more if the price rises. The reason behind this observation is the *law of diminishing returns*. Recall our assumption that the amounts of physical capital and land are constant. If a firm wants to increase output, it has to add more labor to the existing land and capital. As a result, additional workers have access to fewer machines and equipment and therefore, their productivity goes down. To produce additional units of output, the firm has to hire an increasingly larger numbers of workers. Consequently, the cost of additional units of output goes up. In this case the firm will be willing and able to supply more if it receives a higher price for the additional units of output.

Figure 5: Supply Function of a Typical Producer

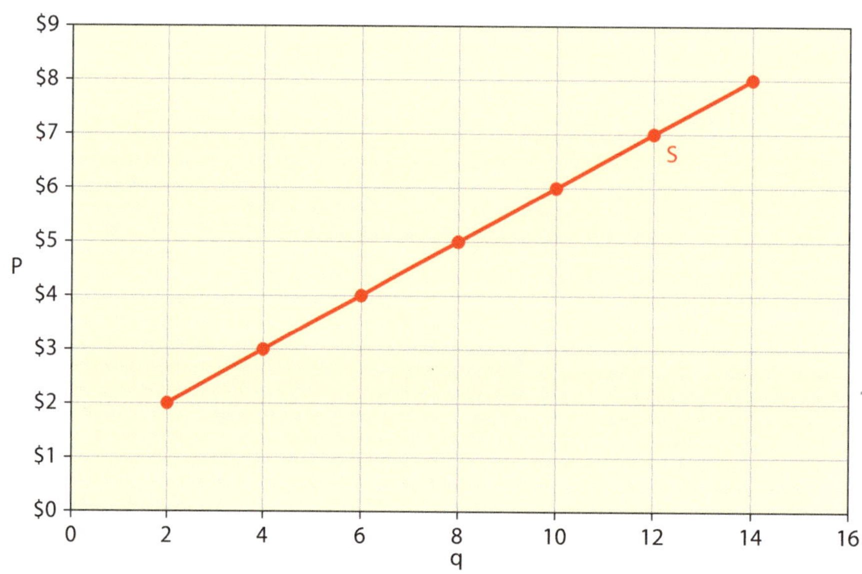

Shifts in the Producer's Supply Function

Changes in any of the determinants of supply that we kept constant while deriving and drawing it will shift the function. If any of these factors changes, the supply curve will shift. We call the result a change in supply. (See Figure 6.)

Input or Resource Prices

If input prices rise, it will cost more to produce the same amount of output. This is because the producer has to pay higher wages, rent, or interest. At the given output price, therefore, the producer cannot afford the same amount of inputs as before; it may lay off labor and produce less.

Technology

Technology is the knowledge of how to produce things. Suppose that the firm learns a better way of producing or its workers become more productive because of learning by doing or on-the-job training. The firm can then produce more at the existing prices and the supply curve shifts to the right.

Taxes and Subsidies

In general, paying taxes to the government is a cost of doing business. Not all kinds of taxes shift the supply curve. However, taxes levied based on the number of units sold or the value of sales will shift the supply curve. Suppose that currently it costs $3 to produce a box of corn flakes. If the government levies a tax of $1 per box sold, the cost per box increases to $4. This will be similar to an input price increase. Therefore, the supply curve will shift to the left.

Subsidies will have the opposite effect. Suppose that for each box of corn flakes produced, the government gives the producers $1 in subsidies. Then the cost of producing corn flakes drops to $2 per box. The supply curve shifts to the right.

Figure 6: Shifts in a Producer's Supply Function

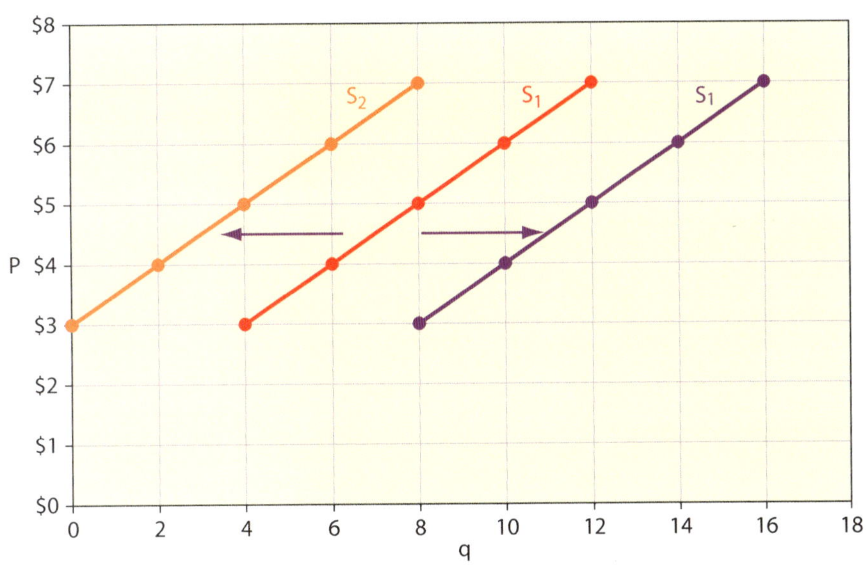

Prices of Related Goods

Substitutes in production are the goods that compete with each other for a producer's resources. This means if the producer increases production of one good, he needs to reduce that of the other good.

A farmer can produce either wheat or barley on his farm. If the price of wheat increases in the marketplace, he will produce more wheat. Since he has only a limited amount of land, he will reduce the barley production. So, substitutes in production have negative cross price effects. In other words, an increase in the price of wheat will cause the supply of barley to shift to the left.

A wheat farm in England

Complements in production are those goods that are produced together. So, if the production of one increases, the production of the other should also increase. They are also called *joint products*. For example, mutton and wool are joint products. If the price of meat increases in the marketplace, more sheep will be slaughtered and the quantity of meat supplied will increase. Simultaneously the supply of wool will also increase.

JOINT PRODUCTS
Two products such that, if the production of one increases, the production of the other also increases.

Expected Future Price

For storable commodities, if producers expect the price to be higher in the future, they will store the commodity to sell in the future. Therefore, the supply in the present period will go down.

Other Factors

Other factors affecting supply include weather conditions, wars, hurricanes, and so on. For instance, in the case of good weather, the supply function by individual farmers will shift to the right.

MARKET SUPPLY FUNCTION

The market supply function is the sum of the individual supply functions. Suppose there are two producers in the market. To derive the market supply function, we add their quantities supplied at different prices. Graphically, we add the supply curves horizontally. Although we generally assume a large number of sellers, for ease of demonstration, let's just take two producers. (See Figure 7.)

The quantity supplied to the market will depend on the same factors that affect an individual producer's supply. However, we will have a larger market supply (shift to the right) if we have a larger number of producers. So here are the determinants of market supply:

1. Own price of the good (+);
2. Input prices (–);
3. Technology (+);
4. Price of related goods (cross prices)
5. a. Substitutes in production (–)
6. b. Complements in production (+);
7. Expected future price (–);
8. Number of producers (+);
9. Other (+ or –).

Figure 7: Deriving the Market Supply Function

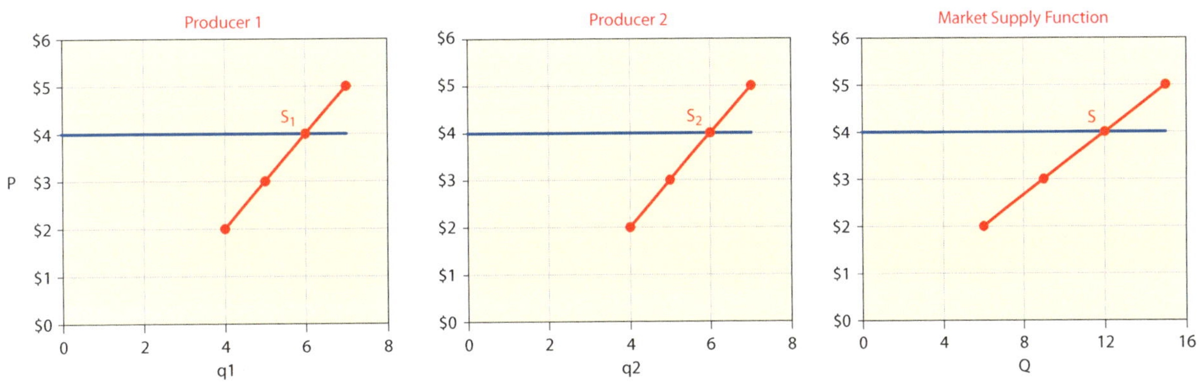

If the amount supplied changes due to a change in the own price, the producer will move on her supply curve from one point to another. So does the market. We call this a movement along the supply curve. We call the resulting change in the amount of supply the *change in quantity supplied*. If the whole supply curve shifts, we call the event a *change in supply*. (See Figure 8.)

Market Demand Function	Market Supply Function
Factor causing movement along the curve (change in quantity demanded)	**Factor causing movement along the curve (change in quantity supplied)**
Own price (–)	Own price (+)
Factors causing a shift in the function (change in demand)	**Factors causing a shift in the function (change in supply)**
Consumers' income Normal goods (+) Inferior goods (–) Tastes (+ or –) Price of related goods (cross prices) Substitutes (+) Complements (–) Expected future price (+) Number of consumers (+) Other (+ or –)	Input prices (–) Technology (+) Price of related goods (cross prices) Substitutes (–) Complements (+) Taxes (–) and Subsidies (+) Expected future price (–) Number of producers (+) Other (+ or –)

Figure 8: Movements Along and Shifts in the Market Supply Function

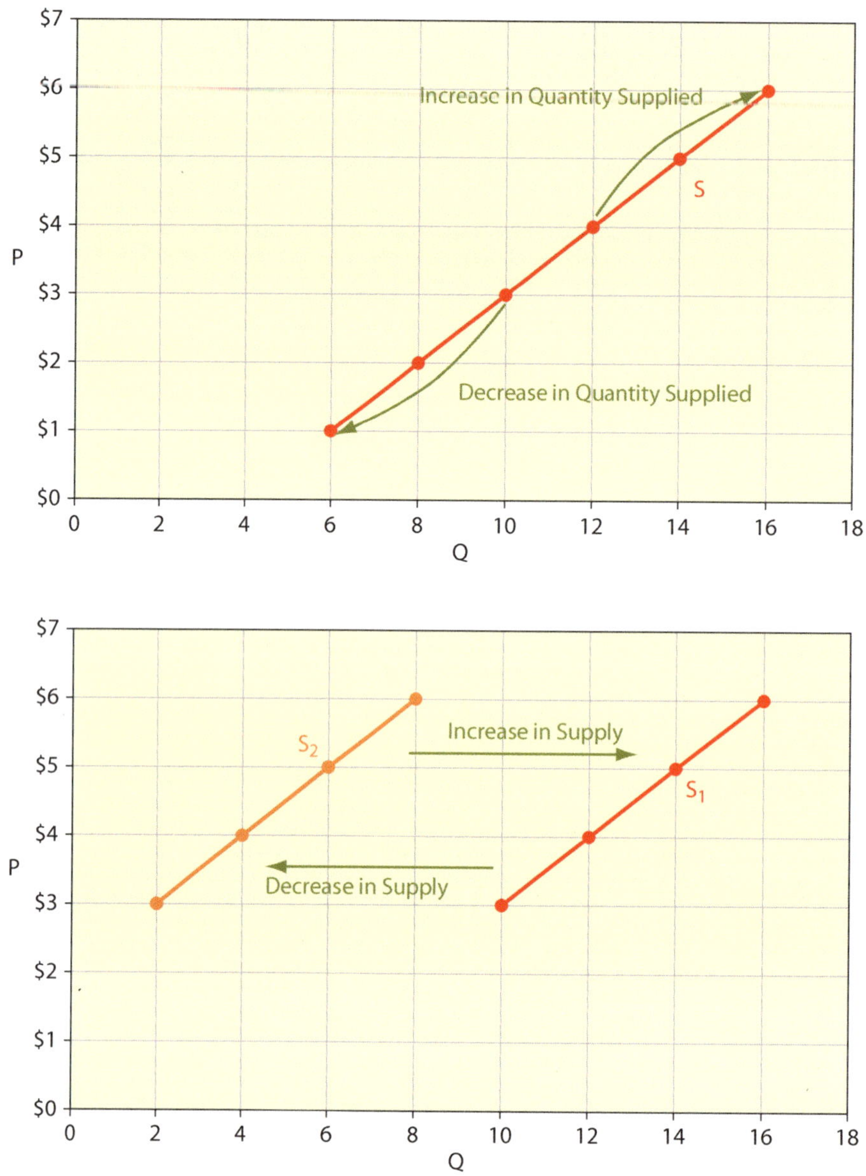

MARKET EQUILIBRIUM

EXCESS SUPPLY/SURPLUS
A situation in which the quantity supplied exceeds the quantity demanded, because actual price is above the equilibrium price. Also called surplus.

Now let's bring the buyers and sellers together in the marketplace. Compare the market demand and supply schedules in Figure 9. For a reason that will become clear shortly, suppose that the price of corn flakes is $7 per box. This price is too steep for consumers, so they are willing and able to buy only 3 boxes per month. For the producers, on the other hand, this is a lucrative price. They are willing and able to supply 21 boxes. However, at this price, they will not be able to sell more than 3 boxes. This is the case of *excess supply* or *surplus* in the market. In this case, each producer will try to lower its price a little bit to move the merchandise. Competition among producers will force the market price to go down.

On the other hand, suppose that for whatever reason, the market price was \$2 per box. This price would be too low for producers and therefore, they would be willing and able to supply only 6 boxes. But since this is such a good price for the consumers, they would be willing and able to buy 18 boxes per month. This would result in an *excess demand* or *shortage* of the product in the market. Competition among buyers would cause the price to go up.

Finally, suppose that the market price is \$4 per box. In this case, the quantity demanded exactly equals the quantity supplied. There are no shortages or surpluses. The amount producers are willing to supply matches the amount consumers are willing to buy. As a result, no competition would arise among sellers or buyers, and the price would remain at \$4. The quantity transacted would settle at 12 units. There would be no reason for either the price or the quantity to change. The market would reach a *state of rest*. This state of rest is called *equilibrium*. The \$4 that equilibrates the demand and supply is called the *equilibrium price* and the 12 units are called the *equilibrium quantity*.

We seem to have the answer to our question at hand. The actual amount of a good produced and consumed in a market economy with no government intervention will be determined by the forces of supply and demand. The market price has an important influence in this process. As we will see shortly, the market price provides both *information* and *incentives* to market participants to make their decisions in such a way as to move toward equilibrium.

The combined information and incentives functions are sometimes called the *rationing function of prices*. In Figure 9, the market system rations the total amount of corn flakes among consumers. When the price is \$6, some people are not willing or able to buy everything producers are willing and able to supply. Therefore, the price starts going down. At lower prices, some producers are not willing or able to supply as much as before. At the same time, a larger number of consumers can afford the good than before. The process continues until the price reaches a level at which there is no surplus. Similarly, when the price is \$2 per unit, consumers are willing and able to buy more corn flakes than are available in the market. Through an increase in price, the market rations the product to those who are willing and able to pay more.

EXCESS DEMAND/SHORTAGE
A situation in which the quantity demanded exceeds the quantity supplied because actual price is below the equilibrium price. Also called shortage.

EQUILIBRIUM/STATE OF REST
If a system is in equilibrium, there are no tendencies on the part of anyone to change anything. For example, if the goods market is in equilibrium, producers will have no incentives to increase or decrease production.

EQUILIBRIUM PRICE
The price at which the supply of a good equals demand.

EQUILIBRIUM QUANTITY
The quantity at which the supply of a good equals demand.

INCENTIVE
A desire to take an action by a decision maker to gain benefits or to avoid costs.

RATIONING FUNCTION OF PRICES
The combined information and incentive functions of the prices that results in the goods and services being rationed among different consumers, in such a way that only those who are willing and able to pay the most get to buy them.

Figure 9: Market Equilibrium

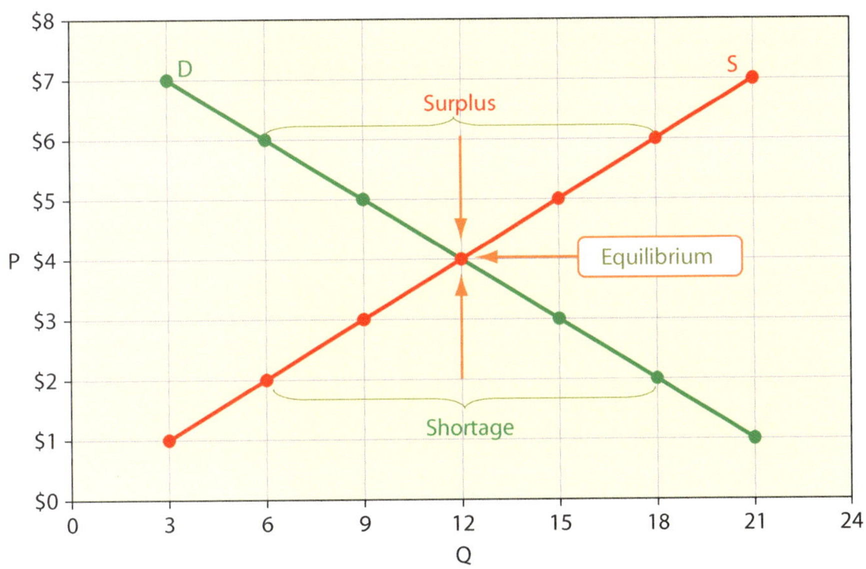

SPECIAL CASES

There are four special cases of supply and demand functions that you should remember. It is hard to find real-life situations that exactly fit these special cases. Most of the time, we utilize these special cases to approximate some extreme scenarios. They are as follows:

Vertical Demand Function

The market demand function for a good would be vertical if the quantity demanded for that good was not sensitive, or responsive, to price. This would be the case if the good was a necessity for which there were no close substitutes. Insulin is a well-known example of this case. Consider Figure 10-A. Regardless of what the price is, consumers will be willing and able to buy only 10,000 units of the drug. As mentioned above, this is an approximation to an extreme scenario. For example, even in the case of insulin or a similar drug, if the price becomes very high, some patients may simply not be able to afford it and may have to stop buying it.

Horizontal Demand Function

This is the opposite of the previous case. Think of a good for which there are plenty of close substitutes. For example, consider the U.S. demand for the homegrown wheat in Figure 10-B. Wheat is wheat, whether produced in the United States or in other countries. Suppose that the price of wheat in the global markets is $3 per pound, and that Americans can buy and sell wheat at that price in foreign countries. Suppose also that foreign countries will not run out of wheat, so Americans can import as much wheat as they want without affecting the world price of wheat. In that case, American consumers will never be willing to pay a penny more than $3 per pound for the U.S. wheat. Why should they? If American producers charge a price even slightly higher than $3 per pound, consumers will buy from foreign producers. Moreover, if they pay less than $3 per pound, they will not get any U.S. wheat, because American producers will choose to sell to the foreign markets at $3 per pound. Therefore, the U.S. demand for the homegrown wheat will be horizontal at the world price of $3 per pound.

Vertical Supply Function

The supply function will be vertical if there is a limited amount of a product in the market and additional production is not feasible. The amount of a perishable fruit that farmers bring to a farmers' market on a Saturday is fixed, so farmers cannot supply more even if consumers' demand increases. Moreover, since it is perishable, farmers may not be able or willing to sell less and take the rest back to their farms if consumers do not buy all the fruits. For all practical purposes, the supply of the product to the market will be vertical. As an exercise, draw the graph of this case.

Horizontal Supply Function

Supply will be horizontal if producers are willing and able to sell any amount at a fixed price. This would happen if the cost of producing additional units of the product is fixed so that producers can produce additional units of the product at the same price. As an exercise, draw the graph of this case.

Market Equilibrium

It is now straightforward to figure out equilibrium prices and quantities for the special cases. Consider Figure 11-A, showing market equilibrium when the demand function is vertical. As you can see, in this case the equilibrium quantity is determined only by the demand function. This is because consumers cannot consume either more or less than this amount, which is 5,000 units in this example. The market supply function only helps determine the equilibrium price, which is \$4 per unit in this example. As we will see later in the book, the location of the supply function is affected by the cost of production. Therefore, in these circumstances, consumers determine the equilibrium quantity and the production costs determine the equilibrium price.

Figure 10-A: Vertical Demand Function

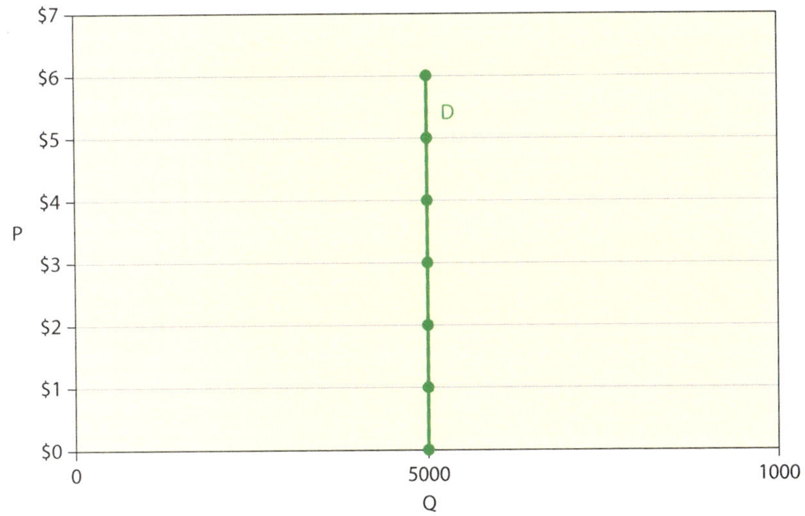

Figure 10-B: Horizontal Demand Function

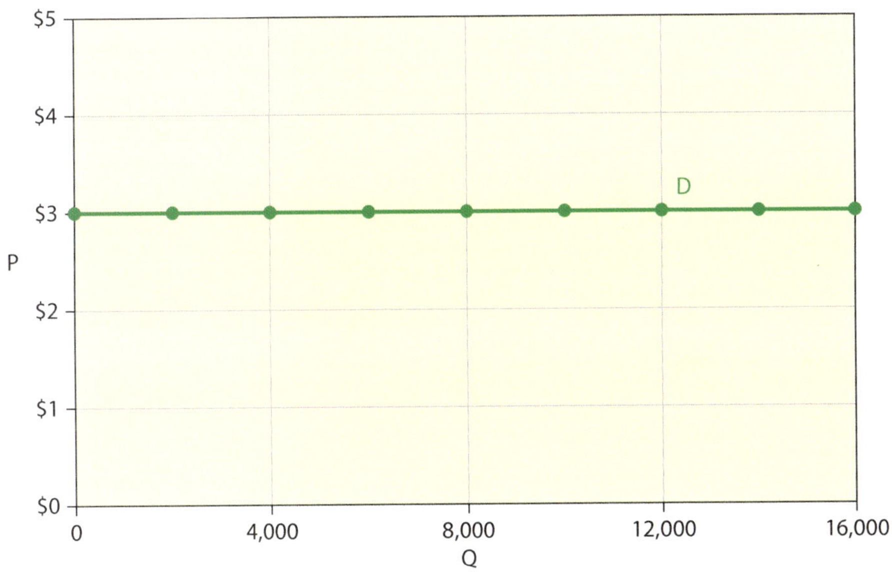

You may wonder that if consumers *have to buy* 5,000 units—regardless of the price—why don't producers charge them the highest price possible, rather than just \$4 per unit? Why not \$6? The answer is, we are assuming that there are a large number of producers in the market, each vying for the consumers' business. If one of them tries to charge a price higher than \$4 per unit, it will lose the market to the other producers. Therefore, each producer will try to charge the lowest possible price it can, which in our example is assumed to be \$4 per unit. Later in the book, we will find out where that \$4 is coming from.

Figure 11-A: Vertical Demand Function

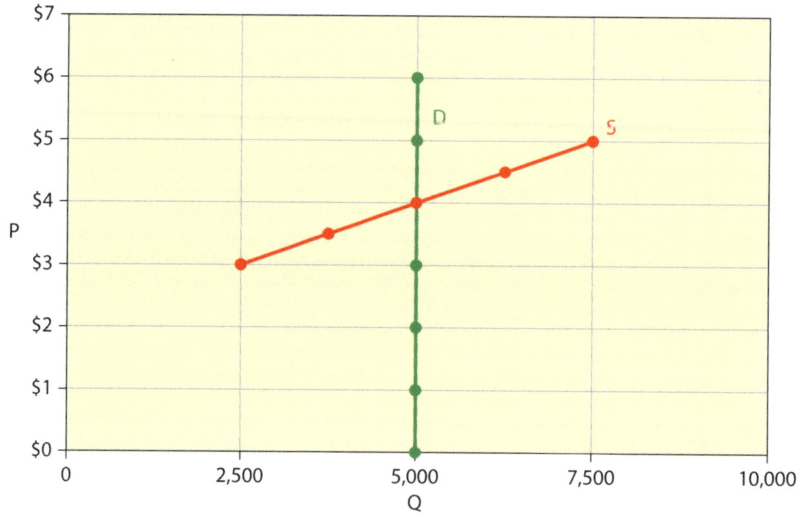

The opposite happens when the demand function is flat and the supply function has a standard shape. In the case of the U.S. wheat market, the price is determined by global competition—assumed to be $3 per pound in this example. Assume that in Figure 11-B, the line labeled S is the supply of wheat to the U.S. market by the American farmers. Figure 11-B shows that 8,000 tons of homegrown wheat will be sold in the United States per year. If U.S. consumers buy a total of 12,000 tons per year, the remaining 4,000 tons must be imported from foreign countries.

Figure 11-B: Horizontal Demand Function

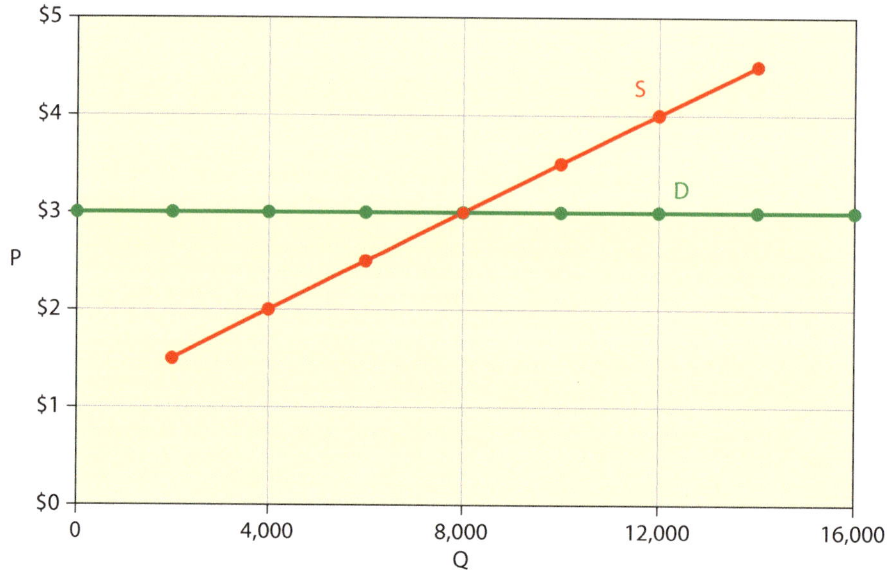

CHANGES IN SUPPLY AND DEMAND

In this section, we will see how market prices play their vital role of providing information and incentives to producers and consumers, and how by doing this, they help the market reach equilibrium. We consider four cases: 1) an increase in demand; 2) an increase in supply; 3) an increase in both demand and supply; and finally 4) an increase in demand, but a decrease in supply.

1. An Increase in Demand

Consider the market for a normal good such as corn flakes, and assume that consumer income increases. (See Figure 12.) Suppose that with the new higher income level, consumers collectively are willing and able to increase their purchases by 6 units at any price level. The demand curve shifts to the right by 6 units to D2.

Initially, producers keep making 12 units, perhaps because they are not aware of the new income changes (point A). At the old price of $4, consumers are willing to buy 18 units (point B). The immediate result of the income change is a shortage of 6 units in the market. As we saw in the previous section, consumers will start bidding against each other to get their hands on a good that is in short supply. This will raise the price of the product.

As the price increases, consumers begin to reduce their quantity demanded for the good. They move from point B to point C along their demand curve. This is the *incentive* effect of prices on consumers. Recall from Chapter 2 that people respond to incentives. So demand increases due to an increase in income, but subsequently the quantity demanded decreases somewhat, due to the resulting increase in price. At the same time, the rising prices give the signal to producers that demand exceeds supply. This is the *information* aspect of the price changes. The higher prices also provide incentives to the producers to increase production. They increase their quantity supplied, moving from point A to point C on their supply curve. The final outcome of the process will be an equilibrium price of $5 and an equilibrium quantity of 15 units

Figure 12: The Effect of an Increase in Consumer Income for a Normal Good

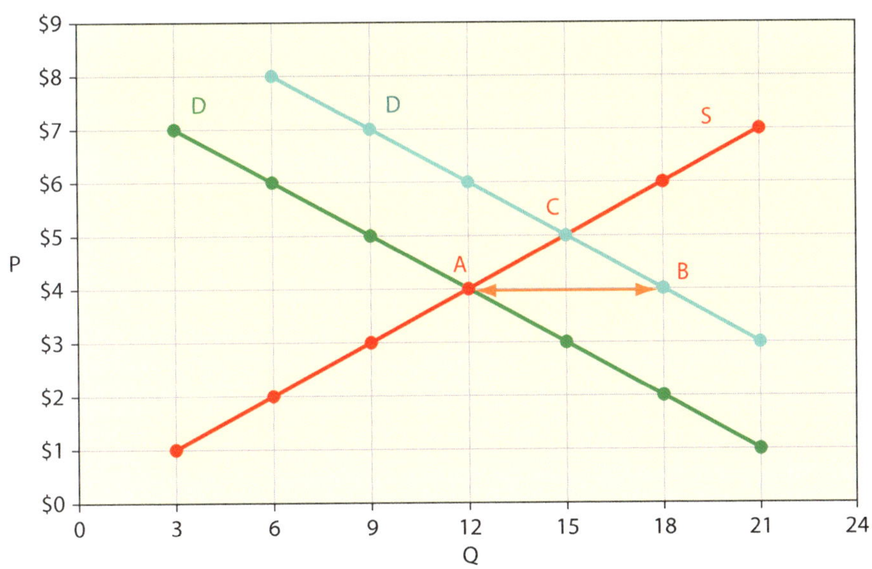

2. An Increase in Supply

This time let's assume that for one of the reasons mentioned previously, the supply of corn flakes increases. As you recall, this could be due to such factors as a reduction in input prices or an improvement in productivity. Suppose that supply increases by 6 units to S2 in Figure 13. Since producers need to pay less for their inputs, they will be willing to produce more at the existing market price of $4. A surplus of 6 units will be generated in the market, and individual producers will find it hard to sell their products. They will start lowering their prices, inducing producers to reduce their quantities supplied. They move on the supply curve from point B to point C. This is the incentive effect of prices.

The news of lower input prices is transmitted to consumers in the form of the falling price of corn flakes. This is the information aspect of prices. This also gives them an incentive to increase their consumption of the good. They move from point A to point C on the demand curve. The new equilibrium price and quantity will be $3 per unit and 15 units of corn flakes.

Figure 13: The Effect of an Increase in Supply

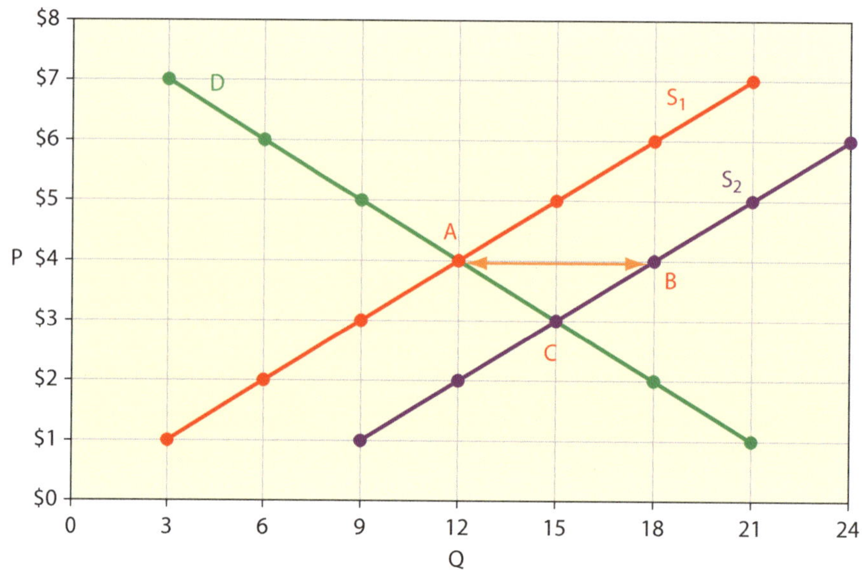

3. An Increase in Demand and Supply

Assume that demand increases due to an increase in consumer income, and supply increases because of a reduction in input prices. It is easiest to consider first the somewhat unrealistic case, in which both the supply and demand increase by the same amount—say 6 units—as in Figure 14. In this case, producers will produce 6 units more, due to input price reduction. However, there will be no excess supply, because consumers will simultaneously increase their demand by 6 units, and hence absorb all the additional supply. Nothing will happen to the equilibrium price, though the equilibrium quantity will increase. The market will move from point A to point B.

Although this case is somewhat unrealistic, it provides us with a benchmark or a starting point. If the increase in demand is greater than the increase in supply, the equilibrium price and quantity will both increase. For example, suppose that demand increases by 12 units and supply by 6 units. (The situation is depicted in Figure 14a.) Similarly, if supply increases more than demand, the equilibrium price will decrease, and the equilibrium quantity will increase. Assume that demand increases by 6 units and supply by 12 units. Then, as Figure 14b shows, the equilibrium quantity will increase, but the equilibrium price will decrease. The point of these examples is that *if demand and supply both increase, the equilibrium quantity will increase for sure, but the equilibrium price may or may not increase.* It depends on which curve shifts more.

Figure 14: The Effect of an Increase in Demand and Supply

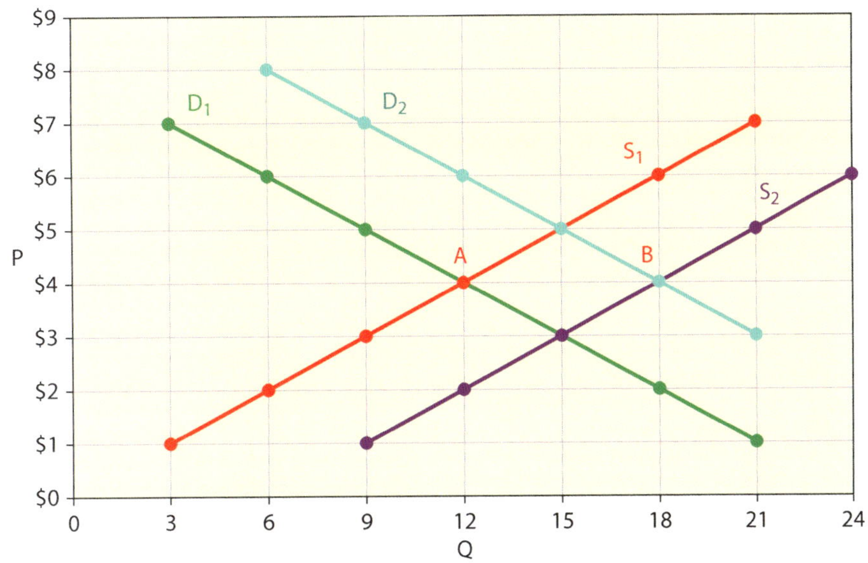

4. **An Increase in Demand and a Decrease in Supply**

Finally, let's consider an increase in demand, but a decrease in supply. Again, start with the benchmark case, in which both changes equal 6 units as in Figure 15. Note that in this case—*and with these specific numbers*—the equilibrium price increases, but the equilibrium quantity remains unchanged. To see this, consider two different cases. First, increase demand by 6 units, but decrease supply by 12 units. In this scenario, the equilibrium price increases to $7, but the equilibrium quantity goes down to 9 units. Second, increase demand by 12 units, and decrease supply by 6 units. You should see the equilibrium price increase to $7, and the equilibrium quantity increase to 15 units. The point of this exercise is that when demand increases but supply decreases, *the equilibrium price will increase for sure, but the equilibrium quantity may or may not increase.* It depends on which curve shifts more.

Figure 14a: Demand Increases More than Supply

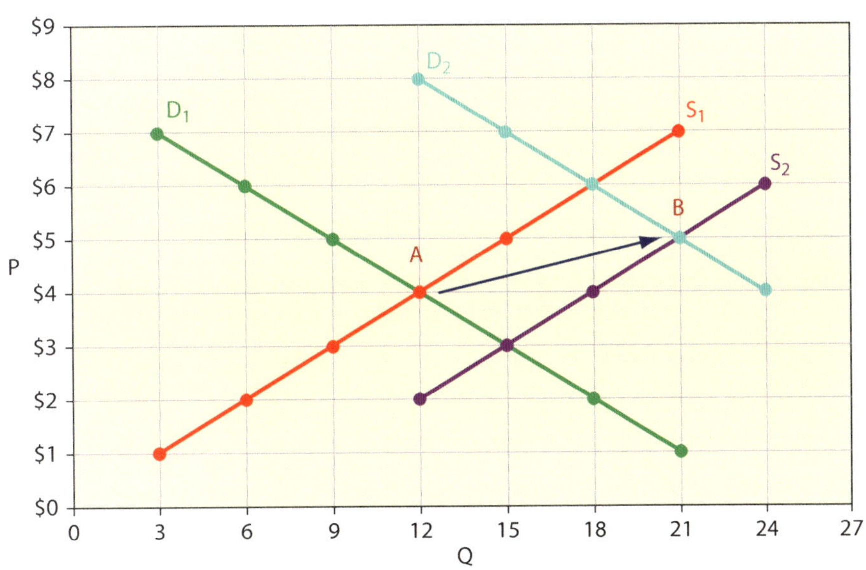

Figure 14b: Supply Increases More than Demand

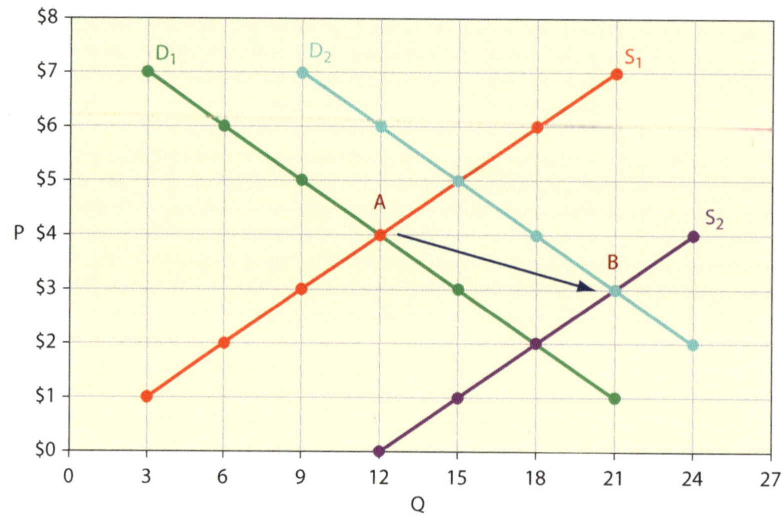

Figure 15 The Effect of an Increase in Demand but a Decrease in Supply

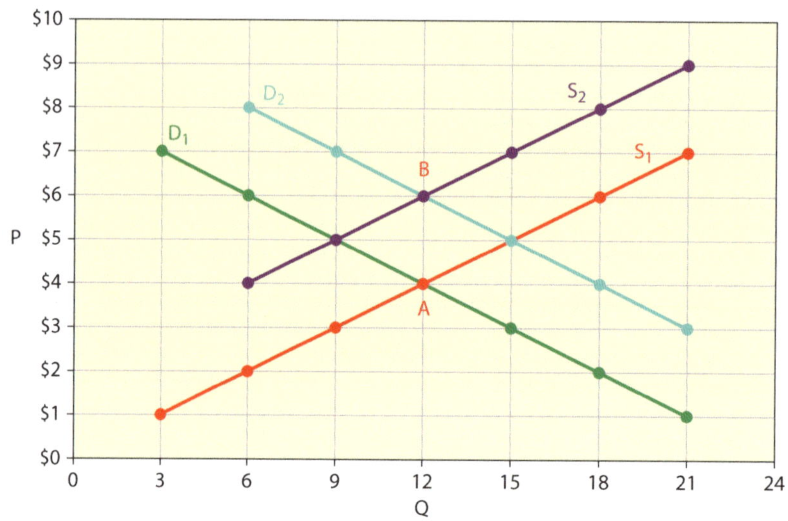

A MISTAKE TO AVOID: THE IDENTIFICATION PROBLEM

In practice, there are no published data on the demand and supply functions for different goods and services. These functions are theoretical, and they indicate consumers' and producers' *willingness* to buy or sell things. What we have in practice are transaction data on the quantities of different goods and their associated prices. Now, the amount of a particular good consumers buy in a year exactly equals the amount producers sell; it cannot be otherwise. Moreover, the prices they pay exactly equal those received by producers. So for any given period of time—say, a year—we have just one number for the quantities traded in the market, and one number for the price agreed upon by both buyers and sellers. In other words, for any given year, we just have one point in our graphs. This point should be the equilibrium point in that year.

To see the problem, suppose you want to estimate the supply function for a product. You go to your local library and find the following data on the price and quantity for two years, 2007 and 2008:

P(2007) = $3 Q(2007) = 9 tons
P(2008) = $5 Q(2008) = 15 tons

You go home and plot these two points and get a figure like Figure 16a. These two points look as if they are coming from a supply function. All you need to do is connect the points and get your function. Actually, you would be right only under one scenario as depicted in Figure 16b: That is, those two points would actually be two points on the supply function, if supply between these two years had not changed, but demand had increased.

Two additional scenarios could also give rise to those two points (as shown in Figure 16c and Figure 16d). In both of these two scenarios, demand increases. However, in one scenario (Figure 16c), supply increases as well; but in the other scenario (Figure 16d), supply decreases. In these two cases, you cannot connect those two points and call the result a supply function. Our general conclusion from these scenarios is: If between two years, the equilibrium price and quantity for a product increase, the demand for this product must have increased for sure, but the supply may have increased, decreased, or remained the same.

Figure 16a: Identification Problem

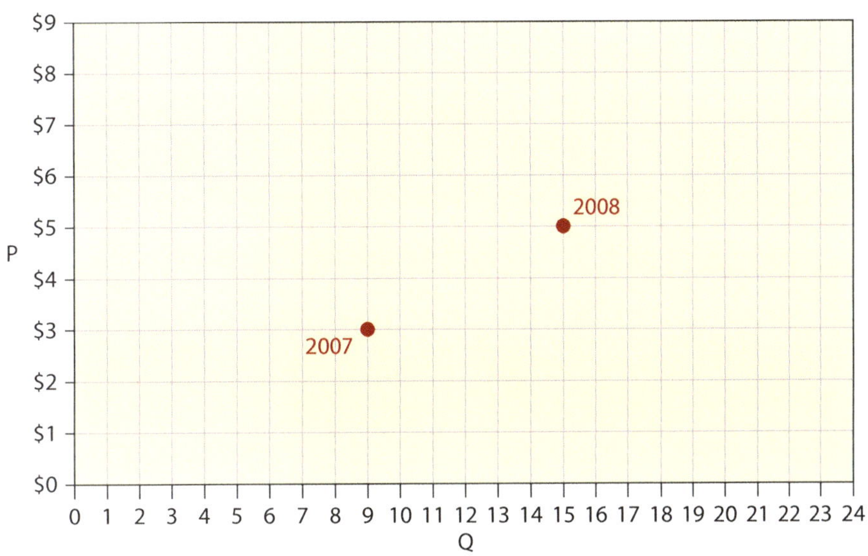

Figure 16b: Demand Increases, Supply Remains Unchanged

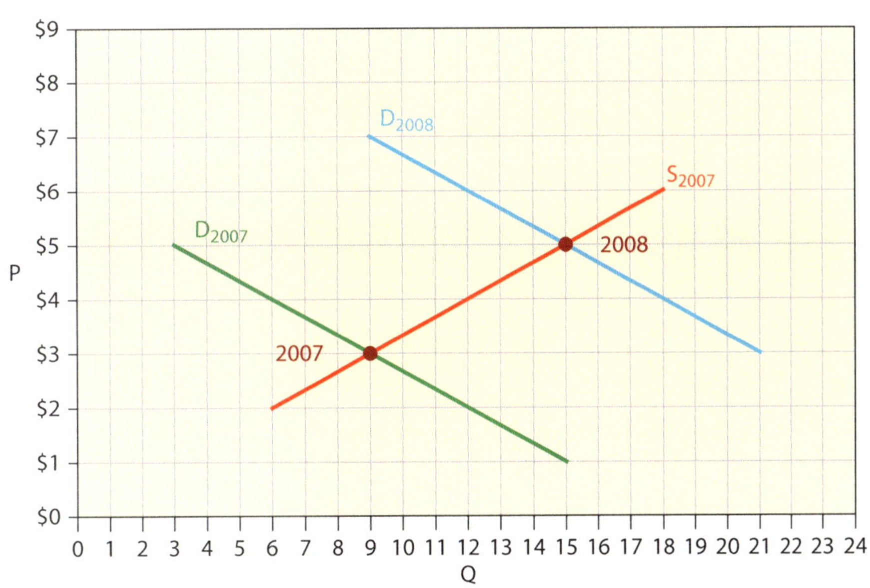

Figure 16c: Demand Increases, Supply Increases

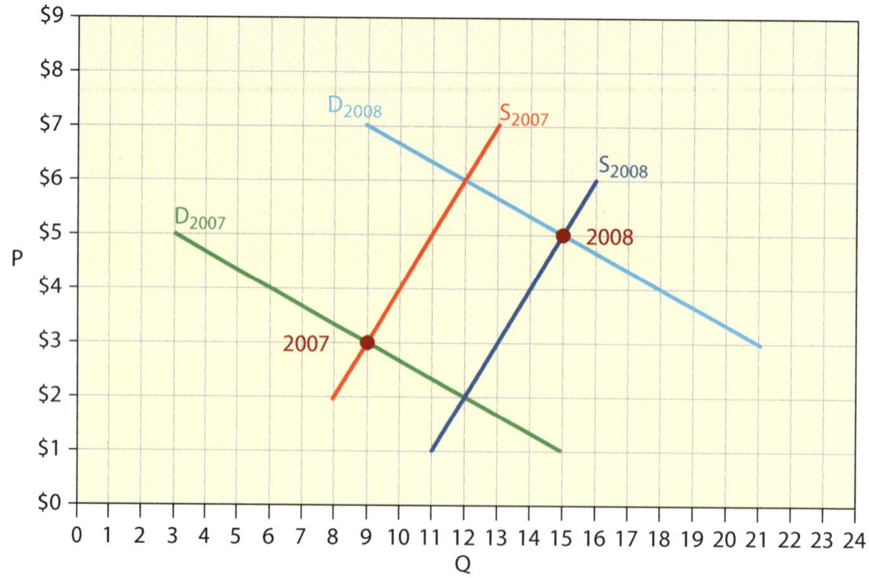

Figure 16d: Demand Increases, Supply Decreases

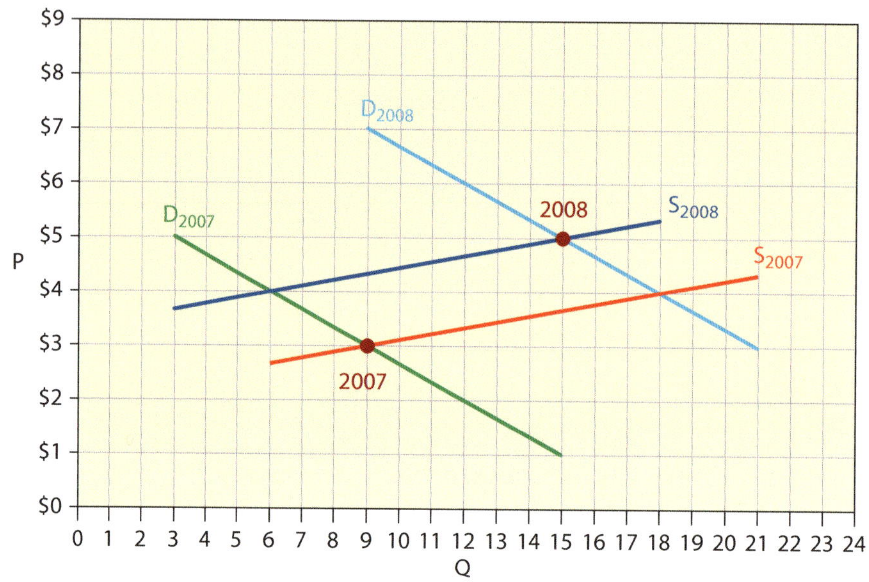

TO SUMMARIZE

1. A *market* is an arrangement, institution, or mechanism that brings buyers and sellers of a good or service together.
2. The *market demand function* for a good or service shows how much consumers are willing and able to buy at different prices.
3. The quantities consumers are willing and able to buy generally depend on the following factors:
    a. Price of the good itself (called own price);
    b. Consumer's income;
    c. Consumer's tastes;
    d. Prices of related goods (called cross prices);
    e. Expected future own price;
    f. Number of consumers;
    g. Other.
4. Suppose the price of a product increases. This will be a movement along the demand function and will result in a decrease in *quantity demanded.* If the price decreases, the there will be an increase in quantity demanded.
5. The *law of demand* says that, all else the same, the relationship between the quantity demanded of a product and its price is negative.
6. This negative relationship is due to the *substitution* and *income effects.*
7. If a determinant of demand changes, the demand function will shift. This shift is called a *change in demand.*
8. If consumer income increases, the demand for normal goods will increase while the demand for inferior goods will decrease.
9. If the price of a product increases, the demand for its substitutes will increase.
10. If the price of a product increases, the demand for its complementary products will decrease.
11. The *market supply function* for a product shows how much producers are willing and able to supply at different prices.
12. The quantity supplied depends on the following factors:
    a. Price of the good (sometimes called own price);
    b. Input prices;
    c. Technology;
    d. Taxes and subsidies;
    e. Price of related goods (called cross prices);
    f. Expected future price;
    g. Number of producers;
    h. Other.
13. Keeping all other determinants of supply constant, as the price of a product increases, the quantity supplied to the market will increase. This is called the *law of supply.*
14. The law of supply is due to the *law of diminishing returns.*
15. Suppose the price of a product increases. This will be a movement along the supply curve, and will result in an increase in *quantity supplied.* If the price decreases, then there will be a decrease in quantity supplied.
16. A change in other determinants of supply will cause a shift in the supply function.
17. When the quantities demanded and supplied in a market are equal, we say that that market is in *equilibrium.* The prevailing price and quantity are called *equilibrium price* and *quantity.*
18. *Equilibrium* means a state of rest.
19. If the market price is above the equilibrium price, a *surplus* will develop. In the opposite case, a *shortage* will develop.
20. Changes in the determinants of supply or demand will cause changes in equilibrium price or quantity, or both.

EXERCISES

Question 1

Show the equilibrium price and quantity when:

a. The supply function is vertical. Which side of the market determines the equilibrium price, and which side the equilibrium quantity?

b. The supply function is horizontal. Which side of the market determines the equilibrium price, and which side the equilibrium quantity?

Question 2

Analyze the effects of the following events on the equilibrium price and quantity. Make sure you understand the information and incentive functions of prices:

a. A decrease in demand.
b. A decrease in supply.
c. A decrease in demand and an increase in supply.
d. A decrease in both demand and supply.
e. A change in demand when demand function is vertical.
f. A change in demand when demand function is horizontal.
g. A change in demand when supply function is vertical.
h. A change in supply when supply function is vertical.
i. A change in demand when supply function is horizontal.
j. A change in supply when supply function is horizontal.

Question 3

What events would cause the price of residential real estate to increase in a region?

Question 4

What events would result in a larger amount of strawberries to be sold in a farmers' market?

Question 5

Suppose that between 2007 and 2008, the equilibrium price of lumber in the United States has increased, but the equilibrium quantity has decreased. What types of events might be responsible for these results?

Question 6

Suppose that between 2004 and 2005, the equilibrium price of pizzas in the United States has increased, along with the equilibrium quantity. What types of events might be responsible for these results?

Question 7

The following graph presents the demand and supply schedules for a good. The questions that follow are independent of each other. Each question refers independently to the following graph.

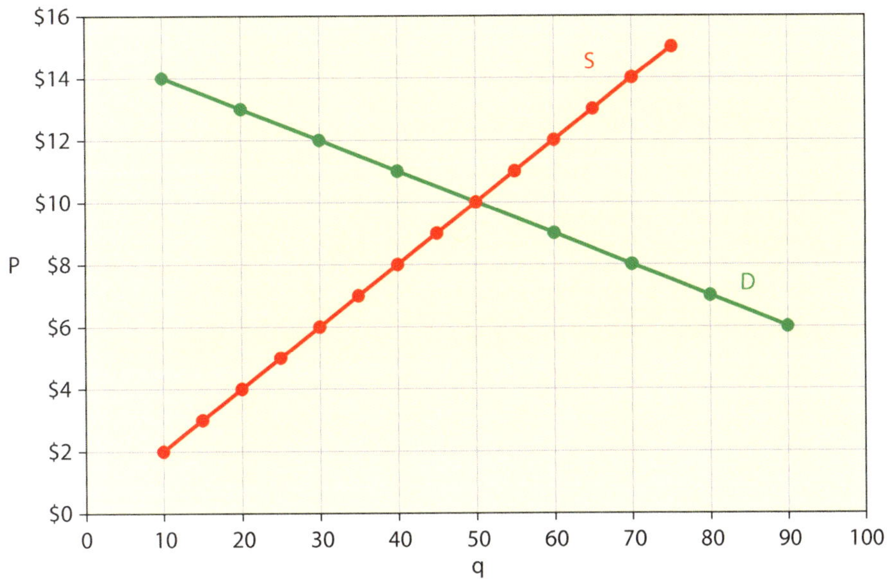

a. What are the equilibrium price and quantity?

b. What would happen in the market if the price of the good was $8?

c. What would happen in the market if the price of the good was $12?

d. Suppose that consumer income increases, so that at each price consumers demand 30 units more than before. Please find the new equilibrium price and quantity.

e. Suppose that technological progress enables producers to supply 30 units more than before at any price. Please find the new equilibrium price and quantity.

f. What will happen to the equilibrium price and quantity if consumers demand 30 units more due to a higher income level, and producers can supply 30 units more due to technological progress?

g. What will happen to the equilibrium price and quantity if consumers demand 30 units more due to a higher income level, and producers can supply 60 units more due to technological progress?

h. What will happen to the equilibrium price and quantity if consumers demand 60 units more due to a higher income level, and producers can supply 30 units more due to technological progress?

i. What will happen to the equilibrium price and quantity if consumers demand 30 units less due to a lower income level, and producers supply 30 units less due to higher input prices?

j. What will happen to the equilibrium price and quantity if consumers demand 60 units less due to a lower income level, and producers supply 30 units less due to higher input prices?

k. What will happen to the equilibrium price and quantity if consumers demand 30 units less due to a lower income level, and producers supply 30 units more due to lower input prices?

Question 8

The following graph presents the supply function for a product, along with two demand functions. The questions that follow are independent of each other. Each question refers independently to the following graph:

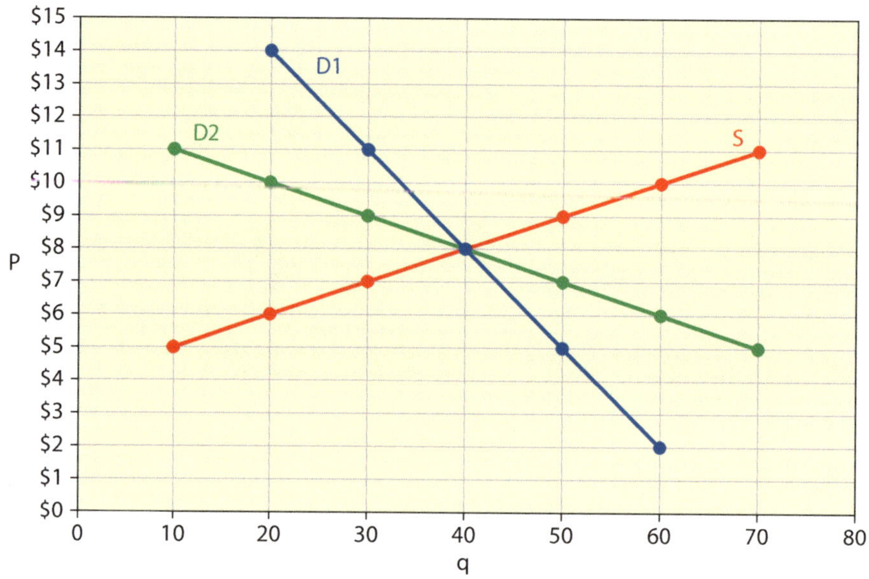

a. What are the equilibrium price and quantity?

b. Suppose that supply increases by 40 units due to an improvement in technology. What would be the equilibrium price and quantity if the demand function was D1? What if the demand function was D2?

c. Suppose that supply decreases by 40 units due to an increase in input prices. What would be the equilibrium price and quantity if the demand function was D1? What if the demand function was D2?

d. Suppose that supply decreases by 40 units due to an increase in input prices. What would be the equilibrium price and quantity if the demand function was vertical? What if it was horizontal?

e. On the basis of your findings above, discuss how the slope of demand function affects the magnitudes of changes in equilibrium price and quantity in the face of supply shifts.

Question 9

The following graph presents the demand function for a product, along with two supply functions. The questions that follow are independent of each other. Each question refers independently to the following graph:

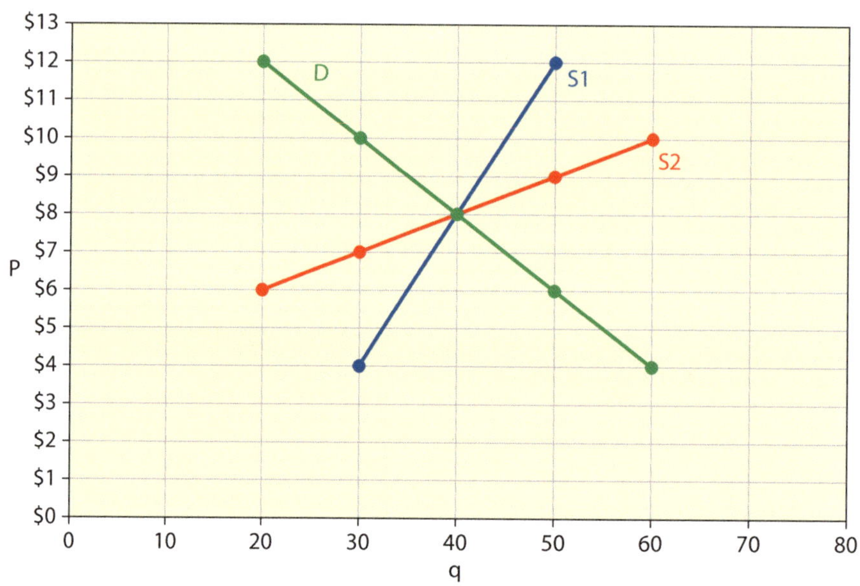

a. What are the equilibrium price and quantity?

b. Suppose that demand increases by 30 units due to an increase in consumer income. What would be the equilibrium price and quantity if the supply function was S1? What if the supply function was S2?

c. Suppose that demand decreases by 30 units due to a decrease in consumer income. What would be the equilibrium price and quantity if the supply function was S1? What if the supply function was S2?

d. Suppose that demand increases by 30 units due to an increase in consumer income. What would be the equilibrium price and quantity if the supply function was vertical? What if it was horizontal?

e. On the basis of your findings above, discuss how the slope of supply function affects the magnitudes of changes in equilibrium price and quantity in the face of demand shifts.

Question 10

You have the following data for a product for the two years 2008 and 2009.

	2008	2009
Price	$10	$14
Quantity	40 tons	30 tons

Describe all the scenarios concerning the demand and supply for this product that could give rise to these two equilibrium points. What general conclusion can you draw from these cases?

Question 11

You have the following data for a product for the two years 2008 and 2009.

	2008	2009
Price	$10	$8
Quantity	40 tons	50 tons

Describe all the scenarios concerning the demand and supply for this product that could give rise to these two equilibrium points. What general conclusion can you draw from these cases?

Question 12

You have the following data for a product for the two years 2008 and 2009.

	2008	2009
Price	$10	$8
Quantity	40 tons	25 tons

Describe all the scenarios concerning the demand and supply for this product that could give rise to these two equilibrium points. What general conclusion can you draw from these cases?

CHAPTER 5

Gross Domestic Product

INTRODUCTION

In Chapter 1, we learned that macroeconomics is mainly concerned with three variables: the aggregate level of output; the general price level; and overall employment. Chapter 4 showed that in a market system, the prices and quantities of goods and services are determined by the interplay of supply and demand in different markets. Therefore, we need to somehow aggregate all the goods and services produced—as well as their prices—into some useful overall indexes to be able to study the overall performance of the economy and make policy decisions. We start by observing that policy makers and economists are interested in the *total* amount of all the goods and services produced in a country. This is because the total amount of goods and services produced by a country affect standards of living and employment possibilities for the citizens of that country. Our standards of living or well-being will improve if we produce more apples, homes, parks, hospitals, or schools. Employment will increase if we produce a larger amount of output, since we will hire more labor; other production factors come into play. If we produce fewer goods and services, employment will decrease.

A log skidder hauls cut timber in Virginia.

Production of all the goods and services in any country takes place with the help of three *factors of production* located in that country. As you remember from the previous chapters, these are labor, land, and capital. Labor is human effort. Land includes all natural resources, such as the land itself, underground resources, underwater resources, forests, lakes, and timberlands. By capital, we mean produced means of production, such as computers, trucks, office spaces, pliers, and screwdrivers. Since these factors of production are scarce, they each command a price: wages for labor; rent for land; and interest and profit for capital. These constitute the incomes of the suppliers of these production factors. Therefore, an increase in production will also result in an increase in the total income received in the society.

For the above reasons, it is important for policy makers and economists to have an index giving them an idea on the amount of *all* the goods and services produced by the factors of production located in the country during a certain period of time—say, a year. Business firms, the government, and households produce these goods and services. Since these three groups produce billions of different types of goods and services, the actual calculation of such an index becomes a daunting task. Thus, we try to count all the goods and services produced to the extent that we can identify them. The result is called *gross domestic product*, or *GDP*.

GROSS DOMESTIC PRODUCT
The total market value of all the goods and services produced by the factors of production located in a country, except those produced by households for household consumption.

The following pages will describe the procedure that national income accountants follow to calculate this index. It is not hard to understand. While reading these pages, ask yourself how *you* would go about calculating GDP. Put yourself in the place of a national income accountant whose assignment is to calculate the GDP for the United States.[1]

Stock and Flow Variables

The first thing you realize is that production takes time. If a firm can produce 1,000 iPods in a week, in ten weeks it can probably produce about 10,000 iPods. Therefore, you need to decide on the period of time over which you want to measure the amount of production. You call your boss and she asks you to calculate the annual GDP for 2007. Macroeconomists say that production is a *flow variable*. This means that we need to specify a time period to describe or measure it. Other examples of flow variables include the amount of money people earn, spend, or save. For example, if I tell you that Melissa makes $5,000, you will not know if this is a lot or not. If she makes that money over a week, then that is a lot; if it is over a year, then it seems too little.

FLOW VARIABLE
A variable that requires a time period to describe or measure its magnitude.

STOCK VARIABLES
Variables that we can measure at any point in time.

Variables that we can measure at any point in time are called *stock variables*. Examples are the number of tractors on a farm or the amount of money in your bank account. You can count them right at this very moment. There is a simple relationship between stock and flow variables. If you save $100 *per week*, then after 5 weeks you will have $500 in the bank. The total amount in the bank is a stock variable, which is the sum of your weekly savings. The amount you save per week is a flow variable. *Stock variables are the accumulation of flow variables.* Suppose that at the end of the sixth week your money in the bank increases to $650. This must be because you have saved $150 in that week. *Flow variables are changes in stock variables.*

COUNT ONLY THE NEW PRODUCTION

Recall that the objective is to find an index that summarizes the total amount of all the goods and services produced in a year, to the extent that you can observe and identify them. All the goods and services in a country are produced by three entities:

1 To expand your knowledge of practical aspects of GDP calculation, you might want to visit the website of the Bureau of Economic Analysis of the Department of Commerce at http://www.bea.gov. This is the government agency in charge of GDP calculations in the United States.

- Business firms produce goods and services, such as computers and haircuts, with an intention to sell them to their customers in different markets.
- Governments produce services such as national defense, education, and health care and render them to their citizens.[2]
- Households produce goods and services such as pancakes, barbecues, and babysitting, mostly for their own consumption.

The first thing you must figure out is which one of these goods and services you should include in the GDP. You call your boss for clarification, and she provides you with the following golden rule of GDP calculation:

> *We count every good and service produced by domestic production factors in the calculation of gross domestic product except those that are produced by households, but are not sold to people outside the households.*

You will have a much easier time reading the rest of this chapter if you keep in mind that every aspect of GDP discussed comes from the simple principle above.

GOODS YOU WILL EXCLUDE FROM GDP

The golden rule will immediately give you a hint as to what to exclude from GDP. There are three categories of such goods.

1. Goods Produced by Households for Household Consumption

You ignore all the goods produced by households that are not sold to people outside the households, for two reasons: First, the production of these goods and services does not generate new employment or income. Second, these activities take place behind closed doors, so there is no way you can measure them. However, if a member of a household produces and sells a good or service to someone else, then you count it in GDP, because income is generated as a result of that transaction.[3] There is some debate among economists as to whether GDP should include the value of household activities. We will come back to this issue later. At this point, I am only describing how the Commerce Department *actually* calculates the GDP numbers.

Consider the following examples. If a landscaping company mows my lawn, that service will count toward GDP, because a firm produces that service. If my neighbor mows my lawn for money, it will also count, because this is a service produced by a household and sold. But if I mow my own lawn, this will not affect GDP, because no market transaction takes place. Note that in all three scenarios, the same lawn is mowed. If you make your own pancakes in the morning, they won't count. If you buy the same pancakes from my restaurant, they will count, because a firm produces those pancakes. This is the case even though both you and my restaurant do exactly the same thing, use the same materials, and make exactly the same number of pancakes.

---

2 Note that for services, production and sale are the same thing. When you get a haircut, a service is produced and sold simultaneously. You cannot produce a service without selling it at the same time. This is because a service is not storable.

3 Illegal activities do not count. We cannot "observe" these, either.

2. Non-Produced Goods

A lot of goods sold during a year are not produced in that year. A very large number of transactions in a given year take place to transfer the ownership of an existing good. You are not interested in such goods, and you should totally disregard them. There are two categories of such goods: second-hand goods and assets. If you buy a new Ford, this will count toward this year's GDP (provided it is produced this year). But if you buy my old one that was produced in 1997, it won't.[4] Forget about those millions of garage sales that take place every weekend. Similarly, you ignore transactions in assets such as land, stocks, and bonds.

3. Imported Goods

Finally, you are interested in the goods and services produced by the factors of production *located in the country*. This is because only the production of such goods would affect the utilization rate of domestic production factors. Therefore, you should ignore those millions of goods imported from foreign countries.

GOODS YOU WILL INCLUDE IN GDP

The golden rule says that you should count only the new production. Therefore, you should remember to include the following categories of goods and services.

1. Unsold and Semifinished Goods

The golden rule does not say anything about purchase or consumption. Therefore, you should include all those goods that are produced in a year, even if they are not sold. So if GM produces 10 million cars in 2008 but can sell no more than 9 million of them, you should include all 10 million cars in the 2008 GDP. This is because the production of those 1 million unsold cars has generated employment for the factors of production involved. Similarly, if GM has some semifinished cars in its assembly lines, you should somehow measure and include them. For example, you count two half-finished cars as one unsold car. We call the unsold and semifinished goods *changes in inventories* and include them in GDP.

2. All the Services Rendered

What if someone buys a used car from a used car dealer? How would you treat that transaction? We already know that you will ignore both the purchase and the subsequent sale of the car by the used car dealer. However, the dealer is providing or producing a *service*. Therefore, you include the services of used car dealers in your calculation. Similarly, you include the services of real estate agents and stock and bond brokers.[5]

4 Again, let's review the logic behind this treatment. If you bought my old Ford, no new employment would be generated. Moreover, since a new good has not been produced, the aggregate standard of living would remain the same: I would lose the car and you would gain it.

5 Capital gains are not included in GDP. If you buy a piece of land in January 2007, sell it in March 2007, and make a profit of $50,000 from the increase in land value, this $50,000 of capital gains will not be included in 2007 GDP. That is because this $50,000 of income has not been generated because of any new production.

CALCULATE THE MARKET VALUE

Now that you have figured out what to include in the GDP, you will need to solve the next problem: How to add linen, wheat, gasoline, health care, and computers together. Remember your sixth grade teacher saying you couldn't add apples to oranges because they have different measurement units? You need to convert them into the same units of measurement. The best solution is to multiply the quantity of each good and service produced by its market price to convert them into dollars, and then add the results. The result will be the market value of these goods and services.

Why should we use market prices rather than, say, weight, to convert the quantities of different goods and services into a common measurement unit? The answer is partly related to the issue of standard of living.[6] As you recall from the previous chapters, in a free market economy, the price of a good or service is the value that the society places on it. Therefore, if a good is valued more highly than another by the society, it will have a higher price, and its production will increase GDP more than production of the other. Moreover, if something is more expensive—such as a car or a house—it generally means that a lot of resources have been used in its production, so the production of this item will increase employment and income a lot.

Suppose that in 2007, a computer company produced 1000 computers and sold each for $1000. A farmer produced 10,000 bushels of wheat and sold them all for $20 per bushel. A landscaping company mowed 1000 lawns each for $10. Then we calculate the contributions of these goods and services to GDP as in Table 1 below:

Table 1

Quantities of Goods & Services (Q)	Market Price Per Unit (P)	Contribution to GDP (P × Q)
1000 computers	$1000	$1,000,000
10,000 bushels	$20	$200,000
1000 lawns mowed	$10	$10,000
		Total = **$1,210,000**

Let's revisit some of the cases we discussed in the previous section. If a used car dealer bought a used car from me for $8000 and sold it to you for $10,000, neither of these two figures will be included in the GDP calculation. The dealer, however, has provided or produced a service for which he has received $2000. So only this $2000, the market value of the service, counts in GDP. Similarly, the fees received by real estate agents and stock and bond brokers count, since they are rewards for performing some services.

Also, we use the market prices of the finished goods sold to value the unsold and semifinished goods. So, if GM sold 9 million cars in 2007 each for $30,000, we use this $30,000 to value the 1 million cars that it could not sell in that year. Similarly, if it had some half-finished cars in its assembly lines, we value them at $15,000 each.

There is an exception to the above general rule. The services provided by the government, such as national defense, education, and health care, are generally not sold, and thus have no market values. We still need to include these in the GDP, because production of these services generates employment and affects our standards of living. The only way you can measure the values

6 Also, of course, the fact that services do not have weight!

of these services is to use their costs. These are basically the costs of providing those services, such as employee wages, costs of purchasing desks, chairs, and blackboards for the schools, and so on.

START WITH FINAL GOODS AND SERVICES

FINAL GOODS
Goods purchased by final consumers or users.

INTERMEDIATE GOODS
Goods that a firm buys from other firms and uses up in production within a production period.

Even though we have excluded a lot of goods from the calculation of GDP, you still have to look for billions of goods and services to include. But being smart, you will find a way of reducing the number of calculations. You will figure that you will save a lot of time and effort if you start counting the final goods and services. *Final goods* are those purchased by final consumers or users. *Intermediate goods* are those goods that a firm buys from other firms and *uses up* in production within a production period—say, a year or quarter. Some intermediate goods are reprocessed to produce the final goods. Examples are flour, eggs, or milk that undergo shape or form change in the production of pancakes or bread. Some other intermediate goods, such as batteries or tires, are placed inside final goods like cars.

You will reason that the values of the final goods already include those of the intermediate goods. The price of a car already includes the price of the seats, tires, battery, alternator, and all the other thousands of weird things you can find under the hood. Once you count the values of final goods, you don't need to count the values of those billions of intermediate goods again, and you can go home early. In fact, if you did, you would count them too many times.

Consider the oldest example in town. Suppose that in 2007, Mr. Farmer plants some seeds that he has carried over from last year and uses only water from his wells to produce wheat—no intermediate goods are purchased. He sells the wheat for $10,000 to Mr. Miller. Mr. Miller gets the wheat and mills it into flour and sells it to Mrs. Baker for $25,000. Mrs. Baker takes the flour and bakes bread. Assume that no other intermediate goods are used. She sells the bread for $100,000. The bread is the final good. (Ignore the last column of the table for the time being).

Table 2

	Value of intermediate goods bought	Value of goods sold	Value added
Farmer	$0	$10,000	$10,000 – $0 = $10,000
Miller	$10,000	$25,000	$25,000 – $10,000 = $15,000
Baker	$25,000	**$100,000**	$100,000 – $25,000 = $75,000
Total			**$100,000**

Note that of the three transactions, the value of bread is all you need to count. If you added the values of the intermediate goods ($10,000 for wheat and $25,000 for flour) to the value of the bread, you would exaggerate GDP—you would count the wheat three times and the flour twice.[7]

Therefore, keep in mind that we start with final goods for two reasons:

- To reduce the number of calculations in practice.
- To avoid multiple counting of the intermediate products.

7 You should be clear about what we are saying here. Conceptually, GDP is the total market value of all the goods and services produced. However, practically, to reduce the number of calculations, we start with the final goods. The end result is still that the value of all the produced goods and services will be included in GDP.

THE GOLDEN RULE AGAIN

The above discussion gives us the following general rule for the inclusion of goods and services in the calculation of GDP:

- A good or service produced by a firm counts, whether sold or not. If not sold, it will be counted as an increase in inventories. If sold, it will be purchased as a final good or an intermediate good. Keep in mind that an intermediate good purchased by a firm, but not used in the production of a final good, is still a good produced and sold by some other firm.
- A service produced by the government counts.
- A good or service produced by a household counts if sold; it does not count if not sold.[8]

DEFINITION OF GDP

Now that you know how to calculate GDP, the formal definition will be quite straightforward.

> *GDP is the total market value of all the goods and services produced in a country during a certain period of time by the factors of production located in that country, except those that are produced by households, but are not sold to people outside the households.*

Note that the definition just adds "the total market value" to the golden rule.

Some books define GDP as the total market value of *final goods* produced in a country. Such definition is a bit misleading, because it indicates that we only count the values of final goods and services. However, as you know by now, we also include the values of the intermediate goods not finished by the end of the year, or finished but not sold. We also include the values of the intermediate goods that are finished and sold, but are not used in the production of final goods. So we actually include *all* goods and services— except, that is, those produced by households that do not come to the marketplace. Furthermore, the phrase "the market value of final goods" might give the impression that we count the values of final goods only if they are finished and are brought to the marketplace. You know that this is not true, either. We also count the values of semifinished and unsold final goods. We start with final goods only to reduce the number of our calculations in practice, and to avoid double counting of intermediate goods. Ultimately, however, we include the value of all the goods and services in GDP calculation. See the appendix for more details on this issue.

THREE FACES OF GDP

As if this were not enough, the next day your boss gives you two more assignments. First, she wants you to calculate the income received by the factors of production located in the country for producing those goods and services. Second, she needs an estimate of the amount of money spent

8 You may ask: How does the Bureau of Economic Analysis (BEA) actually do it? Do they go door to door and ask for the amounts and prices of zillions of goods and services produced by every producer? Well, yes—kind of. They start with some census data collected by the Census Bureau for a certain year. They call it the benchmark year. Then they adjust the numbers every year using some techniques. Sometimes they use other, more frequently conducted censuses to update the figures. Sometimes they use judgmental trend lines, and so on.

to purchase all those goods and services in that year. After the initial shock dissipates, you go to your office, and after some thought—because you are very smart—you make a huge discovery. The GDP number you just calculated also equals the amount of income received by the production factors and money spent on those same goods and services. You don't need to make any new calculations for your boss. This is way cool! In other words, you discover that GDP actually has three faces or aspects:

1. Production aspect.
2. Income aspect.
3. Expenditure aspect

Here is how your reasoning goes.

1. Production Aspect

This is what you have been doing all along: finding the market value of all the goods and services *produced*. So GDP is the value of the aggregate output produced in a country. Let Q_1, Q_2, Q_3, … be the quantities of different goods produced in a country during a certain time period with the corresponding market prices P_1, P_2, P_3, … Then GDP is simply:

$$GDP = P_1 \times Q_1 + P_2 \times Q_2 + P_3 \times Q_3 + \ldots$$

2. Income Aspect

VALUE ADDED
The difference between the market value of output a firm sells and the money it pays for intermediate goods.

The difference between the market value of output a firm sells and the money it pays for intermediate goods is called the firm's *value added*. This is the value that the firm adds to the value of intermediate goods it purchases. You figure that the firm should pay wages, rent, and interest out of its value added. What is left over must become the owner's profit. These payments are the incomes of the production factors: labor, land, and capital.

You first think that you should make a new round of tedious calculations to find all these value added amounts for billions of firms. But then you remember your good friends Mr. Farmer, Mr. Miller, and Mrs. Baker. Revisit the above table. Mr. Farmer bought no intermediate goods and sold the wheat for \$10,000 to Mr. Miller. All of this \$10,000 became the value added generated by Mr. Farmer. He used it to pay wages to his workers, interest to the bank for his loan, rent to the owner of the farm, and the remainder became his profit. This is also Mr. Farmer's contribution to GDP. Mr. Miller's value added was \$15,000, out of which he paid wages to his workers, interest to his uncle for the loan, and rent to the landlord for the shop, and the rest became his profit. This was *his* contribution to GDP. Similarly, Mrs. Baker contributed a value added of \$75,000 to GDP, which became the income of the production factors she used.[9]

The amazing discovery that you made is that the sum of the value added amounts equals the market value of the final goods (\$100,000). Therefore, it must be true that GDP also equals the sum of all the values added in the country by all the firms. This also implies that GDP equals the

9 Note that Table 1 is in terms of goods but Table 2 in terms of economic activities. The contribution of a good to GDP is its market value (price × quantity), while the contribution of an economic activity is the value added it generates. At the end, the values of the contributions of goods and activities should both be equal to GDP.

sum of all the incomes received by the factors of production. This is simply because the value added by any firm equals the sum of wages, interest, rent, and profits paid out by that firm.[10] Therefore,

GDP = Wages received by labor +
Rent received by property owners +
Interest received by creditors +
Profit received by capital owners

The income received by the production factors is called *factor income*.

FACTOR INCOME
Income received by factors of production.

3. Expenditure Aspect

You also figure that GDP must equal the total amount of money spent on the goods and services produced in a country. This is simply because one's income is another person's expenditure. Suppose you walk into a restaurant and buy some pancakes for $5. Three things happen at that very exciting moment. First, $5 of GDP is generated because it is the market value of the pancakes produced (production aspect). Also, as we know by now, $5 of income is made by production factors (income aspect). Finally, you make an expenditure of $5 on those pancakes (expenditure aspect). So no new calculations are required for your boss.

Preparing a pancake breakfast at home will not be included in GDP while eating breakfast at a restaurant will be included in GDP.

NOMINAL GDP, REAL GDP, AND GDP DEFLATOR

So far, we have concentrated on just one year. But what if you want to compare the GDPs from two different years? Suppose that besides Mrs. Baker, there is another shop in town that sells pancakes. In 2007 Mrs. Baker sold 40,000 loaves of bread for $2.50 each. The pancake shop sold 20,000 pancakes for $5 each. Assuming that these are the only firms in the country, the GDP will just equal $200,000. Table 3 shows the calculations (the three trailing zeros are eliminated to save space). This $200,000 is called the *nominal GDP*.

NOMINAL GDP
The monetary value of all the goods and services produced in a country by the factors of production located in that country, except those produced by households for household consumption.

10 Realize that we are measuring the income generated in the production process. Therefore we include in GDP the rent and interest paid by business firms to households. We do not, however, include rent and interest received by firms from households, government, or other firms. The first two are assumed to be already included in the firms' profits. Inter-firm interest and rent payments cancel in the process of aggregation.

Table 3					
Year	Price of Pancakes	Quantity of Pancakes (thousands)	Price of Bread	Quantity of Bread (thousands)	Nominal GDP (thousands)
2005	$3.00	16	$2.00	32	$112
2006	$4.75	18	$1.25	38	$133
2007	$5.00	20	$2.50	40	$200

The table also shows some hypothetical values for 2005 and 2006. Note that nominal GDP has increased in 2006 and 2007.

Have we become better off by these increases? Not necessarily. If these increases were solely due to increases in the quantities of bread and pancakes produced, then we could say that our standards of living have increased. Moreover, we could say that employment has increased, because to produce more goods, we have hired more labor. But note that an important reason for these increases in nominal GDP is the rise in the prices of the two products over time. These price increases do not make us better off. Therefore, we should somehow separate price increases from quantity increases.

The logical way to do this is to calculate the GDP of each year using a fixed set of prices, so that changes in GDP reflect only quantity changes. This is very easy to do. We take a particular year—called the base year—and calculate the GDP of each year, using the prices prevailing in this base year. The resulting GDP is called the *real GDP*. Sometimes it is also called the inflation-adjusted GDP or constant-dollar GDP. Table 4 shows the real GDPs for the three years, using 2005 as the base year.

REAL GDP
A measure of the quantities of goods and services produced in a country by the factors of production located in that country, except those produced by households for household consumption. It is calculated as nominal GDP divided by GDP deflator.

Table 4						
Year	Nominal GDP (thousands)	Growth Rate	Real GDP in 2005 Prices	Growth Rate	GDP Deflator	Growth Rate
2005	$112		$112		$100	
2006	$133	19%	$130	16%	$102	2%
2007	$200	50%	$140	8%	$143	40%

For example, to find the 2006 and 2007 real GDPs in 2005 prices, we carry out the following simple calculations:

$$2006 \text{ Real GDP in 2005 prices} = (\$3 \times 18) + (\$2 \times 38) = \$130$$
$$2007 \text{ Real GDP in 2005 prices} = (\$3 \times 20) + (\$2 \times 40) = \$140$$

Note how growth rates drop compared to those of the nominal GDPs. In fact, the growth rate of real GDP for 2007 is less than that for 2006. This is because a big part of the increase in nominal GDP for 2007 came from a large increase in the price of bread. [11]

11 The growth rate equals (new value – old value) ÷ (old value). So for 2007, the growth rate of nominal GDP = (200 – 133)/133 = .50. We generally multiply this by 100 to turn it into a percentage (0.50 × 100 = 50%).

We have already found a quantity index to measure the total amount of goods and services produced in the economy. That is our real GDP. But it would also be nice to come up with an index showing changes in the prices of these goods and services in the economy. In other words, we want to decompose the nominal GDP into a price index and a quantity index. This will help us understand what portion of the increase in the nominal GDP is due to an increase in the quantity of goods and services, and what part is due to a change in the prices of these goods and services.

This turns out to be an easy thing to do. In general, any nominal magnitude equals a price times a quantity. The quantity is called the real magnitude. For example, suppose you bought 4 loaves of bread from Mrs. Baker for $2.50 each. The nominal magnitude in this transaction is $10, which is equal to a price of $2.50 times a real magnitude of 4 loaves.

We apply the same simple concept to nominal GDP. *Any* nominal thing equals a price times a real thing:

(Nominal Thing) = (Price) × (Real Thing)

We already have the nominal GDP. We also have the real GDP. All we need to do is put them in the same relationship:

(Nominal GDP) = (Price) × (Real GDP)

The only thing left to do is calculate the price from this relationship. The resulting number is called the *GDP deflator*, which is basically a price index. So:

GDP Deflator = (Nominal GDP/Real GDP) × 100

GDP DEFLATOR
An index of general price level calculated as Nominal GDP/Real GDP.

We multiply the result by 100 to convert the fraction into a percentage. The above table calculates the GDP deflators for the three years. For example, the GDP deflator for 2007 is calculated as follows:

GDP Deflator for 2006 = ($200/$140) × 100 = 143

Three things to note:

1. The GDP deflator for 2005 is just 100 because it is the base year.
2. This price index is called the GDP *deflator* because it divides the nominal GDP by this number into a smaller number, which is called the real GDP. So the nominal GDP is reduced in size—it is deflated—by this price index.
3. The GDP deflator is not a good measure of the overall prices faced by households, since it includes the prices of many items that households do not buy. As we know by now, GDP includes purchases of trucks by firms and purchases of tanks by the government. When was the last time *you* bought an anti-aircraft missile? Moreover, since GDP is a measure of all the goods produced inside a country, the GDP deflator does not include the prices of imported goods. For these reasons, policymakers use another index called the *Consumer Price Index* (CPI) that includes baskets of goods purchased by ***households***. We will describe this index in more detail later.

CONSUMER PRICE INDEX
A price index that is calculated by valuing a basket of goods purchased by an average household in 1984, using current prices.

UNIFORM INCREASE IN PRICES

Suppose that the price of every good and service in the economy increases by 5%. What will be the effect on the total factor income? At first this sounds like a difficult question to answer for the following reason. If the price of every good and service increases, the baker will make 5% more money selling bread, but she will also have to pay 5% more for the flour she buys from the miller, and the miller has to pay 5% more to the farmer. However, note from the last column of Table 2 that the values of all these intermediate goods cancel in calculating the total factor income. So the total factor income is the value of the final goods produced. Thus, a 5% increase in the price of all the goods and services will result in a 5% increase in total factor income.

You may complain that in the real world, some incomes are fixed. For example, some workers are under labor contracts that fix their wages. Or, government employees may not get a raise for a few years. Can we still claim that a 5% increase in prices results in a 5% increase in factor income? The answer is yes. If some of the incomes like wages are fixed, then other incomes, such as profits or rents, increase by more than 5%, so that overall the *total* factor income increases at 5%. Please revisit the discussion of the fallacy of composition in Chapter 1. See if that argument makes more sense to you now.

GDP AS A MEASURE OF WELL-BEING

After all this, can we claim that a higher real GDP means a higher level of well-being or welfare?

1. To begin with, a country with a big population may have a large GDP, but each person receives only a very small portion of the GDP. So for purposes of well-being, **per capita** or per head figures are more appropriate. To calculate per capita GDP, we simply divide real GDP by the size of the population.
2. Even per capita figures do not tell the whole story. A country might have a large per capita GDP, but the **distribution** of GDP among people could be paltry. One percent on the top may get almost all the income, and the remaining 99% may live in misery.
3. GDP is also silent about the **kinds** of goods produced. For example, suppose Country A produces a lot of consumer goods such as milk, bread, or beer, while Country B produces a lot of investment goods such as tractors, computers, and factories. The two countries may have the same GDP, but they will have different consumption and growth patterns. Country B will consume less than Country A initially. But since its stock of capital increases, it will be able to produce and consume more than Country A in the future. As another example, a country may produce a lot of "peacetime" goods while another produces "wartime" goods. Again, the well-being of the two countries will be different, even though their GDPs may be equal.
4. A lot of "**bads**" are produced in a country as well as goods. Examples are pollution, noise, etc. We do not count these in GDP. Some economists propose that we should.
5. Many things that affect a nation's well-being are not counted in the GDP. Examples include the level of crime, leisure time, and family stability.
6. **Nonmarket activities** are not included. So a low real GDP may not necessarily mean a lower standard of living. This is a bigger problem for the developing countries, where a lot of production might be carried out by households for household consumption. Nevertheless, some economists propose that all countries should include the value of housework in the GDP to better reflect the level of well-being of the country. If we somehow estimate and

include the market values of lawns mowed and pancakes made by households, the value of GDP would be much higher.[12]

Will GDP be equal to the income generated in the production process if we include the value of housework? The answer is yes, if we redefine the concept of income a bit. By mowing my own lawn, I am saving the money that I would have to pay someone else to do it for me, so I am richer by that amount. Similarly, this is the amount of money I am "paying" myself to mow the lawn. So this is also an expenditure item. Therefore, the three aspects of GDP—production, income, and expenditure—will also apply to GDP if we include the value of housework in its measurement. Note, however, that since there are no market transactions in these cases, the values of these goods and services should be *imputed* on the basis of the observed market transactions on similar goods and services. For this reason, these values are called imputed values. As you might imagine, this might introduce a lot of measurement errors into the GDP figures.

But still, GDP will affect welfare. Higher GDP means more and bigger homes, more parks, more hospitals, better education, and so on.[13] Additionally, nations with higher GDP generally have less pollution. This is because they can afford to clean the air, rivers, and lakes. Since these countries have large GDPs, they have high incomes. High incomes result in a large amount of tax revenue for the government, some of which can be spent to improve their environment. Poorer countries cannot afford most of these.

APPENDIX

This appendix describes several important concepts that are slightly more technical in nature. However, they are not difficult to understand.

ITEMS MISSED IN A FINAL-GOODS CALCULATION

Now that you have used only the values of final goods in your calculations and finished your assignment early, something will nag at you on the way home. If you count only the final goods and services that are sold in the market, you will miss five groups of goods that are produced—but are not among the final goods sold. Since you have missed these goods, you must add them into the 2007 GDP. We call these items *increases in inventories*. They are as follows:

- Semifinished intermediate goods. First, you include intermediate goods that are not finished. Suppose that by midnight on December 31, 2007, a car battery producer had 10,000 semifinished batteries in its assembly lines that were not ready to be sold. The fact that they were "half finished" means that they were "half produced," so they should be included in the 2007 GDP. We only include the portions that are produced by midnight. We value them at 2007 market prices. We call them increases in inventories and include them in the GDP calculation.

12 Estimates of the value of household production range from 35 to 100 percent of GDP. These estimates, however, are very rough. See Katharine G. Abraham and Christopher Mackie, eds., Beyond the Market: Designing Non-Market Accounts for the United States, 2006. The National Academic Press, Washington, DC (p. 56).

13 And yes, Olympic gold medals. If you think about it, the more developed richer countries take home more gold medals. Why do you think this is?

- Unsold intermediate goods. Next, you include intermediate goods that are finished, but not sold. Suppose that at the end of 2007, Mr. Miller had some unsold flour in storage. Suppose also that the 2007 market value of this flour was $12,000. What should you do with this $12,000? Well, you have to count it somewhere in the 2007 GDP, because the miller produced the flour in that year. Recall again that you have to count *everything* produced by all firms, not just those items that are sold. You count this $12,000 toward the 2007 GDP and call it an increase in inventories.
- Unused intermediate goods. Third, you include intermediate goods that are finished and sold, but not used by the buyer. Suppose that Mrs. Baker could not use all the flour she bought in 2007. She carries the unused portion over to 2008. Suppose also that the current 2007 market value of this flour was $5,000. Since it was produced in 2007, you need to include it in the 2007 GDP.
- Semifinished final goods. Fourth, you include final goods that are not finished. Similar to semifinished intermediate goods, suppose that by the end of December 31, 2007, Ford had 100,000 cars on its assembly lines. These "works in progress" are valued at 2007 market prices. We also call these increases in inventories and include them in the GDP calculation.
- Unsold final goods. Finally, you include final goods that are finished, but not sold. If a company produces a certain amount of a final good for sale but cannot sell it all, its inventory of unsold final goods will increase. Suppose that in 2007 GM produced 10,000,000 cars, but could not sell 1,000,000 of them. Then its inventory will increase by these 1,000,000 cars. The value of these cars will be included in the 2007 GDP, even though they were not sold in this year. We evaluate them at current 2007 market prices.

Recall again that we are interested in the final goods and services *produced*, not necessarily sold. When they are sold next year, we don't include their market values in the next year's GDP.[14]

CAPITAL GOODS AND DEPRECIATION

You get an e-mail from your boss asking you whether you took account of capital goods purchases and depreciation charges in calculating the value added amounts. What do these things even mean? You find that firms buy capital goods to produce goods and services, just like intermediate goods. The only difference is that *capital goods* last much longer than a production period, say 10 or 20 years. Examples include trucks, tractors, computers, and ovens. What should you do about these? You cannot subtract the whole purchase prices from the sales revenues as you did with intermediate goods, since not all of these goods are used up in one production period. You should only subtract the portion that is used in that year in the production process. But how do you calculate *that*?[15]

Let's start with a definition. Suppose you buy a new car for $25,000 and drive it for a year. After one year it becomes a secondhand car. You can sell it now for only $20,000. This $5,000 drop

---

14 The issue is a bit more technical. Suppose that a manufacturer produced 10 million cars this year and sold only 9 million of them. We count all 10 million in this year's GDP—9 million as cars sold and 1 million as increase in inventories, both at this year's price. Now if next year the manufacturer sells 8 million cars, we know that 1 million of them are from this year's inventories. We subtract those 1 million from the total sold and call it reduction in inventories. So next year's production equals 8 million sold minus 1 million reductions in inventories. This leaves 7 million cars that are produced next year.

15 You have already included the values of capital goods produced in 2007 if they were produced in that year. No ambiguity here. The question here is how you calculate values added by the firms that purchase these capital goods.

in the market value is called the *depreciation* in the value of the car. Similarly, when a firm buys machines and equipment and uses them in production, they depreciate in value through normal wear-and-tear. Since the depreciation is because of production, it should be regarded as a part of the annual production cost.

DEPRECIATION
The decrease in the market price or value of any good or asset.

The problem is, most of the time a firm cannot determine the amount by which the values of its plants and equipment have depreciated. There might not be any market for some used installed equipment. Even if there is a market, it may not be practical for the firm to appraise the value of its equipment every year. The Internal Revenue Service (IRS) allows business firms to deduct depreciation expenses from their taxable profits. However, for the reasons mentioned above, it is not easy either for the IRS or the firm to estimate how much value each machine has lost in a year in the production process. For this reason, the IRS has come up with some rough percentage depreciation rates for capital goods of different types that firms should use to calculate their tax liabilities.[16]

For example, the IRS rule might say something like "*If you buy a tractor, we will assume that it will have a depreciable life of 10 years and will allow you to deduct 1/10 (or 10%) of its purchase price from your profits for 10 years.*" Since firms generally do not like to keep two sets of books, one for tax purposes and the other for internal decision making, they usually just use the IRS depreciation percentages (10% in the above example) to calculate the amount of depreciation charges for each year. These are percentages of the initial purchase prices of capital goods.[17]

Even if firms report such depreciation expenses in their books, these numbers are not real cash outlays. In a sense, they are phony numbers. Even if an existing old machine loses $100,000 of its value in a year, the firm does not incur any actual cost. All that happens is that the firm's owners subtract that number from their profits and report a smaller amount to the IRS.

Consider the following simple example. Suppose a farmer buys $50,000 worth of intermediate goods in 2007 and produces soy beans. The sales revenue equals $250,000, so the farmer's value added is $200,000. Out of this value added amount, the farmer pays wages, interest, and rent of $100,000, and keeps the remaining $100,000 as his profit. However, at the beginning of 2007 he purchased some farming equipment worth $600,000. The depreciation rate on this type of equipment is 10%, so the farmer can deduct $60,000 from his 2007 income and just pay taxes on the remaining $40,000. The farmer does not really spend that $60,000. It is just an item in the book.

We can therefore write

Reported profit = Profit - Depreciation

In our example,

$40,000 = $100,000 - $60,000

We can rearrange the above relation to read

Profit = Reported profit + Depreciation

In our example,

16 These percentages are regulated by the Internal Revenue Code, which underwent a major change under the Tax Reform Act of 1986. These percentages are called the Modified Accelerated Cost Recovery System, or MACRS for short (pronounced makers).

17 So the depreciation charges calculated using the IRS percentages could be quite different from the true economic depreciation, which is a drop in the market price of capital assets.

$100,000 = $40,000 + $60,000

With the depreciation charges included, the income aspect of GDP takes the following form:

GDP = Wages received by labor +
Rent received by property owners +
Interest received by creditors +
Profit reported by capital owners +
Depreciation of capital

It is the presence of the depreciation charges in the calculation of GDP that makes it "gross." If depreciation is subtracted from GDP, the result becomes *net domestic product*.

CHAIN-WEIGHTED PRICES AND QUANTITIES

What if you took a different year as the base year to calculate the real GDP? Table 5 calculates the real GDP, taking each of the three years at a time as the base year.

Table 5

Year	Real GDP in 2005 Prices	Growth Rate	Real GDP in 2006 Prices	Growth Rate	Real GDP in 2007 Prices	Growth Rate
2005	$112		$116		$160	
2006	$130	16%	$133	15%	$185	16%
2007	$140	8%	$145	9%	$200	8%

Notice an uncomfortable feature of these results. The real GDP growth rates depend on which year you take as the base year. Was the 2006 increase in real GDP 16%, or 15%? To solve this problem, the Bureau of Economic Analysis (BEA) of the U.S. Commerce Department started to use *chain-weighted growth rates* after 1996. BEA analysts take two years—such as 2005 and 2006—and calculate the real GDP growth rate for these two years, using 2005 as the base year (16%) and then taking 2006 as the base year (15%). They then take the geometric average of the two *growth factors*. That is,

CHAIN-WEIGHTED GROWTH RATES
Calculating the growth rates in the real GDP by moving the base year forward one year at a time and calculating the growth rates as the geometric average of the two adjacent growth rates.

$$\sqrt{((1+0.16)\times(1+0.15))}=(1+0.155)$$

They take this 15.5% as the growth rate of real GDP between 2005 and 2006. Next, they take the two years, 2006 and 2007, and repeat the same calculations for these two years to obtain the average growth factor:

$$\sqrt{((1+0.09)\times(1+0.08))}=(1+0.085)$$

The result is a series of chain-weighted growth factors. Finally, they take a year—say 2005 as the base year—and apply these chain-weighted growth factors to the *nominal* GDP in that year to find the chain-weighted *real* GDPs. For example,

Real GDP for 2006 in chained 2005 dollars = (1 + 0.155) × ($112.00) = $129.36
Real GDP for 2007 in chained 2005 dollars = (1 + 0.085) × ($129.36) = $140.35

The chain-weighted GDP deflator is then calculated as usual, by dividing the nominal GDP by the chained-weighted real GDP. (See Table 6.)

Table 6

Year	Nominal GDP	Chained Growth Rate	Chain-Weighted Real GDP	Chain-Weighted GDP Deflator
2005	$112		$112.00	100
2006	$133	15.5%	$129.36	103
2007	$200	8.5%	$140.35	142

TO SUMMARIZE

1. *Gross domestic product (GDP)* is the market value of all produced goods and services, except those produced by households for household consumption. All other details that follow come from this definition.
2. Since production takes time, we need to specify a time period over which to measure GDP. GDP is a *flow variable.* We have both quarterly and annual GDP data.
3. If a good that is sold in a year was not produced in that year, its value will not be included in that year's GDP. This includes:
   - New goods produced in previous years. Example: A purchase in January 2006 of a new Ford produced in December 2005.
   - Used items.
   - Existing assets.
4. If a firm produces a good, its value is included, whether sold or not. So GDP will include:
   - An intermediate good that is produced, but not sold.
   - Semifinished intermediate goods.
   - An intermediate good that is sold, but not used.
   - A final good that is produced, but not sold.
   - Semifinished final goods.
5. No such problems arise with respect to services, because a service is produced at the same time that it is sold and consumed. An example of this is a haircut.
6. The values of services provided by the government are measured at cost and included in the GDP.
7. The goods and services are produced by the *factors of production* located in a country. These are land, labor, and capital.
8. The only produced goods and services whose values are not included in GDP are those produced by households that do not come to the marketplace.

9. GDP has three aspects:
   - Production.
   - Expenditure.
   - Income.

   In other words, the nominal GDP of a country equals the amount of income generated by the factors of production that have produced it. and the total amount of money spent to buy those goods and services.
10. *Nominal GDP* can be decomposed into the product of two variables: the *real GDP* and the *GDP deflator*:

    Nominal GDP = (GDP Deflator) × (Real GDP)

11. The *real GDP* is a measure of the quantity of goods and services produced, while the GDP deflator is an index that attempts to summarize the prices of all the goods and services produced.

EXERCISES

Question 1

The text mentioned that we use market prices of goods and services to convert them into the same measurement units. Why do we not use some other units of measurement, such as weight or the number of hours it takes to produce a good or a service? Relate your answer to the issue of standards of living and employment.

Question 2

Assume Mrs. Baker used up all the flour and baked some bread. But on December 31, 2007, she was left with some unsold bread. She sold these at a reduced price on January 1, 2007. How would national income accountants treat these transactions?

Question 3

Which of the following activities will count toward GDP?

a. The bakery you own bakes a cake worth $10 and sells it.
b. The bakery you own bakes a cake worth $10, but cannot sell it.
c. You bake a similar cake at home and sell it to your neighbor to raise cash for a charity.
d. You bake a similar cake at home and eat it.
e. You bake a similar cake at home and give it as a gift to your chiropractor.

Question 4

What will happen to the GDP if you marry your primary care physician? Would your answer be different if GDP already included the value of housework?

Question 5

Does the concept of value added apply to used car dealers? What are the intermediate goods? How would you calculate the value added?

Question 6

Which of the following transactions will be included in the 2007 GDP?

a. I buy four tires from Big O Tires in 2007 to replace my old ones. The tires were produced in 2007.

b. I buy four tires from Big O Tires in 2007 to replace my old ones. The tires were produced in 2006.

c. GM buys four tires from Big O Tires to put on its 2007 models. The tires were produced in 2007.

d. Big O Tires produced four tires, but could not sell them by the end of the year.

e. My neighbor bought four tires from Big O Tires in 2007, but they did not fit. Since they were the size I needed, I just bought them from my neighbor. Would my purchase count toward 2007 GDP?

Question 7

Suppose a retailer in 2000 buys 11,000 blue jeans from a wholesaler for $15 each. She sells 10,000 of them in 2000 for $25 each. What is the contribution of these activities to the 2000 GDP?

Question 8

Over the past several decades, the participation of women in the U.S. labor force has increased. More women now work outside their homes than before. The result is larger production and a higher GDP. But some economists claim that the effect on the U.S. GDP of women's increased participation in the labor force is overstated. In other words, not all of the increase in GDP is due to a greater amount of production made possible by the additional women in the labor force. Why do you think they say this?

Question 9

On January 8, 2007, you buy a new textbook for $120. At the end of the quarter you sell it back to the bookstore for $40. The bookstore sells it again to some other student for $70. What is the contribution of all these transactions to the 2007 GDP?

Question 10

You buy a nice little piece of land for $100,000 and build a home on it. You hire a foundation company, a framer, an electrician, a plumber, and a roofer to do the job. Once finished, you sell the house for $500,000. The real estate agent gets her 6% commission. All these transactions take place in 2007. The value of which one of these transactions will count in the 2007 GDP?

Question 11

You buy a new 2007 model car in March 2007 for $25,000 and sell it five days later for $22,000. What will be the effect of these transactions on the 2000 GDP?

Question 12

(from a student): Suppose Mrs. Baker bakes some bread, but she cannot sell it all. The unsold bread rots, and she throws it away. How do we treat this bread in our GDP calculations?

Question 13

Suppose our good sister Mrs. Baker sold bread worth $100,000 in 2007. Her revenue and costs are as follows

Revenue =		$100,000
Costs:		
	Materials =	$25,000
	Wages =	$15,000
	Interest =	$10,000
	Rent =	$ 5,000

What is our Mrs. Baker's contribution to GDP? What is the value added of her company? How is this distributed among different income categories?

Question 14

Would the GDP still be equal to total factor income if we could also count the values of goods and services produced by households?

Question 15

What are the annual and quarterly U.S. GDPs? Do we calculate GDP on a monthly basis? Visit the website of the Federal Reserve Bank of St. Louis at http://www.stls.frb.org/fred/ to find out.

Question 16

There have been serious proposals to scrap the current income tax system and replace it with a "consumption-based" tax system. These proposals usually go under the title of "fundamental tax reform."[18] Two such proposals are the value added tax (VAT) and the national sales tax (NST) proposals. In these proposed systems, only business firms would pay taxes. Suppose there are a number of firms in the economy. The final products of these firms are computers, bread, and furniture. The following table shows the market values of the intermediate and final goods in the production chains for a particular year. For example, the computer manufacturer buys memory boards from the board producer, who in turn buys memory chips from the chip producer.

	Market Value		Market Value		Market Value
Memory Chips	20	**Farmer**	10	**Timberland**	10
Memory Boards	50	**Miller**	30	**Wood Producer**	20
Computer Manufacturer	100	**Baker**	60	**Furniture Store**	40

Assume that the producers of the basic materials, the farmer, and the timberland cultivator do not buy any intermediate goods.

a. Calculate the nominal GDP of this country.

b. If the income tax rate in this country is 25%, calculate the total income tax paid by the factors of production.

18 For more information on the fundamental tax reform proposals see the President's Advisory Panel on Tax Reform at http://www.taxreformpanel.gov/index.shtml.

c. The VAT applies to the value added generated by each firm in the production process. If the VAT rate is 25%, calculate the total tax paid by the three businesses.
d. The NST applies only to the final products purchased by consumers. If the NST rate is 25%, calculate the total tax paid by the three businesses.[19]
e. There is an implementation problem you need to avoid. Suppose the VAT is "forward shifted." This means, for example, that the farmer shifts the VAT forward to the miller by charging him $12.50 instead of $10. Similarly, the miller charges the baker $37.50, and the baker sells the bread for $75. If the VAT were shifted forward, what would be the market values observed by government officials? What would be the total value added calculated by the government? What would be the total tax collected? Would this be an overestimation or an underestimation of the true tax liability?
f. Repeat the previous question for an NST system.
g. Suppose that because of fierce competition among sellers of the products, the VAT is "backward shifted." This means, for instance, that the farmer would not be able to sell the wheat for more than $10; therefore, he would have to absorb the whole tax. (Similarly for other producers.) Calculate the total tax collected by the government and comment. Would this be an overestimation or an underestimation of the true tax liability?
h. Repeat the previous question for an NST system.[20]
i. Assuming that the VATs and NSTs are shifted forward, how could the government calculate the true tax liabilities of different businesses?

Question 17

The following table shows the market prices and quantities of three final goods produced in an economy for three years. Calculate the following:

a. The nominal GDP for each year.
b. The real GDP for each year, taking each year as the base year in turn.
c. The chained real GDPs, using 2005 dollars.
d. The GDP deflators, taking each year as the base year in turn.
e. The GDP deflators, using the chained real GDPs.

	Computer		Bread		Furniture	
Year	Price	Quantity	Price	Quantity	Price	Quantity
2005	10	10	2	30	4	5
2006	11	12	3	40	5	7
2007	12	14	4	50	6	9

19 You will obtain the same tax liabilities under the three tax systems. You might then wonder why such proposals are called "consumption based" if they have the same effect as "income based" systems. The answer lies in the treatment of investment spending by firms. In most VAT and NST proposals, the total amounts spent on durable investment goods are treated as intermediate goods and subtracted from sales revenues to obtain the values added. The effect of this "expensing of investment goods" is that the total value of such goods is subtracted from the GDP; the result is the value of the consumption goods. See the next question.

20 For a discussion of forward and backward shifting of VAT and NST, see William P. Orzechowski, Border Tax Adjustments and Fundamental Tax Reform, 2001, The Tax Foundation, http://www.taxfoundation.org.

Question 18

In 2005 a U.S. computer manufacturer buys parts and components, uses equipment, and hires labor to produce laptops. It produces and sells one million laptops. Each laptop sells for $1,000. To produce these laptops, the manufacturer purchases parts and components (such as memory boards and chips) for a total cost of $600 million. It pays $300 million in wages, interest, and rent.

a. What is the contribution of this manufacturer to the U.S. GDP in 2005?
b. What is this manufacturer's value added in 2005?
c. How much total GDP is generated as a result of the production of these laptops?
d. How much total income is generated as a result of the production and sale of these laptops?

Question 19

The value of which of the following will be included in the 2005 U.S. GDP? Provide a brief explanation.

a. GM produced 10 million cars in 2005, but could only sell 9 million of them.
b. A lawn mower manufacturer purchased 100,000 engines from Briggs & Stratton. It used 90,000 of these engines to produce lawn mowers. Of these 90,000 lawn mowers, the manufacturer could only sell 70,000.

Question 20

Suppose there are only two producers in the country. The following table shows the amounts produced and prices per unit for 2003 and 2005.

a. Calculate the nominal GDP for 2005 (current dollars).
b. Calculate the real GDP for 2005 (constant 2003 dollars).
c. Calculate the GDP deflator for 2005.
d. Calculate the rate of growth of real GDP.

	Producer A		*Producer B*	
Year	Price per Gallon ($)	Gallons Produced	Price per Ton ($)	Tons Produced
2003	10	100	22	150
2005	15	200	25	200

Question 21

Do you recall the fallacy of composition and the distinction between microeconomics and macroeconomics? Now that we have learned the definition of GDP, this distinction can be explained more easily. In microeconomics, when the price of a particular good, such as French bread, falls by 5% while the prices of all the other goods remain constant, an individual consumer buys more of it for two reasons. First, she substitutes the now cheaper French bread for some other goods that she consumed before, such as flat bread, oatmeal, muffins, or cereals. This is called the *substitution effect* of a price reduction. Second, if she consumes the same amount of French bread as before, she will have some money left over that she can use to buy more of every good, including French bread itself. It is as if her income has increased. This is called the *income effect* of a price reduction.

Macroeconomics, by contrast, studies the aggregate level of output and the general price level. Suppose the prices of every good and service fall by 5%. Will there be any substitution effect? Will there be any income effect? (Hint: Recall the three faces of GDP).

CHAPTER 6

Growth and Cycles

INTRODUCTION AND REVIEW

WE HAVE LEARNED that macroeconomics is mostly interested in the behavior of three variables: aggregate level of output, general price level, and overall employment. In Chapter 5, we developed two indexes to represent the first two variables: the aggregate level of output is represented by real GDP, and the general price level by the GDP deflator or the consumer price index (CPI), depending on what we are interested in. We also recall from Chapter 1 that overall employment means the total number of people who have jobs.

With respect to these variables, we are mainly concerned with long-run growth and short-run fluctuations in real GDP, inflation, and unemployment. This chapter will define these concepts and describe their costs and benefits. Later chapters will discuss their causes, and whether or not we can do anything to change their levels using macroeconomic policies. We also learned in Chapter 1 that the levels of these variables are determined by the interactions among several macroeconomic markets: the goods and services market, the factor market, the financial markets, and the foreign exchange market. Therefore, we must learn about the functioning of these markets in order to understand how and why these variables change.

ECONOMIC GROWTH

The aggregate level of output produced in a country—the real GDP—has two effects on people's lives. First, it affects the standards of living or well-being of the residents of the country. The standard of living in a nation will be higher if people there can consume larger amounts of goods and services. Second, it affects the level of employment in that country. A country's level of employment will increase if that country produces larger quantities of goods and services. For these reasons, we

Shoppers at a mall in South Africa

like the growth rate to be high, sustained, and stable. In other words, we generally like the aggregate level of output to increase smoothly over time.

The *growth rate* is the rate of increase in real GDP. Growth rates are generally measured on an annual basis. For example, the U.S. real GDPs in 2004 and 2005 were $10.7035 trillion and $11.0486 trillion, respectively. Then we say that the rate of growth in real GDP between 2004 and 2005 was 6.6%. We calculate it as follows:

Growth Rate = (($11.4086 – $10.7035)/$10.7035)) × 100
= 6.6%

GROWTH RATE
Percentage increase in the value of a variable. In economics, it usually refers to the rate of increase in the real GDP.

ECONOMIC GROWTH
Sustained increase in the real GDP over a long period of time.

Keep in mind that we always calculate a rate of change as the new value minus the old value, divided by the old value. We multiply the result by 100 to convert the ratio into a percentage. The reason we are interested in growth *rates*, rather than in actual increases, is easy to understand. If I told you that the real GDP in a country increased by $10 billion over the last year, you would have no sense of whether this was good or bad. If last year the real GDP was $1,000 billion, then this is not a big increase (only 1% growth). But if the real GDP was $100 billion last year, then this is an impressive accomplishment (10% growth).

By *economic growth*, we mean the increase in real GDP in the long run—say, over several decades. Figure 1 shows the actual annual real GDP for the United States for the period 1929–2008. It indicates that the real GDP has been increasing over much of the last century. It is this long-term increase in real output that we define as economic growth. Recall from Chapter 1 that the three production factors—land, labor, and capital—are used to produce output. It stands to reason, therefore, that the long-term growth in real GDP should be due to increases in the quantities and qualities of these production factors. Long-term growth is generally due to one or both of the following reasons:

1. Increases in the amounts of production factors (land, labor, and capital).
2. Technological progress.

By land, we mean all the resources given to us by nature. The amount of "land" can increase by bringing more land into cultivation. Similarly, the amount of natural resources can increase through discovery of new mineral deposits. The quantity of labor can increase through increases in population and migration. The amount of private capital can increase through investment in plants and equipment by business firms. The amount of public capital can increase if governments build more roads, bridges, parks, and schools. Real GDP can also increase, even if there is no increase in the quantity of any of the production factors. This can happen through improvements in technology.

TECHNOLOGICAL PROGRESS
Learning ways of producing new goods or better ways of producing the same goods.

Technology means the knowledge to produce things. An advance in technology, or *technological progress*, means learning better ways of producing the same goods or learning how to produce new or better goods. The quality of land can improve through advancements in farming technology, such as better treatment of land and using more sophisticated agricultural equipment, or the invention of new methods to extract such resources as oil or natural gas. The quality of labor can improve through education, on-the-job training, and learning by doing. Such improvements are called increases in *human capital*. The quality of capital can improve through designing better plants and equipment. This can be achieved in turn through research and development by business firms and academic researchers. In the case of the United States, all these events have taken place in the last century. As a result, the United States has experienced sustained economic growth. For the period 1929–2008, the average annual rate of growth of real GDP for the United States was about 3.5%.

A woman entering line at a state unemployment office.

Figure 1: U.S. Annual Real GDP (1929–2008)

Billions of Chained 2000 Dollars

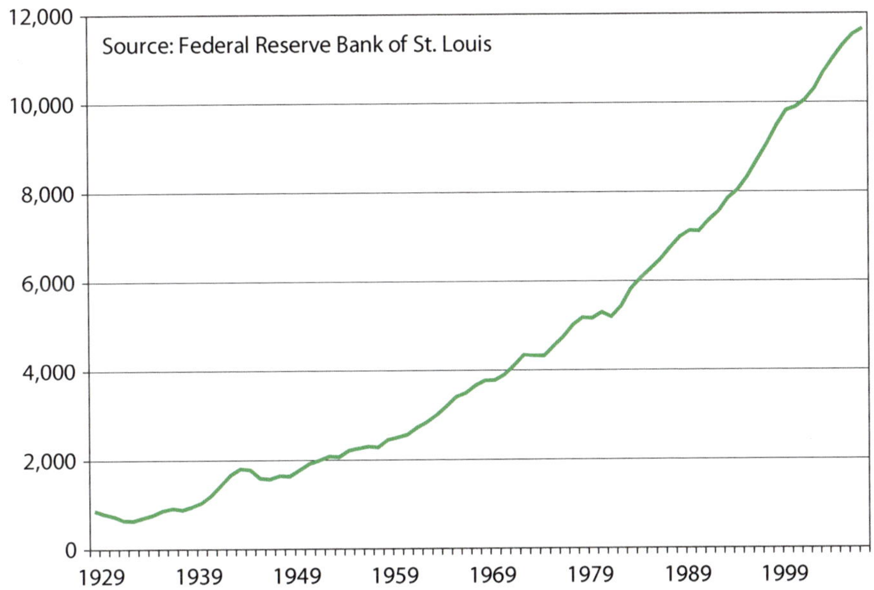

Figure 2 shows the quarterly U.S. real GDP along with what is called the *potential GDP*, from the first quarter of 1950 to the first quarter of 2009. Potential GDP is the total amount of goods and services that *could* potentially be produced, if all factors of production were fully employed. In the case of labor, full employment means that all who are willing to work have a job. Therefore, potential GDP is *not* the *maximum* amount of output that can be produced with the existing resources. It is the amount that *can* be produced in normal conditions when all who want to work have a job. When some of those who want to work don't have a job, we will have unemployment, and the real GDP will fall short of potential. In the opposite case, if demand for labor by business firms is too high relative to normal conditions, then labor will be used more intensively, and the real GDP will be higher than potential.

POTENTIAL GDP
The total amount of goods and services that could potentially be produced, if all factors of production were fully employed.

Figure 2: Actual and Potential Real Quarterly GDPs (1950:1–2009:1)

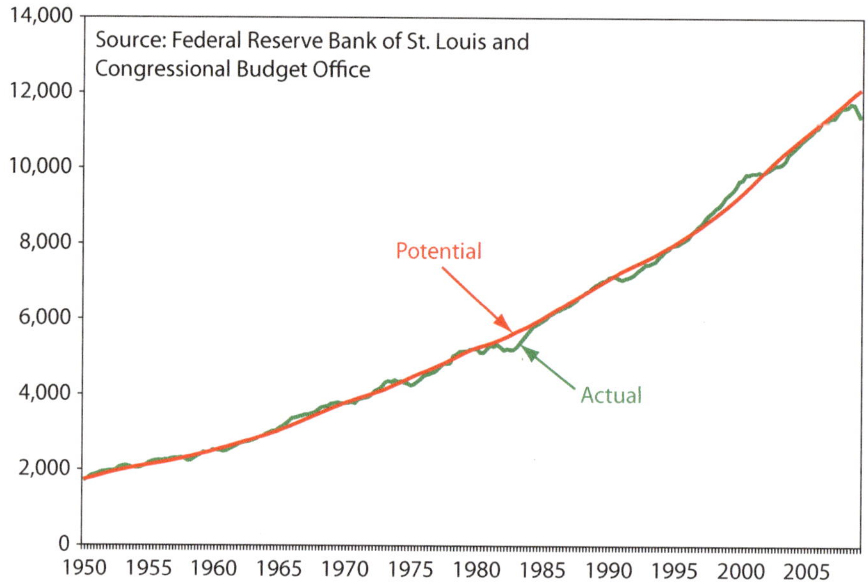

A little example may help clarify the concept. Suppose that at the going wage rate, Abigail and Bartholomew, a nice couple in Colorado, supply a total of 60 hours of labor per week—40 hours by Bartholomew and 20 hours by Abigail. This is the normal supply of labor by this two-earner family. If every household contributed their normal supply of labor, then we would be producing the potential GDP. Now suppose that business firms lay off some workers, and Abigail loses her job. At the current wage rate, the family is still willing to supply 60 hours per week. Since Abigail wants to work but does not have a job, we have unemployment, and the actual GDP is less than potential (the amount that could have been produced if the family supplied 60 hours per week.) After a while, Abigail has to lower her asking wage in order to get hired back.

In the opposite case, suppose that demand for goods and services increases, and as a result firms start hiring additional labor. The problem is that every household, including Abigail and Bartholomew, is supplying its normal amount of labor. However, Bartholomew's contract says that he has to work overtime if the firm asks him to. In this case, the family will supply more than 60 hours of labor, and the real GDP will exceed potential. However, Bartholomew will not take this for long. After a while he will ask for a higher wage. Since the firm's business is good, it will agree to a higher wage.

Note that when the real GDP was less than potential, we had unemployment, and Abigail had to accept a lower wage to get hired back. You know that wages are a part of production costs. Since wages go down, the cost of production will go down and the inflation rate will be reduced. In the opposite case, when the real GDP exceeded potential, Bartholomew asked for a higher wage. In this case, the inflation rate will increase. Therefore, we can have an equivalent definition of potential GDP. *The potential GDP is that level of real GDP at which the inflation rate will not change.*

You can see two patterns in Figure 2. First, the actual and potential GDP were both increasing over time. The reason for the increase in potential GDP is quite straightforward. Over time, the quantities and qualities of the production factors have been increasing. Thus, if we could always fully employ them, we could produce larger and larger amounts of output. Second, the actual real GDP has kept pace with potential quite well. So by and large we have been able to keep our resources fully employed in the long run. This is a very important fact, and we will make great use of it in the following chapters. We will also learn why this is, in fact, the case.

Some may say that the population has also been increasing in the United States, so it is still possible for each person to have received a smaller share of the increased domestic output. But this is not really the case. Indeed, real *GDP per capita* or per head (i.e., real GDP divided by population) has also been increasing over time. This is clearly evident from Figure 3. We will take up the question of the causes of economic growth later in the book.

GDP PER CAPITA
Real GDP divided by population.

Costs of Growth

Possible costs of growth include the damage we could inflict on the environment. By producing more, we could pollute the air, lakes, and rivers. This could cause illnesses and deaths. Some of this pollution could be cleaned up. However, we could also do irreversible damage to the environment. Whole forests and timberlands could disappear, and nuclear waste could permanently render a lake unusable or a town uninhabitable.

Benefits of Growth

The benefits of growth seem obvious. Compare your living standards to those of your grandparents. More people now enjoy better homes, better hospitals, and better schools. As to the issue of pollution, it is interesting to note that more advanced capitalist countries have lower pollution than developing countries. This is because they can afford tough antipollution laws. They have developed technologies to deal with pollution. We have antismog laws, as well as cars that pollute less.

Figure 3: U.S. Real Annual per Capita GDP

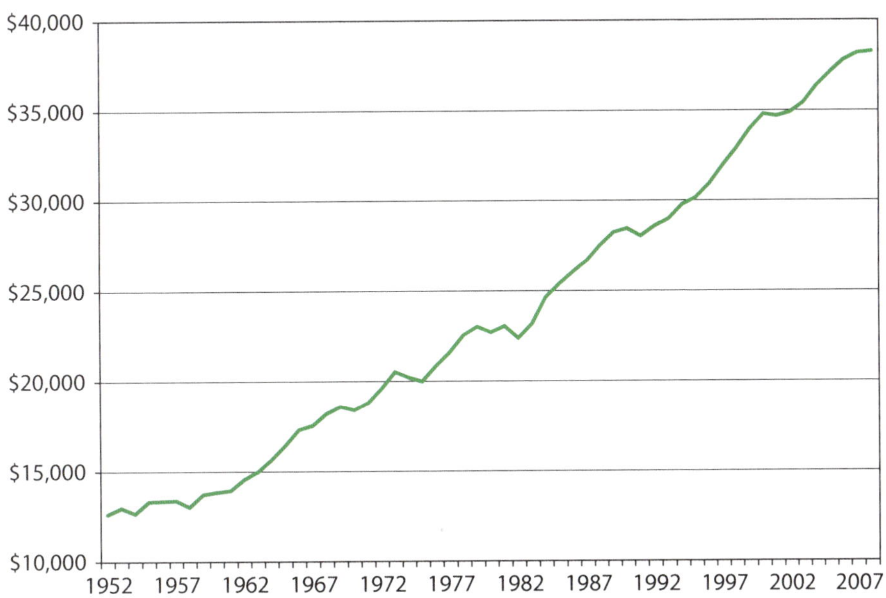

BUSINESS CYCLES

Although real GDP grows over time (as Figure 2 shows), it does not grow along a nice straight line. It goes up and down. Sometimes it lies above the line of potential GDP and sometimes below. These ups and downs constitute what are called *business cycles*. Consider the illustration in Figure

BUSINESS CYCLES
Ups and downs in real GDP.

RECESSION
A fall in the aggregate level of output or real GDP.

PEAK
The point where an expansion phase of a business cycle ends.

TROUGH
The point where a recession ends and the expansion begins.

RECURRENT CYCLES
Business cycles are recurrent in the sense that they keep happening.

PERIODIC CYCLES
Cycles are said to be periodic if they are alike in shape and duration. Business cycles are not periodic.

4. The increase in GDP is called an *expansion*, and the decrease is a *contraction* or a *recession*. The point where an expansion ends is called a *peak*; the point where a recession ends is called a *trough*. Peaks and troughs are called *turning points*. Since the long-run tendency of output is to increase, each turning point is generally higher than the previous turning point of the same type.

Business cycles are *recurrent*, but not *periodic*. They are recurrent in the sense that the up-and-down patterns repeat—i.e., they recur. One *cycle* is defined as the pattern that repeats. You can verify in Figure 4 that this would be from one peak to another, or from one trough to another. Thus, each cycle includes a recession and an expansion. It is this pattern that recurs. The cycles, however, are not periodic, in the sense that they do not occur in equal intervals and do not have equal duration.[1] For this reason, expansions and recessions are hard, if not impossible, to predict.

Figure 4: Phases of Business Cycles

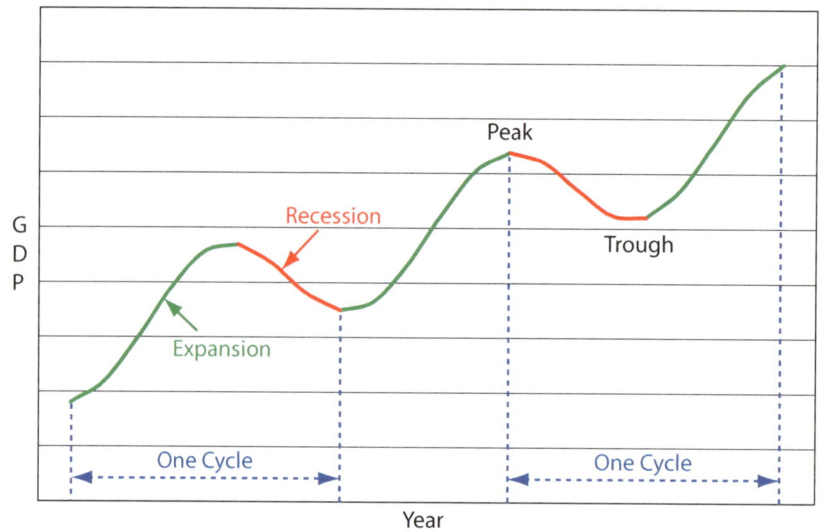

Some define a downward movement in real GDP as a recession if it persists for at least two quarters (six months). This is not, however, generally accepted by economists, for several reasons. For one thing, what if the downturn is quite mild? For another, a recession is not just characterized by the movement of GDP alone. Generally, in a recession several variables, such as unemployment, interest rates, wages, prices, and productivity move with or against GDP. In fact, as we will see, it is possible to have a recession without a big decrease in GDP. Therefore, looking at just one variable would not give the complete picture.

In the United States, a private nonprofit organization of professional economists called the National Bureau of Economic Research (NBER) uses extensive databases to analyze business cycles. NBER's Business Cycle Dating Committee announces the beginnings and ends of business cycles by studying the state of the economy. They announce these turning points after considerable time lags, because they want to analyze all aspects of the economy. For example, on November 26, 2001, the Committee announced that a recession had started in March 2001. The Committee announced on July 17, 2003, that the 2001 recession had ended in November 2001.[2]

GREAT DEPRESSION
A prolonged recession in the 1930s in the United States.

1 This definition of a business cycle is consistent with those provided by Arthur Burns and Wesley Mitchell in *Measuring Business Cycles*, New York, National Bureau of Economic Research, 1946.

2 To learn more about the activities of these economists, visit them at http://www.nber.org.

It is possible to identify several recessions in the figures. First look at the data from the 1920s and 1930s in Figure 1. Those were the years of the *Great Depression*. A prolonged recession is called a depression. To concentrate on the more recent episodes, Figure 5 presents the actual and potential quarterly GDPs for the United States, from the first quarter of 1970 to the fourth quarter of 2008. We can spot five recessions in this period. These happened in 1974–1975; 1980–1982; 1990–1991; March 2001 to November 2001 (as mentioned above); and 2007–2009.[3] The 1980–1982 recession seems the most severe among the five, judging by the size of the *GDP gap*. The GDP gap is the amount by which the actual GDP falls short of the potential GDP. The recessions of 1990–1991 and 2001 were much milder by comparison. The jury is still out on the 2007–2009 recession, but we can see that the fall in GDP is the sharpest among all five. These patterns are consistent with our definition of business cycles—they recur, but are not exactly identical. We will study the causes and consequences of these economic downturns later in the book.

GDP GAP
The amount by which the actual GDP falls short of the potential GDP.

Figure 5: Actual and Potential U.S. Real Quarterly GDPs (1970:1 to 2009:1)

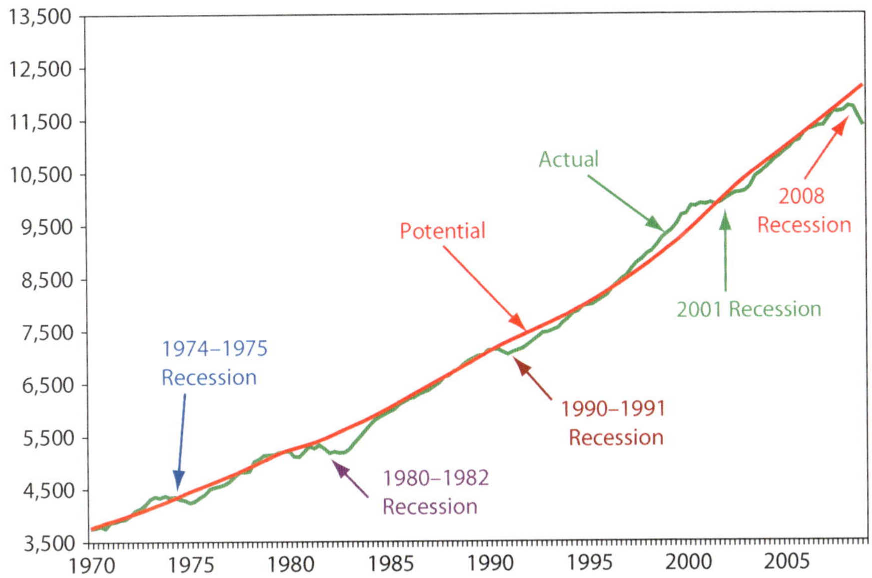

As mentioned, several variables move up or down during the course of a business cycle. For instance, when GDP increases in an expansion phase of a business cycle, interest rates and wages increase as well. Similarly, in a recession they all fall. Such variables that move with GDP are called *pro-cyclical*. If a variable moves against GDP, it is called *countercyclical*. For example, unemployment increases when GDP falls in a recession. Unemployment is thus countercyclical. Of particular interest to economists and policy makers is the behavior of unemployment and inflation during expansions and recessions. This is because of the costs they impose on the society. Therefore, let's turn to a description and discussion of these variables.

PRO-CYCLICAL VARIABLES
Variables that move with the GDP.

COUNTERCYCLICAL VARIABLES
Variables that move against the GDP.

3 At the time of this writing in 2009, the recession was ongoing.

UNEMPLOYMENT

During recessions, some people lose their jobs, and unemployment increases. This is simply because, if we produce fewer goods and services, we need to hire fewer workers. Of course, the same is true for other factors of production. In a recession, the utilizations of land and capital also decrease. As Figure 5 shows, during the four recessions the real GDP was below potential. By the definition of the potential GDP, this implies that some people were unemployed during those recessions. So let's talk about the unemployment problem.

CIVILIAN NONINSTITUTIONAL POPULATION
Civilian population for short; includes persons 16 years of age and older who are not inmates of institutions such as penal and mental facilities or homes for the elderly, and are not members of the armed forces.

We start with the total population of the United States, which includes people of all ages and the members of the armed forces overseas.[4] We subtract from this total all the people who, for one reason or another, are not able to perform civilian (i.e., nonmilitary) work. The result is called the *civilian noninstitutional population*, or just civilian population for short, which includes persons 16 years of age and older who are not inmates of institutions (such as penal and mental facilities or homes for the elderly), and are not members of the armed forces.

Civilian Population = Total Population
- Members of armed forces
- Inmates of penal and mental institutions
- Those in elderly homes
- Those under 16 (minors)

LABOR FORCE
Those who are willing and able to work.

So the civilian population is comprised of all those people who are *able* to perform civilian work. We then divide the civilian population into those who are *willing* to work and those who are not. By definition, the people who are willing to work constitute the *labor force*. The rest of the civilian population is not in the labor force (not willing to work)[5]. Therefore,

Civilian Population = Labor Force + Not in Labor Force

Of those in the labor force (willing to work), some have jobs (are employed) and some do not (are unemployed).

Labor Force = Employed + Unemployed

4 The following description follows the definitions and procedures employed by the U.S. Bureau of Labor Statistics. To learn more, visit their website at http://www.bls.gov.

5 Students are included in this category.

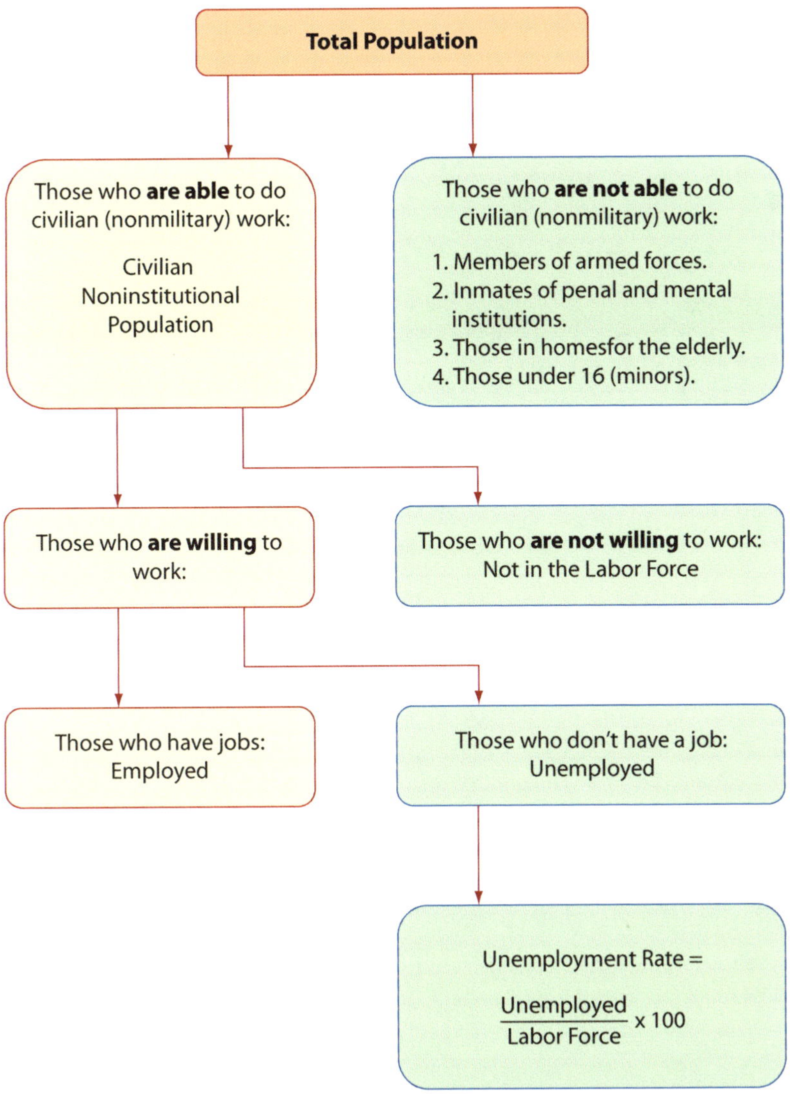

We define

$$\text{Unemployment Rate} = (\text{Unemployed}/\text{Labor Force}) \times 100$$

This measures the percentage of people who are willing to work (labor force), but have no jobs (unemployed). This is a logical variable to focus on, because we should not be concerned about the unemployed who are not willing to work in the first place (are not in the labor force).

Figure 6 shows the quarterly unemployment rate from the first quarter of 1950 through the second quarter of 2009. You can identify the five peaks corresponding to the five recessions in the post–1970 period. The highest unemployment rate occurred in the 1980–1982 recession, which we will have a lot to talk about later. This recession was rather peculiar. The output did not actually fall during this period—it just stopped growing, as shown in Figure 5. However, unemployment soared because of the potential GDP's increase in response to the normal increase in labor force, reaching more than 10% in some months. The 1990–1991 recession was mild by comparison.

If you look carefully at Figure 6, you may be a bit puzzled. Recall that Figure 2 and Figure 5 showed that the actual real GDP traces the potential GDP well in the long run, so we have no unemployment problem in the long run. But this means that the unemployment rate in Figure 6 should average out to zero percent over the entire period. How come the average is more than 4%, then? One of the greatest insights in macroeconomics has been the explanation of this apparent puzzle.[6]

CYCLICAL AND NATURAL RATES OF UNEMPLOYMENT

Consider the following example. Suppose there are 100 people in the labor force (they are willing to work), and there are a total of 100 jobs available out there, filled and unfilled. Of these 100 jobs, 95 have been taken by 95 people. However, there are 5 unfilled jobs, and there are 5 people looking for jobs. You might ask what is going on here. To begin with, by the definition above. we have 5% unemployment rate. But why?

95 jobs filled	5 jobs unfilled
95 people employed	5 people unemployed
Labor Force = 95 employed + 5 unemployed = 100	

Well, some of these 5 people might be new entrants into the job market who are in the process of job hunting. There are jobs available for them. It may just take a few weeks for them to land these jobs. Maybe they have not found those jobs yet, or perhaps they have already found them, but not applied for them yet, or maybe they have applied for and gotten the jobs, but have not started the work yet. We are not too worried about them.

Figure 6: U.S. Quarterly Civilian Unemployment Rate (1950:1 to 2010:1)

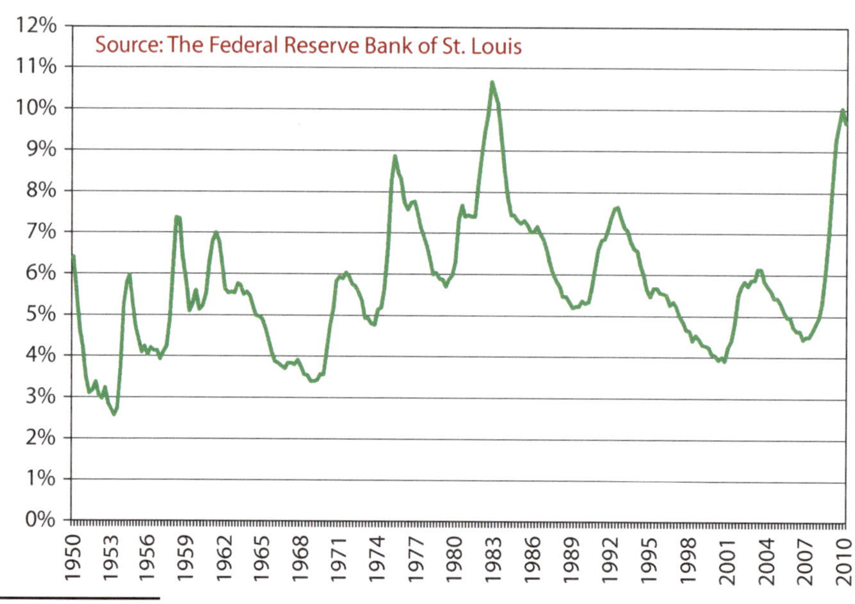

6 The two names associated with this explanation are Edmond Phelps and Milton Friedman, both Nobel laureates.

The second group consists of those who either have been laid off, or have quit their jobs and are searching for a different or a better job. Again, there are jobs available for them, and we hope they will find those jobs soon, after a few phone calls. These two types of unemployment combined are called *frictional unemployment*. They exist due to frictions or imperfections in the labor market. This basically means that finding a job is not an instantaneous process. It takes time and effort to find a job.

FRICTIONAL UNEMPLOYMENT
Unemployment that is due to frictions in the labor market. It is the result of the fact that it takes time to find jobs. In the case of frictional unemployment, there are enough jobs available for the unemployed.

Still, some of those five people may be unemployed for a different reason. Over time, some industries die, and some new ones are born. Some skills become obsolete, and some new ones become popular. Consider the fate of television manufacturers in this country. After the Japanese became efficient in TV production, the United States stopped producing televisions. Workers in these industries gradually lost their jobs, and their skills became obsolete. However, around the same time, the high-technology personal computer and telecommunications industries started to grow. There were still jobs available out there in the economy, but in the new high-tech industries. Similarly, a lot of typists in government and the private sector lost their jobs because word processors made their skills obsolete.

The problem in these situations is that there is a mismatch between the (obsolete) skills of the workers who lose their jobs and the skill requirements in the newly emerging industries. There are jobs available, but not for workers with their certain skills. Such unemployment is called *structural unemployment*—unemployment due to changes in the structure of industries. It naturally occurs in a growing free market economy: you just cannot stop this darn thing called progress. Such unemployment can be dealt with through training.

STRUCTURAL UNEMPLOYMENT
The situation in which there are jobs available, but not for workers with the kinds of skills workers possess.

History has shown that structurally unemployed people have been able to find jobs within one or two years. The sum of frictional and structural unemployment rates is called the *natural unemployment rate*. This is because it is only natural and unavoidable to have this kind of unemployment in a growing free market economy.

NATURAL UNEMPLOYMENT RATE
The sum of frictional and structural unemployment rates.

Natural unemployment exists whenever actual GDP equals potential GDP. This is when we are producing an amount of output sufficient to hire all the labor force. We have enough jobs available for anyone who is willing to work. The only problem is that some of those nice folks have not yet found those jobs. Therefore, *when the economy produces the potential level of output, we will only have natural unemployment*. Economists define this state of affairs as full employment.

We do not have readily available data on the natural unemployment rate. The government estimates it by using some economic models. This rate, though, is generally stable. For example, the estimates of the natural rate for the United States have remained at 5.0% for the last several years. In other words, under the conditions of full employment, 5% of the U.S. labor force would be naturally unemployed. In the following, therefore, we will assume 5% natural rate for the U.S. labor force.

Problems arise when the size of the labor force (those willing to work) exceeds the number of jobs available. Now we are in trouble. Consider the following scenario:

91 jobs filled	5 jobs unfilled
91 people employed	9 people unemployed
Labor Force = 91 employed + 9 unemployed = 100	

In this case, the unemployment rate is 9%. Of these 9 people, 5 are naturally unemployed (frictional + structural). This is under our assumption of 5% natural rate. There are jobs available for these 5 people. The remaining 4 unemployed people will not find any jobs: there are none available for them. These people will remain unemployed until some new jobs are created for them. Such is the case in times of recession, when the economy produces less than potential. Because of this, such unemployment is called *cyclical unemployment*—unemployment due to business cycles.

CYCLICAL UNEMPLOYMENT
Unemployment due to business cycles.

FULL EMPLOYMENT
The situation in which the number of jobs available equals the labor force—those willing and able to work. Therefore, full employment means zero cyclical unemployment.

The moral of this story is that, in a market system, there are always some people unemployed due to labor market frictions. Therefore, *full employment* does not mean zero unemployment. We mean zero *cyclical* unemployment. In other words, in a state of full employment, we will only have natural unemployment. Figure 7 shows the actual and natural unemployment rates for the United States since 1970. Now we have a better understanding of what is going on. During recessions, the total unemployment rate exceeded the natural rate, as in the above example. In other words, we had cyclical unemployment. Using the above hypothetical numbers and some notation,

$u^n =$ natural unemployment rate (5% in our case)
$u^c =$ cyclical unemployment rate (4% in our case)
$u =$ total unemployment rate (9% in our case $= u^n + u^c$)

We should always remember that if we produced the potential level of output, the cyclical unemployment would be zero, but there would still be natural unemployment. The cases are summarized in the following table:

Actual and Potential GDPs	Unemployment Rate
Actual GDP equals potential	$u = u^n + u^c$, $u^c = 0$, therefore $u = u^n$
Actual GDP less than potential	$u = u^n + u^c$, $u^c > 0$, therefore $u > u^n$
Actual GDP more than potential	$u = u^n + u^c$, $u^c < 0$, therefore $u < u^n$

In the last case, when actual GDP exceeds potential, the total number of jobs available exceeds the labor force, so finding jobs becomes very easy. In that case, the actual unemployment will be less than natural. An inspection of Figures 5 and 7 indicates that such cases are rare.

To explain this last case, suppose that due to good economic conditions, there are 8 jobs available, but only 3 people are unemployed. So our overall unemployment rate is 3%. But we know that under normal conditions, we would have a 5% natural unemployment rate. Therefore, the cyclical unemployment rate should be –2% so that we have:

$$u = u^n + u^c = 5\% - 2\% = 3\%$$

Thus, a negative cyclical unemployment rate means that the total number of jobs available exceeds the number of people unemployed.

97 jobs filled	8 jobs unfilled
97 people employed	3 people unemployed
Labor Force = 97 employed + 3 unemployed = 100	

Figure 7: Actual and Natural Quarterly U.S. Unemployment Rates (1970:1 to 2010:1)

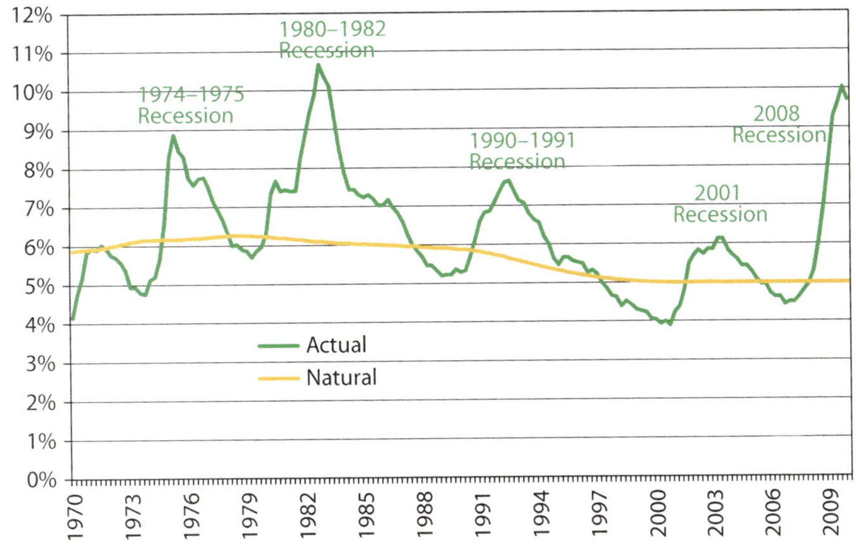

A few things should be mentioned about the natural rate of unemployment. First, it is not a fixed number given to us by nature. In fact, Figure 7 shows that it has been declining in recent years (from about 6% to about 5%). What events or policies do you think could lower the natural rate of unemployment? Think of any event or policy that would help people find jobs faster, if they exist. For example, the government could set up agencies to disseminate job market information faster to both employers and employees. This function has been performed lately by the Internet, which was launched around 1995. This tool has made it easier and less costly for job seekers to find jobs.

Or, it has been observed that frictional unemployment is more prevalent among unskilled labor such as teenagers. They get laid off more easily and find it hard to obtain new jobs due to their low skill levels. So training teenagers may reduce the natural rate. As another instance, minimum wage laws have been cited as a reason why unskilled workers such as teenagers do not get hired fast enough. The value of a teenager to a company might be less than the minimum wage the company has to pay. In that case, the teenager would not get hired even if there was a job available. If this is indeed the case, then the solution would be to either lower the minimum wage or increase the skill level of the unskilled workers.

The following table provides some information on the unemployment situation in the United States for a few selected months. The data for 1982 and 2009 are for the recessionary years with the highest rates of unemployment. You can see that in December 1982, the unemployment rate reached about 10.8%, of which 4.7% was cyclical. By contrast, the year 2000 was not recessionary. In December 2000 the cyclical rate of unemployment was negative. You also see that in October 2009, the overall unemployment was 10.1%. This was actually lower than the unemployment rate in 1982. However, if we compare cyclical unemployment rates, we see that the 2009 unemployment situation was slightly worse than that of 1982.

Year Month	1982 December	2000 December	2009 October
Total Population	233,160,000	283,696,000	308,189,000
Civilian Population	173,199,000	213,736,000	236,550,000
Labor Force	111,083,000	143,248,000	153,854,000
Employed	99,032,000	137,614,000	138,242,000
Unemployed	12,051,000	5,634,000	15,612,000
Unemployment Rate (%)	10.8%	3.9%	10.1%
Natural Unemployment Rate (%)	6.1%	5.0%	5.0%
Cyclical Unemployment Rate (%)	4.7%	–1.1%	5.1%
Source: U.S. Bureau of Labor Statistics and Bureau of Census			

COSTS OF UNEMPLOYMENT

Unemployment involves both economic and social costs.

a. Economic Costs

Lower employment means less output. If you look at Figure 5, you will notice the GDP gaps during recessions. Notice, for example, the huge gap during the 1982 recession. As we saw, output did not drop sharply in 1982. However, the unemployment rate soared. The annual unemployment rate reached u = 9.7%, while the natural unemployment rate was u* = 6.1%. This means a cyclical unemployment rate of u – u* = 3.6%. If the unemployed workers had been hired, the economy would have produced the potential GDP of $5,266 billion. However, the actual real GDP was $4,919 billion. This meant a loss of output equal to $346 billion, or about 7% of potential GDP. This GDP gap is not small potatoes. During the 1991 recession, this gap was $218 billion.

Another problem with unemployment is that workers who lose their jobs may also lose their skills, or have their skills become irrelevant if they don't get hired back soon, or if they cannot return to their previous jobs. Moreover, during the time they are unemployed, they lose the opportunity to improve their skills through training or on-the-job learning. As a result, a temporary recession might have a lasting adverse effect on real GDP.

Social Costs

Unemployment results in such social problems as feelings of idleness, loss of self-esteem, family disintegration, social unrest, spousal abuse, and crime. Recall the 2005 riots in France in the localities populated by North African immigrants. The unemployment rate among these people has been reported to be 40% to 60%, especially among the youth.

Benefits of Unemployment

Some people believe that unemployment and recession have some benefits. I leave it to you to decide.

a. Inflation

During a recession, cyclically unemployed people would be willing to accept lower wages to get hired. This would lower the cost of production. At the same time, firms would be willing to cut their prices to be able to move their merchandise. This will help reduce the general price level and inflation. This is what some economists believe happened during the 1980–1982 recession. Starting in 1979, the U.S. Federal Reserve System under Paul Volcker followed a tight money policy to fight inflation. This resulted in a recession and *disinflation* called *Volcker disinflation*. The problem with this argument is, of course, which one is better—inflation or unemployment? Economists almost unanimously believe that lower inflation is a benefit to the society. However, some might believe that it is not enough of a benefit to justify the cost, which is the resulting unemployment.

VOLCKER DISINFLATION
Starting in 1979, the U.S. Federal Reserve System under Paul Volcker followed a tight money policy to fight inflation. This resulted in a recession and disinflation.

b. Efficiency

Factories that face low demand in recessions lay off workers and seek efficiency in production. This would increase their profits in the long run. For example, during the 1990–1991 recession, companies were laying off workers; at the same time, their stock prices were increasing. Why? Because stockholders were thinking that laying off workers would reduce costs, increase profits, and make firms more efficient. Additionally, less efficient firms are thus eliminated.

The problem with this argument is that it begs the question of why firms were inefficient in the first place, before the recession. Was there something in the free market system that made firms lazy, say, lack of competition? If this is the case, and if we think that this is a serious problem, then why doesn't the government fix the problem somehow using economic policies that address the problem directly? There is a rule in economics called the *specificity rule*: interfere at a place closer to the source of the problem. If we think that the lack of competition is a problem, we should somehow encourage competition in the marketplace through rules and regulations, rather than causing millions to be unemployed. The cure for the lack of competition is not a recession.

c. Balance of Payments

Some say that when a recession hits and people become unemployed, their incomes fall, and they buy fewer goods from foreign countries. Our imports go down, and this is good for the country. This argument is flawed and bogus. If imports were bad for the country, why did we buy goods from foreigners in the first place? Also, if we buy less from foreigners, they will not have enough money to buy from us. Our exports to them will go down and our export sector will suffer: more unemployment at home. Besides, think about the specificity rule again. If we want to lower imports, we can just impose tariffs on imported goods rather than cause unemployment. Finally, as we will see later in the book, under the current international monetary system, the balance of payments always balances. The balance of payments is the difference between what we pay to foreigners to buy their goods and assets, and what they pay us to buy our goods and assets. The two are always equal in the current system of flexible exchange rates. This means that if we buy fewer goods from foreigners, they will buy fewer assets from us.

INFLATION

Finally, we turn our attention to inflation. What is inflation? A one-time increase in the prices of a few goods does not constitute inflation. Inflation is defined as the increase in the general price level: when the prices of almost everything in the society increase. When this happens over a large number of years, we call it sustained inflation.

One way to measure inflation is, of course, to use the GDP deflator. The GDP deflator includes every good and service produced in the economy, including those purchased by firms and the government. Therefore, an increase in the GDP deflator would indicate an increase in the cost of buying goods and services for households, firms, and the government. Sometimes we want to concentrate on the goods consumed by households. For this we have the consumer price index (CPI). The Bureau of Labor Statistic calculates the CPI each month. They take a basket of goods consumed by a typical U.S. urban household in 1982–1984 and ask the question "How much would it cost to buy that basket today?" Every month they walk into stores, take a sample of prices, and use them to calculate the cost of buying that basket in that month. Finally, they divide the number they obtained for that particular month by the cost of buying that basket in 1982–1984, and multiply the result by 100. The fixed 1982–1984 quantity weights cause the CPI to overstate the cost of living. That is because it does not take into account the fact that consumers can substitute low-price goods (such as generic drugs) for the items they used to consume in 1982–1984.

Regardless of which price index you use, the inflation rate between any two periods is defined and calculated as follows, where P_1 and P_2 are the price indexes in periods 1 and 2, respectively.

$$\text{Inflation Rate} = ((P_2 - P_1)/P_1) \times 100$$

They could either be the GDP deflators or CPIs. For example, the CPI indexes published by the Bureau of Labor Statistics for February and March 2006 were 199.1 and 199.8, so the monthly inflation rate between these two months was

$$\text{Inflation Rate} = ((199.8 - 199.1)/199.1) \times 100 = 0.35\%$$

It is customary to multiply monthly figures by 12 to convert them to annual figures. Doing this results in an annualized inflation rate of 12 × 0.35% = 4.2%. So if inflation continued at the fixed monthly rate of 0.35%, then after 12 months it would amount to 4.2%. People annualize monthly inflation rates, mostly to avoid dealing with small numbers.

Figure 8: U.S. Quarterly CPI Inflation Rates (1970:1 to 2010:2)

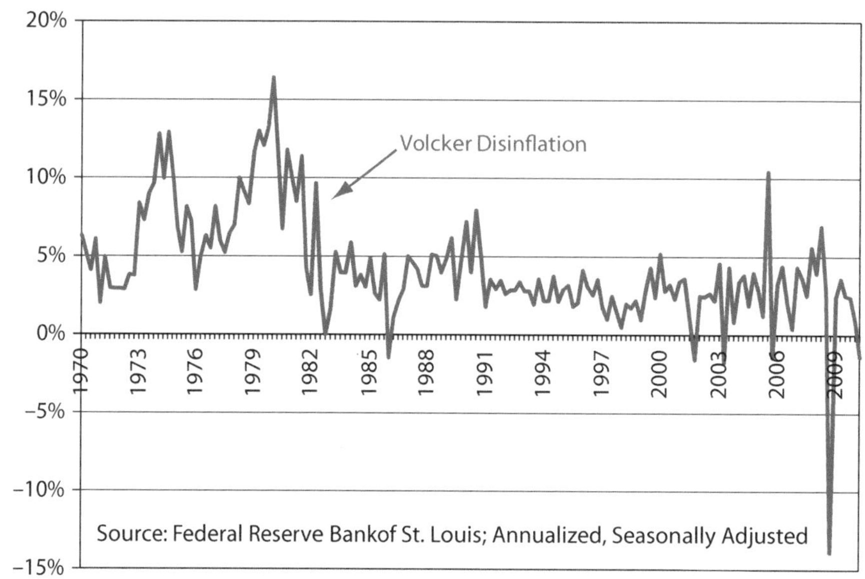

Figure 8 shows the U.S. quarterly CPI inflation rates for the period from the first quarter of 1970 to the second quarter of 2010. We see that the recessions of 1974–1975 and 1980–1982 were characterized by very high inflation rates. We will talk about the reasons for these later in the book. But note how the inflation rate is reduced after 1982, due to Volcker disinflation. Observe also that the variability of inflation has also been reduced since 1982. For now, recall that inflation plus recession is called *stagflation*. We had some inflation in the 1990–1991 recession, but it was not that bad. The increase in the level and variability of the inflation rate toward 2006 was mostly due to the rising oil and gas prices caused by Hurricane Katrina. This hurricane damaged some oil refineries and natural gas facilities in Louisiana, leading to oil and gas shortages and higher prices. Note also the very large negative inflation rate in the 2007–2009 recession. A negative inflation means a drop in the price level, which is the opposite of inflation. A reduction in the general price level is called *deflation*. We will talk about deflation later in the book.

STAGFLATION
Inflation coupled with recession.

DEFLATION
A reduction in the general price level. Deflation results in negative inflation rates.

EFFECTS OF INFLATION ON LENDERS AND BORROWERS

Although inflation means the rise in the general price level, it is easier to understand its effects on lenders and borrowers by considering only one good. Assume it is 2010 and you have $1,000 in your pocket. A good, such as pizza, has a price of $10 per unit. Then you can buy 100 units of that good in 2010:

$$\$1{,}000/\$10 = 100 \text{ units in 2010}$$

Suppose I borrow that $1,000 from you for a year at an interest rate of 5%. After one year, in 2011 I pay you back $1,050, which includes the principal ($1,000) and the interest ($50):

$$\$1{,}000 + .05 \times \$1{,}000 = \$1{,}000 \times (1 + .05) = \$1{,}050$$

How many units of the good can you buy in 2011? That will depend on the price of the good in that year. Suppose that the price of the good increases by 3%, to $10.30. Then you can buy approximately

$$\$1{,}050/\$10.30 = 102 \text{ units in 2011}$$

The amount of goods and services you can buy increases only by 2%, and not by the full 5% interest that I give you:

$$((102 - 100)/100) \times 100 = +2\%$$

This is simply because inflation bites off some of your purchasing power.

The 5% increase in the dollar amount in your pocket is called the *nominal interest rate*. The 2% increase in your real purchasing power is called the *real interest rate*.[7] Note that the real interest rate is *approximately* equal to nominal interest rate minus the inflation rate.[8] In our case

$$\text{Real Interest Rate} = 5\% - 3\% = 2\%$$

NOMINAL INTEREST RATE
This is the stated interest rate on loan documents or bank deposits. This is how much money you will earn if you lend one dollar.

REAL INTEREST RATE
Equals nominal interest rate minus inflation rate. It shows by how much your real wealth or purchasing power will increase if you lend money.

7 Recall the definition of real and nominal variables from the previous chapter. Note again that the nominal thing has units of dollars. The real thing is in terms of quantities of goods.

8 Even though this is only approximately true, we will use the equality sign for ease of exposition.

In the above example, you became better off in real terms by 2%. That is because, instead of buying 10 units of the good now, you lent the money to me and waited for a year. Then, after one year you could buy 10.20 units of the good. However, I became worse off. Why? This is because I borrowed $1,000 from you in 2010 and bought 10 units of the good. After one year, though, I had to sell 10.20 units of the good to pay you back. In a sense, I borrowed 10 units, but had to pay back 10.20 units. The following table summarizes the above story:

	2010	2011	% Change
Amount of Money	$1,000	$1,050	5% (Nominal Interest Rate)
Price of the Good	$10	$10.30	3% (Inflation Rate)
Amount of the Good	100	102	2% (Real Interest Rate)

Let's change some of the numbers in the story. Suppose the price of the good increases by 7% to $10(1 + .07) = $10.70. Then, after one year you can buy

$$\$1{,}050/\$10.70 = 98 \text{ units in 2011}$$

Thus, you become worse off in real terms. But I become better off since I borrow 100 units of the good, but pay back only 98 units. In other words, I borrowed when money was worth more, and paid back when it was worth less. Note that your real well-being has gone down by approximately 2%:

$$((98 - 100)/100) \times 100 = -2\%$$

Again, this -2% is nothing but the real interest rate, and is approximately equal to

$$\text{Real Interest Rate} = 5\% - 7\% = -2\%$$

ANTICIPATED VERSUS UNANTICIPATED INFLATION

As the above story makes clear, lenders and borrowers care about *future* inflation rates. You and I signed our loan contract in 2010, but it was in 2011 that one of us ended up losing in real terms, because of the way inflation turned out. Since neither lenders nor borrowers want to lose purchasing power in the future, they have every incentive to try to predict the future inflation rate and incorporate that prediction into the nominal interest rate at the time of the loan contract.

As another example, assume again that in 2010 I come to borrow $1,000 from you. You have just heard in the news that the inflation rate will be 7% over the next year. So you anticipate a 7% inflation rate for 2011. What nominal interest rate will you charge me? If you charge me just 7%, then you will not expect your real well-being to increase next year. You will lend me 10 units of the good, and I will pay you back 10 units next year.

OPPORTUNITY COST OF WAITING
By lending your money, you lose the opportunity to consume goods and services today.

In the real world, you would want to charge me an interest rate that is higher than the 7% anticipated inflation. This is for two reasons. First, you would want to be compensated for the *opportunity cost of waiting*. By lending your money to me, you lose the opportunity to consume goods and services today, anticipating that if you instead wait for a year, you will be able to consume a larger amount of goods and services then. Otherwise, why would you lend money? Second, the future is uncertain. You will worry that I may not be able to pay back your money in 2011. Therefore, you would want to be compensated for risking your money by lending it to me. Suppose you require a 1% increase in your real purchasing power as compensation for the opportunity cost of waiting and for taking the risk. Then you would charge me 8% nominal interest.

Since I have also heard the same news, I have the same anticipation about the future inflation rate, so I may agree to that 8% interest on the loan. This is because I am borrowing the money to invest in some line of business. If the real rate of return from that business is higher than 1%, then I will be happy to pay 1% in real interest to you. This would be the *real* cost of borrowing from you.

The nominal interest rate minus the *expected* inflation rate is called the *ex-ante real interest rate.* Ex-ante means *before the fact* or *expected*—in this case, before observing the actual inflation rate next year. In the above instance, the ex-ante real interest rate would be 1%, because both parties expect 7% inflation and the nominal rate settles at 8%.

EX-ANTE REAL INTEREST RATE
Nominal interest rate minus the expected inflation rate.

Let r denote the nominal interest rate, π^e the expected inflation rate, and the Greek letter r (Rho, pronounced *row*) the ex-ante real interest rate. Then, approximately

$$r = r - \pi^e$$

When the next year arrives, everyone will observe the actual inflation rate. The nominal interest rate minus the *actual* inflation rate is called the *ex-post real interest rate*. Ex-post means *after the fact* or *actual*. Lenders' and borrowers' decisions are based on the ex-ante rate, rather than the ex-post rate, so this is the rate we will focus on in the future.

EX-POST REAL INTEREST RATE
Nominal interest rate minus the actual inflation rate.

When the next year arrives, I will pay you back $1,080 in principal and interest. If we were both right, and the inflation rate turned out to be equal to 7%, the price of the good would increase to $10.70, and you would be able to buy

$$\$1{,}080/\$10.70 = 101 \text{ units in } 2011$$

In this case we would both be happy, because our expectations of inflation would be realized. Your real purchasing power would increase by the 1% you had required from the loan. I would not become worse off either, because I was willing to pay that 1% to you. Therefore, if we both correctly anticipate the inflation rate and incorporate it into the nominal interest rate, neither of us will get hurt by it. *Correctly anticipated inflation will not hurt either the debtors or creditors.* **This is a very important principle that you should keep in mind.**

Now suppose instead that when the next year arrives, we both realize we were wrong in our inflationary expectations. The inflation rate turns out to be 9%. Then you can buy

$$\$1{,}080/\$10.90 = 99 \text{ units in } 2011$$

This is lower than what you had expected from the loan in 2010. You are thus worse off, and I am better off. By how much? By the percentage by which your actual purchasing power next year (99 units) deviates from your expected one (101 units).

$$((99 - 101)/101) \times 100 = -2\%$$

You are worse off, because not only are you not receiving the 1% additional purchasing power that you were expecting from the loan, but you are actually losing 1% purchasing power, for a total of 2%. I gain, because instead of paying you 101 units of the good (which I was happy to pay), I only pay you 99 units. This 2% percent exactly equals the percentage error in forecasting inflation, which is called *unanticipated inflation*.

UNANTICIPATED INFLATION *The actual rate of inflation in a period minus what people had anticipated in the past. It is nothing but error made in forecasting inflation.*

Anticipated inflation (π^e) = 7%
Actual inflation (p) = 9%
Unanticipated inflation ($p - \pi^e$) = 9% - 7% = 2%

Unanticipated inflation hurts either lenders or borrowers. If actual inflation exceeds the anticipated inflation (as in the above case), then lenders will lose, and borrowers will win. In the opposite case, lenders will win, and borrowers will lose.

Let's put it another way. Next year the ex-post real interest rate will be lower than ex-ante real interest rate.

Ex-ante real interest rate in 2010 = 8% - 7% = 1%
Ex-post real interest rate in 2011 = 8% - 9% = –1%
Difference = Ex Post – Ex Ante = –1% - 1% = –2%

Therefore, lenders' purchasing power will diminish, while borrowers will enjoy a higher purchasing power. The following table summarizes the story:

	Present	Expected		Actual		Difference
	2010	2011	%	2011	%	
Amount of Money	$1,000.0	$1,080.0	8%	$1,080	8%	0%
Price of the Good	$10.0	$10.7	7%	$10.9	9%	2%
Amount of the Good	100.0	101.0	1%	99.0	-1%	-2%

As an exercise, determine what would happen if the actual inflation rate turned out to be 6% next year. What if it equaled 8%?

This simple story has elements of truth to it. In the real world, lenders and borrowers try to predict the inflation rate into the future; on the basis of their predicted inflation rate, they agree on a nominal interest rate. The whole thing happens in financial markets by the interactions of millions of borrowers and lenders. For instance, when banks anticipate a 1% higher inflation rate, they may charge a 1% higher nominal interest rate for their loans. If borrowers forecast the same inflation rate, they would be willing to pay that 1% higher interest rate. When the future comes, the actual inflation rate may turn out to be different than anticipated, in which case one group will become better off and the other group worse off. Therefore, it is the unanticipated inflation that will have undesirable effects.

COSTS OF INFLATION

VOLATILITY *Variability.*

In analyzing the effects of inflation on real economic activity, economists distinguish between the *rate* of inflation and the *volatility*. Volatility means variability. For example, take a look at Figure

8 again. You see that before 1982, both the level and volatility of the U.S. inflation rate was quite high. In some months it was in double digits, and it jumped up and down by large amounts. After 1982 both the level and volatility of the inflation rate have been lower. However, after 2000, the volatility seems to have increased slightly, although the level has not changed much.

Figure 9: Examples of the Level and Volatility of Inflation Rates

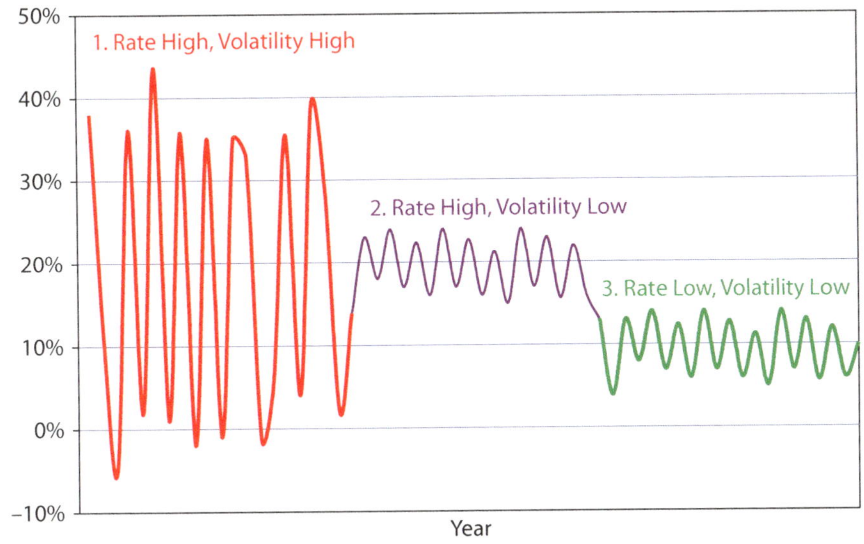

For a sharper picture, consider Figure 9, which shows some hypothetical inflation rates. Period 1 shows very high and volatile inflation rates. The inflation rate jumps between 0% and 40%, averaging about 20%. Period 2 shows inflation rates that are high—averaging 20%—but less volatile. They oscillate between 15% and 25%. In period 3, we have low inflation rates that are also less volatile. They average 10%, and in terms of volatility they are similar to period 2. As we will see, the society prefers period 2 to period 1, but it prefers period 3 to period 2. We like to have both low and less volatile inflation rates.

WHAT IF THE INFLATION RATE IS VERY VOLATILE?

a. Effects on Lenders and Borrowers

When the inflation rate is very volatile—meaning it jumps up and down a lot—it becomes very difficult to forecast the future inflation rate with any degree of accuracy. Figure 8 shows that from 1970 to 1980, this was the case in the United States. In such cases, for example, when people expect the inflation rate to be 2% the next year, it turns out to be 9%. When they expect it to be 7%, it turns out to be 4%. Lenders and borrowers incur large losses because of large errors in forecasting inflation. As a result, due to the fear that they may end up losers, borrowers may not be willing to borrow and lenders may not be willing to lend. Business firms borrow money to buy capital goods. Households borrow to buy homes and appliances. Governments borrow money to spend on such public goods as education, roads, and national defense. If these groups don't borrow money out of fear that inflation may turn against them, investment, productivity—and ultimately GDP—will be adversely affected in the country. Similarly, households who don't lend money out of fear of inflation lose interest income.

On the other hand, if the inflation rate were not very volatile, people would not make large errors in forecasting inflation. You would forecast the inflation rate to be 20%, but it would turn out to be 21%. This small forecast error (1%) would result in small losses for lenders or borrowers. Therefore, the amount of lending and borrowing would be large in the economy, resulting in large investment and high rates of economic growth. This was more or less the case after 1982, as shown in Figure 8. Note that this is true even though the level of the inflation rate is still very high.

b. Higher Risk and Lower Growth

Inflation volatility also creates uncertainty about future price levels. What do you think the inflation rate will be next year? Will it be 4%, 5%, or 4.72%? No one knows for sure; we can only make guesses. Now, firms undertake investment projects with very long horizons. They need to know—with a degree of certainty—what the future prices and costs will be. Will the price of goods I produce exceed the prices of the raw materials I will be buying, or the wages I will be paying? Inflation volatility increases uncertainty about future profits. Firms do not like to take big risks. For this reason, volatile inflation could retard investment spending and, therefore, economic growth.

WHAT IF THE INFLATION RATE IS VERY HIGH?

a. Distributional Effects

The above instances were about inflation volatility. But inflation can have detrimental effects on society, even if it is not very volatile (such as period 2 in Figure 9). Suppose you were spending all your income—$3,000—on two goods, X and Y. You bought 20 units of X and 10 units of Y. When the price of each was $100, you were spending 100(20) + 100(10) = $3,000 on these two goods. Now the prices and your income both rise at 5%. Your income is now $3,150. You can still afford the old bundle at higher prices: 105(20) + 105(10) = $3,150. This example is the essence of the argument that if the prices of all the goods and services and people's incomes rise at the same rate, no one will get hurt by inflation.

Assume instead that the price of X increased at 7%, that of Y at 3%, and your income at 5%. Even though the prices have increased at 5% on average, the same as your income, you have become worse off. You need 107(20) + 103(10) = $3,170 to buy your old favorite bundle. You can no longer afford that bundle. Suppose there was another consumer who consumed 10 units of X and 20 units of Y, and his income also increased by 5%. Now he needs only 107(10) + 103(20) = $3,130 to buy his favorite bundle. He is better off. Thus, one problem with inflation is that not all prices rise at the same rate. Even if your income keeps pace with inflation on average, you may end up a winner or a loser depending on your initial consumption bundle.

The other problem is that many people's incomes don't keep pace with inflation, and therefore, they become worse off due to inflation. These include government employees, fixed-income retirees, and workers with wage contracts. On the other hand, some people's incomes outpace inflation. Therefore, in a sense, inflation distributes GDP from one group to another. Note that inflation will hurt fixed-income families, even if it is correctly anticipated because these families cannot do anything to increase their incomes. Therefore, *overall*, inflation imposes costs on the society whether correctly anticipated or not.

b. Administrative Costs and Inefficiencies

If none of the prices changed over time, a lot of things would be much easier. Companies would not need to print a new catalog every year; restaurants would not need to print a new menu every now and then. Companies would not need to spend a lot of money to buy forecasts of inflation. In some countries, people have to carry baskets of money to buy a few grocery items, simply because inflation has so devalued the currency. Just holding or counting money is a daily hassle.

c. Inflation Creep

Households pay taxes on their nominal incomes. For example, suppose that in 2010 you made $100,000 and you faced an income tax rate of 30%, so that your after-tax income was 70% × $100,000 = $70,000. If the price of a good was $100 per unit, you could buy 700 units of that good. Now, suppose in 2011 both your income and the price level increase at 10%. Suppose also that because of your higher income, you creep into a higher income tax bracket, say 35%. Now your after-tax income is 65% × $110,000 = $71,500, and with the new price of $110 per unit, you can buy only 650 units of the good. So in real terms you become worse off. See the following table:

	2010	2011
Nominal Income	$100,000	$110,000
Tax Rate	30%	35%
After-Tax Income	$70,000	$71,500
Price Level	$100	$110
After-Tax Real Income	700	650

As an exercise, determine what would happen to your after-tax real income if the tax rate did not change.

In summary, high and volatile inflation creates uncertainty about future prices, reduces lending and borrowing, retards investment spending, and disrupts production plans. The end result is reduced national output and diminished national well-being. Moreover, high inflation rates impose costs on the society, even if they are not very volatile and can be correctly anticipated. This is due to their effects on fixed-income families, as well as their administrative and other costs. As such, it is desirable to have low and stable inflation rates (period 3 in Figure 9). For these reasons, some economists advocate *inflation targeting*. This means they favor having the government set a target inflation rate—say 2%—and use monetary policy to maintain the actual inflation rate as close to the target as possible. In other words, these economists desire a *low and stable* inflation rate. You might be thinking "Why 2%? Why not just reduce the inflation rate to 0%?" We will try to address this question later in the book, but the following is a quick answer.

INFLATION TARGETING
A central bank policy aimed at keeping the inflation rate steady and close to a pre-announced target rate.

BENEFITS OF INFLATION

Some argue that mild inflation could serve as a lubricant in the capitalist system. This is because if increases in wages and other production costs lag behind increases in prices—say due to wage contracts—then profits will increase. This will stimulate production and keep the unemployment rate low. Another benefit these economists cite is that, if people saw some mild inflation in the past, they will expect a similar inflation in the future. Therefore, they will spend more now to beat the higher expected future prices. This will stimulate consumer spending, and keep profits and employment from falling.

TO SUMMARIZE

1. *Real GDP*, *real potential GDP*, and *real GDP per capita* have been increasing during the past century.
2. Potential GDP is what the economy can produce with full employment of resources.
3. In the long run, real GDP equals potential GDP.
4. A fall in GDP is called a *recession*, and an increase is called an *expansion*.
5. Total unemployment is the sum of *cyclical* and *natural unemployment*.
6. Natural unemployment is the sum of *frictional* and *structural unemployment*.
7. When actual GDP equals potential GDP, we will only have natural unemployment.
8. When actual GDP falls short of potential, we will also have cyclical unemployment.
9. The economic cost of unemployment is the resulting loss in output.
10. The social costs of unemployment include loss of self-esteem, family breakdown, social unrest, and so on.
11. As for benefits, unemployment leads to lower inflation, greater efficiency, and lower imports. These are all debatable.
12. *Inflation* is an increase in the general price level.
13. *Disinflation* is the reduction in the inflation rate.
14. *Deflation* is the reduction in the general price level (negative inflation).
15. *Volatile inflation* creates uncertainty about future prices. This reduces lending and borrowing, retards investment, and disrupts production, ultimately resulting in lower national output.
16. High inflation rates result in redistribution of real income, administrative costs, higher risk, and lower growth.
17. Unanticipated inflation hurts creditors and benefits debtors.
18. Mild inflation could be a lubricant for the economy if production costs lag behind price increases.
19. The real interest rate is the nominal interest rate minus the inflation rate.

EXERCISES

Question 1

Unemployment benefits are the money that governments pay to workers when they get laid off. What do you think is the effect of unemployment benefits on the natural rate of unemployment? What do you think would happen to the natural rate of unemployment if the government eliminated this program? What would happen if the government gave more generous benefits?

Question 2

Draw a graph showing some recurrent and periodic cycles. Draw another graph that shows cycles that are not periodic.

Question 3

Okun's Law, named after Arthur Okun (who studied the issue), says that a 1 percent increase in the rate of unemployment will be associated with a 3 percent reduction in real GDP, and vice versa. Let's call this 3 percent "Okun's Ratio." This ratio has turned out to be very unstable; you can hardly call this a "law." Consider the data for the fourth quarter of 1982, given in the text.

a. If Okun's Law were credible, then by how many percent would the real GDP increase if we reduced the cyclical unemployment to zero?
b. The real GDP in that quarter was $5,190 billion. If we eliminated the cyclical unemployment, to what level would the GDP increase? What do you call that level of GDP?

c. In the fourth quarter of 1982, the potential GDP was $5,644 billion. Use the above numbers to calculate a new Okun's Ratio.

Question 4

In the last quarter of 2001, the total population of the United States was 286,384,000 people. Of this number, 70,272,000 people were either members of the armed forces, were less than 16 years old, or were institutionalized. Of the total civilian noninstitutional population, 71,890,000 people were not in the labor force. Of those in the labor force, 136,222,000 were employed.

a. Find the unemployment rate for this quarter.
b. The natural rate of unemployment in this quarter was 5.2%. What was the cyclical unemployment rate?
c. The potential real GDP for this quarter was $10,097.4 billion. What would be the actual real GDP predicted by Okun's Law?

Question 5

Let's construct our own consumer price index. Suppose that in 2000, you consumed 10 units of good X, 20 units of good Y, and 25 units of good Z. The prices of these goods in 2000, 2001, and 2002 are in the following table:

Year	X	Y	Z
2000	$ 40	$ 20	$ 44
2001	$ 42	$ 22	$ 46
2002	$ 43	$ 24	$ 50

a. Construct a CPI series for these three years, using 100 as the 2000 CPI.
b. Calculate the inflation rates for 2001 and 2002.
c. Some claim that the fixed-weight CPI overstated the true cost of living, since people may not consume the same goods in the same quantities every year. In particular, suppose that starting in 2001, consumers have found a lower cost generic good (G) that is a substitute for Z, but is cheaper. The prices of G in 2000, 2001, and 2002 were $44, $30, and $25, respectively. Calculate the CPI series, assuming that consumers switched from Z to G starting in 2001.

Question 6

What do you think would happen to nominal interest rates if people expected a 2% higher inflation rate? Who would be the losers and winners if the actual inflation rate turned out to be 5% higher? How much would be the gains and losses?

Question 7

Suppose that both lenders and borrowers are happy with a 2% ex-ante real interest rate. If both expected 5% inflation for the next year, what would be the nominal interest rate? If both heard in the news that the inflation rate would increase to 6%, what would happen to the nominal interest rate? Who will win and who will lose if the actual inflation rate turns out to be 2% lower than expected?

Question 8

In the first quarter of 2000, the total civilian population in the United States was about 211,586,000 people. Of this total, about 69,200,000 people were not in the labor force. Of those in the labor force, 136,619,000 people were employed. In this quarter, the natural rate of unemployment was approximately 5%.

a. Calculate the total unemployment rate.

b. Calculate the cyclical unemployment rate.

c. On the basis of these numbers, would you say that the actual GDP was above or below potential?

Question 9

Assume that the ex-ante real interest is fixed at 2% and will remain fixed forever.

a. In 2005 lenders and borrowers in the financial markets expected 5% inflation over the next year. What was the nominal interest rate in 2005?

b. In 2006 the actual inflation rate turns out to be 8%. What is the ex-post real interest rate in 2006 (given the nominal interest rate you found in part "a" above)?

c. In 2006 the actual inflation rate turns out to be 8%. What is the unanticipated inflation rate in 2006?

d. In 2006 the actual inflation rate turns out to be 8%. Who will gain and who will lose from the unanticipated inflation? By how may percent?

Question 10

What do you think the nominal interest rate would be equal to if the inflation rate had been zero for some time and was expected to be zero in the future?

Question 11

The following table shows the consumer price indexes (CPIs) published by the Bureau of Labor Statistics for the indicated months.

Dec-05	Jan-06	Feb-06	Mar-06	Apr-06
197.7	199.0	199.1	199.8	201.0

Calculate the (annualized) inflation rate between January and February 2006.

CHAPTER 7

The Goods and Services Market

INTRODUCTION AND REVIEW

LET'S REVIEW WHAT we have learned so far. GDP has three faces: It is the market value of all the goods and services produced in a country; it is the total income earned by the production factors that produce those goods and services; and it is the expenditure made on those goods and services. Real GDP, a measure of the quantities of goods and services produced, has been increasing over time. In the long run, it has been tracing the potential GDP, the amount we could have produced if we had fully employed all of our resources. Even if we produced the potential GDP, we would still have some unemployment, called natural unemployment. In the short run, real GDP can deviate from potential GDP. If real GDP falls short of potential, we will have cyclical unemployment, which is the excess of total unemployment over natural unemployment. The last chapter discussed the costs and benefits of growth, unemployment, and inflation. Starting with this chapter, we will explain causes and policy implications.

An objective of policy makers is to try to keep real GDP close to potential, and whenever it falls short, to bring it back up to potential. To that end, they need to understand why GDP goes up and down in the first place. With this chapter, we will begin exploring the causes of the movements in real GDP. Since GDP is an index of goods and services produced, the natural place to start is the goods and services market.

THE NATIONAL INCOME IDENTITY

As you know, the nominal GDP—the dollar value of all the goods and services produced—equals the total dollar value of all the expenditures made on these goods and services:

$$\text{Nominal GDP} \approx \text{Total Expenditure}$$

The identity sign (≡) reads "is identically equal to," and simply means that just because of the way things are defined and measured, the two items are *always* equal. We know this from Chapter 5. The above identity is called the *national income identity*.

NATIONAL INCOME IDENTITY
The total output produced in a country over a certain period of time identically equals the total expenditure on those goods and services. The total expenditure consists of consumption, investment, and government spending, plus net exports.

We are generally interested in the real magnitudes or quantities of goods and services produced and purchased, rather than their nominal values. As you recall, this is because standards of living and employment are affected by actual quantities produced and consumed—not by dollar values. Conversion of nominal magnitudes to real ones is quite straightforward, and you already know it from the chapter on GDP. We simply divide both sides of the above identity by the GDP deflator to get the following:

(Nominal GDP/GDP Deflator) ≡ (Total Expenditure/GDP Deflator)

We know that the left-hand side is the real GDP, which is an index of the quantities of all the goods and services produced in a country during a certain period of time. The right-hand side, therefore, is an index of the quantities of all the goods and services purchased. We call it the *real expenditure*. So we can write

REAL EXPENDITURE
A measure of the quantities of all the goods and services purchased in a period of time.

Real GDP ≡ Real Expenditure

This last identity is also the national income identity, but in real terms. In essence, it says that the total quantities of all the goods and services *produced* in a country (the left hand-side) equal the total quantities *purchased* (the right-hand side).

As it stands, the national income identity is totally useless for economic analysis. In fact, it sounds somewhat unrealistic. It says that, over any given period of time, producers are able to sell any amount of goods and services they produce. So it cannot possibly be a realistic description of the real world. In the real world, sometimes producers produce so much that they cannot sell all they have produced. We call this overproduction. Some other times they produce too little. In that case, they have to sell from past inventories. We call this underproduction.

To resolve this apparent puzzle, you will need to understand a national income accounting convention. Let me give you a simple example. Suppose that in 2006, a computer manufacturer produced 15 million laptops. Since these are items that have been *produced*, they will go to the left-hand side of the identity (1) as part of real GDP. Suppose, however, that the manufacturer could sell only 10 million of these laptops. This is simply because he had made a mistake in predicting the level of demand for his laptops and had overproduced. These 10 million laptops go to the right-hand side of (1) as real expenditures. What happens to the remaining 5 million laptops that he could not sell? He has no choice but to store them to sell in the future.

These 5 million unsold laptops result in an unplanned increase in the level of inventories. Now the national income accountants treat these 5 million laptops as if the manufacturer himself had bought them in order to sell them in the future. In other words, these 5 million laptops also go to the right-hand side of identity (1) as goods purchased by someone—in this case, the manufacturer himself. This explains how the national income identity always holds, even in the case of an overproduction:

15 Million Produced ≡ 10 million purchased + 5 million unplanned inventory increase

Now someone looking at this identity may think that the producer has sold all the laptops in 2006, but you and I know better. We know that 5 million out of those 15 million laptops could not be sold, and the accountants treated them as if the producer himself purchased them. In fact, the above scenario might happen in a recession, where producers have a hard time selling their products. Some go bankrupt for this very reason. Still, the national income identity would hold because of the way they treat unsold goods.

On the other hand, suppose that the producer produces 15 million laptops, but because of a very high demand he sells 16 million. How is this possible? Well, he can do this by drawing down the level of inventories. This is possible if the producer had some unsold goods in the last year that he carried over to the current year. Only 15 million laptops will go to the left-hand side of (1) as the goods *produced in that year*. On the expenditure side, accountants start with the total expenditure of 16 million laptops purchased, and subtract from it the 1 million that were sold from past inventories:

$$\text{15 million Produced} \equiv \text{16 million purchased} - \text{1 million unplanned inventory decrease}$$

Again the two sides become equal, even though the manufacturer has underproduced. So for a single producer, the amount of production over a certain period of time *must* equal demand plus or minus unplanned changes in inventories:

$$\text{Production} \equiv \text{Demand} \pm \text{(Unplanned Changes in Inventories)}$$

GOODS MARKET EQUILIBRIUM

AGGREGATE DEMAND
The sum of planned purchases by households, firms, the government, and foreigners.

If it is true for one producer, it must be true for all of them. So the sum total of all the goods produced in a year—the real GDP—must equal the *aggregate demand* (**AD**) for all those goods and services plus or minus unplanned inventory changes. We will denote the real GDP by the letter **Y**. Now the above story indicated that:

$$Y \equiv \underbrace{AD \pm \text{(Unplanned Changes in Inventories)}}_{\text{Real Expenditure}}$$

If firms produce more than what is demanded, there will be an unplanned increase in inventories. If they produce less than what is purchased, there will be an unplanned decrease in inventories. If firms produce exactly what is demanded, there will be no unplanned changes in inventories. So you see that although the real GDP always equals the real expenditure, it will equal aggregate demand only when there are no unplanned inventory changes.

This last state is called *goods market equilibrium*. Equilibrium is a *state of rest*. If we are in that state, there will be no tendency on the part of market participants to change their prices or quantities.

GOODS MARKET EQUILIBRIUM
A situation in which demand for goods and services equals supply, so that there are no tendencies on the part of market participants to change their prices or quantities.

$$Y = AD \quad \text{Goods Market Equilibrium}$$

Components of Aggregate Demand

Who buys all the goods and services comprising the aggregate demand? Four groups of people, or entities, purchase them: households, business firms, the government, and foreigners. We call the amounts of the goods and services purchased by these four groups *consumption*, *investment*, *government spending*, and *exports*, respectively.

CONSUMPTION
The aggregate amount of goods and services consumed by households.

INVESTMENT
A planned increase in plants and equipment, residential buildings, and inventories.

GOVERNMENT SPENDING
Purchase of goods and services by the government.

EXPORTS
Amount of goods and services sold to foreigners.

The rationale behind this classification is that if a household buys something, it is for household consumption rather than for producing goods for profit. On the other hand, if a firm buys something, it is either to increase the amount of its plants or equipment, or to operate or maintain its existing capital. Therefore, if a household buys a laptop computer, it will be treated as consumption, but if a firm buys that laptop, it will count as investment. There is one exception to this rule. The purchases of new homes by households are classified as investment. Governments buy things like computers and tanks. They also spend money on parks, roads, and education. Government purchases can have consumption or investment aspects. If it buys things like pencils, then it will be a consumption outlay, but spending on education or roads will count as investment. We will not distinguish between these two categories of government spending.

Let's start with households. We will denote the total amount of all the goods and services purchased by households for consumption purposes by the letter **C**. These will include goods produced domestically, such as wheat produced by American farmers, and imported goods, such as cars produced in Japan. We will denote the amount of goods purchased by firms for investment purposes by the letter **I**. This will also include goods produced domestically and those produced abroad. The government buys goods produced by domestic producers, as well as those produced by foreign producers. The government buys goods produced in foreign countries to maintain its embassies and armed forces abroad. We will denote government spending by the letter **G**. Exports are the goods and services that foreigners buy from us. We will denote exports by **EX**.

Now if we add up all the above components, we will get something bigger than the aggregate demand *for the domestically produced goods*. This is simply because those components include goods and services produced in foreign countries. The sum total of all these foreign goods purchased by domestic residents is called imports (**IM**). We need to subtract the imports from the sum of the above components to obtain the aggregate demand for domestically produced goods and services:

$$AD = C + I + G + EX - IM \quad (1)$$

Therefore, the goods market equilibrium condition becomes

$$Y = \underbrace{C + I + G + EX - IM}_{AD} \quad (2)$$

DETERMINANTS OF AGGREGATE DEMAND

The above discussion indicates that aggregate demand will change if any of its components change. Therefore, we should understand what factors cause the values of these components to go up or down in a year. Let's look at them in turn, starting with consumption.

Consumption Spending

The total amounts of goods and services consumed by households in a year depend on a host of variables, as follows:

1. Real Disposable Income. Disposable income is the income you can dispose of, or spend. Recall that GDP equals total factor income (the income aspect of GDP). For instance, it is the wage you receive from the company you work for, the rent you collect from your tenants, the interest you receive from the bank, or the profit you earn from your pizza place. But you cannot spend all of it. You have to pay some of it to the government in *taxes*. We have to subtract taxes from factor incomes. At the same time, the government hands over some money to people *without buying anything from them*. These payments are called *transfer payments*, and include such things as food stamps, unemployment benefits, and social security payments. They should be added to factor incomes.

Now *real* disposable income means the purchasing power of your disposable income—the amount of goods and services you could buy with it. Similarly, real transfer payments means the amount of goods and services you could buy with the dollar amounts of transfer payments you receive from the government. Finally, real amount of taxes means the amount of goods and services you could buy with the dollar amount of taxes that you pay to the government. As you recall, we simply divide nominal magnitudes by a price index to obtain real magnitudes.

In the real world, both taxes and transfer payments depend on the level of GDP. When we do our taxes, we pay the Internal Revenue Service (IRS) a specific percentage of our pretax incomes. If we earn a larger amount of income in a year, we pay a larger amount to the IRS in taxes. The sum of all these pretax incomes is just GDP, as we know by now. Therefore, a larger GDP results in greater tax revenue. Moreover, transfer payments increase in recessions, because more people become unemployed or join the low-income families. To keep things simple, we will assume that taxes and transfer payments are not affected by GDP. We can write the aggregate real disposable income as:

$$Y_d = Y - TX + TR \qquad (3)$$

where TX denotes taxes and TR transfer payments.

We assume that an increase in real disposable income, Y_d, results in an increase in consumption. As the purchasing power of people's take-home incomes increases, they can buy more goods and services. The real disposable income, in turn, can increase if real GDP increases, taxes decrease, or transfer payments increase.

The fraction of the *additional* real disposable income that a household would spend on consumption is called *marginal propensity to consume (MPC)*. Suppose, for example, that the MPC for a household is 0.80. What this means is that if the household's real disposable income increases by 100 units, it will spend 80 percent of that extra disposable income—or 80 units—on consumption, and will save the remaining 20 percent. This concept also works in reverse. If a household's MPC is 0.80 and if that household's real disposable income decreases by 100 units, that household's consumption will decrease by 80 units, saving by 20 units.

MARGINAL PROPENSITY TO CONSUME (MPC)
The fraction of the additional real disposable income that households spend on goods and services.

The concept also applies to national level data. For example, suppose the MPC for the country is 0.80. This means that if the aggregate real disposable income increases by 100 units, then the national consumption will increase by 80 units, and *vice versa*.

2. Expected Future Disposable Income ($Y_d e$). You would expect a higher disposable income in the future if you expect a higher before-tax income, lower taxes, or higher transfer payments. Some economists believe that expected future disposable income is more important for households' consumption decisions than the current disposable income. That is because households usually plan their consumption expenditures ahead of time on the basis of the incomes they expect to receive in the future. Households with high expected future disposable incomes will buy bigger homes, fancier cars, and other consumer durables. This is simply because they will be able to borrow large amounts of money against their future incomes. They will also plan on taking more luxurious vacations, knowing they will have more than enough money in the future to survive. On the other hand, households with low expected future incomes will buy smaller homes and take more modest vacations. The flow of income that you expect to receive in the future is called *permanent income*.

PERMANENT INCOME
The disposable income a household expects to earn in the future.

PERMANENT INCOME HYPOTHESIS
The hypothesis advanced by Milton Friedman that posits that a household plans its consumption expenditures on the basis of its ***permanent income****.*

According to the proponents of the *permanent income hypothesis*, when households expect their permanent income to increase in the future, they modify their consumption plans and increase their consumption in the current year. Suppose that currently you make $100,000 per year, and expect to earn that amount for the foreseeable future. So this is your permanent income. What happens if you find a new, higher-paying job that pays $10,000 more per year? Since your permanent income increases by $10,000, you will afford moving into a bigger house and buying more expensive cars. According to this hypothesis, your current and future consumption will increase by $10,000 per year.

Sometimes households become pessimistic about the future state of the economy and anticipate a recession. They fear that they might lose their jobs in the future. As a result, they reduce their consumption now. Commentators cannot always read people's minds. Thus when consumption falls without any noticeable change in the *current* economic conditions, they attribute it to such factors as "a loss in consumer confidence" or "negative consumer sentiments." And, sometimes they attribute these to consumer irrationality. Many commentators think that the 1990–1991 recession was due to "a loss in consumers' confidence."

The economists who believe in the *permanent income hypothesis* also argue that changes in current disposable income should not have much effect on current consumption expenditure if it is considered transitory by households. In the above example, suppose that you perceived the whole increase in your income as transitory. For instance, that $10,000 was a one-time bonus you got from your company for performing your duties exceptionally well. This transitory increase in income will not make you change your future consumption plan. Instead, you will save the whole $10,000 for future rainy days. Conversely, suppose that due to bad luck, you lose $10,000 in your investments. Again, to maintain your consumption plan, you will draw on your past savings instead of changing your current consumption.

In the permanent income hypothesis, you either consume the whole increase in your income or save the whole thing, depending on whether you think of it as permanent or transitory. In the real world, people may not always know if a change in their income is permanent or transitory. Thus, they may perceive of the change as partly permanent and partly transitory. For this reason, an increase in current disposable income generally leads to some increase in consumption. The hypothesis has an interesting prediction about the relationship between income volatility and consumption. People with stable income, such as salaried government employees, would perceive any increase in their income as permanent, and therefore, would increase their consumption if their income increased. On the other hand, people with volatile income, such as farmers or the self-employed, would tend to regard most of the increases in their income as transitory, and thus, would save most of the increases in their incomes.

3. Real Wealth. Real wealth means the real value, or purchasing power, of the households' financial and physical *assets*.

ASSET
Anything that has value because it will bring some benefits to its owner in the future.

An asset is anything that has value, because it will bring some benefits to its owner in the future.

Financial assets are things like stocks, bonds, and money that people hold. These assets provide their owners with monetary benefits in the future. Physical assets are things like land, homes, and cars that households own. An increase in real wealth would make people wealthier, and as such, is expected to increase consumption. For example, if the overall price level went down, the purchasing power of our financial assets would go up. With the same amount of money that you hold in your pockets, purses, or bank accounts, you can buy more goods and services. Similarly, if we sell our stocks and bonds, we can buy larger amounts of goods and services with the sale proceeds if prices are lower.

Let us denote the total market value of all the assets held by households by letter "**A**" and the general price level by letter "**P.**" Then, the purchasing power of this total amount of wealth is simply

$$\text{Real Wealth} = \frac{A}{P}$$

This is the total amount of goods and services that people can buy with their nominal wealth of A dollars. Our assumption will then be that an increase in real wealth will lead to an increase in consumption.

4. Nominal Interest Rate (r). As you recall from Chapter 6, the interest rate that people and institutions charge for lending money is called the nominal interest rate.[1] If the nominal interest rate increases, the cost of borrowing will increase. Households will find it more expensive to borrow money to buy consumer durables, such as appliances, cars, or homes. In that case, consumption will decrease. If the nominal interest rate decreases, then consumption will increase.

5. Expected inflation rate (π^e). If households expect a higher inflation rate for the future, they will consume more for two related reasons. First, they will hasten their current consumption expenditure to avoid higher future prices. Second, they realize that they will be able to sell their used durable goods at a higher price in the future. This gives them an incentive to buy consumer durables, such as cars.

The two effects above can be described in terms of the ex-ante real interest rate (r), which, you recall, is the difference between the nominal interest rate (r) and people's expectation about the future inflation rate (π^e):

$$r = r - \pi^e$$

1 There are so many interest rates in the economy. We have interest rates on corporate bonds and government bonds, on long-term bonds and short-term bonds, we have mortgage rates, we have rates offered by banks on different types of deposits, and we have rates for car loans. However, all these interest rates move more or less in tandem. We will henceforth talk about "the interest rate" as if there was only one interest rate.

Suppose that the nominal interest rate is r = 7% and you expect the inflation rate to be $\pi^e = 5\%$. Then your ex-ante real interest rate is

$$r = 7\% - 5\% = 2\%$$

Now, if the nominal interest rate increases by 1% with the expected inflation rate unchanged, the real interest rate will increase to 3%, and we know consumption will decrease. If the inflation rate increases by 1% with the nominal rate remaining unchanged, the real rate will decrease to 1%, and consumption will increase. If both the nominal rate and inflation rate increase by 1%, then the real interest rate will remain constant. In this case, the two opposing forces will keep consumption unchanged. We conclude that consumption is negatively related to the real interest rate.

Investment Spending

Although investment spending is not the biggest component of aggregate demand, it is the most *volatile*, as we will see below. This means it jumps up and down more than other components. This is important, because a volatile investment spending would result in volatile aggregate demand. In that case, we need to have a good understanding of investment behavior. In general, business firms undertake investment projects to increase their future profits. For example, if a restaurant buys a new oven or expands its dining area, these expenditures will qualify as investment. Profits from projects are the additional *revenues* made possible from the projects, minus the *costs* of the projects. However, since most of the revenues and costs of a project are realized in the future, they are uncertain as of the date the managers decide whether to undertake the project. So two aspects of future profits are important to the firms' decisions:

a. The expected *levels* of the future profits.
b. The degree of *risk* or *uncertainty* about the levels of future profits.

If for a given level of risk the expected future profits from a project increase, that project becomes more attractive. On the other hand, if for a given level of expected future profit the degree of risk or uncertainty about that level of profit increases, the project becomes less attractive. So any factor affecting the level or riskiness of an investment's revenues or costs would affect the amount of investment spending by business firms. Now, for any firm, the expected future profit is the excess of expected future revenue over cost. Let's look into a few factors that affect revenues and costs of an investment project.

1. Nominal Interest Rate (r). Any factor that increases the cost of capital for the firms would reduce the expected future profits, and so would discourage investment spending. An important factor influencing the cost of capital is the nominal interest rate. Just like households, firms generally borrow to finance investments in their plant and equipment. If the interest rate increases, firms will find it more costly to borrow; as a result, investment spending will go down.

2. Expected Future Inflation Rate (π^e). As in the case of households, if firms expect a higher inflation rate, they will invest more. That is because inflation will increase the value of their plant and equipment. If, for example, the investment did not pay off, the firm can sell the used equipment at a higher price.

As before, the two effects can be combined into the effect of the ex-ante real interest rate on investment spending. Recall that we treat purchases of residential homes as investment spending. If the ex-ante real interest rate fell, more homes would be purchased; if they rose, fewer homes would be bought. Here is why: If the nominal interest rate fell with the inflation rate expected to remain the same, the real interest rate would fall. Since the nominal rate is lower, your mortgage payments to the bank would be lower. With the given level of disposable income that you earn, your interest payments would be a lower fraction of your income. This means that the lending bank would consider you a borrower with a lower default risk and would be willing to lend you money to buy the house.

What if the nominal interest rate was the same, but everyone expected a higher inflation rate in the future? This means that if you bought the house, you would expect to sell it at a higher price in the future and make a profit out of this price increase. This would encourage many people to buy homes. We conclude that, with all else the same, a decrease in the ex-ante real interest rate would stimulate investment spending, and an increase in the ex-ante real interest rate would discourage it.

3. Expected Future Revenues. All else the same, if firms expect higher revenues from investment projects, investment spending will increase. For example, if a "pro-business" president took office, investment spending would increase. This is because the president would try to reduce the rules and regulations. Or, if the government announced lower taxes on corporate profits, the expected future returns on investments would increase, stimulating investment spending. Finally, if the government promises to provide financial subsidies to certain business firms, the expected future profits will increase, encouraging investment spending.

<table>
<tr><td colspan="4">Events That Increase Aggregate Demand
AD = C + I + G + EX – IM</td></tr>
<tr><td>All else the same, a change in the following variable …</td><td>… will cause a change in the following variable, …</td><td>… leading to an increase in the following component of aggregate demand, and therefore, …</td><td>… the level of aggregate demand itself.</td></tr>
<tr><td>Y
TX^{-}
TR ↑</td><td>Y_d ↑</td><td rowspan="4">C</td><td rowspan="9">AD ↑</td></tr>
<tr><td>Y^e
TX^{e-}
TR^e ↑</td><td>Y_d^e ↑</td></tr>
<tr><td>r^{-}
π^e ↑</td><td>P ↓</td></tr>
<tr><td>A
P ↓</td><td>(A/P) ↑</td></tr>
<tr><td>r^{-}
π^e ↑</td><td>P ↓</td><td rowspan="3">I ↑</td></tr>
<tr><td colspan="2">Expected Future Profits ↑</td></tr>
<tr><td colspan="2">Uncertainty about Future Profits ↓</td></tr>
<tr><td colspan="2">Government Spending ↑</td><td>G ↑</td></tr>
<tr><td colspan="2">Net Exports</td><td>(EX – IM)</td></tr>
</table>

4. Riskiness of Investment Projects. Increased uncertainty about the level of future profits would discourage investment spending. For instance, wars, terrorist attacks, or uncertainty about future tax cuts would retard investment spending. You will also recall from Chapter 6 that an increase in uncertainty about inflation would have the same effect.

Government Spending

Government spending is a function of how much the government wants to spend on such things as national defense and education. As we will see later, governments also use their spending power to increase or decrease the level of aggregate demand to affect the employment situation in the country. The government's tax, transfer, and spending programs aimed at changing the level of aggregate demand are called fiscal policy.

Net Exports

NET EXPORTS
The excess of exports over imports.

CURRENT ACCOUNT BALANCE
The difference between the dollar values of the exports in goods and services and the imports in goods and services in a country's balance f payments.

The term (EX – IM) is called *net exports*. It is the excess of the goods and services we sell to foreigners over those we buy from them. In national income accounting, it is called the *current account balance*. If it is positive, we say that the current account is in surplus—we receive more money from exports than we pay for imports. If it is negative, then the current account is in deficit. As we will see, for the United States it has been negative for much of the last several decades. Except for a few instances, we will assume that the economy is closed to international trade so that we have no exports or imports. This is just to make the analysis simple. Later in the book we will give foreign trade due attention.

The above table summarizes the effects of the changes in the variables discussed above on aggregate demand. In this table, a superscript "e" on a variable means the expectation or forecast of the future value of that variable. For example, Y^e means the expected future level of real GDP.

HOW DOES THE GOODS MARKET CLEAR?[2]

Suppose that the goods market was in equilibrium and equation (2) held. What will happen now if the aggregate demand unexpectedly decreases? Since producers did not predict this event, an excess supply of goods will develop in the market, resulting in unplanned inventory increases. To bring the production in line with demand and get rid of unwanted inventories, producers can reduce production. Alternatively, they can reduce their prices to increase their sales. Of course, they can do both at the same time. Similarly, if aggregate demand increases, producers can increase production, increase their prices, or both. We will see in this book that which path they follow depends on circumstances surrounding the goods and resources markets. You will see that such a seemingly simple issue is quite controversial among economists.

In order to keep things simple, we will assume in this chapter that the price level is fixed, so that producers respond to changes in demand by changing their production quantities. This is not a totally realistic assumption, but it will help us understand certain aspects of the goods market more clearly. Later we will relax this assumption. Now take a look at equation (2) again, and assume that aggregate demand increases. For example, suppose that firms become optimistic about future profits, and decide to increase investment spending by 100 units buying some new equipment. This will increase the right-hand side of equation (2) by 100 units. What will be the effect of this event on real GDP—the left-hand side of equation (2)? One might be tempted to say that it will increase by 100 units—but this answer would be incorrect. Here is why.

2 Often economists use the term "clearing" for "equilibrium," probably because it is easier to pronounce! So in this terminology, the phrase "the market clears" would mean "the market reaches equilibrium."

THE MULTIPLIER PROCESS

Assume that the marginal propensity to consume is 0.80, as before. When business firms increase their purchase of equipment by 100 units, the equipment producers experience 100 units of reductions in their inventories, and thus, increase production by 100 units to meet the new demand. This increases GDP by 100 units (the production aspect of GDP), resulting in 100 units of increase in the incomes of factors producing the equipment (income aspect of GDP). Since there is no change in taxes or transfer payments, this increase of 100 units in factor income translates into 100 units of increase in real disposable income.

Households that experience the 100-unit increase in their disposable income spend 80% of it on goods and services. As a result, a new round of demand and income equal to $0.80 \times 100 = 80$ units is generated in the economy. The recipients of these 80 units of income in turn spend 80% of it on goods and services, so a third round of demand equal to $0.80 \times 80 = 64$ units is generated. The process continues. Let's add up all these additional units of real GDP produced:

First round increase in $Y = 100$
Second round increase in $Y = 0.80 \times 100 = 80$
Third round increase in $Y = 0.80 \times 80 = 0.80 \times (0.80 \times 100) = 0.80^2 \times 100 = 64$
Etc.

So the overall increase in real GDP equals:

$$\begin{aligned}\Delta Y &= 100 + 0.80 \times 100 + 0.80^2 \times 100 + 0.80^3 \times 100 + \cdots \\ &= (1 + 0.80 + 0.80^2 + 0.80^3 + \cdots) \times 100\end{aligned}$$

Using the results of the geometric progression from high school for the expression inside the parentheses we get:

$$\Delta Y = (1/1 - 0.80) \times 100 = 5 \times 100 = 500$$

The term $1/(1 - 0.80) = 5$ is called the *expenditure multiplier*. Note that a higher MPC results in a higher expenditure multiplier. For example, if the MPC were 0.90, the multiplier would equal $1/(1 - 0.90) = 10$, and the increase in the real GDP would equal 1,000 units. So in general:

EXPENDITURE MULTIPLIER
A factor by which GDP would increase as a result of an increase in aggregate expenditure.

$$\Delta Y = (1/1 - MPC) \times (\text{Initial Change in Aggregate Demand})$$

Note an important aspect of this story. In each and every round in the multiplier process, the increase in real GDP equals the increase in aggregate demand. (See the following chart.) This is because in each round, producers increase production to meet the increase in demand. So during the whole process, the goods market remains in equilibrium. Keep in mind, however, that these results were obtained under the assumption of fixed prices. Later we will see how things will change when we assume flexible prices.

The same result applies to the case of an increase in consumption spending (C) by households. For instance, suppose that households increase their consumption by 100 units for some reason other than an increase in disposable income. Then, applying the same multiplier formula, the real GDP will increase by 500 units. How about government spending (G)?

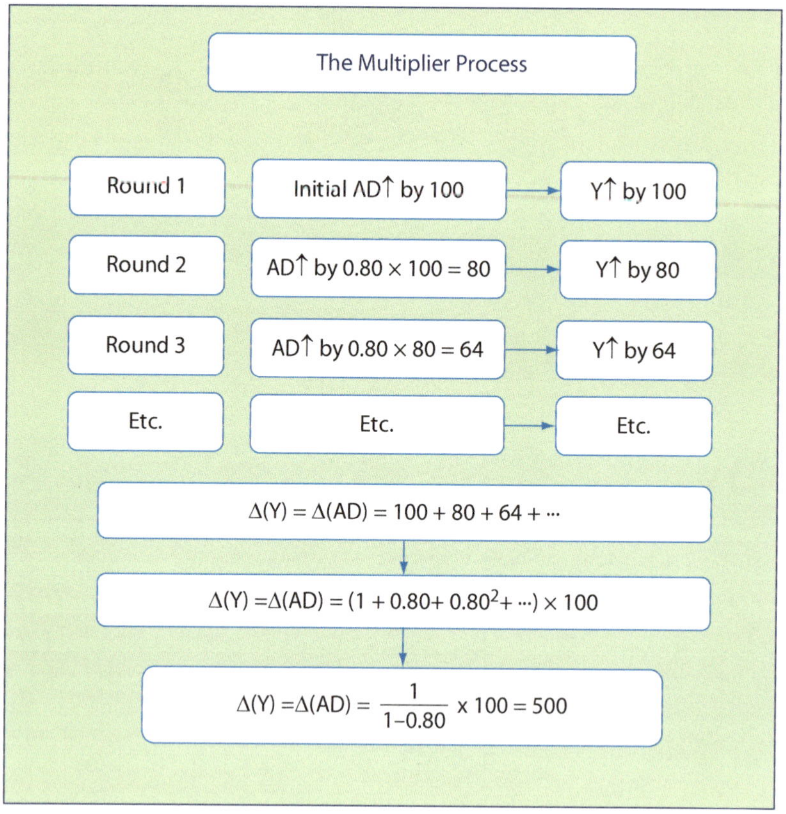

FISCAL POLICY

FISCAL POLICY
A change in government spending (G), taxes (TX), or transfer payments (TR) to change the state of the economy; especially, the real GDP or the unemployment rate.

EXPANSIONARY FISCAL POLICY
An increase in government spending and/or a decrease in taxes, aimed at increasing the level of aggregate demand for goods and services (in order to reduce unemployment).

CONTRACTIONARY FISCAL POLICY
A reduction in government spending and/or an increase in taxes aimed at reducing the level of aggregate demand for goods and services (in order to reduce inflationary pressures).

BUDGET DEFICIT
The amount by which a government's expenditures exceed its tax revenues during a certain period of time.

BUDGET SURPLUS
The amount by which a government's tax revenues exceed its expenditures during a certain period of time.

Fiscal policy refers to changes in government spending, taxes, or transfer payments aiming to achieve a macroeconomic objective. On a yearly basis, every government buys certain amounts of goods and services, collects some taxes, and makes some transfer payments. Not all of these tax-expenditure programs qualify as fiscal policy. For example, every year the government spends money to repair roads and pay for the services of government employees, such as teachers and law enforcement officers. Moreover, every year people routinely pay taxes to the government out of their incomes. These ongoing tax and expenditure activities are necessary to "run the country." Finally, the government provides social security payments and food stamps to help low-income families, and unemployment benefits to help the unemployed. These transfer payments are for humanitarian reasons and have nothing to do with fiscal policy.

We call a change in any of these variables fiscal policy if the sole purpose of the change is to affect the level of aggregate demand in order to achieve a macroeconomic goal. A policy to boost aggregate demand is called *expansionary*; the one that aims to reduce it is called *contractionary*. The goal is generally to increase the level of aggregate demand to fight a recession and increase employment, or to reduce it to fight inflation. At the same time, a change in G, TR, or TX will have the same effect on the real GDP, whether it is the result of an active fiscal policy or not.

The government budget is a record of the government's tax revenue and expenditure for a particular year.[3] If the expenditure (G + TR) exceeds the tax revenue (TX), we say that the government is running a *budget deficit*. In the opposite case, the government would be running a *budget*

3 Let us use the term "government spending" for the government's purchase of goods (G), and "government expenditure" for its total outlays (G + TR).

surplus. If the two are equal, we say that the government's budget is balanced. A government has three options to finance an increase in its expenditure:

a. It can raise taxes of an equal amount to leave the budget deficit or surplus unchanged. This is called a *balanced budget increase in spending*.
b. It can leave the amount of taxes collected unchanged, and instead borrow from the public. In this case, the budget deficit will increase; hence, this method of financing government expenditure is called *deficit spending (or deficit financing)*.
c. Finally, the government can print money to finance its expenditure if it does not want to increase taxes or borrow from the public. A version of this procedure is called *monetizing the debt*. This method of financing will also lead to an increase in budget deficit.

To understand the last two options, we need to know something about the financial markets and monetary policy. In this chapter, we talk about the first option.

BALANCED BUDGET INCREASE IN SPENDING

Suppose that the government wants to increase its spending (G) by 1,000 units and to finance it through an equal amount of taxes (TX). This will leave the budget deficit or surplus unchanged, but will it affect the aggregate demand? The increase in government spending of 1,000 units will directly increase aggregate demand by 1,000 units, because G is a component of aggregate demand—look at equation (1) above. On the other hand, the increase in taxes will reduce disposable income by 1,000 units. Assuming that MPC equals 0.80, households will reduce their consumption expenditures by 800 units. So the net result will be an increase in aggregate demand of 200 units.

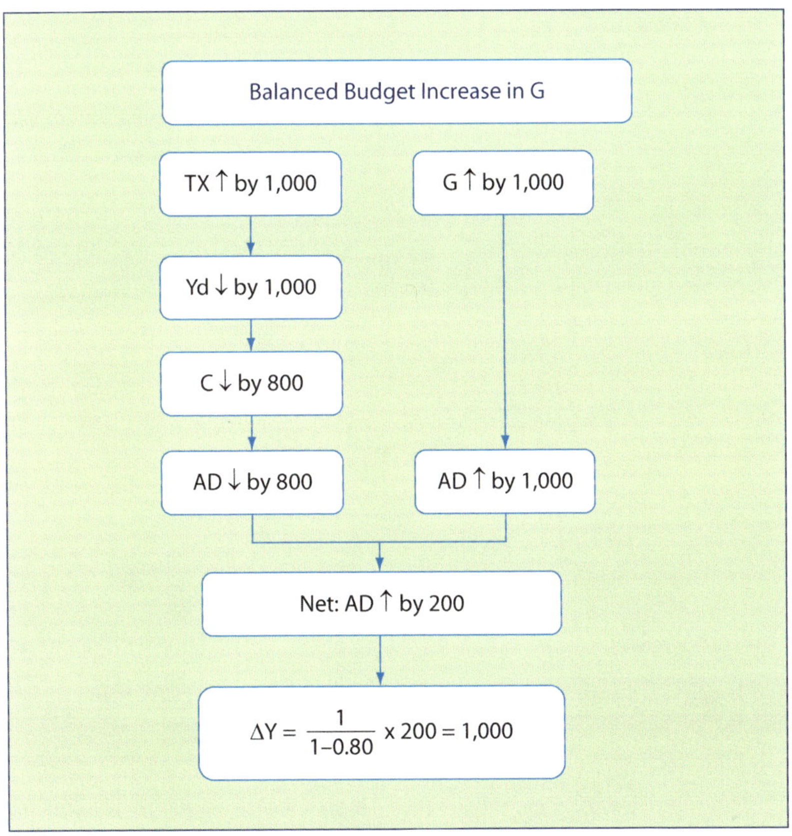

What will be the effect of this expansionary fiscal policy on the economy? Since the initial increase in aggregate demand is 200 units, the real GDP will increase by 1,000 units through the multiplier process as described above. This result is worth remembering. If the government increases spending and finances it by raising an equal amount of taxes, the real GDP will increase by the amount of the increase in government spending. This is called the *unit multiplier* result. Interestingly enough, it does not depend on the size of the multiplier. Suppose, for example, that MPC was 0.90 instead. Then the net increase in the aggregate demand would be (1,000 – 0.90 × 1,000) = 100 and the real GDP would increase by 1,000:

UNIT MULTIPLIER
When the government increases spending and raises an equal amount of tax to finance it, the increase in GDP will equal the increase in spending.

$$\Delta Y = (1/1 - 0.90) \times 10 = 10 \times 100 = 1{,}000$$

BALANCED BUDGET INCREASE IN TRANSFER PAYMENTS

What if the government wants to increase the transfer payments (TR) by 1,000 units and finance it by an equal increase in taxes (TX)? Increases in TR and TX of an equal amount will leave the real disposable income unchanged. This policy, then, will have no effect on aggregate demand. One reason why some governments conduct such a policy in a recession is the belief that those who are taxed generally have lower MPCs than those who receive transfer payments, such as the poor and unemployed. That is because, being poor, this group will spend most the income received on food and other necessities of life. So such an income transfer will increase aggregate demand.

HOUSEHOLD SAVING

What is not consumed is saved. Saving and consumption must therefore add up to disposable income.

$$Y_d = C + S \tag{4}$$

where S stands for saving. This simple concept has two important implications. First, given the level of income, consumption and saving must move in opposite directions and by the same amount. That is, an increase in consumption must be accompanied by an equal decrease in saving, and vice versa. Second, if disposable income increases, both consumption and saving will increase, and vice versa once again. Moreover, there will be a relationship between the increases in these two variables.

Suppose the marginal propensity to consume is MPC = 0.80. Then, if disposable income increases by 1,000 units, consumption will increase by 800 units. What will happen to the remaining 200 units? It will be saved. So if 80% of the increase in disposable income is consumed, the remaining 20% will be saved. The fraction of the increase in disposable income that is saved is called the *marginal propensity to save (MPS)*. In our case MPS = 0.20. We see then that

MARGINAL PROPENSITY TO SAVE
The fraction of the additional real disposable income that households save, rather than spending on goods and services. It is one minus MPC.

$$MPC + MPS = 1 \tag{5}$$

Conversely, if disposable income decreases by 1,000 units and MPC = 0.80, then consumption will decrease by 800 units and saving by 200 units. We will see in later chapters that this simple concept has important implications for the effectiveness of fiscal policy.

LINK TO FINANCIAL MARKETS

We have learned that changes in the interest rate will affect consumption and investment spending. For example, if the interest rate falls, households will find it cheaper to borrow money to buy consumer durables, such as cars and appliances. Similarly, business firms will be able to borrow at a lower interest rate to invest in plant and equipment. And so consumption and investment spending will increase. This will cause an increase in real GDP through the multiplier process.

Thus, if we don't know what the interest rate is, we cannot determine the levels of investment and consumption spending. Without investment and consumption spending, we cannot figure out the level of aggregate demand. If we don't know what AD is, we cannot determine how much GDP we should produce to achieve equilibrium. At this point, we don't know how the interest rate is determined. As a result, we don't know why and how it changes.

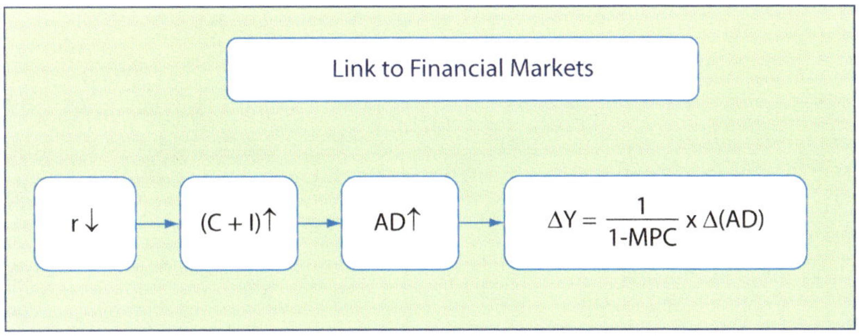

But we know why the interest rate is important. When it drops, the cost of borrowing goes down, and firms and households find it cheaper to borrow money. They borrow money in the financial markets, which play an important role in what is going on in the goods market and the level of real GDP. *The link between these two markets is the interest rate.* For this reason, we should understand what is happening in the financial markets in order to have a better understanding of GDP determination.

Financial markets are also important for a different—but related—reason. Recall that consumption spending depends in part on the level of real wealth, which is the purchasing power of nominal wealth. Nominal wealth is the sum of the market values of financial assets such as stocks, bonds, and money and real assets such as houses, lands, and precious metals. Business firms, households, and the government buy and sell financial assets in these markets. The market values of these assets are determined by their supplies and demands in the financial markets. So we really need to know what is going on in the financial markets in order to understand what is going on in the goods markets.

U.S. Real GDP and Its Components

The following table shows the U.S. real GDP and its components for the years 2000 to 2009. First note that consumption expenditure is the major portion of GDP, about 70%. Second, real gross investment spending is the sum of planned increases in plants, equipment, residential homes, and inventories, as well as unplanned increases in inventories noted above. The government spending is the sum of spending by the federal, state, and local governments. Finally, exports have been less than imports: we have sold fewer goods and services to foreigners than we have bought from them. In fact, for much of the century, the United States has been running a current account deficit.

Observe that, as expected, the real GDP for all the years almost equals the sum of expenditure categories. The slight discrepancy between the two numbers is due to errors and omissions in sampling and calculations of these numbers. Now take, for an example, the year 2008. As mentioned in Chapter 6, this was a recessionary year. Nevertheless, the national income identity holds for this year, like for any other year. Hence the uselessness of this identity.

Figures 1 through 4 present information on the behavior of the components of GDP over the last century. As can be seen, they were all increasing almost *all the time. This observation is related to the issue of economic growth, discussed in the last chapter. As GDP increases, more income is generated—therefore, everyone can buy greater amounts of goods and services.*

It is apparent that consumption expenditures have behaved rather smoothly over time. This makes sense. Households do not change their consumption plans erratically from one year to the next. There seems to be more variation in investment spending. This also makes sense. Business firms' plans to invest in plants and equipment depend on their perceptions of future profitability, as well as the riskiness of these investments. As their perceptions change, they undertake more or less investment in a year. Note in particular the dramatic reduction in investment spending during the 2007–2008 recession.

The government is not in the market to make profits. The government's objective is to provide and produce social capital such as roads and bridges, human capital in the form of education, and certain services such as national defense. Since these objectives do not change abruptly from year to year, government expenditures have smooth behavior over time. However, notice the large increase in government spending in the first half of the 1940s. This was associated with the preparation for World War II.

Finally, both exports and imports have been increasing over time. But imports have exceeded exports most of the time, so the United States has been running current account deficits. Some policy makers worry about this. They feel that if we buy more from foreign countries than we sell to those countries, our employment situation will be adversely affected. These worries are mostly baseless. We know from the previous chapter that in the long run, actual GDP has been tracing potential GDP so that over time, we have had only natural unemployment. Moreover, as we will see later, if our import of goods exceeded our export of goods, it must be true that our "export" of assets exceeded our "import" of assets. In other words, foreigners were buying more of U.S. assets than Americans were buying foreign assets. Thus, on net, our overall balance with foreign countries was not necessarily negative. Note that in the 2007–2008 recession, Americans were buying less from foreigners, but foreigners were buying less from Americans. Such is the result of the global nature of this recession.

Real GDP and Its Components Billions of Chained 2000 Dollars						
Year	Real Gross Domestic Product	Real Personal Consumption Expenditures	Real Gross Private Domestic Investment	Real Government Consumption Expenditures and Gross Investment	Real Exports of Goods and Services	Real Imports of Goods and Services
	Y	C	I	G	EX	IM
2000	11,226	7,608	1,970	2,098	1,188	1,640
2001	11,347	7,814	1,832	2,178	1,122	1,594
2002	11,553	8,022	1,807	2,280	1,099	1,648
2003	11,841	8,248	1,872	2,331	1,117	1,721
2004	12,264	8,533	2,058	2,362	1,223	1,911
2005	12,638	8,819	2,172	2,370	1,305	2,028
2006	12,976	9,074	2,230	2,402	1,422	2,151
2007	13,254	9,314	2,146	2,443	1,546	2,194
2008	13,312	9,291	1,989	2,518	1,629	2,124
2009	12,987	9,235	1,528	2,565	1,472	1,828
Components as Percent of Real GDP						
2000	100%	67.8%	17.6%	18.7%	10.6%	14.6%
2001	100%	68.8%	16.1%	19.2%	9.9%	14.0%
2002	100%	69.4%	15.6%	19.7%	9.5%	14.3%
2003	100%	69.6%	15.8%	19.7%	9.4%	14.5%
2004	100%	69.6%	16.8%	19.3%	10.0%	15.6%
2005	100%	69.8%	17.2%	18.8%	10.3%	16.0%
2006	100%	69.9%	17.2%	18.5%	11.0%	16.6%
2007	100%	70.3%	16.2%	18.4%	11.7%	16.6%
2008	100%	69.8%	15.0%	18.9%	12.2%	16.0%
2009	100%	71.2%	11.8%	19.8%	11.4%	14.1%

Figure 1: U.S. Real Personal Consumption Expenditure

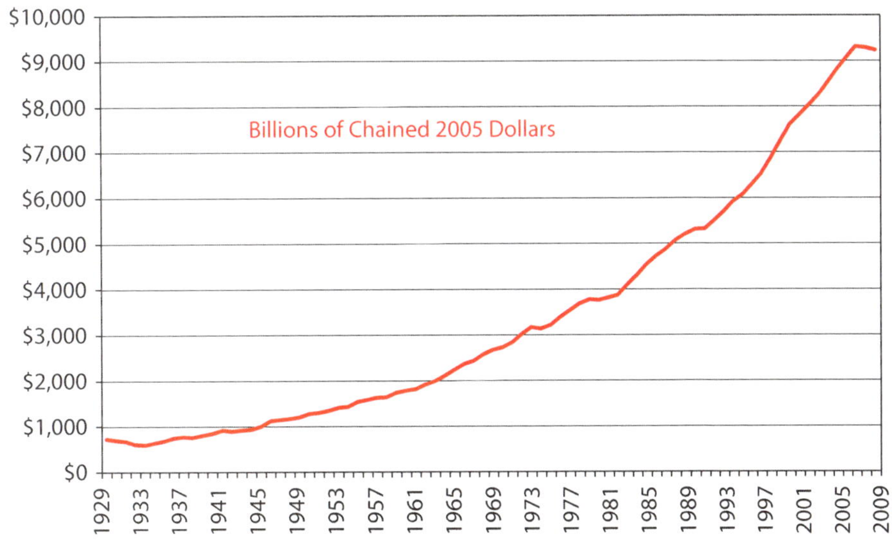

Figure 2: U.S. Real Gross Private Domestic Investment

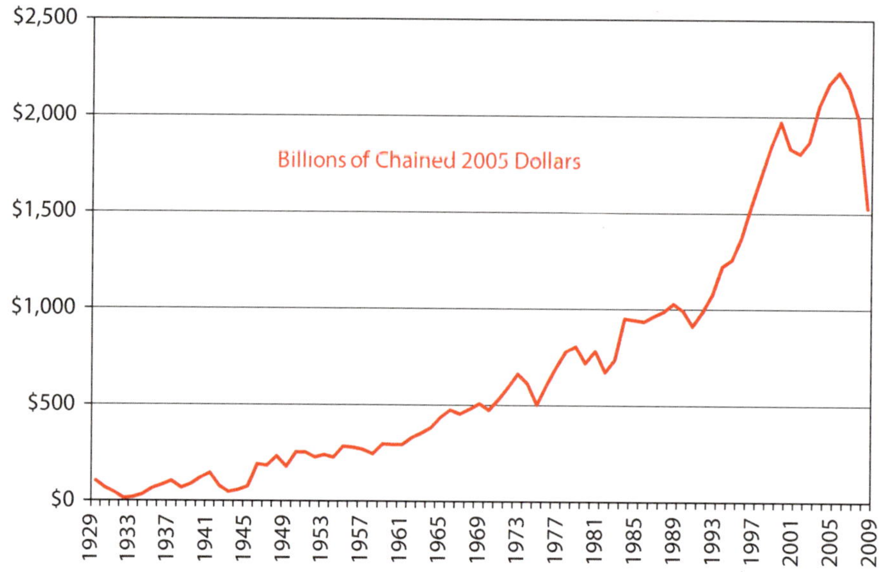

Figure 3: U.S. Real Government Spending

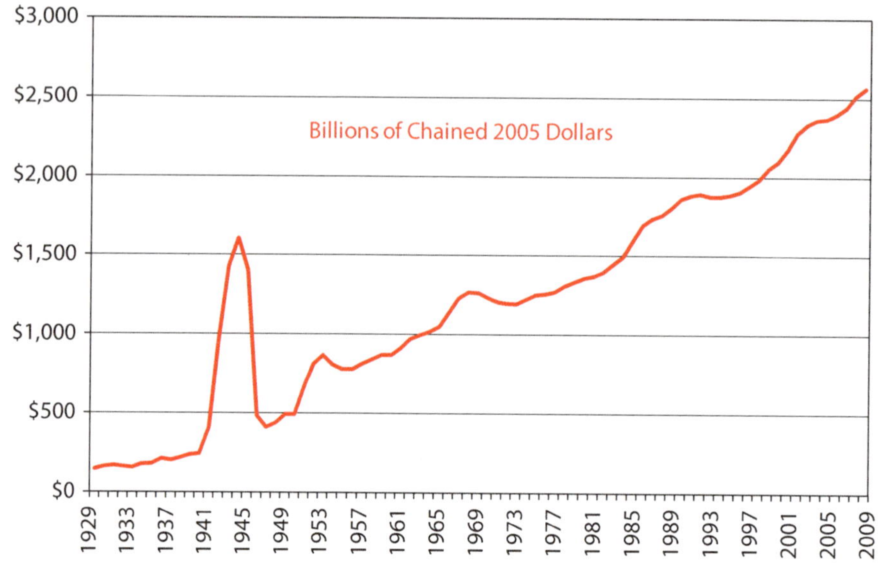

Figure 4: U.S. Real Exports and Imports

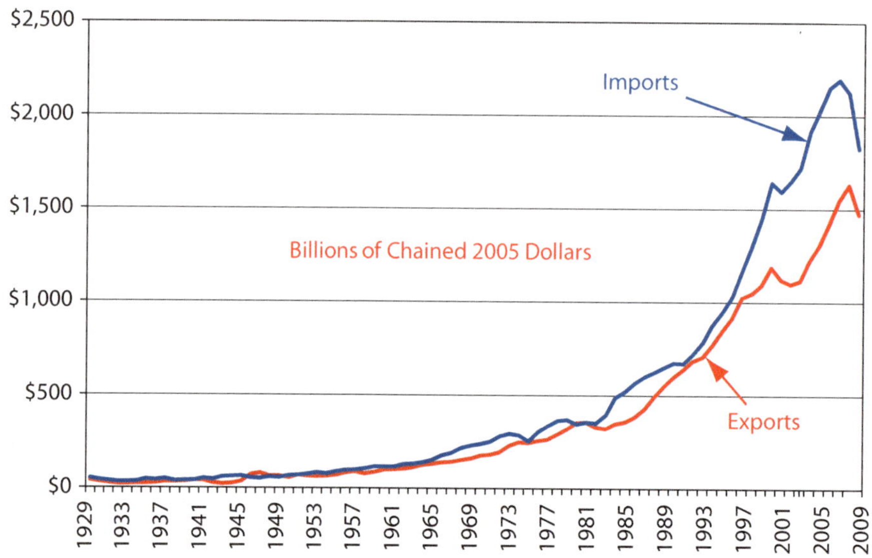

TO SUMMARIZE

1. GDP equals total expenditure, which is the sum of consumption, investment, government spending, and net exports. This is the *national income identity.*
2. In national accounts, investment spending is defined as the sum of planned changes in plants, equipment, and residential buildings, as well as unplanned changes in inventories.
3. Economists define *investment* as the sum of planned changes in plants, equipment, and residential buildings.
4. Unplanned changes in inventories are due to mistakes by business firms in predicting the level of demand.
5. *Aggregate demand* is the sum of desired levels of consumption, investment, government spending, and net exports. It excludes unplanned changes in inventories.
6. The difference between aggregate demand and real GDP is the unplanned changes in inventories.
7. When real GDP exceeds aggregate demand, there will be an unplanned increase in inventories.
8. When real GDP falls short of aggregate demand, there will be an unplanned decrease in inventories.
9. When real GDP equals aggregate demand, unplanned inventory changes will be zero. This state is called *goods market equilibrium.*
10. *Marginal propensity to consume* is the fraction of additional disposable income consumed.
11. An increase in any component of aggregate demand will lead to an increase in real GDP through the *multiplier process*, assuming fixed prices.
12. In general, the government can increase its spending in three different ways: (a) balanced budget increase in spending; (b) *deficit spending*; and (c) through *monetizing the debt.*
13. A *balanced budget increase* in government spending results in an equal increase in real GDP.

EXERCISES

Question 1

Suppose that in a particular year the expenditure categories took the following values in real terms:

C = 700 G = 200 EX = 50 IM = 70 I = 120

The real GDP was Y = 1,000 in that year.

a. Write down the national income identity.
b. Was the goods market in equilibrium in that year?
c. How much was the amount of unplanned changes in inventories?

Question 2

Repeat Question 1, but this time assume that the real GDP was Y = 1,100 in that year.

Question 3

Repeat Question 1, but this time assume that the real GDP was Y = 900 in that year.

Question 4

Explain whether, all else being the same, the following events would increase or decrease aggregate demand. The questions are independent of each other.

a. A recession comes to an end, and the real GDP starts going up.
a. The government provides more generous social security payments.
b. As a result of a new law, the amount of taxes collected by the government increases.
c. Consumers expect a tax hike to take place next year.
d. The nominal interest rate increases by 2%.
e. The nominal interest rate increases by 2%, while the expected inflation rate increases by 1%.
f. The nominal interest rate increases by 2%, while the expected inflation rate increases by 2%.
g. The nominal interest rate increases by 2%, while the expected inflation rate increases by 3%.
h. Firms expect more terrorist attacks in the future.
i. A recession ends in Europe, and Europeans start buying more American goods.
j. The government starts building more schools.
k. Higher-than-normal corporate profits result in higher stock prices.
l. Business firms become optimistic about the future profitability of investment projects.
m. The price level goes down.
n. People expect a recession to come soon.
o. The government provides more generous tax relief for research and development projects.
p. The government imposes a heavy tariff on the import of foreign goods to discourage imports.
q. The government provides a larger amount of food stamps to low-income families.
r. The stock market crashes, and the prices of many stocks plunge.
s. Some good economic news causes stock prices to increase.

Question 5

Assume that MPC = 0.75. What will happen to the real GDP if investment spending falls by 100 units?

Question 6

Suppose that the government increases transfer payments by 100 units. To finance this program, it raises an equal amount of taxes. Analyze the effect of this policy on the real GDP.

CHAPTER 8

The Money Market: Supply of Money

INTRODUCTION AND REVIEW

WE LEARNED IN the previous chapter that we could not fully understand what occurs in the goods market without knowing what is happening in the financial sector of the economy. One reason for this is that both consumption and investment spending—components of aggregate demand for goods and services—depend in part on the interest rate. If the interest rate decreases, then consumption and investment spending will increase, and vice versa. So it becomes important to understand why the interest rate changes, and for this we have to analyze the financial sector. Furthermore, household consumption depends on real financial and non-financial wealth. Real financial wealth is the purchasing power of the financial assets held by households, and the values of these are determined in the financial markets.

In this chapter and the next, we will learn that the government can change the rate of interest by manipulating the quantity of money in circulation. This will then change the aggregate demand and equilibrium GDP. Such a policy is called *monetary policy*. Since both fiscal and monetary policies affect the level of aggregate demand, they are collectively called *demand management policies*. But we are not there yet. We should first learn some introductory information. To begin with, we will learn what money is. We will then learn the meanings of *supply of money* and *demand for money*. They are not really what you might think they are!

MONETARY POLICY
Changes in the money supply by the Fed to affect the interest rate in order to change the level of aggregate demand.

DEMAND MANAGEMENT POLICIES
Fiscal and monetary policies.

SUPPLY OF MONEY
The amount of money people ***actually*** *hold at a point in time in their pockets, purses, and bank accounts.*

DEMAND FOR MONEY
The portion of their total wealth that people wish to hold in the form of money. In other words, it is the amount of money people are willing and able (their wealth permitting) to hold at any point.

DEFINITION OF MONEY

Money plays a huge role in our lives. Actually, it plays more than one role. You use it to buy things. The price of everything you buy is expressed in money: a bottle of carrot juice costs a particular amount of dollars. You hold your savings in the form of money. You pay back your college loans with money. But what exactly *is* money? Let's study money in a few easy-to-follow steps—or your money back!

In economics, money has a specific meaning that differs from some of the day-to-day usages of the term. As they say, *money is what money does*. In other words, we define money by its functions. Anything that performs these functions in a society is money. Here are the four basic functions performed by money:

1. Medium of Exchange. Money is mainly used to buy goods and services. There are very few societies in history without money. All societies have used something as a *medium of exchange*, or *means of payments*, and called it money. This is simply because an economic system without money—called the *barter system*—is enormously inefficient, because of huge *transaction costs* as a result of the problem known as *double coincidence of wants*. We have used many big words here, but they refer to really easy concepts. Suppose you had some biochemistry books you wanted to get rid of, and you also wanted to buy a small round table. Suppose you lived in a barter system with no money in the economy. Then you would have to find a person who wanted exactly the books you wanted to sell, and had exactly the table you wanted to buy. This is the problem of double coincidence of wants. The probability of finding such a person is indeed very small. People wasted an enormous amount of time and effort to find second parties for their transactions. This is what we mean by saying that a barter system is inefficient—it wastes time and effort.

MEDIUM OF EXCHANGE/MEANS OF PAYMENTS
Means of payments. Any object people in a society use to buy goods and services.

BARTER SYSTEM
An economic system without money.

TRANSACTIONS COSTS
The opportunity costs of conducting a transaction.

DOUBLE COINCIDENCE OF WANTS
Finding someone in a barter system who wants to buy what you want to sell, and who wants to sell what you want to buy.

In economics, the time, effort, and money spent to find the parties with whom to enter transactions are called transaction costs. The medium-of-exchange function of money solves the problem of double coincidence of wants. You sell your books for money, and then use the money to buy the table. The person you sell your books to and the person you buy your table from are usually two different people. For this reason, the probability of finding such people is quite high. This function is the most important one. You will see that the importance of the remaining three functions of money is derived from its function as a medium of exchange.

2. Unit of account. Prices of goods and services are expressed in terms of money. For example, a car is $45,000 and a pen sells for $1. This solves two other problems with a barter system: money has a standard value, so the price of any good need be expressed only in terms of money, rather than thousands of other goods. In a barter system, the price of a table should be expressed in terms of all the other remaining goods, depending on what you were getting in exchange. This would be very inefficient. Also, if I said one table was worth 50 books, you would ask "What kind of table? New? Old? Big? Small? Oak? Particleboard?" But when you say a table is worth $500, you don't ask "What kind of dollars, old, new, oak …?" Note that the usefulness of money as a unit of account derives from its usefulness as a medium of exchange. We quote every price in dollars, because dollars are what we use to buy goods and services.

3. Store of Value. The above two functions pertain to a point in time. The next two functions are performed over time. You can save value in the form of money. In other words, money is not only a medium of exchange, but also an asset. If you put $20 under your mattress, one year later you will have $20. Other assets, like stocks, bonds, and houses perform this store-of-value function, but they also yield some returns. Why do people hold their wealth in the form of money, which yields little or no return? Moreover, in the case of inflation, money loses its store-of-value usefulness, because it loses its purchasing power over time. Your $20 next year will buy fewer goods if the prices of goods increase over the next year.

The answer is that people hold money because money is highly liquid. Highly *what*? *Liquidity* is the ease with which you can sell an asset, and it is a relative concept. *One asset is more liquid than another if you can convert it into cash faster, with a smaller loss in value.* Of course, you can convert

LIQUIDITY
Ease with which you can sell an asset.

any asset into cash. You can sell your house in just an hour if you are willing to accept a very low price for it, say $10,000. On the other hand, you can sell a stock or bond in one hour without much loss in their values. Money itself is the most liquid of all assets. Again, the store-of-value function derives its usefulness from the medium-of-exchange function. We want to save in the form of money, because it is what we will use in the future to buy goods and services. If we held all of our wealth in stocks and bonds, then every time we wanted to buy something we would have to sell some of them to get cash for our purchase. This would be too inconvenient and too costly.

4. Standard of Deferred Payments. We pay back our loans with money. Again, the usefulness of this function stems partly from its function as a medium of exchange. I'd like to get back the loan I gave you in the form of money, because that is what I use to buy bread and butter for the family. Moreover, money has a standard value so that both the lenders and borrowers know what they are talking about in loan contracts. If you promise to pay me back your loan in the form of ten chickens, then we have to specify many other things about these chickens such as their weight, age, and health conditions.

WHAT CAN SERVE AS MONEY?

The answer is, basically anything that is accepted by the general public to serve as money can serve as money! So the most important requirement for anything to serve as money is that the general public should accept it in transactions. Take a piece of useless stone. If everyone in the society accepts it in transactions, then it is money. In POW camps, cigarettes were used as money. In some societies, dried fish or salt were used as money. You go to an electronics store and buy a VCR worth $120. You give the seller $120 and walk out with a brand new VCR. Why is it that the seller is willing to part with that fancy and expensive VCR in exchange for some dirty green pieces of paper with some pictures on them? This is because he knows that other people will also accept them, and so he will be able to buy bread and butter with them.

Objects like gold, silver, salt, or dried fish that some societies use as mediums of exchange are called *commodity money*. They have other uses besides being money, so they have some intrinsic value. There are numerous problems with using commodity money. For example, it may be difficult to transport large quantities of them. Some, like gold or silver, may erode over time, and things like fish may spoil if not stored. Also, money must be divisible. You cannot buy something with one and a half chickens. Because of these problems, in today's societies people use *fiat money* in their transactions. Fiat money is something that has no intrinsic value, but is used as a means of payment. This is mainly because of the government's fiat or order. The government decrees that everyone should accept a particular object in their transactions, and it stands ready to accept it in its own transactions. This way the public comes to accept that object as money. In the United States, the bills and coins used in transactions are the fiat money. They are also the *legal tender*—the government mandates their acceptance in repayment of loans and payment of taxes. Unlike dried fish, which can be eaten, or gold, which can be used to make teeth, dollar bills have no intrinsic use or value as a commodity.

COMMODITY MONEY
Objects like gold, silver, salt, or dried fish that some societies use as a medium of exchange. They have other uses besides being money, and therefore have some intrinsic value.

FIAT MONEY
Any object that has no intrinsic value, but is used as a means of payment by a government's order (fiat).

LEGAL TENDER
Anything the government mandates to be accepted in repayment of loans and payment of taxes.

MEASURES OF MONEY SUPPLY

If the government wants to change interest rates by changing the amount of money in the economy, it needs to know what is used as money and how to measure it. What would you count if you wanted to know how much money we have in the economy? First and foremost, you would start with things we use to buy goods and services. Coins and paper money would definitely be in. But so would the money sitting in your checking account. This is the money you can use to buy things. If you have $50 in your purse and $100 in your checking account, you could buy $150 worth of goods and services. However, you can also buy things with the money in your savings account in the bank. Perhaps all you need to do is call your bank and ask them to transfer some money from savings to checking. For some accounts, you don't even need to do that. Banks automatically transfer money from your savings to your checking account whenever your checking account is short of cash.

This is a convenient place to define the concept of money supply. The supply of money is a stock variable. In fact, the supply of money is also called the *stock* of money. We can measure the amount of money at any point in time. Demand and supply for stock variables do not mean the same as flow variables. For a flow variable—such as the quantity of apples bought or sold over a period of time—demand means the amount buyers desire to buy, and supply means the amount sellers desire to sell. The buyers and sellers are two different groups of people. In the case of stock variables, there are no buyers or sellers of anything. By supply we mean the *actual* holdings, and by demand we mean the *desired* holdings. Therefore, *the supply of money is the amount of money people actually hold at a point in time* in their pockets, purses, and bank accounts. *The demand for money is the amount of money people want or desire to hold at any point in time.* We will discuss demand for money in a later chapter. For now, let's define and measure the supply of money.

SUPPLY OF MONEY
The amount of money people actually hold at a point in time in their pockets, purses, and bank accounts.

DEMAND FOR MONEY
The portion of their total wealth that people wish to hold in the form of money. In other words, it is the amount of money people are willing and able (their wealth permitting) to hold at any point.

There are three aggregate measures of money supply in the United States. All consist of currency and some other types of assets thought to function as money, mostly bank deposits. These measures of money supply are called M1, M2, and M3, broadly defined as follows:

M1 = Currency + Travelers' Checks + Demand Deposits

Currency consists of all the bills and coins held outside banks by the non-bank public like you and me. Demand deposits are accounts in banks and other financial institutions on which you can write checks. These are also called checking accounts. This is the narrowest and most liquid definition of money. It is also closest to the medium-of-exchange concept. Think of it this way: the only thing we do with M1 is buy goods and services.

A broader measure of money supply, M2, consists of M1 plus deposits in banks and other financial institutions that are less liquid. These mostly include household holdings of savings deposits, small denomination (less than $100,000) time deposits, and money market mutual fund deposits. Savings deposits are those deposits in financial institutions that you cannot generally write checks on. Time deposits are deposits from which you cannot withdraw for a certain period of time. If you do, you incur a penalty in the form of reduced interest. In the case of money market mutual fund deposits, you deposit your money in a financial institution, and the institution invests it in government bonds. The M2 measure includes M1 plus items that are less liquid, and are used less frequently to buy goods and services.

M2 = **M1** + Savings Deposits + Small Denomination Time Deposits
+ Money Market Mutual Funds Deposits

The last measure, M3, includes M2, as well as items that are much less liquid than those in M2. For example, it includes large-denomination time deposits and institutional (i.e., non-household) money market deposit accounts. So as we go down the list, the aggregate monetary measures become broader and less liquid. They become less of a medium of exchange.

M3 = **M2** + Large-Denomination Time Deposits
+ Institutional Money Market Mutual Funds Deposits
+ Other less liquid deposits

It is easier to keep in mind that money is the sum of all the currency in people's pockets and purses, plus some kind of deposits in banks and other financial institutions, such as credit unions. In this book we will concentrate on M1 only. We will also assume that the amount of travelers' checks is negligible. So for us, money supply will mean the sum of currency in circulation and demand deposits in banks and other financial institutions. Denoting the money supply by the letter M, we have

M = Currency + Demand Deposits

The following table shows M1 and its components for selected months.

M1 and Components Billions of Dollars				
Month & Year	M1 Money Stock	Total Checkable Deposits	Currency Component of M1	Travelers Checks Outstanding
June 1960	140	110	29	0.30
June 1970	208	160	47	0.79
June 1980	389	276	110	3.63
June 1990	809	568	233	7.41
June 2005	1,374	658	709	7.34
June 2007	1,367	605	755	6.50

THE NAME IS BOND, DISCOUNT BOND

To understand the working of monetary policy, we need to have some knowledge of bonds and other similar securities. A bond is a promissory note—it promises to pay a certain amount of money at a certain date in the future. People or institutions that want to borrow money issue bonds. Those who have some money and want to lend it buy bonds. The beauty of bonds and the bond market is that borrowers do not need to go door to door to find lenders. All they must do is issue a bond and sell it in the market at the going market price. The money the seller receives is the amount borrowed. The mechanics of borrowing through selling bonds is somewhat like the following simple story:

Suppose on January 20, 2009, I need some money to buy a refrigerator. I decide to issue and sell a bond to raise the needed cash. I take a piece of paper, as in the figure below, and write on it that whoever brings it to me the next year, on January 20, 2010, I will pay him or her $1,000. This dollar amount is called the *face value*, the *future value*, or the *final value*. The face value, because it is written on the face of the bond. The future value, because it will be paid in the future. The final value, because after that payment is made, the loan will be settled and the bond would cease to exist. The date January 20, 2010, is called the *maturity date*. In this simple example, the bond has a maturity of one year.

FACE VALUE/FUTURE VALUE/ FINAL VALUE
The amount written on the face of a bond that the lender promises to pay in the future. It is also called ***final value.***

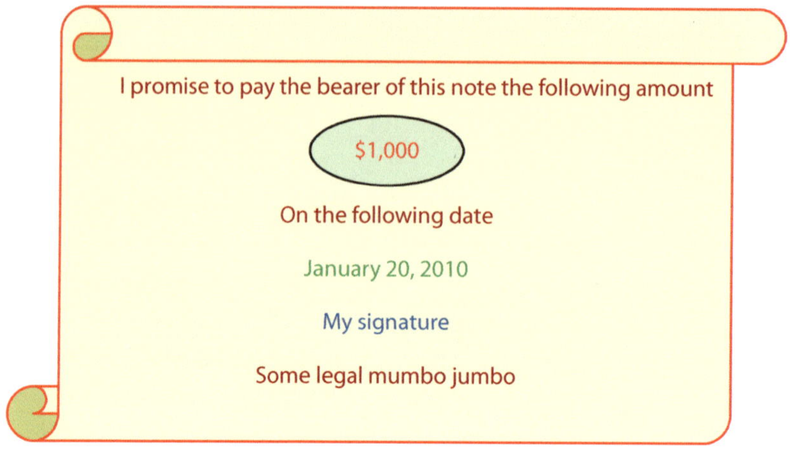

The signature on the bond indicates who the issuer or borrower is. Finally, the bond would come with a great deal of statements defining the legal rights and obligations of the borrower and the lender.

How much would you be willing to pay for this piece of paper? Definitely not $1,000. Why would you pay $1,000 for a piece of paper that will give you $1,000 a year from now? If you did, you would lose interest that you could have earned by investing your money somewhere else, like putting it in a bank. The amount of money people are willing to pay for this bond depends on who the issuer is. For example, the U.S. Treasury Department issues bonds to raise cash to finance the government's expenditures. The Treasury Department is a very trustworthy borrower, since it never defaults on its loans. This is because the government has the power to tax people and use the money to pay back its loans.

Since a bond issued by the Treasury does not carry any default risk, a lot of people would love to buy it. Because of a very high demand for this Treasury bond, its price in the bond market would be high. Still, it would not be equal to $1,000, for the reason mentioned above. Suppose the market price of this bond turns out to be $950. This is how much the Treasury would borrow if it sold this bond. If you bought this bond for this price, you would make a return of $50 over the next year ($1,000 face value – the price of $950). Your rate of return from this investment would be approximately 5.3%, calculated as follows:

$$((\$1{,}000-\$950)/\$950)\times 100=5.3\%$$

This 5.3% is called the *interest rate* on this bond.

INTEREST RATE
The rate of return on bonds.

Now, let's get back to my bond. Suppose I also decide to sell my piece of paper in the bond market, in order to borrow some money. How much would you be willing to pay for *my* bond? Not only would you be unwilling to pay $1,000 for my bond, you would not even want to pay $950 for it. Why not? Well, why would you want to pay $950 to buy my bond when you can use it to buy the risk-free Treasury bond? My bond is risky. I may borrow your money and use it in some risky investments and go bankrupt. In that case, you will lose part or all of your investment. Therefore, you would be willing to pay much less than $950 for my bond. Suppose the best price I could fetch for my bond in the market is $800. The lender who takes a chance and buys it expects to make a rate of return of 25% on it, calculated as follows:

$$((\$1{,}000-\$800)/\$800)\times 100=25\%$$

We learn two lessons from this simple story. First, a riskier bond would have a higher required rate of return than a risk-free bond. In the above story, the investors required a rate of return of 25% from the risky bond compared to the 5.3% they required from the Treasury bond. Second, for the same face value, the higher the price of the bond, the lower the interest rate on it.

COUPON BONDS

In the real world, bonds are more complicated than the one described above. The types of bonds depicted above are called *discount bonds*, because they sell at a discount (e.g., $950) relative to their face value (e.g., $1,000). Most bonds have maturities longer than just one year. They make periodic payments every year or every six months called *coupon payments*. Such bonds are called *coupon bonds*. They might have maturities ranging from 5 years to 30 years.

DISCOUNT BOND
A bond that promises just one payment in the future, called face value. They sell at a discount relative to their face value, so that the buyer can earn an interest out of the difference.

COUPON BONDS/COUPON PAYMENTS
Bonds that have maturities longer than one year and make periodic payments called coupon payments every year, or every six months.

Let's suppose that in January 2000, the Treasury Department issued and sold some 30-year bonds, promising to pay $1,000 per year from January 2001 through January 2030. If Adam bought one of these bonds in January 2000, he would receive coupon payments of $1,000 per year for 30 years, starting with January 2001. If he sold the bond to Barbara in March 2004, then Barbara would receive these annual coupon payments. The bond will cease to pay coupons after the maturity date of January 2030. In any particular year, households and firms hold bonds issued by the government in prior years that will mature in some future years.

Corporations and households also issue bonds to borrow money. Corporations borrow to invest in plants and equipment and households to buy homes. It is slightly more complicated to calculate the annual interest rate for coupon bonds. Nevertheless, two features are common to both discount and coupon bonds, namely:

1. Riskier bonds carry higher interest rates; and
2. The higher the price of the bond, the lower the interest rate on the bond.

These facts are worth remembering. In this book, we will only consider Treasury bonds.

THE FEDERAL RESERVE SYSTEM

The central bank of the United States is called the Federal Reserve System, or "the Fed" for short. The Fed has two major functions. The first is to make sure the banking system is functioning smoothly. For example, it wants to prevent widespread bank failures. This occurs when a large

The Federal Reserve headquarters in Washington, D.C.

number of people try to withdraw their deposits, but find out there is not enough money in the banks. If people thought that the banking system was not sound, bank panics would spread. Larger and larger numbers of people would want to withdraw their deposits, causing financial trouble for the banking system.

You see, banks are in business to make profits. Their profits come from the difference in the interest rates they pay their depositors and the interest rates they charge to borrowers. The more money a bank lends, the more profit it will make. This gives banks an incentive to lend as much money as they can. Suppose that a bank pays 2% interest on its deposits and charges an average of 12% on its mortgage and other loans to households and firms. So if you deposit $1,000 in this bank, it will make a profit of $100 if it lends the whole thing out.

$$\text{Bank Profit} = (12\% - 2\%) \times \$1{,}000 = 10\% \times \$1{,}000 = \$100$$

However, if it lends only $500 out, its profit will be $50. So the bank will want to loan out the whole $1,000.

If a bank lends most of its deposits to maximize its profits, it may not have enough money to pay the depositors who want to withdraw money from the bank. Suppose you go to your local bank to withdraw some money and the bank teller says to you, "We are sorry, we don't have enough money today to pay you. Please come back tomorrow." This would sound very bizarre to you. You call your friend and tell her your story, and pretty soon the news will spread. Worrying that the bank may be in financial trouble, people will rush to withdraw their money from this bank. Since banks loan out a large portion of their deposits, no bank has enough money on hand to satisfy all its depositors simultaneously. So in the case of a deposit outflow, the bank may go bankrupt, in which case a lot of people may lose their savings.

There is another problem that arises from the very nature of banking. The bank essentially plays with other people's money. This fact dulls the banks' incentives to be careful with the money they lend. Suppose an investor comes to borrow $100 million for a risky investment. Since the investment is too risky, the investor offers to pay 25% interest on the loan. The owners of the bank would probably not lend their own money to this investor. But since the money they are lending belongs to you, they may not worry too much about losing it. If the investor's project takes off and he pays the promised 25% interest, the bank will make $23 million. If the project goes bust and he defaults on the loan, the bank may file for bankruptcy in which case *you* lose. So for the bank this is a win/no-lose situation.

For these reasons, banking is one of the most tightly regulated industries in all countries. The Fed has three tools at its disposal to prevent bank panics and bank failures. All three aim at maintaining liquidity in the banking system by ensuring that enough money exists in the banks.

REQUIRED RESERVES
The amount of the total reserves that banks are required to keep by law.

1. Required reserves. The Fed—and other government regulators—requires banks to keep a fraction of their deposits on hand at all times. These are called *required reserves*. This is to prevent excessive lending. The aim is to ensure that at any point, enough reserves are available in the banking system in case a large number of people want to withdraw their deposits from the banks.

2. Discount loans. The Fed acts as a bank for the other banks. Banks hold some of their reserves at the Fed, and the Fed extends loans to banks that are in trouble. These loans are called discount loans. The Fed charges interest on these loans at a rate called the *discount rate*. If there is an unexpected deposit outflow and a bank does not have enough money to pay its depositors, the Fed extends temporary loans to this bank to save it from bankruptcy and to protect people's deposits.
3. Bank capital regulation. Finally, the Fed regulates the amount of bank capital. It requires shareholders to maintain a minimum amount of their own money in the bank. This is for two reasons. One is to prevent excessive risk taking mentioned above. If bank owners have some stake in the bank, they will be more careful in lending money. Second, it is to ensure that if borrowers default on their loans, the bank has enough cushion money to stay solvent.

DISCOUNT RATE
The interest rate that the Fed charges on its discount loans.

The second function of the Fed is to conduct monetary policy, which means changing the amount of money in the economy to achieve certain goals. For example, in a recession the Fed may want to increase the money supply to ease credit conditions so business firms find it less costly to borrow money for their investments. Or when there is a fear of inflation, the Fed may want to reduce the amount of money in circulation in order to bring down the inflation rate. The Fed can change the money supply using one or more of three tools:

1. Open market operations. *Open market operations* refer to buying and selling of government bonds by the Fed.
2. Discount rate. The Fed can increase or decrease the amount of discount loans by changing the discount rate it charges banks.
3. Required reserve ratio. As we saw above, the Fed requires banks to keep a certain percentage of their deposits in the banks in the form of reserves. This percentage is called the *required reserve ratio*.

OPEN MARKET OPERATIONS
Buying and selling of government bonds by the Fed to change the interest rate.

REQUIRED RESERVE RATIO
The fraction of the total deposits the Fed requires banks to keep on hand in the form of reserves.

We will see shortly how the Fed can change the money supply using these tools. To understand how this can be done, we need to learn about the bank balance sheet.

BANK BALANCE SHEET

To see how monetary policy works, we must have some basic understanding of the concept of a balance sheet. This concept is based on a simple idea. You buy anything with either the money that belongs to you or the money that you have borrowed from someone else. What you have borrowed from other people are your *liabilities* and what belongs to you is your *net worth*. Thus, at any point in time, the market value of all the assets you have must equal the sum of your liabilities and your net worth. For obvious reason, the liabilities and net worth are also called the *sources of funds*; the values of total assets are called the *uses of funds*. Therefore, we have:

$$\text{Assets} = \text{Liabilities} + \text{Net Worth}$$

For instance, suppose I used $20,000 of my own money and borrowed $80,000 from a bank to buy a house worth $100,000. The total market value of my assets ($100,000) is then equal to my liabilities ($80,000) plus my net worth ($20,000). It cannot be otherwise. If the next day the

LIABILITIES
What you owe to other people.

NET WORTH
What you own. Excess of your assets (what you have) over your liabilities (what you owe).

SOURCES OF FUNDS
Sources of financing the purchase of an asset. An asset can be purchased by borrowed money (liabilities), or by the buyer's own money (net worth).

USES OF FUNDS
Values of assets held in a company or by a household.

market price of the house increased to $150,000, my liabilities would remain at $80,000, but my net worth would increase to $70,000.

Now let's look at a simplified version of a bank balance sheet. What concerns us here are six major items in the balance sheet. Look at the following hypothetical example:

Bank Balance Sheet				
Assets Uses of Funds			**Liabilities + Net Worth** Sources of Funds	
Reserves		$150	Deposits	$1,000
Required @ 10%	$100			
Excess	$50		Borrowing	$120
Treasury Bonds		$250		
Loans		$900	Net Worth	$180
	Total	$1,300	Total	$1,300

On the liabilities side, the deposits ($1,000) are the money that people (the public) have deposited in the bank. These are the depositors' assets, but the bank's liabilities. They belong to the depositors, and the bank must hand them over whenever the depositors come to withdraw these funds. Banks also borrow money. Usually, when a bank is short of cash, it can borrow money either from other banks or from the Fed. Our bank has borrowed $120 from these two sources.

At any time, some banks have excess money that they want to lend, and some other banks are short of money and thus want to borrow. Banks borrow from each other overnight in what is called the *federal funds market*.[1] The interest rate on these loans is called the *federal funds rate* and is closely watched by financial analysts and investors. Banks also borrow from the Fed. Such loans are called discount loans. The interest rate the Fed charges on them is called the discount rate. The Fed does not have to lend any money to any bank—in fact, it is generally reluctant to do so. However, whenever it feels that a bank is temporarily out of cash and in risk of bankruptcy, it may rescue that bank by lending some money to it. We say that the Fed acts as a *lender of last resort*. Another reason the Fed extends loans to commercial banks is to change the supply of money. We will shortly see the effects of such loans on the money supply.

FEDERAL FUNDS MARKET
The market in which banks borrow from each other overnight.

FEDERAL FUNDS RATE
The interest rate banks charge on the loans borrowed in the federal funds market.

LENDER OF LAST RESORT
Whenever the Fed realizes that a bank is temporarily out of cash and in risk of bankruptcy, it may rescue that bank by lending some money to it.

The net worth is the amount that belongs to the bank's shareholders. It is also called bank capital. The amount of net worth in a bank cannot drop below a certain level. Banks are required by law to hold a minimum amount of bank capital. This is for the two reasons mentioned above: to prevent excessive risk taking, and to ensure that the bank has enough money to pay its depositors or creditors in case some of the bank loans default. The bank will become bankrupt when the net worth drops below zero. At that point, the government would shut down the bank, fire its managers, and administer bankruptcy procedures.

Now let's study the asset side of the balance sheet. What do banks do with our money? They take our money and pay us some interest on our deposits, and turn around and lend that money to someone else at a higher interest rate. The balance sheet shows that our bank has $900 of loans outstanding. This loan amount is a part of the bank's assets, and it will receive interest on it in the future. These loans are generally made to households to buy homes or to businesses to invest

1 The reason for this terminology is that banks have accounts at the Fed. When Bank A borrows $100 from Bank B, Bank B deposits $100 in Bank A's account at the Fed.

in plants and equipment. Banks also invest in Treasury bonds. Our bank holds $250 worth of Treasury bonds.[2]

For the reasons mentioned above, the Fed requires banks to keep a certain percent of their total deposits in the bank or in their accounts at the Fed. Banks can only loan out the rest. That percentage is called the required reserve ratio (rrr). It depends on the size of the bank and the type of deposit. Assume it is 10%. Then in the above example, banks are required to keep 0.10 × $1,000 = $100 of their deposits in the banks. This amount is called the *required reserves*.

REQUIRED RESERVES
Reserves that are required by law to be kept in the banks, and not loaned out.

Reserves just mean the physical cash held by the banks. In the above example, the bank is holding total reserves of $150. Of this, $100 is required by the Fed and the remaining $50 constitutes the *excess reserves*—those held in excess of what is required. Our bank can loan out this $50. If a bank does not have any excess reserves, we say that the bank is *fully loaned out*.

EXCESS RESERVES
Reserves held by banks in excess of what is required by law.

FULLY LOANED OUT
A situation in which banks have loaned out all their excess reserves.

TOOLS OF MONETARY POLICY

We are now ready to learn how the Fed can change the money supply using the three tools it has at its disposal. Keep in mind while reading the following pages that in all three cases, some additional excess reserves are generated that the banks will be able to lend. The borrowers will deposit the loaned amounts in the banks. This lending will result in multiple deposit creation.

Open Market Operations

If the Fed buys anything, the supply of money will increase, because the Fed would pay with money that was sitting inside the Fed's vault and thus out of circulation. Recall that money is what *people* hold as currency in their pockets, purses, and bank accounts. However, the Fed doesn't buy just anything. It generally buys things like bonds, foreign currency, or gold. The Fed's purchases and sales of U.S. Treasury bonds are called *open market operations.* A purchase is called an *open market purchase* and a sale an *open market sale*.

OPEN MARKET OPERATIONS
Buying and selling of government bonds by the Fed to change the interest rate.

OPEN MARKET PURCHASE
Buying of government bonds by the Fed to change the interest rate.

OPEN MARKET SALE
Selling of government bonds by the Fed to change the interest rate.

Let's consider an open market purchase of bonds, in which the Fed buys Treasury bonds worth $300,000. The Fed does this by offering a price higher than the current market price for bonds. If no seller is found, the Fed increases the price offered a little. It continues this process until it has bought $300,000 worth of Treasury bonds. There are always people out there who will be induced to sell at some high price. Suppose the seller is a bank called the First Global Bank. The Fed receives the bonds from First Global, and deposits $300,000 in First Global's account at the Fed. Now First Global has $300,000 of additional reserves.

Such transactions cause changes in the bank balance sheets, shown by what are called T-accounts. These accounts just show the segments of the balance sheets affected by the transactions, in order to save space. A plus sign in these tables means an increase and a minus sign a decrease. Since the balance sheets must balance at all times, for any change in an item, you need to find another offsetting change in the balance sheet to make the sum of the two sides equal. The following is the T-account showing the effect of the Fed buying $300,000 worth of bonds from First Global:

2 Banks are not allowed to invest in stocks. This is because the government does not want banks to use our savings in risky investments. What if banks were allowed to invest in stocks, and the stock prices went down substantially in a recession? A lot of people could lose their life savings in that case.

First Global Bank (After Selling Treasury Bonds)	
Changes in Assets	Changes in Liabilities + Net Worth
Excess Reserves +$300,000 Treasury Bonds -$300,000	

Note that no new demand deposits have been generated in the bank. This means two things. First, no additional money has been created yet, because money by definition equals currency in the hands of the public plus demand deposits. Second, First Global is not required to keep any part of this $300,000 in the bank as required reserves. That is because it is not a demand deposit, and thus is not affected by the required reserve ratio. The whole amount constitutes excess reserves that the bank can lend out.

Discount Loans

Discount loans are loans that the Fed makes to the banks at an interest rate called the discount rate. Suppose that the Fed wants to make a discount loan of $300,000. The Fed does this by lowering the discount rate it charges the banks. Banks find it profitable to borrow from the Fed at the new low discount rate and lend it to the public to increase their profits. Suppose First Global borrows from the Fed. Then its reserves increase by $300,000 as shown in the following T-account.

First Global Bank (After Taking a Discount Loan)	
Changes in Assets	Changes in Liabilities + Net Worth
Excess Reserves +$300,000	Discount Loans +$300,000

Again, no demand deposits are generated, and the whole $300,000 constitutes excess reserves that can be loaned out. Note that the outcome of the discount policy is less certain than that of an open market operation. This is because the Fed cannot force banks to borrow. If the banks feel that there are not many profitable investment opportunities, or they think they cannot find low-risk borrowers, they may decide not to take the discount loan from the Fed.

The Required Reserve Ratio

Finally, the Fed can create additional excess reserves by lowering the required reserve ratio. This is easy to understand. Take a look at the bank's balance sheet, assuming that the system is fully loaned out. Suppose that initially, the required reserve ratio is 20%. Since the bank has deposits of $3,000,000, it must hold $600,000 of reserves (0.20 × $3,000,000).

First Global Bank Balance Sheet Before Change			
Assets		Liabilities + Net Worth	
Reserves	$600,000	Deposits	$3,000,000
Required @ 20%	$600,000		
Excess	$0		
Loans	$3,400,000	Net Worth	$1,000,000
	$4,000,000		$4,000,000

Now suppose that the Fed reduces the required reserve ratio to 10%. Immediately, $300,000 of the required reserves are released, and become excess reserves that the banks can lend to the public. Changing the required reserve ratio is a very powerful tool, because it affects all banks in the system. Therefore, small mistakes and miscalculations on the part of the Fed or the bank regulators can have huge consequences. For this reason, the Fed does not change this ratio often.

First Global Bank Balance Sheet After Change			
Assets		Liabilities + Net Worth	
Reserves	$600,000	Deposits	$3,000,000
Required @ 10%	$300,000		
Excess	$300,000		
Loans	$3,400,000	Net Worth	$1,000,000
	$4,000,000		$4,000,000

For the above reasons, open market operations are the Fed's favorite policy tool. As a result, we will solely concentrate on this monetary policy tool in our book. But what happens to the money supply? In all three cases above, $300,000 dollars of excess reserves were created in the banking system. We now need to know how this $300,000 becomes money.

MULTIPLE DEPOSIT CREATION

The $300,000 of excess reserves will generate additional money in the economy because of the banks' lending process. Suppose that the Fed increases the amount of excess reserves through an open market purchase. What happens to the money supply from now on depends on the following three factors:

1. How much money banks want to lend.
2. How much money people want to borrow.
3. How much of the borrowed money people want to hold as cash.

To make the story simple, we will assume that banks want to loan out all their excess reserves, which people will borrow completely, and people don't want to hold any cash.

Assume that First Global Bank lends the whole $300,000 of excess reserves to Adam. Assuming Adam does not want to hold any cash, he deposits the whole $300,000 in Second Global Bank. At this point, the money supply has increased by $300,000, because bank deposits are part of the money supply—Adam can buy goods and services with this money. Second Global Bank now has $300,000 of additional reserves, which is the physical money sitting in the bank vault. The bank is required to keep 20% of this $300,000 (or $60,000) in the bank. The remaining $240,000 is the excess reserve that it can legally loan out. At this point the Second Global is losing money, for the simple reason that it must pay interest to Adam on the $300,000, but the $300,000 itself is sitting idle in the bank earning no interest. So the bank has every incentive to loan out as much of that $240,000 of excess reserves as it can.

Federal Reserve Chairman Ben Bernanke

By our assumption, it lends out the whole $240,000 to Becky. After these two transactions, Second Global's balance sheet changes to the following:

Second Global Bank After Receiving $300,000 from Adam and Lending $240,000 to Becky			
Changes in Assets		Changes in Liabilities + Net Worth	
Reserves	+$60,000	Deposits	**+$300,000**
Required @ 20%	+$60,000		
Excess	$0		
New Loans	+$240,000		
	+$300,000		+$300,000

Becky will deposit the whole $240,000 in her bank, Third Global Bank. Now the money supply has increased by $540,000, of which $300,000 belongs to Adam and $240,000 to Becky. Third Global will keep 20% of this inside the bank as required by law, and loan out the remaining $192,000 to Carolyn.

Third Global Bank After Receiving $240,000 from Becky and Lending $192,000 to Carolyn			
Changes in Assets		Changes in Liabilities + Net Worth	
Reserves	+$48,000	Deposits	**+$240,000**
Required @ 20%	+$48,000		
Excess	$0		
New Loans	+$192,000		
	+$240,000		+$240,000

Carolyn will deposit the whole $192,000 at Fourth Global Bank. The process will continue. How much money will be generated at the end? Remember that the money supply is the sum of currency held by the public and demand deposits in the banks. By our assumption, people deposit all the borrowed money in the banks, and do not hold any of it as currency. Therefore, the increase in money supply will just equal the sum of all the demand deposits created in the banking system:

$$\begin{aligned}\Delta M &= \$300{,}000 + \$240{,}000 + \$192{,}000 + \ldots \\ &= \$300{,}000 + 0.80 \times \$300{,}000 + 0.80^2 \times \$300{,}000 + \ldots. \\ &= (1 + 0.80 + 0.80^2 + \ldots) \times \$300{,}000\end{aligned}$$

The expression inside the parentheses is the familiar geometric progression. Therefore we can write the expression above as:

$$\Delta M=(1/(1-0.80)) \times \$300{,}000 = 1/0.20 \times \$300{,}000 = \$1{,}500{,}000$$

Table 1 summarizes the whole process. In the above expression, the $300,000 is the initial excess reserves that the Fed injected into the banking system. Let's call it DER. The 0.20 is nothing but the required reserve ratio (rrr). So we can write the above expression as:

$$\Delta M = (1/rrr) \times \Delta ER$$

The above formula is called the multiple deposit creation formula. What happened to the $300,000 of excess reserves that the Fed injected into the system at the very beginning? As Table 1 shows, it was just apportioned among different banks. For obvious reasons, the ratio 1/rrr is called the *money multiplier*.

Note finally that the open market operation resulted in an additional loan amount of $1,500,000—exactly equal to the increase in the money supply. In other words, the whole increase in money supply is brought about by the banks' lending process. That is why the popular press generally refers to an increase in money supply by the Fed as "easing credit conditions" or "injecting credit into the system."

MONEY MULTIPLIER
The ratio of money supply to monetary base. It shows by how much the money supply will change if the monetary base changes by one dollar.

Be aware that the money-multiplier formula above gives you the *maximum potential* amount of money that can be created if the Fed injects some reserves into the banking system. That is because of the three assumptions we made at the beginning. Let's quickly analyze the effects of these assumptions.

Table 1

	Demand Deposits ($)	Required Reserves ($)	Excess Reserves ($)	New Loans ($)
First Bank				300,000
Second Bank	300,000	60,000	0	240,000
Third Bank	240,000	48,000	0	192,000
Fourth Bank	192,000	38,400	0	153,600
Fifth Bank	153,600	30,720	0	122,880
Sixth Bank	122,880	24,576	0	98,304
Seventh Bank	98,304	19,661	0	78,643
Eighth Bank	78,643	15,729	0	62,915
etc.	etc.	etc.	etc.	etc.
Total	**1,500,000**	**300,000**	**0**	**1,500,000**

We assumed that banks will lend all of their newfound excess reserves. If some banks decide to keep part of the new reserves in the bank instead of lending them out, the increase in money supply will be less than indicated by the above formula. The same will be true if banks want to lend, but people do not want to borrow. Finally, if people do not deposit all the borrowed money in the banks and instead hold some of it as currency, the increase in money supply will be less than potential.

We see then that three groups of people and entities can change the supply of money in the economy.

1. The Fed is the most important entity in the money supply process. It can change the supply of money through one of the three monetary policy tools described above.

2. Banks can affect the supply of money by changing the amount of reserves they hold in their vaults. If they decide to hold more reserves, fewer loans will be made and the money supply will decrease.
3. The public also has a role in the money supply process. If people decide to withdraw their money from the banks and hold more cash, banks will be left with less money to loan out. Since money is created through bank lending, the money supply will go down.

To give you an example, during the Great Depression a lot of people lost their faith in the banking system. They withdrew large amounts of money to hold under their mattresses. As a result, the money supply was sharply reduced in 1930 and 1931, creating many problems that we will see in later chapters. As another case, after the September 11 terrorist attacks, uncertainty about the state of the economy grew. The fear arose that more attacks might happen. As a result, the Fed was concerned that banks might hold larger amounts of reserves, because they would be hesitant to lend money to businesses. The public could also hold more cash out of a fear of recession and bank failures. Both events would reduce money supply, causing problems for the economy. Therefore, the Fed injected $45 billion into the banking system through discount loans to counteract such possibilities.

In this book we will make two simplifying assumptions about the money supply. First, we will assume that only the Fed has control over the money supply. We will ignore the effects that the behaviors of the banks and the general public have on money supply. You know from the story above that if the public decides to hold less currency or the banks decide to hold fewer excess reserves, the money supply will increase. However, the Fed has the most important role in the money supply process. Therefore, our first assumption is realistic.

Second, we will assume that the Fed changes the money supply only through open market operations. This also makes sense, since this is actually the way the Fed generally conducts monetary policy. As mentioned above, a discount policy has a rather uncertain effect on the reserves, and the required reserve policy is too powerful. So our second assumption is also realistic.

A More Realistic Money Supply Process

This appendix gives you a more realistic picture by modifying two of the assumptions in the above story about the money supply process. First, we assume that banks do not loan out all their excess reserves, for two reasons: either they don't want to; or they want to, but the public does not want to borrow all that money. Banks may not want to loan out all their excess reserves, either because they may anticipate deposit outflows in the near future, or they may perceive some of the loans as too risky. The public may not want to borrow because they may not have sufficient profitable investment opportunities, or they may believe it is too risky to invest under the existing economic conditions. For example, they may be waiting to learn about the outcome of the upcoming election a few months down the road. Second, we assume that the public wants to hold some cash. This is because they need it for their day-to-day transactions.

Assume that the required reserve ratio is 20%, and that banks want to hold 5% of their deposits as excess reserves. Moreover, suppose the public wants to maintain a currency/deposit ratio of 50%. The Fed injects $300,000 of excess reserves into the banking system through an open market purchase of bonds from First Bank. Adam borrows this $300,000, keeps $100,000 in his pocket, and deposits $200,000 in Second Bank.[3] Second Bank keeps 20% of this amount as required ($40,000), and another 5% as excess reserves ($10,000). It lends the remaining $150,000 to Becky. Becky also wants to maintain a currency/deposit ratio of 50%; therefore, she keeps $50,000 of this loan in her purse, and deposits the remaining $100,000 in Third Bank. Continuing this way, the total amount of money created in the economy at the end will be $600,000. Of this amount, $200,000 will be the currency in the hands of the public, and $400,000 in demand deposits. See Table A below. Now I explain how to calculate these numbers.

Note that the total amount of excess reserves created by the Fed at the beginning was $300,000. This physical amount remains the same. It is just apportioned between the currency in the hands of the public and the reserves in the banks. People hold part of it in their pockets and purses as currency. Banks hold some of it as required by law, with the remaining as excess reserves.

The sum of currency and reserves is called *monetary base*. It is the base upon which money supply is "built" through the bank loan process. So:

MONETARY BASE
The sum of currency and reserves in the banking system.

$$B = CU + RR + ER$$

where B is the monetary base, CU is the currency held by the public, and RR and ER are the required and excess reserves. The Fed can increase the monetary base by increasing the excess reserves, as we have seen above.

3 Thus, Adam has a currency/deposit ratio of 50% (=$100,000/$200,000). So does everyone else in the story.

Table A							
	Currency Held by Public ($)	Demand Deposits ($)	**Required Reserves ($)**	**Excess Reserves ($)**	**Total Reserves ($)**	New Loans ($)
First Bank						300,000
Second Bank	100,000	200,000	40,000	10,000	50,000	150,000
Third Bank	50,000	100,000	20,000	5,000	25,000	75,000
Fourth Bank	25,000	50,000	10,000	2,500	12,500	37,500
Fifth Bank	12,500	25,000	5,000	1,250	6,250	18,750
etc.	etc.	etc.	etc.	etc.	etc.	etc.
Total	**200,000**	**400,000**	**80,000**	**20,000**	**100,000**	**600,000**

Money supply, on the other hand, is the sum of currency and demand deposits:

$$M = CU + DD$$

where DD is the amount of demand deposits. Dividing this by monetary base we get:

$$M/B = (CU + DD)/(CU + RR + ER)$$

Since we have information about the ratios of these amounts to demand deposits, we divide the numerator and the denominator by DD:

$$\frac{M}{B} = \frac{\frac{CU}{DD} + \frac{DD}{DD}}{\frac{CU}{DD} + \frac{RR}{DD} + \frac{ER}{DD}}$$

Let us denote the currency/deposit ratio by "cu". The ratio RR/DD is just the required reserve ratio (rrr)/ and the ratio ER/DD is the excess reserve ratio. Let's denote it by "err". Then we can write the above equation as

$$M = \left(\frac{cu + 1}{cu + rrr + err}\right) \times B$$

MONEY MULTIPLIER
The ratio of money supply to monetary base. It shows by how much the money supply will change if the monetary base changes by one dollar.

The expression inside the parentheses is called the *money multiplier*. Assuming that the ratios are constant, the money multiplier will be constant. Note that it reduces to the simple money multiplier in the text when cu = err = 0.

This equation is important, because it shows how the actions of the three groups can change the money supply. The **public** decides on the currency/deposit ratio (cu). All else being the same, an increase in cu causes a reduction in money supply. This makes sense. If people hold more currency and fewer deposits, fewer reserves and loans will be generated. **Banks** and the public decide on the excess-reserve ratio (err). All else being the same, if banks decide to hold more reserves, or if the public decides not to borrow, err will increase, and the money supply will decrease. All else being the same, if **the Fed** sets a higher rrr, the money supply will go down. This is because the banks will not be able to lend as much as before. Finally, all else being equal, if the Fed increases the monetary base (B) through one of its three monetary policy tools, then money supply will increase. Of the three groups, the Fed is the most important one. Using the numbers in our example above:

$$(0.50+1)/(0.50+0.20+0.50)=2$$

So

$$M = 2 \times B$$

Since the money multiplier is constant, we can also apply the formula to *changes* in the base and money supply.

$$\Delta M = 2 \times \Delta B = 2 \times \$300{,}000 = \$600{,}000$$

Now we have all the information to find the other unknowns. First, from the definitions of money supply and the currency/deposit ratio, we have:

$$M = CU + DD = cu \times DD + DD = (1 + cu) \times DD$$

Since (1 + cu) is constant, we can apply this formula to changes in DD and M:

$$\Delta(DD) = \frac{\Delta M}{1+cu} = \frac{\$600{,}000}{1+0.50} = \$400{,}000$$

The rest of the calculations are now straightforward:

$$\Delta(CU) = cu \times \Delta(DD) = 0.50 \times \$400{,}000 = \$200{,}000$$
$$\Delta(RR) = rrr \times \Delta(DD) = 0.20 \times \$400{,}000 = \$80{,}000$$
$$\Delta(ER) = err \times \Delta(DD) = 0.05 \times \$400{,}000 = \$20{,}000$$

Note finally the important fact that the whole increase in money supply comes from new loans.

TO SUMMARIZE

1. "Money is what money does." What does money do? It performs four functions as: *medium of exchange*, unit of account, store of value, and standard of deferred payments.
2. An asset is more *liquid* than another asset if it can be converted into money faster and with lower cost.
3. *Fiat money*, unlike *commodity money*, has no intrinsic value but is used as a means of payment, because the public accepts it as money.
4. *Legal tender* is anything the government mandates is acceptable in payments of loans and taxes.
5. M1 = Currency + Demand Deposits.
6. M2 = M1 + savings deposits + small denomination time deposits + money market mutual fund deposits.
7. M3 = M2 + large denomination time deposits + institutional money market mutual fund deposits.
8. The *supply of money* is the total amount of money that people actually hold at a point in time.
9. One of the Fed's functions is to make sure that the banking system has sufficient liquidity. It regulates banks by requiring banks to hold reserves, extending *discount loans*, and requiring banks to maintain a certain level of bank capital.
10. Another function of the Fed is to conduct *monetary policy*.
11. The Fed can change the money supply through: i) required reserve ratio; ii) discount rate; and iii) open market operations. In all cases, additional excess reserves are generated in the banking system, setting off the process of multiple deposit creation.
12. In every case, the maximum potential amount of money created in the system will be given by the *money multiplier* formula, $\Delta M = \frac{1}{rrr} \times \Delta R$, where ΔR is the level of reserves injected by the Fed.
13. The required reserve ratio (rrr) is the fraction of deposits that banks must hold by law.
14. Open market operations are the tool most widely used by the Fed.
15. If banks loan out all their excess reserves, the banking system is said to be fully loaned out.
16. The supply of money is affected by the actions of the Fed, banks, and the non-bank public.
17. In the more realistic formula, the change in money supply equals the change in the *monetary base* times the *money multiplier*.
18. Monetary base = CU + RR + ER.
19. Money multiplier = (1 + cu)/(cu + rrr + err).

EXERCISES

Question 1

Rank the following assets in order of liquidity: my house; your car; Treasury bonds.

Question 2

A discount bond with a face value of $1,000 is selling for $980. What is the interest rate on the bond?

Question 3

If you required a rate of return of 8% from a discount bond with a face value of $1,000, how much would you be willing to pay for it?

Question 4

During the Great Depression, many people lost their faith in the U.S. banking system and withdrew their money from the banks.

a. What would be the effect of this event on the bank reserves?
b. What would be the effect of this event on the money supply?

Question 5

Assume that the required reserve ratio is 5%. The Fed conducts an open market purchase worth $100,000.

a. Calculate the money multiplier.
b. Analyze the effect of this policy on the money supply.
c. How many additional loans will be created following this policy?

Use the balance sheet below to answer Question 6. Assume a required reserve ratio of 10%.

Bank Balance Sheet			
Assets Uses of Funds		Liabilities + Net Worth Sources of Funds	
Reserves	$200	Deposits	$1,000
Treasury Bonds	$300	Borrowing	$120
Loans	$800	Net Worth	$180
Total	$1,300	Total	$1,300

Question 6

Analyze the effect of the following transactions on the above balance sheet. These questions are independent of each other. Write a new balance sheet for each.

a. Is this bank fully loaned out?
b. Someone deposits $500 in the bank.
c. Someone borrows $50 from the bank.

d. The bank borrows $150 from another bank.
e. The market value of Treasury bonds increases to $500.
f. A borrower defaults on his loan and cannot payback the $100 he owes to the bank.
g. Someone withdraws $100.
h. Someone withdraws $200. As the bank manager, you need to make a decision. How many ways can you solve this problem? (What *is* the problem?)

Question 7

Show that the money multiplier formula reduces to the multiple deposit creation formula when cu = 0 and err = 0.

Question 8

Assume the following:

cu = 0.20
rrr = 0.15
err = 0.05

a. The Fed increases the monetary base by $80. Calculate the increase in M, CU, DD, RR, and ER.
b. Suppose instead cu was equal to 0.80. Calculate the increase in M, CU, DD, RR, and ER for the same increase in monetary base. Explain your findings.
c. Suppose instead we had cu = 0.20, rrr = 0.25, and err = 0.05. Calculate the increase in M, CU, DD, RR, and ER for the same increase in monetary base. Explain your findings.
d. Suppose instead we had cu = 0.20, rrr = 0.15, and err = 0.45. Calculate the increase in M, CU, DD, RR, and ER for the same increase in monetary base. Explain your findings.
e. Suppose instead we had cu = 0.20, rrr = 0.15, and err = 0.05. Calculate the increase in M, CU, DD, RR, and ER, assuming that the Fed increases the monetary base by $120. Explain your findings.

Question 9

What do you expect to happen to the money supply in a recession—even though the Fed does not conduct any monetary policy?

Question 10

Explain how an action by one group can affect the values of all the other variables in the banking system. For example, assume that all else the same, people decide to withdraw some of their deposits from the banks and hold them under their mattresses. What will be the effect of this decision on M, B, CU, DD, RR, and ER? What if, ceteris paribus, banks decide to hold more excess reserves?

CHAPTER 9

The Money Market: Demand for Money

INTRODUCTION AND REVIEW

WE LEARNED IN the last chapter that the supply of money is the total amount of currency and demand deposits people hold at any time. For example, these days if you count the amounts of coins and dollar bills in people's pockets and purses—as well as the money sitting in all the checking accounts in the United States—the total will be around $1,500 billion, or $1.5 trillion. This is the total supply of money in the economy.[1] We also learned that the Fed can change this in three different ways: changing the required reserve ratio; changing the discount rate it charges on its loans to commercial banks, and open market operations. What is the effect of monetary policy on the interest rate? To answer this question, we will learn about theories of interest rate determination.

In the real world, there are actually many interest rates. Banks offer different interest rates on different types of deposits. Bonds carry different interest rates, depending on the creditworthiness of the issuer, term to maturity, and tax treatment. Corporate bonds have higher required interest rates than Treasury bonds, long-term bonds have different interest rates than short-term bonds, and some bonds—such as municipal bonds—are tax free. All of these rates, though different, move together. Therefore, we will assume that there is only one interest rate out there and refer to it as *the* interest rate.

There are several theories that try to explain the movements in the interest rate. We will consider two of them in this book. The first theory posits that the interest rate is determined by the interplay between demand for and supply of money. We will call this theory the *liquidity preference* theory.

LIQUIDITY PREFERENCE
The amount of money (liquidity) people want to hold.

LOANABLE FUNDS THEORY
The theory that posits that the interest rate is determined by the demand for and supply of loans.

1 We know that this is actually the amount of M1, the only kind of money we have in this book (recall that we assume the amount of travelers' checks to be negligible, or they would also be included). If you add savings and other saving-type accounts to M1, you get M2. M2 is close to $5 trillion. Here is food for thought: We know that the U.S. GDP is about $10 trillion. How can we, as a nation, buy $10 trillion worth of goods and services with only $1 trillion of money? We will provide an answer to this question shortly.

The second theory hypothesizes that the interest rate is determined by the demand for and supply of loans. This is called the *loanable funds theory.* Most of the time, the two theories give the same prediction about the direction of the movements in the interest rate. There are occasions where they differ from each other, though. Additionally, sometimes one theory cannot explain the effect of an event on the interest rate, while another can. So which theory we use will depend on the circumstances. We start off with the liquidity preference theory. We will discuss the loanable funds theory in the next chapter.

DEMAND FOR MONEY

In this theory, the interest rate is determined by the interaction of demand for money and supply of money—i.e., *liquidity*. We know what the supply of money is, but what is demand for money? Demand for anything is a *desired* magnitude. In the case of flow variables such as the quantity of apples, demand is the amount consumers are willing and able to buy during a certain period of time. Supply is the amount the producers are willing and able to sell during a certain period of time. Moreover, demanders and suppliers are two different groups of people. How about stock variables such as money? In this case, no one is actually buying or selling anything. By *supply*, we mean actual holdings; by *demand*, the desired holdings. Therefore, *demand for money* should be the total amount of money people are *willing* and *able* to hold. This statement requires some elaboration.

DEMAND FOR MONEY
The portion of their total wealth that people wish to hold in the form of money. In other words, it is the amount of money people are willing and able (their wealth permitting) to hold at any point.

Recall that by the terms demand and supply, we always mean the effective magnitudes (note: willing and *able* to hold). In the case of demand for goods, it means demand backed by money. Your demand for anything will affect its price and quantity produced if you have enough money to buy it. This eliminates wishful thinking. In the case of demand for money, the term *able* means that the amount of money people want to hold does not exceed their total wealth. Suppose that the market value of all your assets, including your house, the furniture, the car, the stocks, and bonds, is $900,000. Suppose also that you already have $100,000 in cash. Then your demand for money is the portion of this $1,000,000 total that you want to hold in the form of money (currency and demand deposits). Obviously, you cannot hold 2 million dollars in cash. So by *demand for money*, we mean this:

> *Demand for money is the portion of their total wealth that people want to hold in the form of money at any point.*

To keep our story simple and to concentrate on open market operations, we'll assume that money and bonds are the only assets available for people to hold. Later in the book we will introduce other kinds of assets into the picture.

THE CLASSICAL APPROACH TO DEMAND FOR MONEY

Why do people want to hold the amount of money they do? Why don't they hold all their wealth in the form of interest-bearing bonds, rather than idle cash or checking accounts? We assume that checking accounts do not pay interest. Even if they did, the interest they pay is much less than the interest on bonds. So the question still remains: Why do people put their money into checking accounts, when they can earn higher interest by holding bonds? We will come back to this issue later. A group of economists, including Alfred Marshall and A. C. Pigou of Cambridge, England, began looking into this question around the turn of the 20th century. Irving Fisher of Yale also made major contributions to this field. The resulting approach is called the classical, or Cambridge, approach to demand for money.

The Cambridge economists argued that people want to hold money predominantly to buy goods and services. Therefore, if the prices of goods and services rise by 10 percent, people will want to hold 10 percent more money. Similarly, if the quantities of goods and services produced increase by 10 percent, people will want to increase their money holdings by 10 percent. So the classical demand for money function takes the following simple form:

A young woman shopiping

$$M^d = k \times P \times Y$$

where k is a constant coefficient called the *Cambridge k*, P is the general price level, and Y is the real GDP. Recall that P × Y is the nominal GDP.

To see how the equation works, assume that k = 0.20, P = \$10, Y = 20. Then

$$M^d = 0.20 \times \$10 \times 20 = \$40$$

What will happen to demand for money if the price level increases by 10 percent? Since the only reason you want to hold money is to buy the existing quantities of goods and services, you will want to hold 10 percent more money:

$$M^d = 0.20 \times \$11 \times 20 = \$44$$

Similarly, suppose that at the current level of prices, the real GDP increases by 10 percent. Again you will want to increase your money holdings by 10 percent:

$$M^d = 0.20 \times \$10 \times 22 = \$44$$

In general, if either P or Y increases, the demand for money will increase proportionately. So let's remember:

> *All else being the same, an increase in the price level will result in a proportionate increase in the demand for money; similarly for a decrease in the price level.*
> *All else being the same, an increase in real GDP will result in a proportionate increase in demand for money; similarly for a decrease in real GDP.*

The Cambridge economists Marshall and Pigou thought that the amount of money people want to hold as a fraction of their total expenditure depends on the level of institutional, technological, and financial development of the society. This fraction is the Cambridge k. Since these factors do not change readily from year to year, they concluded that k must be fairly constant. For example, in the old days when financial institutions were not well developed, people held most of their money needed for transactions under their mattresses or in their bank accounts. So k was rather high. On the other hand, people in advanced capitalist countries with well-functioning financial markets and institutions—and an abundance of investment opportunities—do not hold a lot of money. They hold most of their wealth in the form of stocks and bonds. This is because they can always sell these assets easily when they need money. In these countries, therefore, k must be relatively low. On the other hand, residents of developing countries who do not have access to modern financial institutions hold most of their wealth in the form of money. In those countries, k must be relatively high.

MONEY MARKET EQUILIBRIUM IN THE CLASSICAL MODEL

Money market will be in equilibrium if the supply of money equals the demand for money—if people hold the amount of money they want to hold. In other words, if

$$M = M^d$$

Substituting for M^d we get:

$$M = k \times P \times Y$$

This simple equation has an important implication for monetary policy. It implies that the rate of growth of money supply equals the rate of growth of nominal GDP.

To see this, suppose that k = 0.20, P = 10, and Y = 20 as before. Then, the nominal GDP equals P × Y = 10 × 20 = 200 resulting in the demand for money of M^d = 0.20 × 200= $40. Assuming equilibrium, the supply of money will also be M = $40. Now if M increases by 10 percent to $44 and k remains at its current value of 0.20, the nominal GDP has to increase to P × Y = 220. This is because in this theory people hold money only to buy goods and services. Therefore, they will use the extra money to buy additional goods and services. Producers will respond by either increasing their production, or their prices, or both. At this point we don't know at what rate P or Y will increase individually, but we know that the product will increase at 10%. In later chapters, we will solve this mystery.

This theory gives us an easy and nice way to understand why prices change in an economy. Simply solve the money market equilibrium condition for the price level:

$$P = M/(k \times Y)$$

Thus, given k, you will have a higher price if M is large or Y is small. If the government pumps more money into the economy without the real GDP growing, the prices will increase. This is popularly called *too much money chasing too few goods*. On the other hand, if you keep the money supply under control and design policies to grow your real GDP, then your price level will decrease. Keep in mind that all these predictions are under the assumption that k is constant.

VELOCITY OF CIRCULATION

VELOCITY OF CIRCULATION *The number of times a dollar changes hands in a period of time. It is the inverse of* ***Cambridge k.***

The Cambridge k is related to another concept called the *velocity of circulation* of money. Suppose you pay one dollar and buy a chocolate bar. Where did you get that dollar? The government did not print that one dollar specifically for you so you could buy that chocolate bar. In all likelihood, you got that dollar from someone else in the society. The point is that a dollar changes hands many times during the course of a year. Clearly, one dollar plays the role of more than one dollar. The number of times a dollar bill changes hands in a period of time is called the velocity of circulation of money.

Suppose that on January 1, 2010, you pay Abigail one dollar to buy that chocolate bar from her. Abigail pays that dollar to buy a can of soda from Brad. So far, with one dollar, two things have been purchased, each worth a dollar, for a total of two dollars. Assume that this dollar changes hands a total of five times by December 31, 2010. (See the graph above.) Then we say that the velocity of circulation is five: one dollar plays the role of five dollars. We denote velocity by the letter V. Then V = 5.

Now, assume that in 2010 the general price level is P = \$10 and the real GDP is Y = 20, so the nominal GDP equals P × Y = \$10 × 20 = \$200. This, as you recall, is the total value of all the goods and services produced in the country in 2010. How much money must people have to be able to buy \$200 worth of goods and services? Since one dollar plays the role of five dollars, then \$40 will play the role of \$200 (\$40 × 5). So people need to have only one-fifth of \$200 in circulation, calculated as follows:

$$\$40 \times 5 \equiv \$10 \times 20$$
$$\$40 \equiv 1/5 \times \$10 \times 20 \equiv 0.20 \times \$10 \times 20$$

In symbols,

$$M \times V \equiv P \times Y$$
$$M \equiv 1/V \times P \times Y$$

Denoting the inverse of velocity by the letter k, we can write the above formula as

$$M \equiv k \times P \times Y$$

In our example, since V = 5, we have k = 0.20, meaning that the amount of money people need to hold to buy all the goods and services produced in 2010 is only a fifth of the nominal GDP.

Note that we have used an identity sign in the above relationships. This is because these relationships hold by definition. For any particular year, if you divide the amount of money in circulation (such as M1, or M2) by the nominal GDP of that year, you get a number that is simply k. For example, in 2006 the U.S. nominal GDP was \$13,195 billion. The average of the monthly M1 figures over the year was \$1,375 billion, so that V = \$13,195/\$1,375 = 9.60 and k = 1/V = 0.10. In other words, each dollar played the role of about 10 dollars. In this way, Americans held only about 10% of nominal GDP as currency and demand deposits (M1) to be able to buy all the goods and services produced in 2006.

Being an identity, the above relationship is of no use for economic analysis. Why not? Well, suppose that the real GDP increases. What will be the effect of this on the amount of money holdings? As things are right now, we cannot tell. The answer depends on what happens to k when Y increases. If k goes down at the same time, then M might remain the same or may even decrease. If it stays the same or increases, then M will increase. So by assuming that k is constant, the classical economists turn this identity into a theory. This is because k may or may not be constant. But if it were constant, as classics claim, then this theory would give us a very useful tool to predict the effect of money supply on nominal GDP. Well, is it constant?

EMPIRICAL EVIDENCE ON CAMBRIDGE K

During the time classical economists were writing about monetary issues, there were no good data on economic aggregates. Even if k danced around, they would not notice. Later, as data became available on such variables, it became increasingly clear that k was, in fact, not constant. Figure 1 shows the values of k using the U.S. annual nominal GDP and M1 data for the period spanning from 1960 to 2006. The M1 data are the annual averages of the monthly data. As can be seen, k is anything but constant.

Figure 1 shows two kinds of variations in k: a long-term trend and short-term movements. As can be seen, k had been going down until 1980. From 1981 to 1995, it behaved rather erratically, stabilizing again somewhat after 1994. We know that k is the ratio of the amount of money people want to hold to the value of goods they want to buy. This, as Cambridge economists correctly argued, could depend on a host of institutional factors. For example, as mentioned above, financial institutions were not well-developed, so people held most of their wealth in the form of non-interest bearing cash or demand deposits. This resulted in a large k. Over time, financial markets became more efficient, and a large number of different alternative financial instruments were developed. People could hold a lot of assets that could easily be converted into money. These days, people also use credit cards to buy goods and services. As a result of all these financial market developments, people do not need to hold a lot of money to carry out their transactions. These developments have resulted in a general downward long-term trend in k, as seen in Figure 1. But how would you account for short-term variations in k?

Figure 1: The Quarterly Cambridge k for the United States (1960:1 to 2009:1)

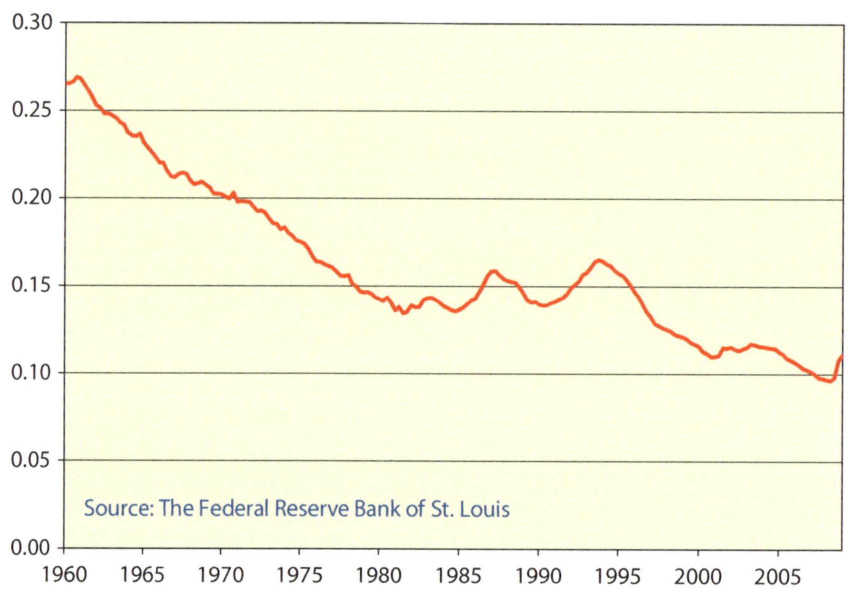

KEYNESIAN LIQUIDITY PREFERENCE THEORY

John Maynard Keynes

John Maynard Keynes argued that the story told by the Cambridge economists neglected the role of interest rate in demand for money. Cambridge economists only focused on the role of money as a medium of exchange, and ignored the store-of-value function of money as an asset. The fact is, money is an asset, and it competes with bonds in people's portfolios. People will compare the liquidity they will enjoy if they hold money to the interest income and capital gains that they will earn if they hold bonds. Liquidity in this context means having enough money on hand to be able to pay for both routine and unforeseen expenses. People always prefer to have some liquidity, so that they don't have to sell their bonds or other assets every time they make a payment for something.

So two opposing forces affect the amount of money people want to hold: interest on bonds and the convenience of liquidity. People will hold less money and more bonds if bonds offer a higher interest rate. This is for two reasons. First, they will enjoy a higher interest income from bonds. Second, an increase in the interest rate means a reduction in bond prices. (Remember the negative relationship?) So some people might think that bond prices will rebound in the future and they will make capital gains if they buy bonds now and sell them in the future. Therefore, they will be willing to sacrifice some liquidity now in exchange for a higher interest income and capital gains in the future. On the other hand, if the interest rate on bonds goes down, people will lose less interest income if they hold money. Thus, they will increase their money holdings to enjoy a higher degree of liquidity.

For example, assume that currently r = 10%, P = \$10, Y = 20, and k = 0.20. Then the demand for money equals:

$$M^d = 0.20 \times \$10 \times 20 = \$40$$

Now suppose that, all else the same, the interest rate rises to 12%. In that case, bonds become more attractive and people decide to hold only M^d = \$20 of money. Given that P and Y have not changed by assumption, the Cambridge k must have decreased to k = 0.10:

$$M^d = 0.10 \times \$10 \times 20 = \$20$$

On the other hand, suppose that the interest rate drops to 9% and as a result people increase their money holdings to M^d = \$60. Then, you can verify that the Cambridge k increases to k = 0.30. Therefore, the Cambridge k and demand for money are negatively related to the interest rate. These hypothetical cases are summarized in Table 1.

Table 1

r	k	P×Y	Md = k × P × Y
12%	0.10	\$10×20	\$20
10%	0.20	\$10×20	\$40
9%	0.30	\$10×20	\$60

THE KEYNESIAN DEMAND FOR MONEY FUNCTION

The above discussion indicates that k changes with r. So let's write it as k(r) to remember this fact. In that case, our demand for money function becomes:

$$M^d - k(r) \times P \times Y$$

This function shows that changes in r, P, or Y will cause changes in demand for money. Figure 2 shows the graph of the demand for money function, using the hypothetical numbers in Table 1. To draw this function, we keep P and Y unchanged, and trace the effect of changes in the interest rate on the demand for money.

Table 2			
r	k	P×Y	Md = k × P × Y
12%	0.10	$10×40	$40
10%	0.20	$10×40	$80
9%	0.30	$10×40	$120

Figure 2: Demand for Money Function

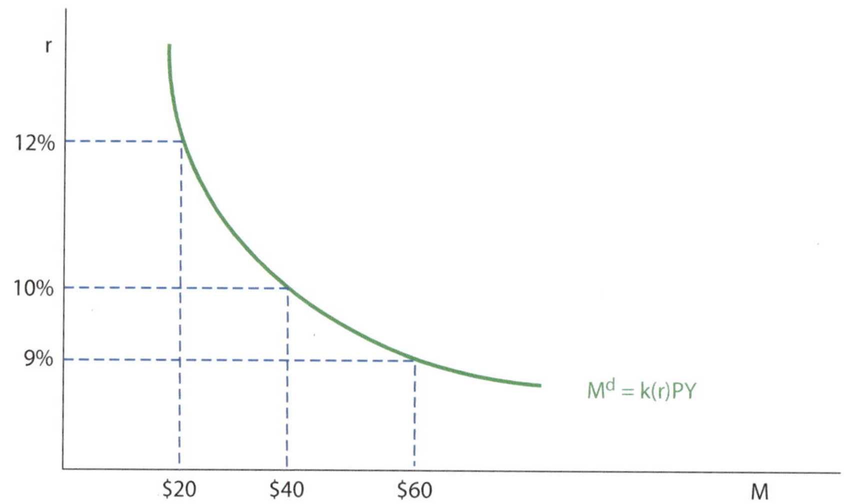

Now, what would happen if at the given interest rate, the real GDP increased? We know that since r has not changed, k would remain constant. Therefore, demand for money would increase proportionately. For example, if Y doubled to Y = 40, then at any interest rate, the demand for money would double (as in Table 2). In that case, the demand for money function would shift to the right as in Figure 3. Similarly, the function would shift to the left if real GDP went down. You realize that a doubling of the price level P would have exactly the same effect on demand for money.

So let's summarize the Keynesian theory of demand for money.

Given the nominal interest rate, an increase in the price level or in the real GDP will cause a proportionate increase in demand for money, and vice versa.

Given the level of prices and real GDP, a rise in the interest rate will result in a decrease in demand for money, and vice versa.

Figure 3: The Effect of an Increase in GDP on Demand for Money Function

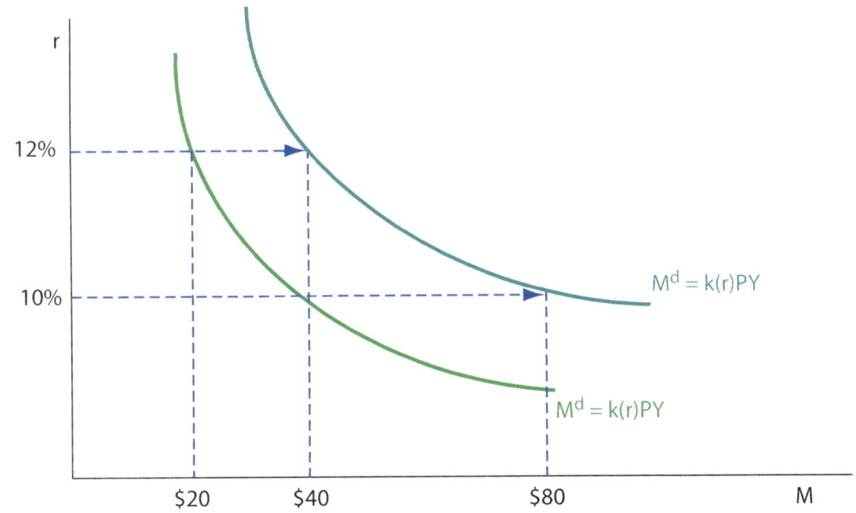

MONEY MARKET EQUILIBRIUM IN THE KEYNESIAN MODEL

Consider Figure 4. Suppose that currently, the total supply of money in circulation is $40 billion. This is shown by the vertical line labeled M. Figure 4 shows that demand equals supply; the money market, then, reaches equilibrium when the interest rate equals 10%. This 10% is called the *equilibrium interest rate*. To see what this means, assume that—for whatever reason—the interest rate was 12% instead. Then for the reasons we already know, people would want to hold less money and more bonds. They would want to hold only $20 billion of money, while they were actually holding $40 billion. There would be an excess supply of money. As a result, people would start buying bonds. This would push up the price of bonds and lower the interest rate. The lower interest rate would make people want to hold more money. They would move along the demand curve, until demand equaled supply at an interest rate of 10%.

EQUILIBRIUM INTEREST RATE
The interest rate at which demand for money equals supply of money (in the liquidity preference theory), or demand for loanable funds equals supply of loanable funds (in the loanable-funds theory).

Note that in the end, there was no change in the amount of money holdings. This is because the demand for money equals the supply of money, and the Fed determines the supply of money. But by our assumption, there was no change in the supply of money by the Fed. In effect, what happened is that everyone in the society was trying to buy more bonds. But the Fed had fixed the total amounts of money and bonds in the society. You tried to buy my bonds and I tried to buy yours. By doing this, we pushed up the price of bonds and reduced the interest rate. However, in the end, you and I together held the same amount of money and bonds as before.

Figure 4: Money Market Equilibrium

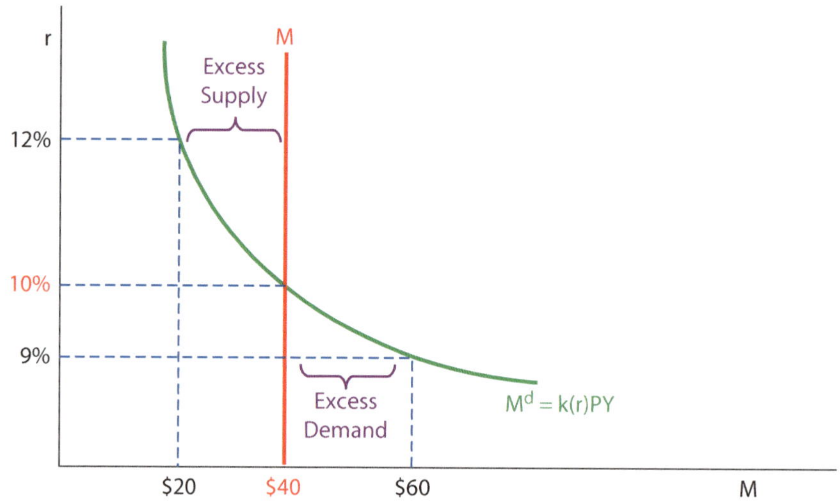

What if the interest rate was 9%, for whatever reason? Then the demand for money would exceed supply—people would want to hold more money than they were actually holding. They would start selling their bonds to get more money. The price of bonds would go down and the interest rate would rise. As the interest rate rose, people would reduce their demand for money. This would continue until the demand for money equaled the existing supply at an interest rate of 10%. If the interest rate equaled 10%, the demand for money would equal the supply, and people would no longer try to buy or sell bonds. The money market will be in a state of rest—equilibrium.

THE EFFECT OF AN INCREASE IN P OR Y

Suppose that currently the money market is in equilibrium, with the interest rate at r = 10% as in Figure 5. What will happen if Y increases, due to an increase in aggregate demand for goods and services in the expansion phase of a business cycle? Although this almost never happens in an expansion, to have a sharper picture, assume that the real GDP doubles. Or assume that the price level doubles. We know these two events have the same effect on the demand for money. People will demand more money to buy the additional, or more expensive, goods and services. As we learned above, the demand for money function will shift to the right and people will want to hold $80 billion. At the existing interest rate, there will be excess demand for money: people will want to hold more money. They will try to sell their bonds to get more money. The price of bonds will go down and the interest rate will rise. As shown in Figure 5, it will increase to 12%. In the opposite case, a decrease in Y or P will cause a reduction in the interest rate. Note again that in the end, people will hold the same amount of money as before, as this amount is determined by the Fed ($40 billion).

INTEREST RATES OVER BUSINESS CYCLES

The Keynesian liquidity preference theory explains why the interest rate increases during an economic expansion. During an expansion phase of a business cycle, the real GDP goes up (Y↑). People want to hold more money than before, because there are more goods and services to buy. Demand for money goes up as in Figure 5. As a result, the interest rate increases. Conversely, in a recession, the interest rate declines for the opposite reasons. In a recession, the real GDP goes down, reducing demand for money and interest rate. So this model provides a satisfactory prediction of the behavior of the interest rate over the course of business cycles. This explains, for instance, the 1981–1982, 1990–1991, and 2007–2009 decreases in the interest rate. The situation is shown in Figure 6.

How about the stagflation of 1974–1975? As you recall from Chapter 6, higher oil prices caused this stagflation. Oil is an input in many manufacturing processes. For example, the transportation sector is heavily oil intensive. Of course, higher oil prices would cause production costs to increase. For instance, bus and trucking companies would start charging higher fares. An increase in the prices of oil-intensive goods and services would result in a reduced demand for them, so the level of output would go down.

During a stagflation, a higher P will shift the demand for money to the right, while a lower Y will shift the demand to the left. The end result on the interest rate would depend on which one of these two effects is stronger. The price effect must have been stronger during the 1974–1975 stagflation, because the interest rates were quite high during this period.

How do higher oil prices affect you?

Monetary Policy

We are now just a short step away from understanding the effects of monetary policy. We define monetary policy as an increase or decrease in the money supply by the Fed. As you recall, the Fed can do this using one of three tools: required reserve ratio; discount rate; or open market operations. We will generally assume that monetary policy is conducted through open market operations. Suppose that currently, we have equilibrium in the money market with r = 10% and M = $40 billion. (See Figure 7.) Now suppose the Fed increases the money supply to M = $60 billion through an open market purchase of bonds. The Fed does this by coming to the bond market and offering a high price for bonds. Assume that some banks sell the bonds to the Fed and receive money for them. As you recall from the previous chapter, this money becomes excess reserves in the banking system.

Figure 5: The Effect of an Increase in P or Y on the Interest Rate

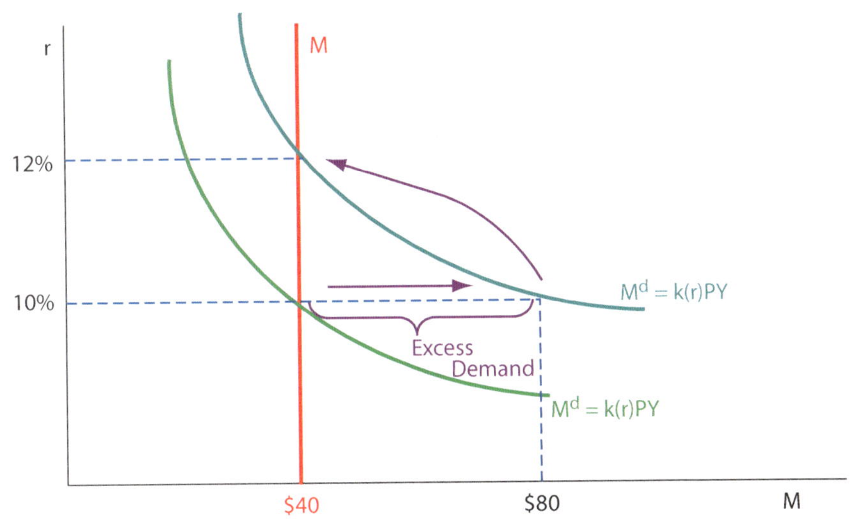

Figure 6: The Interest Rate in a Recession

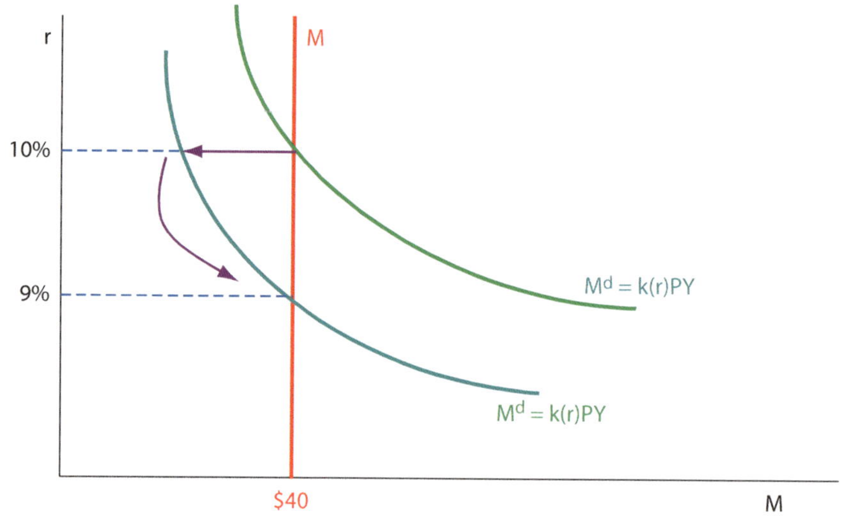

Since the Fed offers a high price for Treasury bonds, the interest rate on these bonds declines. This is due to the well-known negative relationship between the bond prices and interest rates. Now that there is more money in the economy ($20 billion more), the prices of Treasury bonds are high, and their interest rates are low. Therefore, people who wanted to have bonds in their portfolios start buying the other, less expensive bonds such as corporate bonds—those issued by corporations. As a result, the prices of all kinds of bonds increase, and the interest rates in the economy decline. The final result will be that the interest rate will be lower (9% in Figure 7) and people will hold a larger amount of money ($60 in Figure 7).

Figure 7: An Expansionary Monetary Policy

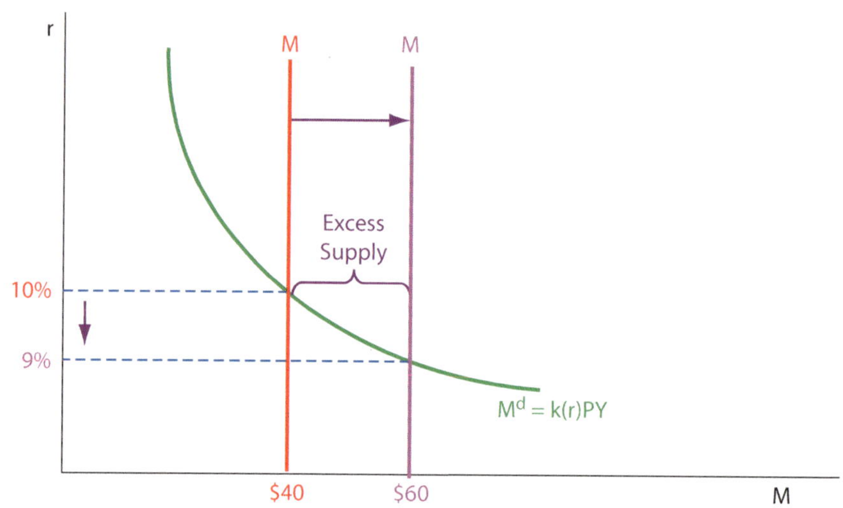

As an exercise, analyze the effect of an open market *sale* of bonds by the Fed on the interest rate.

MONEY SUPPLY GROWTH RATE

There is one aspect of monetary policy that we should learn now, because we will encounter it quite often in the future. In the real world, the Fed is mostly concerned with the rate of growth of the money supply, not the level. That is because of its concern with the inflation rate, which is the rate of increase in the price level. We will distinguish between three cases as follows.

Case 1 First, what if both the money supply and the price level increase at the same rate? Assume that initially P = \$10, Y = 20, k = 0.20, and M = \$40 billion. So the money market is in equilibrium with r = 10%. (See Figure 8.) Suppose the price level doubles to P = \$20 (it increases by 100%). As we know, the demand for money function shifts to the right, and at the 10% interest rate, people want to hold twice as much money as they held before, i.e., M^d = \$80. What happens to the interest rate if at the same time the Fed doubles the money supply to M = \$80? As Figure 8 shows, nothing happens to r.

When the price level doubled, people doubled their demand for money to buy the now more expensive goods. Without the Fed's action, they would sell some of their bonds to get the needed additional \$40 billion. This would cause the interest rate to increase to 12% because the supply of money in the economy is fixed. You would try to sell your bonds to me and I would try to sell to you. Competition among us to get rid of our bonds would push down the price of bonds and push up the interest rate, but ultimately, we would end up holding the same amount of money as before—\$40 billion. Now if the Fed enters the bond market with a deep pocket and starts buying all those bonds, we wouldn't need to reduce the prices of our bonds in order to sell them. As a result, the interest rate remains unchanged.

Case 2 As the second case, assume that the rate of growth of the money supply is less than the rate of increase in the price level. For example, assume that the price level increases by 100% to P = \$20, but the money supply increases by only 50% to M = \$60. In this case, the Fed does not inject enough money into the banking system, so people must reduce their bond prices to be able to sell them for cash to buy the now more expensive goods and services. As a result, the interest rate increases. (Figure 9 shows this case.)

Case 3 For the last case, assume that the rate of growth of money supply is higher than the rate of increase in the price level. In this case, the Fed injects more money than needed to keep the interest rate unchanged. As a result, the interest rate goes down. Draw the graph of this case as an exercise.

Figure 8: Money Supply Growth Rate Equals Inflation Rate

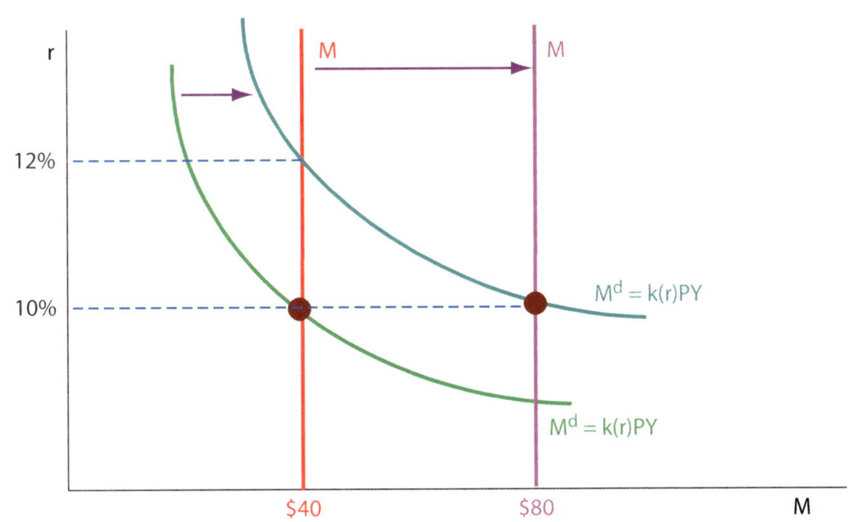

Figure 9: Money Supply Growth Rate Is Less than Inflation Rate

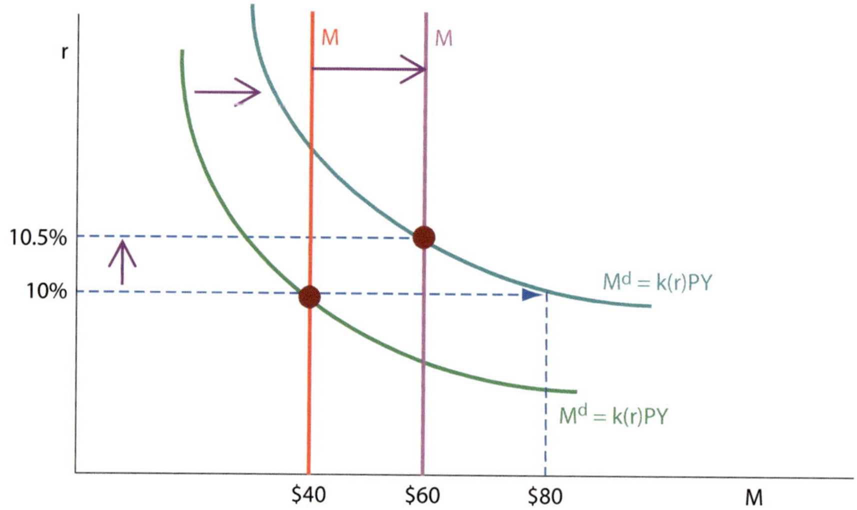

KEYNES ON THE EFFECTIVENESS OF MONETARY POLICY

Keynes believed that in a severe recession, the interest rate could be so low that few people would think it could go any lower than that. The flip side of the same argument is that the bond prices could be so high that most people would believe they could not go any higher. In that case, not many people would want to hold bonds, because they would not see any prospect of earning capital gains. They would rather hold most of their wealth in money. The demand for money would become too large and the bottom portion of the demand for money function would become flat, as in Figure 10. In that figure, we assume that the function becomes flat at the interest rate of 1%. Keynes called this situation the *liquidity trap*. People want a lot of liquidity (money), so the interest rate is trapped in that segment of the function and cannot move.

LIQUIDITY TRAP
The notion proposed by Keynes that, in a recession, the interest rate could go so low that the monetary policy could not reduce it any further.

Figure 10: Liquidity Trap

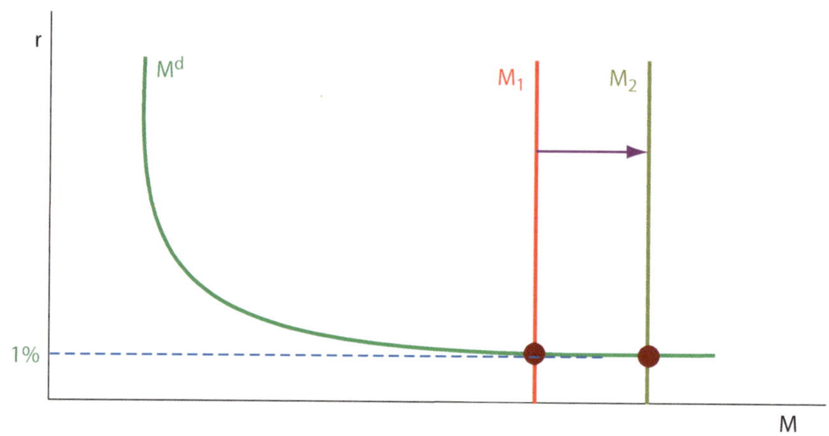

Now what happens if the Fed increases the money supply using an open market purchase of bonds? Since lots of people want to get rid of their bonds, the Fed will have an easy time buying

them at their current prices. Therefore, bond prices will not increase, and the interest rate will not decrease. As a result, consumption and investment will not be stimulated, and aggregate demand will not increase. This was one reason why Keynes did not advocate the use of monetary policy in recessions.

There are two ways an economy can fall into the liquidity trap, as is shown in Figure 11. During normal times, the demand for money would equal the supply of money at a point like point A. However, as the price and GDP levels fall in a recession, the demand-for-money function will shift to the left. If the recession continues long enough, the demand-for-money function will keep shifting, until ultimately the supply of money will intersect the demand for money at the flat portion of the latter at point B.

Figure 11: Falling into the Liquidity Trap: A Shift in Demand for Money

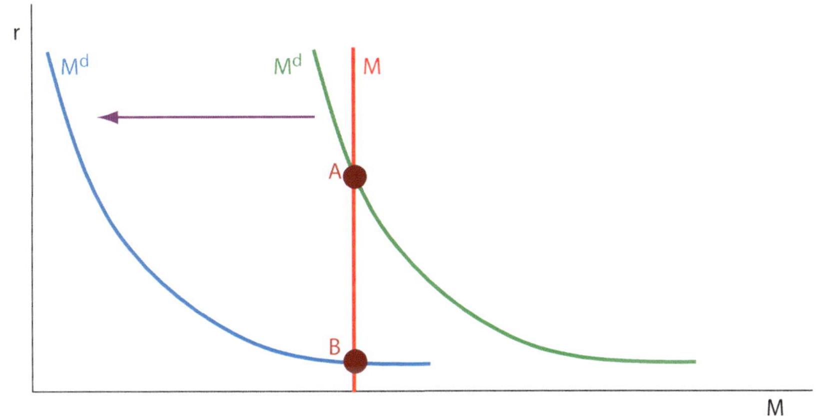

Figure 12: Falling into the Liquidity Trap: An Increase in Money Supply

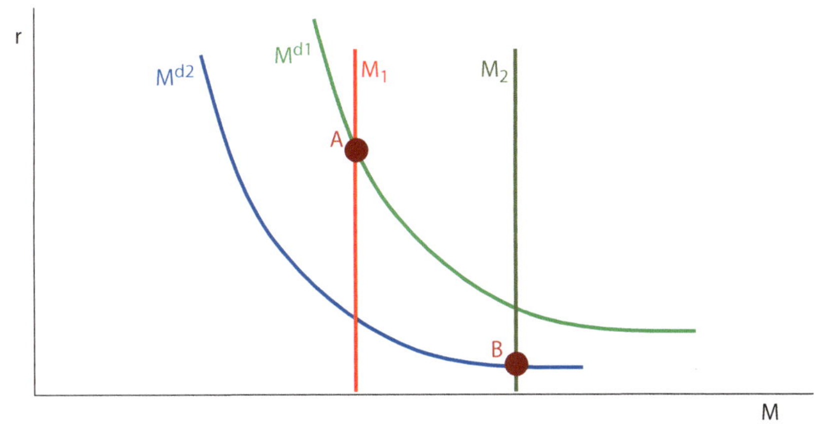

Another way for the economy to fall into the liquidity trap is for the Fed to increase the money supply by a large amount to fight a recession. In Figure 12, the demand for money decreases from M^{d1} to M^{d2} due to a reduction in the general price level and real GDP as before. However, the economy does not fall into the liquidity trap—the Fed increases the money supply from M_1 to M_2, so that the equilibrium interest rate is trapped at point B. Some economists believe this is what happened in the 2007–2008 recession.

Many economists believe that the liquidity trap is either an irrelevant theoretical curiosity, or that it was a possibility in the Great Depression of the 1930s (but has not been observed since). However, Paul Krugman, an MIT economist, argues that the Japanese interest rate had been trapped for several years in the 1990s due to a prolonged recession in Japan. See Paul Krugman, "It's Baaack! Japan's Slump and the Return of the Liquidity Trap," Brookings Paper in Economic Activity 1998. Krugman also believes that the U.S. economy was in a liquidity trap in the 2007–2008 recession.

There is another reason why Keynes did not believe monetary policy would be very effective in increasing aggregate demand. Even if the Fed is successful in reducing the interest rate in a recession, the investment and consumption spending might not increase much. This is because firms and households may not be optimistic about the future state of the economy. No matter how low the interest rate is, if firms believe that there might not be enough demand for their products in the future, they will not invest in new plants and equipment. Similarly, if households believe they might not have their jobs in the future to be able to pay back bank loans, they will not borrow to buy homes no matter how low the interest rate is. For these reasons, Keynesians believe that fiscal policy is more effective in getting the economy out of recession.

TO SUMMARIZE

1. Economists define *demand for money* as the portion of their total wealth that people want to hold in the form of money (currency plus demand deposits).
2. Total wealth is the market value of all the assets held by a household.
3. Excess demand for money means that people would like to hold more money than they are actually holding.
4. An excess demand for money implies an excess supply of bonds: people are holding more bonds than they would like to hold.
5. *Velocity* is the number of times a dollar changes hands over a given period of time.
6. The ratio of demand for money to total expenditure is called the *Cambridge k*.
7. Velocity is the inverse of Cambridge k.
8. Cambridge economists argued that k was constant.
9. Therefore, in the Cambridge approach, demand for money was a constant fraction, k, of nominal GDP.
10. According to Keynes, k depends negatively on r. Demand for money, therefore, depends positively on P and Y, and negatively on r.
11. We can thus write the demand for money function as $M^d = k(r)\ PY$.
12. In equilibrium, the demand for money equals the supply of money ($M^d = M$).
13. An increase in P or Y will cause a proportionate increase in M^d, and an increase in the interest rate.
14. An increase in the riskiness of bonds increases the demand for money and hence the interest rate.
15. An expansionary monetary policy means an increase in the money supply by the Fed.
16. An increase in money supply will reduce r, and vice versa.
17. Three cases concerning the rate of growth of money supply:
    a. If the rate of growth of money supply equals the rate of increase in the price level, the interest rate will remain unchanged.
    b. If the rate of growth of money supply falls short of the rate of increase in the price level, the interest rate will increase.
    c. If the rate of growth of money supply exceeds the rate of increase in the price level, the interest rate will decrease.

EXERCISES

Question 1

The following table shows the U.S. nominal GDP and M1 money supply for the years 1996 and 1997:

Year	Nominal GDP ($ Billion)	Real GDP (Billions of Chained 2000 Dollars)	M1 Money Supply ($ Billion)
1996	7,817	8,329	1,107
1997	8,304	8,704	1,070

a. Calculate the GDP deflators for the two years (use these as the price levels).
b. Calculate the rates of change of the money supply and the price level for these two years.
c. On the basis of these two rates of change, what would be your best guess as to whether the interest rate had increased or decreased in 1997?
d. On the basis of your guess in the previous part, would you say the Cambridge k had increased or decreased in 1997?
e. Calculate the Cambridge k and the velocity for these two years. Was the behavior of the Cambridge k consistent with your guess in the previous part?

Question 2

Assuming money market equilibrium, write an expression relating the velocity to the interest rate. How do changes in the interest rate affect velocity? What do you think will happen to velocity during different phases of business cycles?

Question 3

What will happen to the interest rate if the money supply increases by 5%, while the price level increases by 6%?

Question 4

Suppose that the demand for money function jumps up and down because of changes in the price level.

a. What will happen to the interest rate if the Fed keeps the money supply constant? Will the price level and the interest rate move in the same direction, or the opposite direction?
b. What will happen if the Fed tries to keep the interest rate constant by changing the money supply in response to price changes? Will the price level and the money supply move in the same direction, or the opposite direction?

Question 5

Suppose that in a country the real GDP has been growing at a rate of 2% per year, and the inflation rate has been zero. What do you think will happen to the real GDP growth if the Fed keeps the money supply constant? What kind of monetary policy would you suggest the Fed to follow to keep the rate of growth of GDP from falling below 2% per year?

Question 6

Suppose that in a country the real GDP has been growing at a rate of 2% per year, and the annual inflation rate has been 3%.

a. What has been the approximate annual rate of increase in the demand for money?
b. What do you think will happen to the real GDP growth if the Fed keeps the money supply constant?
c. What do you think will happen to the real GDP growth if the Fed increases the money supply by 2% per year?
d. What kind of monetary policy would you suggest the Fed to follow to keep the rate of growth of GDP from falling below 2% per year?

Question 7

a. What will happen to the inertest rate under the following scenarios?

b. Both money supply and the price level increase by 5%.

c. Money supply increases by 5%, and the price level increases by 7%.

d. Money supply increases by 5%, and the price level increases by 4%.

CHAPTER 10

The Loanable Funds Market

INTRODUCTION AND REVIEW

OUR LAST CHAPTER described the liquidity preference theory of interest rate determination. In that theory, the interest rate is determined by the demand for and supply of money. Demand for money means the portion of their total wealth that people want to hold in the form of money. Supply of money means the actual stock of money in existence in people's pockets, purses, and bank accounts. This chapter will discuss the loanable funds theory. Both theories are useful, and each describes a part of the reality. For example, the effect of an increase in money supply on the interest rate can be easily described using the liquidity preference theory. On the other hand, the effect of an increase in expected inflation or the government budget deficit can more easily be analyzed in the loanable funds framework.

THE LOANABLE FUNDS THEORY

In this theory, the interest rate is determined by the demand for and supply of the amounts of loans, or loanable funds. Irving Fisher, an American economist, made major contributions to the development of this theory. Unlike the liquidity preference theory, the loanable funds theory is expressed in terms of flow variables. The amount of loans that you take or make is a flow variable. For example, if you borrow \$100 this week and \$150 next week from a bank, then in two weeks you will have borrowed \$250. So the total amount borrowed depends on the amount of time. The accumulation of all these borrowed amounts at the end of the period is your liability, which is a stock variable. At the end of the second week, you will owe \$250 to the bank. You can measure this at one point in time. You also remember that a change in a stock variable relates to a flow variable. That is, if at the end of the third week your liability is \$350, then you must have borrowed another \$100 the third week.

LOANABLE FUNDS MARKET
The market in which borrowers borrow money from lenders.

Unlike the liquidity preference theory, in the loanable funds theory there are actually people who demand loanable funds, and there are other people who supply them. This is an important difference from the liquidity preference theory. Households, firms, and the government can be on the lending or borrowing side of the *loanable funds market*. Households borrow funds to buy homes and consumer durables such as cars and appliances. Firms borrow to invest in plants and equipment. The federal, state, and local governments borrow to finance their budget deficits. They borrow to provide such services as education, national defense, law and order, and to make transfer payments. Households also lend directly—by buying corporate bonds—or indirectly, by depositing their savings in commercial banks. Similarly, firms lend occasionally when they have excess idle cash. Banks and other financial institutions are the major players in this market. They put together the small deposits of households and make loans to other households or to business firms. We saw this in the chapter on the supply of money.

The historic Savings Union Bank Building located at the intersection of Grant Avenue and Market Street in San Francisco, California was constructed in 1910.

DEMAND FOR AND SUPPLY OF LOANABLE FUNDS

Both the demand and supply of loanable funds depend on the nominal interest rate. If the interest rate decreases, lenders realize that lending is not as attractive as before. Some lenders reduce the amount of loans they make because they think that the lower interest rate is not worth sacrificing current consumption, lending, and waiting for a whole year to consume a little more then. They may also think that the reduction in the interest rate is only temporary, and perhaps in the future it might increase. Thus, if they lend now and tie their funds up in loans, they might miss out on future opportunities should the nominal rate increase. We can conclude that:

> *All else the same, if the nominal interest rate decreases, the quantity of loanable funds supplied will decrease.*

The opposite will happen if the nominal interest rate increases.

How about demand for loanable funds? If the nominal interest rate goes down, borrowing will become more attractive. As you remember from the discussion in Chapter 7, business firms will find it less expensive to borrow for their investment projects when the nominal interest rate is low. Households will also find it more affordable to borrow money to finance their purchases of homes, cars, and appliances. We therefore conclude that:

> *All else the same, if the nominal interest rate decreases, the quantity of loanable funds demanded will increase.*

The opposite will happen if the nominal interest rate increases.

EQUILIBRIUM INTEREST RATE

After all this, how would the nominal interest rate itself be determined? It would be determined by the demand for and supply of loanable funds. Consider the hypothetical example presented in Table 1 and the corresponding Figure 1. They show the demand (D^{LF}) and the supply of loanable funds (S^{LF}).

Table 1 Demand for and Supply of Loanable Funds		
Nominal Interest Rate r	Amount of Loanable Funds Demanded DLF	Amount of Loanable Funds Supplied SLF
12%	$80	$120
11%	$90	$110
10%	**$100**	**$100**
9%	$110	$90
8%	$120	$80

Figure 1: Loanable Funds Market

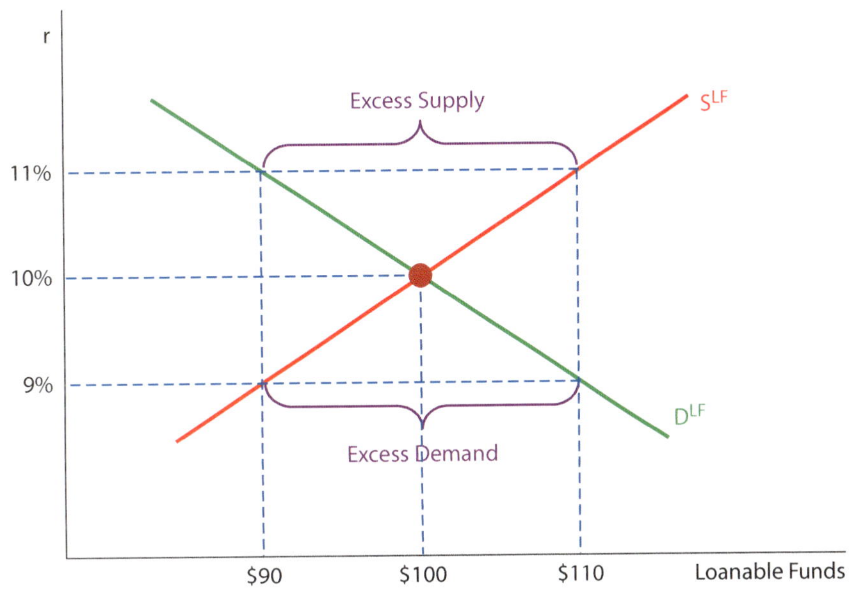

Consistent with the above story, we assume that as the nominal interest rate decreases, the amount of loanable funds demanded increases, and the amount supplied decreases. Now assume that the interest rate is 9%. At this rate, the amount of loanable funds demanded will be $110, and the amount supplied will be $90. There will be an excess demand for loanable funds by households and businesses. The shortage of loanable funds in the market will cause the nominal interest rate to increase. If, on the other hand, the nominal interest rate was 11%, the amount of loanable funds demanded would be $90, and the amount supplied would be $110. The excess supply of loanable funds in the market would cause the interest rate to drop. If the interest rate was 10%, the amount of loanable funds demanded would equal the amount supplied. This would be the equilibrium situation, in the sense that the rate would stay at 10% if nothing else changed in the economy. This would be a state of rest.

Once again, we need to emphasize that demand for and supply of loanable funds are flow variables. As such, they should be measured over a certain period of time. Let's pick a year as our time frame. What we are saying in the above example is that when the interest rate is 10%, the amount of loans demanded *in a year* will be $100, which will exactly match the amount of loans supplied *in that year*. If the interest rate falls to 9%, then the annual demand for loanable funds will exceed the annual supply of loanable funds.

CHANGES IN THE EQUILIBRIUM INTEREST RATE

The nominal interest rate is not the only thing borrowers and lenders care about. A host of other variables affect the demand for and supply of loanable funds. Changes in any of these other variables would cause the demand or supply curves to shift, as discussed below.

SHIFTS IN THE DEMAND FOR LOANABLE FUNDS

The following factors would cause the demand for loanable funds to shift.

1. Expected inflation rate. Suppose that currently the nominal interest rate is 10% and the expected inflation rate is 4%, so that the ex-ante real rate is 6%. Now, for whatever reason, borrowers increase their inflation expectations to 5%. Perhaps they have heard in the news that higher oil prices will lead to an increase in the future inflation rate. In that case, the real rate drops to 5%. Borrowers realize that the cost of borrowing in real terms is lower. If they borrow some money today, they will pay back their loans when the prices of goods and services are higher and money is worth less. This will increase the demand for loanable funds.
2. Expected future interest rate. If borrowers expect the interest rate to increase in the future, they will borrow more today, increasing the demand for loanable funds. Conversely, if they expect the interest rate to decline, they will wait to borrow in the future, causing the demand for loanable funds to go down.
3. Expected future economic conditions. We recall from Chapter 7 that if business firms expected the level of their profits to be higher in the future due to better economic conditions, they would invest more. As a result, they would borrow more money to finance the purchase of plants and equipment. Moreover, if households expected better economic conditions in the future, they would borrow more money to buy houses. This is because they would expect to have jobs in the future, and thus be able to pay back the loans. If people expect economic conditions to get worse in the future, the demand for loanable funds will decrease.
4. Uncertainty about the level of future profits. If firms became uncertain about the future state of the economy or the level of their own profits, they would be more hesitant to invest in plants and equipment, and the demand for loans would be reduced. If, on the other hand, firms became less uncertain about future profits, the demand for loanable funds would increase.
5. Tax policy. Changes in tax policy could also affect the demand curve for loanable funds. For instance, if the government reduced taxes on profits, the expected level of future after-tax profits would increase, and business firms would have stronger incentives to borrow and invest in plants and equipment. As a result, the demand for loanable funds would increase.

6. Government budget deficit. If the government's tax revenues were not sufficient to cover its spending and transfer payments, the budget would be in deficit. If the government could not reduce its expenditures to the level of its tax revenue, or increases its tax revenues to match its expenditures, it would either have to borrow in the financial markets (called deficit financing) or print money (called monetizing the debt). The government borrows by selling bonds. Deficit financing results in an increase in the demand for loanable funds by the government.

An increase in demand for loanable funds will result in a rightward shift in the demand curve. Similarly, a decrease will result in a leftward shift. Suppose, for example, that for one of the above reasons, borrowers want to borrow $20 more than before *per year* at any nominal interest rate. Then, the demand curve for loanable funds would shift to the right by $20. See Figure 2.

Figure 2: An Increase in the Demand for Loanable Funds

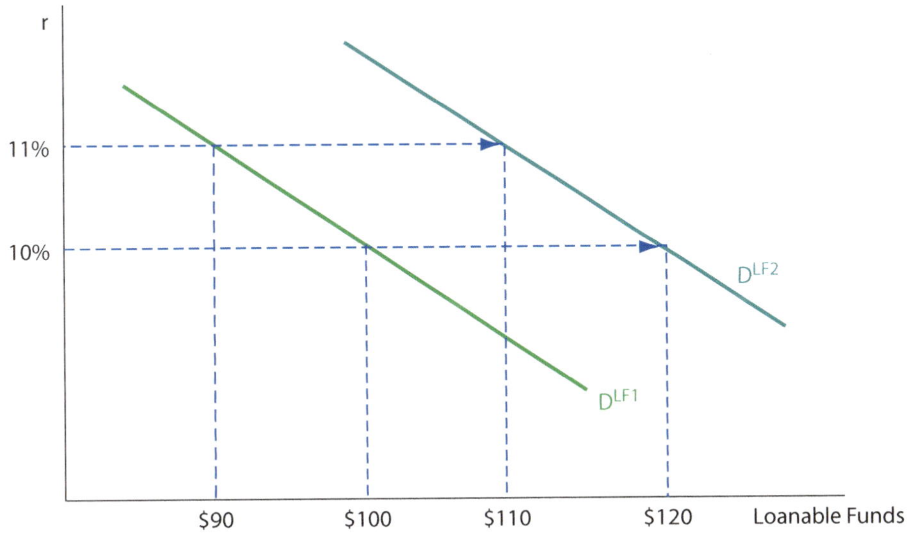

SHIFTS IN THE SUPPLY OF LOANABLE FUNDS

The following factors would cause the supply of loanable funds to shift. Keep in mind that households, firms, and the government lend money by buying bonds.

1. Expected inflation rate. Suppose again that currently the nominal interest rate is 10%, and the expected inflation rate is 4%, so that the ex-ante real rate is 6%. Lenders expect to be able to buy 6% more goods and services in the future if they lend money today. Now, for whatever reason, lenders increase their inflation expectations to 5%. In that case, the real rate drops to 5%. Now lenders expect their standards of living to increase by only 5% if they lend. Therefore, some people will be discouraged from lending, and the supply of loanable funds will shift to the left.
2. Expected future interest rate. If lenders expect the interest rate to increase, they will wait to lend in the future. This will cause a reduction in the supply of loanable funds. Conversely, if

they expect the interest rate to fall in the future, they will try to lend more today. As a result, the supply of loanable funds will increase.

3. Income and wealth. As the income and wealth of households increase, they can save more and, thus, lend more. They can lend more in one of two ways. First—directly, by buying the bonds issued by corporations or the government. Second—indirectly, by depositing their savings in banks and other financial institutions. In the second case, the financial institutions lend those funds to borrowers. In either case, the supply of loanable funds increases.
4. Business risk. If households perceive that business firms may not be able to pay back their loans due to bad economic conditions, they will be inclined to lend less. and the supply of loanable funds will decrease. On the other hand, if economic conditions improve and loans become less risky, the supply of loanable funds will increase.

An increase in the supply of loanable funds means that people want to supply more loans at any level of the interest rate. Let's suppose that at any interest rate, lenders are willing to lend $20 more than before *per year*, as in Figure 3. In that case, the supply of loanable funds shifts to the right.

Figure 3: An Increase in the Supply of Loanable Funds

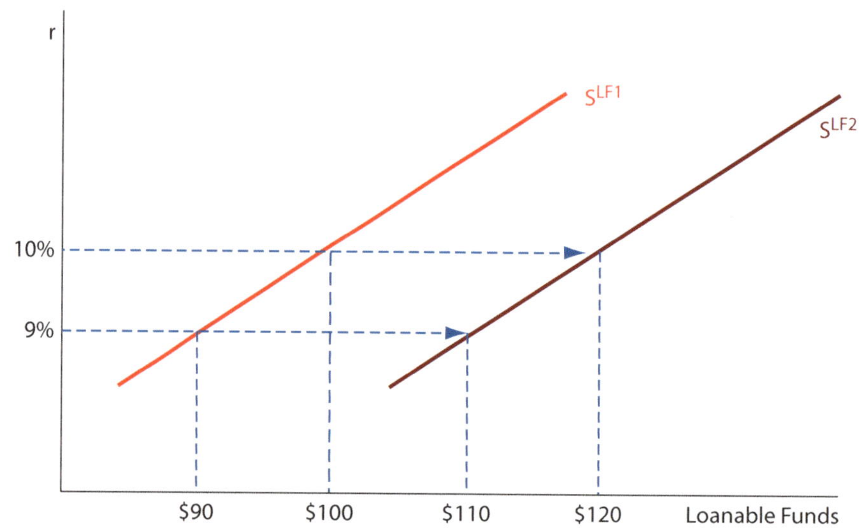

FAVORABLE CHANGE IN TAX POLICY

We are now ready to analyze changes in the equilibrium interest rate. We start with a couple of easy cases. Suppose the government reduces the tax rate on profits. As a result, firms expect to earn higher after-tax profits in the future. We know that this policy causes an increase in demand for loanable funds. Suppose that demand increases by $20, as in Figure 4.

At the current interest rate of 10%, there is now an excess demand for loanable funds by business firms equal to $20 per year. As firms compete against each other to borrow the limited funds available in the market, the nominal interest rate will rise. It will rise until the demand equals supply. In our example, the nominal interest rate will increase to 11%. Assuming that expected inflation remains constant, the increase in the nominal interest rate will equal the increase in the ex-ante real interest rate. For example, if $\pi^e = 4\%$, then the real interest will increase from $r = 10\% - 4\% = 6\%$ to $r = 11\% - 4\% = 7\%$.

Figure 4: A Favorable Tax Policy

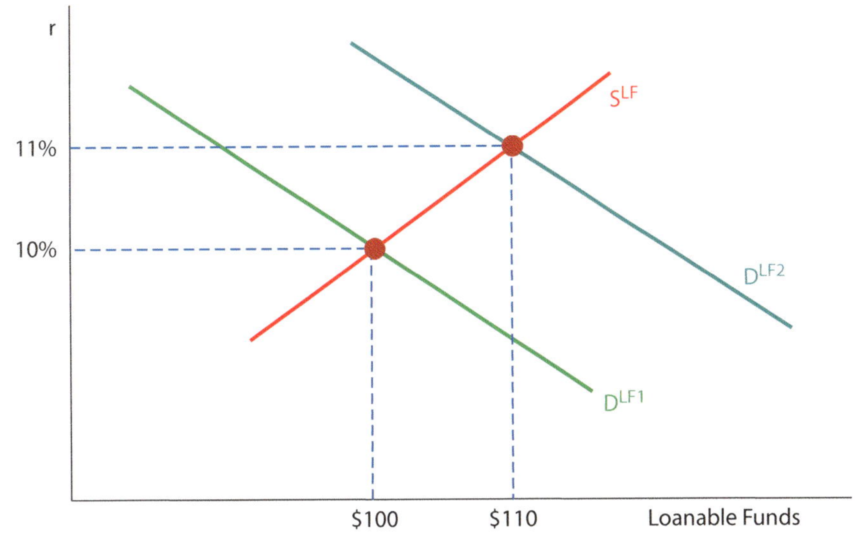

THE INTEREST RATE OVER BUSINESS CYCLES

How do you think the nominal interest rate behaves over the course of business cycles? As a recession ends and the expansion phase of the business cycle begins, the real GDP starts to go up. Business firms predict better economic conditions and higher profits in the years ahead. As we know from the discussion above, they increase their demand for loanable funds to finance their investments in plants and equipment. The demand curve for loanable funds shifts to the right, as in Figure 5. At the same time, households begin to earn higher incomes, and can afford to save and lend more. Thus, the supply of loanable funds also shifts to the right.

Since both curves shift in the same direction, the effect on the real interest rate is uncertain in general. It depends which curve shifts more. However, empirical evidence shows that the interest rate increases during an expansion phase of the cycle. This is consistent with Figure 5, in which the demand curve shifts more than the supply curve, and the interest rate increases to 10.5%. Conversely, in a recession, the interest rate will go down. We see that both the liquidity preference and the loanable funds theories give the same prediction about the behavior of the interest rate over the course of business cycles.

Figure 5: The Loanable Funds Market in an Expansion

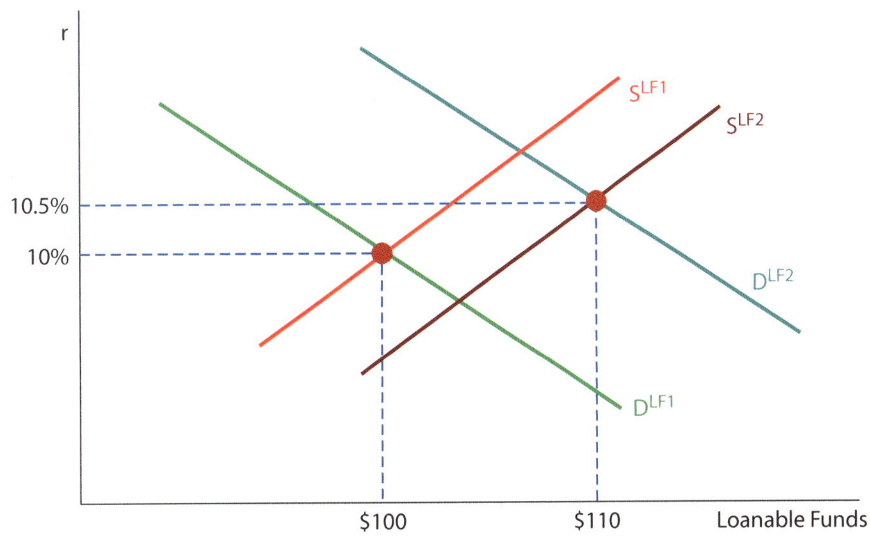

AN INCREASE IN CREDIT RISK

CREDIT RISK
The chance that a borrower may not be able to pay back (a part) of his or her loan to the lender.

Credit risk is the risk that borrowers may default on their loans. Suppose that lenders begin to worry about the ability of the borrowers to pay back their loans. The supply of loanable funds will decrease, as in Figure 6. At the existing equilibrium interest rate of 10%, an excess demand for loanable funds will develop. Competition among borrowers to get loans will push up the nominal interest rate until it reaches 11%, at which supply again equals demand.

If a lot of banks worry about the credit risk of the borrowers, they may severely curtail the amount of money they lend. As a result, the interest rate soars and many firms and households cannot borrow money to buy equipment, homes, or other durable goods. Such a severe reduction in the loanable funds is called a *credit crunch*. Many economists believe this is what happened in the 2007–2008 recession.

Figure 6: The Effect of an Increase in Credit Risk

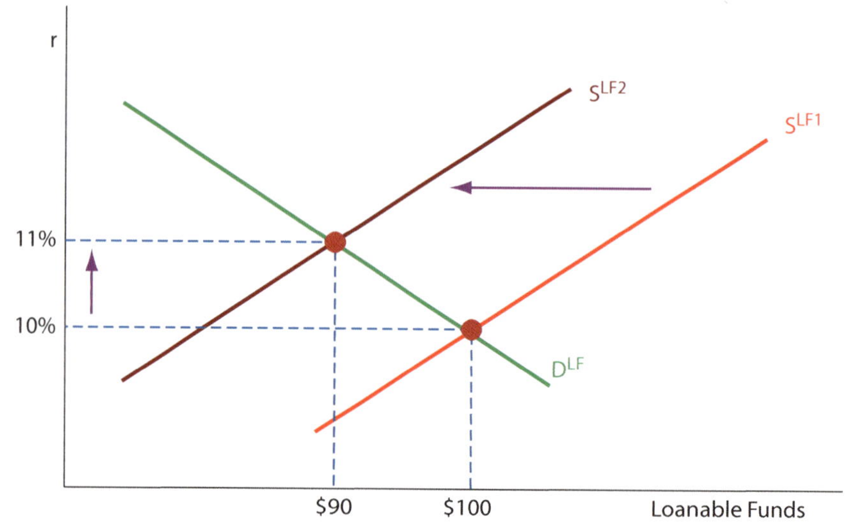

Irving Fisher

AN INCREASE IN EXPECTED INFLATION RATE

Suppose that both lenders and borrowers expect a higher inflation rate in the future. As we know by now, business firms will increase their borrowing to invest in plants and equipment. This will result in a rightward shift in the demand for loanable funds. (See Figure 8.) At the same time, households will require a higher interest rate on their loans. This means that the supply of loanable funds will shift up and to the left. In this case, the interest rate on loans will increase.

FISHER EFFECT
The increase in the interest rate, as a result of an increase in the expected inflation.

This increase in the interest rate as a result of an increase in the expected inflation is called the *Fisher Effect*. This effect was named after Irving Fisher of Yale University, one of the major contributors to the theory of the determination of bond prices described in this chapter. The Fisher Effect states that when people expect a higher inflation rate, the interest rate will increase, and vice versa. The Fisher Effect actually makes a stronger statement. Note that in Figure 7, both the supply and demand curves shifted by the same amount so that the equilibrium amount of loanable funds remained the same. What is the rationale behind this assumption?

According to this theory, people care about the ex-ante real interest rate rather than the nominal interest rate. Suppose that the current nominal interest rate is 10%. People expect 4% inflation for the future, so the ex-ante real rate equals r = 10% - 4% = 6%. Therefore, lenders think that if they lend money at the 10% interest rate, their purchasing power will increase by 6%. Borrowers believe that if they borrow at 10%, the real cost of borrowing is only 6%. This is because those who borrow are mostly households wanting to buy homes and firms wanting to buy plants and equipment. These borrowers think that the inflation will make the values of their homes, plants, and equipment increase by 4%. Although they will pay an interest of 10%, in real terms they will only pay 6%. Suppose that both groups are happy with this 6% ex-ante real interest rate.

Figure 7: An Increase in Expected Inflation (Fisher Effect)

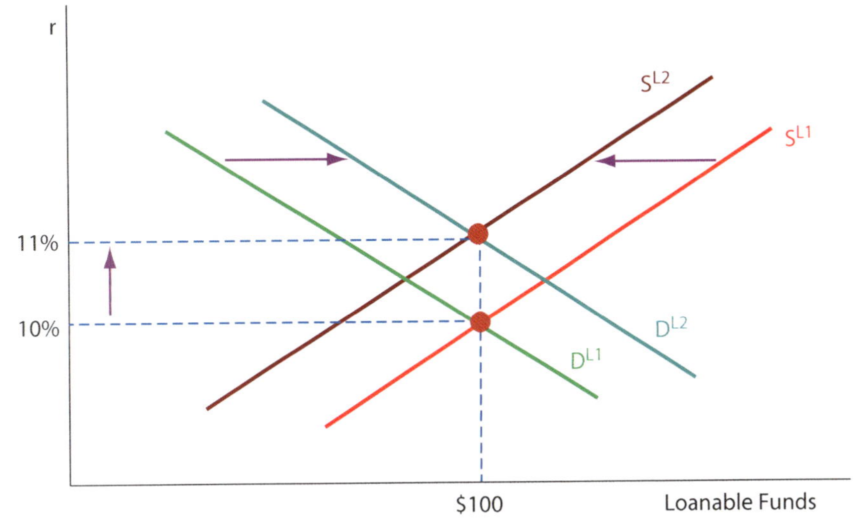

Now suppose that they both expect the inflation rate to increase to 5%. At the current nominal interest rate of 10%, the ex-ante real interest rate drops to r = 10% - 5% = 5%. Since borrowers and lenders are both happy with a 6% real interest rate, both supply and demand will shift up by 1%. Lenders will demand a 1% higher interest rate (supply will shift up by 1%) and borrowers will be happy to comply (demand will shift up by 1%). As a result, the interest rate will increase by 1% to 11%, and the ex-ante real rate will remain constant at 6% (11% – 5%).

AN INCREASE IN THE EXPECTED FUTURE INTEREST RATE

If both lenders and borrowers expect the interest rate to increase in the future, demand for loanable funds will increase and supply will decrease, increasing the equilibrium interest rate. There is an element of self-fulfilling prophecy here. If the market expects the rate to increase in the future, it will increase now. The converse is also true. If the market expects the rate to fall in the future, it will fall now. Figure 7 can also be used to present this case.

THE CLASSICAL THEORY OF SAVING, INVESTMENT, AND FISCAL POLICY

The loanable-funds framework can be used, with a little modification, to shed light on two important macroeconomic issues: the relationship between saving and investment and the effect of fiscal policy on the real GDP. We need to switch from nominal variables to real variables, to be consistent with the rest of the book. Since real variables are in terms of some base-year prices (and for the story to be more intuitive), we will refer to the real variables in terms of dollars.

THE SAVING-INVESTMENT RELATIONSHIP

Recall the goods market equilibrium condition:

$$Y = C + I + G$$

Recall also the definition of disposable income:

$$Y_d = Y - TX + TR$$

Substituting the first equation into the second, we get

$$Y_d = C + I + G - TX + TR$$

Rearranging this equation further yields

$$(Y_d - C) = I + (G + TR - TX)$$

The term on the left-hand side $(Y_d - C)$ is the excess of household disposable income over household consumption. It is called saving (S), as we saw in Chapter 7. So the equation can be written as:

$$S = I + (G + TR - TX)$$

The second term on the right hand side (G + TR - TX) is the excess of government's outlays over its tax revenue. This equation is the saving-investment relationship. It says that in equilibrium, the amount of funds supplied to the financial market by households in a year from their savings must equal the sum of demands *for these funds* by firms and the government. So (G + TR - TX) is the demand by the government for the loanable funds supplied by households through their savings.

BUDGET DEFICIT
The amount by which a government's expenditures exceed its tax revenues during a certain period of time.

Suppose that the sum of the government's outlays, G and TR, exceeds its tax revenue, TX. The government is then running a *budget deficit*. One way for the government to finance the deficit is to borrow an amount equal to the deficit from households. For example, let the amount of funds supplied to the market by households be S = \$100, the demand for these funds by firms I = \$80, and by the government to finance its deficit (G + TR - TX) = \$20. Then

$$\$100 = \$80 + \$20$$

Another way of looking at this equation is that households are supplying \$100 to the market. However, since the government is borrowing \$20 of that amount, business firms get to borrow only the remaining \$80. Hence, the larger the amount of funds borrowed by the government, the smaller the amount left for the business firms in the private sector to borrow. For instance, if the government borrows \$30, then the private sector gets to borrow \$70.

BUDGET SURPLUS
The amount by which a government's tax revenues exceed its expenditures during a certain period of time.

On the other hand, when the government runs a *budget surplus*, (G + TR - TX) becomes negative. This means the government has some additional cash it can provide to the financial system by depositing it in commercial banks, so that not all the supply comes from households. For example, suppose (G + TR - TX) = - \$20. Then

$$\$60 = \$80 - \$20$$

In this case, the supply of loanable funds to the market by households equals what firms demand, minus what the government provides to the firms.

The financial system channels savings from households to firms and the government in one of two ways. In the case of *indirect finance*, households deposit some of this money in commercial banks, and these banks lend it to firms and the government. In the case of *direct finance*, households provide the money to firms directly by buying their bonds. They lend money to the government by buying government bonds.

We saw in Chapter 7 that consumption depends negatively on the interest rate. If the interest rate rises, the cost of borrowing will increase, and households will reduce their purchase of consumer durables such as appliances or cars. Since saving is left over from consumption, this means that an increase in the interest rate will increase the quantity of saving. This is shown in Table 2 using some hypothetical numbers, and Figure 8 as the upward sloping function labeled S. We also know from Chapter 7 that investment spending depends negatively on the interest rate: an increase in the interest rate will discourage investment spending. Table 2 shows this using some hypothetical numbers.

Table 2 assumes that the government budget deficit is $200. The budget deficit is not related to the interest rate. That is because the government is not in business to make money. It runs budget deficits for reasons unrelated to interest rates. For example, it has to spend on national defense, law and order, education, roads, and bridges, regardless of what the interest rate is in the market. The sum of investment demand and budget deficit must therefore be negatively related to the interest rate, only because of the negative relationship between investment spending and the interest rate. In Figure 8, the supply of saving by households equals the demand for saving by firms and the government at the interest rate of 10%.

Table 2

Equilibrium Saving and Investment

r	S	I	G + TR - TX	I + (G + TR - TX)
12%	1,200	600	200	800
11%	1,100	700	200	900
10%	**1,000**	800	200	**1,000**
9%	900	900	200	1,100

Figure 8: Equilibrium Saving and Investment

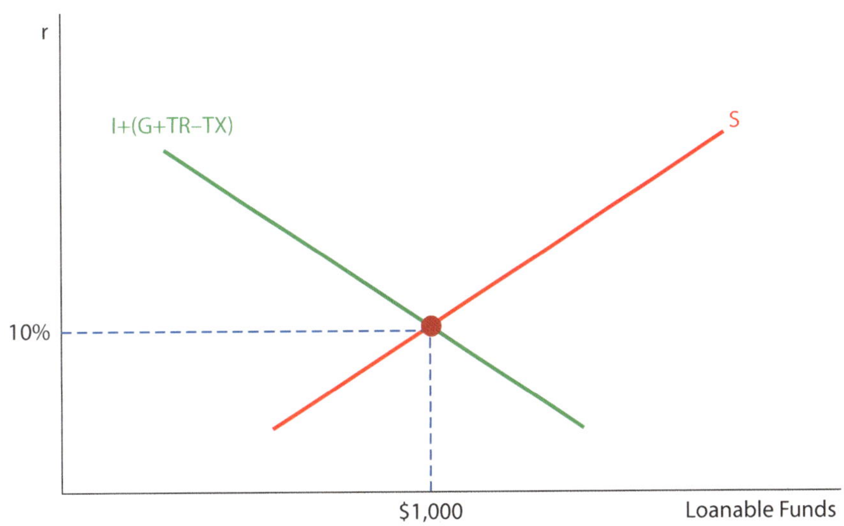

We know that any change in the interest rate will cause saving and investment to change along the two functions. Keep two things in mind. First, any movement along the I + (G + TR – TX) function in Figure 8 should be due to changes in the investment spending, because the deficit does not depend on the interest rate. Second, along the saving function, if the amount of saving increases, the amount of consumption should decrease, and vice versa. This is because that function assumes a constant disposable income.

AN INCREASE IN INVESTMENT SPENDING

What will happen if the investment spending increases for reasons unrelated to changes in the interest rate? Let's say that business firms become optimistic about future profits and decide to buy more equipment. Therefore, they increase their demand for loanable funds by $200 at every interest rate. This scenario is shown in Table 3 and Figure 9.

Table 3				
The Effect of an Increase in Investment Spending				
r	S	I	G + TR - TX	I + (G + TR - TX)
Original Investment				
12%	1,200	600	200	800
11%	1,100	700	200	900
10%	**1,000**	800	200	**1,000**
9%	900	900	200	1,100
Increased Investment				
12%	1,200	800	200	1,000
11%	**1,100**	900	200	**1,100**
10%	1,000	1,000	200	1,200
9%	900	1,100	200	1,300

Figure 9: An Increase in Investment Spending

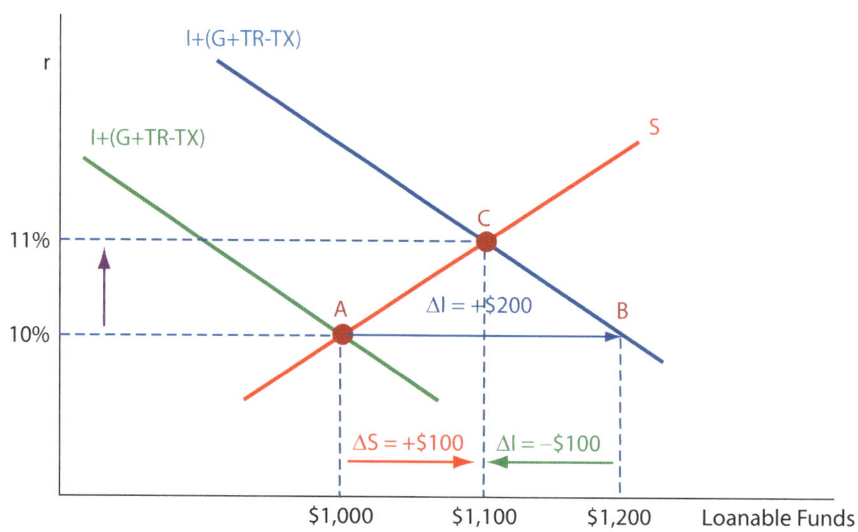

The increase in investment demand for loanable funds causes the demand curve to shift to the right by $200 units. At the current interest rate of 10%, the total demand for funds will be $1,200 (point B in Figure 9), so there will be an excess demand for loanable funds equal to $200. Competition among firms to obtain the scarce funds in the market will push up the equilibrium interest rate to 11%. As the interest rate rises, some firms will reduce the amount of money they want to borrow. This will be the movement from point B to point C. In our hypothetical situation, this reduction in investment equals $100. So the investment demand for loanable funds increases by $200 due to investor optimism about future profits, but subsequently decreases by $100, due to the increase in the interest rate. The net increase in investment, therefore, is $100.

On the other hand, the higher interest rate encourages households to save and lend more. In Figure 9, saving increases by $100 from point A to point C. However, as we know from Chapter 7, this also means that consumption decreases by $100. Altogether, then, investment increases by $100, while consumption decreases by $100. So the investment demand for goods replaces the consumption demand "dollar for dollar."

AN INCREASE IN SAVING

What if saving increases for reasons unrelated to the interest rate? Suppose saving increases by $200 because of an increase in disposable income. Table 4 and Figure 10 show that the saving function shifts to the right by $200; at the current interest rate, the amount of saving equals $1,200 (point B). This saving glut causes the interest rate to go down to 9%. The lower interest rate causes investment spending to increase by $100, from point A to point C. On the other hand, it discourages saving somewhat, and the quantity of saving decreases by $100, from point B to point C. In other words, this lower interest rate encourages consumption by $100. Remember that along the saving function, if saving decreases, consumption will increase by the same amount. We see then that, as households bring an additional saving of $200 to the financial market, consumption and investment will increase by exactly $200. Note finally that the net increase in saving equals $100 (= $1,100 – $1,000).

Table 4				
The Effect of an Increase in Saving				
r	S	I	G + TR - TX	I + (G + TR - TX)
Original Saving				
12%	1,200	600	200	800
11%	1,100	700	200	900
10%	**1,000**	800	200	**1,000**
9%	900	900	200	1,100
Increased Saving				
12%	1,400	600	200	800
11%	1,300	700	200	900
10%	1,200	800	200	1,000
9%	**1,100**	900	200	**1,100**

Figure 10: An Increase in Saving

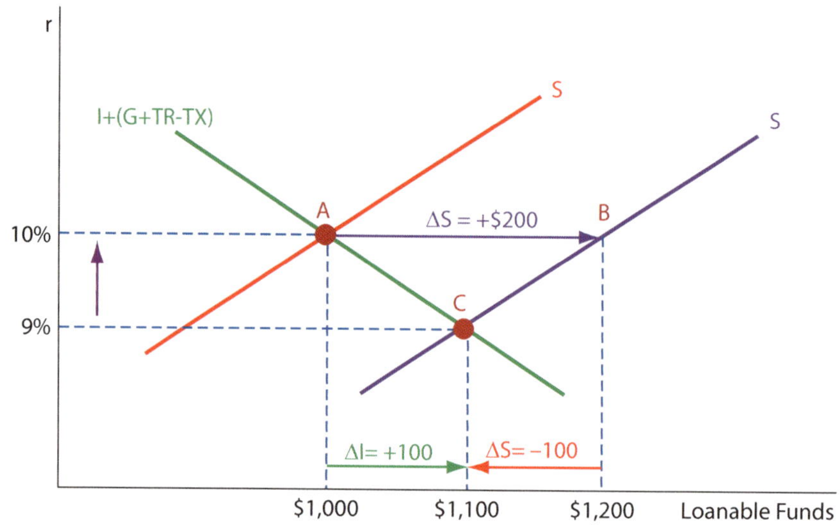

BUDGET DEFICITS AND CROWDING OUT

Recall from Chapter 7 that the government can pay for an increase in its expenditures in three different ways: raising an equal amount of taxes; borrowing; and printing money. The first is called balanced budget increase in spending; the second, deficit spending (or deficit financing); and the third, monetizing the debt. We will now talk about these financing methods in light of what we have learned about the loanable funds market.

BALANCED-BUDGET INCREASE IN SPENDING

We talked about this issue in Chapter 7. We learned that if the government increases its spending (G) through an equal increase in taxes, and the price level is fixed, the real GDP will increase by the amount of the increase in government spending. We called this the ***unit multiplier*** result. Now you will be surprised to see how this result changes, once we introduce the loanable funds market into the picture. You will benefit from reviewing the materials in Chapter 7 before proceeding.

Three Ways to Finance Government Expenditures

Balanced Budget Increase
Raise an Equal Amount of Taxes
$\Delta(G + TR) = \Delta(TX)$

Deficit Financing
Borrow an Equal Amount of Money
$\Delta(G + TR) = \Delta(D^{LF})$

Monetizing the Debt
Print an Equal Amount of Money
$\Delta(G + TR) = \Delta(M)$

As in Chapter 7, assume that the government raises taxes by 1,000 units to finance its spending of an equal amount. As a result of the reduction in disposable income, consumption decreases by 800 units. This is under the assumption that MPC = 0.80. What the story left out was that the reduction in disposable income of 1,000 units would also cause household saving to decrease by 200 units. What is the effect of this on our story? Well, it will be just the opposite of the case above when saving increased.

Table 5 and Figure 11 show that the financial market is initially in equilibrium at point A, with r = 10%. Suppose that saving decreases by $200 at every interest rate. This will cause an increase in the interest rate to 11%. The increase in the interest rate will cause investment spending to go down by $100, from point A to point C. It will also attract $100 of savings to the financial market, shown by a movement from point B to C. This increase in saving means a reduction in consumption of an equal amount. So the reduction saving of $200 leads to a reduction in consumption and investment of $200.

We see, then, that a balanced-budget increase in government spending of 1,000 units will cause consumption spending to decrease by 800, due to the increase in taxes to pay for the increased spending. Then, the increase in the interest rate will cause consumption and investment to decrease by 200 units, so that aggregate demand for goods and services will remain unchanged. We say that an increase in government spending crowds out private spending. More specifically, this result is called complete or dollar-for-dollar *crowding out*. In this case, fiscal policy is totally ineffective in changing the level of aggregate demand.

CROWDING OUT
A reduction in private spending (investment and consumption) resulting from an increase in government spending.

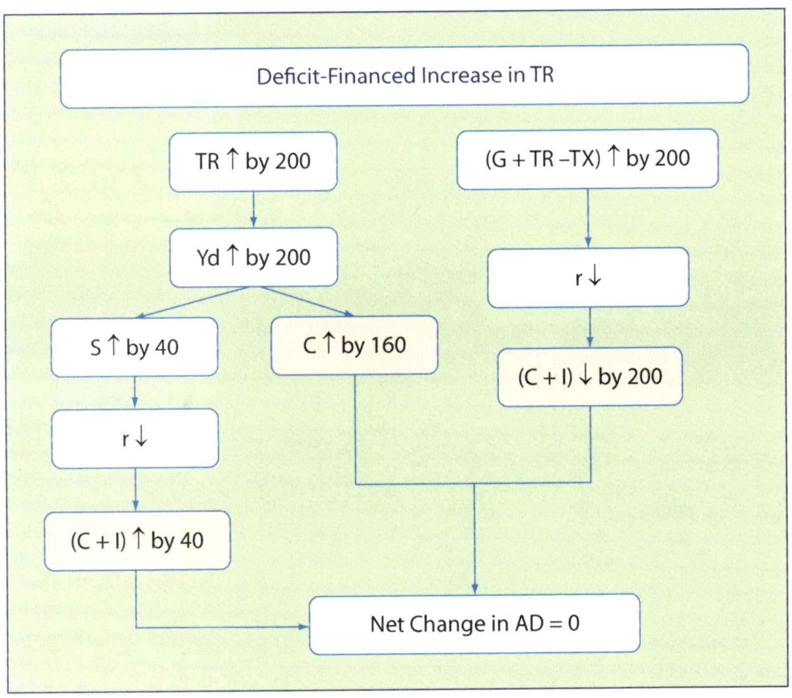

Table 5				
The Effect of a Reduction in Saving				
r	S	I	G + TR - TX	I + (G + TR - TX)
Original Saving				
12%	1,200	600	200	800
11%	1,100	700	200	900
10%	**1,000**	800	200	**1,000**
9%	900	900	200	1,100
Reduced Saving				
12%	1,000	600	200	800
11%	**900**	700	200	**900**
10%	800	800	200	1,000
9%	700	900	200	1,100

Figure 11: A Reduction in Saving

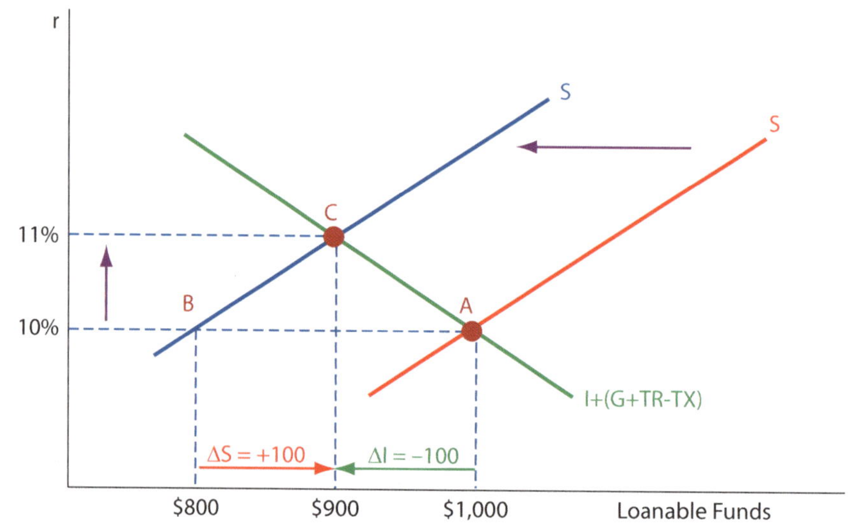

DEFICIT SPENDING

A government budget deficit can increase in two different ways:

1. An increase in (G + TR) without an equal increase in TX.
2. A decrease in TX without an equal reduction in (G + TR).

Suppose that the government's budget deficit increases by $200 to (G + TR - TX) = $400, because of an increase in government spending (G). (See Table 6 and Figure 12.) This increases the total demand for loanable funds by $200 so that at the current interest rate, the total demand for loanable funds equals $1,200 (point B). The equilibrium interest rate increases to 11%. The higher interest rate encourages additional savings by households, and the amount of loanable funds supplied to the market increases by $100 (from $1,000 at point A to $1,100 at point C). The demand by the government increases by $200, and the supply by households increases by only $100. What happens to the remaining $100? This is the amount by which business firms reduce their demand for funds for investment purposes (from $1,200 at point B to $1,100 at point C). This reduction in investment spending is due to the increase in the interest rate. The increase in saving of $100 means a reduction consumption of the same amount. So the increase in government spending ($200) will equal the sum of the reductions in consumption ($100) and investment ($100). The deficit-financed increase in government spending will crowd out private spending dollar for dollar, leaving the aggregate demand unchanged. Such a policy will not be expansionary.

Remember that capital is one of the production factors. The amount of capital in an economy can increase through investment in plants and equipment, as well as in research and development. If firms cannot raise cash to finance their investment projects because of high interest rates, the amount of capital in the economy and the rate of growth of GDP will be lower. As a result, future generations will receive a smaller amount of capital and a lower GDP. This reduced standard of living for future generations is the most important adverse consequence of government budget deficits.

Table 6

The Effect of an Increase in Budget Deficit

r	S	I	G + TR - TX	I + (G + TR - TX)
Budget Deficit = 200				
12%	1,200	600	200	800
11%	1,100	700	200	900
10%	**1,000**	800	200	**1,000**
9%	900	900	200	1,100
Budget Deficit = 400				
12%	1,200	600	400	1,000
11%	**1,100**	700	400	**1,100**
10%	1,000	800	400	1,200
9%	900	900	400	1,300

Figure 12: An Increase in Budget Deficit

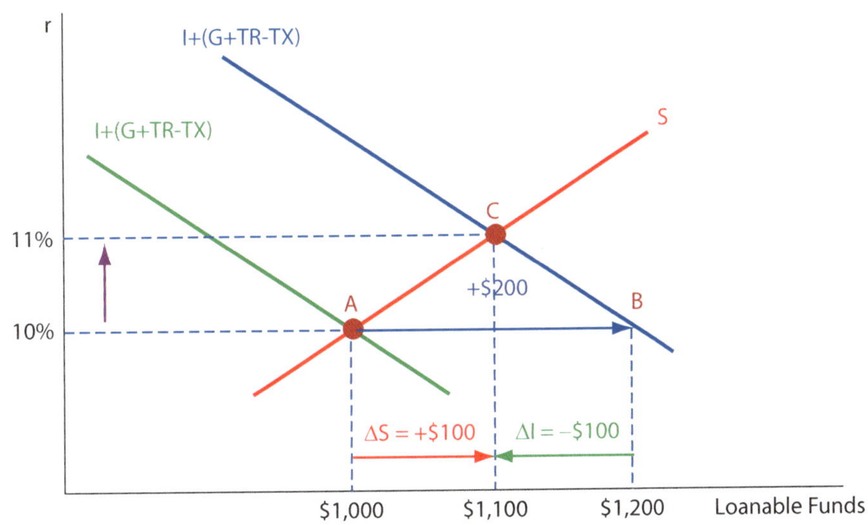

CHANGES IN TAXES OR TRANSFERS

What if the government increases transfer payments by $200 without raising taxes? This policy will increase the budget deficit by $200, and will thus crowd out private spending (C + I) by $200, as in Figure 12. But this $200 will be given to some people as unemployment benefits, Food stamps, welfare payments, and so on. This will increase their disposable income by $200, pushing up the aggregate demand. This is, of course, the intent of the policy. Assume that the marginal propensity to consume is 0.80. Therefore, increasing transfer payments will cause household consumption to increase by $160 (0.80 × $200) and household saving by $40 (0.20 × $200). As we know from above, the increase in saving of $40 will lead to an equal amount of increase in consumption and investment spending. The net result of the policy is that aggregate demand will remain unchanged—dollar-for-dollar crowding out. Note finally that we would get exactly the same result if the government reduced taxes by $200 without reducing its expenditures.

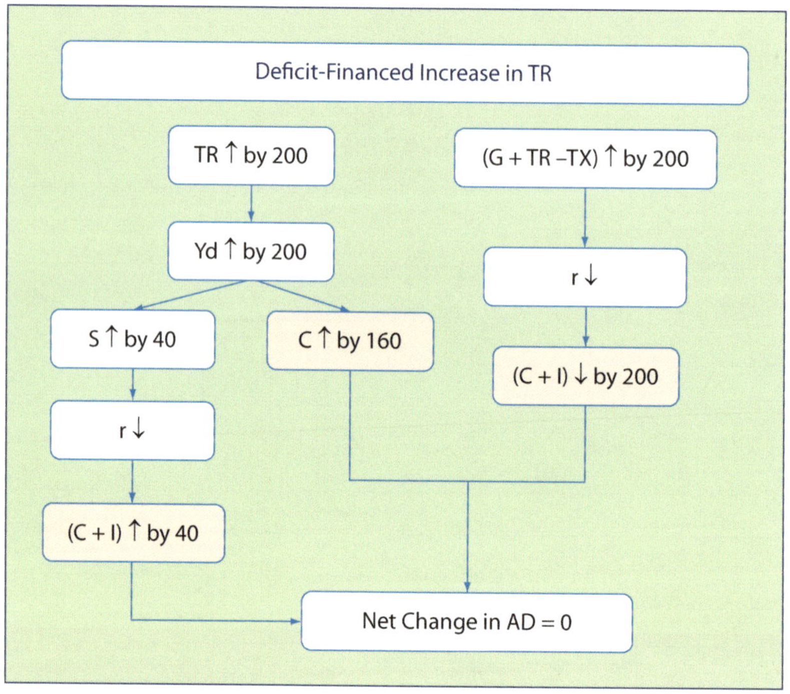

MONETIZING THE DEBT

MONETIZING THE DEBT
The purchase of the bonds by the Fed that the Treasury has sold to the public to finance the government's budget deficit. It is effectively printing money to finance the deficit.

The mechanics of debt monetization is as follows. The Treasury Department sells bonds in the loanable funds market to borrow money to finance the deficit. Then, the Fed buys these Treasury bonds and injects reserves into the banking system through an open market operation. So the Fed collects the Treasury bonds from private hands and replaces them with money. That is why this process is called *monetizing the debt*. It is pretty much like printing money to finance the deficit. So let's just assume that the government buys some goods and services in the goods market and prints money to pay for them.

To begin with, this policy will have no effect in the loanable funds market, because no new loan demand is generated by the government. Recall that the term (G + TR – TX) in the saving-investment relationship is the government budget deficit *financed from household savings*. In this case, though, the government does not increase its demand for private-sector loans. Therefore (G +

TR – TX) remains unchanged. Since saving does not change either, nothing happens in the above graphs. So, we cannot use the graphs in this chapter to analyze this case.

Nevertheless, the effect of this policy is not hard to understand. The policy will be quite expansionary, because it will be a combination of fiscal and monetary policies: the government will increase spending (G) financed by an increase in money supply by the Fed (M). However, if the government keeps printing money to buy goods and services, at some point the economy will reach its maximum production capacity, and the increases in aggregate demand will no longer raise the real GDP. It will only create inflation.

WHO PAYS FOR GOVERNMENT EXPENDITURES?

Who pays for all the goods and services the government buys? The answer: all of us, ultimately through some kind of tax. A government can increase its spending either by increasing taxes, borrowing, or printing money. Consider the budget equation again:

$$\text{Budget} = G + TR - TX$$

In the case of a balanced budget increase in spending, the government increases spending (G) and finances it through an equal increase in taxes (TX). So both spending and taxation take place contemporaneously.

The second way for the government to increase spending is to borrow money. In the budget equation, (G + TR) increases more than TX, resulting in an increase in the deficit. But there is more to the story. Suppose the government borrows $100 billion that it will pay back at annual installments of $10 billion for the next 20 years. It does this by issuing and selling 20-year U.S. Treasury coupon bonds. Over the course of the next 20 years, the government will have to pay back the whole $100 billion—plus another $100 billion in interest. Where will it get this money from? The answer is, taxes collected from future generations. So whether the government finances its spending through taxes or borrowing, at some point it has to raise taxes to pay for them. The only difference is in the timing of the increase in taxes.

How about printing money? In this case, taxes are not increased; however, monetizing the debt has its own problems. As we will see in subsequent chapters, printing excessive amounts of money to pay for government spending will, at some point, create inflation. Inflation will erode the purchasing power of money. This particularly adversely affects those people such as retirees, government employees, or workers with fixed-wage contracts whose incomes do not keep pace with the rate of inflation. The effect of losing purchasing power to inflation is similar to that of losing income to taxes: reduced ability to buy goods and services. For this reason, losing purchasing power due to inflation is sometimes called the *inflation tax*. We see then that in all three cases, ultimately people pay for the government's spending through *some kind of tax*.

INFLATION TAX
A reduction in purchasing power as a result of inflation.

Who Pays for Government Expenditures

Balanced Budget Increase
Spend Now, Tax Now

Deficit Financing
Borrow and Spend Now, Tax Later

Monetizing the Debt
Print Money and Spend Now, Inflation-Tax Later

TO SUMMARIZE

1. The interest rate is determined by the demand for and supply of *loanable funds*.
2. An increase in the money supply would reduce the interest rate by increasing the supply of loanable funds.
3. The interest rate increases during expansions and decreases during recessions.
4. An increase in expected inflation, all else the same, will cause an equal increase in the nominal interest rate, leaving the ex-ante real interest rate unchanged. This is called the *Fisher Effect*.
5. An increase in the expected future interest rate will result in an increase in the current interest rate.
6. In equilibrium, the flow of saving to the loanable funds market equals the demand for these funds by firms to finance their investment spending and the government to finance its deficit.
7. *Budget deficits* cause an increase in the interest rate.
8. In the classical model, deficit-financed increases in government spending always crowd out household consumption and private investment, dollar for dollar. The same is true for deficit-financed reductions in taxes.
9. Increases in government expenditures are always financed by some kind of taxes.
10. In the case of a balanced-budget increase in spending, taxes are raised in the same year as the spending increases. In the case of deficit financing, the government borrows now and then raises taxes in the future to pay back its loan with interest. In the case of printing money, some people become subject to the inflation tax in the future.

EXERCISES

Question 1

What do you think would happen to the nominal rate in a recession? Use both the liquidity preference and loanable funds theories to analyze the question.

Question 2

Suppose that bonds become more risky and at the same time, the government changes the tax code in favor of businesses. What will be the combined effect of these two events on the interest rate?

Question 3

Suppose that business firms become pessimistic about the future profitability of investment projects; at the same time, the Fed conducts an open market purchase. What will be the combined effect of these two events on the ex-ante real interest rate?

Question 4

Consider the following table. The following questions refer independently to the information given in the table.

Hypothetical Loanable Funds Market		
Interest Rate	Amount of Loanable Funds Demanded	Amount of Loanable Funds Supplied
20%	$2,000	$2,800
16%	$2,200	$2,600
12%	$2,400	$2,400
8%	$2,600	$2,200
4%	$2,800	$2,000

a. Draw the supply and demand functions.
b. What is the equilibrium interest rate?
c. Suppose that people currently expect the inflation rate for the next year to be 4%. What is their expectation of the real interest rate?
d. Assume (for this part only) that the expected inflation rate increases to 8%. If people want to keep the real interest rate at the same rate as in part c, what will happen to the nominal and real interest rates? Show this graphically.
e. Suppose that the supply of loanable funds decreases by $400, and expected inflation remains the same. What will be the new real and nominal interest rates?
f. Suppose a recession comes and the demand for loanable funds goes down by $800, but the supply of loanable funds goes down by $400. Find the new interest rate.

Question 5

Consider the following table that shows saving, investment, and the budget deficit in a country. Note that saving is assumed to be insensitive to changes in the interest rate. In the following, each question is independent of the previous one.

a. Draw the graph of the loanable funds market and find the equilibrium interest rate.
b. Suppose that the government conducts a balanced-budget increase in spending of 1,000 units ($\Delta G = 1{,}000$), and assume that the marginal propensity to consume is MPC = 0.80. Analyze the effect of this policy in the graph. Discuss the crowding out effect.
c. What will happen in this market if household saving increases by 200 units?
d. What will happen in this market if investment spending increases by 200 units?
e. What will happen if the government budget deficit increases to 400 units? Discuss the crowding out effect.
f. What will happen if the government budget deficit is reduced to zero?

r	S	I	G + TR – TX
12%	1,000	600	200
11%	1,000	700	200
10%	1,000	800	200
9%	1,000	900	200
8%	1,000	1,000	200

Question 6

Consider the following table that shows saving, investment, and the budget deficit in a country. Note that investment spending is assumed to be insensitive to changes in the interest rate. In the following, each question is independent of the previous one.

a. Draw the graph of the loanable funds market and find the equilibrium interest rate.
b. Suppose that the government conducts a balanced-budget increase in spending of 1,000 units ($\Delta G = 1{,}000$), and assume that the marginal propensity to consume is MPC = 0.80. Analyze the effect of this policy in the graph. Discuss the crowding out effect.
c. What will happen in this market if household saving increases by 200 units?
d. What will happen in this market if investment spending increases by 200 units?
e. What will happen if the government budget deficit increases to 400 units? Discuss the crowding out effect.
f. What will happen if the government budget deficit is reduced to zero?

r	S	I	G + TR – TX
12%	1,200	800	200
11%	1,100	800	200
10%	1,000	800	200
9%	900	800	200
8%	800	800	200

Question 7

Under which of the following two scenarios do you think the future generations will suffer more from a government deficit spending:

a. Saving is insensitive to interest rate changes,
b. Investment is insensitive to interest rate changes.

Question 8

Consider the following table that shows saving, investment, and the budget deficit in a country. Suppose that the government balances its budget. What will be the effect of this event on the equilibrium interest rate, saving, and investment?

r	S	I	G + TR - TX
12%	1,200	600	200
11%	1,100	700	200
10%	1,000	800	200
9%	900	900	200

Question 9

Consider the following table that shows saving, investment in a country. Currently, the government is running a budget deficit of 150 units. In the following, each question is independent of the previous one.

r	S	I
12%	600	150
11%	550	250
10%	500	350
9%	450	450
8%	400	550

a. Draw the graph of the loanable funds market and find the equilibrium interest rate.

b. Suppose that the government conducts a balanced-budget increase in spending, and as a result saving is reduced by 300 units. What will be the effect of this on the equilibrium interest rate, saving, and investment?

c. What will happen in this market if household saving increases by 300 units?

d. What will happen in this market if investment spending increases by 150 units?

e. What will happen if the government budget deficit increases by 150 units? Discuss the crowding out effect.

f. What will happen if the government budget deficit is reduced to zero?

CHAPTER 11

Labor Market and the Classical Model

INTRODUCTION AND REVIEW

MACROECONOMICS STUDIES THREE broad economic issues: long-run economic growth; unemployment; and inflation. Economic growth is the increase in the real GDP over a long period of time, say a decade or more. Unemployment exists whenever the economy produces an amount of output that falls short of potential GDP. Inflation is the increase in the general level of prices over several time periods. The first two issues relate to the level of real GDP, and the third to the price level. This is why it is important to understand the changes in the real GDP. We will deal with the question of long-term economic growth later in the book. For now, we concentrate on the other two issues: inflation and unemployment.

In this chapter, we will discuss the production side of the economy. In previous chapters, we have learned that the real GDP equals the total amount of goods and services produced in the economy, but we have not discussed how firms decide on the level of production. Firms are in business to make money. That money in economics is called profit, and it is the excess of sales revenue over production cost. Cost of production is the total amount of money a firm pays for its factors of production, which include land, labor, and capital. The prices of these factors are determined in the *factor markets*. A firm's objective is to maximize profits. Therefore, we need to understand how a firm decides how much of each factor to hire in order to maximize its profits. Since labor cost is a very large portion of production costs for most firms—and since our primary interest at this point is analyzing employment issues—we will solely concentrate on the labor market.

FACTOR MARKETS
The market, such as the labor market, in which firms demand production factors, and households supply these resources to the firms.

DEMAND FOR LABOR BY FIRMS

Firms want to hire an amount of labor that will maximize their profits. That amount depends on the relationship between the wages they pay their workers (the cost side), the price of the output

NOMINAL WAGE
Or money wage; the dollar amount workers receive from business firms per unit of time such as an hour or a year. See also real wage.

they are producing (the revenue side), and the productivity of labor. Let L denote the amount of labor hired, and W the nominal wage rate per worker. The *nominal wage* is the dollar amount workers receive from business firms. Then the aggregate level of profits over a period of time equals:

$$\text{Profit} = P \times Y - W \times L \times \text{Other Costs}$$

where P is the price and Y is the level of output produced. At the macro level, you can think of (P × Y) as the nominal GDP and (W × L) as the total nominal amount of wage income received by workers. Other costs include items like rent, interest, and payments for parts and components. Assume that these other costs do not change.

The unit of labor is the person-hour. If I tell you that a firm hires 50 workers, you won't be able to tell how much labor it uses. If each worker works 10 hours per day, the amount of labor in the firm will be 500 person-hours. If each worker works 8 hours a day, the amount of labor will be 400 person-hours per day. To make the story more intuitive, we will assume that every laborer works the same number of hours. In that case, we can use the number of people as the unit of labor.

Consider the following simple hypothetical example. Suppose you are producing backpacks in Los Angeles. If you hire your first worker, that worker will produce 6 backpacks per day. If you hire a second worker, the two workers together will produce 11 backpacks per day. Note that two workers can produce less than twice what the first worker produced, so that hiring the second worker adds 5 backpacks to your daily production. The additional production amount made possible by the next worker hired is called the *marginal product of labor (MPL)*. Similarly, if you hire a third worker, your total production will increase to 15 backpacks per day. So the marginal product of the third worker is 4 backpacks. (See Table 1.)

MARGINAL PRODUCT OF LABOR (MPL)
The additional production amount made possible by the next unit of labor hired.

We generally assume that the marginal product of labor declines as the firm hires additional labor. This is called the law of diminishing marginal product of labor, or the *law of diminishing returns* for short. The reason for this assumption is that as the firm hires more and more labor, the additional workers will use a smaller share of the plant, equipment, and office space. Therefore, the contribution of additional workers to production diminishes as the firm hires more labor.

LAW OF DIMINISHING RETURNS
The idea that, given a fixed amount of capital, the marginal product of labor declines as the firm hires additional labor.

Table 1

Labor L	Total Product of Labor	Marginal Product of Labor MPL	Value of Marginal Product P×MPL	Nominal Wage W	Real Wage W/P
1	6	6	$600	$300	3
2	11	5	$500	$300	3
3	15	4	$400	$300	3
4	18	3	$300	$300	3
5	20	2	$200	$300	3
6	21	1	$100	$300	3

Suppose the price of backpacks in the market is $100 per unit. In that case, the first worker hired will bring a revenue of $100 × 6 = $600 to the firm. Similarly, hiring the second worker will increase revenue by $100 × 5 = $500, and so on. The quantity P × MPL is called the *value of marginal product (VMP)* of labor. These values for our hypothetical firm are shown in the fourth column of Table 1.

VALUE OF MARGINAL PRODUCT (VMP)
The market value of the output produced by the next (marginal) unit of labor. It is calculated as the price of output (P) times the marginal product of labor (MPL): VMP = P × MPL.

How many workers you hire depends on the nominal wage rate. Suppose the wage rate per person per day is $300. Then you will hire 4 workers. You will hire the first worker, since she will bring in $600 of revenue but will only cost $300 to hire, increasing your profit by $300. Similarly, you will hire the second worker, because he will increase your profit by $200. Continuing this way, you will hire the fourth worker, but not the fifth one. In other words, you will hire up to the point where

$$P \times MPL = W$$

You hire the next worker if that worker adds to your profit, and stop hiring workers when hiring an additional worker would reduce your profit. Hence, the above rule will maximize your profit from hiring labor. In the real world, you may stop at the fourth worker, since the fifth worker does not add anything to your profits. In this book, we will assume that you will hire the fifth worker. This will provide a more definitive theory and a more elegant graphical presentation. This assumption will not affect any of our conclusions.

There is another equivalent way of saying the same thing. Dividing the above equation by P, we get

$$MPL = W/P$$

The right-hand side is the *real wage*. Like any other real thing, it is the nominal wage divided by the price level and is in terms of quantities of goods. In the above example, you are paying a real wage of $300/$100 = 3 units to your workers. What does this mean? With the nominal wage you are paying and the price of your backpacks, each of your workers can buy 3 backpacks per day. In a sense, you are paying a real wage of 3 backpacks to each of your workers per day. Now look at Table 1 and Figure 1. The first worker produces 6 backpacks, but receives only 3 backpacks in real wage. Therefore, you will hire her. Continuing with this reasoning, you will hire 4 workers. You see that the MPL schedule is nothing but the demand for labor function by an individual firm. If you know the real wage, you can determine the amount of labor the firm will hire using this schedule.

REAL WAGE
The purchasing power of nominal wage calculated by dividing the nominal wag by the price level.

Now we need a simple way of moving from a single firm to the economy as a whole. Assume that there are 100 identical firms in the economy, each facing the same MPL schedule as in Figure 1. Adding these individual firms' MPL curves horizontally, we get the aggregate demand for labor function shown in Figure 2. Therefore, if the real wage is 3, each firm will hire 4 workers and the economy as a whole will hire 4 × 100 = 400 workers. Note that the demand for labor depends only on the ratio of W to P. For example, if the nominal wage increases to $600 and the price of output increases to $200, the real wage will still be 3, and the firms will hire the same 400 workers. If the nominal wage increases to $400 while the price level increases to $200, the real wage will go down to 2, and firms will hire 500 workers.

Figure 1 Demand for Labor by a Firm

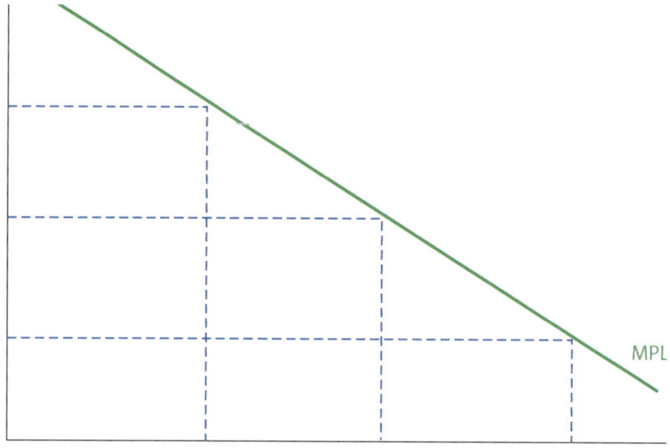

Figure 2 Aggregate Demand for Labor

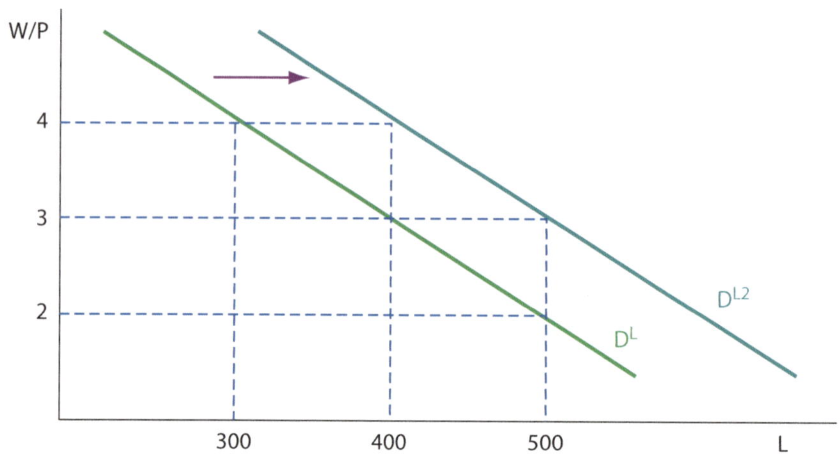

Two events could cause firms to demand more labor at the existing real wage. Both events result in an increase in labor productivity (MPL), making labor more desirable for the firms. These events are

1. An increase in the amount of capital available. If we have more trucks, tractors, and assembly lines, each laborer gets to work with a larger amount of capital. Thus, labor productivity increases.
2. Technological progress. As you recall, technological progress means learning ways of producing new goods, or better ways of producing the old goods. Technological progress generally improves workers' productivity, making them more attractive to firms.

These events could happen only over a long period of time. There might also be some factors that could increase or decrease the demand for labor in the short run. We will talk about them later. For the time being, note that the above factors would cause a shift in the curve to the right, so that firms would want to hire more workers at any level of real wage. Suppose that initially, the demand for labor was D_L. Now, for whatever reason, producers want to hire more labor at any given real wage. If before they wanted to hire 300 workers at the real wage of 4, now they want to hire 400.

If before they wanted to hire 400 workers at the real wage of 3, they now want to hire 500. So the whole curve shifts to the right.

SUPPLY OF LABOR BY HOUSEHOLDS

Households supply their labor services to firms in return for the wages they receive from them, which constitute their incomes. By the supply of labor, we mean how much of their services households are willing and able to supply to the firms. *Supply of labor is the same as the labor force.*

In principle, the supply of labor would also depend on the real wage. Who cares how many *dollars* you receive from your company; what matters is the amount of *goods and services* you could buy with those dollars. For example, suppose that the nominal wage is $200 per day and the price level is $100, so that the real wage is $200/$100 = 2 units. At this real wage you'd like to work only four days a week. If the nominal wage increases to W = $2,000 and the price level jumps to P = $1,000, you will still want to work four days a week, because the real wage has not changed.

Will the supply of labor increase or decrease with the real wage? It could go either way. Would you like to work more or less if the real wage increased? If the real wage increased, the opportunity cost of leisure would increase. You would lose a lot of goods and services that you could buy if you did not stay in bed Saturday morning and instead worked somewhere. As a result, you would be inclined to work more at a higher real wage. Therefore, an increase in the real wage would increase the supply of labor. This is called the *substitution effect*—you would substitute labor for leisure. By leisure, economists mean non–work-related activities.

SUBSTITUTION EFFECT
When real wage decreases, workers substitute leisure for labor, so that the quantity of labor supplied decreases. The substitution effect results in a positive relationship between the real wage and the quantity of labor supplied.

On the other hand, if the real wage increased, your real income would be higher. If you needed to work six days a week with the lower real wage to make ends meet, now with the higher real wage, you need only work five days a week. As a result, you would reduce your supply of labor. This is called the *income effect*.

INCOME EFFECT
When the wage rate increases, the worker may decide to supply less labor, because now she can earn the same income as before by working fewer hours.

Economists seem to agree that the income effect dominates for permanent changes in the real wage and the substitution effect for transitory changes. Here is the logic. Suppose you are making $100,000 per year and the price level is $100, so that your real annual wage is 1,000 units. You expect that both your income and the price level will rise at 5% per year so that your real wage will remain unchanged. So your *permanent* real wage is 1,000 units. At this real wage, you plan to buy your dream home, a couple of cars, certain appliances, and take a number of annual vacations. Now if you unexpectedly receive a raise and your permanent real wage jumps to 1,200, you can achieve the same long-term consumption goal by working less. On the other hand, what if you receive an unexpected and permanent wage reduction? This is what a lot of employees experienced during the 2007–2008 recession. Then you will work harder, perhaps looking for a second job, to be able to maintain your long-term consumption plan.

Suppose now your permanent real wage is the same, but your company is offering a higher wage to any worker who is willing to work over weekends for the next three months. You will take advantage of this short-term offer to make more money now so that you can relax or take more vacation later, and still meet your long-term consumption goal. By the same token, suppose your company gives its employees a temporary wage cut due to hard financial conditions. In that case, you might think that the pay is too lousy to work such long hours. You will take some leisure now, knowing that you can still work longer hours later at your permanent wage and make up for the lost income. Since we will mostly talk about recessions and expansions—short-run phenomena—we will assume that the substitution effect dominates. So the supply of labor is upward sloping.

These employees have opted to work weekends now to earn extra money. They may later choose to take a restful vacation. (McWay Falls, Big Sur, Caifornia pictured at right)

Figure 3 shows such a relationship. The figure shows that households care about the real wage. If the real wage is 3 units, 400 workers would be willing to supply their services to the labor market. If the real wage increased to 4 units, the number of workers willing to work would increase to 500. If it decreased to 2 units, only 300 workers would be willing to work.

The supply of labor curve shifts to the right if more labor is offered to firms at any real wage. The most important reasons for this are increases in the size of population and in the *labor force participation rate*. The latter is defined as the fraction of the population who are willing to work

LABOR FORCE PARTICIPATION RATE
The fraction of the population that is willing to work, calculated as the ratio of the labor force over population.

Labor Force Participation Rate = Labor Force/Population

Cross-multiplying, we get

Labor Force = (Labor Force Participation Rate) × (Population)

Then for any given participation rate, the larger the size of the population, the larger the labor force will be. Population can increase either through birth or migration. Moreover, if for any given population size a larger share of that population decides to work, then the supply of labor will increase. For example, the increase in the participation rate of women in the labor force in the United States in the last century has increased the labor supply for any given population size. Figure 3 shows how the supply of labor (S^L) shifts to the right (to S^{L2}), as a result of a larger labor force.

Note that these events take a long time to happen—the population of a country cannot change overnight. The participation of women in the work force has also gradually increased, as a result of change in social and cultural norms after both World Wars. As many men were recruited to go overseas with their positions in the workforce vacant, the resulting labor shortage left a responsibility for women to carry out many of the contemporary tasks previously held only by men. Consequently, society's view of gender and its role in labor has dramatically changed. Finally, the invention of many labor-saving home appliances drastically reduced the amount of time women spent at home in household drudgery. Once freed from running the households, women began to run the corporations.

Figure 3 Aggregate Supply of Labor

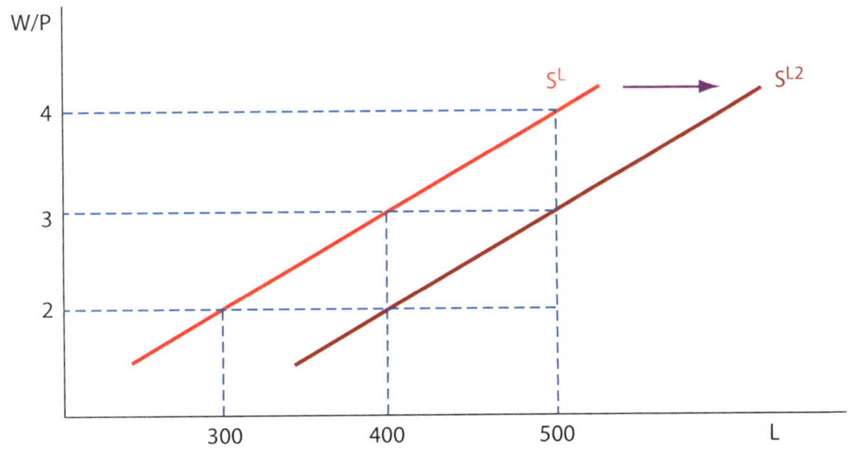

LABOR MARKET EQUILIBRIUM AND POTENTIAL GDP

The labor market will be in equilibrium if the demand for labor equals the supply of labor. All we need to do is put the two previous curves together. Figure 4 does just that. Equilibrium in this figure occurs at point E, when the real wage is W/P = 3. If the nominal wage rate is $300 and the price level is $100, the real wage will be 3 units and firms will want to hire 400 workers, just equal to the number of people who are willing to work.

$$D^L = S^L \quad \text{Labor Market Equilibrium}$$

The demand for labor by firms is nothing but the total number of filled and unfilled jobs in the economy. As mentioned above, the supply of labor is the same as the labor force—the number of people who are willing and able to work. Therefore, the labor market equilibrium is nothing but our good old friend full employment. You also recall that when the labor market is in equilibrium, only natural unemployment will exist.

What if, for whatever reason, the price level went down to $75, pushing up the real wage to 4 units? At this higher real wage, firms would demand only 300 workers but households would supply 500. We would have an excess supply of labor of 200 workers. Now there are not enough jobs for everyone who is willing to work—we have unemployment. Would the situation persist? The outcome would depend on our assumptions about the behavior of nominal wages.

A group of economists called the *classical economists* assume that wages and prices are fully flexible, both upward and downward. If you look at the published wage and price data, you will notice that they are quite variable. So why do we need to *assume* that they are flexible? The answer is that "variable" is not the same as "flexible." Economists define wage and price flexibility as follows:

CLASSICAL ECONOMISTS
The economists who wrote before John Maynard Keynes, and the present day economists who make similar assumptions and reach similar conclusions.

Wages and prices are said to be flexible if they change fast enough and in sufficient magnitude to instantly restore equilibrium in the labor market.

Figure 4 Labor Market Equilibrium

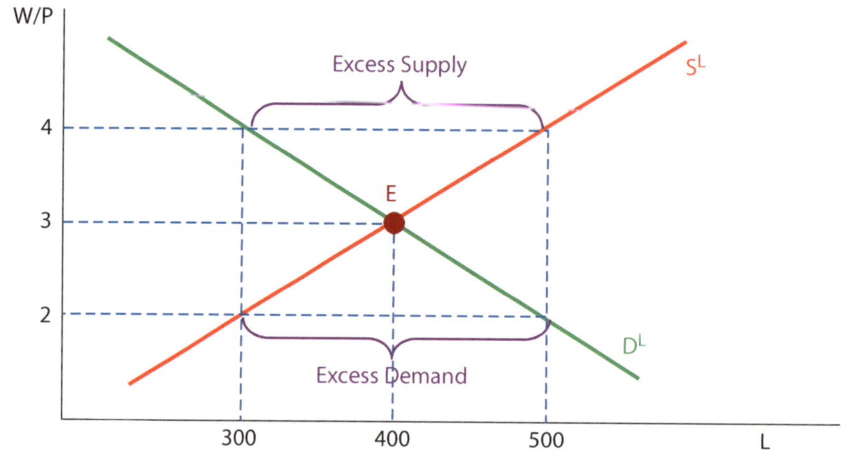

In our case, the 200 unemployed people would compete against each other to get the scarce existing jobs. They would accept lower wages, and as a result, the nominal wage would drop to \$225, resulting in a real wage of 3. The labor market will clear again.[1]

The opposite would happen if the price level went up to P = \$150. The real wage would decrease to 2 units, and we would have an excess demand for labor of 200 workers. Firms would compete against each other to hire the existing scarce workers. They would offer higher wages, pushing the nominal wage up to \$450 and the real wage to 3 units so that the labor market would clear again.

In the *classical model* of the labor market, all these adjustments take place instantly, so the labor market is always in equilibrium. The economy never leaves the intersection point of the two curves. This basically means that in the classical model, due to the assumption of wage and price flexibility, we never have unemployment. This is something worth emphasizing:

> *In the classical model, nominal wages and prices are fully flexible, so we always have full employment.*

This is also true of the other factors of production, land and capital.

CLASSICAL AGGREGATE SUPPLY FUNCTION

CLASSICAL AGGREGATE SUPPLY FUNCTION
The function that gives the combinations of price level and real GDP that clear the labor market.

From here it is a short step to derive what is called the *classical aggregate supply function* for goods and services. This is the function that gives the combinations of price level and real GDP that clear the labor market. All you need to realize is that since nominal wages are fully flexible in this model, the labor market will always clear, and there will be no unemployment in the economy. Moreover, since the demand-for-labor and supply-of-labor functions do not change in the short run due to reasons mentioned above, both the level of employment and the real wage are fixed. In Figure 3, the level of employment is 400 workers, and the real wage is 3 units.

In the real world, neither prices nor nominal wages stay put for long. In practice, they both rise over time. However, if the real wage is fixed, then they should both rise at the same rate. For

1 As you know, often economists use the term "clearing" for "equilibrium," probably because it is easier to pronounce! So in this terminology, the phrase "the market clears" would mean "the market reaches equilibrium."

example, suppose that currently the nominal wage is W = \$300 and the price level is P = \$100, so that the real wage is \$300/\$100 = 3. What if the price level increases by 20% to P = \$120? Then the real wage will go down to \$300/\$120 = 2.5, and there will be an excess demand for labor. Because of the assumption of nominal wage flexibility, the nominal wage will immediately increase by 20% to W = \$360, so that the real wage will go back to \$360/\$120 = 3, and the excess demand will be eliminated. Similarly, if the price level decreases by 20% to P = \$80, then the nominal wage will also decrease by 20% to W = \$240, so that the real wage will remain at 3.

You see that in this model, prices and nominal wages increase at the same rate so that the real wage remains unchanged at its equilibrium level and the labor market always clears. We call the rate of increase in prices *inflation*. So in this model, the nominal wage always increases at the rate of inflation, and the labor force is fully employed. Now the fully employed labor force produces a level of output that is called potential GDP, denoted Y_P. In the above example, we will have full employment if there are 400 jobs in the economy, all taken by 400 workers. Suppose that these workers can produce 10,000 units of output. Then our potential GDP will equal Y_P = 10,000.

In the classical model, we will always produce the potential level of GDP, regardless of the price level.

Deriving the classical aggregate supply function is quite easy. Suppose the price level is P = \$100. We know that since the real wage is fixed at 3 units, the nominal wage must be W = \$300. There are 400 workers employed in the economy, producing Y_P = 10,000 units of output. This combination of price level and potential GDP is shown as point A in Figure 5. If the price level was P = \$120 instead, then the nominal wage would be W = \$360 to keep the real wage fixed at 3 units. At this real wage, 400 workers would be employed, producing Y_P = 10,000 units. This would give us point B in Figure 5. Connecting all such points, we get the classical aggregate supply function (AS).

Figure 5 Classical Aggregate Supply Function

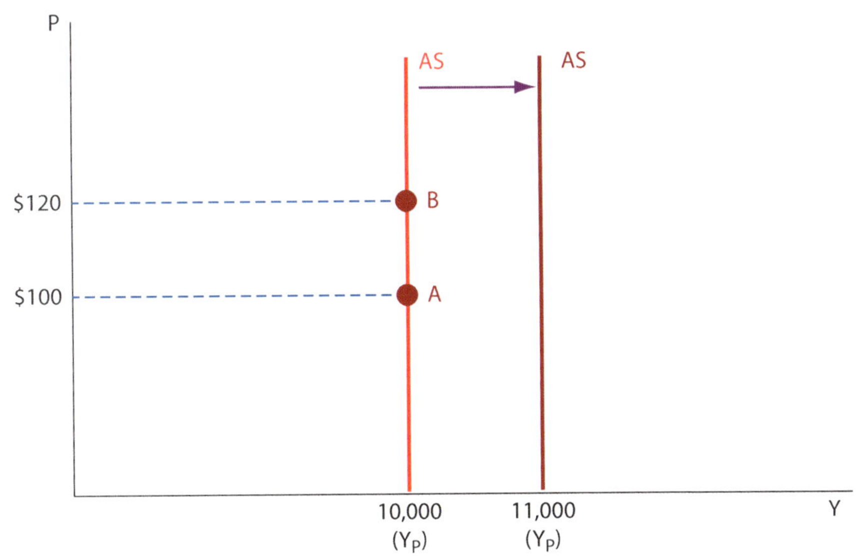

We already know all the features of this supply function:

1. The classical aggregate supply function gives all the combinations of price level and real GDP that clear the labor market.
2. The classical aggregate supply function is vertical at the level of potential GDP, due to the assumption of nominal wage and price flexibility.
3. In the classical model, the economy will always be on the aggregate supply function.
4. At any point on the classical aggregate supply function, the rate of inflation equals the rate of increase in nominal wages.

SHIFTS IN THE CLASSICAL AGGREGATE SUPPLY FUNCTION

Two factors would shift the classical aggregate supply (AS) function to the right: an increase in the supply of labor and an increase in demand for labor. If the supply of labor increases, either due to an increase in population or an increase in the labor force participation rate, there will be more productive people in the society, increasing the total amount of production. This will cause a rightward shift in the supply-of-labor function in Figure 4 (shift the function as an exercise). In that figure, an increase in the supply of labor brings down the real wage and increases employment. Note that, due to nominal wage flexibility, we still do not have any unemployment. Because of the increase in the number of people employed, the potential GDP will increase.

With the given supply of labor, an increase in the demand for labor would cause the D^L function to shift to the right in Figure 4 (shift this curve as an exercise). Both the real wage and the total employment will increase. As mentioned above, the increase in demand for labor is usually the result of an increase in the amount of capital or improvements in technology. All these events would increase the productivity of labor, so not only would more people be employed, but the employed workers would be able to produce more due to the increase in productivity.

In both cases, since the number of workers employed increases, the potential GDP also increases. This results in a rightward shift in the aggregate supply function as shown in Figure 5.

THE GENERAL PRICE LEVEL

For the first time, we are ready to figure out how the general price level is determined. Recall from Chapter 9 that classical economists believe that the only reason people hold money is to buy goods and services. Therefore, demand for money bears a constant relationship to nominal GDP:

$$M^d = k \times P \times Y$$

In equilibrium, demand for money will equal supply of money, M, so that:

$$M = k \times P \times Y$$

Recall also that the classical economists assume that the Cambridge k is constant. We now learn they also believe that the real GDP is constant and equal to potential GDP. Solving the above equation for P and replacing Y with Y_p, we get:

$$P = M/(k \times Y_p)$$

Given that k and Y_p are constant, the price level is solely determined by the level of money supply. Suppose, for example, that k = 0.10 and M = \$100,000, and Y_p = 10,000. Then:

$$P = 100{,}000/(0.10 \times 10{,}000) = 100$$

The price-output combination is shown in Figure 6 as point E.

Figure 6 The Classical Model of P and Y

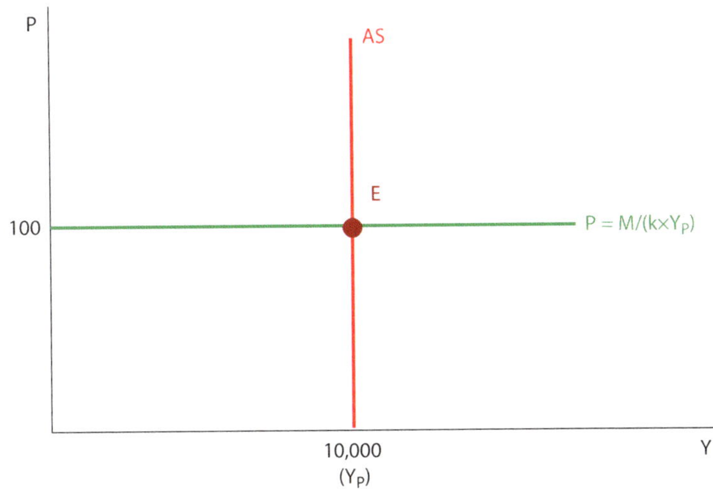

We are now ready to ask you-know-what-kinds of questions. What are the effects of monetary and fiscal policies in the classical world? After learning the above arguments, you will find the answers to these questions pretty straightforward.

MONETARY POLICY AND INFLATION

What happens if M increases by, say 10% through an open market purchase of bonds? The answer to this question should be eminently clear from the discussion and formula above. Since people hold money only to buy goods and services, if money supply increases by 10%, they will just spend the additional amount of money. Households and firms will borrow from the banks, through the multiple deposit creation process, and buy equipment, homes, and consumer durables. But since the real GDP is fixed at the potential level, this increased demand for goods and services will only push up prices. By how much will the general price level increase?

In the price equation above, increase the money supply by 10% to get:

$$P = 110{,}000/(0.10 \times 10{,}000) = 110$$

So the price level will increase by 10%. (See Figure 7.) What will happen to the nominal wage? Well, since the real wage is constant, the nominal wage will also increase by 10%. We say that in the classical model *money is neutral*: it only affects the nominal variables, but not the real variables. By injecting more papers with pictures on them into the banking system, you cannot increase production and employment. You just create inflation.

MONEY IS NEUTRAL
The idea that changes in the level of money supply will not affect the real variables such as real GDP or employment.

Figure 7 An Expansionary Monetary Policy

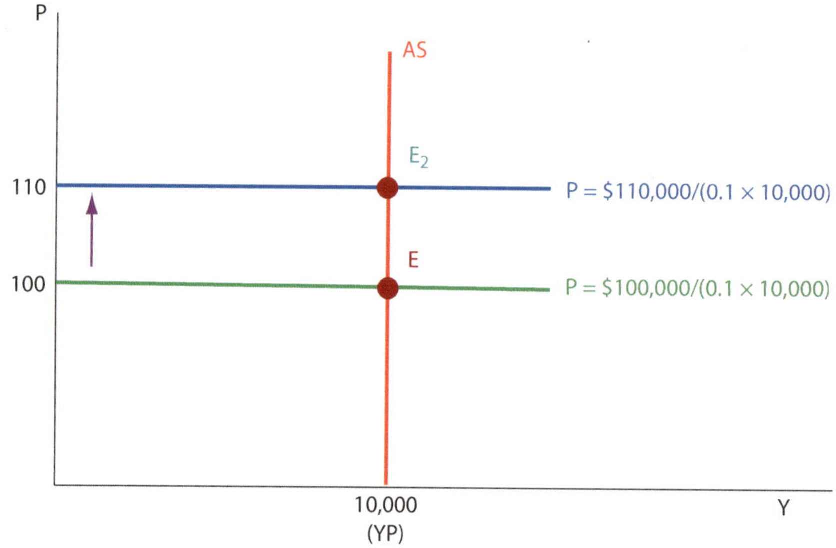

FISCAL POLICY AND CROWDING OUT

We saw in Chapter 10 that the classical model fiscal policy, if not financed by printing money, is totally ineffective in changing the level of aggregate demand and real GDP. For example, an increase in government spending financed through raising taxes or borrowing will crowd out private spending dollar for dollar. Interestingly enough, this conclusion does not depend on whether the economy is in a recession or not. Whenever the government raises taxes or borrows to finance its spending, it deprives the private sector of financial resources. Thus, consumption and investment decreases dollar for dollar. As you recall, this is called *financial crowding out.*

In fact, in the classical model there is no recession! Nevertheless, we now have a new case for complete crowding out. If the real resources of the economy (land, labor, and capital) are fully employed and utilized, an increase in government spending will crowd out private spending, because national production cannot increase. So if the government buys more, the private sector will get to buy less. To see this, recall the goods market equilibrium condition, and replace the real GDP with the potential GDP:

$$Y_P = C + I + G$$

REAL CROWDING OUT
Reduction in private spending, as a result of an increase in resource prices that is due to an increase in government budget deficit.

Since the left-hand side is constant, an increase in G must reduce (C + I) by the same amount. Crowding out caused by the full employment of real resources is called *real crowding out*.

How about monetizing the debt? Monetizing the debt is a combination of fiscal and monetary policies. Suppose the government prints money to buy some military equipment for the army. The purchase of the military equipment will cause a real crowding out of private spending due to the full employment of resources. Printing money, meanwhile, will cause inflation.

SUMMARY OF THE CLASSICAL MODEL

We now have the complete classical model summarized as follows:

1. Wages and prices are fully flexible so that the labor market is continuously in equilibrium. The economy always produces the potential level of GDP, and there are no recessions.
2. The velocity of circulation—and hence the Cambridge k—is constant.
3. Because of the previous two assumptions, money is neutral and inflation is a monetary phenomenon. An increase in money supply will push up prices and nominal wages proportionately, leaving the real variables such as the real GDP and employment unchanged.
4. Fiscal policy is totally ineffective in changing the level of aggregate demand and real GDP. An expansionary fiscal policy will completely crowd out private spending.

We have come a long way. We finally seem to have answered all the questions about determination of the GDP and price levels. If wages and prices are fully flexible, then the labor market will always clear, and we will produce an amount of output that will generate enough jobs for everyone in the labor force. This output level will also maximize the profits of the firms. We will produce the potential level of GDP, no more and no less. We will never have unemployment. The aggregate demand side will only cause changes in the price level, not in the amount of output produced. Government spending will only displace private spending, and monetary policy will only cause inflation.

THE CLASSICAL MODEL IN THE LONG RUN

Is the classical model a realistic description of the real-world economies? Given that capitalist economies go through cycles of recessions and expansions, why would anybody believe in a model that continuously produces the potential level of GDP? The answer is, even though the classical model may not work in the short run, it describes the long-run tendencies of free-market capitalist systems reasonably well. We present two pieces of empirical evidence; one of them you have already seen before.

GDP in the Long Run

Revisit Figure 2 of Chapter 6. That figure showed that the U.S. real GDP traces the potential GDP quite well in the long run. In other words, in the long run, the U.S. economy has been on the AS function in Figure 6. That is why this function is called the *long-run classical aggregate supply function*. Therefore, in the long run, wages and prices must be sufficiently flexible for us to get this result.

LONG-RUN CLASSICAL AGGREGATE SUPPLY FUNCTION
A vertical line that indicates that with wage and price flexibility an economy would produce the ***potential GDP*** *regardless of the level of the prices. In other words, along this function the labor market would be in equilibrium.*

Inflation Rate in the Long run

How about the conclusion that inflation is a monetary phenomenon? Many economists believe that this result also holds in the long run. However, the name most closely associated with this proposition is Milton Friedman, a University of Chicago non-Keynesian economist, who won a Nobel Prize partly for his work on monetary economics.

Figure 8 shows the quarterly U.S. inflation and money supply growth rates for the period 1959 through 2005. The inflation rates have been calculated using the GDP deflator series. The money supply growth rates are the quarterly growth rates of the M2 money supply.[2] It appears that there had been a positive relationship between the two series up until the 1990s. The rate of growth of the M2 money stock and the inflation rate moved in the same direction until around 1990. After 1990, though, the relationship seems to have broken down somewhat. Note finally that the money growth rates have almost always been greater than the inflation rates. I will also explain this phenomenon shortly.

Figure 8 The U.S. Quarterly Inflation and M2 Money Growth Rates

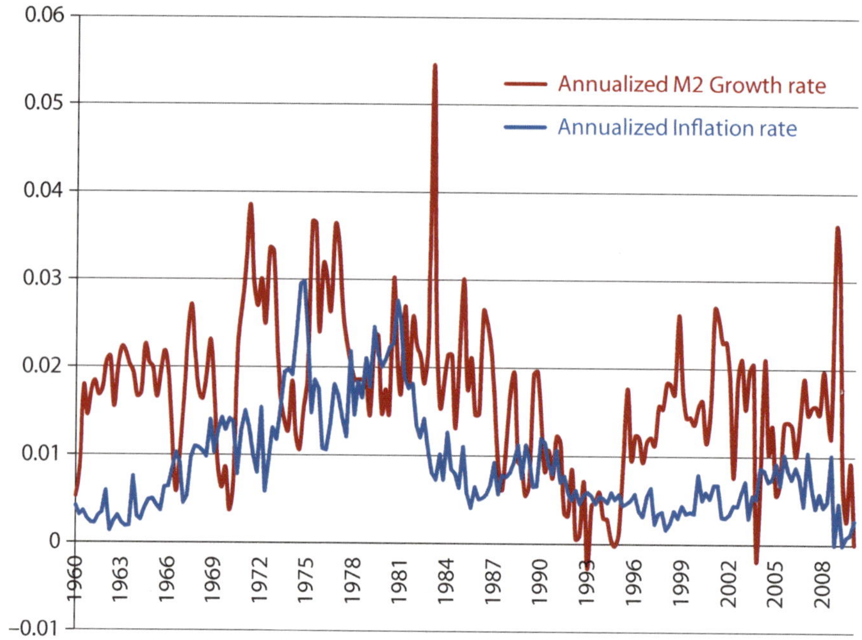

Since so many random shocks hit the economy from one quarter to the next, we should examine the *averages* of money growth and inflation rates to have a better picture of the long-run relationship between these two variables. This is because, by taking averages, positive and negative random shocks cancel, and we get a purer picture of the long-run relationship. Figures 9a and 9b show the 5-year and 10-year averages of growth rates of money supply and inflation rates over the last fifty years.

These figures clearly point to a positive relationship between the rate of growth of money supply and the inflation rate. The 10-year figure shows even a sharper picture. In any decade in which the money growth rate was higher, we had a higher inflation rate. Consistent with the pattern we saw in Figure 8, these figures also show that this tight relationship has been weakened somewhat after 1990. You are probably thinking that the observed positive relationship does not constitute equality. Again, consistent with Figure 8, we see that in all decades, the money growth rates have exceeded the inflation rates. We need to resolve this last puzzle.

2 All the data used in this chapter have been obtained from the FRED database of the St. Louis Federal Reserve Bank. The result for M1 was less tight. As an exercise, you can construct the graphs for M1 by visiting FRED's website of the St. Louis Federal Reserve Bank.

Figure 9a The U.S. Inflation and Money Growth Rates: Five-Year Averages

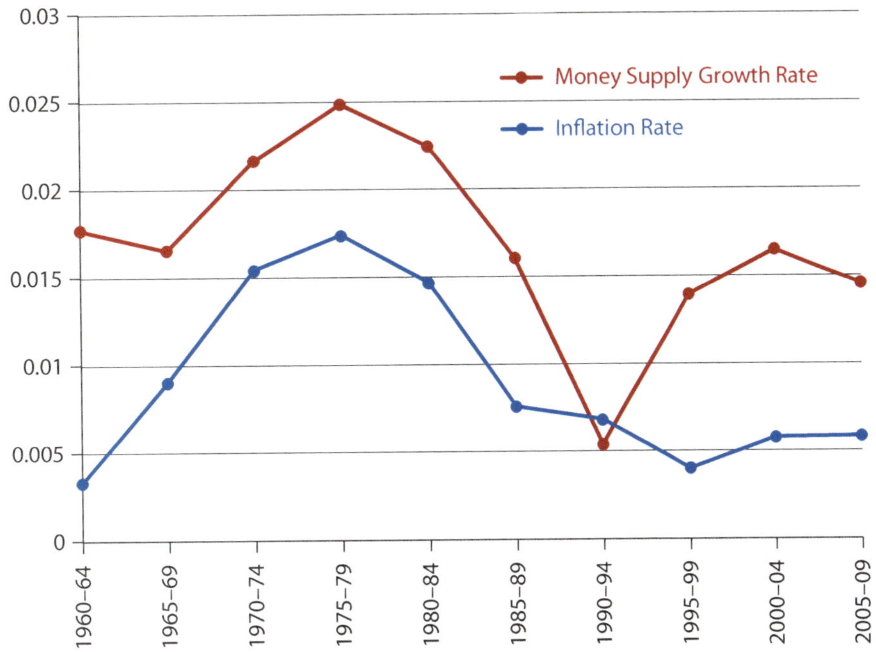

We know that the inflation rate will equal the rate of growth of money supply if the Cambridge k and real GDP are constant. Consider again the money market equilibrium condition in the classical model:

$$M = k \times P \times Y$$

It is easy to verify that, for small percentage changes, this equilibrium condition implies that the rate of change of the left-hand side equals the sum of the rates of changes of the variables on the right-hand side:[3]

$$\frac{\Delta M}{M} = \frac{\Delta k}{k} + \frac{\Delta P}{P} + \frac{\Delta Y}{Y}$$

Solving this equation for the percentage change in the price level we get:

$$\frac{\Delta P}{P} = \frac{\Delta M}{M} - \frac{\Delta k}{k} - \frac{\Delta Y}{Y}$$

Thus in the real world, we should never expect the inflation rate to equal the money growth rate exactly. However, if k is more or less stable in the long run, its rate of change will be small and the inflation rate will *approximately* equal the money growth rate, minus the growth rate of real GDP:

$$\frac{\Delta P}{P} = \frac{\Delta M}{M} - \frac{\Delta Y}{Y}$$

3 *Recall again that ΔM means the change in M and so ΔM/M is the rate of change of M. Realize also that ΔP/P is nothing but the inflation rate p and ΔM/M is the money supply growth rate.*

Figures 10a and 10b show the inflation rates and the differences between the money supply and GDP growth rates. In other words, they show the two sides of the above equation. We see that the two series move together very closely.

Figure 9b The U.S. Inflation and Money Growth Rates: Ten-Year Averages

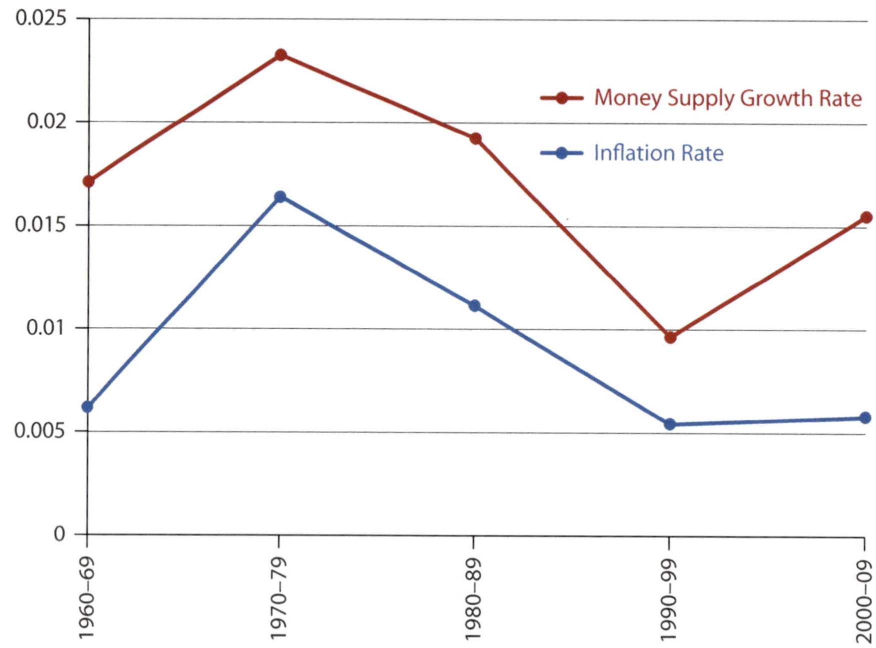

Figures 10a and 10b perform two tricks at once. First, they solve the puzzle above: namely, why the inflation rates were less than the money supply growth rates. The differences were the GDP growth rates. Second, since the two series now move rather closely, it must be that the rate of change of the Cambridge k is close to zero in the long run. To further verify this last hypothesis, Figure 11 shows the quarterly rates of change of the Cambridge k for the period that starts in the second quarter of 1959, and ends in the first quarter of 2009. Note that the rate of change of k does not have an upward or a downward trend. Even though it jumps around in the short run, it revolves around a constant value in the long run. That constant value is the long run mean of the series and is equal to +0.01%. Figures 9a through 10b support our hypothesis that the rate of change of k is close to zero in the long run.

Figure 10a U.S. Inflation and GDP-Adjusted Money Growth Rates: Five-Year Averages

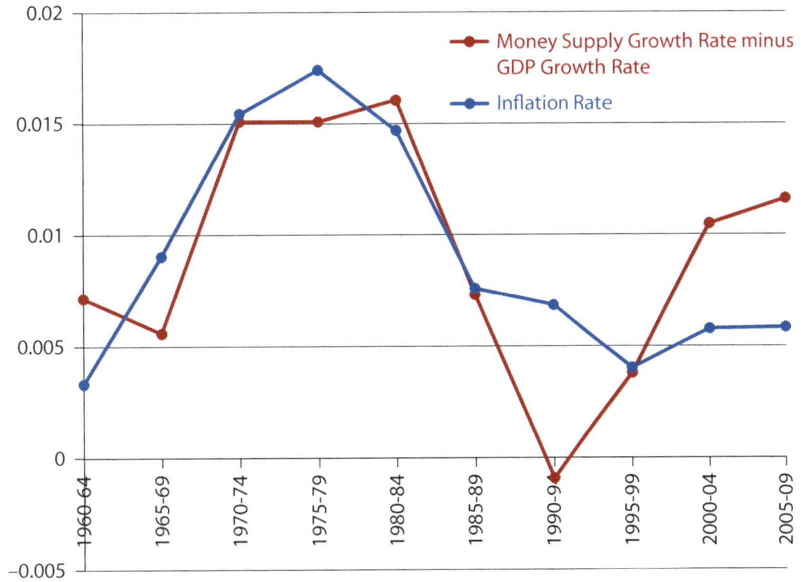

Figure 10b U.S. Inflation and GDP-Adjusted Money Growth Rates: Ten-Year Averages

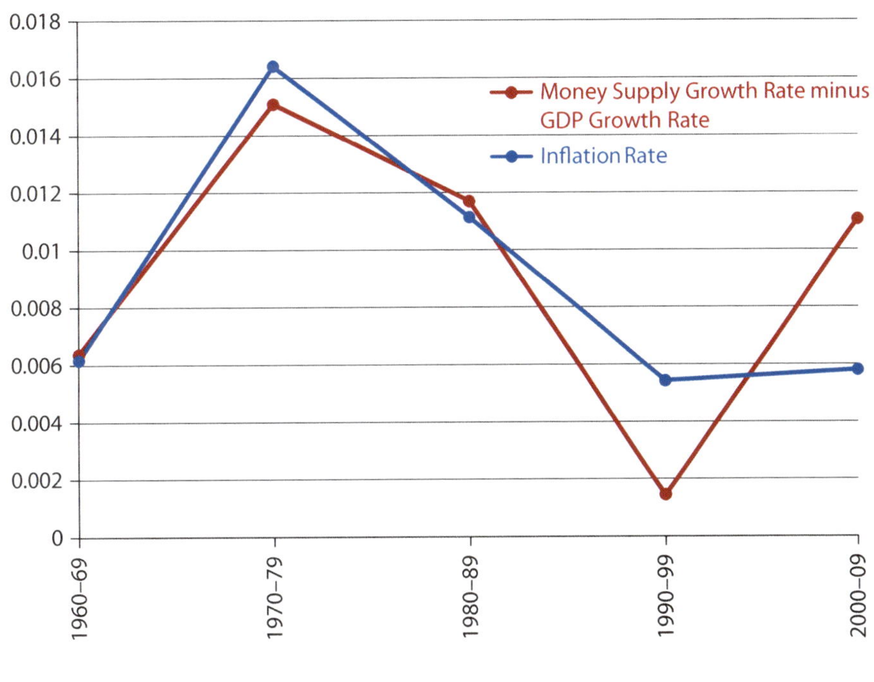

The following table presents the mean values of the quarterly growth rates of the GDP deflator, M2 money supply, the real GDP, and the GDP-adjusted money supply for the whole period 1960 through 2009.

Variable Name	Average Growth Rate (1960–2009)
M2 Growth Rate	1.69%
Real GDP Growth Rate	0.78%
GDP-Adjusted Money Supply Growth Rate	0.91%
Inflation Rate of GDP Deflator	0.90%
Rate of Change of Cambridge k	0.01%

We see that for the whole period, the average of the inflation rate (0.90%) almost equals the GDP-adjusted money supply growth rate (0.91%). The difference between these two averages is the rate of change of Cambridge k (+0.01).

We conclude that inflation is, in fact, a monetary phenomenon in the long run. The rate of inflation in the long run approximately equals the rate of growth of money supply, less the rate of increase in national output. If real GDP did not grow, the inflation rate would equal the money growth rate. In our models we assume that in the long run, the level of real GDP is constant and equal to potential GDP. This is only to make the models simple so they can help us organize our thoughts. As a final piece of empirical evidence, we should mention that countries with high money growth rates experience high inflation rates. In view of the above discussion, we will assume that in the long run, the rate of inflation equals the rate of growth of money supply.

Figure 11 Quarterly Rates of Change of Cambridge k: 1959 through 2010

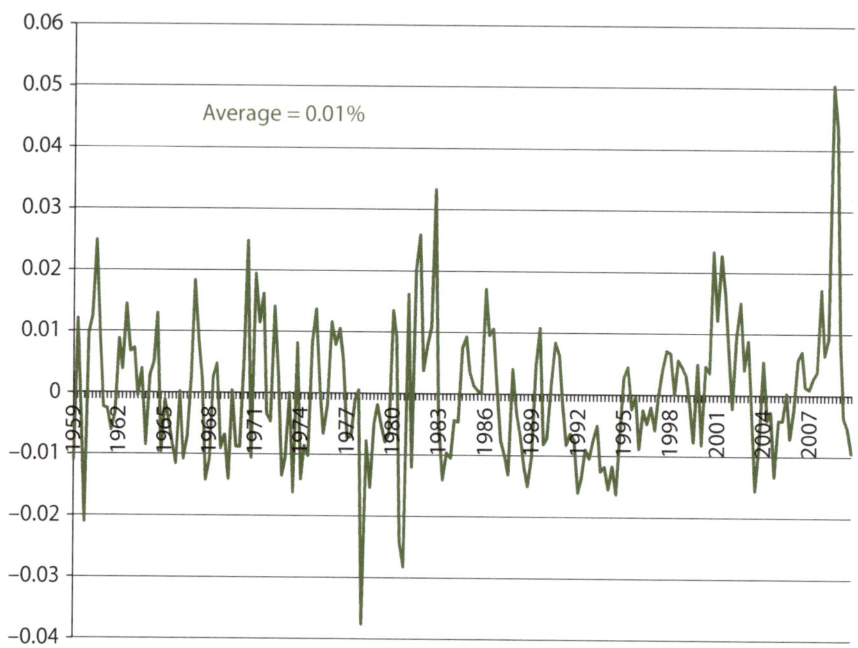

On the basis of the above discussion, we will define two "runs" as follows:

1. Short run A period of time that is too short for some wages and prices to adjust to market conditions.
2. Long run A period of time that is long enough for all wages and prices to adjust to market conditions.

So these "runs" are not measured in calendar time, such as a year or a quarter. Moreover, they may be different from one country to another and from one era to another.

The Labor Market and Unemployment Data

Even though there is no unemployment in the classical model, it is useful for future reference to relate the labor market graph to the unemployment data we have talked about all along. The demand for labor is the total number of jobs in the economy, filled and vacant. Now we know that this is not a fixed number. It depends on the real wage. In Figure 2, if the real wage were 3 units, there would be a total of 400 jobs in the economy, filled and unfilled. If the real wage increased to 4, firms would want to downsize their labor to 300, eliminate 100 jobs, and lay off 100 workers. Then only 300 jobs would exist in the economy. If the real wage were to decrease to 2, firms would create an additional 100 jobs, and the total number of jobs would increase to 500.

The supply of labor is the same as the labor force—the number of people who are willing to work. In Figure 3, when the real wage is 3, the labor force consists of 400 workers. In this case, the number of jobs equals the number of people who are willing to work. We have full employment. Does this mean that every one of those 400 workers has a job? You know that the answer is no. Some of those 400 workers will be naturally unemployed. Suppose, for example, that the natural unemployment rate is 5% of the labor force. Then 20 people will be looking for the 20 available jobs (.05 × 400 = 20).

If the wage rate jumped to 4, the number of total jobs would decrease to 300, but the labor force would increase to 500. Two types of unemployment would be created. We know that of these 300 jobs some will be vacant due to natural unemployment. If we assume that the natural rate of unemployment is 5% of the labor force, then 25 people would be unemployed, but there would be jobs available for them (0.05 × 500 = 25). This means that of the 300 jobs, 25 would be vacant, and only 275 would be filled. However, there are 200 people who are cyclically unemployed—they are willing to work but there are no jobs available for them (500 – 300). The cyclical unemployment rate would be (500 – 300)/500, or 40%. The total unemployment rate would then be 5% + 40% = 45%.[1]

Unemployed = Labor Force - Employed

Unemployed = 500 - 275 = 225 = 200 Cyclical + 25 Natural

Unemployment Rate = Unemployed/Labor Force =((200+25)/500) × 100 = 40% +5%"

If the real wage dropped to 2 units, we would have an excess demand for labor equal to 200. We would not have any cyclical unemployment, but some natural unemployment would be unavoidable. Although there would be 500 jobs out there, only 300 people would be willing to work. Therefore, the actual employment would not exceed 300—the size of the labor force. Of this, 5%, or 15 people, would be naturally unemployed. So of the 300 people who are willing to work, only 285 would have jobs.

1 *Needless to say, these percentages are only for expository purposes, and bear no relation to real-world unemployment rates.*

TO SUMMARIZE

1. We assume that the demand for and supply of labor depends on the real wage.
2. Classical economists assume that wages and prices are fully flexible upward and downward, so that we always have equilibrium in the labor market.
3. What this means is that the economy always produces the potential level of GDP and there are no recessions.
4. Since the level of real GDP is independent of the price level, the aggregate supply function in the classical model is vertical at the level of potential GDP.
5. In the classical model, *money is neutral*: it only affects the nominal variables such as prices and nominal wages, but not the real variables such as real GDP, employment, consumption, or investment.
6. In the classical model, the inflation rate is equal to the rate of change of money supply—inflation is a monetary phenomenon.
7. Since the real wage is constant, the rate of price inflation equals the rate of nominal-wage inflation.
8. Fiscal policy will crowd out private spending dollar for dollar, leaving the aggregate demand and real GDP unchanged. We have both financial and real crowding out.

EXERCISES

Question 1

Consider a country where labor is the only scarce factor of production. All the workers in this country are identical in terms of skill level and productivity. The following table shows the marginal product of labor for a typical firm:

L	MPL
1	14
2	13
3	12
4	11
5	10
6	9
7	8
8	7
9	6

There are 1,000 identical firms in the country producing an identical product. The natural unemployment rate is zero. The following table shows the supply of labor in this country:

W/P	SL
14	9,000
13	8,000
12	7,000
11	6,000
10	5,000
9	4,000
8	3,000
7	2,000
6	1,000

Graph the demand-for-labor function for a typical firm.

a. Graph the demand-for-labor and the supply-of-labor functions for the whole economy.
b. What is the equilibrium real wage?
c. At this real wage, how many people will have jobs?
d. Suppose that each worker can produce 2,000 units of output. What is the potential GDP?
e. Assume that M = $100,000,000 and k = 0.10. Find the price level and the nominal wage.
f. If the price level increases by 1%, what will happen to the nominal wage, the real wage, and the potential GDP?
g. What will happen if the Fed increases the money supply by 5%?
h. What will happen if the government reduces taxes?

Question 2

Consider the following table, which assumes that the labor supply is independent of the real wage. Suppose that each worker can produce 10 units of output. The natural rate of unemployment equals 5%. The expenditure multiplier is 10. Make all the classical assumptions. The questions are independent of each other, unless explicitly stated otherwise.

W/P	DL	SL
7	800	1,000
6	900	1,000
5	1,000	1,000
4	1,100	1,000
3	1,200	1,000

a. Graph the demand-for-labor and the supply-of-labor functions.
b. What is the equilibrium real wage?
c. At this real wage, how many people will have jobs?
d. How many jobs will be vacant?
e. What will be the level of real GDP?
f. Suppose that, for whatever reason, the price level doubles. What will happen to the nominal wage?
g. Suppose that W/P = 6. What is the cyclical unemployment rate? How many people are cyclically unemployed? How many people are naturally unemployed? How many jobs have been taken?

h. Answer question (g) for $W/P = 3$.
i. Draw the aggregate supply function.
j. Assume that $M = \$100,000,000$ and $V = 5$. Find the general level of prices, as well as the nominal wage rate.
k. Find the general price level, the nominal wage, the real wage, and the real GDP if the money supply increases by 10%.
l. What will happen if the government increases its spending (G) by 5,000,000 units?

CHAPTER 12

Keynesian Economics: The Aggregate Demand Function

INTRODUCTION AND REVIEW

Classical economists assume that wages and prices are fully flexible downward and upward, so we never have recessions or unemployment in the economy. The fully employed labor produces a level of output equal to the potential GDP, regardless of the level of prices. This constitutes the vertical aggregate supply function. Moreover, an expansionary fiscal policy is totally ineffective in changing the amount of GDP. It just raises the interest rate, and leads to a complete crowding out of private spending. Similarly, money turns out to be neutral: monetary policy does not affect real variables such as GDP or employment. It just causes inflation.

Keynesian economists argue that these conclusions are at odds with the empirical evidence. As we saw in Chapter 6, in the five recessions since 1970, the actual rate of unemployment has far exceeded the natural rate. For example, during the recession of 1980–1982, unemployment reached 11% of the labor force. It is hard to imagine that the whole 11% (about 12 million people) were frictionally or structurally unemployed. We also saw that the actual real GDP was below the potential GDP during these recessions. These two empirical observations tell essentially the same story, because we know that whenever the actual GDP is less than potential ($Y < Y_p$), the unemployment rate will exceed the natural rate ($u > u^n$).

Applicants in line at an unemployment office in California

According to the classical economists, if demand for labor decreases, wages and prices fall quickly so that no unemployment will occur. Keynesian economists argue that the very fact that recessions and unemployment exist indicates that wages and prices are not fully flexible. They assume that wages and prices are *rigid* or *sticky*, especially in the short run. Therefore, when the demand for labor falls, firms lay off workers instead of reducing wages or prices. But why does the demand for labor fall in the first place? According to Keynesians, the main reason is the reduction in the aggregate demand for goods and services by households and firms. When aggregate demand falls, firms cannot reduce their prices, and workers do not accept lower wages, the only option available for the firms would be to reduce their production and lay off some workers. The next chapter will discuss the reasons for wage and price stickiness. This chapter will derive the aggregate demand function, an important component of the Keynesian model.

Does this mean that the classical model is useless? Not at all. First, it provides us with a benchmark, or a starting point. It gives us the conditions under which recessions and unemployment will not occur—namely, wage and price flexibility. Second, as we saw in Chapter 11, over time the actual real GDP traces the potential GDP rather well. Equivalently, the unemployment rate oscillates around the natural rate, so that recessions and unemployment seem to be temporary phenomena. In the long run, we have full employment. Moreover, inflation rate approximately equals the money supply growth rate. This indicates that the classical model of the last chapter is in fact relevant for the long run, although not for the short run. It cannot tell us why we have recessions and unemployment. For the short run, we need another model that is capable of generating these phenomena. Third, some new models of business cycles are based on the classical model, so it is important to understand this model.

DEMAND MANAGEMENT POLICIES

A little review of what we know is in order. We know that one of the goals of economic policy makers is to keep the level of employment high. We have learned that the way to do this is to try to keep real GDP close to potential, in order to have zero cyclical unemployment. So a successful policy requires an understanding of the causes of changes in real GDP. Real GDP is an index of all the goods and services produced in a country by the factors of production located in that country. Producers in a market system produce to satisfy consumer demand, so ultimately real GDP will equal aggregate demand, which is the sum of demands by households, firms, the government, and residents of foreign countries. So the government may be able to manipulate the level of aggregate demand through changes in spending, taxes, or transfer payments.

Changes in government spending (G) affect aggregate demand directly, because G is a component thereof. However, changes in taxes (TX) and transfer payments (TR) affect consumption spending (C) through their effects on household disposable income. Changes in government spending, taxes, and transfer payments made to affect the state of the economy is called fiscal policy.

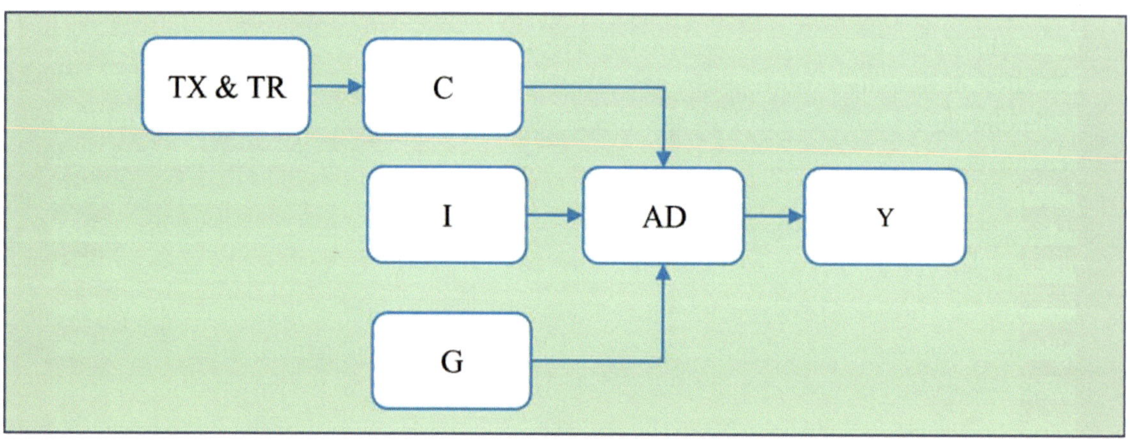

We have also learned that demands by households and firms depend on the interest rate. If the interest rate is high, the cost of borrowing will be high, and households will find it too expensive to borrow to buy consumer durable goods, automobiles, or homes. Similarly, firms will find it cost ineffective to borrow for undertaking investment projects. If the interest rate falls, on the other hand, firms will increase their investment spending, and households will be encouraged to buy homes and consumer durables. So to understand why GDP changes, we should also understand why the interest rate changes.

To find out why the interest rate changes, we should go to the money and financial markets. The interest rate is determined by the interaction of the supply of money and demand for money. Therefore, it seems that once we figure out what determines the supply of money and demand for money, we can find the interest rate and use it to figure out the level of our aggregate demand and GDP. We learned that the interest rate is also affected by what is going on in the loanable funds market. So events in the loanable funds market could also affect aggregate demand and real GDP.

The Fed controls the supply of money through changes in the required reserve ratio, the discount rate, and open market operations. This is called monetary policy. The demand for money depends on the price level, the level of real GDP, and the interest rate. Banks and households also have some control on the supply of money. We have learned that if banks decide to keep more excess reserves and lend less, money supply will decrease. Similarly, if households decide to hold more money in cash and less in bank deposits, money supply will decrease. This is because banks will have less money to loan out. Changes in money supply will affect the interest rate, and hence, consumption and investment spending.

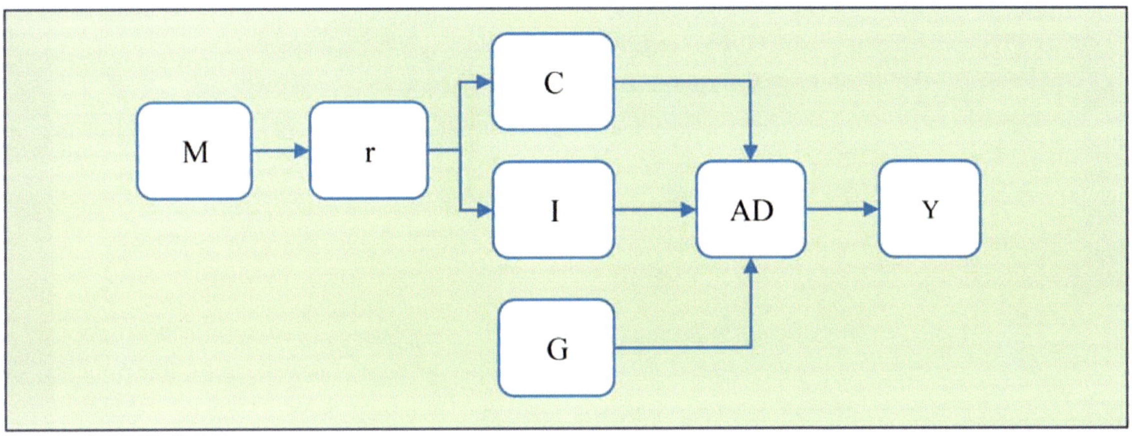

Recall that in Chapter 7 we assumed that the price level was fixed in order to concentrate on the effect of quantity changes in the goods market. This chapter will relax that assumption and will explore the relationship between the general price level and the equilibrium real GDP. We will denote the price level by the letter P, as before. We will take P to be the GDP deflator, which, as you recall from Chapter 5, is an index of the prices of all the goods and services produced in the economy.

AGGREGATE DEMAND FUNCTION

AGGREGATE DEMAND FUNCTION *The combinations of the price and GDP levels that equilibrate (clear) the goods and money markets.*

We are now ready to describe one of the most important functions in macroeconomics called the *aggregate demand function*, which is a relationship between the price level and the level of real GDP that equals aggregate demand for goods and services. It is based on a simple idea—you will find the arguments quite familiar. We will start by asking a simple question. Suppose that the goods market is in equilibrium and we have (see Chapter 7):

$$Y = C + I + G + (EX - IM)$$

Now what will happen to the equilibrium real GDP if, for whatever reason, there is a change in the general price level? The change in the price level will affect the equilibrium real GDP through three channels, as follows:

1. Real Wealth Effect

All else the same, a reduction in the price level will lead to an increase in households' real wealth, resulting in a higher level of consumption and aggregate demand. This will set off the multiplier process, and the equilibrium real GDP will increase by the amount of the increase in consumption demand times the multiplier. Conversely, an increase in the price level will cause a reduction in the real wealth and hence aggregate demand. This will cause a reduction in equilibrium real GDP through the multiplier process. So the relationship between the price level and the equilibrium real GDP is negative.

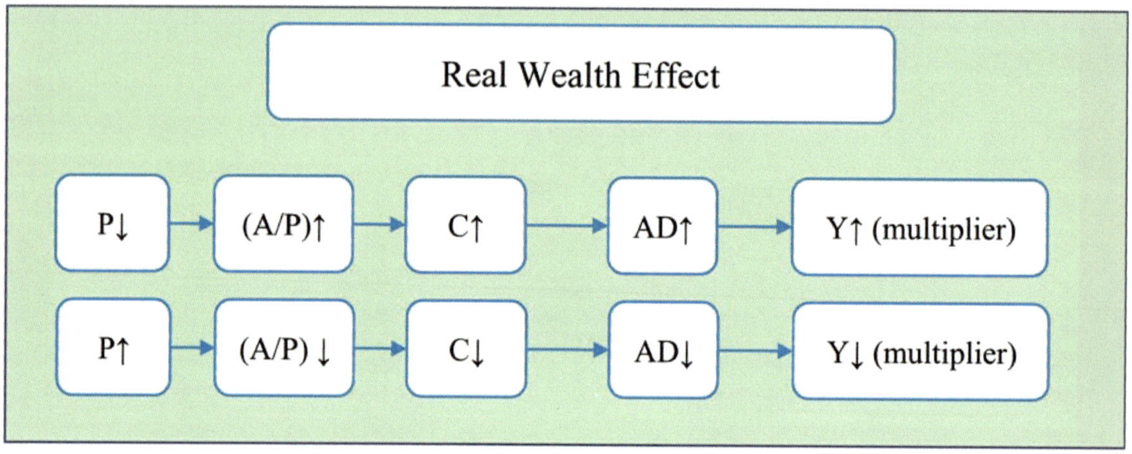

Figure 1 shows a hypothetical AD function. Currently, the price level is P = 100 and the level of aggregate demand is 10,000 units. Assuming that the goods market is in equilibrium, the real GDP will also be 10,000 units, and the economy will be at point A. Now assume that the price level falls to $75, and as a result of consumption spending, increases by 500 units. Suppose that the expenditure multiplier is 4. As we know from Chapter 7, ultimately both the aggregate demand and real GDP will increase by 4 × 500 = 2,000 units, and the economy will move to point B. So at point B, the goods market is again in equilibrium. As you recall from Chapter 7, at every step of the multiplier process, producers increase production to meet the increase in demand so that the goods market clears all the time. Therefore, *at any point on the aggregate demand function, the goods market is in equilibrium.*

2. Foreign Trade Effect

Even though we have thus far ignored foreign trade, this effect is quite easy to understand. When the level of domestic prices falls in the United States, American goods become cheaper relative to foreign goods. Americans buy more domestic goods and less foreign goods. This reduces imports. Foreign residents also buy more American goods. This increases exports. The combined effect is an increase in net exports. Net exports are a component of aggregate demand for goods and services. Therefore, an increase in net exports increases aggregate demand and the equilibrium real GDP through the multiplier process. Figure 1 applies to this

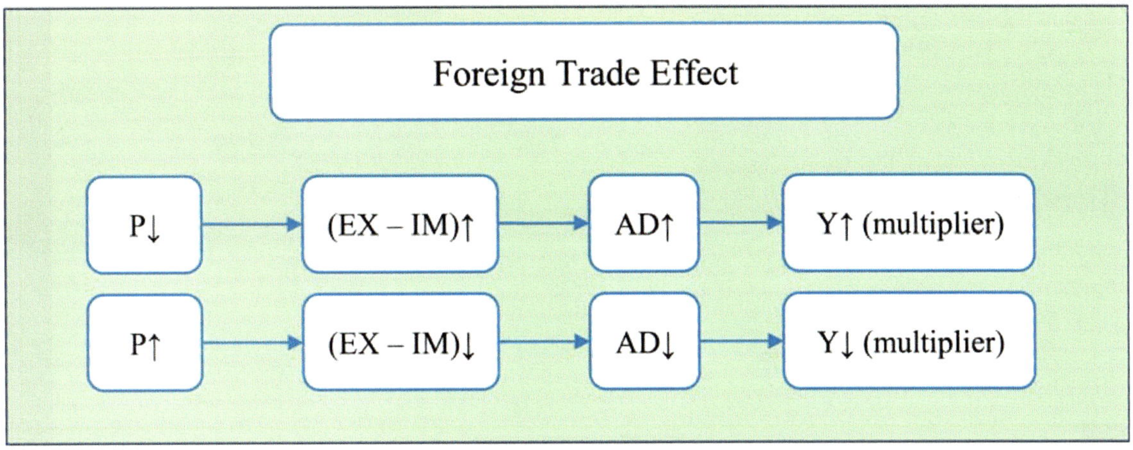

3. Interest Rate Effect

This effect works through the money market. A decrease in the price level would result in a decrease in demand for money. Since the supply of money is fixed by the Fed, the money market would reach equilibrium with a lower interest rate. (Please see Chapter 9.) This lower interest rate would stimulate consumption and investment spending, causing an increase in aggregate demand. As in the previous cases, the increase in aggregate demand would cause the equilibrium real GDP to increase through the multiplier process. The opposite would take place if the general price level increased. Figure 1 also applies to this case.

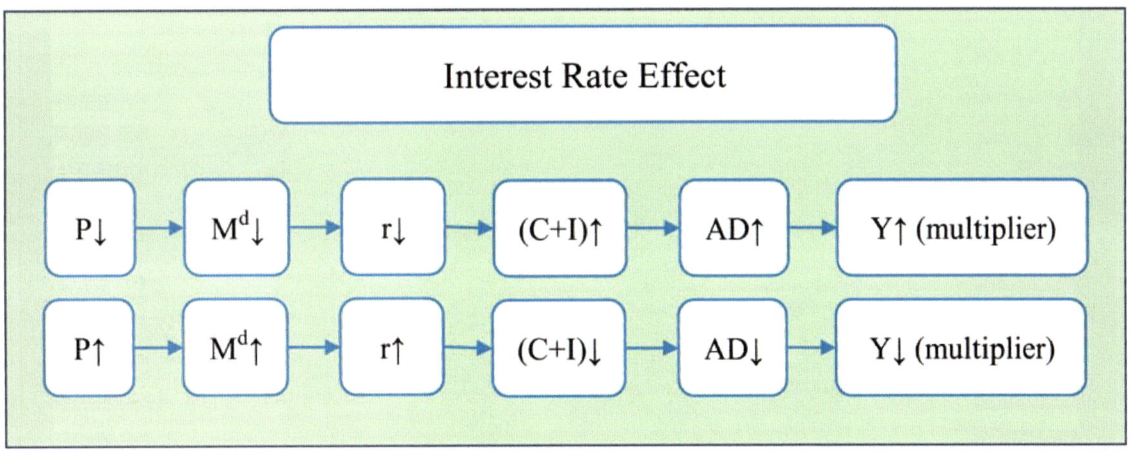

The interest rate effect adds a new insight into the AD function. It indicates that along the AD function, not only is the goods market in equilibrium, the money market is also in equilibrium. This is well worth remembering:

Along the aggregate demand function, both the goods and money markets clear.

We will use this fact quite often in the rest of the book. The following diagram demonstrates all three effects for a reduction in the general price level:

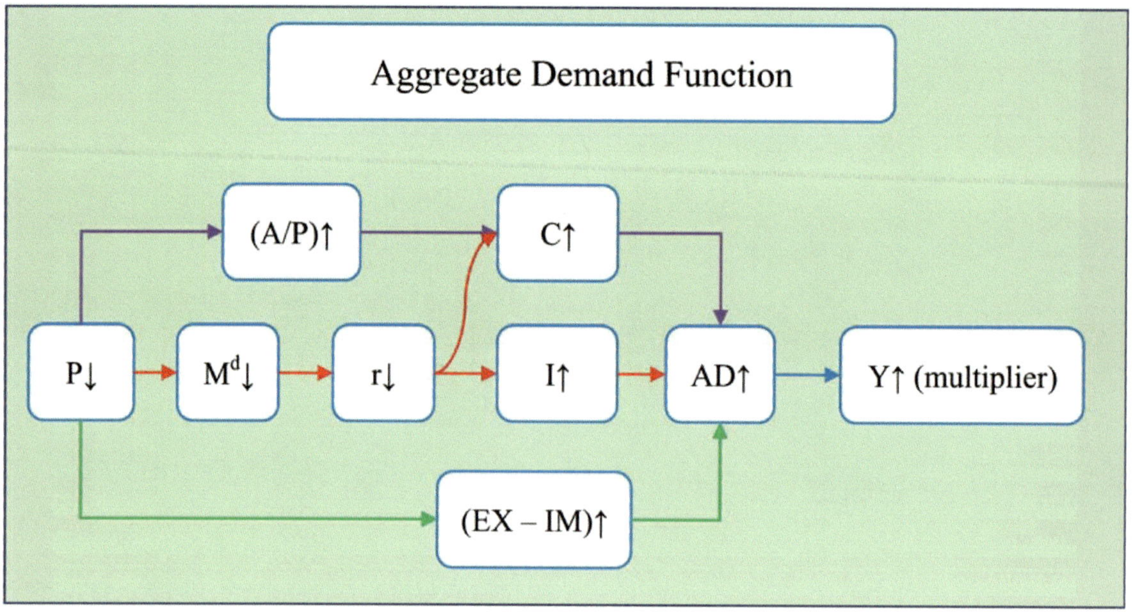

Figure 1 Aggregate Demand Function

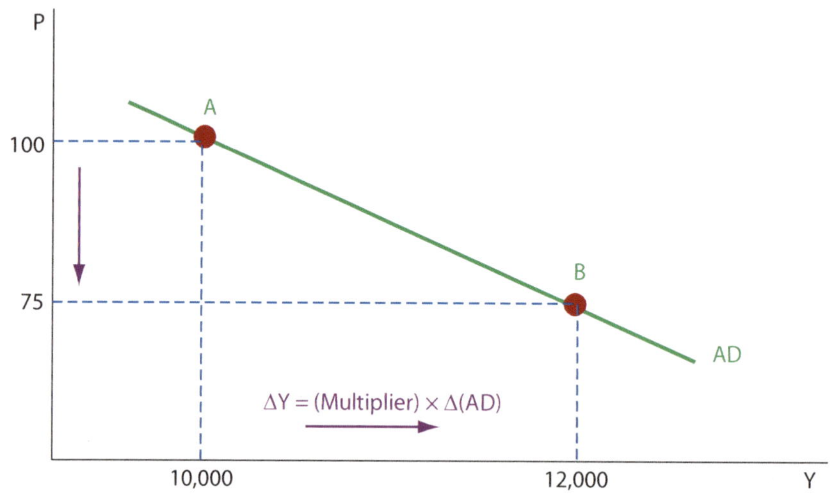

Points off the Aggregate Demand Function

If on the aggregate demand function both the goods and money markets clear, at any point off the function, one or both of the markets would be out of equilibrium. We will assume that the money market is always in equilibrium. Here is why. Demand for money is the portion of total wealth people want to hold in the form of money, as opposed to bonds. If people decide to hold more money and less bonds, all they need do is call their brokers and ask them to sell some of their bonds. If they decide to hold more bonds and less money, they can instruct their brokers to buy some bonds. All these transactions can take place within a short period of time.

The goods market, on the other hand, would take time to clear. That is because it may take time for producers to realize that the demand has increased. It may take additional time for them to schedule new production and bring the additional products to the market. They may also need to buy additional intermediate goods and hire additional labor. For these reasons, we will assume that if the economy is off the aggregate demand function, it must be the goods market that is out of equilibrium.

Now consider Figure 2. When the price level is $100, aggregate demand equals 10,000 units as before. Real GDP is a measure of all the goods and services produced. So if the real GDP also equals 10,000 units, then the goods market will be in equilibrium. What if the real GDP equals 9,000 units so that the economy is at point A? At point A, the quantities of all the goods and services produced are less than aggregate demand. At point A, therefore, we have *excess demand* for goods and services, and inventories are being depleted unplanned at a rate of 1,000 units per year. Similarly, at point B, the real GDP exceeds aggregate demand. At that point, we have an *excess supply* of goods, and inventories are piling up at a rate of 2,000 units per year. We conclude that:

At any point to the left of the aggregate demand function, there will be an excess demand for goods and services. At any point to the right of the AD function, there will be an excess supply of goods and services.

Shifts in the Aggregate Demand Function

The rule to shift the AD function is quite straightforward and is consistent with what was said in the mathematical appendix to Chapter 1. That is, if a variable changes, and if that variable is already measured on one of the two axes, then we will have a movement along the curve. But, if that variable is not measured on any of the two axes, then the whole curve will shift. We start with the price level, which is measured along the vertical axis.

The components of aggregate demand—such as consumption, investment, or net exports—can change, either because of changes in the price level, or because of reasons unrelated to price changes. If the change in any of the components of aggregate demand is due to a change in the level of prices, then the economy will move along the AD function. If the change is due to a reason other than a change in the price level, then the whole curve will shift.

Here are some examples. Consider Figure 3; assume that currently the price level is 100, and the real GDP equals 10,000. The economy is at point A on the AD function, and thus, the goods market and money markets clear. First, suppose that the price level goes down to 75. In that case, the consequent increase in aggregate demand—due to the three effects mentioned above—will cause the economy to move on the AD function to a point like point B. This means that to clear the goods market, the real GDP needs to increase to 12,000.

Figure 2 Positions off the Aggregate Demand Function

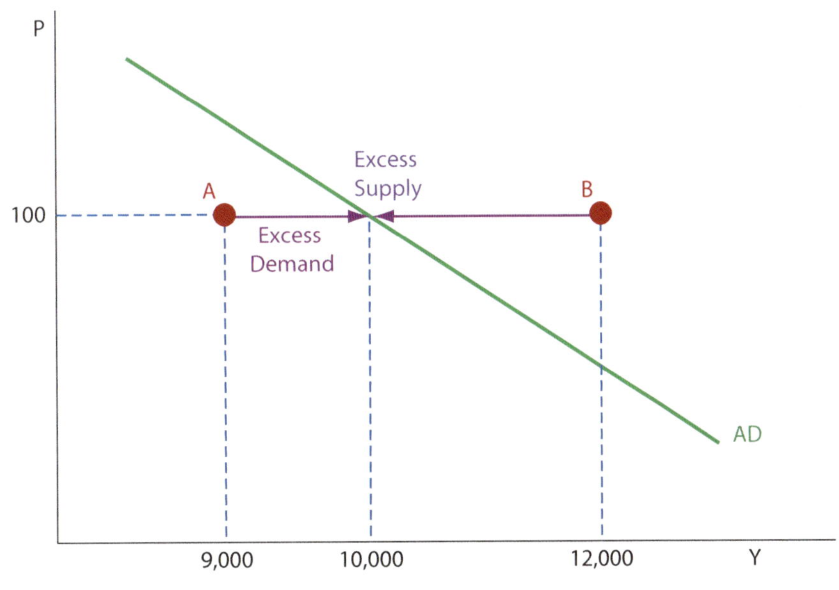

Now suppose we are at point A again. What will happen if, at the given price level of 100, firms come to expect better future economic conditions and increase their purchase of equipment for investment purposes? This increase in investment spending is not due to a price change. Therefore, the AD function will shift to the right to AD2. Similarly, an increase in consumption spending or net exports for reasons unrelated to changes in the price level will cause a rightward shift in the AD function.

What will be the extent of the shift in the AD function? You actually know the answer. It will equal the initial increase in investment spending times the expenditure multiplier. For instance, suppose the marginal propensity to consume is MPC = 0.75, so that the multiplier equals 4. If investment spending increases by 1,000 units due to producer's optimism about future profits, the AD function will shift by 4 × 1,000 = 4,000 units, as in Figure 3. The logic of this argument should be familiar to you from Chapter 7. In that chapter, we kept the price level fixed, and increased aggregate demand by a certain amount. As a result, producers responded by increasing production; this started the multiplier process. Here we are doing the same thing. We are increasing the investment demand by 1,000 and as a result, *at any given price level*, the equilibrium real GDP increases by 4,000 units.

Figure 3 Shifts in the AD Function

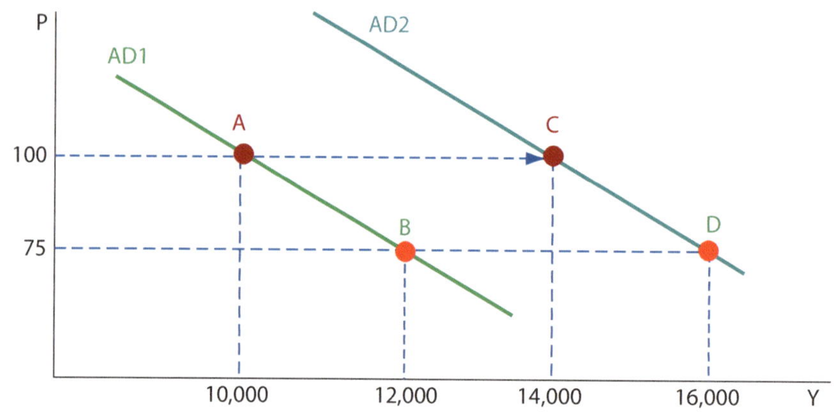

FISCAL POLICY

Recall from Chapter 7 that fiscal policy refers to changes in government spending, taxes, or transfer payments that aim at achieving a macroeconomic objective. Recall also that a government can increase its spending in three different ways.

a. *Balanced budget increase in spending*. In this case the increase in the government's outlays is financed by an equal increase in taxes.
b. *Deficit spending*. In this case, the increase in the government's outlays is financed through borrowing in the loanable funds market.
c. *Monetizing the debt*. Here, the increase in the government's outlays is financed by printing money.

According to classical economists, the first methods of financing a government spending will crowd out private spending, and the third method will cause inflation. Keynesian economists, on the other hand, do not believe in the concept of financial crowding out, especially in a recession. The following is a brief discussion of their view.

KEYNESIAN VIEW OF THE CROWDING-OUT EFFECT

The classical analyses of saving, investment, and fiscal policy of Chapter 10 indicated that *everything crowds out everything else dollar for dollar!* An increase in investment crowds out consumption, an increase in consumption crowds out investment, and an increase in government spending, if not financed by printing money, crowds out consumption and investment. The reason for this result is that there is a limited amount of saving that comes to the financial market by households each year. Saving is left over from disposable income after consumption, and the amount of disposable income in a year is more or less given. So, if some people in the economy borrow more, the interest rate will increase, and other people will reduce their borrowing. This is called *financial crowding out*: crowding out due to a higher interest rate because of limited financial resources.

Things look hopeless. It seems that aggregate demand for goods and services, and real GDP, can never increase. An increase in demand by one group of people or industries will reduce demand by some other group, and by the same amount. The converse is also true. If one group of people or industries reduces its demand for goods and services, the interest rate will drop. Some other group will increase its demand so that the aggregate demand will remain unchanged. We can never have recessions due to deficient aggregate demand. So we need to ask if any of these analyses are realistic.

The Keynesian critiques of the theory, such as that of J. Bradford DeLong of the University of California–Berkeley, point to the significant increase in the real GDP and employment during the high-tech bubble of the 1990s. Take a look at the GDP graph in Chapter 6. Moreover, DeLong mentions the huge increase in employment during the housing bubble of the 2000s. He argues that the tremendous increase in investment spending in these sectors did, in fact, increase aggregate demand and GDP. He also argues that the Great Depression of the 1930s was due to a reduction in aggregate demand for goods and services, a fact inconsistent with the above theory.[1]

You might be interested in a little bit of history. During the Great Depression of the 1930s, some economists—notably John Maynard Keynes—were arguing for an expansionary fiscal policy to boost the aggregate demand and lift the British economy out of the recession. The staff of the Chancellor of the Exchequer (Britain's Treasury Department) put out reports attacking this idea. They basically argued that an expansionary fiscal policy would be ineffective, because it would merely shift financial resources from one industry to another. This argument came to be known as the *Treasury view*. This view was later criticized and ridiculed by Keynesian economists. It is interesting to note that the same argument was put forward in 2009 by two University of Chicago professors of finance, Eugene Fama and John Cochrane, stirring yet another debate among economists.

In the 1930s, the FSA employed several photographers to document the effects of the Great Depression on the population of America. The March, 1936 photograph by Dorothea Lange commonly called ***Migrant Mother****. The photograph depicts the 32-year-old Florence Owens Thompson with three of her children in Nipomo, California.*

The biggest sin committed by the staff of the Chancellor of the Exchequer was that they based their argument on the national income identity you saw in Chapter 7. The national income identity is true by definition, and it cannot tell us anything about the economic behavior of consumers and firms. The analysis in Chapter 10 did not make the same mistake, as it was based on the goods market

1 J. Bradford DeLong, "The Modern View of the Treasury View," January 18, 2009, DRAFT.

equilibrium condition, which describes economic behavior of households, firms, and the government. Nevertheless, it reached exactly the same conclusion.

There must be some element of truth in the crowding-out result, otherwise it would not endure this long in history (and would not occupy a few pages of this book.) However, the strict dollar-for-dollar crowding-out result is probably suspect; otherwise this would be the end of our book. The following summarizes the reasons why the complete financial crowding-out effect is probably a strong conclusion.

Available Funds for Investment

The saving-investment relationship says that in equilibrium, the flow of saving in a year to the financial market should equal the amount of investment and budget deficit in that year *financed by this saving*. As you know, saving is disposable income left over after consumption. But disposable income is the "take-home" *factor income* in a year. This factor income excludes capital gains, as you remember from Chapter 5. So the actual flow of saving to the financial market could be more than $S = Y_d - C$.

But even more important, the saving-investment relationship looks at the amount of saving generated by households over just one year. The total supply of funds to the financial market could be much more than the annual saving flow, plus capital gains. Households save every year. Through the years and decades, those savings accumulate into their total wealth. As you recall, they hold some of it in the form of money, which we call the supply of money. So if the government increases demand for loanable funds to finance its deficit, households can supply the needed amounts from their money holdings without having to reduce their consumption. Moreover, during a recession, when the economic activity is down, households might have a lot of idle money holdings they can lend to the government. As a *very* rough approximation, in 2009 the flow of saving in the United States was about \$1.5 trillion, and the M2 money supply was about \$8.5 trillion. Adding the amount of money in the money market mutual funds accounts of close to \$2.5 trillion, one can get an approximation to M3 of \$11 trillion. This is much more than the flow of saving in 2009.[2]

Similarly, if in a year the supply of saving to the financial market decreases because of a balanced budget increases in spending, the amount of investment *financed by this saving* will go down—not all the investment. Even though saving may go down in a year, people can still lend from their accumulated past savings—their total wealth.

The Flow of Funds Argument

The money that the government borrows to finance its deficit does not evaporate into thin air. It comes back to the system. Say that I have \$1 million in my bank account. Abigail, who owns an export-import company, wants to borrow that money to upgrade the computer system in her company. So this is the investment demand for that \$1 million. Instead, the government borrows that money and spends it on some road repair. Abigail then is deprived of those one million dollars. This is the essence of dollar-for-dollar financial crowding out.

However, when the government spends that money on road repair, some people receive that money, and their incomes increase by \$1 million. Assuming that the marginal propensity to consume is 90%, they will spend \$900,000 of that money and save the remaining \$100,000. People who receive that \$900,000 spend \$810,000 and save the other \$90,000. The process continues.

2 In 2006 the Fed stopped publishing the M3 data.

Does this remind you of the expenditure multiplier process? How much additional saving will be generated in the financial system? Using the multiplier formula, a total of $10 million of income will be generated in the system. This will result in an additional saving of $1 million. So my $1 million of saving will be replenished dollar for dollar!

Increase in Money Supply

If deficit financing increases the rate of interest, banks will find it more lucrative to reduce their excess reserves and lend more to the public and the government. As you know from Chapter 8, this will increase the supply of money. More important, these loanable funds will not come "out of households pockets," so will not cause a reduction in consumption.

Time Lag between Deficit Spending and Demand Reduction

Suppose the government increases its expenditure in 2010 through deficit financing. This will increase aggregate demand in 2010. We also know that this will also increase the interest rate, resulting in a reduction in consumption and investment. However, most probably these reductions will not be in 2010. This is because it takes time for households and firms to make decisions to change their purchase of consumer durables and equipment. So on net, the aggregate demand will increase in 2010, and this policy will be expansionary. Moreover, if deficit spending ends in 2010, the interest rate will return to normal in 2011—in which case, the crowding out in consumption and investment will be very small.

Permanent Income Hypothesis

Remember that under the permanent income hypothesis, consumption is affected by permanent disposable income, not by current disposable income. If the government raises the taxes of its citizens in one year to finance its additional expenditure, consumption may not go down at all. This is because households will perceive the reduction in their disposable income as transitory.

Liquidity Trap

Finally the interest rate might fall into the liquidity trap. People generally hold bonds for two reasons: to earn interest income while holding the bond, and to make a capital gain when selling it. A capital gain, as you recall from the GDP chapter, is the excess of sale price over the purchase price of an asset. You also remember from the Keynesian theory that bonds compete with money in people's portfolios. Finally, you remember the negative relationship between bond prices and interest rates.

In a recession, the interest rate may go down so much that investors may think it cannot possibly go any lower. In that case, investors will come to believe that the interest rate can only go up in the future. But then it would be quite irrational to hold bonds for speculative purposes. Why? Because if you expect the interest rate to go up in the future, you will also expect the price of bonds to go down in the future. Remember the negative relationship? Therefore you will expect to make *capital losses* if you hold bonds. In this case, the demand for money will be huge, and the interest rate will fall into the liquidity trap (see Chapter 9). But if the interest rate is in the liquidity trap, a deficit spending will not affect it, and fiscal policy will be effective.

CAPITAL LOSSES
An asset holder makes a capital loss if the sale price of the asset is less than the purchase price. The opposite of capital gains.

After all this, you need to realize that there are some elements of truth in the theory. In particular, it is a realistic description of the *long-run* tendencies of economies. Recall once again that this is a flow theory. It essentially says, for instance, that if in the long run the level of investment in a country is high year after year, its level of consumption will be low, and vice versa. So the country should decide between achieving high investment or consumption targets. Higher investment involves sacrifice of current consumption, and results in larger amounts of productive capital for future generations—leading to greater output and standards of living for them. On the other hand, if we consume more today, there will be less capital formation for future generations.

Similarly, if a government keeps borrowing to pay for its expenditure year after year, it will ultimately crowd out consumption and investment, to the detriment of both current and future generations. However, for reasons mentioned above, the theory cannot be a realistic description of the effect of a one-time deficit spending when the economy is in a recession.

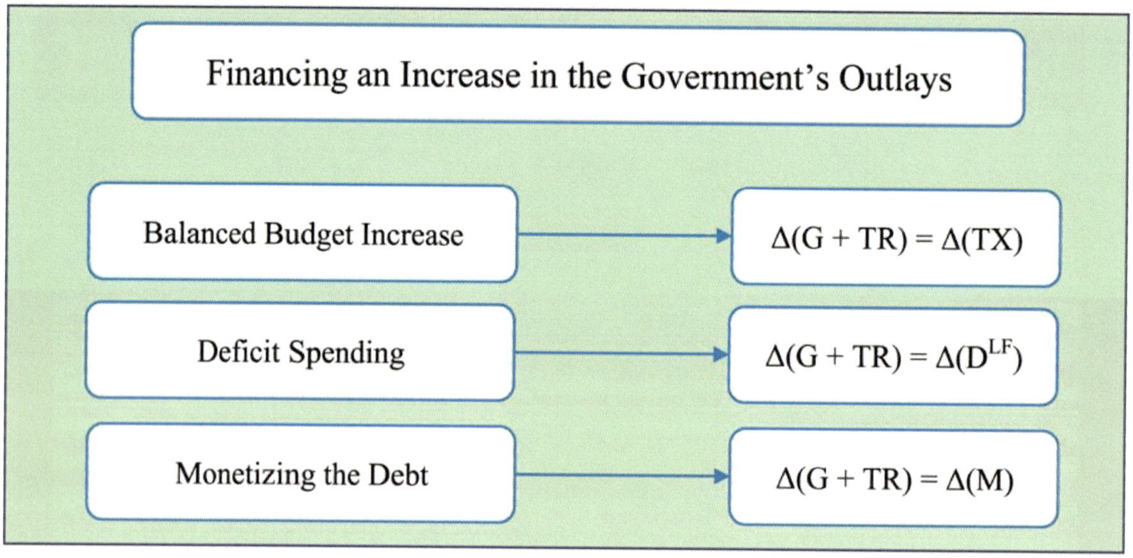

THE MULTIPLIER EFFECT

Therefore, Keynesians believe that changes in G, TX, or TR will have their full multiplier effects on aggregate demand. Let's elaborate.

A Balanced-Budget Increase in G or TR

As we saw in Chapter 7, a balanced budget increase in government spending will cause an equal increase in the equilibrium real GDP, regardless of the size of the marginal propensity to consume. This means, then, that if the government increases spending by 4,000 units and finances it through raising an equal amount of taxes, the aggregate demand function will shift to the right by 4,000 units, as in Figure 3. This is called the unit-multiplier result. Similarly, a balanced budget increase in transfer payments will have no effect on aggregate demand, because it will leave the disposable income unchanged.

Deficit Spending

Keynesians believe that deficit-financed changes in G, TR, or TX will affect aggregate demand through the multiplier process. Here are some examples. An increase in G will directly cause AD to increase through the multiplier process, as G is a component of aggregate demand. So the aggregate demand function will shift to the right by the amount:

$$\Delta Y = (\text{Expenditure Multiplier}) \times \Delta G$$

Effect of Fiscal Policy on the AD Function

Balanced Budget Increase in G

If $\Delta(G) = \Delta(TX)$, then $\Delta(Y) = \Delta(G)$

If $\Delta(TR) = \Delta(TX)$, then $\Delta(Y) = 0$

Deficit Spending

G↑ with No Change in TX, or TR → $\Delta(Y) = (\text{Multiplier}) \times \Delta(G)$

TR↑ with No Change in TX, or G → $\Delta(Y) = (\text{Multiplier}) \times MPC \times \Delta(TR)$

TX↓ with No Change in TR, or G → $\Delta(Y) = -(\text{Multiplier}) \times MPC \times \Delta(TX)$

Monetizing the Debt

Combination of Deficit Spending and Monetary Policy

An increase in transfer payments affects disposable income first. Households consume a portion of that, determined by MPC, on goods and services. So consumption increases by $\Delta C = MPC \times \Delta TR$. Aggregate demand then increases through the multiplier process. So the aggregate demand function will shift to the right by the amount:

$$\Delta Y = (\text{Expenditure Multiplier}) \times MPC \times \Delta TR$$

An increase in taxes reduces disposable income. As a result, consumption decreases by MPC, and the aggregate demand function shifts to the left by the amount:

$$\Delta Y = -(\text{Expenditure Multiplier}) \times MPC \times \Delta TX$$

Notice the negative sign in the equation: an increase in taxes reduced aggregated demand.

Monetizing the Debt

Printing money to finance an increase in government spending is most expansionary, because it is a combination of a deficit-financed fiscal policy and an expansionary monetary policy. This policy will shift the AD function to the right twice. Once as G increases; the next as M increases.

A change in G, TR, or TX to increase aggregate demand is called an *expansionary fiscal policy*; the one to reduce it is a *contractionary fiscal policy*. Therefore,

An expansionary fiscal policy will shift the aggregate demand function to the right.

Similarly:

A contractionary fiscal policy will shift the aggregate demand function to the left.

EXPANSIONARY FISCAL POLICY
An increase in government spending and/or a decrease in taxes, aimed at increasing the level of aggregate demand for goods and services (in order to reduce unemployment).

CONTRACTIONARY FISCAL POLICY
A reduction in government spending and/or an increase in taxes aimed at reducing the level of aggregate demand for goods and services (in order to reduce inflationary pressures).

MONETARY POLICY

Recall from Chapter 9 that in the Keynesian model, demand for money depends on the price level, real GDP, *and the interest rate.* (It is a good idea to review that chapter.) An increase in money supply will push down the equilibrium interest rate, stimulating consumption and investment spending, and hence aggregate demand. Since this increase in aggregate demand is for a reason other than a reduction in the general price level, the effect will be a rightward shift in the aggregate demand function, as in Figure 3. Such a policy is called an *expansionary monetary policy*. Conversely, *a contractionary monetary policy* (a reduction in M) will cause a leftward shift in the AD function. So we have another rule:

An expansionary monetary policy shifts the aggregate demand function to the right.

As an exercise, try to verify the following rule:

A contractionary monetary policy shifts the aggregate demand function to the left.

Note that these are very similar to the effects of fiscal policy. Since both fiscal and monetary policies affect the level of aggregate demand, these two policies are often referred to as *demand management policies*. The above rules are summarized in Figure 4.

EXPANSIONARY MONETARY POLICY
An increase in the money supply aimed at reducing the interest rate and increasing the level of aggregate demand for goods and services (in order to reduce unemployment).

CONTRACTIONARY MONETARY POLICY
A reduction in money supply aimed at increasing the interest rate and reducing the level of aggregate demand for goods and services (to reduce inflationary pressures).

DEMAND MANAGEMENT POLICIES
Fiscal and monetary policies.

Figure 4 Demand Management Polices and the AD Function

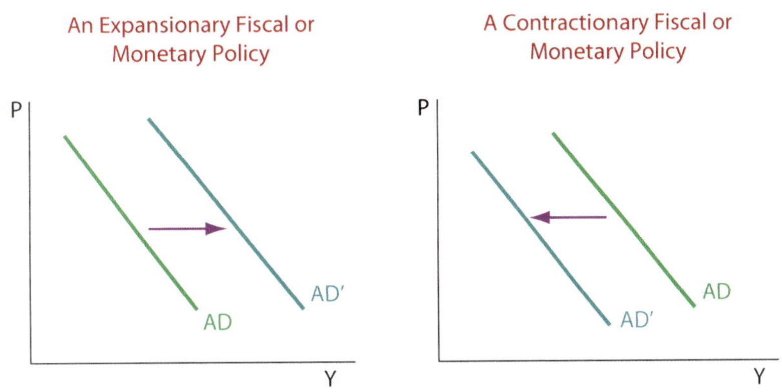

ECONOMIC UNCERTAINTY

We will now put together a lot of things we have learned to analyze the effect of uncertainty on aggregate demand. This problem became particularly acute during the recession of 2007–2008. We will analyze the effects, both in the money and loanable funds markets.

The Money Market

You know that money is defined as the currency in people's pockets and purses, plus the amounts in bank deposits. In this book we concentrated on demand deposits or checking accounts only, although the argument applies to any kind of deposit. So supply of money is the total *actual* amount of currency and bank deposits belonging to the non–bank public. Similarly, demand for money is the total amount of currency and bank deposits that people *want to hold.*

$$M^d = \text{Currency} + \text{Deposits}$$

Sometimes during recessions, households and firms begin to worry about the health of the banking system. As you know from Chapter 8, this is because banks are in the business of lending depositors' money to firms and households, making profit out of this activity. In bad economic times, many firms that have borrowed from banks may experience losses and go bankrupt. Similarly, a lot of householders who have borrowed from banks to buy consumer durables and homes may lose their jobs. As a result, these firms and households may not be able to pay back their bank loans. If this happens, banks may go bankrupt, and depositors may lose their deposits.

The fear of losing their deposits induces people to withdraw their money from the banks and hold them in currency until the bad times are over. This does not mean that people increase their demand for money. What it means is that they want to hold more of their money under their mattresses, and less in banks. For example, suppose that currently, people want to hold \$1,000 of money, \$100 in currency, and \$900 in bank deposits:

$$M^d = \text{Currency} + \text{Deposits} = \$100 + \$900 = \$1{,}000$$

As uncertainty about the banking system increases, people may want to hold \$800 in cash and only \$200 in banks:

$$M^d = \text{Currency} + \text{Deposits} = \$800 + \$200 = \$1{,}000$$

So nothing happens to the total demand for money—only its composition changes. In terms of our graphs, the demand for money function stays put.

Figure 5 The Effect of Uncertainty in the Money Market

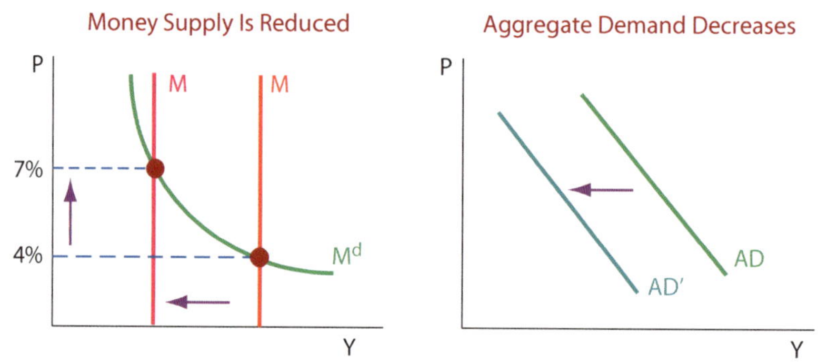

However, you know from Chapter 8 that when people hold more currency and fewer deposits, banks lose reserves. Since there is less money to loan out, the supply of money decreases. This is shown in Figure 5. This reduction in money supply pushes up the interest rate, causing a reduction in consumption and investment, and ultimately, aggregate demand. The fall in aggregate demand makes the bad economic condition worse by increasing unemployment and bankruptcies. This further reduces the money supply, and so on and so forth.

Known as a "run" on a bank, anxious depositors wait to withdraw their savings outside a bank during the Great Depression.

Actually, this is not the end of the story. During bad economic times, banks also become hesitant to lend money, and for the same reason: they are afraid that borrowers may not be able to pay the loans back. Thus, they would hold more excess reserves, and the supply of money would decrease. Note that the supply of money would decrease for two reasons: fear on the side of both households and banks. The result would be a dramatic reduction in aggregate demand.

The above scenario worries governments and policy makers quite a bit, because the situation could easily get out of control. Therefore, the governments usually try to restore confidence in the economy by reassuring people that their deposits are safe. The slogan, *the only thing to fear is fear itself* came out during the Great Depression. These words were said by President Franklin D. Roosevelt during his first inauguration in 1933. Roosevelt said this to allay people's fears, and to stop bank deposit withdrawals—and the avalanche of bank bankruptcies. The sole purpose of establishing government deposit insurance agencies such as FDIC has been to reassure depositors and prevent the kind of bank runs described above.

Moreover, this is the reason why the Fed injects lots of money into the banking system in a severe recession. This increase in money supply works to calm the economy in two ways. First, by shifting the money supply to the right in Figure 5, the Fed would lower the interest rate and restore consumption and investment spending. Second, the Fed would signal to the worrying depositors that there is enough money in the banking system; thus, there is no need to worry about banks going under. In other words, the second purpose of increasing the money supply is to build confidence in people. For example, in the 2007–2008 recession, the Fed injected more than a trillion dollars into the banking system, to prevent bankruptcies and build confidence.

The Loanable Funds Market

During bad economic times, a similar thing happens on the supply side of the loanable funds market. Since during such times firms lose money and people lose jobs, *credit risk* increases. Credit risk is the risk that a borrower may not be able to pay back the loan. In such circumstances, banks generally become reluctant to lend money. Therefore, they significantly reduce the supply of loanable funds to the market, and increase their holdings of excess reserves. We saw this in Chapter 10. The significant reduction in the supply of credit to the economy is called a *credit crunch*. As shown in Figure 6, a credit crunch would cause a leftward shift in the supply of loanable funds and an increase in the interest rate. This would, in turn, cause a reduction in consumption and investment spending. The aggregate demand function would shift to the left. Many believe that credit crunch happened during 2007–2008, and was a major cause of the recession.

CREDIT RISK
The chance that a borrower may not be able to pay back (a part) of his or her loan to the lender

CREDIT CRUNCH
A dramatic reduction in the supply of loanable funds due to a substantial increase in credit risk.

Figure 6 The Effect of Uncertainty in the Loanable Funds Market

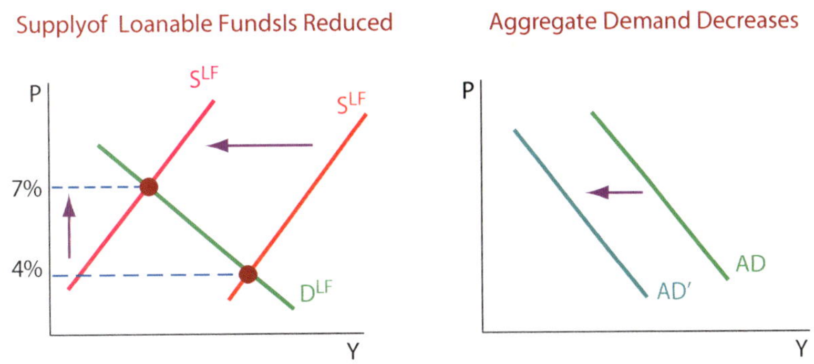

TO SUMMARIZE

1. The *aggregate demand function* gives the combination of all the price levels and real GDP quantities that are consistent with equilibrium, in both the goods and money markets.
2. It is downward sloping for three reasons:
   a. A fall in the price level leads to a higher purchasing power of household wealth. This increases consumption, and leads to excess demand for goods. To clear the market, GDP must increase.
   b. A fall in the price level leads to larger exports and smaller imports, resulting in excess demand for goods. To clear the market, GDP must increase.
   c. A fall in the price level leads to a reduction in the interest rate, resulting in higher consumption and investment, which generates excess demand for goods and services. To clear the market, GDP must increase.
3. At any point below and to the left of the AD curve, we will have excess demand for goods and services. To the right and above, we will have excess supply.
4. A change in the price level will cause a movement along the AD function.
5. A change in any other variable affecting aggregate demand will cause a shift in the function.
6. *Expansionary fiscal* or *monetary policies* cause the AD function to shift to the right. *Contractionary policies* shift the curve to the left.
7. Bank panics would cause the AD function to shift to the left.
8. A significant increase in *credit risk* that causes a *credit crunch* would shift the AD function to the left.

EXERCISES

Question 1

What will happen to the AD function if there is a reduction in taxes?

Question 2

What will happen to the AD function if there is a balanced-budget increase in spending?

Question 3

Suppose that the economy is at a point like point A in Figure 2, so that we have excess demand for goods. To clear the goods market, we must increase GDP (move to the right to reach the AD function). But as the graph shows, we can also move up to get to the AD function. Explain why the goods market will clear if you move up.

Question 4

Repeat the previous question for point B of Figure 2.

Question 5

Suppose there is an open market purchase of bonds by the Fed. Show that the magnitude of the shift in AD function will be greater when the demand for money function is steeper. If the demand for money function is relatively flat, the AD function will not shift that much. What is the reason for this? Give an economic interpretation.

Question 6

Suppose there is an open market purchase of bonds by the Fed. Show that the magnitude of the shift in AD function will be greater when consumption and investment are more sensitive to changes in interest rates.

Question 7

There are two countries—Country A and Country B—that are nearly identical. The only difference between the two countries is that Country A has a larger expenditure multiplier. Which country would have a steeper AD function? In which country would fiscal policy be more effective in shifting the AD function? How about monetary policy?

Question 8

Although we don't have stocks in our model, it is not hard to answer this question. Suppose that the stock market goes down drastically. What will be the effect on the AD function?

Question 9

Suppose the government encourages exports by providing financial incentives to exporters. What will be the effect of this on the AD function?

Question 10

Suppose that the government imposes a high tariff on foreign goods to reduce imports. What will be the effect of this on the AD function?

Question 11

Suppose the interest rate is in the liquidity trap.

a. What would be the effect of an expansionary monetary policy on the aggregate demand function?

b. What would be the effect of an expansionary fiscal policy on the aggregate demand function?

Question 12

Consider the following two AD functions:

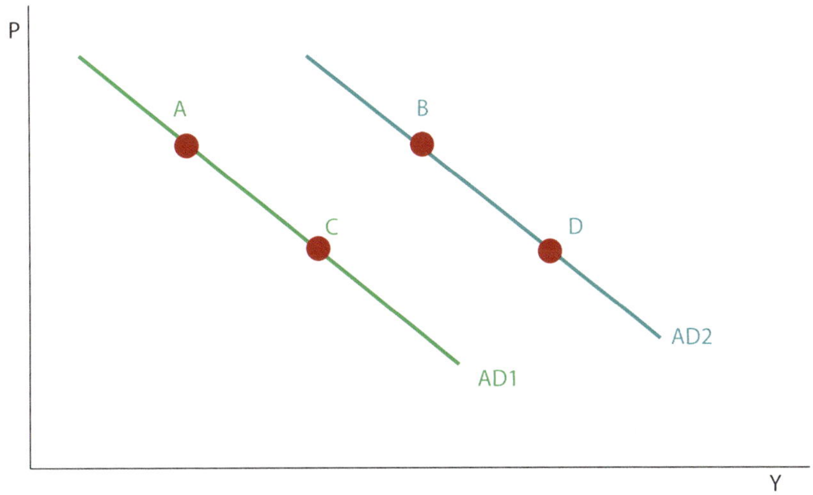

Which one of the following statements is true (we can claim with certainty); wrong (we know for sure it is not true); or ambiguous (we just can't tell without more information)? In all cases, explain why.

a. At point C, the price level is lower than at point A. (Okay, this was a joke to get you warmed up.)
b. At point C, the amount of taxes collected by the government is the same as at point A.
c. At point A, the money supply is the same as at point C.
d. At point A, the government spending is the same as at point C.
e. At point A, the interest rate is the same as at point C.
f. At point A, the amount of money demanded is the same as at point C.
g. At point A, the investment spending is the same as at point C.
h. At point A, the nominal wealth is the same as at point C.
i. At point A, the real wealth is the same as at point C.
j. If currently the aggregate demand function for the economy is AD_1, then at point B we have excess demand for goods.
k. If currently the aggregate demand function for the economy is AD_2, then at point C we have excess demand for goods.
l. Suppose that the aggregate demand function has shifted from AD_1 to AD_2 due to an increase in government spending. Then at point D, the amount of money demanded is larger than at point A.
m. At point C, the interest rate is lower than at point B.

n. Assume that the money supply has not changed. Then at point C, the interest rate is lower than at point B.

o. Assume the money supply has not changed. Then at point C, people are holding more money than they want to hold.

p. Assume that the money supply has not changed. Then at point B, people want to hold more money than at point C.

q. Suppose the aggregate demand function has shifted from AD_1 to AD_2 due to an open market operation. Then at point B, people want to hold more money than at point C.

r. Suppose that the aggregate demand function has shifted from AD_1 to AD_2 due to an open market operation. Then at point B, people want to hold more money than they are actually holding.

s. Suppose the aggregate demand function has shifted from AD_1 to AD_2 due to an open market operation. At point B, the interest rate is lower than at point A.

t. An increase in investor optimism about the future will shift the aggregate demand curve from AD_1 to AD_2.

u. Suppose that a new president takes office, and participants in the bond market become nervous (don't ask me why). Portfolio investors expect that bond prices will go down in the future. They believe bonds are too risky to hold now. Therefore, they start selling their bonds today to hold more money. As a result, the aggregate demand curve shifts from AD_1 to AD_2.

v. A loss in consumer confidence (whatever it means) causes a shift in the aggregate demand function from AD_1 to AD_2.

w. At point D, the disposable income is higher than at point C.

x. At point C, the disposable income is higher than at point A.

y. At point B, the transfer payments are higher than at point A.

z. At point C, the transfer payments are higher than at point A.

CHAPTER 13

Keynesian Economics: Wage and Price Rigidity

INTRODUCTION AND REVIEW

According to the classical economists, wage and price flexibility ensures that the labor market always clears, and we don't have recessions and unemployment. Keynesian economists argue that the existence of recessions indicates these assumptions are suspect. There are two propositions at the heart of Keynesian economics:

1. Demand shocks are the main cause of business cycles.
2. Wages and prices are rigid or sticky in the short run.

Keynesians believe that a reduction in aggregate demand causes a reduction in the demand for labor. This would not cause a recession if wages and prices were flexible. However, since firms cannot cut their prices—and since workers resist wage cuts—firms are left with no other choice but to lay off some workers. So the main trigger for recessions in the Keynesian theory is a reduction in aggregate demand. But the reason for the resulting unemployment is wage and price rigidity. In our last chapter, we derived the aggregate demand function. In this chapter, we will use it to analyze recessions.

There are two more features of this theory related to economic policy.

1. Money is not neutral. The interest rate is determined in the money market. Changes in money supply affect the rate of interest, which in turn affects consumption and investment, and hence, aggregate demand.
2. There is no financial crowding out, especially in a recession. For the reasons mentioned in Chapter 12, there will be plenty of financial resources for the government to borrow without retarding the private consumption and investment spending. Therefore,

a. A balanced-budget increase in spending has a unit-multiplier effect described in Chapter 7.
b. Deficit spending will be expansionary. For example, an increase in G will cause an increase in aggregate demand through the multiplier process.
c. Monetizing the debt will be the most expansionary demand management policy, as it is a combination of fiscal and monetary policies.

WAGE AND PRICE RIGIDITY

According to Keynesians, we can have unemployment and recessions if nominal wages, prices, or both, are rigid or sticky—*they do not move fast enough and in sufficient magnitude to instantly clear the labor market.* We need to address a question at the beginning: Why do economists *assume* that wages and prices are either flexible or not flexible? Can they not just look at the published data to see if they are flexible or not? The answer is that there is a difference between wage and price *variability*, as seen in the published data, and wage and price *flexibility*, as defined by macroeconomists. Wages and prices can be variable without being flexible; they may vary, but not fast enough to clear the labor market. The main reason we need to make assumptions about wage and price flexibility is that it is not possible to know whether the labor market clears by just looking at wage and price data, or by observing current market behavior. The labor market, like any other market, is in a state of flux. Every day, some people enter the market and some leave; some new jobs appear and some existing jobs disappear. For this reason, we often make assumptions that we believe are realistic characterizations of the markets.

Why would wages be sticky in the first place? As discussed in Chapter 1, economics is based on the assumption that the decision-making units act rationally in their own self-interest. This means that they take an action if the benefit of that action exceeds the cost of that action, and they don't take the action if the cost exceeds the benefit. However, the assumption of sticky wages is contrary to this widely accepted principle. Why would a worker who has just lost his job resist a wage cut and remain unemployed for many months? Having no job is worse than having a low-paying job.

Similarly, suppose that the demand for the products of a producer goes down. If the producer lowers its price, it can increase sales and satisfy its customers. Why would the producer instead decide to keep the price at the current level, or reduce it only slightly, and lose sales and customers? A more intriguing question is, Why would the producer not increase his price when the demand for the product increases? So we need to explain why wages and prices are sticky—while at the same time the decision-making units are acting rationally. To put it differently, we need to understand why we can have cyclical unemployment while people are acting in their own self-interest.

REASONS FOR NOMINAL WAGE RIGIDITY

Labor Contracts

COST-OF-LIVING ADJUSTMENT (COLA)
Increases in wages by employers to adjust for increases in prices.

There are two kinds of labor contracts: explicit and implicit. Explicit contracts are written contracts between firms and labor unions that fix workers' wages for one to three years. Some contracts include the effect of inflation on wages. For example, they include phrases such as: the wage rate for the next three years will be so and so, *plus* the percentage change in the consumer price index (CPI). This is called *cost of living adjustment (COLA)*. However, even with COLAs, wages do not adjust quickly. That is because there are time lags between the times CPI figures are published and the times wages are adjusted. Also, not all COLAs adjust wages for inflation on a one-to-one basis.

Another feature of contracts is that they usually fix the nominal wage, but they do not fix the amount of labor hired. In fact, producers can lay off workers if their sales drop. Furthermore, the labor contracts usually promise to provide additional hours to the firms and allow the firms to hire additional labor during times of high demand.

The future state of the economy is not known. Why do firms and workers commit themselves to three-year wage contracts? Why do you commit yourself to a fixed wage rate for the next three years, if you don't know what the price will be then? Isn't this irrational? Not really, say the Keynesians. Entering into wage negotiations is costly for both the firms and the unions. Sometimes they have to hire lawyers and economists or CPAs for these negotiations. To minimize these costs, they do this every two to three years. During this time period, wages remain rigid.

Implicit labor contracts are for sociological or cultural reasons. There are no written or explicit contracts between workers and employers. For example, firms often try not to cut workers' wages. They cut wages only in severe cases such as severe recessions or bankruptcies. They would rather lay off some workers than make all their workers mad by cutting their wages. This is rational behavior, since firms are basically buying workers' loyalty.

Efficiency Wage Theory

This theory is becoming popular among economists. Suppose that the going market-clearing wage rate is $60, and that if you pay $60 per day to your workers, you will be able to hire all the workers you need. But instead, a lot of firms may choose to pay $80 per day. Why? Are they acting irrationally? No, they do this because with that extra $20 they pay each worker, they buy their loyalty and increase their morale. Additionally, since this is higher than the going wage in the market, workers do not want to lose their jobs and land in a lower-paying job. Therefore, the extra $20 reduces shirking and increases productivity. This increase in labor productivity results in a lower overall average cost of production and higher profits. Such above-equilibrium wages are called *efficiency wages*. As you can see, this is a rational behavior on the part of the firms.

EFFICIENCY WAGES
Wages paid by a firm that are above-equilibrium wages in order to improve productivity and increase productive efficiency.

The way in which efficiency wages result in sticky wages is as follows: Suppose that currently the going market-clearing nominal wage is $60, but you are paying an efficiency wage of $80 per day. Now if the going wage in the market place goes up to $65 or down to $55, you will not care that much and will continue paying $80 per day to your workers. Of course, if the going wage changes to $80 or $30, then you will think of changing your wage. To that extent, nominal wages will be sticky.

A famous example of an efficiency wage is Henry Ford's $5-per-day wage. This was twice the going wage rate of the time. A lot of workers lined up in the Ford factory to get hired. Why did Henry Ford do it? He introduced assembly line production for cars. Workers were mostly low skilled and were doing repetitive simple tasks. The jobs were boring, resulting in shirking, low morale, many "sick leaves," and low productivity. Moreover, the productivity of any one worker depended on the productivity of the worker before him on the assembly line. If worker number 12 did not tighten the screw on time or properly, worker number 13's job would be compromised. This would result in delays and other production problems. By offering $5 per day, Henry Ford got rid of all these problems. The number of people quitting their jobs dropped and labor productivity improved—as a result, Ford's production costs actually went down!

Workers at a Ford assembly line in 1913

Federal and State governments enact minimum wage laws.

Minimum Wage Laws

If your value to a company is only $4 an hour, but the minimum wage is $6.25 per hour, then you will not get hired. This argument affects a small fraction of the labor force—teenagers and some unskilled workers. Note that in this case, unemployment among teenagers and unskilled workers would not lower the minimum wage.

Insider-Outsider Model

Some economists argue that when there is a recession, people lose their jobs and become unemployed. People who are unemployed would probably be willing to work for less to get hired, so there is no irrationality on the part of the unemployed workers. However, the problem is that they are unemployed and outside the company. They are *outsiders* and therefore don't sit at the bargaining table. They have no power. Firms negotiate wages with workers who are employed, and are inside the company. Now, the firm can threaten the *insiders* that they could get laid off and join the outsiders if they don't accept a lower wage. But this strategy is not quite effective. This is because it could lower morale and loyalty, resulting in reduced worker productivity. So even if there are unemployed workers outside, firms try to make the workers inside happy by offering them good wages. This is a rational behavior on the part of the firms, as a result of which there can be unemployment and rigid wages.

REASONS FOR PRICE RIGIDITY

Price Contracts

The most obvious reason for price rigidity is the presence of contracts between producers and their major suppliers and customers. For instance, a computer producer might have a long-term contract with its suppliers, such as producers of memory boards and other parts and components, as well as with its customers such as major retail outlets. Such contracts ensure price stability for both buyers and sellers over a certain period of time.

Menu Costs

The menu cost argument proposed by Gregory Mankiw of Harvard University is that changing prices is costly. Firms have to publish new menus or catalogs, inform their distributors about the new prices, and so on. Therefore, when the demand for their products goes down, they don't rush to lower their prices. Instead, they sell fewer items at the existing high prices. After a while, however, they realize that the small cost of changing the prices is less than the loss in profits due to lost sales, because of charging high prices. At that point, they lower their prices and publish new catalogs.

Empirical evidence shows that prices are, in fact, rigid. A 1986 study by Dennis Carlton of the University of Chicago showed that prices were more rigid (changed less frequently) in more monopolistic industries. Anil Kashyap (1995) studied the prices of 12 industrial items listed in the catalogs of L.L. Bean, Orvis, and Recreational Equipment, Inc. over a 35-year period. He found both large and small changes in prices. He also found that prices in general were rigid. He concluded that small changes in prices are against the menu cost argument. If menu costs were important, then we would observe a long period over which the price of an item was fixed, and then we would witness a big change in its price. That is because it would not be cost effective to print a new menu every time the price increased by a few cents. The fact that there were many small price changes indicated that menu costs were not really the cause of rigid or sticky prices. In other words, he found that prices were rigid, but not due to menu costs.

Coordination Problem

In 1994 Alan Blinder of Princeton University conducted a survey with the help of his graduate students. They sent questionnaires to several producers asking them about their pricing policies. About 50% of the respondents said they changed their prices only once a year or less. Only 22% of producers said they changed their prices four times a year or more. Blinder found that menu costs were of some relevance. However, there was a more important reason for price rigidity.

Many respondents said they did not change their prices for strategic reasons. They did not want to be the first firm in the industry to change prices. "If we raised our price," they said, "we would be afraid that our competitors might not follow suit. We would then lose a lot of market. But if we lowered our price, our competitors would do the same to protect their market share. As a result, we would not gain much from lowering our price." In other words, producers have a *coordination problem*. If they could just talk to each other, they could reduce or increase their prices together. But this is not feasible or even legal.[1]

COORDINATION PROBLEM
The notion that producers cannot coordinate their pricing policies. A producer is hesitant to raise its price, fearing that others will not follow suit and it will lose sales. The producer is also hesitant to reduce its price, thinking that others will follow suit and it will not gain any advantage from doing that.

GENERAL EQUILIBRIUM OF THE ECONOMY

Figure 1 puts together the aggregate demand and the classical aggregate supply functions. Along the aggregate demand function, the goods and money markets clear. Along the aggregate supply function, the labor market clears. So if the economy is on the AS function, there will be no unemployment, and the real GDP will equal potential. Therefore, at point E_0, all three markets clear—we have a *general equilibrium* in the economy.

GENERAL EQUILIBRIUM
A situation in which all three markets—goods, money, and labor— are in equilibrium.

1. *Goods market equilibrium* (Y = C + I + G). Aggregate demand for goods and services equals aggregate supply or real GDP. There are no unwanted inventory changes.
2. *Money market equilibrium* ($M = M^d$). The amount of money people hold equals what they want to hold.
3. *Labor market equilibrium* ($S^L = D^L$). Supply of labor equals demand for labor so that we have full employment. In other words, the total number of jobs available in the economy, filled and unfilled, equals the number people who want to work—the labor force.

In a free market economic system, all three markets clear sooner or later, because markets cannot stay in a state of disequilibrium for long. So point E_0 describes a long-run situation. Note finally that the real GDP is determined by the AS function (the labor market) and the price level by the AD function (goods and money markets).

1 The strategic price behavior in oligopolistic markets is discussed more fully in the micro portion of the text.

Figure 1 The General Equilibrium of the Economy

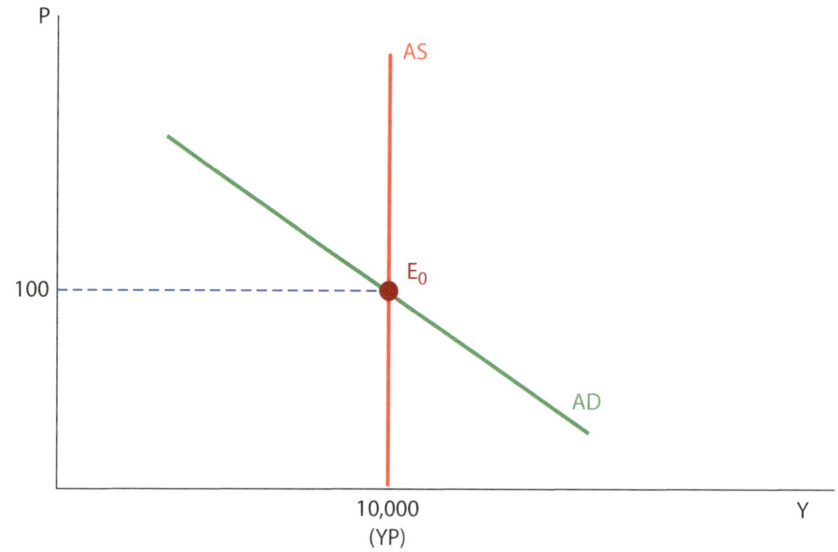

THE SHORT-RUN MODEL

To understand the implications of demand shocks combined with wage and price rigidity, consider Figure 2. Suppose that initially, the economy is in the state of general equilibrium at point E_0,where the aggregate demand function, AD_0, intersects the classical supply function, AS. The price level is P = 100, and the real GDP is at the potential level Y_P = 10,000. As a result of a reduction in consumer confidence or an increase in producer pessimism, aggregate demand decreases to AD_1.

At the current price level of P = 100 there will be an excess supply of goods equal to 1,000 units (10,000 – 9,000). Under the classical assumption of wage and price flexibility, the price level would immediately drop to P = 80 to clear the goods market. Wouldn't producers lose money if they reduced their prices? No, because nominal wages would also drop at the same rate to keep the real wage constant and to clear the labor market. The economy will instantly move to point E_1. To summarize the classical result:

Items on sale at a Wal-Mart in China

1. Producers would cut the price level to P = 80 to restore sales to the previous level of Y_P = 10,000 on the new demand function, AD_1.
2. Workers would accept a proportionately lower nominal wage so that the real wage would remain the same, and no unemployment would develop.
3. The economy would move to point E_1 immediately.
4. Since wages and prices drop at the same rate, firms do not lose any profits and workers do not suffer any reductions in the purchasing power of their wages.

Figure 2 The Short-Run Model

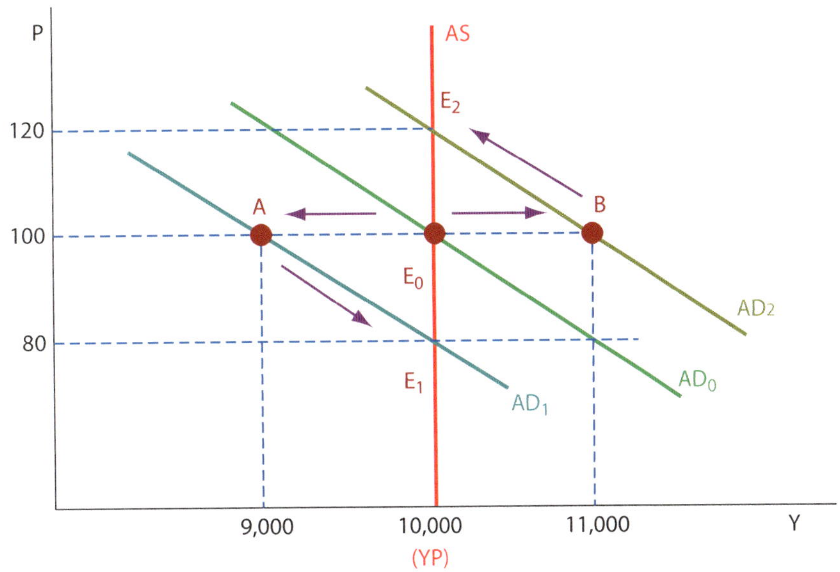

With wage and price stickiness, the above scenario is not feasible anymore, at least not in the short run. Wages are rigid because of contracts and some other reasons. Producers will lose money if they reduce their prices while paying their workers high contract wages. Separately, prices are sticky for the reasons mentioned above. As a result, producers keep prices at their current levels, but reduce production to match consumer demand. The economy moves to point A, producing 9,000 units at the current price level. Now since actual real GDP is less than potential ($Y < Y_P$), we have a recession with cyclical unemployment. At point A, goods and money markets clear, but we have unemployment. Keynes called this situation *unemployment equilibrium*.

UNEMPLOYMENT EQUILIBRIUM *The situation in which the goods market is in equilibrium, but some people are still unemployed.*

Keynes lived and wrote during the Great Depression of the 1930s. He saw a lot of unemployment over a long period of time. Keynes blamed the downward rigidity of nominal wages for the persistence of unemployment. According to Keynes, since market forces are not capable of reducing nominal wages to eliminate unemployment, we need the government to interfere in the marketplace. He advocated fiscal policy because of its direct effect on aggregate demand.

The economy cannot stay at point A forever. At point A, there is unemployment, and the unemployed need jobs to support their families. Sooner or later, contracts will expire and workers will start accepting lower wages. As wages go down, producers can reduce their prices. Three things happen as prices fall. First, households' real wealth (A/P) increases, encouraging consumption. Second, net export rises, increasing the demand for domestic goods. Finally, demand for money is reduced, reducing the interest rate and stimulating consumption and investment. As you recall from Chapter 12, these are the reasons for the negative slope of the AD function. As aggregate demand increases, producers step up production and real GDP increases. The economy moves down the new AD function. The process continues for as long as there are unemployed resources, and stops as soon as full employment is restored at point E_1.

Consider next an increase in aggregate demand. Suppose that the economy was in equilibrium at point E_0, but then the aggregate demand increased to AD_2. In the classical model, prices would increase to $120, wages would rise just as fast, and the economy would move to the new equilibrium point, E_2, instantly. Now, however, wages and prices are rigid. Producers are reluctant to increase prices for the reasons described above. They try to satisfy the new high demand by producing 11,000 units at the current price level, and the economy moves to point B.

At point B, real GDP exceeds potential ($Y > Y_P$). This situation cannot last long. A lot of workers are working overtime, and sooner or later they ask for higher wages as contracts expire. At that point, producers have to increase their prices. As prices rise, aggregate demand is reduced for the familiar three reasons, and the economy moves up the AD_2 function. As aggregate demand is reduced, real GDP starts to fall, until the economy reaches point E_2, at which the price level is $120 and real GDP equals potential.

You could say that the Keynesian model is the classical model in slow motion. Therefore, all the classical results hold in this model, too, with the only difference being that in the short-run model, it takes time for wages and prices to change. For example, a loss in consumer confidence (as happened in the 1990–1991 recession) would cause the AD function to shift down, resulting in unemployment (point A). Over time, though, the economy would move to point E_1, and full employment would be restored. Or, an expansionary demand management policy would shift the AD curve to AD_2. This would expand output in the short run (point B), but the resulting pressure in the labor market would cause the prices to rise, and the economy would move to point E_2. As in the classical model, an expansionary fiscal policy would crowd out private spending, and monetary policy would only cause inflation.

ANALYSIS OF A RECESSION

SELF-CORRECTING MECHANISM
The idea that a recession will end by itself without the help of the government. This is because, even though wages and prices may be rigid in the short run, they will adjust over time to clear the labor market.

This model has the same answer as the classical model, but for the long run. This is because of the *self-correcting mechanism* inherent in the economy. In essence, when a recession hits for whatever reason, unemployment results. This is due to sticky wages and prices. But unemployment cannot last forever. Workers need to eat. So over time, as contracts expire, wages go down and the unemployed get hired. Prices go down, lowering the interest rate, so that households and firms start buying more goods and services. The recession comes to an end.

Should the government step in at any time to stimulate aggregate demand in order to get the economy out of recession? The answer depends in part on how long the long run is. How long *is* the long run? We don't know. (How is that for an answer?) We have had short recessions lasting about two years (the 1973–1974 and 1990–1991 recessions), and long ones (the Great Depression). The answer also depends on the severity of the recession—whether it's shallow, with mild unemployment (1990-–1991), or deep, with a high unemployment rate (1980–1982).

Arguments Against Active Policy

The opponents of active stabilization policy make several arguments against government intervention. First, they argue that the self-correcting mechanism will ultimately get the economy out of recession, so a government policy intervention would be unnecessary. Second, an expansionary fiscal policy would only crowd out private spending, and thus be ultimately ineffective. Moreover, an expansionary monetary policy may only cause inflation. That is because firms are pessimistic about future profits in a recession, so an increase in money supply may reduce the interest rate, but may not increase investment spending. Pumping more money into the economy just raises prices.

Third, there is the issue of lags in the implementation and effects of demand management policies. Suppose a recession comes. It takes time for the policy makers to recognize that a recession is going on. Then it takes time to formulate a policy response. Should the government increase spending, cut taxes, provide more generous transfer payments, or increase the money supply? In either case, what should be the size of these changes? Suppose the government decides to increase spending to stimulate the economy. Obviously, it takes time for this policy to take effect. Suppose that due to the lags in recognition and decision, the government increases spending six months before the end of the recession, but it takes one year for the multiplier process to have the full effect. Then the policy will have its full effect six months after the recession has already ended. Now the aggregate demand will increase when real GDP is already equal to potential. This policy will then exacerbate the fluctuations in GDP.

Fourth and finally, these lags are both long and variable. In other words, in one recession it may take only one year for the policy to have its full effect. In another recession, it may take two years. Because of this problem, the lengths of these time lags cannot be accurately predicted ahead of time. This makes the outcome of the policies quite uncertain, and reduces the net benefits of the policies. Chapter 22 discusses the lags in fiscal policy in a slightly more detailed fashion.

Arguments for Active Policy

The proponents of government intervention believe that if the recession lasts long and the unemployment problem is severe, then some government intervention is justified to reduce the pain and suffering endured by the families of the unemployed. First, the self-correcting process could be long and painful. Since unemployment is a kind of market failure that results from sticky wages and prices, an expansionary demand management policy is justified to boost aggregate demand and reduce unemployment.

Volunteers prepare food packages at the San Diego Food Bank. Food Banks provide much needed food assistance to low-wage and unemployed individuals and families.

As you recall, Keynes believed that fiscal policy is generally more effective to get the economy out of a recession. If the government conducts an expansionary fiscal policy, then AD_1 shifts up in Figure 1, and the recession may end sooner. Between a balanced-budget increase in spending (as in Chapter 7) and running a budget deficit (as in Chapter 10), Keynesians favor the latter. This is because the former has only a multiplier of one, while the latter, which relies on borrowing rather than taxation, is more expansionary.

How about the crowding-out effect? Keynesians argue that crowding out could happen during normal times. Recessionary times are not normal times. These are times in which consumption and investment are already down. Firms are not buying due to uncertainty about the state of the economy and future profitability of investment projects. Households are not buying, because they have either lost their jobs or fear that they might in the future. So there isn't much private spending to be crowded out in the first place. Moreover, in a recession, the interest rate may fall into the liquidity trap, so a deficit financing by the government may not increase the interest rate. If the interest rate does not increase, there will be no crowding-out effect. Moreover, in a recession, there is plenty of idle cash in the banking system that the government can tap into to increase its spending.

According to Keynesians, monetary policy may not be effective during a recession, because one or more of the links in the monetary policy process may be weak or broken. An increase in money supply may not reduce the interest rate if the interest rate is in the liquidity trap. Even if the interest rate is reduced, consumption and investment may not be stimulated due to general uncertainty in the economy. Finally, even if consumption and investment increase, aggregate demand may not increase much due to a small expenditure multiplier during a recession. This is because of a small marginal propensity to consume during a recession.

How about lags in the implementation of fiscal policy? Proponents point to the fact that consumption spending depends in part on the expected future disposable income. Even if there are lags in fiscal policy, if households know that taxes will decline in the future, they will increase consumption today, somewhat eliminating the effects of lags on GDP. Moreover, once business firms realize that demand will rise in the future due to an increase in government spending, they may increase their investment spending today in expectation of higher profits. Therefore, fiscal policy also works through increasing people's confidence in the future state of the economy.

SUPPLY SHOCKS

ADVERSE SUPPLY SHOCK
Any event that results in higher prices and lower quantities supplied with the given demand conditions.

An *adverse supply shock* is any event that results in higher prices with the given demand conditions. As the name implies, the shock should originate from the supply side, rather than the demand side. The event should cause an increase in the cost of production unrelated to the level of output produced. For example, all else the same, if labor unions ask for and receive a higher wage, the cost of production will increase. Business firms will try to pass the additional cost on to their consumers. This will increase prices. Labor is not the only production factor and wages are not the only cost of production. Firms buy other inputs such as raw materials, parts, and components. They also buy oil and natural gas as production inputs. Some firms like transportation companies, airlines, or electricity producers are heavy users of oil and gas products.

What happens if the prices of such production inputs increase? What happens if OPEC comes with a higher oil price? Many economists believe that the recession of 1974–1975 was because of higher oil prices caused by Saudi Arabia's oil embargo. The higher oil prices of 1979 and the subsequent recession of 1980–1982 were also partly blamed on the rise in oil prices, brought about by the Iranian Revolution and the resulting disruptions in oil production. Moreover, some blame the Iraqi invasion of Kuwait and the resulting oil price increase as a factor contributing to the 1990–1991 recession.

Their reasoning can be explained using Figure 3. The figure shows that the economy is in a state of long-run equilibrium at point E_0. Consider a one-time-only increase in the price of crude oil brought about by OPEC. The resulting increase in the cost of production will cause prices of goods and services to rise, as producers try to pass the higher costs to consumers. Since the price level is already on the vertical axis, there will be no shift in the AD function. The economy will move on the AD function from point E_0 to a place like point A. The higher prices will result in a higher interest rate, reducing consumption and investment. Moreover, higher prices will reduce consumption through the real wealth effect. During the time the economy is moving from point E_0 to point A, prices will be rising and the real GDP falling. During this time we will have inflation coupled with cyclical unemployment. This situation is called *stagflation* (stagnation + inflation).

STAGFLATION
Inflation coupled with recession.

INFLATIONARY EXPECTATIONS
Expectations about the future inflation rates.

During the period in which prices are rising, workers, firms, and households will come to expect that the rising prices will continue into the future. These *inflationary expectations* will lead to further actual inflation in the future. This is for a simple reason: In anticipation of higher future prices and in order to protect their real wages, workers will ask for higher nominal wages in their wage negotiations. Since producers also expect higher prices in the future, they will be willing to accept these wage demands. Therefore, the inflationary expectations will be built into the wage contracts, and in the following years, wages and prices will increase for this secondary reason.

Since this was just a one-time increase in the price of oil, the effect on the U.S. goods prices cannot go on forever. After a while, the economy will reach a point like point A, with a high price level and a high unemployment rate. Goods prices stop rising, and unemployment finally starts pushing nominal wages down. The economy starts to move down the AD function until it reaches E_0 again. An increase in one component of production costs—oil prices—results in a decrease in the other: nominal wages. In the end, the price level goes back to where it was before, and unemployment is eliminated. What happens to the real wage? Since the price level is back to its initial level and we have no unemployment, the real wage must be the same as before. So supply shocks, like economic polices, do not have a permanent effect on the economy.

Supply shocks, though, pose several policy dilemmas for the government. First, should the government interfere when the economy is suffering from inflation and unemployment, or should it wait for the self-correcting mechanism to solve both problems over time? Second, assuming that the government decided to interfere, what should it do? Consider Figure 3 again. Suppose that as a result of the supply shock, the economy moves to point A. If the government decides that inflation is the more serious problem, it may reduce the aggregate demand through a contractionary fiscal or monetary policy to AD_1. Then the economy will move to point B. The price level will be brought back to the level it was before the OPEC shock, but now we will suffer from an even worse unemployment problem. On the other hand, if the government decides that unemployment is a bigger problem, it can conduct an expansionary demand management policy, increasing the aggregate demand to AD_2. This policy will solve the unemployment problem at the cost of higher prices.

Figure 3 A Supply Shock

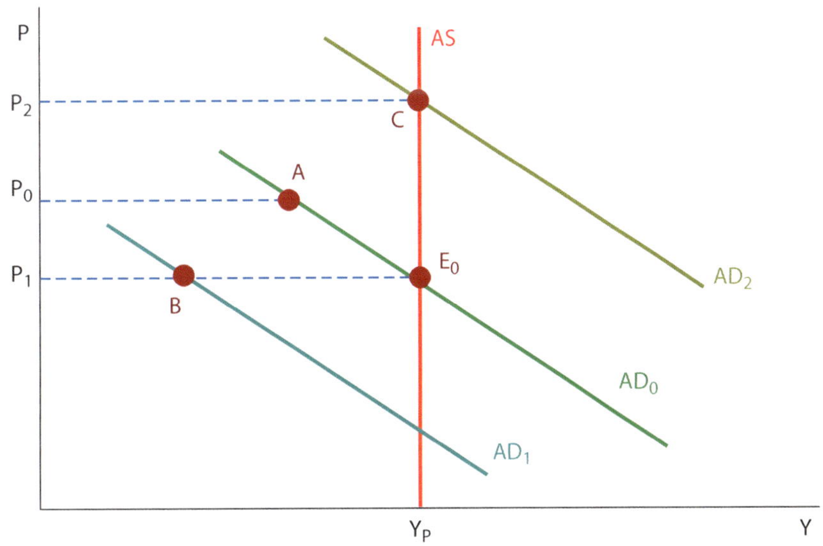

The Four Post–1970 Recessions: A Summary

Our discussion of the four post–1970 recessions has been scattered all over the book. Since we have now developed the complete macro model, this is a good place to briefly describe the four recessions. You should, however, note that there are still some disagreements among economists about the exact causes of some of these recessions.

Recession of 1974–1975

As you recall, this recession is associated with an increase in the price of crude oil from the Middle East. From 1973 to 1975 the Organization of Petroleum Producing Countries (OPEC) doubled the price of oil exported to the West. The increase in the price of oil affected the U.S. economy through several channels.

1. *Oil is an input into many industrial and commercial activities. For example, the transportation sector is heavily oil dependent. An increase in the price of oil would push up the cost of producing many products, reducing consumer demand for these products. For instance, the prices of airline and bus tickets would increase, resulting in fewer trips taken by households. As a result, firms would lay off workers. The combined higher general price level and low unemployment is called stagflation. This would be a movement along the AD curve in the north-west direction.*

2. *Demand for gasoline by households is price inelastic in the short run. This means that when the price of gasoline increases, households cannot drastically reduce their driving. As a result, gasoline takes a big chunk of household expenditures, leaving less money to be spent on other goods and services. This further reduces aggregate demand, and encourages workers to ask for higher wages. The higher wages further push up production costs and the goods prices, creating additional inflation.*

3. *These events make workers and capitalists expect higher inflations in the future. These inflationary expectations are built into wage contracts creating more inflation in the future. Such a process is described in more detail in Chapter 18.*

In 1975 the Congress passed the Tax Reduction Act to stimulate the economy. This expansionary fiscal policy shifted the aggregate demand function to the right. At the same time, the Fed increased the money supply to keep the interest rate down. This expansionary monetary policy prevented the crowding out of private spending that would otherwise result from the reduction in taxes.

After all this, you may find it interesting that some economists do not believe that the oil price hikes of the 1970s were the main reason for the stagflations of the time. Expenditure on oil and oil-related products comprises less than 10% of total U.S. expenditures on all the goods and services. Therefore, they ask, how could oil have such a huge effect on the economy?

They point out that the recession of 1974–1975 began in November 1973, but oil prices jumped in January 1974. Barsky and Killian argue that the stagflations of the 1970s were mostly the results of monetary policies alternating between being expansionary and contractionary. Finally, Bernanke, Gertler, and Watson argue that postwar recessions have been preceded not only by higher oil prices, but also by contractionary monetary policies. This means that empirically, it has been difficult to isolate the separate effects of oil price hikes and tight monetary policies on the GDP and, as a result, the effect of oil on GDP has been exaggerated. For a short and readable paper and references to the above studies, see Bharat Trehan, "Why Hasn't the Jump in Oil Prices Led to a Recession?" Federal Reserve Bank of San Francisco Economic Letter, Number 2005–31, November 18, 2005.

Recession of 1980–1982

The high oil prices of the 1970s—combined with expansionary demand-management policies of the decade—had resulted in very high inflation rates. Another oil price hike came in 1979, when the Iranian revolution resulted in the disruption in oil supplies. At some point, the inflation rate was running at 10% per year or higher. Around 1980 Paul Volcker, then chairman of the Fed, decided to bring the runaway inflation under control by following a contractionary monetary policy. This resulted in very high interest rates at the time. The high interest rates reduced the aggregate demand through the channels we already know. The demand for housing was particularly hit hard, as this sector is very sensitive to changes in interest rates. This episode is famous as the Volcker disinflation.

It must be noted that this disinflation was taking place during the time President Reagan was increasing budget deficits, and hence, aggregate demand. This would have an effect on inflation and prices opposite to a tight monetary policy. In the long run, though, as our model predicts, the monetary policy won the battle, and the inflation rate was brought under control.

Recession of 1990–1991

The recession of 1990–1991 began in July 1990. Many commentators at the time blamed the loss on consumer confidence as the cause of this recession. Nevertheless, commentators had a hard time explaining the reasons for this loss in consumer confidence in the economy. The Iraqi invasion of Kuwait took place late in the summer of 1990, and oil prices jumped in August of that year. So oil prices were not the main reason for the recession, although they were the contributing factors.

The recovery came in the second half of 1991. But there was something peculiar about this recovery. The recovery took place without much increase in employment. This recovery came to be known as the "jobless recovery." President George H. W. Bush had inherited large deficits from his predecessor President Reagan, as we saw above. For this reason, he was reluctant to increase government spending further to stimulate aggregate demand. Such a move, he thought, would increase interest rates and crowd out private spending. Additionally, it would increase an already high national debt—the sum total of money borrowed by the government in the past. President Bush was not reelected, mostly because of his inaction to effectively combat the recession.

Recession of 2001

As you recall, this was a mild recession that started in March 2001 and ended after eight months in November 2001. The following are the factors that caused this recession:

1. *During the second half of the 1990s, the prices of high-technology stocks soared. Investors had a great deal of optimism about the future of "dot-com" companies such as telecommunication and Internet firms. These events were self propelling. Business firms, whose stock prices had increased, found an easy way of raising funds for their investments by selling stocks. Households also experienced an increase in their real wealth as the prices of the high-tech stocks they were holding increased. Finally, federal and state governments' tax revenues increased sharply because of the increase in the capital gains taxes, which was the result of higher stock prices. Households are taxed on the profits (called capital gains) they realize from selling stocks. Governments then increased their spending on goods and services. Therefore, the aggregate demand was increasing because of the increases in C, I, and G.*

   Around the year 2000 investors realized that most of the optimism they held about the hi-tech companies was not warranted. In the middle of the year 2000, the prices of these companies started to decline sharply. The reduction in stock prices had an effect on the aggregate demand opposite of what is described above. Households, in particular, reduced their consumption because of the reduction in their real wealth. The reduction in aggregate demand set off the recession.

2. *The terrorist attacks of September 11, 2001, also had some effect on stock prices. These attacks shook investors' confidence in the future of the economy, as they expected more attacks to come. Transportation, tourism, and the related industries were particularly hit hard as households reduced their demands for these services out of fear of terrorism. The result was a reduction in stock prices, and lower consumption and investment. This event, though, was not big enough—relative to the size of the U.S. economy—to have a significant effect on the GDP. Moreover, the Fed conducted a massive expansionary monetary policy to keep the interest rates low and get the economy going. The Fed's action alleviated the effect of the terrorist attacks on the economy.*

3. *Finally, there were some corporate scandals in 2001 and 2002 that played a role in the 2001 recession. In particular, it came to be known around this time that some corporations like Enron and WorldCom had been inflating their profits through accounting gimmicks and manipulating their financial statements. They were doing this to pretend they were more profitable than they actually were, and to raise funds for investments through artificially inflated stock prices. Once investors learned about these fraudulent accounting practices, they lost faith in the profitability of other corporations as well. As a result, stock prices fell, reducing consumption and investment.*

4. *As mentioned above, the Fed responded to these events by an expansionary monetary policy. Some economists believe that this was the most aggressive expansionary policy the Fed had ever followed. The policy was apparently effective in ending the recession, thus making it one of the most short-lived recessions in U.S. history.*

TO SUMMARIZE

1. In the Keynesian model, deficient aggregate demand coupled with sticky nominal wages and prices, results in recessions.
2. The government can get the economy out of recession with an expansionary demand management policy.
3. Nominal wages are rigid due to labor contracts, efficiency wages, imperfect information, minimum wage laws, and the insider-outsider problem.
4. Prices are rigid due to menu costs, coordination problems, and sticky information.
5. A recession starts due to a fall in aggregate demand.
6. The resulting unemployment puts downward pressure on wages and prices. As prices fall, interest rates fall, aggregate demand rises, and the recession is eliminated.
7. Thus, a recession is a temporary phenomenon.
8. For the same reason, demand management policies only have temporary effects.
9. The same is true for supply shocks such as oil price hikes.
10. Surges in oil prices have generally been blamed for the stagflations of the 1970s through the 1990s. However, some economists have recently argued that inflationary expectations and monetary policy actions by the Fed were also part of the explanation.

EXERCISES

Question 1

Consider the following aggregate demand data. Assume that the expenditure multiplier is 10. The potential level of output equals Y_p = 10,000 units.

Aggregate Demand Data	
P	Y
80.0	7,000
67.5	8,250
65.0	8,500
62.5	8,750
60.0	9,000
50.0	10,000
47.5	10,250
45.0	10,500
42.5	10,750
40.0	11,000
30.0	12,000
20.0	13,000

a. Find the equilibrium price level.

b. Suppose that investment spending decreased by 300 units. What would happen to the equilibrium price level and the real GDP in the classical model? What if investment spending increased by 300 units?

c. Suppose that investment spending decreased by 300 units, but wages and prices were sticky. Find the short run values of Y and P. Show this graphically. What would happen in the long run?

d. Repeat part (c) for the case where investment spending increases by 300.

e. Calculate the percentage GDP gap in the short run in part (c) above.

f. Suppose that the Fed reduces money supply by 20%. What will be the effect of this policy on P and Y in the short run and the long run?

g. Repeat part (f) for the case where money supply increases by 25%.

h. Start with the equilibrium situation of part (a). Assume that OPEC comes with a higher price of oil, and as a result the price level increases by 20%. What will be the effect of this supply shock on Y and P in the short and long runs?

i. Repeat part (h) for the case of a drop in the price of oil by 20%.

j. Start with the equilibrium situation of part (a). Assume that OPEC comes with a higher price of oil, and as a result the price level increases by 20%. To combat the resulting unemployment, the Fed immediately increases the money supply by 20%.What will be the effect of these two events on Y and P in the short and long runs?

k. Start with the equilibrium situation of part (a). Assume that OPEC comes with a higher price of oil, and as a result the price level increases by 20%. To combat the resulting inflation, the Fed immediately reduces the money supply by 20%.What will be the effect of these two events on Y and P in the short and long runs?

l. Suppose that investment spending is reduced by 100 units. To fight the resulting recession, the Fed increases the money supply by 25%. Discuss the short run and long run effects of these two policies on P and Y.

Question 2

Starting from a situation of equilibrium, analyze the short run and long run effects of a once-and-for-all decrease in the price of oil.

Question 3

Suppose that a recession hits as a result of a loss in consumer confidence. As the economic advisor to the government, would you propose an expansionary demand management policy to get the economy out of the recession? What factors would you take into consideration in deciding for or against such a course of action?

Question 4

Suppose a stagflation comes as a result of an OPEC action. Would you, as the economic advisor to the government, propose any demand management policy to get the economy out of the mess? What kind of policy would you suggest? What factors would you take into consideration in suggesting such a course of action?

CHAPTER 14

Expectations and Economic Fluctuations

INTRODUCTION AND REVIEW

Before discussing some new models of business cycles, it is useful to summarize what we have learned so far. For several reasons (including things such as labor contracts), nominal wages and prices are sticky in the short run—they do not change fast enough or in sufficient magnitudes to clear the goods and labor markets. We assume that the money market is always in equilibrium. Wage and price rigidity are the main reasons why recessions can occur. A recession is a situation in which actual real GDP is less than potential so that some workers are cyclically unemployed. In other words, the supply of labor exceeds the demand for labor. The assumptions of wage and price rigidity result in what is called the Keynesian model. The assumptions themselves are called the Keynesian assumptions.

We are interested in knowing two things:

1. What causes the real GDP to deviate from the potential GDP?
2. Could—or should—the government interfere when this happens?

To see how the real GDP can deviate from the potential GDP under the conditions of wage and price rigidity, we first assume that the two are equal. Then we change a variable that causes either the aggregate demand or the price level to change, and trace the effect on the real GDP. As you recall, Keynes believed that changes in aggregate demand are the main reasons for recessions. Therefore, let's generate a recession in the spirit of Keynes, by assuming that aggregate demand decreases due to a loss in consumer or producer confidence in the future of the economy.

As these two groups reduce their consumption and investment spending, the aggregate demand for goods and services goes down. Inventories start to pile up, and business firms realize that they are producing too much. If nominal wages were flexible, business firms could lower their prices quickly and by a sufficient amount, to restore the original sales volume. This is because they would know that the nominal wage would drop immediately to restore the original real wage, following the price reduction. This nominal wage flexibility would have two very important implications. First, firms could afford to lower their prices. Lowering prices would reduce their revenues, but the immediate reduction in wages would reduce their costs so that their profits would remain unchanged. Second, the labor market would instantly clear, and no unemployment would arise. Therefore, the only effect of a lower demand would be lower nominal wages and prices. Such a result is called the classical result.

The rigidity of wages and prices would change the whole story. For two reasons, producers would not be able to lower their prices sufficiently to restore the previous sales volume. First, because of contracts and other reasons, they would know that if they lowered their prices, nominal wages would not fall, and as a result they would lose money. Second, even the firms that did not have wage contracts with their workers might not lower their prices. This is partly because they believe that if they did so, their rivals would follow suit, and they would not be able to restore the sales volume to the original level. Moreover, they might not have the most updated information about demand conditions. Therefore, they keep charging prices that were good for the previous market conditions.

As a result of wage and price rigidity, business firms would not be able to restore their original sales volume. Consequently, they would not need to employ as many workers as before, and thus would lay off some workers. The economy would slip into a recession. Unemployment, though, cannot last forever. As contracts expired, workers would accept lower wages in their new contracts. Moreover, some unions might renegotiate new contracts before the old ones expired to prevent further unemployment and suffering among their members. Therefore, as time passes, wages would decrease and firms would find it financially feasible to lower their prices. As wages and prices decline, the economy moves out of recession and full employment is gradually restored. The period of time that it takes for the recession to be over is called the long run. In the long run, therefore, we will have the classical outcome.

The adjustment of wages and prices to get the economy out of recession is called the self-correcting mechanism of the capitalist system. Keynes lived during the Great Depression, which took a long time to end. During this period, many people were out of jobs. There was a great deal of suffering in both Europe and the United States. Keynes believed that the self-correcting mechanism was too slow, and that it would take a long time for it to put an end to the recession. He mostly blamed nominal wage rigidity for the failure of the self-correcting mechanism. Because of this, he advocated the use of demand management policies, especially fiscal policy, to push the economy out of recession.

CHALLENGES TO KEYNESIAN ECONOMICS

By the 1960s Keynesian economics reigned supreme. Economists and policy makers generally (although not unanimously) believed that recessions start due to demand shocks, and linger due to nominal wage and price rigidity. To solve the problem, all they had to do was conduct an expansionary fiscal or monetary policy to push the aggregate demand back up and get the economy out of the recession. Similarly, when the level of aggregate demand was too high, policy makers would reduce spending or the money supply to reduce the inflationary pressure. Such polices were called *leaning against the wind*.

LEANING AGAINST THE WIND
Conducting an expansionary demand management policy in a recession and a contractionary policy in an expansion.

The events of the 1970s and 1980s led some economists and policy makers to question the Keynesian model's conclusions and policy prescriptions. The stagflations of the 1970s and 1980s were believed to be due to adverse supply shocks, not demand shocks. They were mostly thought to be due to oil price shocks brought about by the oil embargo by Saudi Arabia in 1973 and the Iranian revolution that ended in 1979. These events posed two challenges to the Keynesian model. First, unlike the Keynesian diagnosis, the source of the recessions was not demand shocks, but rather supply shocks. Second, the recessions were accompanied by severe inflation. Such a combination had not been observed in practice or anticipated by the Keynesian model.

Moreover, even though Keynes himself had talked about expectations, later Keynesian economists had by and large ignored the role of expectations in economic events. This is mostly because Western economies did not experience any severe inflationary episodes after the Second World War. However, the high inflation rates of the 1970s and 1980s led people to expect more inflation down the road. These inflationary expectations resulted in further inflation. That is because labor unions built these inflation forecasts into their wage contracts, pushing up production costs and prices. Moreover, expectations of higher inflation rates would reduce real interest rates, and encourage consumption and investment. The resulting increase in aggregate demand would further increase the inflation rate. On top of all this, demand management policies were thought to be ineffective in dealing with these problems.

On the theoretical side, some economists questioned the Keynesian assumptions of wage and price rigidity. They argued that these assumptions imply irrational behavior by firms and workers. To take account of these realities, some economists developed new models that radically departed from the Keynesian paradigm. They assumed self-interest and wage and price flexibility. For this reason, their models looked more like the classical model. However, unlike the classical model, the new models could generate business cycles. Nevertheless, the new models yielded the result that demand management policies do not always successfully end recessions. Since they resemble the classical model, these new models are called *new classical economics*. We first talk about the *rational expectations hypothesis*. We then turn our attention to the *real business cycle* model.

NEW CLASSICAL ECONOMICS
The two post–Keynesian models that make the classical assumptions of rational economic behavior and wage-price flexibility. These are the rational expectation models and the real business cycle models.

RATIONAL EXPECTATIONS HYPOTHESIS

This model revolves primarily around the work of Robert Lucas Jr. of the University of Chicago, who introduced it through a series of influential papers in the 1970s. Lucas won the Nobel Prize in economics in 1995 for his work. The following is a brief description of his model. Lucas wanted to show how we can have business cycles even with flexible wages and prices, and why sometimes economic policy does not have the intended effect. Lucas started by assuming that individuals act in their own self-interest, as in the classical model. This implies that wages and prices are fully flexible, because wage and price rigidity are not consistent with economic rationality. For example, a worker who has been laid off will be better off accepting a lower-paying job than asking for his previous wage and remaining unemployed. A producer will benefit if he increases his price in response to an increase in demand rather than keeping it unchanged. How can GDP deviate from potential with wage and price flexibility?

RATIONAL EXPECTATIONS HYPOTHESIS
Proponents of this hypothesis believe that wages and prices are flexible, and that individuals and firms take all the relevant information into account in making decisions and predicting the future. Business cycles happen because unanticipated events create misperceptions about relative prices. Anticipated events do not create misperceptions, and thus do not affect the GDP.

The problem is that producers and workers know the prices of what they sell but have a fuzzy idea about the prices of all the other goods and services in the economy. This is because the other goods are too many in number and they don't buy them regularly. However, the prices of these other goods are important for their economic decisions. A producer calculates his profit as the difference between his revenue, which depends positively on the price of what he is selling, and his costs, which depend positively on the prices of all the inputs he is buying that include parts, components, and labor services. Moreover, he also wants to know whether the increase in the

REAL BUSINESS CYCLE
The theory positing that business cycles are the effects of technological shocks that affect the demand for labor and potential output. In this theory, all unemployment is voluntary.

Determining the sale price of a product includes considering the prices of materials and labor as well as the demand for the product itself.

price of the product is due to an increase in the demand for his product, in which case he will produce more, or to an overall increase in all the prices in the economy, in which case he will not increase production. Similarly, a worker will calculate his real wage using his nominal wage and the prices of all the goods and services he buys.

UNANTICIPATED POLICY

Suppose that the economy was at point E_1 in Figure 1 and all three markets cleared. Suppose also that the nominal wage was W = \$200 and the price level was P = \$100, so that the real wage equaled 2 units. Now suppose that the Fed increases the money supply by 10% without announcing it to the public beforehand. The aggregate demand curve shifts to the right to AD_2. Prices and wages go up by 10% as in the classical model due to the assumption of wage and price flexibility. The real wage remains the same. Producers mainly notice the increase in the prices of their own products, even though all prices and wages have risen by 10%. So they mistakenly believe that the prices of their own products have increased *relative to the prices of other products*. They mistakenly believe that this is because of an increase in the demand for their products. "My marketing efforts have finally paid off," they think to themselves. So they produce more output.

Figure 1 The Effect of an Unanticipated Expansionary Policy

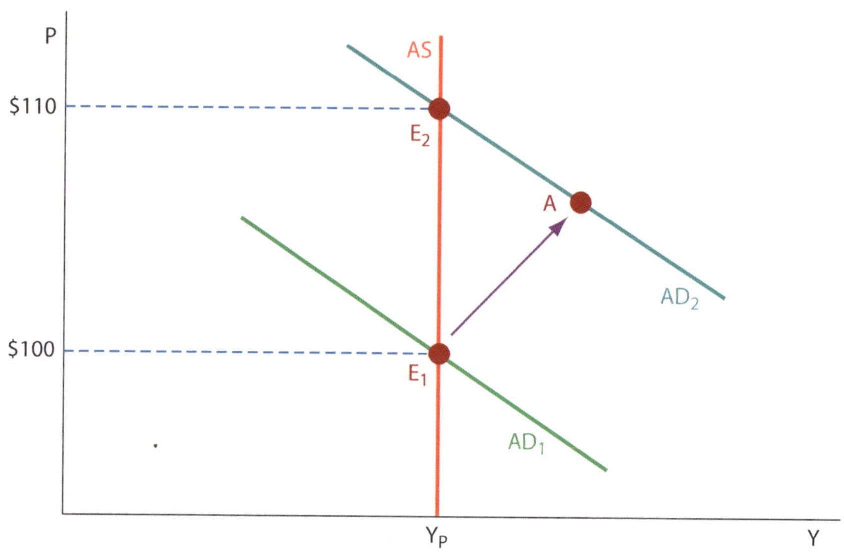

But why are workers willing to supply the additional labor to enable the additional production if their real wage has not changed? They, too, see the 10% increase in their nominal wage because that is the price of what they are selling. However, they do not realize that the prices of all the goods they buy have increased by 10% on average, so that their real wage has remained the same. They think that their nominal wage has increased relative to the prices of goods and services. So they mistakenly think that their real wage has increased. As a result, they supply more labor. This enables producers to hire more workers to produce more output. The economy moves to point A.

So when the AD shifts rightward due to an unanticipated or unannounced increase in money supply, output increases and the real GDP exceeds the potential GDP. Similarly, if AD decreases unexpectedly, prices and wages decline. However, producers notice the decline in their own prices and perceive it as a reduction in the demand for their products and produce less. Workers see the reduction in their wages and supply less labor services. Therefore, real GDP falls short of potential, and a recession starts. It is worth remembering that, in the rational expectations model:

Unanticipated changes in the aggregate demand will cause business cycles.

This conclusion is due to misperceptions about relative price changes by producers and workers. That is why this model is also sometimes called the *misperceptions model*.

MISPERCEPTIONS MODEL
The idea that people and firms have a better idea about the prices of what they sell than the prices of all the other goods in the economy.

ANTICIPATED POLICY

Now start with the same premise as in the previous case, but this time suppose that in 2008, the Fed announces it will increase money supply by 10% in 2009. Since this policy is widely publicized, there will be no misperceptions about relative prices. People will use this information to form their rational expectations of the future price level. Since they have taken a macro class, they will predict that the prices of all the goods and services, including nominal wages, will increase by 10% next year. Therefore in 2008 they will expect the aggregate demand curve in 2009 to be AD_{2009}^{e}, as in Figure 2.

Rational expectations mean the best possible forecasts of the future course of events using all the relevant information currently available. Advocates of this theory believe that since wrong forecasts are costly, people will make every effort to take into account all the information relevant to their forecasts. Recall from Chapter 6 that wrong forecasts of inflation would hurt either borrowers or lenders. In the above example, both producers and workers will take into account the fact that the Fed will increase the money supply by 10%, and therefore, will predict—rationally expect—10% higher wages and prices in the future.

RATIONAL EXPECTATIONS
The best possible forecasts of the future course of events, using all the relevant information currently available.

When the year 2009 comes, the Fed increases the money supply by 10%, as promised. Prices and wages increase by 10%, and the real wage remains unchanged. Since there are no misperceptions about relative prices, producers know that the increase in the prices of their products is just a part of the overall price increase. Workers also know that their real wage has not changed. Therefore, the economy will keep producing Y_p and employment will remain the same at point E_{2009}. So we have the following conclusion:

Anticipated policy is totally ineffective in moving the real GDP. It just creates inflation.

Figure 2 Policy Is Announced in 2008 and Implemented in 2009

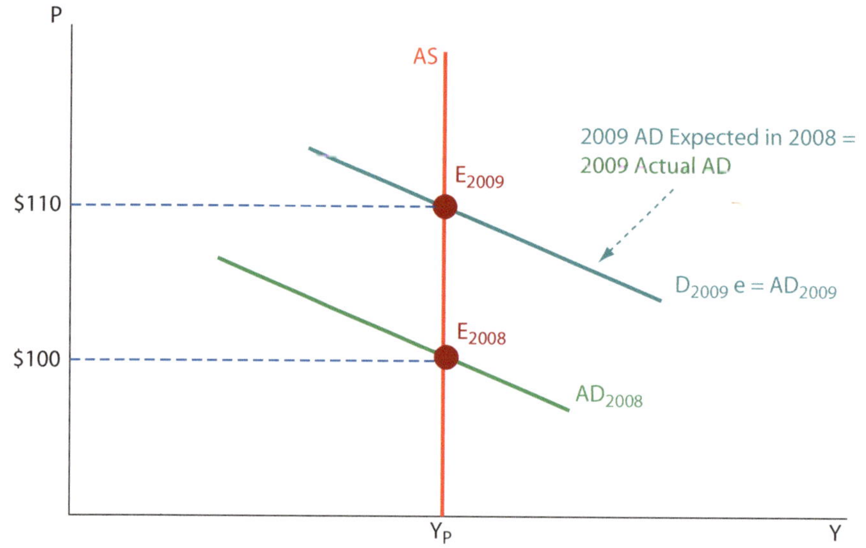

POLICY SURPRISES

There is one interesting case that we should analyze now. What if the Fed announces that it will increase the money supply by 10%, but it actually increases it by 15%? We can answer this question by combining the above two cases. In this case, the money supply will increase by more than anticipated. Nominal wages and prices will increase by 15% to P = $115 and W = $230, so that the real wage will remain unchanged at 2 units.

Look at Figure 3a. In 2008 the Fed announces that the money supply will increase by 10% in 2009, so everyone expects the AD function to shift to AD_{2009}^{e} and the price level to jump to $110 in 2009. When 2009 comes, the AD curve actually shifts more than anticipated, to AD_{2009}. This creates misperceptions, as in the previous case. Producers realize that the prices of their products have increased to $115. They think that perhaps other prices have increased to $110, but not theirs. They mistakenly come to believe that the demand for their products has increased and thus increase production. Similarly, workers expected to receive $220 in wages, but receive $230. They also mistakenly believe that their real wage has increased, so they work more. The economy moves to point E_{2009}. We now have an expansion, with real GDP greater than potential. Again, only the unanticipated part of the policy is effective.

Figure 3a Policy Surprise: Money Supply Increases More than Anticipated

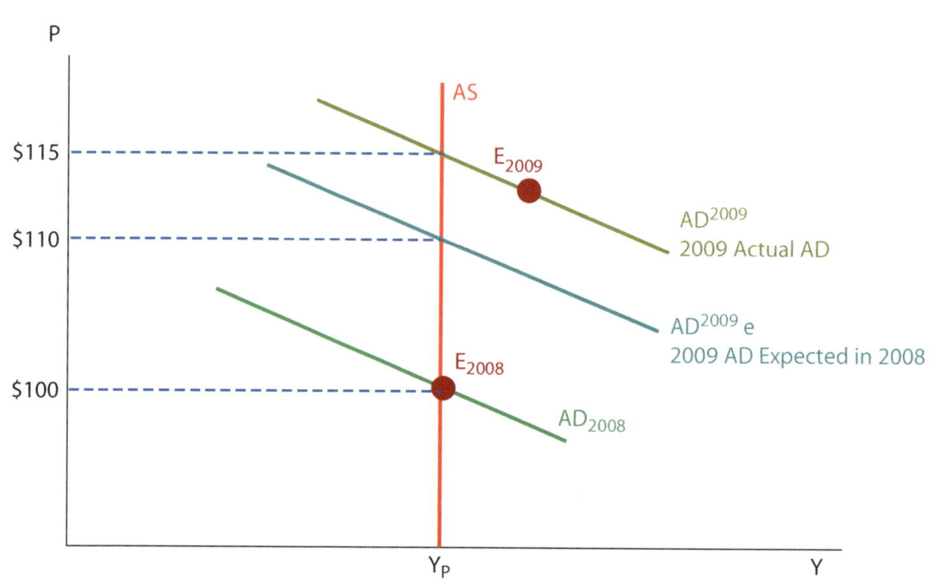

Now let's analyze the opposite case. Suppose in 2008 the Fed announces that it will increase the money supply by 10% in 2009, but it increases it only by 5%. Everyone was anticipating the price level to be P = \$110 and the wage rate W = \$220. But now the price level increases to P = \$105 and the money wage to W = \$210, so that the real wage equals 2. We will have a misperception problem again. Producers will think that the lower than expected price is due to the fall in demand for their products, and thus will produce less. Workers will also think that the lower than expected nominal wage means a lower real wage, so they will supply less labor. The economy will move to point E_{2009}, and a recession will ensue.

Note how perverse the result is. What we see in 2009 is that the *increase* in money supply results in a *reduction*, rather than an increase, in real GDP. In the past, analysts found such a case mysterious. But we now know that there is no mystery about it. Although AD has increased, it has increased less than expected.

Figure 3b Policy Surprise: Money Supply Increases Less than Anticipated

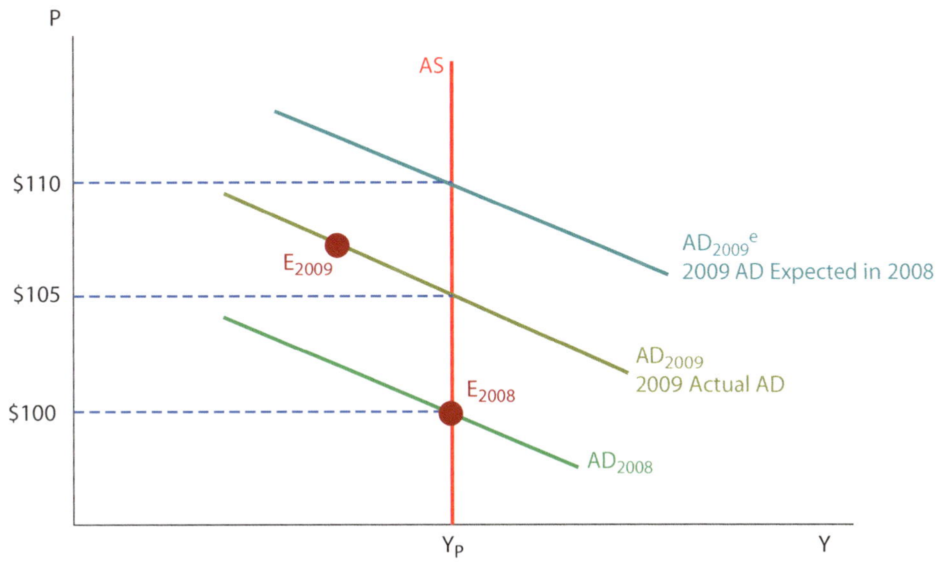

POLICY IMPLICATIONS

The most important implication of this theory is that the government can change the real GDP only if it surprises people. Anticipated policy is ineffective. For this reason, all kinds of antirecession policies, such as Keynesian-type fine tuning and leaning against the wind, will be ineffective. If the Fed follows a policy of increasing money supply during recessions to raise aggregate demand, people will learn about this pattern and anticipate this policy when the economy moves into a recession. They thus neutralize the effect of this policy. This, according to the rational expectations economists, accounts for the policy failures of the 1970s.

By the same token, *credible* anti-inflationary policies will be effective. Just announce that you will lower the money supply by 5%, and then do so. The inflation rate will go down without causing any unemployment. That is because, in this case, everyone will know about the policy and form rational expectations about it. So when the next year comes, prices will be lower, with no change in employment and output.

But then you may ask, "Why did the Volcker disinflation take so many years to reduce the U.S. inflation rate even though the Fed's policy had been well publicized?" The answer that the economists in the rational expectations camp give us is that the Fed was not a credible inflation fighter at that time. Before Paul Volcker took office, the Fed was mostly fighting unemployment at the cost of generating huge inflation, so people did not quite believe that the Fed was serious about its fight against inflation. If the Fed had been more believable as an inflation fighter, the inflation rate would have been reduced much earlier.

Now that we have expectations in our model, we should keep in mind a new relationship between the AS and AD functions as follows:

1. If in 2009 the aggregate demand function intersects the aggregate supply function at the 2008 expected price ($110), then actual GDP in 2009 will equal potential GDP. This is the case of the correctly anticipated price as in Figure 2.
2. If in 2009 the AD function intersects the AS function at any other price, then the actual GDP will deviate from potential GDP. Examples of this case are provided in Figure 3a and 3b.

CRITICISMS OF THE THEORY

The following are some of the criticisms that have been advanced against the rational expectations hypothesis.

1. If the story were true, recessions would be short lived, because they would be due just to misperceptions about prices. Critics point out that the government publishes price data monthly, so recessions should not last more than a couple of months. Once people see the new published prices, they should not have any more misperceptions. The rational expectations economists respond that even though we learn about our forecast errors within a month, it takes time to adjust our production plans.
2. The theory assumes that people know the above model and know exactly what the price will be next year. Many people are not that sophisticated. Even if they are, they may not agree on the "right" model. Even economists do not agree on a single universal model, so why should we expect the general public to do so?

Despite these criticisms, the rational expectations hypothesis has been very influential. The notion that people act in their self-interest and try to forecast the best they can is appealing. Therefore, almost all economists these days assume that expectations are rational. Moreover, there is some empirical support for the argument that an anticipated policy may be ineffective. This is especially true in the financial markets, where news is incorporated in stock prices when they are announced.[1]

REAL BUSINESS CYCLE THEORY

The second theory in the spirit of classical economics is the *real business cycle theory* (RBC). The theory was developed by two economists, Finn Kydland and Edward Prescott, for which they won

1 We will talk about this issue in the chapter on financial market. The rational expectations hypothesis in financial markets is called the efficient markets hypothesis.

the 2004 Nobel Prize in economics. As in the classical and rational expectations models, the RBC theorists assume that

1. People act in their own self-interest.
2. Wages and prices are fully flexible.

Since wages and prices are flexible, the labor market always clears, so there is no unemployment in the economy. This means that the economy is constantly on the vertical long-run classical supply function. The RBC theorists also assume that aggregate demand shocks are not the major cause of business cycles. Now I know you are a bit puzzled. If we are always on the vertical aggregate supply function and if the AD shocks are not important, then how can GDP change? How can we generate business cycles? The answer is that it is in fact the vertical supply function that shifts and causes business cycles. But what causes the supply function to shift?

TECHNOLOGY SHOCKS AND BUSINESS CYCLES

The main difference between the RBC and the previous theories is that the RBC economists believe that randomly occurring *technology shocks* are the major causes of business cycles. Some might argue that technological innovations take decades or centuries to materialize. How can technological shocks be random, temporary, and frequent? The answer is that RBC theorists include a lot of events in this category. A sudden oil price hike, an unexpected discovery of a natural resource, deregulation of an industry, imposition of stricter air quality standards, a new industrial innovation improving labor productivity—all are examples of technological shocks in the RBC model.

TECHNOLOGY SHOCKS *Events that affect the relationships between inputs and outputs and hence the productivity of inputs.*

In Figure 4, the equilibrium happens to be at a real wage of 2 units. The employed workers will produce an amount of output equal to Y_{P1}. This is shown in the lower panel of the graph. Remember from Chapter 13 that technological shocks shift the demand-for-labor curve up and down by affecting the marginal product of labor. For example, when the price of oil increases, production falls, and firms demand less labor. The demand-for-labor curve shifts to the left, from D^{L1} to D^{L2}. This is an adverse technological shock, the same as an adverse supply shock. However, in the RBC model, this event causes a shift in the AS curve. Since demand for labor is reduced, the real wage goes down to 1 unit. Workers decide that it is not worth supplying as much labor as before, so they voluntarily stay home and employment goes down to 400 workers. As a result, the AS curve shifts to the left. The potential GDP falls to Y_{P2}, and the price level increases from \$100 to \$120.

Note that even though the real GDP has gone down, there is nothing the government can do to increase it. This is because the economy is now on the new vertical classical supply function, AS_2. Suppose that the government observes the reduction in GDP and employment and "mistakenly" believes that there is a recession. If it increases spending or the money supply, AD will shift up, but Y will not change. This policy only creates more inflation, as in the classical model. This should remind you of the stagflation of the 1970s due to oil price shocks and the inflationary policies of the Fed to reduce unemployment.

Figure 4 Labor-Market Equilibrium and Aggregate Supply Function

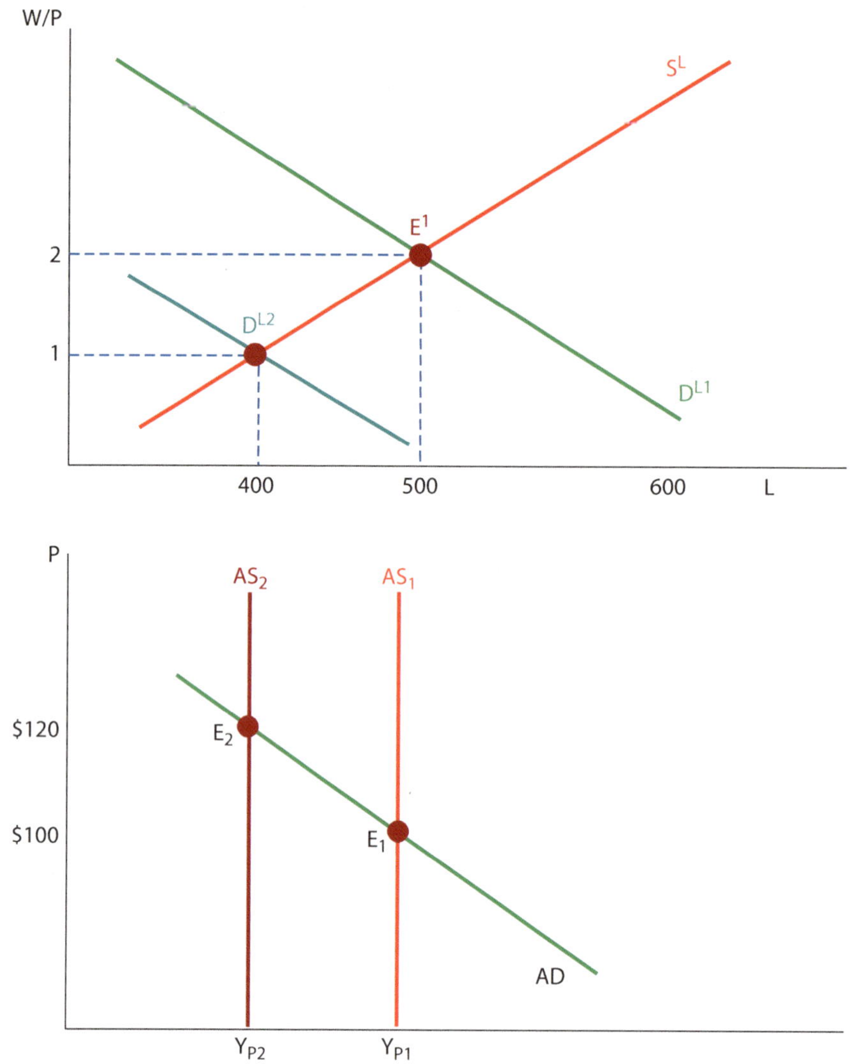

DISCUSSION

Note that the RBC model does not generate recessions in the ordinary sense of the word. There is no unemployment during an economic slowdown. When output goes down, workers voluntarily stop working. One criticism leveled against this model is that in a recession, many people lose their jobs and register as unemployed. Why do those people call themselves unemployed if they voluntarily chose not to work? The response by the RBC theorists is that perhaps they do it just to collect unemployment benefits. They are "officially" unemployed, not involuntarily. But was this true of all 12 million of them in 1982? The RBC theorists respond that the other reason they may call themselves unemployed is that they mean a different thing by that word. What they probably mean is that "I am unemployed in the sense that I cannot find a job that I like and that pays the same wage as before."

Moreover, the RBC theorists argue that in a recession caused by technology shocks, the industries that experience the negative technology shocks shrink, and some others expand. Workers who are laid off from these industries enter the pool of unemployed and start looking for jobs in other industries. There might in fact be jobs available for them, but the cost of job search and the mismatch between the obsolete skills of the workers and the requirements of the new jobs prolong the unemployment spell. In other words, these workers are *structurally unemployed*, not cyclically. Recall from Chapter 6 that structural unemployment is a part of natural unemployment. Therefore, according to the RBC theorists, the whole increase in the unemployment rate during a recession is just an increase in the natural unemployment rate.

Empirical evidence only partially supports the RBC economists' claim. Some studies show that, in line with RBC theorists' argument, during a recession structural unemployment increases, and that some laid-off workers from an industry find jobs in other industries. But they also find that some of those laid-off workers find jobs in the same industries after a period of unemployment. This means that some unemployment is cyclical—workers temporarily lose their jobs due to deficient demand.

Critics also have problems with the technology shocks explanation of the RBC model. First of all, they say that we only had a couple of major oil price shocks. These are the only noteworthy major technology shocks that caused two stagflations. Can you name any other major event? The RBC theorists respond that although a lot of shocks are small, the sum of them can result in big cycles. Opponents, however, point out that this argument can also go the other way. Small positive random shocks in one industry can cancel small negative random shocks in another industry, so that on average there will be no technology shock. However, proving these assertions empirically one way or another is not easy.

Consider Figure 4 again. In the RBC, model a small change in the real wage would generate a large change in employment and GDP. This means that the labor supply function has a very small slope (it is rather flat). However, many economists believe that the labor supply function is not very flat. In fact, they believe that it is very steep, almost vertical. This is simply because most workers do not have the option of voluntarily increasing or decreasing their work hours whenever they desire in response to changes in wage rates. In most jobs you have to work a fixed number of hours per year and you don't have the flexibility to stay home for four months and work doubly hard the next four months.

The opponents have pointed to numerous studies showing that monetary policy is effective. An increase in the money supply, they argue, has resulted in a subsequent increase in output through the channels we have seen in this book. RBC economists respond that these studies do not necessarily prove that monetary policy is effective. In other words, the increase in the money supply could be *the result of* the increase in output, and not the other way around. *What?* Well, suppose that businesses correctly anticipate that demand and output will increase in the near future, so they demand more money to buy materials and hire workers to increase output in the near future. The increase in the demand for money pushes up the interest rate. At this point, the Fed is afraid that the high interest rate could result in an economic slowdown (remember why?), so it increases the money supply to keep the interest rate from rising. Now, the researcher observes a rise in money supply and then a rise in output. He mistakenly concludes that the increase in M has caused the increase in Y. But we know that it is really the rise in Y that has caused the rise in M, and not the other way around.

THE FOUR THEORIES COMPARED

Here is a quick summary of all the models we have learned so far.

The Classical Theory

1. People act in their own self-interest.
2. Wages and prices are flexible.
3. There are no business cycles.
4. Government intervention is neither effective nor needed.

The Keynesian Theory

1. People act in their own self-interest.
2. Wages and prices are sticky.
3. Aggregate demand shocks are the major cause of recessions.
4. The government has a role to play to get the economy out of recession. Fiscal policy is more effective than monetary policy for this purpose.

The Rational Expectations Theory

1. People act in their own self-interest.
2. Wages and prices are fully flexible.
3. Only unanticipated aggregate demand shocks cause business cycles.
4. The government should not intervene. First, if people learn about the pattern of the policy, the policy will fail to be effective, because it will always be anticipated. Second, the policy could have the wrong result.

The Real Business Cycle Theory

1. People act in their own self-interest.
2. Wages and prices are fully flexible.
3. Technology shocks are the major cause of business cycles.
4. Demand management policies are ineffective in changing the level of output.

TO SUMMARIZE

Rational Expectations Hypothesis

1. People act rationally in their own self-interest.
2. Therefore, wages and prices are fully flexible.
3. Business cycles are because of misperceptions of workers and producers about relative prices: the prices of what they sell relative to the prices of what they buy.
4. Unanticipated policy is effective in changing real GDP, because it generates misperceptions about relative prices.
5. People need forecasts of future economic conditions for their employment decisions and wage negotiations.
6. Wrong forecasts are costly, both for the firms and the workers.
7. Therefore, they try to make the most accurate forecasts of future economic conditions, especially the future price levels.
8. To do this, they take into account all the available relevant information to form their best guesses about future price levels.

9. These best guesses are called rational expectations.
10. For this reason, an anticipated demand management policy will be totally ineffective. If producers and workers expect the price level to increase in the future as a result of the policy, they will not have any misperceptions about relative prices when the price level actually increases. Moreover, they will factor this information into their wage contracts. When the future comes, the real wage will remain the same. So will employment and output. Only the price level will increase.
11. For the same reason, it is very easy to get rid of inflation without causing unemployment. Just announce that you will reduce the money supply in the future. Expectations will adjust fast. The price level will be reduced. There will be no change in output and employment.
12. Only unanticipated policy can affect the level of output.
13. Business cycles are generally caused by unanticipated demand shocks.
14. Therefore, countercyclical demand management policies (increasing AD during recessions and reducing it during expansions) will lose their effectiveness, since people will learn about their pattern and will "neutralize" them.

Real Business Cycle Theory

1. People act rationally in their own self-interest.
2. Therefore, wages and prices are fully flexible.
3. There is no unemployment. Those who call themselves unemployed are not really *involuntarily* unemployed, they just choose not to work.
4. Business cycles are caused by random technology shocks. In the case of an adverse technology shock, demand for labor does down, reducing the real wage. At the lower real wage, workers voluntarily decide to work less and take more leisure. As a result, employment and output go down. The reduction in output causes the inflation rate to increase.
5. In the case of a favorable technology shock, demand for labor goes up, increasing the real wage. At the higher real wage, workers voluntarily decide to work more and take less leisure. As a result, employment and output go up.
6. For these reasons, demand management policies do not work. In fact there is not even a need for such policies, since the observed unemployment is voluntary.

EXERCISES

Question 1

Use the rational expectations model to analyze the effects of the following events on the price and output levels.

a. In 2008 the Fed announces that it will decrease the money supply by 10% in 2009. When 2009 comes, it keeps its promise and reduces the money supply by 10%.
b. In 2008 the Fed announces that it will decrease the money supply by 10% in 2009. When 2009 comes, it reduces the money supply by 5%.
c. In 2008 the Fed announces that it will decrease the money supply by 10% in 2009. When 2009 comes, it reduces the money supply by 15%.

d. In 2008 the Fed announces that it will decrease the money supply by 10% in 2009. When 2009 comes, it does not change the money supply at all.

Question 2

Use the previous question as a hint to answer this question.

a. Explain how an increase in money supply could result in a recession.
b. Explain how a decrease in money supply could result in an expansion.

Question 3

Sometimes prices and interest rates change *because of* the Fed's decision *not to change* the money supply. Can you explain why? To be more concrete, provide an explanation for each of the following two occurrences using the rational-expectations model:

a. The aggregate demand function in 2009 does not shift relative to 2008, but the price level increases and the real GDP declines (along the AD function).
b. The aggregate demand function in 2009 does not shift relative to 2008, but the price level decreases and the real GDP increase (along the AD function).

Question 4

In the rational expectations model, the Fed can reduce the price level by announcing a lower money supply. Analyze the following two scenarios, assuming that in 2008 the economy is in equilibrium with $Y = Y_p$ and P = $100.

a. In 2008 the Fed announces that it will increase the money supply by 5% in 2009, but people don't believe the Fed. They think the Fed will not change the money supply. However, when 2009 comes, the Fed keeps its promise and increases the money supply by 5%.
b. In 2008 the Fed announces that it will decrease the money supply by 5% in 2009, but people don't believe the Fed. They think the Fed will not change the money supply. However, when 2009 comes, the Fed keeps its promise and decreases the money supply by 5%.

Question 5

One of the criticisms of the RBC model is that in the real world, the supply of labor function is not as flat as the one assumed by the RBC theorists. Analyze the effect of a technology shock, assuming that the supply of labor function is vertical.

CHAPTER 15

Inflation and Unemployment

INTRODUCTION AND REVIEW

THE MODEL PRESENTED in Chapter 13 is the standard macroeconomic model; it is used widely by both policymakers and academic economists to understand the effects of economic events on the state of the economy and to conduct policy analyses. The model gives Keynesian results in the short run, and the classical results in the long run. Demand or supply shocks create recessions or expansions due to wage and price rigidity, although they are short-run phenomena. As time passes, wages and prices adjust to clear the goods, money, and labor markets, and recessions or expansions come to an end. So recessions and expansions are temporary phenomena. Chapter 14 added rational expectations to the model, and concluded that demand shocks would create recessions or expansions if they are not anticipated by the public. This is because an anticipated policy does not create misperceptions about relative prices; thus, employment and output remain the same.

These models are very useful in explaining directly and intuitively how demand and supply shocks create recessions and expansions, and how wage and price adjustments bring the economy to the full employment path over time. There are, however, two things in the model we need to modify to make it more useful and more realistic. First, the model is in terms of price and GDP *levels*. As you recall from Chapter 6, we are more interested in inflation and unemployment *rates*. Second, the model indicates that the price level goes down during a recession. A decrease in the price level results in a negative inflation rate. However, as Figure 8 of Chapter 6 shows (and as we will see below), in only a handful of quarters did the CPI inflation rate become negative. Generally, the inflation rate goes down without becoming negative. This means that—with some notable exceptions—the price level increases during a recession, but at a slower pace.

Figure 1 shows the relationship between the U.S. (annualized) quarterly inflation and cyclical unemployment rates for the period 1970:01 through 2010:01. The inflation rates have been calculated using the GDP deflators. I use the GDP deflator because it includes the prices of all the goods produced in the economy—see Chapter 6 for the explanation. As you know, the cyclical unemployment rate for any quarter is the excess of the actual unemployment rate (u) over the natural unemployment rate (u^n). Cyclical unemployment ($u - u^n$) becomes positive in a recession. You have seen these data in Chapter 6.

Figure 1 shows some interesting facts about these two series. First, the inflation rate as measured by the GDP deflator has never become negative since 1970, even in the severe recessions of 1980–1982 and 2007–2008. Second, in the stagflation of 1974–1975, both the inflation and unemployment rates were quite high—hence the name *stagflation*. So in this period, there was a positive relationship between the two variables. Later, though, the high unemployment rate caused the inflation rate to go down. Third, in the remaining recessions there seemed to be a negative relationship between the inflation and unemployment rates. When the cyclical unemployment rate was positive and high—when we had a recession—the inflation rate was going down. Between 1976 and 1980, the cyclical unemployment rate was low and at times negative, meaning economic expansion. During this period, the inflation rate was increasing. In the 1980–1982 and 2007–2008 recessions, the economy experienced very high cyclical unemployment rates compared to the other recessions since 1970. During these times, the inflation rate was going down. You can see similar patterns in other recessions and expansions. Note also that even though there was a CPI deflation in 2008 (see Chapter 6), the GDP deflator did not actually go down.

Figure 1: U.S. Quarterly Inflation and Cyclical Unemployment Rates 1970:01 through 2010:01

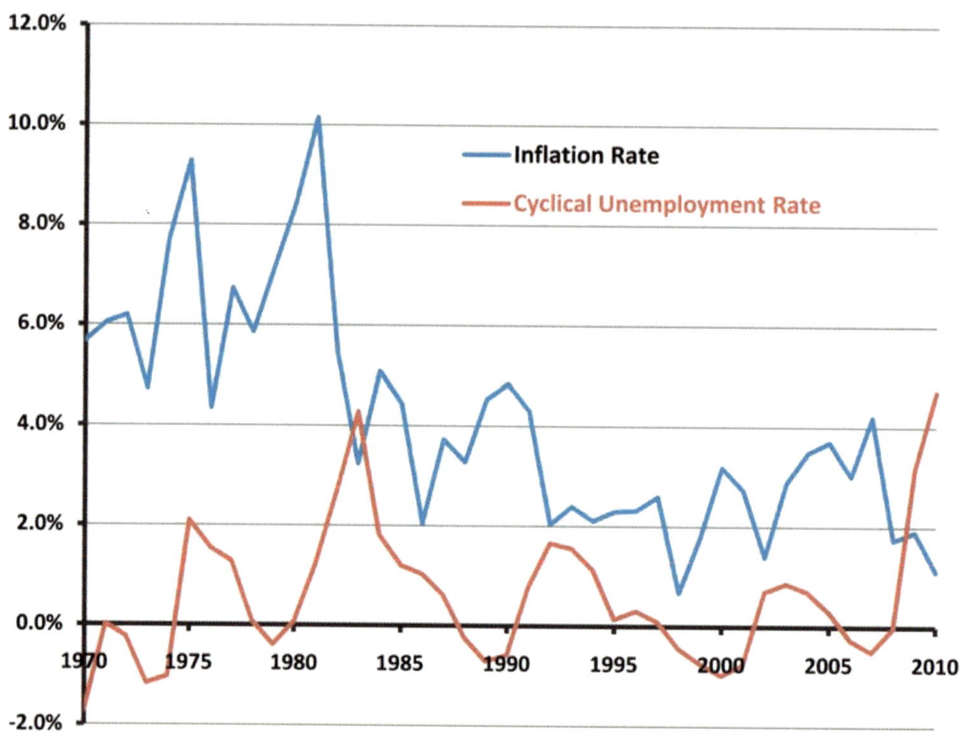

This chapter will remedy both of these deficiencies. We will develop a model in terms of inflation and unemployment *rates*—two of our macroeconomic concerns. We will take the model of the last chapter and tweak some of its assumptions to get the new model. Most of the material in this chapter will sound familiar to you. Moreover, I will present a lot of actual data to build your confidence in the model. But first, we need to have a good grasp of the difference between price level and inflation rate.

PRICE LEVEL AND INFLATION RATE

To understand the relationship between the inflation rate and the price level, recall that the inflation rate is the rate of change in the price level such as the CPI or GDP deflator. For example, suppose that in 2006 the price level was P_{2006} = \$109, and in 2007 it was P_{2007} = \$112. Then the inflation rate for 2007 was about 3%, calculated as follows:

$$\Pi_{2007} = \frac{P_{2007} - P_{2006}}{P_{2006}} \times 100 = \frac{112 - 109}{109} \times 100 = 3\%$$

If the price level went down in 2007, the inflation rate for that year would turn negative. For example, let P_{2007} = \$106. Then

$$\Pi_{2007} = \frac{P_{2007} - P_{2006}}{P_{2006}} \times 100 = \frac{106 - 109}{109} \times 100 = -3\%$$

A constant inflation rate and a constant price level are two different things. If the price level is constant, then the inflation rate is zero. If the inflation rate is a constant different from zero, then the price level is increasing. If prices rise for several years, we call the resulting situation sustained inflation. The following table depicts several hypothetical scenarios concerning the relationship between the price level. P and the inflation rate. Π.

	Scenario 1		Scenario 2		Scenario 3		Scenario 4	
Year	P	Π	P	Π	P	Π	P	Π
2004	100		100.00		200.00		100.00	
2005	100	0	105.00	5%	210.00	5%	110.00	10%
2006	100	0	110.25	5%	220.50	5%	121.00	10%
2007	100	0	115.76	5%	231.53	5%	133.10	10%

In the first scenario, the price level is constant, implying zero inflation rates. In scenarios 2 and 3, we have a constant inflation rate of 5%. However, scenario 3 has a higher price *level* compared to scenario 2 in every year. Now compare scenarios 2 and 4. They both start with the same price level in 2004. But scenario 4 has a higher inflation rate. Under this scenario, then, the price level increases much faster than the price level in scenario 2.

You can also calculate the price level from knowledge of last year's price level and the inflation rate between the two years. For example, in 2004 the price level was \$100. If the inflation rate from

2004 to 2005 were 5% as in scenario 2, then the price level in 2005 would equal \$105, calculated as follows:

$$P_{2005} = P_{2004} \times (1 + \pi) = \$100 \times (1 + .05) = \$105$$

If instead the inflation rate were 10% as in scenario 4, then the price level in 2005 would be \$110:

$$P_{2005} = P_{2004} \times (1 + \Pi) = \$100 \times (1 + .10) = \$110$$

Therefore, given last year's price, the higher the inflation rate between the two years, the higher this year's price will be. Conversely, the lower the inflation rate between the two years, the lower this year's price will be. You can see this relationship easily by comparing scenarios 2 and 4.

UNEMPLOYMENT RATE IN THE LONG RUN

Our objective in this chapter is to develop a simple model in terms of inflation and unemployment rates. We do this in a few straightforward steps. It is easier to start with the long-run classical case. The unemployment rate is the easiest to figure out. In fact, you already know the answer. Recall from the classical and Keynesian models that in the long run, the economy produces the potential level of output so that we only have natural unemployment. Now consider Figures 5 and 7 of Chapter 6; they indicate that in the long run, the real GDP equals potential GDP, and the unemployment rate equals the natural rate. Therefore, we have our first lesson:

> *In the long run, regardless of the rate of inflation, the unemployment rate equals the natural rate.*

This conclusion is depicted in Figure 2.

Figure 2: The Unemployment Rate in the Long Run

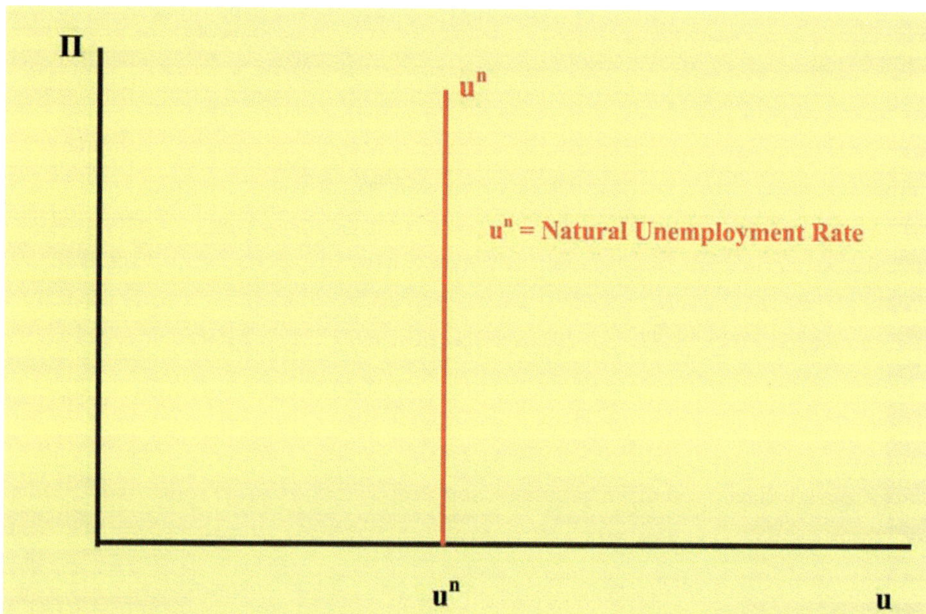

INFLATION RATE IN THE LONG RUN

In Chapter 11 we saw that in the long run, the rate of inflation approximately equals the rate of growth of money supply. Figure 3 puts together two pieces of information we have learned about the long run. In the long run, the unemployment rate will equal the natural rate and the inflation rate will equal the rate of growth of money supply. We will denote the rate of growth of money supply by the letter m. In Figure 3, the long run equilibrium occurs at point E. The economy will gravitate to that point in the long run. So we have our second lesson:

In the long run, the rate of inflation equals the rate of growth of money supply.

Figure 3: Inflation and Unemployment Rates in the Long Run

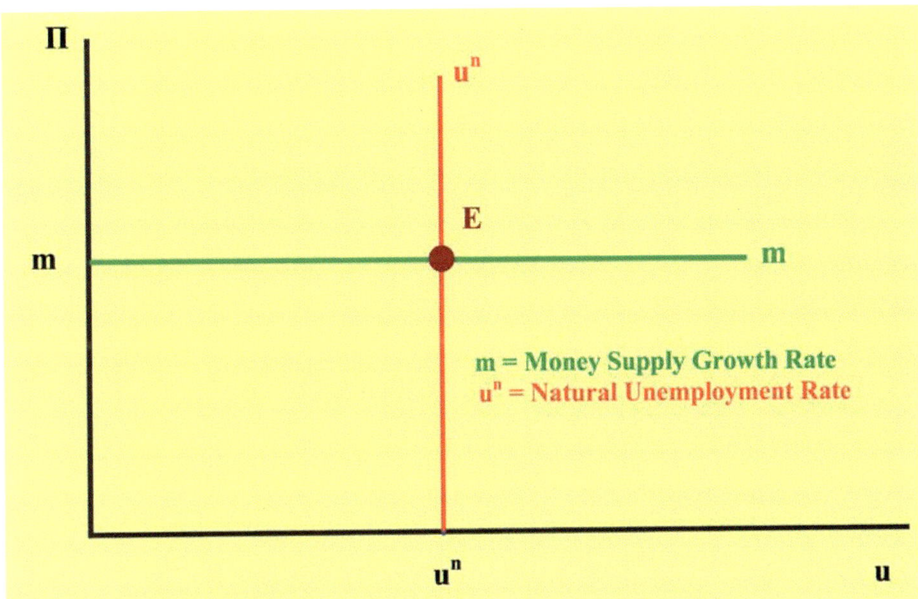

INFLATION AND UNEMPLOYMENT IN THE SHORT RUN

We now turn to the relationship between the inflation and unemployment rates in the short run. It turns out that the relationship between these two variables could be either positive or negative, depending on the source of the disturbance in the economy. Demand shocks result in a negative relationship between the inflation rate Π and the unemployment rate u. Supply shocks result in a positive relationship. We explain these in turn.

DEMAND SHOCKS: NEGATIVE RELATIONSHIP BETWEEN Π AND U

This relationship is quite straightforward to understand. We only need to think in terms of inflation *rates* rather then price *levels*. Suppose that currently, the inflation rate is 5% and the unemployment rate is 4%, so that the economy is at point A in Figure 4. What happens if the money supply or government spending increases? We know that in either case, the result will be an increase in the aggregate demand for goods and services. This will have two effects on the economy. First, producers will experience unplanned decreases in inventories. They will thus hire more labor and step up production. For this reason, unemployment will decrease. At the same time, producers will change their pricing policies. Up until now, they were increasing their prices at a rate of 5% per year. Now with this high demand, they will start increasing their prices at 6% per year. Therefore, the economy will move to point B in Figure 4, and we will get a negative relationship between Π and u.

Figure 4: Demand Shocks and Negative Relationship Between Π and u

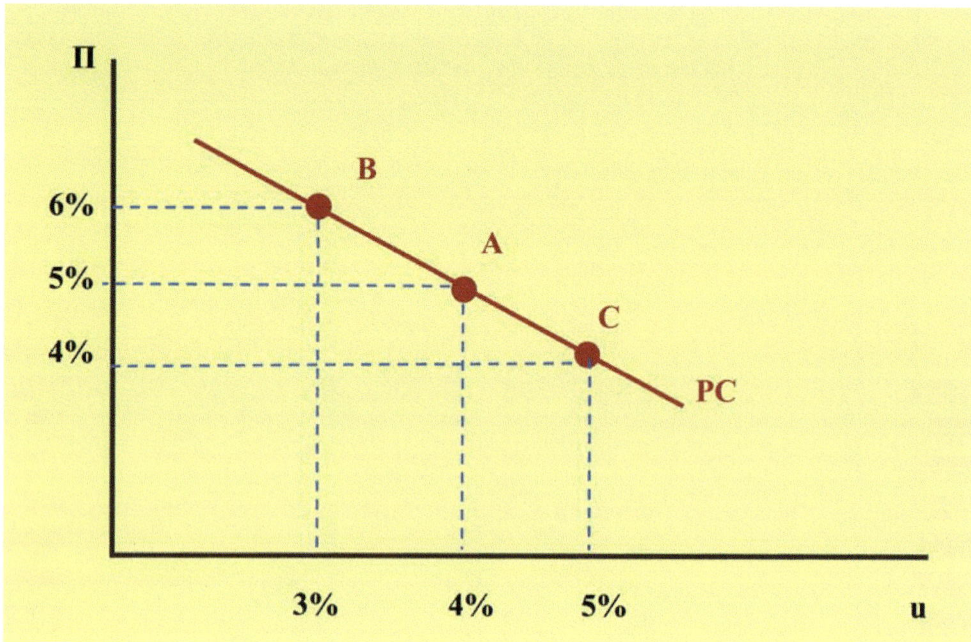

On the other hand, suppose that the aggregate demand for goods and services goes down, perhaps due to a loss in consumer confidence. Producers experience unplanned increases in inventories. Two things happen as a result. First, they reduce production and lay off some workers. Second, they increase their prices at a lower rate than before to be able to sell their merchandise. In Figure 4, the unemployment rate increases to 5% and the inflation rate decreases to 4%, and the economy moves to point C.

PHILLIPS CURVE
A negative relationship between inflation and unemployment rates.

Connecting all such points, we get a negative relationship between π and u. This negative relationship is called the *Phillips Curve (PC)* in honor of the British economist A. W. Phillips, who first observed it in the British economy. We will talk about the history of this curve in a later chapter. We have our third lesson:

Demand shocks result in a negative relationship between the inflation rate and the unemployment rate.

Lower demand due to the recession reduces sales and puts downward pressure on the inflation rate. The resulting bankruptcy increases unemployment.

SUPPLY SHOCKS: POSITIVE RELATIONSHIP BETWEEN Π AND U

Supply shocks result in a positive relationship between Π and u. A supply shock is an event that affects the cost of production for business firms. Recall that production cost is comprised of the payments firms make to production factors. Therefore, an increase in the prices of production factors would increase the production cost. For example, an increase in the prices of inputs such as raw materials used by business firms would qualify as a supply shock. We will concentrate on two important sources of supply shocks:

1. An increase in the price of oil by oil-producing countries.
2. An increase in the nominal wage rate that is not the result of an increase in the price level.

For an event to qualify as a supply shock, it must be independent of current demand conditions. For example, OPEC increases the price of oil for reasons related to their own economies or for political reasons, not the U.S. economy.[1] Or, if workers *expect* that goods prices will be high *in the future*, they may ask for—and receive—a higher nominal wage. This increase in nominal wage is not related to demand conditions *today*.

Figure 5: Supply Shocks and Positive Relationship Between π and u

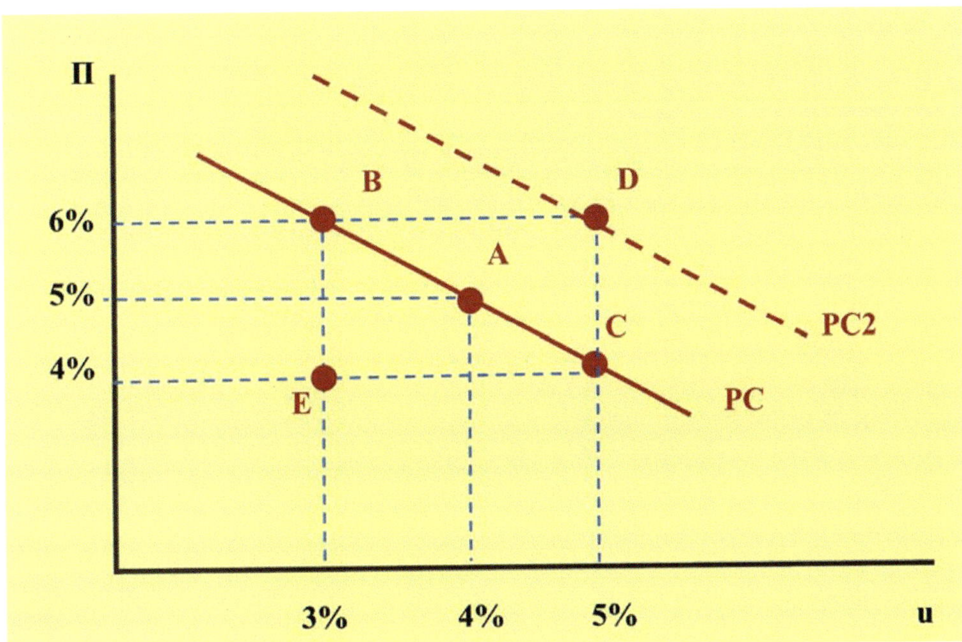

Suppose that the economy was at point A in Figure 5. OPEC suddenly increases the price of oil. Oil is an input to many manufacturing processes. Consider, for example, the transportation industry, which is heavily dependent on oil. The resulting increase in the cost of production will cause the prices of goods and services to increase faster than before, as producers try to pass the higher costs to consumers. Therefore, the inflation rate will increase. Now, since the inflation rate is higher than the rate of increase in the money supply, the interest rate will increase, reducing

1 OPEC stands for the Organization of Petroleum Exporting Countries, a group of countries that coordinates their policies concerning the price and quantity of crude oil they export.

consumption and investment, and hence aggregate demand. (See Figure 3 of Chapter 13 to refresh your memory.) The resulting decrease in aggregate demand will cause the real GDP to decrease and unemployment to increase. So the economy will move to a point like point D, with higher inflation and unemployment rates. This situation is called stagflation (**stag**nation + in**flation**), as you recall. Graphically, what this means is that the Phillips Curve will shift out to pass through point D. This is shown as PC2.

Figure 6: Inflation and Unemployment Rates

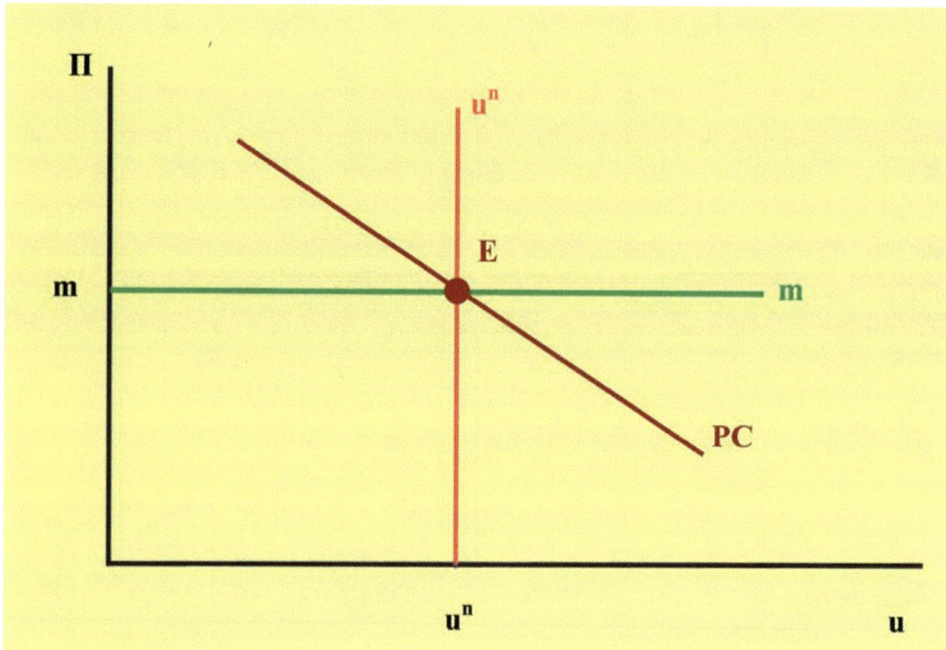

Similarly, if there is a sudden, unexpected reduction in the price of oil, both the inflation and unemployment rates will decrease, and the economy will move to a point like point E in Figure 5. The Phillips Curve will shift down and to the left. So we have our fourth and last lesson:

> *Supply shocks generate a positive relationship between the inflation and unemployment rates and cause the Phillips Curve to shift.*

Figure 6 puts together everything we have learned in this chapter. In the long run, the economy will be at the intersection point of two lines, one representing the natural rate of unemployment (u^n) and the other the money growth rate (m). This is point E. In the short run, though, the economy could be somewhere else. In the case of a demand shock, it will move to a point on the PC curve different from point E. In the case of a supply shock, the whole PC curve will shift up or down. In the next chapter we will use this powerful model to conduct economic analysis.

THE PHILLIPS CURVE

In 1958 British economist A. W. Phillips published a paper showing that there had been a negative relationship between the rate of change of nominal wages and the unemployment rate for Britain over the period 1861–1957. Since policy makers were more interested in the general price inflation rather than changes in nominal wages per se (and since the two moved rather closely), pretty soon they replaced the wage inflation with price inflation. Figure 7 shows the inflation and the unemployment rates for the United Sates for the period 1960–2005.[2] You can easily identify a negative relationship for the 1960–69 period. Because of these findings, during the 1960s economists and policy makers thought there was a negative relationship between inflation and unemployment.

Figure 7: U.S. Inflation and Unemployment Rates: 1960–2005

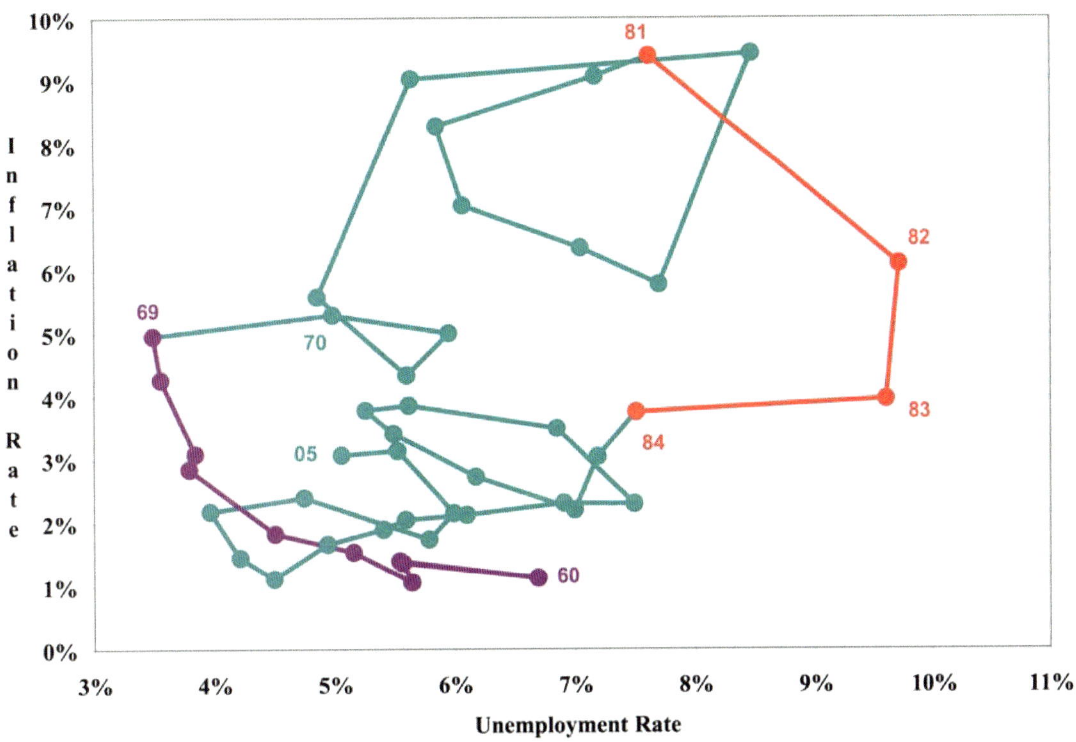

This was a very important finding at the time, since it implied a menu of choices for the policy makers: you could either reduce the inflation rate (∏) or the unemployment rate (u), but not both. For example, consider Figure 4. Suppose the economy was at point C, with 5% unemployment and 4% inflation. The policy makers could reduce the unemployment rate to 3%, at the cost of increasing the inflation rate to 6%. If the economy was at point B, then they could reduce inflation rate to 4%, if they were willing to let the unemployment rate increase to 5%. However, they could not reduce both the inflation and unemployment rates. The economy could not go to a point with 4% inflation and 3% unemployment. This option was not on the "menu."

Just as an aside, realize that both of these options are painful and unpopular. Which alternative would you choose if you were a policy maker? Would you reduce unemployment at the cost of inflation, or would you lower inflation and let go of unemployment? This is a subjective matter; it requires normative judgments. Some economists and policy makers prefer reducing inflation and letting unemployment increase. This is not because they are cold-hearted people. Rather,

2 The annual data are the quarterly averages of the unemployment rate and the percentage changes in the GDP deflator.

they believe in the self-correcting mechanism of the free market capitalist system—they know the classical model. They believe that the system will take care of the unemployed in the long run. But inflation is something created by the government through increases in money supply. So the government could and should reduce inflation. Other economists and policymakers believe that "the long run is too long" and the unemployed need a helping hand, so they would rather see a reduction in unemployment.

Starting in 1970 the situation changed. The point for 1970 was not on the 1960–1969 Phillips Curve, and after that year the whole thing became chaotic. (See Figure 7 again.) This was a big mess. What was going on? How could we make sense of this seemingly erratic behavior? Interestingly enough, Milton Friedman had provided the answer to this question in his presidential address to the American Economic Association in 1968—two years before this wild behavior![3] Friedman and another economist, Edmund Phelps, had argued that there was a series of short-run Phillips curves that were shifting over time.[4] Later, more work was done to understand this whole inflation-unemployment trade-off. Let's proceed in small steps to see if we can create order out of this chaos and solve this mystery. Actually, you know most of the answers already, and the whole argument will sound pretty straightforward to you. Just keep in mind the four lessons mentioned in the introduction.

AN INCREASE IN THE RATE OF GROWTH OF THE MONEY SUPPLY

This section analyzes the effect of an increase in the rate of growth of the money supply (m) on inflation and unemployment. The analysis will closely follow Friedman's 1968 argument. Consider Figure 8. Suppose that initially, the Fed had been increasing the money supply at a rate of m = 2% per year, and hence the economy was in the long-run equilibrium at point E_1 on the Phillips Curve, PC1, with Π = 2%. The natural rate of unemployment is assumed to be u^n = 5%.

Now the Fed decides to increase the money supply growth rate to m = 6%. We know what happens to the Phillips Curve. Since this causes an increase in the aggregate demand, the inflation rate increases and the unemployment rate falls. The economy moves on PC1 to the left, say to point A. At point A, we have 4% inflation and 3% unemployment. In the short run, the economy will stay at point A. But two things are happening at that point. First, since unemployment is less than natural, we have excess demand for labor. Moreover, workers were expecting 2% inflation, so they were building only a 2% increase in nominal wages into their wage contracts. But now prices are rising at 4%, and the workers' purchasing power is going down. Workers and firms have made a forecasting error of 2% about the inflation rate. As you recall from Chapters 6, this 2% is called unanticipated inflation. Since workers observe 4% inflation now, they adjust their expectations of inflation upward to 4%. They then ask for 4% higher wages in the future. Come next year, wages rise at 4% because of this new contract. As you know by now, this causes the Phills Curve to shift up.

3 See Friedman's "The Role of Monetary Policy," *American Economic Review, 1968. This is one of the most influential papers ever written in economics. Friedman won a Nobel Prize for his work in monetary economics.*

4 Edmund Phelps won the Nobel Prize in economics in 2006, mostly for his work on these issues.

Figure 8: An Increase in the Rate of Growth of Money Supply

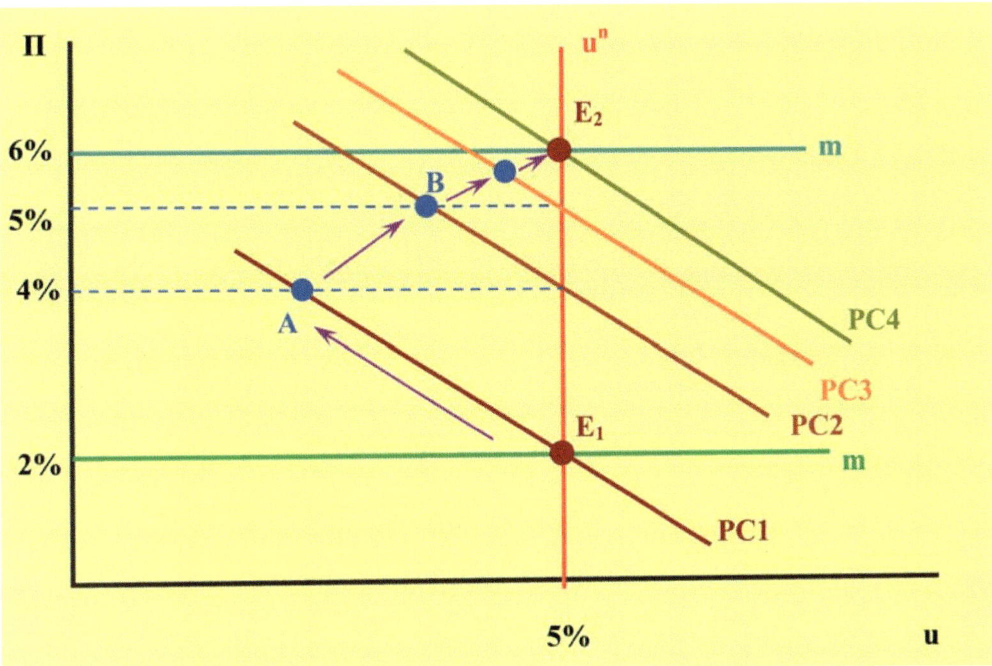

The Phillips Curve shifts up by 2% to PC2. This is simply because nominal wages have increased by 2%, and producers will try to pass this wage increase on to their consumers. However, they will not be successful in increasing their prices by a full 2%. This is because, as the inflation rate rises, the aggregate demand falls, for reasons we know. This puts downward pressure on the inflation rate, so the inflation rate increases by less than the full 2% increase in wages. The economy moves to point B on PC2, so the inflation rate increases by only 1%. Now the inflation rate is $\Pi = 5\%$. Note that unemployment increases. This is due to the reduction in output produced because of the higher prices, as just mentioned.

At point B, history is repeated. Workers were expecting 4% inflation but the actual inflation rate turned out to be 5%. They again have made a forecasting error, this time equal to 1% (5% – 4%). Having observed 5% inflation for some time, they revise their expectations upward to 5%, and the Phillips Curve shifts to PC3. This is because workers ask for 1% higher wages. For a similar reason, the inflation rate will increase only by 0.7% to 5.7% (not shown on the graph). The process will continue.

Note that every time, the workers' forecasting error gets smaller. First they made an error of 2% (4% – 2%). The next year they made an error of 1% (5% – 4%). The following year they made an error of 0.7% (5.7% – 5%). So as time goes by, the workers learn more and more about the process and make better predictions of the future inflation rate. When does the process end? It ends when the workers' forecasting error is reduced to zero. This happens graphically when the Phillips Curve shifts all the way until it intersects the u^n line at point E_2. At that point, the expected inflation rate again equals the actual rate ($\Pi = \Pi^e = 6\%$) and they are both equal to the rate of growth of money supply ($m = 6\%$). Moreover, at point E_2, we only have natural unemployment ($u = u^n$). At point E_2, wages and prices are rising at the same rate (6%), so that the real wage is constant.

So what caused the Phillips Curve to shift in the 1970s? During the 1960s, the inflation rate was low, and people had come to expect low and stable inflation rates. Since people did not change their inflationary expectations, the Phillips Curve did not shift much. Moreover, most of the shocks to the economy were from the demand side. With demand shocks and unchanging inflation expectations (and hence a non-shifting Phillips Curve), we had a negative relationship between Π and u (movement along the curve). After 1970, there were two major oil price shocks. These inflation shocks caused the Phillips Curve to shift up. The resulting inflation made people expect even more inflation down the road. These inflationary expectations further contributed to the shifts.

Let's summarize the story so far:

1. There will be a negative relationship between the rates of inflation and unemployment if demand shocks are the major cause of the movements in real GDP. These negative relationships are called short-run Phillips curves.
2. The short-run Phillips curves can shift in the case of supply shocks. These include increases in nominal wages or the prices of raw materials such as oil.
3. The location of the short-run Phillips Curve depends on expectations of the future inflation rate (Π^e). An increase in Π^e shifts the curve up by the amount of the increase in Π^e. That is because workers ask for higher wages.
4. In the long run, there is no trade-off between Π and u. In the long run, the unemployment rate equals u^n, regardless of the inflation rate. Some people call the vertical line at u^n the long-run Phillips Curve.
5. At the intersection of the short-run and long-run Phillips curves, $\Pi = \Pi^e$ and $u = u^n$.
6. Moreover— this is important—at the intersection point of the two curves, the rate of growth of the money supply, the actual rate of inflation, the expected rate of inflation, and the rate of growth in nominal wages are equal. For example, at point E_2 in Figure 8, the money supply is growing at 6%, the inflation rate is 6%, people expect the inflation rate to be 6% in the future, and the nominal wage is increasing at 6% to keep the real wage unchanged.

A DECREASE IN THE RATE OF GROWTH OF THE MONEY SUPPLY

We can now reverse the above arguments to analyze the effect of a decrease in money growth rate on inflation and unemployment. Suppose that currently, the rate of growth of the money supply averages out to 8% per year, creating 8% inflation. The economy is at point E_1 in Figure 9. At that point, people expect the inflation rate to be 8% in the future. The Fed now comes to the realization that this rate of inflation is too high for the country, and decides to reduce it to a lower level. Thus, it reduces the money growth rate to 3% per year. This causes an increase in the interest rate, and consequently, a decrease in aggregate demand. The economy then moves along the PC curve to a point like point A. The inflation rate goes down to 5%, but the unloyment rate soars to 7%.

Figure 9: A Reduction in the Rate of Growth of the Money Supply

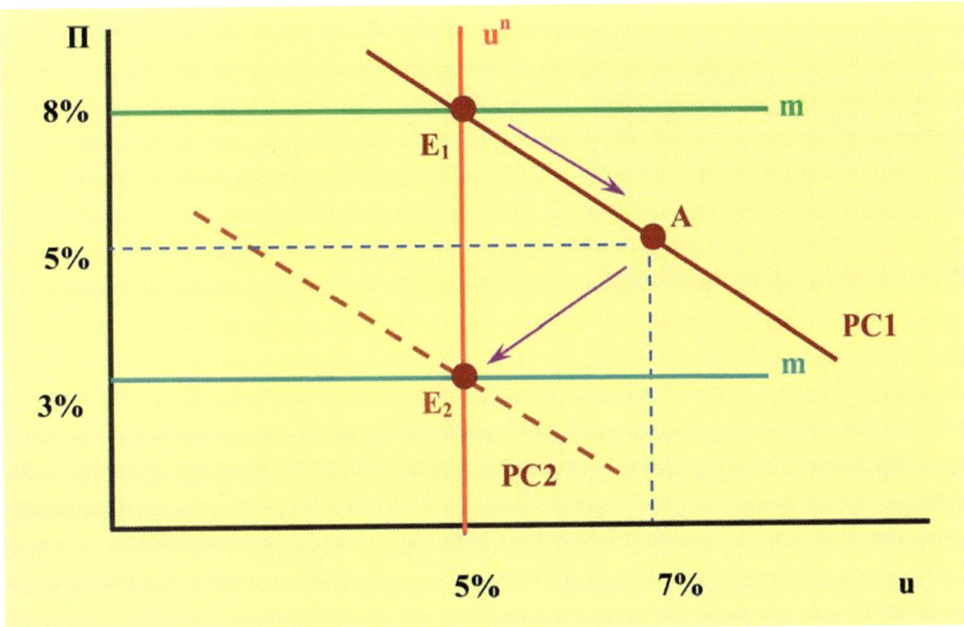

At point A, workers and employers realize they had made a forecasting error in predicting the rate of inflation. They were expecting 8% inflation, but they got only 5%. The recession and unemployment that exists at point A puts a downward pressure on the rate of increase in wages and prices. Employers can no longer afford to give workers an 8% raise in wages due to a low aggregate demand. Workers also begin to accept lower wages due to unemployment. Since both groups expect the inflation rate to be 5%, they agree to a 5% increase in wages. As a result, the Phillips Curve starts shifting down. The economy will move to a new long-run equilibrium point (E_2), because we now have a lower money supply growth rate. In the long run, the inflation rate will be reduced, with no change in the unemployment rate.

The policy just described is what the Fed followed under Paul Volcker starting in 1979. At the time, the inflation rate was running at double digit rates, and the Fed decided to reduce it to a more reasonable level. During the 1970s, there were two oil–price-related inflation shocks. Recall that inflation shocks create stagflation. Figure 1 indicates that this is in fact what happened then. The U.S. economy experienced very high inflation rates (higher than 10% in some months) and unemployment rates (close to 10%). Remember that inflation shocks are a source of headaches for policy makers (please review Chapter 12 on the Keynesian model). If you try to get rid of unemployment through an expansionary demand management policy, you will create more inflation. If you try to reduce inflation, you will end up with higher unemployment. During much of this time, the Fed tried to reduce unemployment. The result, as you can predict, was high inflation rates. The Fed was not famous as an inflation fighter at that time.

When Paul Volcker became the chairman of the Fed, he decided to get rid of inflation. He substantially reduced the growth rate of the money supply. This policy caused the interest rate to increase, resulting in lower investment and consumption. The aggregate demand function shifted to the left, causing a recession. The housing market was in particularly dire straits. This was the 1980–1982 recession that we've been talking about all along. This was the most severe recession of the postwar era, with an unemployment rate of about 10%. The Fed deliberately created this reces-

DISINFLATION
A reduction in the inflation rate.

sion to combat inflation. The inflation rate was dropped to about 3%. This reduction in inflation is called the Volcker *disinflation*, and for good reason.[5]

Look also at Figure 7 to see how the inflation-unemployment points traveled over time between 1981 and 1984 and beyond. Note that the movement of the economy from 1981 to 1984 in Figure 1 closely resembles the movement in Figure 9 from point E_1 to point A to point E_2.

INFLATION REDUCTION UNDER RATIONAL EXPECTATIONS

In Friedman's story, it takes a long time for workers and capitalists to learn about their forecasting errors. Advocates of the rational expectations hypothesis argue that such behavior is not rational. Since both groups are interested in maximizing their well-being, they will have every incentive to learn about the monetary policy and adjust their expectations accordingly. For the same reason, they argue, it should not be too painful to reduce inflation in a country. If the Fed announces loud and clear that it will conduct a tight money policy to fight inflation, both workers and capitalists will factor that information into their wages and prices. If the Fed follows through on its promise, then no forecasting errors will be made: the real wage will remain unchanged, and no unemployment will result. This is simply because of the rational expectations result that anticipated policy does not change the level of output; it only affects the inflation rate.

Consider Figure 9 again, and assume that initially, the economy is in equilibrium at point E1 with 8% inflation and 4% unemployment. The Fed perceives the 8% inflation as too high, and decides to reduce it through tight monetary policy. In the short run, the economy moves to a point like point A, unemployment increases to 7%, and the inflation rate goes down to 5%. The increase in unemployment as a result of bringing down inflation by 1% is called the *sacrifice ratio*. In this case, the sacrifice ratio is one 0.67 increase in unemployment for each one percent reduction in the inflation rate:

SACRIFICE RATIO
The ratio that indicates by how much unemployment rate will increase if the government reduces inflation rate by one percent.

$$\frac{\Delta u}{\Delta \Pi} = \frac{7\% - 5\%}{5\% - 8\%} = -0.67$$

Under the rational expectations hypothesis, the sacrifice ratio may well be zero. If the Fed announces the policy beforehand—and if the Fed is credible—then the Phillips Curve will shift to PC2 immediately, the inflation rate will drop to 3% in an instant, and the economy will move from point E_1 to E_2 quickly, with no increase in unemployment or reduction in output. Although there is no empirical evidence for this strong version of the theory, economists agree that the adjustment process could be faster and the sacrifice ratio smaller if the Fed were more transparent and credible.

This is the reason that economists cite for why it took so long for Paul Volcker's tight money policy to reduce the inflation rate in the United States during the 1980s. At the time, the Fed was not known as a credible inflation fighter. Therefore, when the money supply growth rate was reduced, many people did not believe in the permanency and seriousness of this policy. As a result, they did not change their expectations of inflation for some time. The Phillips Curve finally started to shift as people came to the realization that tight money was there to stay because the Fed was serious in combating inflation.

So far, we have demonstrated that the only event affecting the inflation rate in the long run is a change in the rate of growth of the money supply. We now consider the effects of other kinds of

DEFLATION
A reduction in the general price level. Deflation results in negative inflation rates.

5 *Disinflation* means a reduction in the rate of inflation. *Deflation* means a reduction in prices, i.e., a negative inflation.

policies and events on Π and u. You can guess the answers already. For as long as the rate of growth of the money supply remains unchanged, nothing will happen to Π or u in the long run. In the short run, though, both Π and u can change due to wage and price rigidity.

ANALYSIS OF A RECESSION

We begin with the analysis of a recession. Consider Figure 10, and assume that the economy is in the long-run equilibrium at point E. The supply of money is increasing at a rate of 5% per year, so the inflation is running at a rate of 5% per year. We only have natural unemployment of 5%. We also know from Chapter 9 that at this state of full employment, the nominal wage is also increasing at the same rate of 5% per year, so that the real wage is constant.

Suppose that, as in the 1990–1991 recession, households lose confidence in the economy and consume less. Or assume that firms become pessimistic about future profits and invest less. At the current rate of inflation, the aggregate demand goes down. In Figure 10, the economy moves to point A. Since contracts force the nominal wage to increase at the old rate of 5%, the real wage increases, and some workers lose their jobs. Unemployment increases to 7%.

The economy cannot stay at point A for long. Two events will cause the economy to move toward point E again. First, at point A the inflation rate is running at 4%, but the money supply is increasing at 5%. Therefore, the interest rate keeps going down, and at some point households and firms will find it attractive to borrow money for consumption and investment purposes. As a result, aggregate demand will increase, and economy will move along the PC curve toward point E.

Figure 10: A Recession

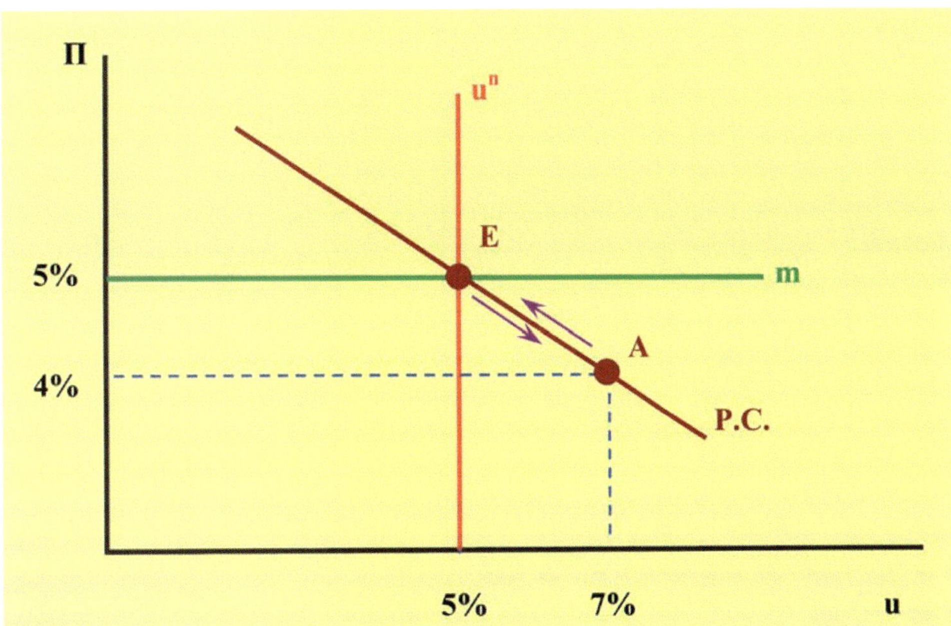

Second, at point A we have cyclical unemployment. Workers cannot remain unemployed forever. Sooner or later, as contracts expire and as workers realize there are not enough jobs to go around, they will reduce their asking wages in order to get hired back. In this way, wages will increase at a lower rate than before. As a result, unemployment will be reduced. The process just described is called the self-correcting mechanism of a market economy, which was introduced in

Chapter 12. That chapter also discusses arguments for and against active government policies in such cases. The same arguments apply here as well.

EXPANSIONARY DEMAND MANAGEMENT POLICIES

An expansionary fiscal or monetary policy is quite straightforward to analyze. This is just the opposite of the previous case. Suppose that currently, the money supply is increasing at a rate of 5% per year, and the economy is in equilibrium at point E of Figure 11. The natural unemployment rate is 5%. Now the government increases the level of spending or the stock of money. As a result, the economy moves to point A. However, point A is not sustainable. There is a shortage of labor, so firms find it harder and harder to find qualified workers. They begin offering higher wages to attract them. Firms also pay overtime to their existing workers. These events cause nominal wages to increase faster than before. Therefore, prices start rising faster than before.

At point A, the inflation rate (6%) is higher than the money growth rate (5%). Therefore, the interest rate increases, aggregate demand falls, GDP goes back to equal Y_p, and u moves towards u^n again. These are all movements along the PC curve.

Figure 11: An Expansionary Demand Management Policy

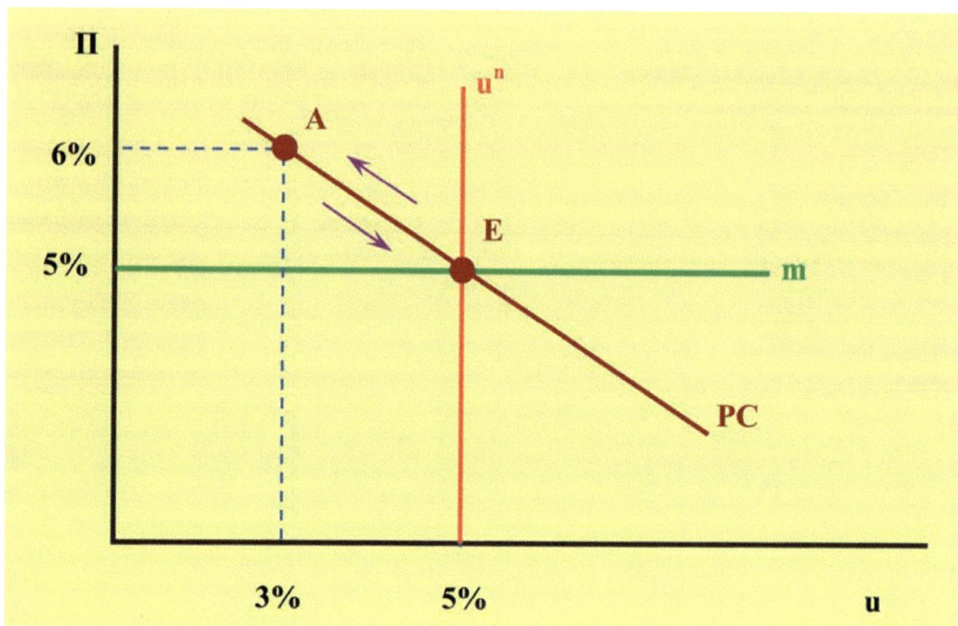

There is an important lesson in the above analysis that will be repeated later in the book. The government cannot reduce the unemployment rate below the natural rate for long by using fiscal and monetary policies. The task of these policies is to reduce the unemployment rate when it temporarily exceeds the natural rate. Contrary to some common beliefs, demand management policies cannot permanently reduce the unemployment rate. In other words, they cannot reduce the natural rate of unemployment. If a government tries to reduce unemployment year after year by stimulating aggregate demand, it will only cause inflation.

A SUPPLY SHOCK

A supply shock is any event that results in higher inflation rates because of its effects on production costs. As the name implies, the shock originates from the supply side rather than the demand side. For instance, if all else the same labor unions ask for and receive higher wages, the cost of production will increase. Business firms will try to pass the additional costs on to their consumers, causing an increase in the inflation rate. Labor is not the only production factor, and nominal wage is not the only cost of production. Firms buy other inputs such as raw materials, parts, and components. They also buy oil and natural gas as production inputs. Some firms, like transportation companies, airlines, or electricity producers, are heavy users of oil and gas products. What happens if the prices of such production inputs increase? What happens if OPEC sets a higher oil price? Many economists believe that the recession of 1974–1975 was caused by higher oil prices resulting from Saudi Arabia's oil embargo. The higher oil prices of 1979 and the subsequent recession of 1981–1982 were also partly blamed on the rise in oil prices brought about by the Iranian revolution, which resulted in disruptions in oil production. Moreover, some blame the Iraqi invasion of Kuwait and the resulting oil price increase as a factor contributing to the 1990–1991 recession.

Figure 12: A Supply Shock

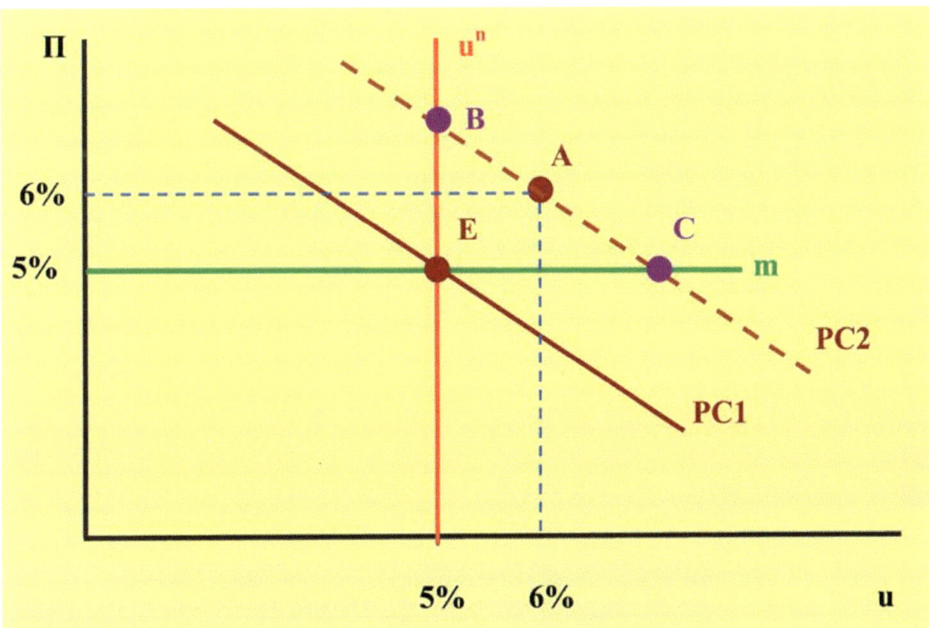

Their reasoning can be explained using Figure 12. The figure shows that the economy is in the state of long run equilibrium at point E. Consider a permanent increase in the price of crude oil brought about by OPEC. The resulting increase in the cost of production will cause prices of goods and services to increase faster than before, as producers try to pass the higher costs to consumers. The Phillips Curve will shift out, and the economy will land in a place like point A on the new PC. The higher inflation rate will result in a higher interest rate reducing consumption and investment. Moreover, higher prices will reduce consumption through the real-wealth effect. During the time the economy is moving from point E to point A, both the inflation and the unemployment rates will be rising. During this time, we will have stagflation.

During the period in which prices are rising, workers, firms, and households will come to expect that rising prices will continue into the future. These inflationary expectations will lead to further actual inflation. This is for a simple reason. In anticipation of higher future prices and in order to protect their real wages, workers will ask for higher nominal wages in their wage negotiations. Since producers also expect higher prices in the future, they will be willing to accept these wage demands. Therefore, the inflationary expectations will be built into the wage contracts, and in the following years, wages and prices will increase for this secondary reason.

Since this was just a one-time increase in the price of oil, the effect on the U.S. goods prices cannot go on forever. After a while, the economy will reach a point like point A, with high inflation and a high unemployment rate. Once the effect of the higher oil price is fully built into goods prices, the inflation rate will stop rising. Moreover, at some point the unemployment starts pushing the inflation rate down. This is because wages begin to rise at a lower pace than before. As the pace of the increase in nominal wages is reduced due to unemployment, the cost of production begins increasing at a lower rate, and the Phillips Curve starts shifting back. In the end, the inflation and unemployment rates go back to where they were before, and the stagflation is eliminated. So inflation shocks—like economic polices—do not have permanent effects on the economy.

As you recall from Chapter 12, supply shocks pose several policy dilemmas for the government. The government may decide to take no action and let the self-correcting mechanism get the economy out of the stagflation, as discussed above. If it decides that inflation is the worse of two evils, it can follow a contractionary demand management policy when the economy is at point A. This will drag the economy down the PC2 curve to point C. The inflation rate will get back to 5%, but at the cost of a much higher unemployment rate. On the other hand, if the government decides that unemployment is a bigger problem, it can conduct an expansionary demand management policy. This would cause the economy to move to point B. The unemployment will be eliminated at the cost of a higher inflation rate. Finally, all the problems mentioned previously about any economic policy, such as the existence of long and variable lags, apply to this case too. Therefore, some economists believe that the best course of action is to let the self-correcting mechanism work itself out rather than to create an even bigger mess.

TO SUMMARIZE

1. The price level, especially the GDP deflator, seldom decreases during a recession.
2. It is the inflation rate that goes down in a recession and goes up in an expansion. A realistic model of the economy should incorporate this fact.
3. In the long run, the unemployment rate equals the natural rate of unemployment no matter what the inflation rate is.
4. In the long run, the inflation rate equals the rate of growth of the money supply. This implies that the Cambridge k is constant in the long run.
5. In the short run, a demand shock will result in a negative relationship between the inflation and unemployment rates. This relationship is called the *Phillips Curve.*
6. In the short run, a supply shock will result in a positive relationship between the inflation and unemployment rates. This will be a shift in the Phillips Curve.
7. Only a change in the rate of growth of the money supply will affect inflation in the long run.
8. However, even a change in the rate of growth of money supply will not affect employment in the long run.
9. All other events will only have a short-run effect on inflation and unemployment.
10. A decrease in aggregate demand will cause a recession and lower inflation in the short run, but will have no effect on inflation and unemployment in the long run.
11. A permanent increase in aggregate demand will cause higher inflation and lower unemployment in the short run, but will have no effect on inflation and unemployment in the long run.
12. A supply shock will cause temporary stagflation.

EXERCISES

Question 1

In a country, the Cambridge k is constant, the money supply grows at a rate of 5% per year, and real GDP grows at a rate of 3% per year. What is the inflation rate in this country?

Question 2

In a country, the Cambridge k declined by 1% over a certain year, the money supply grew at a rate of 5%, and real GDP grew at a rate of 2%. What happened to the inflation rate in this country over this year?

Question 3

After reading the discussions and studying the graphs presented in this chapter, do you think the following proposition is true: *The government cannot change the rate of unemployment in the long run, using fiscal or monetary policies.*

Question 4

After reading the discussions and studying the graphs presented in this chapter, do you think the following proposition is true: *The government cannot change the rate of inflation in the long run, using fiscal or monetary policies.*

Question 5

After reading the discussions and studying the graphs presented in this chapter, do you think the following proposition is true: *The government cannot change either the rate of inflation or the rate of unemployment in the short run, using fiscal or monetary policies.*

Question 6

After reading the discussions and studying the graphs presented in this chapter, do you think the following proposition is true: *The government can reduce both the inflation and unemployment rates in the short run using, fiscal or monetary policies.*

Question 7

After reading the discussions and studying the graphs presented in this chapter, do you think the following proposition is true: *In the long run, the rate of growth of nominal GDP equals the rate of growth of money supply.*

Question 8

What is the relationship between the rate of change of Cambridge k and the velocity of circulation?

Question 9

After reading the discussions and studying the graphs presented in this chapter, can you describe the behavior of the velocity of circulation in the long run?

CHAPTER 16

Economic Growth

INTRODUCTION AND REVIEW

WE HAVE COME a long way. Recall that throughout the book, we have been chasing three macroeconomic goals: low and stable inflation, low unemployment, and long-term economic growth. The first two goals pertain to short run. They are about business cycles, deviations of GDP from its long-term trend—which is nothing but the potential GDP. The last goal is about long-run trends in GDP itself, the subject of this chapter.

WHAT CAN CAUSE LONG-TERM GROWTH?

As you recall, economic growth is the long-run increase in real GDP. You also remember that in the long run, we employ all the production factors fully and efficiently so we do not have unemployment. Thus, the only way to increase output is to increase the amount of production factors, or make the existing ones more productive. We can conclude, then, that the following events will cause economic growth:

Population growth. Population growth has two opposing effects on growth. On one hand, more people mean a larger labor force, and a greater amount of production. On the other hand, a larger population means, ceteris paribus, smaller GDP per capita, and lower standards of living. Population can increase either through net birth (births minus deaths) or net migration (immigration minus emigration).

Capital accumulation. Capital goods are produced means of production. Physical capital includes both private capital—such as trucks, tractors, and computers—owned by private citizens, and public capital—roads, parks, bridges, and schools—owned by the public. *Human capital* is all the knowledge, skills, and expertise that a person has accumulated over time through education, training, or learning by doing.

HUMAN CAPITAL
All the knowledge, skills, and expertise acquired and possessed by an individual.

Increase in the amount of natural resources. This can happen, for example, if a nation discovers new underground resources or it improves the quality of arable land.

Technological progress. Technology means knowledge of how to produce things. Technological progress means that a nation learns ways of producing new goods, or better ways of producing existing goods. Technology is a subset of human capital that is directed to production of goods and services.

ISN'T GDP PER CAPITA MORE IMPORTANT?

Real GDP per head (or per capita) is more important as far as standards of living are concerned, which is what economic growth is all about. Population is a double-edged sword. If we have more people in the country, they can produce more, but they also "eat" more. So as far as the well-being of the people is concerned, the question is why and how GDP *per head* increases over time. In other words, even if the size of the overall economic pie has been increasing, the increase in the population over time could mean a smaller share of this growing pie for each person. As Figure 1 shows, this is clearly not the case. The real GDP per capita for the United States has been increasing over the last century.

Figure 1: U.S. Real GDP per Capita and per Labor

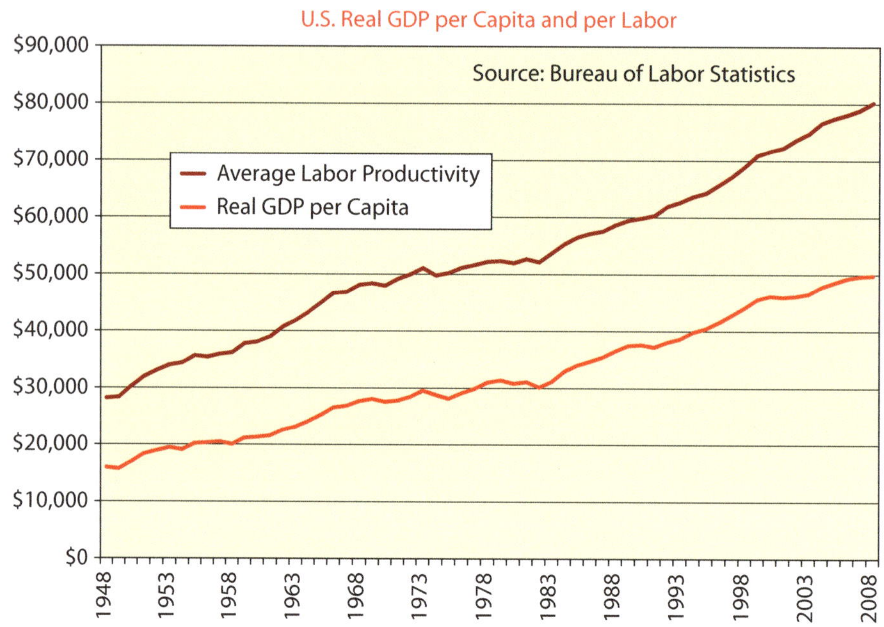

WHAT CAUSES GDP PER CAPITA TO INCREASE?

To answer this question, we perform a simple mathematical trick. Let N stand for population (Number of people). Note that GDP per head can be written as:

$$\frac{Y}{N} \equiv \left(\frac{LF}{N}\right) \times \left(\frac{L}{LF}\right) \times \left(\frac{Y}{L}\right)$$

where, as before, Y is the real GDP, L is the number of workers employed, and LF is the labor force. The labor force is defined as the number of people (over 16) who are willing and able to work. The GDP per head, Y/N, will increase if any of the ratios on the right-hand side increases, all else remaining the same. The above identity says: what fraction of the population wants to work (LF/N), what percent of those who want to work have jobs (L/LF), and how much each of those who have jobs produces on average (Y/L).

Table 1 shows these ratios for the United States for selected years over the past several decades.[1] The ratio (LF/N) is called the *labor force participation rate*: the percentage of the population who are willing and able to work. If, *everything else the same*, a larger percentage of the population wanted to work, the real GDP per capita would increase. This ratio has increased mildly in the last century, mostly due to the increased participation of women in the labor force. Figure 2 shows that the overall participation rate has increased from around 59% in 1950 to 66% in 2008. It also shows that the main reason for this increase has been the increase in the participation of women in the labor force, which has doubled from around 30% to about 60%. However, the participation of men in the labor force has decreased. This is partly for mathematical reasons. If the share of women in the labor force increases, that of men should go down, even if the number of participants—both men and women—increases. There may also be more substantive reasons behind this trend. The older men retire earlier nowadays, and the younger men go to school rather than work "on the farm." The participation rate depends partly on cultural and socioeconomic factors such as the rise of feminism. It also depends on technological progress. For example, the production of home appliances such as clothes washers and dryers has substantially reduced the number of hours women work at home, enabling them to participate in the labor force.

Women entered the workforce in large numbers in World War II. This wartime propaganda poster depicts the cultural icon known as Rosie the Riveter. The increase in women in the workplace drove the labor force participation rate in the last century.

LABOR FORCE PARTICIPATION RATE
The fraction of the population that is willing to work, calculated as the ratio of the labor force over population.

Table 1
GDP per Head and Its Components

Year	Y/N	LF/N	L/LF	Y/L
1950	16,927	0.59	0.95	30,179
1960	21,338	0.59	0.94	38,030
1970	27,515	0.60	0.95	47,947
1980	30,771	0.64	0.93	51,979
1990	37,600	0.67	0.94	59,872
2000	46,181	0.67	0.96	71,693
2005	48,870	0.66	0.95	77,887
2008	49,817	0.66	0.94	80,203

But by itself, increased labor force participation would not increase GDP per capita if the new entrants into the labor force could not find jobs and remained unemployed. This would reduce L/

1 Verify that the above identity holds for the numbers in Table 1. The source of data for Table 1 is the Bureau of Labor Statistics.

LF, leaving Y/N unchanged.[2] Therefore, we look at the ratio L/LF. But this is nothing but our good old friend the employment rate—the percentage of people who are willing to work who actually have jobs. We know by now that this ratio is fairly constant in the long run. It is one minus the unemployment rate: L/LF = 1 – u. We know that in the long run, the unemployment rate equals the natural rate, say about 5%. So L/LF jumps up and down over expansions and recessions, but it settles around a constant ratio (say 95%). Table 1 shows that this ratio has, in fact, stayed steady around 95% over the past several decades. In a sense, we don't have an unemployment problem in the long run.

Figure 2: Labor Force Participation Rates for the U.S.

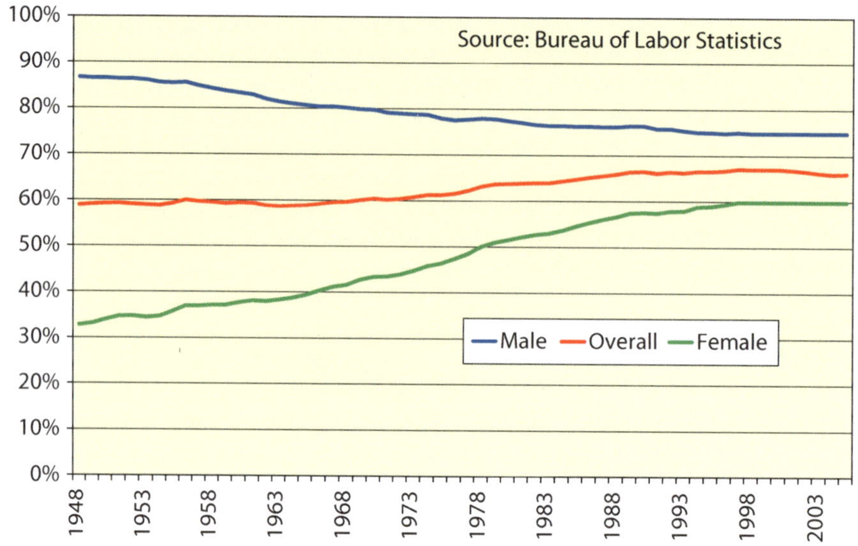

AVERAGE LABOR PRODUCTIVITY
The amount of output produced by a unit of labor.

This leaves the first ratio, (Y/L), which is called *average labor productivity*. This is how much output each employed worker can produce on average. If each employed worker produces more output over time, then everything else the same, (Y/N) will increase. There is ample evidence that (Y/L) has been increasing for the United States over the past century. Look at Figure 1 again. This figure clearly shows that the average labor productivity has been increasing over time.[3] The reason for this increase is the increase in the amount of physical and human capital over time, as well as improvements in technology. As a result of an increase in physical capital, each worker gets to use more and better equipment, thereby producing more output.

So far we have learned that GDP per head will increase if 1) the labor force participation rate increases, 2) the employment rate increases, or 3) the labor productivity increases. As mentioned above, the participation rate depends partly on sociological and cultural factors such as the rise of feminism. We will not consider these here. Moreover, the overall participation rate has not had a very strong trend. The second ratio, the employment rate, is fairly constant over time. Therefore,

2 To see this, assume that N = 100, LF = 60, L = 57, and Y = 114, so that Y/N = (114/57)(57/60)(60/100) = 2×.95×.60 = 1.14. Now suppose that someone enters the labor force, but cannot find a job. Then Y/N = (114/57)×(57/61)×(61/100) = 2×.93×.61 = 1.14. However, if she can find a job, then Y/N = (116/57)×(58/61)×(61/100) = 2×.95×.61 = 1.16. This assumes that each worker can produce 2 units of output on average.

3 Note that during the 1970s, the average labor productivity did not increase much. This phenomenon is called the productivity slowdown of the 1970s. It's a puzzle. The same thing happened in most European countries at the time. Economists do not quite agree on the possible causes of the slowdown.

increases in labor productivity seem to have been the main engine of economic growth in the United States in the last century. So for the question of economic growth, we need to figure out what determines labor productivity. We start with the simple relationship that indicates the importance of this question. We saw above that, all else the same, higher labor productivity results in a larger output per head:

$$\frac{Y}{L}\uparrow \rightarrow \frac{Y}{N}\uparrow$$

WHAT DETERMINES LABOR PRODUCTIVITY?

There are two main reasons for the increase in labor productivity: increases in capital per worker and improvements in technology. We start with the first one. It should be intuitively obvious that labor productivity will be higher if each worker gets to work with a larger amount of capital. Let's denote capital by the letter K. Then capital per worker is K/L. If a worker gets to use a larger amount of machines and tools, that worker will be able to produce more output. Therefore, the whole population will enjoy more food, shelter, and clothing. Consequently,

$$\frac{K}{L}\uparrow \rightarrow \frac{Y}{L}\uparrow \rightarrow \frac{Y}{N}\uparrow$$

WHAT CAUSES CAPITAL PER WORKER TO INCREASE?

The answer to this question is pretty straightforward.[4] The ratio K/L will increase if the numerator, K, increases at a higher rate than the denominator, L. As an example, suppose that K = 200 computers and L = 100 workers, so that K/L = 200/100 = 2 computers per worker. If K increases at 4% and L at 1%, then the next year we will have K = 208 and L = 101 so that K/L = 208/101 = 2.06 computers per worker. But if K increases at 1% as well, then the next year, K = 202 and K/L = 202/101 = 2 computers per worker. To put it simply, if next year we have 2 more workers but 6 more computers, then the number of computers per worker will increase.

Capital, the numerator of K/L, increases through investment. Every year we, as a nation, earn some income. We spend part of it on goods and services. This is called consumption. What is left over is called saving. What happens to our savings? We put them in a bank and the bank lends them to firms that want to buy machines and equipment, and to households that want to buy homes. So our savings become investment. If we save more, more investment will be generated. If we save less, less investment will be generated. We can thus conclude that a larger saving per worker in a country results in a higher investment per worker—hence, a higher capital per worker.

The increase in L, on the other hand, is the result of an increase in population, which is affected by the rates of net birth and migration. From the relative stabilities of the labor force participation rate and the employment rate in the long run, we can safely assume that the rate of increase in L equals the rate of increase in population. This rate is called the *natural growth rate*.

NATURAL GROWTH RATE
The rate of growth of the population in the long run.

If the natural growth rate in a country were too high, that country would find it hard to increase its capital per worker. This is because, as you know by now, for K/L to increase, K should increase at a higher rate than L. If a country could not increase its savings per worker sufficiently in order

4 The following is the essence of the model developed by Robert Solow of MIT in the 1960s.

to increase its stock of capital at a rate at least equal to the population growth rate, its capital/labor ratio would go down over time. This could create a vicious circle of economic decline in that country. Lower K/L would lead to a lower Y/N, which in turn would result in lower savings and investment. The main lesson of the chapter so far is that if a country wants to enjoy a high output per capita over time, it must increase its savings per worker and try to control its population growth.

WHAT IS THE ROLE OF TECHNOLOGICAL PROGRESS?

Technology is the knowledge to produce things. Technological progress means learning ways of producing new things, or better ways of producing the same things. If labor becomes more productive through training, education, or research and development, (Y/L) will be higher for any given (K/L). In other words, each worker on average will produce more than before, with the given amount of capital per worker. So we will have a second route to increase output per head as follows:

$$\text{Technological Progress} \rightarrow \frac{Y}{L}\uparrow \rightarrow \frac{Y}{N}\uparrow$$

The above growth model goes by the name of the *neoclassical growth model*. Economists working on this model did not analyze the question of what causes technological progress in a country. In this model, technological progress is *exogenous*—it just somehow happens because of reasons *outside* the model. For instance, someone suddenly discovers a new way of producing chocolates.

A new branch of growth theory called the *new growth theory* tackles this issue head on. This theory is associated with Paul Romer of Stanford University. According to his theory, technological progress does not "just happen." Rather, it is *endogenous*—explained within the model itself. Entrepreneurs following their own self-interest and trying to maximize their profits spend substantial amounts of resources on research and development activities, in order to develop new products or to find better ways of producing existing products. Because of the assumption of endogenous technological progress, this theory is also called the *endogenous growth theory*. Therefore, according to this theory, economic growth can take place for reasons unrelated to an increase in capital per worker.

Investing in research and development is like investing in physical capital. In the latter case, the firm acquires additional physical capital by spending money and/or effort to buy or build it. In the case of research and development expenditures, the firm spends resources to acquire additional knowledge to produce things. Romer calls the sum total of all such knowledge the stock of *knowledge capital*. Just as with physical capital, the larger the stock of knowledge capital, the higher labor productivity will be. This, in turn, will result in greater output per head.

If this is so, then why emphasize the role of knowledge capital as distinct from physical capital? An important reason for this is the presence of positive spillover effects associated with knowledge capital. If a farm spends money to buy a tractor, only that farm will own and use that tractor. On the other hand, if a firm spends money on research and development and discovers new products or better ways of producing existing ones, word will spread, and other firms will benefit from this firm's innovations. This is the case of a *positive externality*: a decision made by one person benefits others, without any monetary compensation being made from the beneficiary to the person causing the externality.

NEOCLASSICAL GROWTH MODEL
The growth theory originally proposed by Robert Solow, which posits that the rate of growth of national output in the long run depends positively on the rate of growth of capital per labor. The latter can increase through additional savings.

NEW GROWTH THEORY
The theory advanced by Paul Romer, which argues that endogenous technological progress is the main engine of economic growth.

ENDOGENOUS GROWTH THEORY
A theory that posits that economic growth takes place because entrepreneurs, trying to maximize their profits, spend substantial amounts of resources on research and development activities in order to develop new products, or to find better ways of producing existing products.

KNOWLEDGE CAPITAL
The sum total of all knowledge in a society.

POSITIVE EXTERNALITY
An externality situation in which a decision made by a decision maker benefits other people. Positive externality: An externality situation in which a decision made by a decision maker benefits other people.

PRINCIPLE OF DIMINISHING RETURNS (LAW OF DIMINISHING RETURNS)
The idea that, given a fixed amount of capital, the marginal product of labor declines as the firm hires additional labor.

Moreover, in the case of physical capital, as capital per worker increases, output per worker generally increases at a decreasing rate. This is called the *principle of diminishing returns*. If you give more and more computers to a given number of workers, at first the amount of output will increase at an increasing rate. But how many computers does a worker need? Once every employee gets to have a computer, additional computers purchased will not add much to production. Because of this phenomenon, some economists in the past thought there must be a *limit to growth*.

The endogenous growth theory challenges this view. There are no diminishing returns to knowledge capital, especially at the level of the economy. At the firm level, additional dollars spent on research and development may not be as fruitful as previous dollars. However, at the national level, as knowledge expands, there are always people who can put the know-how to profitable use. Even though additional dollars spent on research and development may bring less profit to the firm undertaking these investments, the resulting knowledge could be very beneficial to other, free-riding firms.

WHY DO GROWTH RATES DIFFER ACROSS COUNTRIES?

The above analysis should provide you with the answer to this question. All else the same, a country with more capital per worker will have higher labor productivity and a higher growth rate. Investment is the way to increase capital stock. Therefore, a country whose economic environment is conducive to investment will have a higher growth rate. For example, political instability and despotism are the enemies of investment. Investors prefer stable environments. They don't want to invest in countries whose governments change frequently, or whose governments can confiscate properties randomly and at will. These factors create uncertainty about the future rates of return on investment and, as we know, retard investment spending.

All else the same, countries with open economies who are not hostile to foreign investment will experience higher growth rates. For instance, many African countries have a negative view of foreign investment in their countries because of their colonial past. The situation is exacerbated by the fact that these countries may also have unstable political systems. These factors have resulted in low levels of investment and economic growth in these countries.

Google, Inc., based in Mountain View, California, has realized phenomenal growth in part because of the United States government's policies pertaining to technological progress, free markets, and property rights.

All else the same, according to the above analysis, a country with a higher savings rate is expected to experience a higher growth rate. Larger savings result in greater amounts of investment and capital per worker. The greater capital per worker makes workers more productive. In the 1970s and 1980s, the high Japanese savings rates (more than 10% per year) were the reasons for the high Japanese growth rates. Later, the Japanese performance deteriorated somewhat. Some economists blamed inefficient financial markets in Japan for the slowdown in growth. In other words, the financial markets were not able to channel savings to investment efficiently.

The analysis also indicates that countries whose institutions encourage technological progress will have higher growth rates. That is, higher incomes, respect for property rights, and free markets in the United States provide a great deal of incentives for firms to take risks and try to bring new products to the market. Moreover, new technologically advanced machines and equipment are built to make the new products. These technological improvements, along with an efficient education system in the United States, have resulted in larger and larger amounts of capital per worker—and a higher GDP.

Finally, all else the same, countries with lower population growth rates are expected to experience higher growth rates of GDP per capita. Population is a rather tricky factor. If the size of the population is too small, firms may not have a large enough domestic market to sell their products. For this reason, many small, developed counties advocate free and open trade with other countries.

HOW CAN WE INCREASE GDP PER HEAD?

So far we have been discussing growth *theory*. Now it is time to talk about economic policies that encourage economic growth. The above theoretical discussion should provide you with ample hints as to what these policies should be. The policies should aim at increasing the savings rate, increasing investment spending, encouraging technological progress, and reducing population growth.

Policies to Increase the Propensity to Save

An increase in the marginal propensity to save will result in greater savings for any level of GDP. If these savings turn into investment, then the stock of capital per worker will increase. This, as we have seen above, will increase labor productivity and output per head. Many countries know this savings-growth link and have implemented or proposed policies to increase their savings rates. In the United States, for example, the government encourages creation of tax-deferred retirement accounts. If you open such an account, part of your monthly income is deposited in this account and the interest earned on the money is not taxable until you withdraw it after retirement. The tax-deferral feature of these accounts makes them attractive for working people, increasing the amount of money they put into these accounts. Financial institutions, such as banks, credit unions, or pension funds, lend these funds to the firms that need them for investment purposes.

Some economists in the United States and elsewhere propose to scrap the current income tax system and replace it with a consumption tax system. Under this system, you are taxed on the amount you consume, not on the amount you earn. The rationale for this proposal is that if you tax people on their consumption, then they will have incentives to reduce their consumption in order to pay fewer taxes. This increases their savings, which can turn into investment. A variant of this proposal is a national sales tax. Imposing a tax on most consumer items will reduce consumption and increase savings.

Policies to Increase Investment

The problem is that for several reasons, increases in savings may not result in increases in investment if certain other conditions are not satisfied. Countries need efficient financial systems to channel funds from savers to investors. In many developing countries, financial markets are not well developed. Hence, there are no ways of channeling the funds from savers to investors. Most of these savings just become household wealth such as expensive jewelry, antiques, and the like.

Even if there is an efficient financial system in a country, firms may not want to undertake investments for other reasons. For example, investors may fear that if their investment becomes successful, the government may levy a heavy tax on the profits. In general, democratic political systems provide better economic environments for investment. In nondemocratic countries, there is always concern that the government may randomly tax companies or confiscate their properties. Generally, stable political systems and pro-business tax laws are more conducive to business investment.

Finally, we have the "Asian Miracle" of the 1980s and 1990s, which refers to a period of extremely high economic growth in several East Asian countries. This growth was mostly due to foreign investments in East Asian countries such as Indonesia and Malaysia. Pro-business countries that open their doors to foreign trade and investment generally have higher investment rates and more capital per worker. Foreign companies bring not only their capital, but also their know-how, work ethics, workplace discipline, and so on. All these factors could have positive impacts on the economies of the recipient counties.

The south side of the James Madison Building in Alexandria, Virginia. It is one of the five buildings that forms the headquarters of the United States Patent and Trademark Office.

Policies to Encourage Technological Progress

The new growth theory argues that technological progress is even more important than an increase in capital per worker. A lot of developed, industrialized countries have policies in place to encourage risk-taking and innovation. A business firm will take risk and invest in new lines of business if it knows that it can reap the fruits of its efforts. No firm would be foolish enough to spend a lot of money and resources to invest in new products or production processes if its owners did not expect to receive their required rates of return from the investment. Imagine if a pharmaceutical company invented a new drug and other firms learned about the formula, and started to produce and market it. Then the company would have no incentive to invest money to find new drugs. For this reason, many countries have *patent laws,* which give exclusive rights to the inventor of a new product to produce and sell it. In the United States, patents run for 20 years, during which time only the inventor of the new product can market it.

PATENT LAWS
Laws giving exclusive rights to the inventor of a new product to produce and sell it.

Tax systems are also important in encouraging risk-taking and innovation. To begin with, firms pay taxes to the government when they make a positive profit. However, they don't receive a refund from the government if they make a loss. For example, suppose you invest in a new product. You succeed, and make $100 million from it. If you are in the 40% tax bracket, you have to pay $40 million to the government. But, if you lose $100 million dollars, the government does not pay you $40 million. If you gain, your gain is reduced, but if you lose, your loss is not reduced. This asymmetric treatment of your profits and losses reduces the expected after-tax rate of return on your investment.

To somewhat alleviate this problem and encourage risk-taking and innovation, the U.S. tax system allows firms to carry their losses back five years and forward 15 years. For instance, suppose your firm makes a profit of $30 million in 2005. If you are in the 40% tax bracket, you pay a tax of $12 million to the government. In 2006 you incur a loss of $100 million. You can now carry this $100 million back to 2005 and subtract it from your 2005 profit of $30 million. In other word in 2006 you go back and adjust your 2005 profit to zero. Since you have paid $12 million of tax on that profit, the government returns that $12 million to you in 2006. Now you still have $70 million of loss ($100 million incurred in 2006 - $30 million profit in 2005). You carry forward this $70 million to 2007. If in 2007 you make a profit of $50 million, then you subtract that $70 from the 2007 profit, wiping it out altogether. You don't pay any tax on 2007 income. You still have $20 million of 2006 loss remaining that you can carry forward to 2008. So this tax system tries to treat profits and losses symmetrically, thereby encouraging risk-taking.

Another feature of the U.S. tax system that encourages research and development is to *expense* the research and development expenses. This means subtracting all of the research and development expenses from your revenue in calculating your taxable income. If you buy a physical asset for your company in 2006, you cannot subtract its full purchase price from your revenue to calculate your profit. Suppose you buy a machine for $10 million and your 2006 revenue is $14 million. Suppose your other 2006 costs amount to $3 million. In this case, as we have learned from the GDP chapter, your profit will *not* equal $14 – $3 – $10 = $1 million. You only get to deduct the portion of the machine that depreciates in 2006. Suppose it is 10% of the purchase price, or $1 million. Then you have to calculate your profit as $14 – $3 – $1 = $10 million, and pay a tax of $4 million (0.40 × $10 million) to the government. On the other hand, if you spend $10 million on research and development activities, you can subtract the whole figure from your revenue, reducing your taxable income to $1 million and paying only $400,000 in taxes.

Finally, some economists argue that there are a lot of positive externalities in the high-tech industries. The information about an innovation by one firm spreads to other firms through informal chats by the employees of different firms in cafés or by workers quitting one firm and going to work for another. As a result, firms may not reap the whole fruits of their own investments. For example, there is always fear that your competition could bring the new product you are working on to the market sooner than you. For this reason, there are some proposals to provide economic subsidies to these firms to reduce their costs of spending money on new products, and to spur innovation in that sector of the economy.

Policies to Control Population

As we noted above, population is a tricky issue. Too many people in the country may divert resources from savings and investment to consumption. By contrast, if the population of a country is too small, there will not be large enough markets for firms to sell to and gain economies of scale. Additionally, excessively low population growth may cause problems. For example, Russia's population is declining—it has a negative growth rate. The problem with this scenario is that, if the trend continues, the future population of the country will be old and not very productive. A small percentage of young people will have to support a large percentage of old people. This could result in very low savings and investment in the future, threatening economic growth.

TO SUMMARIZE

1. Economic growth means the increase in real GDP in the long run. This is important for a nation's standard of living.
2. The real GDP can increase in the long run for two reasons:
    a. The amounts of production factors such as labor, capital, or natural resources increase. Increases in labor come from increases in population. Capital increases through investment.
    b. The existing factors become more productive through technological progress.
3. To improve your economic well-being, you should try to increase GDP per head (Y/N). This can happen if, everything else the same,
    a. Your *labor force participation rate* increases (LF/N).
    b. Your employment rate increases (L/LF).
    c. Your labor productivity (Y/L) increases.
4. Labor force participation depends mostly on sociological and cultural factors.
5. The employment rate is constant in the long run.
6. Therefore, to increase your Y/N, you should try to increase your Y/L.
7. To increase your Y/L, you should try to increase your K/L.
8. To increase your K/L, you have to encourage larger investment per worker.
9. How large? Large enough that it results in an increase in capital that is greater than the increase in the number of workers. This way, each worker will get to work with larger and larger amounts of capital over time.
10. How can we do this? Three ways:
    a. Increase savings per worker. This results in a higher investment per worker.
    b. Increase labor productivity through education and R&D spending.
    c. Reduce the population growth. With a lower *natural growth rate*, the same amount of investment per worker leads to a greater K/L, a higher Y/L, and a larger Y/N.
11. According to the *new growth theory*, technological progress is the main engine of growth. To increase economic growth, governments should follow policies that encourage research and development, as well as other activities that result in innovation.

EXERCISES

Question 1

Consider a country in which the amount of capital in a year and the number of people employed are K = 500 and L = 200, respectively. In this country, L grows at a constant rate of 2% per year and investment equals saving.

a. What should be the amount of investment per worker in the next year for the capital/labor ratio to remain unchanged?
b. What will happen to the capital/labor ratio next year if savings equal 20 units?

Question 2

Suppose there are three countries: A, B, and C. Currently, in all three countries K = 1000 and L = 10. Moreover, in all three economies the following relationship exists between capital per worker and output per worker:

$$\frac{Y}{L} = \sqrt{\frac{K}{L}}$$

In Country A, both capital and labor will grow at 20% per year. In country B, capital will grow at 20% per year, but labor at 10% per year. Country C's capital will grow at 10% per year, but labor at 20% per year. Calculate output per worker in each country after three years. Which country would you like to live in?

Question 3

Consider the three countries in the previous question. We have the following data on the labor force participation and employment rates for these countries:

	Country A	Country B	Country C
LF/N	0.70	0.50	0.70
L/LF	0.90	0.80	0.95

Calculate output per capita in each country after three years.

Question 4

In a country, K = 10,000, L = 100, and the following relationship exists between capital per worker and output per worker:

$$\frac{Y}{L} = \sqrt{\frac{K}{L}}$$

a. Suppose labor force participation and unemployment rates are 60% and 5%, respectively. Calculate the GDP per capita.

b. The natural growth rate is 5%. By how much should K increase to leave GDP per capita unchanged?

c. Suppose that saving increases by 1,000 units. If saving equals investment, what will be the GDP per capita next year?

CHAPTER 17

The Stock Market and the Economy

INTRODUCTION AND REVIEW

So far, we have learned how the interactions between three markets determine the equilibrium level of output, employment, and inflation rates. These three markets are the goods market, the money market, and the labor market. In this chapter, we will take a look at the stock market and its interactions with the rest of the economy. Every day the news has something to say about stock prices rising or plummeting. What causes these fluctuations? What are their consequences on the rest of the economy? This chapter will examine these questions while building upon previously learned concepts.

DIVIDENDS
The profits distributed to shareholders by a corporation.

STOCK PRICES

Predicting which way a stock price will go in the future is a tricky business. Conceptually, however, it is very easy to understand why stock prices move from day to day. Stocks are ownership rights in corporations. If you own some stocks in a corporation, you own part of that corporation, and are entitled to a portion of the profits earned by that corporation. Suppose a corporation has issued 1,000 shares of common stock. This means that to own the whole corporation, you would have to own all 1,000 shares. Let's say you purchase 100 of these shares. Then you own 10% of the assets of this corporation, and are entitled to 10% of the corporation's profits. If the corporation makes a profit of $1 million next year, you are entitled to $100,000 of that profit. The profits distributed to shareholders are called *dividends*.

The New York Stock Exchange

The difference between stocks and bonds is that, unlike bonds, corporations are not obligated to pay you any dividends. There are three reasons why a corporation may not give you any dividends. First, the corporation may decide to plow the whole profit back into the corporation, buying machines and equipment or investing in a new line of business. Second, the corporation may lose money, in which case it will have no profits to distribute. Third, the corporation may go bankrupt altogether. So dividend payments are inherently uncertain.

To make the story simple, we will begin by assuming that the buyer of a stock is planning to hold it only for one year and will sell the stock at the end of the year. Although this assumption is not realistic, it works well for our purpose. Once we learn this simple case, we can easily generalize it to the case of multiple holding periods. Our investor buys the stock in the hope of selling it the next year and making some money. Investors would like to receive dividends before selling the stocks. However, there is no guarantee that they will receive any dividends. So unlike bond investors, stock market investors should guess two things: amount of dividends next year, and the stock prices.

Consider the stock of XYZ Corporation. What price are you willing to pay it? In forming your opinion, you will consider two basic things: Will the company pay any dividends; and what will the market price of the stock be next year? You will consider a few factors in answering these questions. Is the company enjoying good management? How fierce are the domestic and foreign competition? Does the company have a good relationship with its labor? Is the company at the cutting edge of innovation, and will it bring new successful products to the market soon? On the basis of the answers to these questions, you will form an opinion about the future profitability of the corporation. If a corporation is perceived to be profitable, many people will expect it to pay good dividends and its stock to sell at a high price in the future.

Risk is also important. Given the expected future dividends and stock price, not very many people would want to buy the stock of a corporation if they perceive it to be too risky. For example, if a company's profits jump up and down a lot, it is regarded as more risky than another whose profits are more stable. This is because the chance that the first company may go bankrupt is greater than that of the second company. For this reason, you are willing to pay a lower price for it. As you will see below, this means that you require a higher rate of return from the stock of the more risky company.

Stock prices, like the prices of any other assets, are determined in the market by what are called *marginal investors*. These are the investors who are willing to pay the highest price for the stocks. Suppose the XYZ Corporation is selling its stock in the market. Investors expect that the corporation will pay a dividend of $30 next year, and that the price of the stock will be $90 then. So if they buy this stock, they will receive an expected $120 next year: They will collect the dividend of $30, and sell the stock for $90. Both of these numbers are, of course, inherently uncertain. In fact, the corporation may decide not to pay any dividends, and the price of the stock could be higher—or lower—than $90.

MARGINAL INVESTORS
Investors who are willing to pay the highest price for assets, and therefore are the ones who get to determine their prices.

Now, some people will be willing to pay no more than $75 for this stock. Some others may be willing to pay $80 for it, and someone else might pay $100. If $100 is the highest price offered, the stock will sell at that price. People who offer the highest price for an asset, thus ultimately determining its market price, are the marginal investors. They either have more information about the corporation, or are less risk averse than other investors.

What rate of return do the marginal investors expect to earn from buying this stock and selling it next year? They expect to make 20%, calculated as follows:

$$\frac{\$30 + \$90 - \$100}{\$100} = 0.20 \qquad (1)$$

We can solve this equation for the current price of the stock as follows:

$$\$100 = \frac{\$30 + \$90}{(1 + 0.20)} = \frac{\$120}{1.20} \qquad (2)$$

Although the math is easy, equations (1) and (2) tell us a very important story. The marginal investors are willing to pay \$100 for the stock. In other words, these investors *require* a rate of return of no less than 20% from this stock—see equation (1). Equation (2) says the same thing in reverse. Since the marginal investors require a rate of return of 20% from the stock, they are willing to pay no more than \$100 for it. This is because at any higher price, their rate of return would be less than 20%. *This \$100 is the value of the stock to them.* The 20% is called the *required rate of return* by the marginal investors.

Let's denote the price of a stock in the current year by P_{S0}. Let's also denote the expected dividends and the future price of the stock by d_1^e and P_{S1}^e, respectively. Finally, let the marginal investors' required rate of return from this stock be R. Then the stock price formula becomes similar to the bond price formula:

$$P_{S0} = \frac{d_1^e + P_{S1}^e}{(1 + R)} = \frac{d_1^e}{(1 + R)} + \frac{P_{S1}^e}{(1 + R)} \qquad (3)$$

People who were more risk averse required a higher rate of return from the stock, and so were willing to pay a smaller price for it. For example, one group required a 50% rate of return from it. They were willing to pay no more than \$80 for it:

$$\frac{\$30 + \$90}{(1 + 0.50)} = \$80$$

Note that the higher the required rate of return from the stock, the less people are willing to pay for it. This is similar to the negative relationship between interest rates and bond prices.

Suppose news reports indicate that the corporation's research and development efforts have been successful, and that next year it will bring a new product to the market. People will expect the company to be more profitable and its stock price to be higher next year. Suppose they expect the stock price to increase to \$126 next year. Then, if the marginal investors' perception of the riskiness of the company has not changed, they will be willing to pay \$130 for it:

Usually, when investors expect a corporation to be more profitable in the future, they may also expect higher dividend payments by the corporation. This also results in a higher stock price today. We conclude that:

$$P_{S0} = \frac{\$30 + \$126}{(1 + 0.20)} = \$130$$

If market participants expect a corporation to be more profitable in the future, the price of its common stock will increase today.

Suppose instead that the company gets into trouble with the regulators or the labor union, and people become more uncertain about its future profits. Then they will require a higher rate of return from the company. Suppose the marginal investors now require a 25% rate of return. Then they are willing to pay no more than $96 for the stock:

$$P_{S0} = \frac{\$30 + \$90}{(1 + 0.25)} = \$96$$

We conclude that:

The required rate of return on a stock will increase, and its price will decrease, if investors perceive the corporation to become riskier.

GOING FROM ONE YEAR TO MANY

What if the marginal investors want to hold the stock for two years and sell it then? They expect to collect two dividends, one at the end of each year, and sell the stock at the end of the second year.

Current Year (Year 0)	After One Year (Year 1)	After Two Years (Year 2)
P_{S0}	d_1^e	$d_2^e + P_{S2}^e$

In that case, we use equation (3) to determine the price of the stock after one year, and use this price to find the current price. The price of the stock next year is determined on the basis of the dividends expected to be paid and the stock price expected to emerge in the second year:

$$P_{S1}^e = \frac{d_2^e + P_{S2}^e}{(1 + R)} = \frac{d_2^e}{(1 + R)} + \frac{P_{S2}^e}{(1 + R)}$$

Substituting this into equation (3), we get

$$P_{S0} = \frac{d_1^e}{(1 + R)} + \frac{1}{(1 + R)}\left[\frac{d_2^e}{(1 + R)} + \frac{P_{S2}^e}{(1 + R)}\right] = \frac{d_1^e}{(1 + R)} + \frac{d_2^e}{(1 + R)^2} + \frac{P_{S2}^e}{(1 + R)^2}$$

For example, suppose people think that the corporation will pay dividends of $30 and $35 in the next two years, and that the stock price will equal $95 after two years. If the marginal investors require a rate of return of 20% from this corporation, the price of the stock will be

$$P_{S0} = \frac{\$30}{(1+0.20)} + \frac{\$35}{(1+0.20)^2} + \frac{\$95}{(1+0.20)^2} = \$115.28$$

Continuing this way, and assuming that the stock will not be sold any time soon, the stock price formula becomes

$$P_{S0} = \frac{d_1^{\,e}}{(1+R)} + \frac{d_2^{\,e}}{(1+R)^2} + \frac{d_3^{\,e}}{(1+R)^3} + \frac{d_4^{\,e}}{(1+R)^4} + \dots \qquad (4)$$

This equation is called the *present value formula*. Note that the cash flows that occur in the more distant future are divided by larger numbers, and become less important than those that occur in the near future. For this reason, we ignore the future stock price in the formula. To see this, suppose that a stock is expected to pay \$30 of dividends in each of the next 20 years and sell for \$100 in year 20. Assuming that R = 20%, the price of this stock today will be

PRESENT VALUE FORMULA
The formula that calculates the present value of an asset on the basis of the cash flows the asset is expected to generate in the future.

$$P_{S0} = \frac{\$30}{(1+0.20)} + \frac{\$30}{(1+0.20)^2} + \dots + \frac{\$30}{(1+0.20)^{20}} + \frac{\$100}{(1+0.20)^{20}}$$

$$P_{S0} = \$25 + \$20.80 + \cdots + \$0.80 + \$1.30 = \$147.70$$

In this example, the value to the marginal investors today of that \$30 they expect to receive next year is only \$25. The value of the \$30 they expect to receive after two years is \$20.80. Note that the value of the \$100 they expect to receive from selling the stock after 20 years is only \$1.30.

You are willing to pay less for the cash flows that occur in the distant future for the two reasons we saw in Chapter 6. First, you would want to be compensated for the opportunity cost of waiting. By buying the stock of XYZ Corporation, you lose the opportunity to consume goods and services today—anticipating that, if you wait a year instead, you will be able to consume a larger amount of goods and services then. Otherwise, why would you invest? Second, the future is always uncertain. You are not really sure that you will, in fact, receive those dividends. Moreover, if the corporation goes bankrupt, you will be unable to sell the stock. So you would want to be compensated for risking your money. It is for this reason that, if investors perceive a corporation to be more risky, they require a higher rate of return. Consequently, its price goes down in the market.

Equation (4) is not operational, since the expected dividends go on forever. Therefore, sometimes practitioners make some simplifying assumptions about the dividend streams to get an approximation of the stock price. One popular assumption is that dividends will grow at a constant rate of g forever. In that case, equation (4) reduces to the following

$$P_{S0} = \frac{d_1^{\,e}(1+g)}{(R-g)} \qquad (5)$$

For instance, suppose investors expect the next dividend to be \$30, and to grow at 5% per year afterward. Then, assuming R = 20%, the price of the stock equals

$$P_{S0} = \frac{\$30 \times (1+0.05)}{(0.20-0.05)} = \$210$$

For this formula to work, note that R must be larger than g, as otherwise the stock price becomes negative, which is not possible. The above equation is sometimes called the Gordon formula in honor of the economist who derived it. However, you can derive it from (4) and the results of geometric series you learned in sixth grade. The equation says that the stock price will be higher if the corporation is expected to pay a high dividend (d_1^e is high); if the dividends are expected to grow faster (g is high); or if the corporation is not very risky (R is low).

ASSET DEMAND AND PORTFOLIO CHOICE

The above discussion concentrated on stocks in isolation. To understand the relationship between the financial markets and the economy as a whole, we also need to have some basic understanding of the factors affecting an individual's demand for an asset in relation to other assets. In this section, we will present a simple theory of asset demand that will help you understand the financial and economic news.

An asset is anything that brings some future benefits. The key word is *future*. An apple brings some benefits, but only when you are eating it right now. Stocks, bonds, or homes, on the other hand, are valuable because they give you some benefits in the future. Stocks and bonds provide you with monetary benefit, while a house provides you with a service called shelter, which is not monetary. We will assume that there are 3 kinds of financial assets:

1. Money;
2. Bonds;
3. Stocks.

We will ignore foreign currencies for the time being. Financial assets are pieces of paper that entitle you to some future benefits. Bonds promise future payments, stocks give you dividends, and money enables you to buy goods and services. As we know, people hold money instead of stocks or bonds because of its liquidity. We also have physical assets, such as gold and land, which bring some future benefits to their owners. People hold gold partly for cosmetic reasons and partly to enjoy future price appreciation. Land is owned either for agricultural production or for speculative reasons.

What determines how much of each asset people want to hold in their portfolios? There are four major determinants of asset demand, as follows:

1. Wealth;
2. Expected relative rates of return;
3. Relative riskiness;
4. Relative liquidity.

1. Wealth

The total wealth of an individual is the sum of the market values of all the financial and physical assets that the individual owns. We saw this concept in the chapter on demand for money. An investor's wealth increases over time through savings. simply because people hold their savings in the form of some type of asset. As you save more, you can buy and own more stocks, bonds, and physical assets. So as wealth increases, it must be held in the form of one of these assets. Therefore,

All else the same, an increase in wealth results in an increase in demand for assets.

2. Expected Relative Rates of Return

As we saw above, rates of return on some assets like stocks depend on their future prices, which are not known when individuals make their investment decisions. Therefore, they should base their decisions on the rate of return they *expect* to receive in the future. Moreover, people care about the expected rates of return on an asset *relative* to that on other assets. If the expected rates of return on all the assets increase by 5%, there will be no increase in demand for any of them. If, however, people expect only the price of Microsoft stock to go up in the future, they will dump some of their other assets to buy the Microsoft stock. Or, if the rates of return on all the assets are expected to increase by 5%, but that of the Microsoft stock by 7%, people again will try to sell the other assets and buy Microsoft stock. We will therefore make the following assumption:

All else the same, an increase in the expected rate of return on an asset relative to others will increase the demand for that asset.

3. Relative Riskiness

RISK AVERSE
Everything else the same, a risk-averse investor prefers less risk to more risk.

Risk is the chance that the actual rate of return on an asset might deviate from the expected rate of return. The more volatile the rate of return of an asset, the more risky it is. We assume that people are generally *risk averse*, meaning that, everything else the same, they prefer less risk to more risk. For example, if you offer them two assets with the same expected rates of return, they will prefer the one with less risk. Therefore, we will assume that:

All else the same, an increase in the riskiness of an asset relative to other assets will reduce the demand for that asset.

4. Relative Liquidity

Liquidity is the ease with which you can sell an asset. Of course, you can sell any asset quickly if you accept a very low price for it. You can sell your car in five minutes if you accept $10 for it. So the term “ease” in the definition of liquidity means how fast you can sell your asset without incurring a substantial price reduction. Liquidity is only a relative concept. Some assets are more liquid than others. Money is the most liquid of all assets. Stocks and bonds are also highly liquid, because you can sell them quickly without any loss in value. You can sell an asset, or anything else for that matter, faster if there are a large number of people willing to buy it.

Suppose, for example, there is a company in a town producing gadgets. Not very many people know about this company. If you buy the bonds of this company, you may not be able to sell them easily. Now if the company becomes famous through advertising, many people will learn about it. Once the business is well known, it would be easier to sell the bonds issued by this company. The bonds become more liquid, and thus more attractive. We assume that:

Everything else the same, an increase in the liquidity of an asset relative to others will increase the demand for that asset.

Physical Assets

The rate of return on a physical asset is the percentage increase in its price since the time you purchased it. If you buy some gold coins for \$100 and sell them a year later for \$120, your rate of return from this investment will be 20%. Generally, the prices of commodities such as gold and silver increase with the overall rate of inflation. All else the same, when investors anticipate higher inflation rates in the future, they will expect a higher rate of return on physical assets. Therefore, consistent with our relative return rule, they sell some of their stocks and bonds and buy gold and silver.

SPILLOVER EFFECTS IN FINANCIAL MARKETS

If an asset becomes more attractive for one of the reasons mentioned above, the investor has to sell some of his other assets in order to buy more of this now-more-attractive asset. As a result, the prices and the rates of returns on all the assets will be affected.

A Wal-mart store entrance in China

Suppose for example that a free-trade agreement is signed with China. As the cost of doing business with China is reduced, American firms are expected to make more profits in the future selling in the Chinese markets. This event increases the expected rate of return on stocks (R), and makes stocks more attractive relative to other assets. Investors sell bonds and physical assets to buy stocks. As people sell bonds, bond prices fall and interest rates on bonds increase. Similarly, as people sell physical assets to buy stocks, the prices of physical assets—such as gold and silver—fall. For a given expectation of the future price level, therefore, the rates of return on physical assets increase. As a result, the expected rates of return on all assets increase.

Similarly, suppose that people revise upward their expectation of future inflation rate (π^e). In other words, they expect a higher rate of return from buying physical assets now and selling them in the future. Therefore, they sell their stocks and bonds to buy physical assets. This reduces the prices of these assets, and increases their expected rates of return. Again, all the rates of return on all assets move in the same direction. Note that this result is similar to the Fisher Effect we saw in Chapter 11 on the loanable funds theory: an increase in expected inflation results in an increase in the interest rate.

THE STOCK MARKET AND THE ECONOMY

Why is the stock market always in the news? We already know one answer to this question from previous chapters. Changes in stock prices affect the values of wealth held by households. This in turn affects households' consumption expenditures and aggregate demand for goods and services.

There is another reason for the importance of stock prices. If a corporation's stock price is high in the market, the corporation can raise cash more easily. A corporation can raise cash from two different channels: selling bonds and selling stocks. In the first case, the corporation borrows from people. In the second case, it sells a portion of the corporation to other people, and entitles them to future profits of the corporation. We know about the first channel from previous chapters. If the interest rates decrease, firms find it cheaper to borrow money for their investment spending. Another way of saying the same thing is that when interest rates drop, bond prices increase, and firms can raise more cash selling bonds.

The case for raising cash through selling stocks is similar. Corporations can raise more cash with greater ease when the price of their stocks is higher. We already know why the price of a particular stock could be high. When marginal investors expect the corporation to make more profits in the future or they perceive the corporation's stock to be less risky, the stock of this corporation becomes more attractive and commands a higher price in the stock market.

MONETARY POLICY

You can use any of the above formulas and the theory of asset demand to analyze the effects of different events on the stock prices and the economy. We demonstrate this point using the case of an expansionary monetary policy. Suppose that the Fed increases the money supply through an open market purchase of bonds. As we know, the increase in the demand for bonds by the Fed increases their price and lowers the interest rate. The reduction in the interest rate causes an increase in stock prices through three channels.

Prefabricated home interior side walls are prepared for delivery.

1. Since bonds are now more expensive, investors turn to stocks. This raises stock prices. Another way of saying the same thing is that, as the interest rates on bonds decrease, stocks become more attractive to investors. The resulting increase in demand for stocks pushes up their prices.
2. People receive cash from the Fed for the sale of their bonds. They can either hold these as idle cash or invest them in some assets. As a result, demand for stocks increases.
3. The fall in interest rates reduces the cost of borrowing for corporations. Corporations sell bonds to borrow money, and use the proceeds to increase their investment in plants and equipment. As a result, investors expect corporations to make higher profits because of these investments. This causes stock prices to increase. Moreover, households find it cheaper to borrow money to buy homes. This increase in the demand for homes results in an increase the profits of corporations that either build homes or supply materials for homebuilders. As the stocks of these corporations become more attractive, their prices increase in the market.

The increase in stock prices further increases economic activity through two channels:

1. As stock prices increase, corporations find it easier to raise cash by selling stocks, so investment in plants and equipment increases, further pushing up the aggregate demand.

2. As stock prices increase, households find that they are wealthier. This is because, as you recall, the market values of stocks are part of their total wealth. Therefore, they increase their consumption, and aggregate demand increases.

EFFICIENT MARKETS HYPOTHESIS

We saw above that the stock market affects, and is affected by, the rest of the economy. Current prices are always affected by expectations about future prices and dividends. These expectations are formed on the basis of the information that investors posses. It is therefore important to ask whether the stock market is efficient in processing the information that is relevant for stock price determination. In other words, do investors possess all the relevant information to predict future prices and dividends? If investors do not have all the relevant information, if they use the wrong information, or if they have the correct information, but don't know how to use it to correctly predict future stock prices and dividends, then current prices will not be right. As a result, decisions made based on them could have detrimental effects on the economy.

EFFICIENT MARKETS HYPOTHESIS
Financial markets are said to be efficient in Fama's sense if asset prices fully reflect all the available relevant information.

The well-known *efficient markets hypothesis* is mostly associated with Eugene Fama of the University of Chicago. This is nothing but the rational expectations hypothesis, applied to financial markets.

Financial markets are said to be efficient in Fama's sense if asset prices reflect all the available relevant information.

I will describe the implications of this theory in both stock and bond markets.

EFFICIENT MARKETS HYPOTHESIS AND THE STOCK MARKET

Consider the stock price determination story above. We saw in equation (3) that the current price of a stock is determined by the following formula:

$$P_{S0} = \frac{d_1{}^e + P_{S1}{}^e}{(1 + R)}$$

Now, according to the efficient markets hypothesis, $P_{S1}{}^e$ is the best forecast of the future price formed by the financial market participants, based on all the available information in the current period. But how do they come up with this best forecast? They know that next year, the demand and supply for the asset will determine its equilibrium price. So in their minds, they set $P_{S1}{}^e$ equal to the expected future equilibrium price of the asset. To this end, the market participants form their best guesses of the future demand and supply curves for the asset—along with all the factors affecting these curves—and find the equilibrium price. Based on this best forecast of the future equilibrium price and the best guess about the dividend, $d_1{}^e$, the market determines the current price, P_{S0}. It is in this sense that asset prices reflect or embody all the available relevant information—market participants use all the relevant available information to predict future stock prices and dividends.

There is much literature testing whether the efficient markets hypothesis holds in financial markets. The evidence is mixed. We will not concern ourselves with those issues. Since the main objective of this chapter is to provide you with the tools to understand financial market behavior, we will discuss an aspect of the hypothesis that has been supported by empirical observation. We have already seen a different version of the issue in Chapter 15, which introduced rational expectations.

The first implication of the theory should come to you as no surprise, because it is a variation of what you saw above. It is this:

> *Implication 1: If market participants expect the price of the stock to increase in the future, it will increase today.*

This is obvious from equation (3) and our previous discussion. However, there is a little more to this conclusion in the efficient market hypothesis. Under this hypothesis, the current stock price incorporates all the available information relevant to this stock.

The theory implies that there will be no unexploited profit opportunities in the market. In other words, you cannot make a rate of return on any asset that is too high relative to its risk. In our example, the market expects the future price to be P_{S1}^{e}. You cannot beat this prediction, since it is based on all the information possessed by millions of investors. You cannot possibly have any information about this stock that the market is not aware of and has not already incorporated in the stock price. Now, on the basis of the expected future price, expected future dividend, and the required rate of return, R, the market determines the current stock price, P_{S0}.

But whose required rate of return? We know from the previous discussion that it should be the required rate of return of the *marginal investors*: those who are well informed, are less risk averse, and have enough money to affect prices. On the basis of these factors, the market price turns out to be P_{S0}. If you buy this asset, you will only make a rate of return of R that is the lowest possible consistent with the risk of the asset. You cannot beat the market. You don't have any information that the market does not already possess, and you are competing with the marginal investors that have the lowest R.

But what is the process of getting there? Suppose that for a particular stock, the future economic factors will result in some supply and demand conditions. The expected supply and demand will determine the expected equilibrium price of the stock to be $P_1^e = \$90$ and $d_1^e = \$20$. Suppose also that due to the kind of risk this stock has, the marginal investors have a required rate of return of $R = 0.10$, or 10%. The efficient markets hypothesis says that these investors will push the current price to equal $P_0 = \$100$.

Now take the above price formula and solve it for R:

$$R = \frac{d_1{}^{e} + P_{S1}{}^{e} - P_{S0}}{P_{S0}}$$

Since the expectations on the right-hand side embody all the information, so is this rate of return. Therefore, if markets were efficient, the stock would yield a return of 10%:

$$R = \frac{\$20 + \$90 - \$100}{\$100} = 0.10$$

Suppose instead that for whatever reason, the current price is \$90. This current price is too low. What do we mean by *too low*? We mean it will result in an expected rate of return that is too high:

$$R = \frac{\$20 + \$90 - \$90}{\$90} = 0.22$$

This 22% is too high, in the sense that for the kind of risk the stock carries, the marginal investors are willing to make only 10% on it. So for them, this stock is way too attractive. They will buy the stock, pushing up the price to $100, and reducing the expected return to R = 10%. By the time you wake up at 8:00 a.m., the profit is already gone! We thus have our second implication of the theory:

> *Implication 2: In efficient capital markets, no one will earn above-normal risk-adjusted rates of return.*

At least not for a long time.

Now suppose in 2007, news breaks out that the corporation has invented a new product expected to hit the markets next year, in 2008. Therefore, the market will expect the company to make higher profits in the future. As a result, they will expect the stock price to be higher in 2008. As we know by now, the stock price will jump up today, in 2007. Now when 2008 arrives and the new product is introduced to the market the way it had been anticipated, there will be no change in the stock price in that year. The price had already been adjusted last year in anticipation of this event—why should it increase again? So we have our third implication:

> *Implication 3: Sometimes when an event occurs that affects the profitability of corporations, stock prices do not move. This is because this event was anticipated in the past, and its effect had already been incorporated into the prices.*

Finally, as in the case of rational expectation, we could have seemingly paradoxical results. Continuing with our previous story, suppose that when the year 2008 arrives, the corporation does *not* introduce any new product to the market. But the stock price is high in 2008 because of last year's anticipation of the introduction of a new product. Therefore, the current stock price is not consistent with the reality of this corporation. Because of this, the stock price will go down to reflect this adjustment in the investors' view of the profitability of the corporation.

The opposite of the above scenario can also happen. Suppose that last year, the market participants expected a bad thing to happen to a corporation. Let's say they expected the corporation to lose a class action lawsuit, or they expected a workers' walkout. This could cause the stock price to go down last year. However, if these events do not materialize in 2008, the stock price will adjust upward to incorporate this new reality. Thus, we have our fourth and final implication of the efficient markets hypothesis:

> *Implication 4: Sometimes stock prices move, even though there is no significant news affecting the profitability of corporations. This happens when previous anticipations about current market conditions are not realized.*

The previous two implications can be summarized into the following general statement. If current events had been exactly predicted in the past, then the stock prices will not change. If current events are different from what people anticipated in the past, then stock prices will move.

They will increase if the event is more favorable than expected; they will decrease if it is less favorable.

EFFICIENT MARKETS HYPOTHESIS AND THE BOND MARKET

Now I will describe the implications of the efficient markets hypothesis for the bond market. These are very similar to those we saw in the stock market. Suppose that on the basis of some information that they have, market participants expect the Fed to increase the money supply by 2% next month. Perhaps the Fed has announced that it will do so. On the basis of this prediction, they determine that next month, the interest rate will decrease and bond prices will increase.

In the loanable funds market, borrowers will wait until next month to borrow money at a lower rate. This will reduce the demand for loanable funds. Lenders, however, will try to lend more today by issuing new bonds in order to avoid the lower interest rates next month. An increase in the supply of loanable funds and the reduction in the demand will force down the interest rates today. You will get the same result in the general bond market, which is the market for both new and old bonds. Since people expect higher bond prices next month, they will buy bonds today in order to sell them at a higher price next month. As a result, bond prices will increase, and interest rates will decrease today.

This new bond price reflects all the available relevant information mentioned above about the future conduct of monetary policy. So the first implication of the theory is as follows:

> *Implication 1: When market participants expect the interest rate to fall in the future, it falls today.*

Note also that since the current bond prices already incorporate all the relevant information about the bond market and the stance of monetary policy, you cannot make above-normal, risk-adjusted rates of return from speculation in bonds. So just as in the case of stocks, we have the second implication for bonds:

> *Implication 2: In efficient bond markets, no one will earn above-normal, risk-adjusted rates of return from buying and selling bonds.*

We enter the next month with a lower interest rate on bonds. This low interest rate already incorporates the expectation that the Fed will increase the money supply by 2%. If the Fed does, in fact, increase the money supply by 2%, then nothing will happen to the interest rat—since it was already adjusted last month as if the Fed had already increased the money supply. Our third implication:

> *Implication 3: Sometimes when the Fed increases the money supply, nothing happens to the interest rates. This happens when the Fed's move had already been anticipated in the past.*

Now suppose that when next month comes, the Fed increases the money supply by only 1% or it does not increase it at all. The bond market did not predict this. The low interest rate inherited from last month is consistent with a 2% increase in money supply, not 1% or lower. With a lower than expected amount of money supply in the system, the interest rate will increase. See how paradoxical this result looks. Even though the Fed increases the money supply next month, the interest rate increases. This is the opposite of what we have seen in the previous chapters. Or, even if the Fed does not change the money supply at all, the interest rate still increases. Such interest rate behavior has puzzled economists and commentators in the past. But the efficient markets (or rational expectations) hypothesis provides an explanation for it. Our fourth conclusion:

> *Implication 4: Sometimes when the Fed increases the money supply or when it does not change the money supply at all, interest rates increase. This happens when the increase in the money supply is less than the amount market participants had expected.*

As a practice, assume that the Fed announces that it will reduce the money supply by 2% next month. What will happen to interest rates today? What will happen to interest rates next month if the Fed reduces the money supply by 2%? What will happen to interest rates next month if the Fed does not change the money supply? What will happen if it reduces the money supply by more or less than 2%?

TO SUMMARIZE

1. Prices of financial assets are determined by *marginal investors*—those who have more information about assets or are less risk averse.
2. Stocks are ownership rights in corporations.
3. The price of a stock is determined by the expected future *dividends*, the future price of the stock, and the *required rate of return* of the marginal investors.
4. All else the same, an increase in expected future profits increases the price of a stock.
5. Similarly, an increase in the riskiness of a stock reduces its price.
6. Demand for an asset depends on investors' wealth, the expected rate of return on that asset relative to other assets, the riskiness of the asset relative to other assets, and the liquidity of the asset relative to other assets.
7. The rate of return on physical assets is the percentage appreciation of their prices.
8. According to the efficient markets hypothesis, asset prices reflect all the available relevant information.
9. When market participants expect something to happen to the stock prices in the future, stock prices change today.
10. In efficient capital markets, no one will earn above-normal, risk-adjusted rates of return.
11. Sometimes when an event occurs that affects the profitability of corporations, stock prices do not move. That is because this event was anticipated in the past, and its effect had already been incorporated into the prices.
12. If current events had been exactly predicted in the past, then the stock prices will not change. If current events are different from what people had anticipated in the past, then stock prices will move. They will increase if the event is more favorable than expected; they will decrease if it is less favorable.
13. When market participants expect the interest rate to fall in the future, it falls today.
14. Sometimes when the Fed increases the money supply, nothing happens to the interest rates. This happens when the Fed's move had already been anticipated in the past.
15. Sometimes when the Fed increases the money supply, interest rates increase. This happens when the increase in money supply is less than the amount market participants had expected.

EXERCISES

Question 1

You want to borrow some money to buy a new car. You issue a bond that promises to pay $25,000 a year from now. You auction it among five friends of yours, with the following required rates of return from your bond:

Investor	Required Rate of Return
Abe	12%
Chris	10%
David	13%
Gabriel	14%
Peter	11%

Which one of your friends will buy the bond? Which one is the marginal investor?

Question 2

A common stock is expected to sell next year for $125. It is not expected to pay any dividends. The marginal investors' required rate of return from this stock is 40%. What will be the price of this stock in the market?

Question 3

Suppose that market participants expect the Fed to conduct an expansionary monetary policy next year. What will happen to the interest rates today? What will happen to stock prices?

Question 4

Suppose that, all else the same, market participants expect a higher inflation rate in the future. What will happen to stock and bond prices today? What will happen to the price of gold? Why?

Question 5

Analyze the effect of a contractionary monetary policy on stock prices.

Question 6

News breaks that some accounting firms have been exaggerating the profits of their client corporations. In other words, the actual profits made by these corporations have been lower than were presented to shareholders in the annual reports. What do you think will be the effect of this news on stock prices? [This is similar to what happened in the Enron scandal.]

Question 7

News breaks that the U.S. government is going to hit corporations with new environmental regulations. The new regulations will significantly increase the cost of doing business. What will happen to bond prices and interest rates? What will happen to the price of gold?

Question 8

Some very rich gold mines are discovered in Congo. This discovery will significantly increase the supply of gold in the international markets in the next several years. Analyze the effect of these discoveries on interest rates and stock prices in the United States.

Question 9

Brokerage firms increase their fees for stock transactions, but charge the same fee for bond transactions. This makes stocks less liquid relative to bonds. What will happen to stock and bond prices?

Question 10

Suppose that due to some recent corporate restructuring, GM stocks become less risky. What will be the effect of this on the prices of Ford and Chrysler stocks?

Question 11

What will happen if the Fed announces it will increase the money supply by 1%, but it actually increases it by 2%?

Question 12

Sometimes interest rates increase *because* the Fed does not change the money supply. Why do you think this happens?

Question 13

A stock is expected to pay a dividend of $d_1^e = \$10$ next year. The dividends are expected to grow at a rate of $g = 2\%$ per year. The marginal investors' required rate of return is $R = 25\%$. What is the price of the stock? What would be the price if $g = 0$?

Question 14

Suppose in 2009, the market expected the XYZ Corporation to lose a lawsuit in 2010 that would significantly reduce its profit potential.

a. What will happen to the price of the stock today?
b. What will happen to the price of the stock next year, if indeed the corporation loses the way the market had anticipated?
c. What will happen to the price of the stock next year if the corporation wins the court battle?

Question 15

Suppose the Fed announces that it will reduce the money supply by 5% next month.

a. What will happen to the interest rate this month?
b. What will happen to the interest rate next month if the Fed reduces the money supply by 5%?
c. What will happen to the interest rate next month if the Fed reduces the money supply by 2%?
d. What will happen to the interest rate next month if the Fed reduces the money supply by 7%?

CHAPTER 18

The Foreign Exchange Market

INTRODUCTION AND REVIEW

UNTIL THIS CHAPTER, we have ignored foreign transactions. This was merely done to keep our stories simple. It is now time to introduce transactions with other countries into the picture. You don't need to look too far to see the importance of these transactions. Globalization has occurred at an amazing speed in the last few decades. You can hardly find a country that does not buy goods, services, and assets from other countries. You are probably writing with a pen and using a laptop made in China, wearing clothes made in Taiwan, driving a car made in Japan or Germany, using gasoline purchased from Saudi Arabia, and may end up working in a company headquartered in England at some point in the future. An economy that closes its doors to international trade is called a *closed economy*. Most economies these days can be described as *open economies*.

Why do we need a different field to study open economies? Why is it that we don't have a separate field to study the economic relationships between California and Arizona, but we need one to analyze the relationships between the United States and the United Kingdom? The reason is simply that the two countries have different national governments and different currencies. The United States and the United Kingdom have independent monetary and fiscal policies. The conduct of a demand management policy in one country could affect the economy of the other country. Such issues are nonexistent in the relationships between states or provinces of the same country.

North Korean police automobile on patrol while residents hurry along on their business in a suburb of Pyongyang. Do you think North Korea is a closed economy?

THE FOREIGN EXCHANGE MARKET

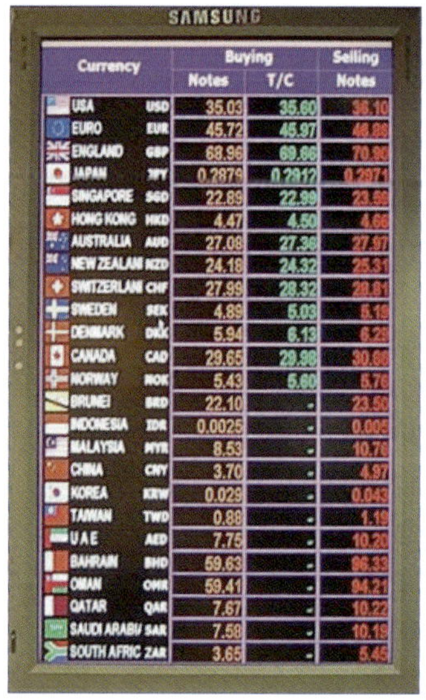

An electronic display of exchange rates

We start with a description of the foreign exchange market. This is the market in which foreign currencies are bought and sold. This market is probably the largest market in the world, always awake, and always active. More than $1 trillion of foreign currencies are transacted in this market *per day*. How big is that? Note that the U.S. nominal GDP in 2009 was a little more than $14 trillion, *annually*—this was the value of all the goods and services produced in the United States in that year.

As usual, we need to make some assumptions to make our story simple. Here they are:

1. There are two countries: the United States and Europe (the European countries that use euros as their domestic currency).[1] We will treat all the European countries that use euros as their national currency as one country. You can substitute any other country for Europe, and the results of the analysis will be the same.
2. Americans use dollars in their domestic transactions. They don't accept euros. Europeans use euros in their domestic transactions. They do not accept U.S. dollars. This is a fair assumption. Although in some countries people may accept foreign currencies in their day-to-day transactions, this practice is not common.
3. Americans have dollars in their possession, but not euros. Europeans have euros, but not U.S. dollars. This assumption will make our story less complicated, but will have no effect on the results. This assumption is not totally realistic, because most international firms—those with international transactions—have some foreign currency that they use to settle foreign transactions. However, the size of these funds relative to the rest of the economy is small, so for practical purposes, this is a good assumption to make.
4. Americans buy *goods*, *services*, and *assets* from Europeans. Europeans buy *goods*, *services*, and *assets* from Americans. This assumption basically says that we are now dealing with open economies. For example, Americans buy foreign automobiles and Europeans buy U.S.-made medical equipment. As for services, American companies pay European insurance companies to insure their ships and airplanes. Or, American professional firms provide consulting services to European firms and governments. As for assets, Americans buy European stocks, bonds, land, and factories; Europeans buy similar U.S. assets.
5. Transactions are settled in the currencies of the sellers. Even though this is not totally true, it will make our model easier to follow, and will not have any effect on the results. In practice, transactions are usually settled in the currency of the party with the greater economic power. For example, if IBM or HP purchases some parts and components from a foreign country, chances are it will pay for these goods with U.S. dollars. The reason is that these are large, reputable, and stable companies, and any foreign firm would love to do business with them. Therefore, they would be willing to accept U.S. dollars from these companies rather their own local currency.

---

1 Twelve European countries have adopted the euro as their common currency: Finland, Ireland, the Netherlands, Germany, Belgium, Luxembourg, France, Austria, Portugal, Spain, Italy, and Greece.

How can the residents of the two countries carry out transactions if they don't have or accept each other's currencies? The answer is that they use the foreign exchange market to convert one currency into the other. The foreign exchange market does not operate in a single physical location. Rather, it is the interconnection of all the banks and financial institutions around the world, through telephone wires and Internet lines. If you are planning to go to Germany, you may walk into your local branch of a large bank and buy some euros for the trip. You have just completed a transaction in the foreign exchange market. In some countries, you might see individuals selling foreign currencies on sidewalks. They are also a part of this huge market. Therefore, like any other market, *the foreign exchange market is an institution that brings buyers and sellers of foreign currencies together*.

The Euro

Consider Figure 1, which shows the use of the foreign exchange market by American and European residents. The symbol for the euro is €. An American buys goods, services, and assets from a European resident. The American buyer has dollars, but the European seller accepts only euros for the sale of the merchandise. The American buyer, therefore, takes her dollars to the foreign exchange market, buys the needed euros, and sends them to the European seller. The European buyer of American goods, services, and assets does the opposite. Generally, banks are involved in these transactions as intermediaries. So the American buyer takes her dollars to her local bank, pays them to buy euros, and sends the euros to the European seller. Or, even more realistically, she takes her dollars to the bank and the bank delivers euros to the European seller.

Figure 1 Transactions in the Foreign Exchange Market

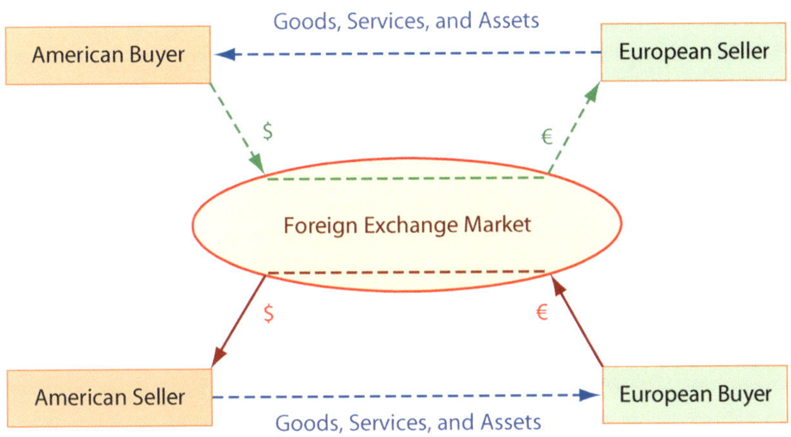

With all of its simplicity, Figure 1 contains a lot of useful information. Who demands euros in the market? Answer: Those who need them but don't have them—i.e., Americans, to buy European goods, services, and assets. Who supplies the U.S. dollars to the market? Answer: Those who have them and want to spend them to buy euros in order to buy European goods, services, and assets—i.e., Americans again. So the supply of dollars and demand for euros come from the same people and to the same end. By the same token, the supply of euros and demand for dollars come from Europeans to buy U.S. goods, services, and assets. So we only need to study half of the market: either the demand for and supply of euros, or the demand for and supply of dollars. We will concentrate on the demand for and supply of dollars.

Now the question is, if the American buyer wanted to buy €1,000,000 from her bank, how many dollars would she have to pay for them? Similarly, if a European buyer needed to buy

$1,000,000 from his bank, how many euros would he have to pay? The answer is: It depends on the *foreign exchange rate.*

FOREIGN EXCHANGE RATE
This is the amount of units of a domestic currency that the residents of a country must pay to buy one unit of a foreign currency.

WHAT IS THE FOREIGN EXCHANGE RATE?

An exchange rate is just the price of a foreign currency. This rate is the number of units of a domestic currency the residents of a country must pay to buy *one unit* of a foreign currency. Suppose Americans have to pay $0.50 to buy *one* euro. Then we say that the exchange rate for Americans is $0.50/€. This is no different from the price of any other good. The price of an iPod is how many dollars we have to pay to buy one iPod. Similarly, from the viewpoint of Europeans, the exchange rate is how many euros they have to pay to buy one dollar. In the above example, they have to pay 2 euros to buy one dollar. So this is the dollar exchange rate for them. We will use the exchange rates from the viewpoint of Europeans. Let's use the letter "e" for the exchange rate. So in the above example, the exchange rate will be e = €2/$.

Let's learn the basic relationship between prices and exchange rates. Suppose there is a T-shirt in a New York shop selling for $10. How many euros does a European have to pay to buy it? If the exchange rate is €0.80/$, then she has to pay ($10) × (€0.80/$) = €8 for that T-shirt. Note how the currency signs cancel. If the price of the T-shirt goes down to $8 in New York, while the exchange rate remains the same, then the European buyer will have to pay fewer euros: ($8) × (€0.80/$) = €6.40. If the exchange rate goes down to €0.70/$, while the price of the T-shirt remains the same, then she will have to pay fewer euros: ($10) × (€0.70/$) = €7. *To convert dollars into euros we multiply the dollar amounts by the exchange rate, e.*

In Figure 1, what guarantees that the amount of euros Americans want to buy from the market equals the amount that Europeans want to sell to the market? The answer is that, like any other market, exchange rates adjust to equilibrate supply and demand.

FOREIGN EXCHANGE MARKET EQUILIBRIUM

Like the price of any other commodity, the interplay of supply and demand for a currency determines the exchange rate. Movements of the exchange rate guarantee that supply always equals demand. Consider Figure 2. On the vertical axis we measure the €/$ exchange rate, which we denote by letter e. As we know, this is nothing but the price of U.S. dollars in terms of euros—the number of euros a European has to pay to buy one dollar. Similar to any other commodity, the horizontal axis measures the quantity of the good whose price is on the vertical axis. This should be the quantity of the dollars, Q($). The demand for dollars by Europeans is drawn with a negative slope. A fall in the exchange rate results in a larger quantity of the dollars to be demanded by Europeans. This is because a fall in the exchange rate makes American goods cheaper for the Europeans to buy (recall the above T-shirt example), so they decide to buy more American goods. To do that, they need to buy more dollars.

The supply of dollars by Americans is upward-sloping. This is because when the exchange rate goes up, the European goods become cheaper for Americans to buy. Consider the T-shirt example again. Let the exchange rate be e = €0.80/$, and assume that the price of a T-shirt in Europe is €8. Then an American buyer has to pay (€8) ¸ (€0.80/$) = $10 for the European T-shirt. Now suppose that the exchange rate goes up to €0.90/$. Then, for the same T-shirt, the American buyer has to pay only (€8) ¸ (€0.90/$) = $8.89. Note that when the exchange rate goes up, the euro becomes cheaper for Americans.

Figure 2 Foreign Exchange Market Equilibrium

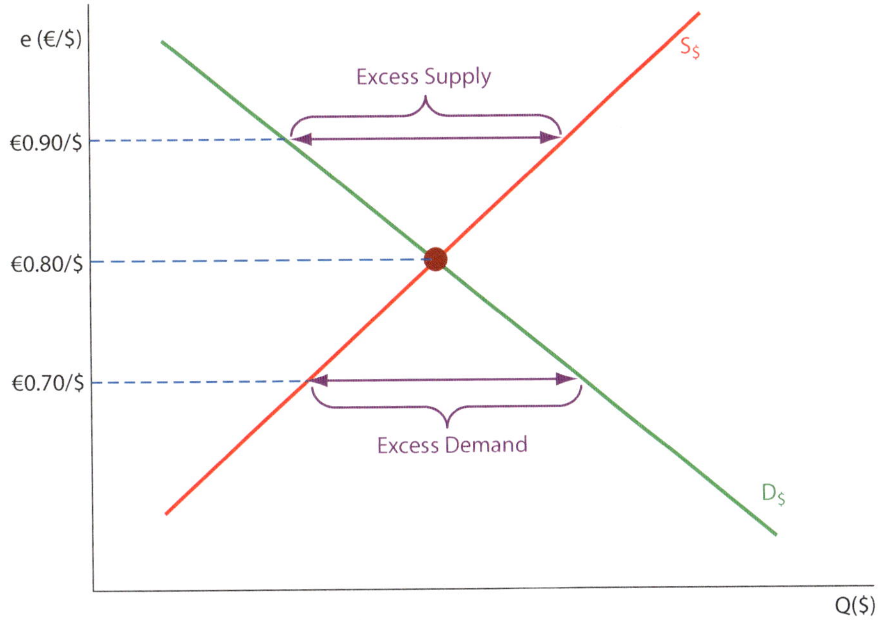

In Figure 2, the equilibrium exchange rate is €0.80/$. If for whatever reason the exchange rate increases to €0.90/$, then the supply of dollars by Americans would exceed the demand by Europeans. There would be an excess supply of dollars in the market. At this high exchange rate, European goods would become less expensive for Americans to buy. Therefore, Americans would want to sell a lot of dollars to buy euros in order to buy European goods. At the same time, American goods would become more expensive for Europeans to buy. Therefore, they would reduce their demand for American goods and, thus, demand fewer dollars. This excess supply would force down the price of dollars to €0.80/$. Again, this is no different from the market for any other commodity.

If, on the other hand, the exchange rate decreases to €0.70/$, there would be an excess *demand* for dollars. Europeans would find American goods less expensive. They would bring a lot of euros to the market to buy dollars in order to buy American goods. This demand would exceed the amount of dollars that Americans would be willing to supply to the market. This excess demand for dollars would push up the price of dollars to €0.80/$.

In case you are wondering, Figure 3 shows a graph of euro-dollar exchange rates from January 1999 through August 2006. As you can see, during the 2004–2006 period, the value of the dollar on average was about €0.80. However, the €/$ exchange rate has fluctuated somewhat. We will next learn why exchange rates change all the time.

SHIFTS IN SUPPLY AND DEMAND

Like any other commodity, if the demand for a currency increases, its price will go up. If the supply increases, its price will go down. When the price of a currency goes up, we say that the currency has *appreciated*. When it goes down, we say it has *depreciated*. First let's start with the demand for dollars by the Europeans. Any event, *except a change in the exchange rate itself,* causing Europeans to buy more American goods, services, and assets results in an increase in demand for U.S. dollars: therefore, a rightward shift in the demand for dollars. Conversely, any event that leads Europeans

APPRECIATION
The increase in the market price or value of any good or asset.

DEPRECIATION
The decrease in the market price or value of any good or asset.

to buy less American goods, services, and assets results in a leftward shift in the demand for dollars. These factors are easy to figure out. They are as follows:

1. National income. If the level of GDP rises in Europe, Europeans will enjoy higher income levels. They can buy more of everything, including American goods. Therefore, demand for dollars increases.
2. Prices of goods and services. If American goods become cheaper relative to European goods, Europeans will buy more American goods. Therefore, demand for dollars will increase.
3. Tastes. If it becomes more fashionable in Europe to wear American clothes or drive American cars, demand for dollars will increase.
4. Expected relative rates of return. Remember that people also buy assets from foreign countries. If the rates of return on American assets are expected to be higher than those on European assets, Europeans will try to sell some of their own assets to buy American assets. This will cause an increase in demand for dollars. Also, if Europeans expect the dollar to appreciate in the future, they will buy U.S. dollars and hold them in anticipation that they would sell at a higher price in the future. Recall that money itself is an asset.
5. Relative riskiness of assets. If for some reason American assets are perceived to be less risky relative to European assets, Europeans would want to buy and hold more American assets. This will increase the demand for dollars.
6. Government policies. Two types of government policies can affect the foreign exchange market. First, a government can impose a trade restriction on the imports or exports of goods and services. For instance, suppose that the European governments impose a heavy tariff on the import of American goods. This means that importers must pay a tax to the European governments when they import American goods into Europe. This makes American goods more expensive for Europeans to buy, and as a result, reduces their demand of dollars. Second, sometimes governments come to the foreign exchange market directly to buy and sell currencies to smooth out the fluctuations in exchange rates. This is called *government intervention*. If a European government buys U.S. dollars in the market, the demand for U.S. dollars will increase.

GOVERNMENT INTERVENTION
Generally, this refers to any government interference in a market. Specifically, it refers to a government's buying and selling of currencies in the foreign exchange market to smooth out the fluctuations in exchange rates.

Figure 3 The Euro-Dollar Exchange Rates (€/$)

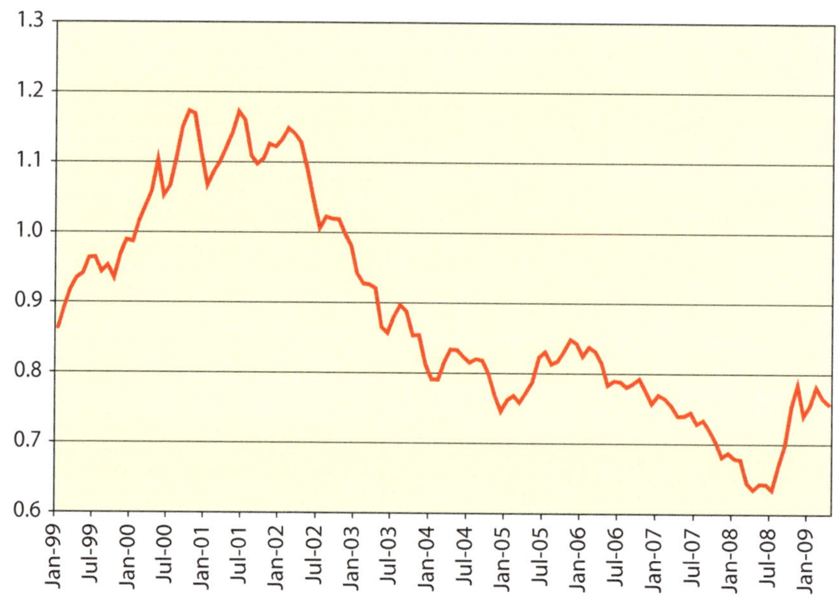

Similarly, any event that causes Americans to buy to buy more European goods, services, and assets will increase the supply of dollars. These events would be the same as those listed above. For example, a higher U.S. income, a lower European price level, or a relatively higher expected rate of return on European assets would cause a rightward shift in the supply of dollars. Often, an event causes both supply and demand to shift simultaneously. For example, a decrease in the prices of American goods and services makes Europeans buy more American goods, increasing the demand for dollars. At the same time, this event makes Americans buy more of their own goods and less of European goods. As a result the supply of dollars decreases. The same will be the case if, for instance, the expected rates of return on U.S. assets increase. Let's analyze a few of these cases.

AN INCREASE IN FOREIGN INCOME

Consider the foreign exchange market depicted in Figure 4. Suppose that the market is in equilibrium, with the equilibrium exchange rate at e = €0.80/$. What happens if European income increases? Let's imagine that Europe has been in a recession for some while; it reaches the trough of the recession, and its GDP starts to rise. As Europe begins the expansion phase of its business cycle, European employment and income increase. As European consumers' purchasing power increases, their demand for American goods increases. As we know by now, this results in an increase in European demand for dollars. At the current exchange rate of €0.80/$, an excess demand for dollars develops, pushing up the exchange rate to €0.90/$. We see then that the European recovery results in a dollar appreciation.

Figure 4 An Increase in Foreign Income

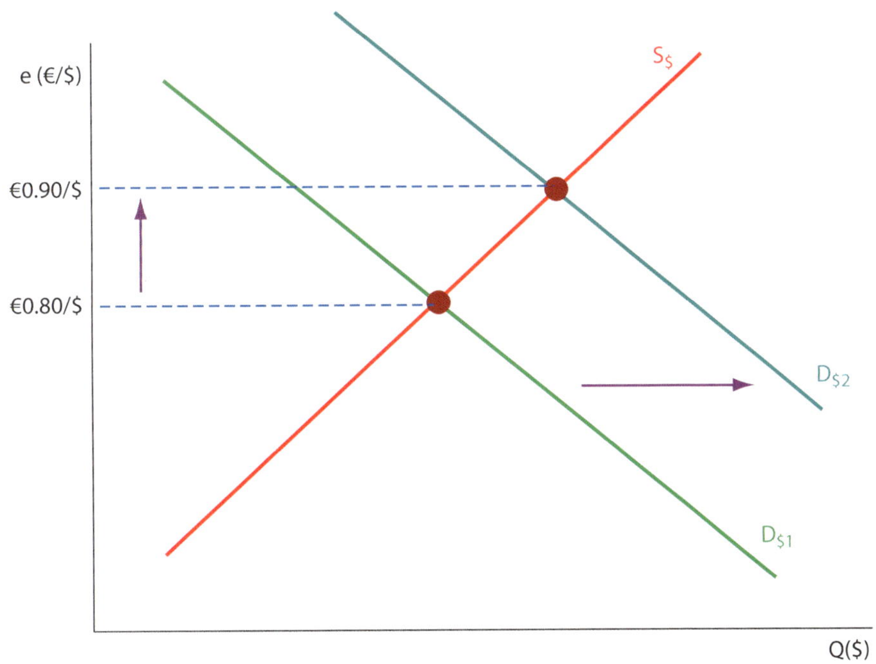

Needless to say, the story is symmetric with respect to the American income. An increase in U.S. income results in a higher American demand for European goods and services. Americans supply more dollars to the market to buy euros in order to buy those goods and services. Therefore, the supply of dollars shifts to the right as in Figure 5, and the dollar depreciates. Some commentators may think that this dollar depreciation is a sign of weakness in the U.S. economy. But you know that this is not true. Whenever the U.S economy expands, all else the same, the dollar depreciates, because Americans become better off and buy foreign goods and services.

Figure 5 An Increase in Domestic Income

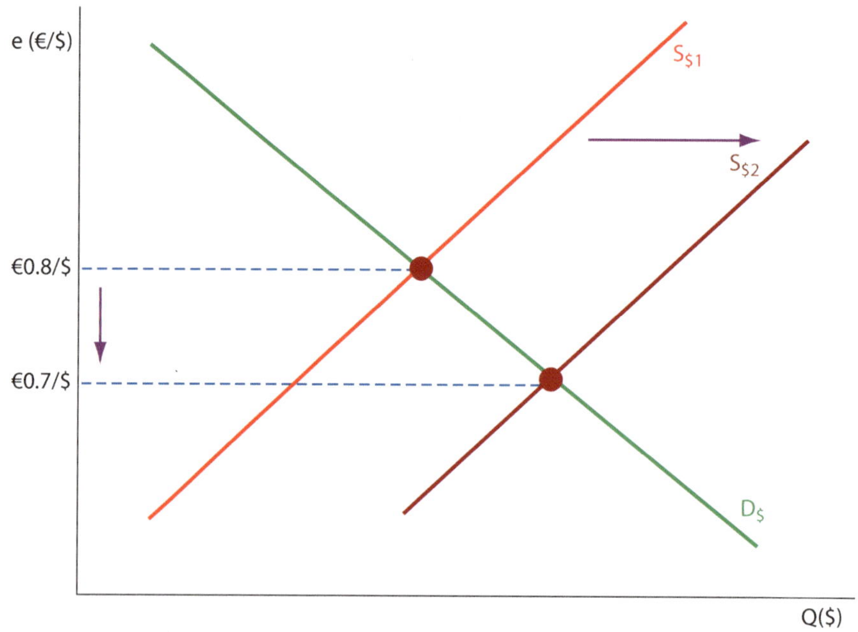

AN INCREASE IN DOMESTIC PRICES

Suppose, all else the same, that the prices of American goods and services increase, and they become more expensive relative to European goods and services. Europeans reduce their demand for American goods and services. This results in a leftward shift in the demand-for-dollars curve in Figure 6. At the same time, Americans start buying the now-cheaper European goods. This shifts the supply-of-dollars curve to the right. At the current exchange rate, an excess supply of dollars develops in the market, pushing down the exchange rate; the dollar depreciates.

It is generally the case that countries with high prices have weak exchange rates—meaning they are worth less in terms of other currencies. In Figure 6, one dollar was worth €0.80 before the rise in the U.S. price level, but its value declined to only €0.60 afterward. Similarly, countries with high inflation rates have exchange rates that depreciate over time. As we have seen in previous chapters, in the long run inflation is mostly a momentary phenomenon. Therefore, it is safe to say that countries with loose and irresponsible monetary policies have weak currencies that get weaker still over time. As an example, the governments of some developing countries print money to pay for their development projects such as building roads and schools. Such policies increase the amount of money in circulation without a corresponding increase in the production of consumer goods and services—the case of too much money chasing too few goods. Residents of the countries who have received a lot of domestic currency turn to foreign countries to buy their goods and services. This raises their demands for foreign currencies and weakens their domestic currencies.

Figure 6 An Increase in Domestic Prices

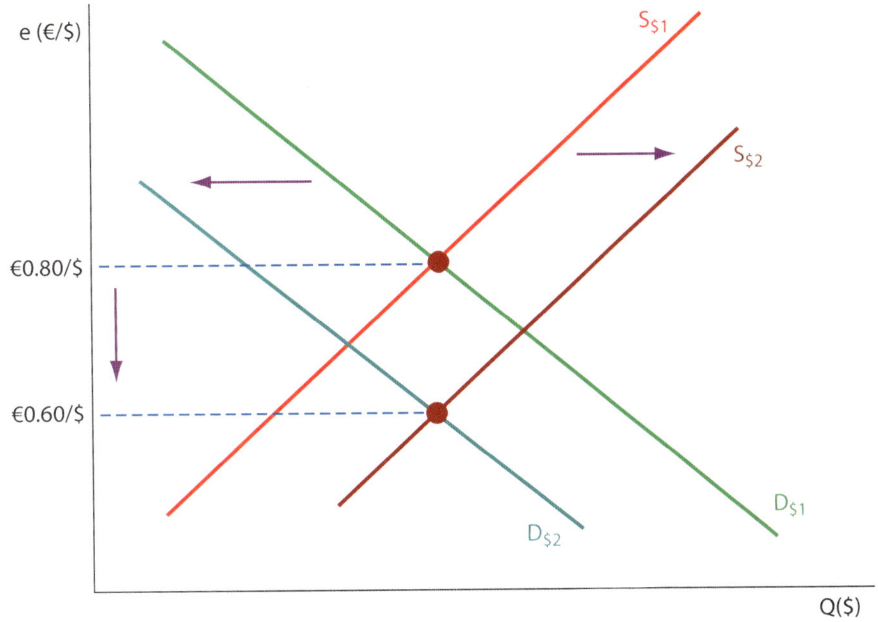

AN INCREASE IN DOMESTIC INTEREST RATES

Suppose that the Fed reduces the supply of money, and as a result U.S. interest rates increase relative to European interest rates. (See Figure 7.) The rise in U.S. interest rates makes American assets more attractive for Europeans. For example, if U.S. bonds pay higher interest compared to European banks or bonds, then many European investors will want to put their money in U.S. banks or buy U.S. bonds. But since American banks do not accept euros, Europeans must convert their euros to dollars in order to carry out these transactions. As a result, the demand for dollars increases. At the same time, American investors will find that it is now more lucrative to deposit their money in U.S. banks or invest in U.S. bonds. They reduce their demand for European assets, and as a result, the supply of dollars decreases. The combined effect of these actions is an appreciation of the dollar.

The analysis shows that a decrease in the U.S. money supply results in a dollar appreciation. Moreover, since financial investors constantly change their expectations of relative rates of return on the basis of new information that arrives very frequently, exchange rates are very volatile—they jump up and down all the time. Investors analyze information such as the states of monetary policies in different countries, budget deficits, oil prices, and so on. Recall from our chapter on financial markets that all such events move the interest rates and rates of return on assets. Recall also that the rates change whenever the Fed does something different from what investors had anticipated in the past. Since expected relative rates of return change all the time, and since they affect the demands and supplies in the foreign exchange market, foreign exchange rates are among the most volatile among all the prices.

Figure 7 An Increase in U.S. Interest Rates

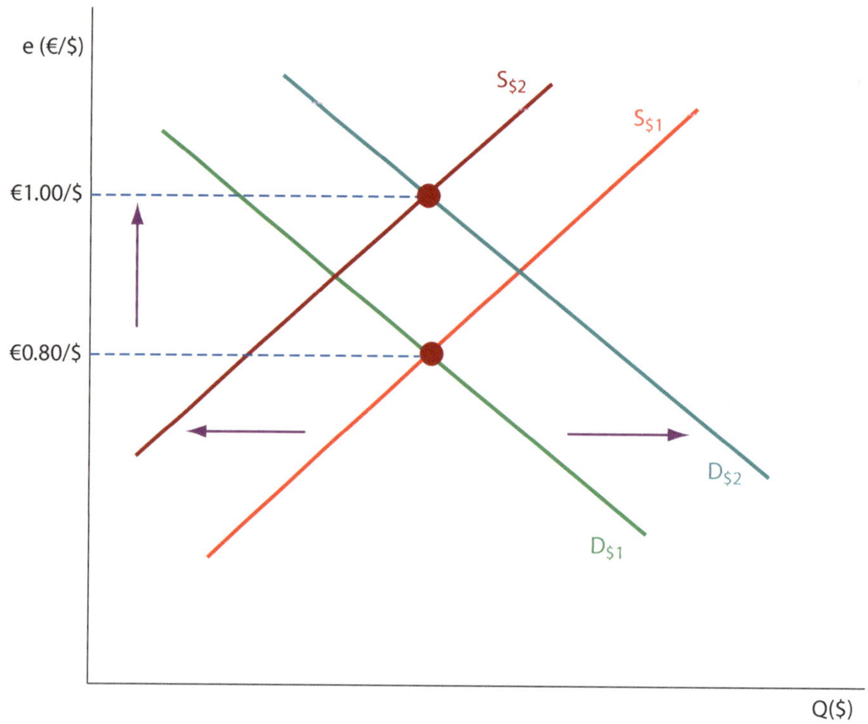

THE FIXED EXCHANGE RATE SYSTEM

FLEXIBLE EXCHANGE RATE SYSTEM
An exchange rate system in which exchange rates are determined by the free interplay of demands and supplies for currencies.

FIXED EXCHANGE RATE SYSTEM
An exchange rate system in which governments of different countries keep exchange rates fixed, by standing ready to buy and sell foreign currencies at fixed, previously agreed upon prices.

The foreign exchange system, in which exchange rates are determined by the free interplay of demands and supplies for currencies, is called the *flexible exchange rate system*. In the above analysis, we had assumed such a system. Before 1973, the industrialized countries were under a *fixed exchange rate system*. Under such a system, the governments of the countries stand ready to buy and sell foreign currencies in the market at a fixed, previously agreed upon price.

The main reason for adopting such a system is the belief that keeping the exchange rates fixed would eliminate price uncertainties for exporters and importers, which would promote international trade in goods and services. If exchange rates fluctuate often, the price of the U.S. T-shirt for Europeans will be very volatile, even though its dollar price is quite stable. Moreover, fixed exchange rates eliminate a source of uncertainty about relative rates of return on assets, encouraging investment in foreign countries. This is also easy to see. Suppose you put some money in a European bank for a year to take advantage of high European interest rates relative to U.S. rates. After one year, when you want to convert your euro proceeds to dollars, the exchange rate might change in such a way as to wipe out all your gains.

These are, in fact, a few of the reasons why some European countries decided to adopt a common currency, which they called the euro. Adopting a common currency means that you fix the exchange rates between the currencies at one. In other words, different countries become like states or provinces within a single country. In the United Sates, for example, one "California dollar" will exchange for exactly one "Arizona dollar." Traders and investors in these states do not need to worry about changes in the exchange rates between the currencies of these different states. Similarly, by adopting a common currency, Europeans hope that different countries will act like just one country: the resulting increase in trade and investment will cause faster economic growth and greater prosperity for the member countries.

They also hope that greater economic power will lead to greater political power in the world. The downside is, of course, that the member countries lose their economic independence. For example, suppose that there is unemployment in California. The California government cannot conduct monetary policy to pump more money into the economy. First of all, it does not have such power. Second, even if it could pump some money into the California economy, that money could move to other states to finance investment projects in those states. The California government has no mechanism to keep that money inside California. Similarly, if a euro country increases its money supply (which is in euros), that money could flow to some other euro countries.

Consider Figure 8. Assume that at some point in the past, the equilibrium exchange rate was €0.70/$ and that the United States and Europe decided to fix the exchange rate at that level. Now, suppose that the demand for dollars increases for one of the reasons mentioned above. At the fixed exchange rate of €0.70/$, the demand for dollars equals $320 and the supply $280, so an excess demand of $40 develops in the market. Under the flexible exchange regime, the exchange rate would go up to €0.80/$. In the fixed exchange rate system, on the other hand, one of the two governments should supply $40 to the market in order to keep the exchange rate fixed at €0.70/$.

We see that under the flexible exchange rate system, the exchange rates are determined in the market, and governments have no control over them. By contrast, in a fixed exchange rate system, the exchange rates are fixed, but the governments must constantly worry about buying and selling foreign currencies in the market. Moreover, governments must maintain reserves of foreign currencies for this purpose. This then results in two related problems. First, as in Figure 8, some countries must supply foreign currencies to the market in the case of excess demand for foreign currencies. When the situation lasts for a long period of time, they run out of foreign currency reserves. Second, in the opposite case of excess supply of foreign currencies, governments have to buy foreign currencies. If the situation lasts for a long time, they accumulate a lot of unwanted foreign currency reserves that could have been spent on goods and services. Because of such problems, the Western countries abandoned the fixed exchange rate regime and adopted the flexible exchange rate system in 1973.

Figure 8 Fixed Exchange Rate System

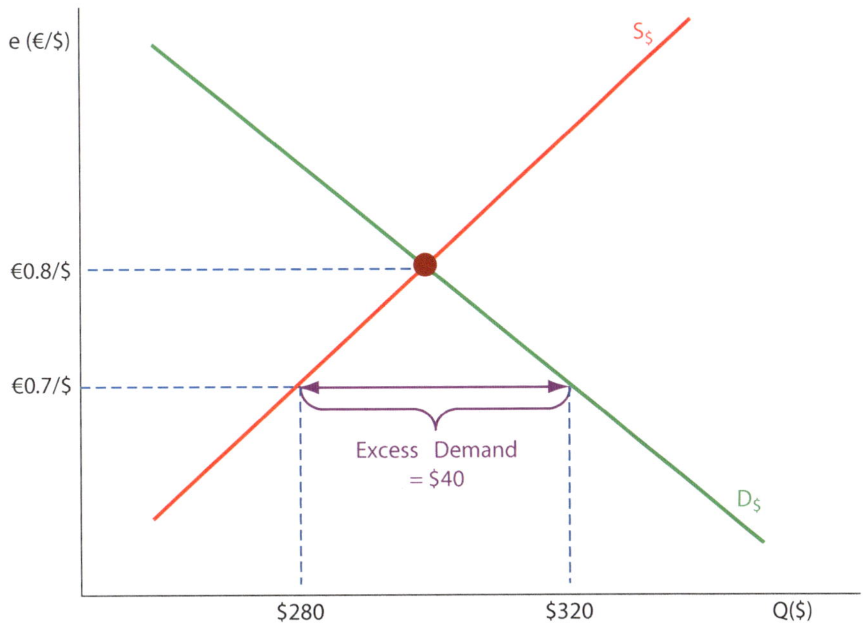

TO SUMMARIZE

1. A *foreign exchange rate* is the price of one currency in terms of the other.
2. Under the flexible exchange rate regime, the foreign exchange rate is determined in the foreign exchange market by the forces of supply and demand.
3. Demand for dollars comes from foreigners wanting to buy U.S. goods, services, and assets. Supply of dollars comes from Americans wanting to buy foreign goods, services, and assets.
4. Demand for dollars will increase if: foreign incomes increase; American goods and services become relatively cheaper; tastes change in favor of American goods; U.S. assets are expected to yield higher rates of return relative to foreign assets; U.S. assets become comparatively less risky; or if a foreign government purchases dollars to smooth out fluctuations in the foreign exchange rate.
5. The supply of dollars by Americans will increase for similar reasons.
6. An increase in the value of a currency is called *appreciation*; a decrease is called *depreciation.*
7. All else the same, an increase in demand for dollars or a decrease in supply will result in dollar appreciation. A decrease in demand or an increase in supply will cause the dollar to depreciate.

EXERCISES

Question 1

Some questions about exchange rates and goods prices:

a. If the equilibrium €/$ exchange rate is e = €0.80/$, what is the $/€ exchange rate? What is the meaning of this?
b. If the dollar appreciates, do European goods become cheaper or more expensive for Americans to buy?
c. If the euro depreciates, do European goods become cheaper or more expensive for Americans to buy? Do American goods become cheaper or more expensive for Europeans to buy?

Question 2

More questions about exchange rates and goods prices:

a. Suppose the price of the British pound is $2/£. If a car is worth £10,000 in London, how many dollars should an American pay to buy that car?
b. Suppose the price of the British pound is $1.50/£. If a VCR is worth $75 in New York, how many British pounds should a British resident pay to buy it?

Question 3

Consider Figure 2. What will happen in this figure if:

a. The U.S. price level decreases?
b. The European price level increases?

c. The rates of return on European assets are expected to increase by 3%, while those on U.S. assets are expected to increase by 1%?
d. The rates of return on European assets are expected to increase by 3%, while those on U.S. assets are expected to increase by 4%?
e. The rates of return on European assets are expected to increase by 3%, and those on U.S. assets are expected to increase by 3% as well?
f. The U.S. assets are perceived to be relatively more risky?
g. European governments buy dollars to stabilize the euro?
h. The U.S. government imposes a tariff on the import of European goods?
i. Europeans expect the dollar to appreciate in the future?
j. Europeans expect the dollar to depreciate in the future?

Question 4

Draw the foreign exchange market graph with the demand for and supply of *euros*. What should be measured on the vertical and horizontal axes?

a. What will happen in this graph if the U.S. income level increases?
b. What will happen in this graph if the U.S. price level increases?
c. What will happen in this graph if the rates of return on U.S. assets are expected be higher than those on the European assets?

CHAPTER 19

Open Economy Macroeconomics

INTRODUCTION AND REVIEW

Our last chapter looked at the foreign exchange market between two economies—the United States and Europe. The foreign exchange markets link the economies of the countries together. The foreign exchange rate is determined in this market through the interplay of supply and demand for currencies. Residents of a country want to buy goods, services, and assets from other countries. In order to do this, they need to purchase the currencies of the other countries with their own domestic currencies. Demand for foreign goods and services depends on their relative prices, and demand for assets depends on their relative rates of return across countries. Therefore, demand for and supply of foreign currencies are modified in response to changes in relative goods prices and asset returns. As a result, exchange rates differ in response to changes in these variables. In this chapter, we will learn about macroeconomic policies in economies that are open to international trade in goods, services, and assets. However, before we can do that, we should learn a concept called the balance of payments.

BALANCE OF PAYMENTS

Balance of payments is just the record of a country's transactions with the rest of the world. We will only concentrate on the U.S. balance of payments. Balance of payments has two main features:

1. Any transaction that leads to a payment of money to Americans is recorded as a credit item (positive). Conversely, any transaction that leads to a payment of money to foreigners is recorded as a debit item (negative).
2. Balance of payments always balances. This means that the sum of all the credit items equals the sum of all the debit items.

DOUBLE-ENTRY BOOKKEEPING
The conventional accounting system followed in developing balances of payments, resulting in an equal amount of a debit (negative) item for each credit (positive) item.

CURRENT ACCOUNT
A subaccount of the balance of payments of a country that records transactions in goods and services (exports and imports), those that are consumed in the "current period.

CAPITAL ACCOUNT
A subaccount that records transactions in assets of the balance of payments of a country.

The first feature is just a bookkeeping convention. The second feature follows from the first. The conventional accounting system followed in developing balances of payments is called *double-entry bookkeeping*. All you need to know is, in this system, for every credit item there is a corresponding debit item of equal value. This results in the sum of credits being equal to the sum of debits.

A balance of payments is divided into separated accounts, the most important of which are the *current account* and the *capital account*. Current accounts record transactions in goods and services, those that are consumed in the "current period"—usually meaning one year. Current account balance is the same thing as net exports (EX – IM), which we saw in Chapter 8. Capital accounts record transactions in assets. Assets are also called capital assets, hence the name. As you know, these are things that last for more than the "current period," and provide some benefits to their owners in the future.

Consider a hypothetical and condensed balance of payments for the United States *for a particular year* in Table 1.

Table 1
A Hypothetical Balance of Payments

Transaction/Account	Credit ($)	Debit ($)
Exports of goods and services	140	
Imports of goods and services		170
Current account balance		30
Capital inflow	160	
Capital outflow		130
Capital account balance	30	
Total	**300**	**300**
Balance of payments	0	

CURRENT ACCOUNT DEFICIT
The amount by which imports exceeds exports in a country's current account of the balance of payments.

CAPITAL INFLOW
The amount of money that a country receives from foreigners—money flows in—from the sale of assets to them.

CAPITAL OUTFLOW
The amount of money that a country pays foreigners—money flows out—for buying their assets.

CAPITAL ACCOUNT SURPLUS
The amount by which capital inflows exceed capital outflows in a country's capital account of the balance of payments.

In this example, the Americans exported some goods and services for which they received $140, and imported $170 worth of goods and services. The United States thus had a *current account deficit* of $30 ($140 – $170) in that year. Americans paid more to foreigners to buy their goods and services than they received for selling goods and services to them.

In the same year, foreigners paid $160 to buy American assets. These assets included both financial assets—such as stocks and bonds—and physical assets—such as agricultural lands and factories. Similarly, Americans paid $130 to buy foreign assets. Note that a capital account transaction results in a *capital inflow* if as a result of that transaction, the country receives *money* from foreigners—money flows in. Such a transaction is recorded as a credit. A capital account transaction results in a *capital outflow* if as a result, the country pays money to foreigners—money flows out. Such a transaction is recorded as a debit. In the above example, the United States had a *capital account surplus* of $30 (=$160 – $130).

Note that the current and capital accounts are equal in magnitude, but have opposite signs. If one account is in deficit, the other must be in surplus, so that their sum equals zero. So if we have a current account deficit, we must have a capital account surplus of equal magnitude. This makes sense simply because, as I said above, the balance of payments always *balances*. In the above example, the sum of all the credit items is $300, the same as the sum of all the debit items. All in all, the country has paid the same amount of money to foreigners that it has received from them.

Therefore, the sum of the two subaccounts must be zero, as demonstrated by the following simple math:

$$\$140 + \$160 = \$170 + \$130$$
$$(\$140 - \$170) + (\$160 - \$130) = 0$$

Therefore, in general we can write

Current Account Balance + Capital Account Balance = 0

Although this relationship is quite straightforward, its importance should be emphasized. First, as you will see below, it only holds in a flexible exchange rate system. Second, as should be clear from the discussion above, this relationship shows that when one of the two accounts is in deficit, the other must be in surplus. If, on net, we have paid more to buy foreigners' goods, they must have paid more on net to buy our assets.

Finally, in the hypothetical example, Americans have paid more to buy foreign goods and services than the foreigners have paid to buy American goods and services. That is why the current account is in deficit. Since people and media understand trade in goods and services better than trade in assets, and since they think that the former has implications for employment, they generally concentrate only on this portion of the balance of payments. The evening news usually reports the balance on the current account, not the overall account. There is nothing to report on the overall account: it is always zero! But now you know that these emphases are misplaced. If we pay more to buy "their" goods, "they" pay more to buy our assets.

Soldiers from the 2nd Infantry Division conduct an area reconnaissance mission in Baghdad. How do the wars in Iraq and Afghanistan increase the current account deficit?

Figure 1 shows the U.S. quarterly current and capital account balances for the period 1960:01 through 2008:04. As we can see, they are *almost* mirror images of each other. When one is negative, the other is positive by almost the same amount. But why almost—and not exactly—are they calculated as indicated by the above simple math? This is because of the statistical discrepancies described below. Note also the increase in current account deficits starting in the 1980s. We will explain these below. In later years, the current account deficit has been even larger than before, partly due to the two Middle Eastern wars, and partly due to the overall increase in U.S. income.

Table 2 shows the U.S. balance of payments data for selected years. As in Figure 1, it shows that the current account slipped into a deficit in the 1980s, and stayed in deficit thereafter. The statistical discrepancy arises out of the fact that collecting data on all international transactions is a daunting task, and very often the accounts don't balance due to errors and omissions. Moreover, illegal activities might create a wedge between the current and capital account transactions. If someone smuggles some goods into the United States, sells them, and sends the proceeds legally to a foreign country, only half of these transactions—the legal parts—will be recorded in the balance of payments accounts.

There is an obvious relationship between the balance of payments accounts and the transactions in the foreign exchange market. This is simply because, as described earlier, all international transactions must go through the foreign exchange market. Consider Table 1. In that table, the sum of all the credit items ($300) is the total amount of dollars Americans have received from the sale of goods, services, and assets to foreigners. But foreigners must have purchased this amount in the foreign exchange market, since they generally don't posses dollars. Therefore, the sum of all the credit items corresponds to demand for dollars in Figure 2 of Chapter 18.

Figure 1 U.S. Quarterly Current and Capital Account Balances ($Billion) 1960:01 to 2008:04

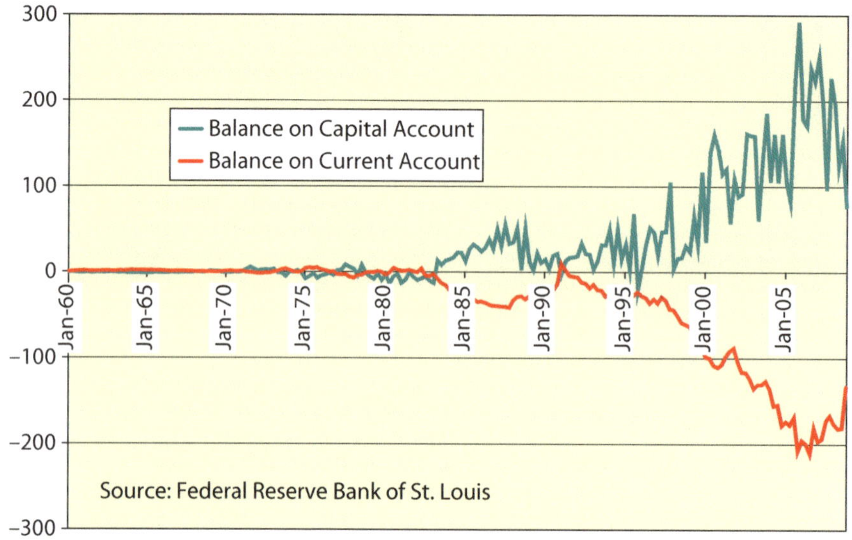

Table 2
Balances on the U.S. Current and Capital Accounts

Year	Balance on Current Account ($Billion)	Balance on Capital Account ($Billion)	Statistical Discrepancy ($Billion)
1970	2.3	-2.1	-0.2
1975	18.1	-22.8	4.7
1980	2.3	-24.9	22.6
1985	-118.2	99.5	18.7
1990	-79.0	58.1	20.8
1995	-113.6	82.8	30.7
2000	-417.4	477.7	-60.3
2005	-729.0	700.7	28.3
2008	-673.3	546.6	126.7

Similarly, the sum of the debit items is the total amount of dollars Americans have paid to buy foreign goods, services, and assets. This must correspond to the supply of dollars to the foreign exchange market by Americans. However, there is a major difference between the balance of payments accounts on the one hand, and the supply-demand functions on the other. The former is the record of transactions after the transactions have already taken place. But, as you know, the supply and demand functions are the amounts of currencies people were *willing* and able to buy.

Finally, recall that under the flexible exchange rate regime, supplies and demands for currencies determine the prices of currencies, so the demand for dollars equals the supply of dollars. Translated into the balance of payments accounts, this means that the sum of credit items equals the sum of debit items (except for statistical discrepancies noted above). Therefore, under the flexible exchange rate regime, balance of payments always balances, without any government intervention in the market. We will ignore the fixed exchange rate systems in this chapter.

DETERMINANTS OF CURRENT AND CAPITAL ACCOUNT BALANCES

Combining the discussions of Chapter 18 and those presented above, you can easily figure out what could cause movements in the two accounts. Let's start with current account balance.

Current Account Balance

The current account balance is nothing but our good old friend net exports:

$$\text{Current Account Surplus} = NX = EX - IM$$

All else the same, any event that causes foreigners to buy more U.S. goods and services will increase the current account surplus or net exports. All else the same, any event that causes Americans to buy more foreign goods will decrease the current account surplus or net exports. For ease of exposition, we will think of foreign countries as Europe. However, our theory is more general and applies to all foreign countries. Here is the list of such events:

1. An increase in U.S. income. If the U.S. GDP increases, the disposable income in the United States will increase and Americans will be able to buy more foreign goods and services. This will result in an increase in imports, and a reduction in current account surplus.
2. An increase in foreign income. For the same reason, if foreign income increases, foreigners will buy more U.S. goods and services. This will result in an increase in our exports and current account surplus.
3. An increase in the U.S. price level. All else the same, if the U.S. price level increases, U.S. goods and services become relatively more expensive for foreigners to buy. Conversely, foreign goods and services become relatively cheaper for Americans to buy. The resulting decrease in U.S. exports and the increase in U.S. imports will lead to a reduction in the U.S. current account surplus.
4. An increase in the foreign price level. For a similar reason, an increase in the foreign price level will result in an increase in the U.S. current account surplus.
5. An increase (appreciation) of the U.S. dollar. We have seen in the last chapter that when the U.S. dollar appreciates, U.S. goods become more expensive for foreigners to buy, and foreign goods become cheaper for Americans to buy. For example, Europeans must pay more euros to buy dollars in order to buy U.S. goods. Revisit the T-shirt example of Chapter 18.

Capital Account Balance

The capital account records transactions in assets. Investors buy assets in anticipation of making a return on them in the future. Recalling the theory we discussed in Chapter 17, if they expect the rate of return on an asset to be higher, they will sell some of their other assets to buy more of this asset. Here is the list of variables that will affect the capital account surplus.

1. An increase in the U.S. interest rate. All else the same, if rates of return on U.S. assets increase relative to foreign assets, foreigners will buy more U.S. assets, and Americans will buy fewer foreign assets. This will increase the U.S. capital account surplus. An example is the increase in U.S. interest rates relative to foreign interest rates.
2. An increase in the foreign interest rate. For a similar reason, if the rates of return on foreign assets increase, the U.S. capital account surplus will decrease.
3. Expected appreciation of dollar. If foreigners expect the U.S. dollar to appreciate in the future, they will buy more U.S. dollars for speculative reasons. Suppose that the exchange rate is currently e = €1.00/\$, but investors expect it to appreciate to e = €1.02/\$ next month, so the expected appreciation rate is 2%:

   $$d^e=(1.02-1.00)/1.00\times100=2\%$$

   This means that if a European buys dollars, holds them for a month, and sells them after one month, he will make a speculative profit of 2%.

We are now ready to conduct economic analyses.

SHIFTS IN THE AGGREGATE DEMAND FUNCTION

An event that causes a shift in the aggregate demand function in a closed economy will also cause a similar shift in an open economy. In open economies, though, some additional factors will cause shifts in the aggregate demand function. Keep in mind that any event not related to a change in the price or GDP levels will shift the aggregate demand function. Also, the effects of these events will be through the current account. We mention two examples.

Figure 2 Shifts in the AD Function

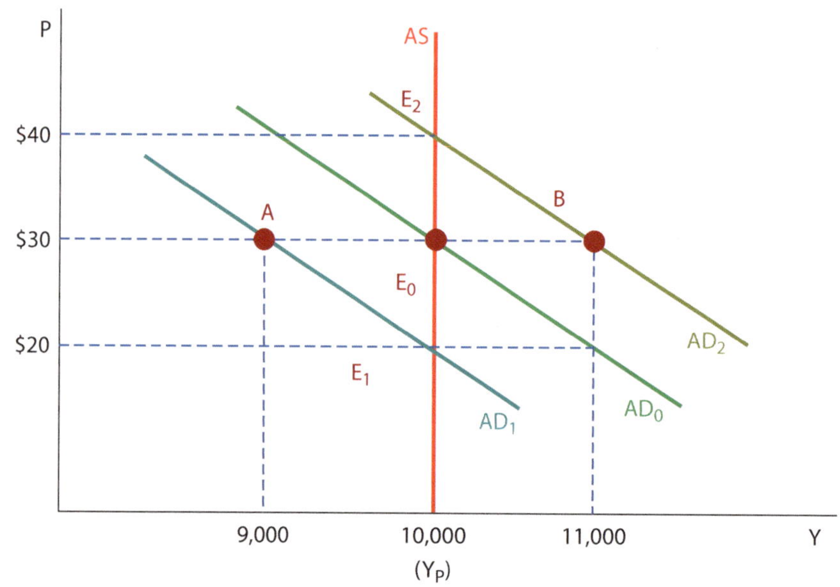

Consider Figure 2, which you saw in Chapter 12. Assume that the economy is at point E_0, with P = \$30 and Y = 10,000. What will happen if foreign countries slip into a recession and foreign income decreases? In that case, net exports will decrease as foreigners buy fewer U.S. goods and services. But we know that

$$AD = C + I + G + (EX - IM)$$

Therefore, the AD function will shift to the left to AD_1, and the economy will move to point A. The result will be a recession in the United States. In the long run, the economy will move to a new equilibrium point E_1 with a new, lower price level. However, we also know that in the long run, the inflation rate will stay put since the rate of growth of the money supply remains unchanged by assumption.

In the opposite case, when foreign income increases, the U.S. aggregate demand function will increase, and the U.S. economy will move to point B in the short run, and point E_2 in the long run. We conclude that business cycles in foreign countries could create business cycles at home. However, you should be aware that this conclusion depends on the relative sizes of the economies. A small economy will be more severely affected by foreign events than a large country. For instance, a recession in Britain may not affect the U.S. aggregate demand function appreciably, but a recession in the United States could have a severe impact on the British economy.

Another example is a change in the exchange rate. Suppose that, for whatever reason, the dollar appreciates. As we saw above, this will make U.S. goods more expensive for foreigners to buy—and therefore, the current account surplus, AKA net exports, will decrease. This will result in a leftward shift in the aggregate demand function. If the dollar depreciates, then the aggregate demand function will shift to the right.

MONETARY POLICY

As in the case of a closed economy, monetary and fiscal policies will have no effects on the level of GDP in the long run. In the long run, the level of GDP is determined in the labor market, the price level by the amount of money supply, and the rate of inflation by the growth rate of the money supply. The short-run effects, though, could be different. Monetary policy would have a stronger effect on the GDP if the economy were open. Here is the simple reason why. In an open economy, there is an additional channel through which an increase in money supply would affect the aggregate demand and real GDP: the exchange rate channel.

Figure 3 Monetary Policy in an Open Economy

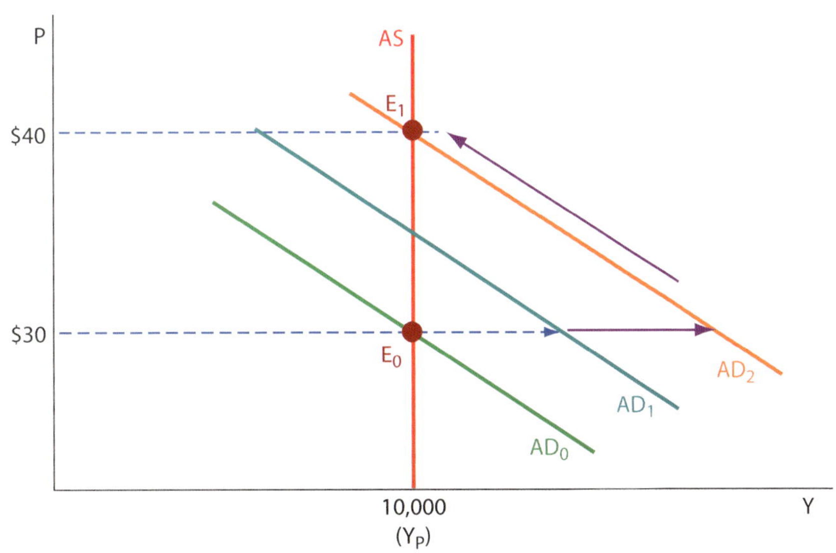

Suppose the Fed increases money supply through an open market purchase of bonds. This causes a reduction in the domestic interest rate and an increase in investment spending, as we know by now. The AD function will shift to AD_1 in Figure 3. In an open economy, the decrease in the interest rate will make domestic assets less attractive relative to foreign assets. This would cause a reduction in the demand for U.S. dollars by foreigners, as they reduce their purchase of U.S. assets. This would also result in an increase in the supply of U.S. dollars, as Americans try to buy the now more attractive foreign assets. As a result, the dollar will depreciate against foreign currencies, as we saw in Chapter 20.

The depreciation of the U.S. dollar would make U.S. goods and services cheaper for foreigners to buy, and foreign goods more expensive for Americans to buy. This would cause the U.S. net exports (EX – IM) to increase, further pushing up the aggregate demand. In Figure 3, the AD function would shift to AD_1 if the economy were closed. It will, however, shift to AD_2 in an open economy due to the additional current account effect.

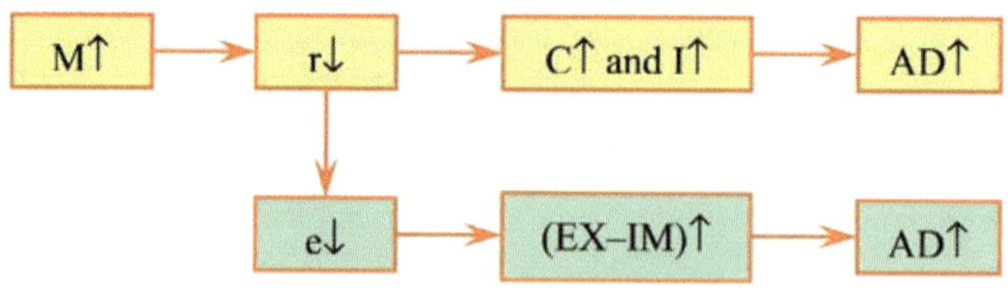

In the long run, the economy will move to point E_1, for reasons we already know well. However, the price level at the end will be higher if the economy is open than if it were closed.

FISCAL POLICY

Fiscal policy will be less effective in the short run in an open economy. Suppose that, all else the same, government spending increases. As we know by now, this causes an increase in aggregate demand and real GDP in the short run. We also know that the higher GDP results in a larger demand for money, and thus the U.S. interest rate increases. The rise in the U.S. interest rate makes U.S. assets more attractive. The analysis of Chapter 18 indicates that the dollar will appreciate against other currencies. The dollar appreciation will make U.S. goods and services more expensive for foreigners to buy, reducing next exports. The reduction in net exports will cause the aggregate demand function to shift less than it would in a closed economy, as in Figure 4.

In Figure 4, the AD function would shift to AD_1 if the economy were closed. It will, however, shift only to AD_2, due to dollar appreciation. For this reason, the real GDP will increase less than it would if the economy were closed. In the long run, the economy will move back to point E_1, with a higher price level. We also know that in the long run, the rate of inflation will equal the rate of growth of the money supply.

Note that in the long run, government spending will crowd out not only domestic investment and consumption, but also net exports.

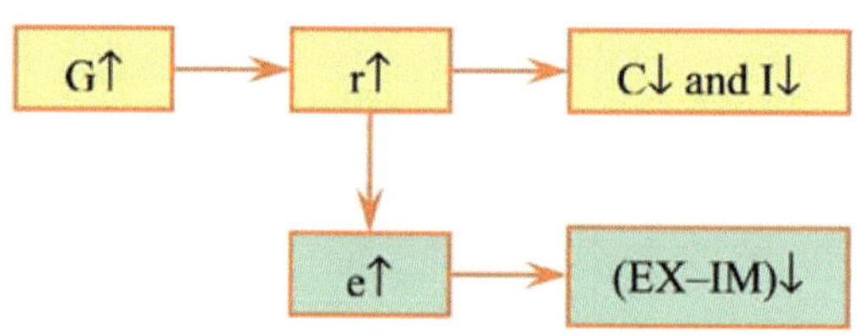

Figure 4 Fiscal Policy in an Open Economy

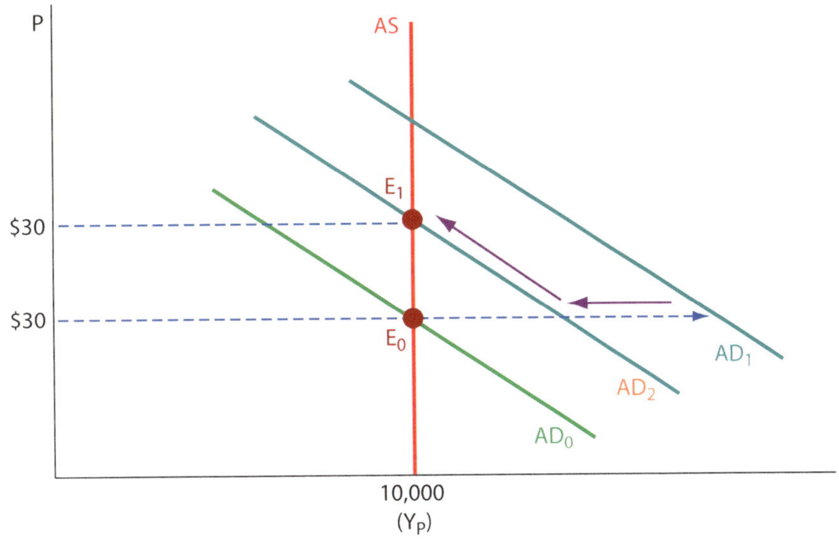

THE TWIN DEFICITS

Now suppose that the U.S. government increases its spending and transfer payments, but does not have enough tax revenue to pay for its outlays. It therefore comes to the loanable funds market to borrow from the private sector. We have already seen the effect of budget deficits on interest rates in Chapter 11. The increase in the demand for loanable funds by the government causes the real and nominal interest rates to increase.

The increase in the U.S. interest rates makes American assets more attractive for foreigners, and foreign assets less attractive for Americans. Because of this, demand for U.S. dollars increases, and the supply of U.S. dollars decreases. As Chapter 20 shows, this results in an appreciation of the U.S. dollar against foreign currencies. As the dollar appreciates, American goods and services become more expensive for foreigners to buy. Foreign goods are then cheaper for Americans to buy. As exports decrease and imports increase, the current account slips into a deficit.

Consider an example from the real world: President Ronald Reagan ran huge budget deficits during the 1980s, mostly because of military spending. To finance the deficits, the U.S. government borrowed in the financial markets by issuing and selling U.S. Treasury bonds. The increase in government demand for loanable funds resulted in very high nominal and real interest rates in the United States This is what the loanable funds theory predicts. The high U.S. interest rates attracted a lot of foreign capital into the United States. For instance, the Japanese famously purchased a lot of Treasury bonds during this period. As our model predicts, the result was an appreciated dollar.

This is not the end of the story. Consistent with our explanation above, an expensive dollar resulted in expensive American goods for foreigners, and cheaper foreign goods for Americans. As a result, U.S. exports of goods and services to foreign countries decreased, and imports increased. This resulted in a current account deficit, or negative net exports. The budget deficit and the resulting current account deficit were called the *twin deficits* at the time.

TWIN DEFICITS
The budget deficit and the current account deficit. During the Reagan years, some economists believed that the former was the cause of the latter, hence the name.

Negative net exports meant that aggregate demand was lower than what it could have been in the absence of these policies. Some feared that low aggregate demand could lead to unemployment. It did not happen simply because the large government spending outweighed the effects of current account deficits. In fact, the economy was growing at a robust rate during most of that time.

Figures 5 through 7 demonstrate this case. Figure 7 shows that during the 1980s, U.S. budget deficits increased sharply relative their past values. Recall that a budget deficit is the excess of government spending, G, and transfer payments, R, over its tax revenue, T. Government borrowing to finance these deficits resulted in an increase in interest rates, as shown in Figure 7. This figure shows the interest rates on ten-year U.S. Treasury bonds.[1] As can be seen, the rates were quite high during the first half of the 1980s. In certain weeks, the rates were over 15%. Figure 7 shows that the value of the dollar, in terms of the currencies of America's major trading partners, was quite high. These numbers are not really exchange rates. Rather, they are indexes that are calculated by weighting the exchange rate of each country by the amount of foreign trade the country carried out with the United States. These high values were because of the elevated U.S. interest rates mentioned above. The result of the appreciated dollar on the current account is evident in Figure 1, which shows that this account was in deficit for most of the 1980s.

Figure 5 shows that there were also large deficits in the first halves of the 1990s and 2000s. The first was due to the Gulf War; the second was due to the Iraq War. Nevertheless, the exchange rate during these periods was not as high as in the 1980s. The reason is, during this period, if you recall, the Fed was pursuing a policy of low and stable inflation rates under Greenspan. This resulted in low and stable interest rates through the Fisher Effect described in Chapter 11. This can be seen in Figure 6. The low and stable interest rates, in turn, resulted in low and stable trade-weighted exchange rates. There is another reason for the low interest rates of the 2000s that I will explain later.

Figure 5 U.S. Government Budget Deficits (–) and Surpluses (+) ($Million)

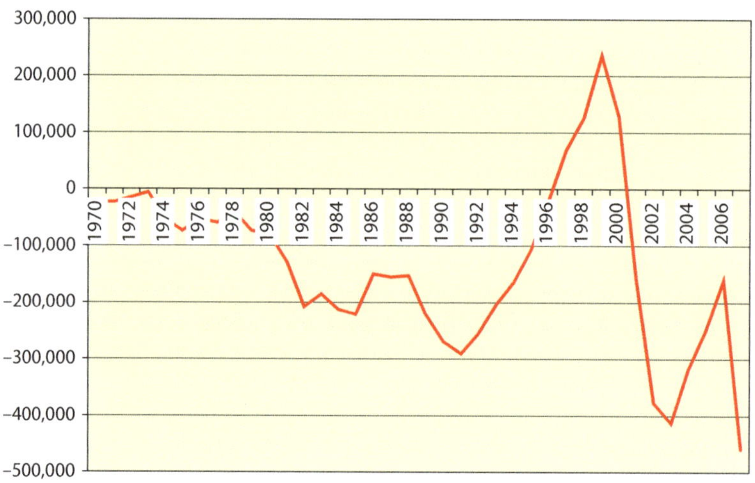

1 The interest rates are the averages of weekly interest rates over the calendar years. All the data used in this chapter have been obtained from the St. Louis Federal Reserve Bank's economic data (FRED) at http://research.stlouisfed.org.

Figure 6 Interest Rates on Ten-Year U.S. Treasury Bonds

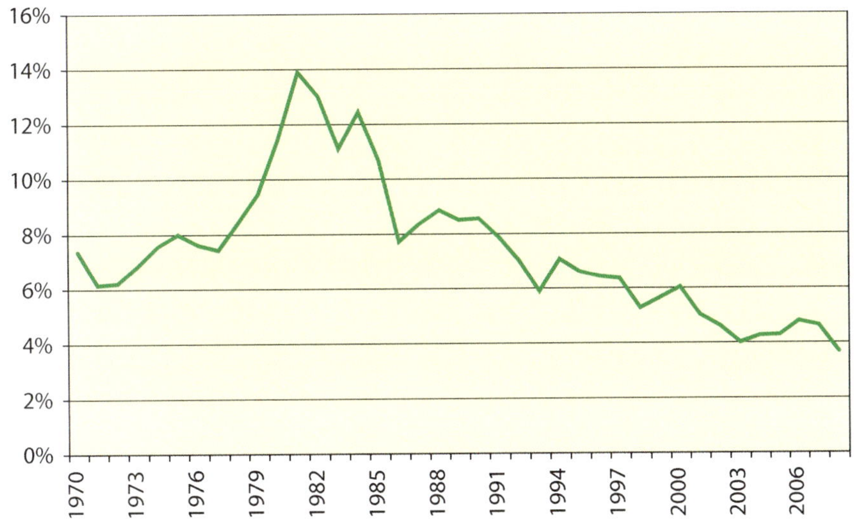

Figure 7 Trade-Weighted Exchange Index: Major Currencies

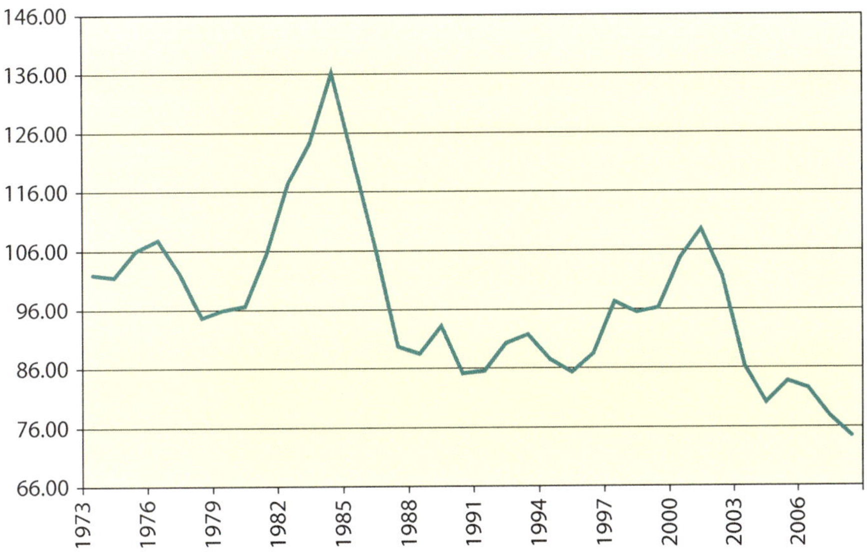

DEFICIT FINANCING IN AN OPEN ECONOMY

Recall from Chapter 11 that deficit financing by the government crowds out private spending, by pushing up the interest rate. Does this conclusion also hold in an open economy? To answer this question, let's go through the same math—assuming this time that the economy is open to trade. We start with the goods market equilibrium condition:

$$Y = C + I + G + NX \qquad (1)$$

Substituting this in the definition of disposable income we get:

$$Y_d = Y - T + R = C + I + G + NX - T + R \quad (2)$$

Rearranging this equation further, we get

$$(Y_d - C) - NX = I + (G + R - T) \quad (3)$$

We know that Y_d - C equals private sector saving, S. We also know that balance of payments balances. Using net exports for its equivalent, current account balance, in the balance-of-payment equation above we get:

$$NX + \text{Capital Account Balance} = 0$$

So that

$$\text{Capital Account Balance} = - NX$$

With these two modifications equation (3) becomes

$$S + \text{Capital Account Balance} = I + (G + R - T) \quad (4)$$

This equation says that the funds needed by firms for their investment projects (and by the government to finance its deficit) come from two sources. The first is the domestic savings, as before. The second is the funds provided by foreign savers/lenders. For example, when the Chinese buy U.S. bonds, they pour money into the U.S. financial system that is channeled to U.S. borrowers/investors. Since the U.S. saving and the capital account balance (CAB) are a positive function of the U.S. interest rate, the left-hand side of equation (4) depends positively on the U.S. interest rate.

Figure 8 An Increase in Budget Deficit

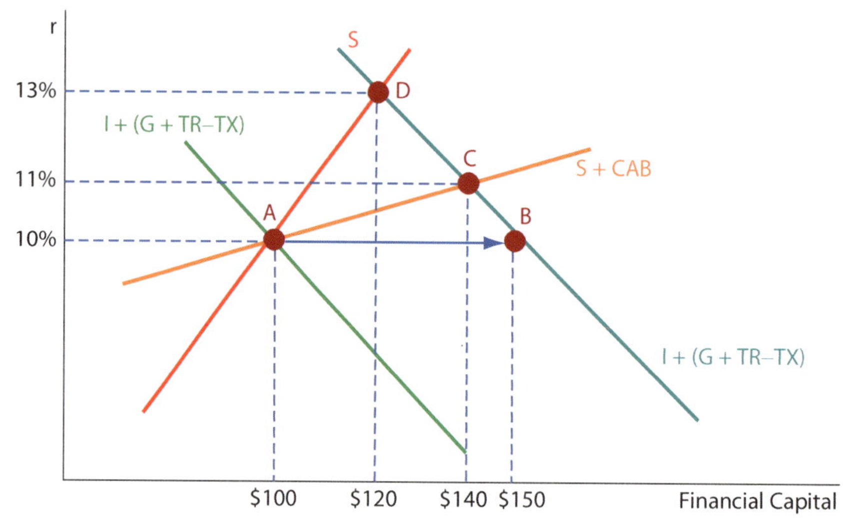

Consider Figure 8, which is similar to Figure 9 of Chapter 10. It is a good idea to refresh your memory of the crowding-out effect by reviewing that chapter. In a closed economy with no capital inflows from abroad, the economy would be at point A, with an interest rate of 10%. If the budget deficit increased by $50, the I + (G + TR - TX) line would shift to the right by $50, and the economy would move to point D. The interest rate would increase to 13%, and $20 of additional saving would be forthcoming from domestic households (point A to point D). At the same time $30 of private investment would be crowded out, because of this higher interest rate (point B to point D). Consumption would also decrease because of the increase in saving.

Now assume that the economy is open to international transactions. To have a sharper picture, let's assume that it is at point A—as before—with 10% interest rate. The supply-of-funds line S + CAB is drawn flatter than the S line, because there is a large amount of financial capital outside the United States that Americans can tap into. If the U.S. interest rate increases, large sums of money would flow in, much larger than what U.S. households could supply. For instance, compare in Figure 8 the amount of additional financial capital supplied to the market along the S and S + CAB lines, when the interest rate increases from 10% to 11%.

Now when the budget deficit increases by $50, the economy moves to point C, the interest rate increases only by 1%, and $40 of additional capital is provided to the government, most of it from foreign sources (point A to point C). Since the interest rate does not rise as much as before, private spending is crowded out by only $10 (point B to point C). So in an open economy, deficit spending would still increase the interest rate and crowd out private spending. However, since foreigners would finance some of the government spending, the domestic interest rate would not rise as much as it would if the economy were closed. Crowding out would also be less severe.

TO SUMMARIZE

1. Balance of payments is the record of a country's transactions with the rest of the world.
2. Any transaction leading to the payment of money to domestic residents is recorded as a credit item; any transaction that leads to the payment of money to foreigners is recorded as a debit item.
3. Balance of payments always balances.
4. *Current accounts* record transactions in goods and services.
5. The current account is said to be in deficit if the import of goods and services exceeds the export.
6. *Capital accounts* record transactions in assets. Purchase of U.S. assets by foreigners causes capital (money) inflows. Purchase of foreign assets by Americans causes capital outflows.
7. The capital account is said to be in deficit if domestic residents pay more to buy foreign assets than foreigners pay to buy domestic assets.
8. In a flexible exchange rate regime, the sum of current account and capital account balances is always zero.
9. Monetary policy is more effective in the short run in an open economy than in a closed economy.
10. Fiscal policy is less effective in the short run in an open economy than in a closed economy.
11. Budget deficits lead to high interest rates, an appreciated dollar, and current account deficits. These results may not happen if the Fed keeps the inflation rate steady.
12. In an open economy, a budget deficit would still increase domestic interest rates and crowd out private spending. But these effects would be much weaker due to the influx of foreign capital.

EXERCISES

Question 1

Explain how each of the following transactions will be recorded in the U.S. balance of payments accounts.

1. You buy a Japanese camera.
2. A British resident buys 100 Ford stocks.
3. Your firm hires a Norwegian computer programmer to write some programs for your firm.
4. An American resident buys an oil field in South America.
5. You buy a German factory.
6. A French resident buys some California wines.
7. You do some economic consulting for an Italian firm.
8. You buy some Swiss chocolates.

Question 2

What will happen to the current account surplus in the following cases?

1. A decrease in U.S. income.
2. A decrease in foreign income.
3. A decrease in U.S. price level.
4. A decrease in foreign price level.
5. Dollar depreciation.
6. Domestic and foreign prices both rise at 5%.

Question 3

What will happen to the capital account surplus in the following cases?

1. A decrease in U.S. interest rate.
2. A decrease in foreign interest rate.
3. The U.S. interest rate increases by 2%, and the foreign interest rate increases by 5%.
4. The dollar is expected to depreciate in the future.

Question 4

If the Fed unexpectedly decreases the money supply, what do you think will happen to the €/$ exchange rate? Analyze the effect of this policy on the current and capital accounts balances.

Question 5

If the U.S. government unexpectedly decreases its spending, what do you think will happen to the €/$ exchange rate? Analyze the effect of this policy on the current and capital accounts balances.

Question 6

If the U.S. government unexpectedly increases taxes, what do you think will happen to the €/$ exchange rate? Analyze the effect of this policy on the current and capital accounts balances.

Question 7

Some argue that one reason for the housing bubble in the United States during 2000–2006 was that Asian countries were buying U.S. Treasury bonds. This was partly to keep their own currencies depreciated, and partly to invest in U.S. assets.

1. Use the foreign exchange market graph to analyze the effect of this policy on the exchange rate between U.S. and Asian currencies. How do you think Asian policy makers thought this course of action would benefit their economies? (Hint: Recall the T-shirt example of the last chapter.)
2. Use a graph similar to Figure 8 to analyze the effect of this policy on U.S. interest rates.
3. Now explain why such a policy would increase the demand for housing in the United States.

Question 8

Consider Figure 8. If the United States were a small economy relative to the rest of the world, an infinite amount of foreign financial capital would be available to U.S. investors at a given interest rate. The (I + CAB) line would be horizontal.

1. What would be the effect of an increase in the budget deficit? How much would be the amount of crowding out?
2. If the interest rate did not change, could the government run large amounts of deficits indefinitely?

CHAPTER 20

Fiscal Policy: A Closer Look

INTRODUCTION AND REVIEW

WE HAVE LEARNED in this book that the government has two major policy tools to affect the level of GDP and the rate of inflation. These are fiscal and monetary policies. In this chapter, we will take a closer look at fiscal policy. Fiscal policy is related to the government's expenditures and financing of these expenditures. The government can finance its expenditures in two different ways: raising taxes and borrowing money from the public. We will study both of these alternatives. We will analyze the U.S. tax system and the government's tax revenues. If in any year the amount of tax revenue is not sufficient to pay for all the government's expenditures, the government is said to run a *budget deficit*. In that case, it has to borrow money to finance its spending. The accumulation of these borrowings is called *national debt*, which we will also discuss.

BUDGET DEFICIT
The amount by which a government's expenditures exceed its tax revenues during a certain period of time.

NATIONAL DEBT
The accumulation of past borrowings to finance government spending. The amount of borrowing in each year equals the budget deficit for that year.

WHAT IS FISCAL POLICY?

We learned in Chapter 7 that fiscal policy refers to deliberate increases or decreases in government spending or taxes *in order to achieve a particular macroeconomic goal.* This goal is generally to change the level of the GDP or the rate of inflation, though the former is more common than the latter. The rate of inflation is usually controlled by monetary policy.

The definition of fiscal policy brings out two points about the government's tax and expenditure activities. First, state and local governments have the authority to tax their residents and spend the proceeds to build roads and bridges, to pay state and local employees (including teachers), and to make transfer payments to low-income families. However, none of these activities aim at changing the national aggregate demand or achieving some macroeconomic objective. So by and large, these state and local government activities do not qualify as fiscal policy. Therefore, we will focus on the activities of the federal government.

AUTOMATIC STABILIZERS
Factors that automatically cause the aggregate demand to increase (or at least not to decrease) in a recession, without any expansionary demand-management policy. Automatic stabilizers act in the opposite direction in an expansion.

Second, there are built-in *automatic stabilizers* in the government's taxes and expenditures. What this means is that because of some well-defined and relatively fixed rules, the government's expenditures increase and taxes decrease automatically during a recession. As a result, the aggregate demand decreases by less than it would in the absence of these automatic changes in spending and taxes. For example, during a recession certain people lose their jobs and automatically become eligible to receive the government's unemployment payments. Also, since households pay taxes on the basis of their incomes—and since households' incomes are decreased during a recession—they automatically pay fewer taxes to the government.

Similarly, during the expansion phase of a business cycle, unemployment decreases and household income increases. As a result, the government's unemployment payments are reduced, and tax revenues increase. These automatic changes in expenditures and taxes slow down the increase in aggregate demand during an economic expansion. Because of these automatic changes in taxes and expenditures, the government would appear to be following a countercyclical fiscal policy, even though it might not be following *any* policy at all. Because of this, we need to find a way of distinguishing between a *discretionary fiscal policy* and the automatic changes in the government's spending and taxes. We will return to this issue later.

DISCRETIONARY FISCAL POLICY
Changes in the government spending or taxes that are the results of the deliberate actions of the governments, rather than due to automatic stabilizers.

An example of discretionary policy is the deliberate increase in spending and cuts in taxes by the Japanese government during the 1990s. During this decade, called the *lost decade* by some, the Japanese economy was not performing well. As a result, the government decided to follow an expansionary fiscal policy to boost aggregate demand and get the Japanese economy out of recession. During this period, the Japanese government spent large sums of money to undertake projects of dubious economic value. For instance, the government built large bridges, long roads, and fancy airports whose economic benefits were not large enough to justify their costs. Whether these expansionary fiscal policies were successful in getting the Japanese economy out of recession is a matter of dispute among economists.

Japan's Akashi-Kaikyo Bridge, also known as the Pearl Bridge, has the longest central span of any suspension bridge, at 1,991 metres (6,532 ft). It is located in Japan and was completed in 1998.

THE FEDERAL BUDGET

Table 1 shows the receipts and outlays of the U.S. government for the fiscal years 2000 and 2008. A fiscal year is the 12-month period over which the government calculates its receipts and outlays. The fiscal year for the U.S. government runs from October 1st through September 30th. On the receipt side, we see that close to half of the tax revenues come from individual income taxes. Individuals must pay a specific percentage of their total incomes from all sources to the government. Payroll taxes, also called social insurance and retirement receipts, are levied on wages only. Usually employees pay half of these taxes, and their employers pay the other half. These taxes are to finance social security and unemployment payments. In 2008 these two taxes accounted for 36% of the federal government's revenue.

With all the media coverage and public debates, corporation taxes were only about 10% of the government's tax revenue. Because of this, some economists believe that the social costs of corporate taxes outweigh their social benefits and thus they should be abolished. Social costs arise partly because these taxes may distort economic incentives. Moreover, because of the complexity of business operations, both the taxpayers and the government need to hire an army of tax professionals to calculate and audit corporate taxes. On the other hand, for all the effort spent on corporate tax administration, these taxes comprise only about 10% of the government's total revenue. So doing away with this source of tax revenue might do more good than harm. Not all economists agree with this assessment, however. Finally, less than 10% of the tax revenue comes from other sources such as sales taxes.

Table 1

Federal Government Receipts and Outlays

	2000 Fiscal Year		2008 Fiscal Year	
	Billions of Dollars	Percent	Billions of Dollars	Percent
Total Tax Revenue	2,025.6	100%	2,523.8	100%
Individual income taxes	1,004.5	50%	1,145.7	45%
Corporation income taxes	207.3	10%	304.3	12%
Payroll taxes	652.9	32%	900.4	36%
Other	160.9	8%	173.4	7%
Total Expenditure	1,789.1	100%	2,978.6	100%
National defense	294.4	16%	624.1	21%
International affairs	17.2	1%	28.8	1%
Health	154.5	9%	280.6	9%
Medicare	197.1	11%	390.8	13%
Income security	253.7	14%	432.7	15%
Social security	409.4	23%	617.0	21%
Net interest	222.9	12%	248.9	8%
Other	239.9	13%	355.7	12%
Budget Surplus (+) or Deficit (–)	+236.5		-454.8	

Source: The Economic Report of the President, 2009, Table B80.
The 2008 numbers are estimates.

On the expenditure side, defense spending comprised 21% of the expenditures in 2008. One percent of the total expenditure was spent on international affairs such as maintaining foreign embassies. Sixty percent of total expenditures were transfer payments, which comprise health and Medicare payments, as well as social security and income security payments. About 10% of the total budget went toward payment of interest on the national debt. Net interest means payment of interest on the national debt minus the receipt of interest on such loans as student and farm loans. The category "other" could include both purchases of goods and services and transfer payments.

Finally, note that in 2000 the U.S. government was running a budget surplus of $236.5 billion, while the budget was in deficit in 2008. Since there were not enough tax revenues to cover its expenditures in 2008, the government had borrowed this much money in the financial markets from the public. The accumulation of budget deficits is called the national debt. If you borrow $10 from a friend in one week and $20 in another, your total debt to him would be $30. If in week 3 you borrow another $5, your total debt will increase to $35. If, on the other hand, you pay back $5 then you owe only $25. Similarly, when in any year the government runs a deficit, the resulting borrowing increases the national debt. If it runs a *budget surplus*, it pays back some of the loan, and the national debt goes down by that amount.

BUDGET SURPLUS
The amount by which a government's tax revenues exceed its expenditures during a certain period of time.

Figure 1 shows the U.S. government's deficit and debt over time. The deficits in the 1940s were related to the increases in expenditures in connection with the Second World War. The increase in deficits in the 1980s was the result of the tax cuts and increases in military spending by President Reagan. The second increase in deficits came in the 1990s, because of the Iraqi invasion of Kuwait and the ensuing Gulf War. Because of the Clinton tax increase in 2000, the budget turned into surplus. The deficit increased again in 2003 due to the Iraq War. Note that, corresponding to the deficits graph, the national debt has been increasing after the 1980s. The debt was reduced somewhat in 2000 thanks to the brief Clinton budget surplus, but increased afterward due to the Iraq War.[1]

It must be realized that it is not the dollar amount of the debt that is important, but its size relative to national income or GDP. This is similar to a household debt. Suppose a family owes a bank one million dollars. This debt would be overwhelming if the household income was only a hundred thousand dollars per year, but it would not be a big deal if the annual family income were ten million dollars. Similarly, the same amount of national debt would be a smaller problem if the nominal GDP were higher. It would be easier to pay off the debt if the nominal GDP was high. This is because by increasing the tax rate just a little, the government could raise a large amount of tax revenue to pay off the debt.

Figure 2 shows the ratio of the national debt to the nominal GDP for the United States since 1940. This picture is much less scary. It shows that the debt/GDP ratio was quite high during the 1940s, but it's now around 40%. The ratio declined in 2000 because of President Clinton's deficit reduction effort. It is, however, increasing due to the spending for the Iraq and Afghanistan Wars.

1 The national debt in Figure 1 is the portion of the total debt held by the public. The other portion of the debt is held by other U.S. government agencies, notably the Federal Reserve Bank and the Social Security Administration. The Fed owns some of the bonds due to open market operations. The Social Security Administration has purchased some government bonds for investment purposes.

FULL-EMPLOYMENT BUDGET

We saw above that the government's budget will change because of the presence of built-in automatic stabilizers. In an economic recession the budget deficit will automatically increase, and in an expansion it will decrease. To see why this happens, realize that taxes are a function of GDP. The income tax levied on each individual is a fraction of that individual's income. Consequently, as the aggregate household income is reduced during a recession, the government's tax revenue goes down as well. In the same way, as some individuals lose their jobs, the amount of payroll taxes is reduced. As a simple example, suppose that the government's tax revenue (TX) has two parts. One part (TX_0) does not depend on GDP.

Figure 1 U.S. Government Budget Deficit and National Debt: 1940–2009

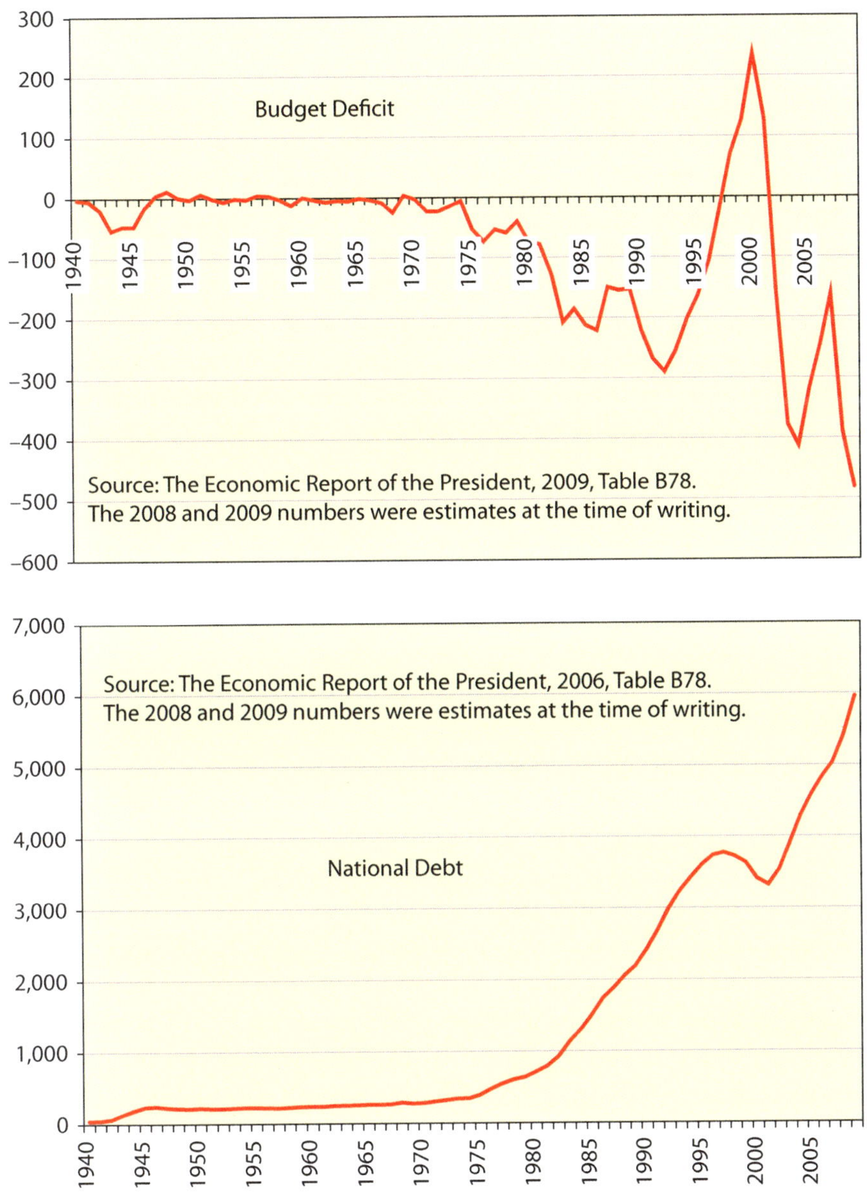

Figure 2 National Debt as a Percent of GDP: 1940 to 2009

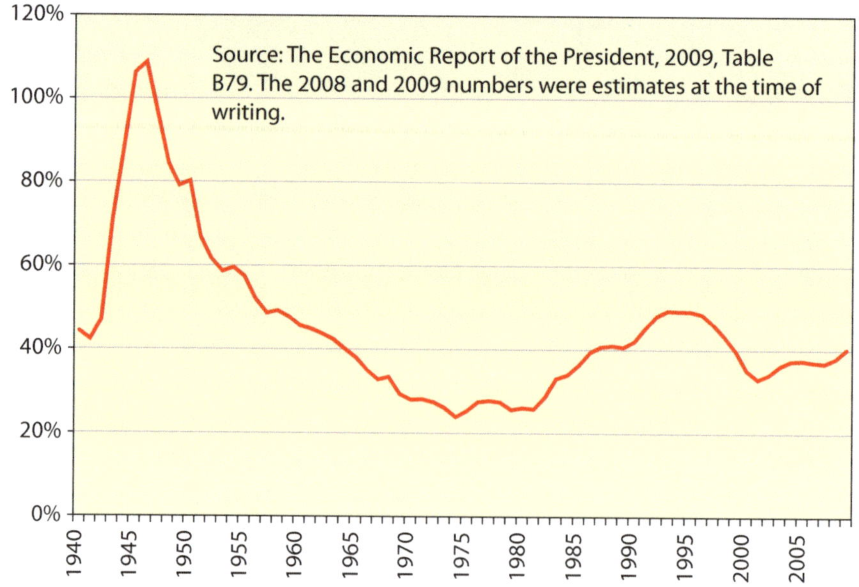

The other portion is a constant fraction (t) of real GDP. Then the tax function can be written as

$$TX = TX_0 + tY$$

where Y is the real GDP, as before.

Similarly, assume that transfer payments (TR) consist of two portions. One portion (TR_0) does not depend on real GDP. For example, the government makes social security payments to the elderly, regardless of the state of the economy. The other portion depends on real GDP. It increases in recessions and decreases in expansions. Suppose that the second portion is a constant fraction (h) of real GDP. Therefore, the transfer payments function takes the following form:

$$TR = TR_0 - hY$$

Finally, we assume that government spending does not depend on real GDP. So we denote it by G_0. We define the budget surplus (B) as the excess of tax revenues over government expenditures:

$$B = TX - G - TR$$

Substituting our new definitions into the budget equation, we get

$$B = (TX_0 + tY) - G_0 - (TR_0 - hY)$$

Or, collecting the terms,

$$B = (TX_0 - G_0 - TR_0) + (t + h)Y$$

The budget function is shown in Figure 3. It is upward sloping, because as income increases, tax revenues increase and transfer payments decrease—resulting in a larger budget surplus or a lower budget deficit. The figure assumes that at the potential level of output, the budget is in deficit. This budget deficit, shown by the distance AB in the figure, is called the *full-employment budget deficit*. Now, suppose that the economy slips into a recession, and the real GDP declines to point D. Since the real GDP is lower, tax revenues will decline and transfer payments will increase, As a result, the budget deficit will widen. The new budget deficit is shown by the dashed arrow. Note that this increase in budget deficit is solely due to the effect of automatic stabilizers. There has been no deliberate increase in spending or cut in taxes.

FULL-EMPLOYMENT BUDGET DEFICIT/CYCLICALLY ADJUSTED DEFICIT
A measure of the government budget deficit that removes the effects of automatic stabilizers on the budget. The result is a budget deficit that is solely the result of an active fiscal policy. It is also known as the full-employment deficit.

The effect of discretionary changes in spending or taxes is more accurately measured by the full-employment budget deficit. These discretionary changes affect T_0, G_0, and R_0, all of which are in the intercept. In other words, a discretionary change in any of these variables would cause a shift in the budget function. If the budget function shifts, the distance, AB, will change. In the above example, since the distance, AB, did not change, policy observers would conclude that there had been no discretionary increases in spending or cut in taxes.

Figure 3 The Full-Employment Budget Deficit

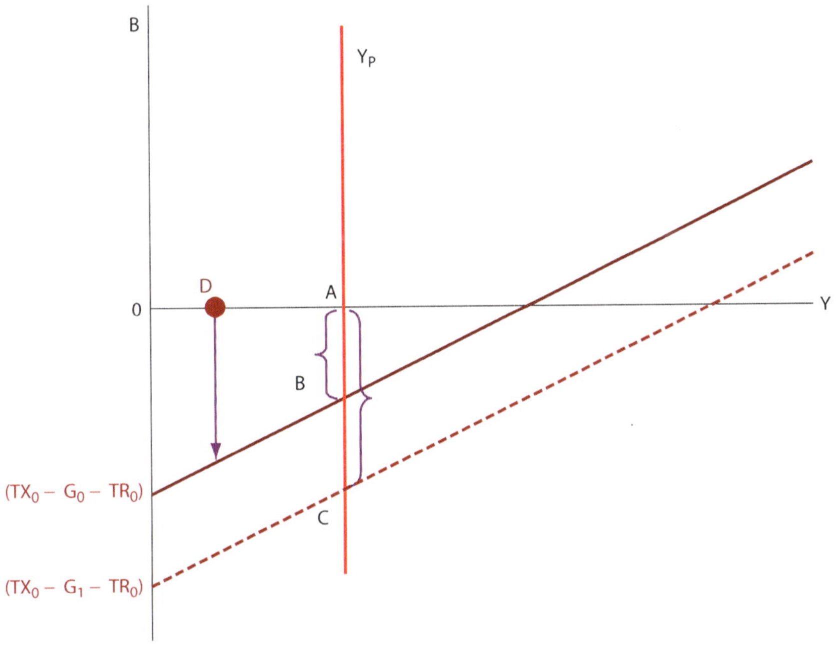

Now suppose that we are at point A again, and the government increases its purchase of goods and services to G_1. In that case, the budget function shifts down, and the full-employment deficit increases to AC. So by observing the full-employment deficit, we can tell whether the government is actively changing its taxes or spending.

Note that in the above discussion, we avoided the term "discretionary fiscal policy." As you recall, fiscal policy is defined as the deliberate change in spending or taxes to achieve a macroeconomic goal such as full employment. The full-employment budget deficit, on the other hand, shows the effect of *any* discretionary change in spending or taxes, even if it is not aimed at furthering a macroeconomic goal. In other words, all it does is remove the effect of automatic stabilizers from the total budget surplus or deficit. For instance, the decision to go to war results in a discretionary increase in spending as the government purchases more military goods. This is not really a fiscal policy. Nevertheless, it increases the full-employment deficit.

The Congressional Budget Office (CBO) estimates the full-employment surpluses and deficits for the U.S. government. It calls the full-employment deficit the *cyclically adjusted deficit*, since it removes the effects of automatic stabilizers from the total budget deficit. In other words, as in Figure 3, it calculates the surplus or deficit assuming full employment. Figure 4 shows the total and cyclically adjusted deficits for the United States from 1962 to 2009 estimated by CBO. As can be seen, they are close to each other, and the latter incorporates the effects of such events as the invasion of Iraq and Afghanistan—wars that cannot be considered a fiscal policy.

SHOULD THE BUDGET ALWAYS BE BALANCED?

Occasionally, you hear about proposals mandating the government to continuously balance its budget. So far, such proposals have been rejected. The problem with such schemes is that they tie the hands of policy makers in conducting discretionary fiscal policy. Moreover, such a policy would exacerbate business cycles. Suppose a recession comes and the real GDP falls. This will cause a reduction in taxes and an increase in transfer payments. The budget will go into deficit. Is this the time to balance the budget? To balance the budget, the government needs to reduce government spending and/or transfer payments, or increase taxes. All such polices will further reduce aggregate demand, and prolong the recession.

An alternative proposal is to balance the budget in the long run: After a few years of deficits, try to reduce spending or increase taxes, so that over a certain period of time the sum of deficits and surplus equals zero. But then the problem is to agree on the number of years over which we should balance the budget.

PROBLEMS WITH FISCAL POLICY

LONG AND VARIABLE LAGS
The idea that it would take a long time for the effects of fiscal and monetary policies to take effect and that these time lags vary from recession to recession so that they are generally unpredictable.

RECOGNITION LAG
The time it takes for government officials to recognize that there is a recession by studying the available data.

DECISION LAG
The amount of time it takes for the government to decide on the appropriate course of action after determining that the economy is in a recession.

LEGISLATIVE LAG
The amount of time—several months, or even years—it may take for both houses of Congress to pass a bill approving a proposed fiscal policy initiative.

There are several problems inhibiting the frequent use of discretionary fiscal policy as a stabilization tool. The first problem is that it is quite inflexible. This is very different from monetary policy, which can be used to change the stock of money on short notice. A lot of government programs have come into existence by acts of Congress to achieve certain socioeconomic objectives. For example, the social security program was designed to reduce the level of poverty in the United States. The goal of the Medicare and Medicaid programs is to reduce the burden of health care costs on low-income families and the elderly. The amount of money spent on these programs would depend on such factors as the number of low-income families and elderly in the economy. Therefore, the government cannot readily change the level of spending on these programs.

The second problem with fiscal policy is the presence of *long and variable lags*, from the time the government decides to initiate a discretionary policy and the time the policy actually takes effect. Government officials must first recognize that there is a recession going on by studying the available data. It may take several weeks or months for the relevant data to be collected and become available. This is called the *recognition lag*. Once it has judged that the economy is in a recession, the government must decide on the appropriate course of action. Suppose it finally decides to pursue an expansionary fiscal policy. This lag is called the *decision lag*.

Any expansionary fiscal policy is either in terms of an increase in spending or a decrease in taxes. Both of these require an act of Congress. A member of Congress usually introduces a bill proposing to increase spending or cut taxes. It may take several months for both houses of Congress to pass a bill approving the proposed expansionary fiscal policy. Once a bill is passed, it becomes law. This lag is called the *legislative lag*.

Once the bill is passed, the government must choose how to implement it. For example, if the bill directs the government to reduce certain tax rates, the appropriate government department—such as the Treasury—will be informed about the new bill. Then the Internal Revenue Service, a branch of the Treasury, will get to work on publishing new tax forms and informing taxpayers about the new tax rules. The cut in the tax rate will not have any effect on people's disposable income until the following year, when they actually calculate and pay their taxes using the new tax rates. If the bill authorizes the government to increase spending by a certain amount, then the government has to find ways of doing it. For instance, the government has to draw up plans and hire contractors to build roads or bridges. All these delays in implementing the new bill result in what is called the *implementation lag*.

President Barack Obama signing the Helping Families Save Their Homes Act and the Fraud Enforcement and Recovery Act in May 2009. The recession was already well under way when this legislation was enacted.

Because of all these lags, the government does not use fiscal policy very frequently. That was a reason for the emphasis on monetary policy in this book. As you might imagine, the lags are not only long, but also variable. In one recession, it may take four months for government spending to increase following an initial decision, and in another it may take two years. For this reason, it becomes very difficult to predict the timing of fiscal policy. The government may implement an expansionary fiscal policy that only starts to affect the GDP after the recession is already over. Such a policy would actually destabilize the economy.

Finally, as we have seen repeatedly in this book, an expansionary fiscal policy might crowd out private spending, especially in the long run. However, the effect of crowding out on the economy would depend on the circumstances. For example, if in a recession the level of private spending is low in the first place, then a temporary increase in government spending to get the economy out of the recession may not crowd out any private spending. Moreover, to the extent that the government spending results in an increase in productive social capital—such as roads, bridges, and schools—then private investment may actually increase in the future, because of these new economic infrastructures.

PROBLEMS WITH BUDGET DEFICITS

Is it bad for the government to run budget deficits? Some argue that in the same way a household should not spend too much beyond its means, a government should try to spend amounts close to its tax revenues. A government, though, is different from a household: While a household may default on its loans, the chances of a government doing so are slim. The government has the power to tax people and pay its debts in the future. This is not to say that governments never go bankrupt. If a government borrows excessively, then at some point it might have so much debt on its hand that it cannot be repaid by normal amounts of tax increases.

How about moderate amounts of deficits and debts? Since future generations need to be taxed to pay for the debt, some people argue that they bear the burden of the debt incurred by current generations. This argument, however, does not stand up to close scrutiny. In the future, one group of citizens will be taxed to pay another group, so that the nation as a whole will not bear any burden.

It is nevertheless true that future generations may suffer from the deficits incurred by present governments. You already know the argument, which is called crowding out. If government spending exceeds its tax revenues, it must borrow in the bond market to cover its deficit. This will put an upward pressure on the real interest rate, reducing investment spending by the private sector. Because of this, future generations receive smaller amounts of capital stock such as factories, machines, and equipment. This reduces the productivity and well-being of future generations.

This argument should be countered by observing that some of the government's spending goes toward construction of productive physical public capital such as roads, bridges, and schools. If, for example, the government borrows at 10 percent from the public to build the social capital—and the rate of return on the capital is 25 percent—then the overall well-being of the nation will increase over time. The problem will arise when the government wastes the borrowed funds in unproductive endeavors.

Should we propose a law mandating that the government continually balance the budget on a yearly basis? Even though this question arises periodically in the political arena, not many economists like the idea. The problem with this proposal is that it will exacerbate fluctuations in the GDP. Suppose, for example, that the economy slips into a recession. We know that the budget will move into deficit because of the effect of automatic stabilizers. Now if the government tries to balance the budget, it will either have to reduce spending, or increase taxes. Both of these policies will reduce aggregate demand, further reducing GDP and making the recession worse.

CAN DEFICITS CAUSE INFLATION?

You might hear a lot in media commentaries that government budget deficits would cause inflation somewhere down the road. Can deficits cause inflation? Well, it depends. We saw in Chapter 15 that a once-and-for-all government policy cannot cause inflation. Suppose the Treasury wants to increase spending by $100 million to boost aggregate demand, without raising taxes. It has to borrow this money from the public by issuing and selling bonds. This expansionary fiscal policy will increase aggregate demand and the level of prices, but it will not cause a sustained inflation. As you recall, inflation is a monetary phenomenon. Only continuous increases in the money supply can cause inflation. In this case, the money supply does not increase. The government borrows $100 billion from the public, and returns it to the public through the purchase of goods and services.

Now consider a different scenario. Suppose the Treasury borrows $100 billion every year to finance its expenditures. This increases the national debt, and people accumulate a lot of government bonds over time. Suppose that, to keep the national debt from increasing, the Fed enters the market and buys $100 billion worth of government bonds every year. This open-market purchase will increase the amount of excess reserves in the banking system by $100 billion, and the money supply will increase. Now *this* will cause inflation. Such purchasing of government debt by the Fed is called *monetizing the debt*. In a sense the government is printing money—$100 billion each year—to pay for its expenditures, but indirectly.

MONETIZING THE DEBT
The purchase of the bonds by the Fed that the Treasury has sold to the public to finance the government's budget deficit. It is effectively printing money to finance the deficit.

This is the reason why some developing countries experience huge inflations. In these countries, bond markets are not well developed, and people may not trust their governments to pay back the loans. Moreover, the governments may not be able to collect taxes for two reasons. First, people may be so poor that they cannot afford to pay taxes. Second, the governments do not have the experience or the institutions to collect taxes. Therefore, the only way open for them to spend money on their economic development projects (and keep their workers employed) is to just print money. And this causes inflation.

If you think about it, inflation caused by printing money is a form of taxation. Since in such environments prices rise faster than people's incomes, the purchasing power of people's incomes (their real income) is eroded over time. They can buy fewer goods and services over time due to inflation, so that the government can buy more goods and services through printing money. So in

INFLATION TAX
A reduction in purchasing power as a result of inflation.

a sense the government taxes away their real incomes, and spends it on development projects. This erosion in people's purchasing power caused by inflation is called the *inflation tax*.

IS DEFICIT SPENDING EXPANSIONARY?

This question sounds a bit weird, especially since we have always talked of an increase in government spending as an expansionary fiscal policy. You have seen one aspect of this argument in Chapter 11, where we talked about the crowding-out effect of deficit spending by the government. If the government increases spending without increasing taxes, it has to borrow money to pay for it. This increases the real interest rate, and crowds out consumption and investment spending. So aggregate demand may not increase at all.

RICARDIAN EQUIVALENCE
The idea that a deficit-financed increase in government spending would not be expansionary because people would expect the government to raise taxes in the future to pay off its debt. This would reduce the expected future disposable income, and hence current consumption.

Some economists put forward an argument indicating a deficit spending by the government will have no effect on aggregate demand. This argument is called the *Ricardian equivalence*. Suppose the government borrows $100 million to finance a bridge construction project. The government must pay back this money, plus interest, in the future. Where does the government bring the money to pay for all this in the future? You know the answer: it has to tax people. As I said in Chapter 11, all government expenditures are ultimately financed through taxes. In the case of a balanced budget increase in spending, taxes increase at the time of the increase in spending. In the case of deficit financing, taxes increase in the future to pay off the debt. We also know that even printing money is a form of taxation.

Now people will realize that the government will tax them in the future to pay off its debt. They will thus predict a reduction in their future disposable incomes. As we know from Chapter 7, this will cause a reduction in their current consumption. This is perhaps because they will save more today to make up for the deficiency in their future income, or just to set aside money to pay for the expected increase in future taxes. Many economists are skeptical of the relevance of this argument in the real world. They argue that most people may not be sophisticated and farsighted enough to relate a current increase in government spending to a possible future increase in taxes. Further, at least some of the taxes will be collected far in the future from generations yet to come, and not from the current generation lending money to the government. This dulls people's incentives to reduce their current consumption in order to pay the future taxes. Therefore, these economists argue, deficit spending is expansionary.

TO SUMMARIZE

1. Fiscal policy refers to deliberate increases or decreases in government spending or taxes, in order to achieve a particular macroeconomic goal.
2. Built-in *automatic stabilizers* in the government's taxes and expenditures cause spending to increase and taxes to decrease in a recession. The opposite happens in an expansion.
3. By contrast, *discretionary fiscal policy* is the deliberate act of changing government spending or taxes to achieve some macroeconomic objective, such as full employment.
4. A *budget surplus* is the excess of the government's tax revenues over its expenditures.
5. National debt is the accumulation of *budget deficits*.
6. The *full-employment budget* surplus or deficit measures the effects of deliberate changes in government taxes and spending on the budget. It eliminates the effects of automatic stabilizers. It is also called the cyclically adjusted budget surplus or deficit.
7. There are three main problems with fiscal policy: (1) It is inflexible; (2) it involves long and variable lags; and (3) it can crowd out private spending.
8. The main problem with budget deficits is their crowding-out effect. However, this problem is mitigated by the fact that some of the government's spending goes toward construction of productive physical capital.
9. Supply-side economists argue that lower taxes provide incentives for individuals to work harder and longer, and for firms to increase their investment spending. This policy would increase output and reduce inflation rate.
10. There is disagreement among economists as to the magnitude of the effects of supply-side policies.

EXERCISES

Question 1

Assume the following magnitudes:

$T_0 = 220$
$G_0 = 50$
$R_0 = 200$
$t = 0.20$
$h = 0.10$

a. Write down the budget function using the above magnitudes, then graph it.
b. At what level of GDP would the budget balance?
c. Suppose that currently, the real GDP equals potential and $Y_P = 80$. Calculate the full-employment budget surplus or deficit.
d. Suppose that the real GDP drops to $Y = 70$. Calculate the actual and full-employment budget surplus or deficit.
e. Suppose instead that the government increases its spending to $G_0 = 60$, and as a result, the real GDP increases to $Y = 120$. Calculate the actual and full-employment budget surplus or deficit.

f. Suppose instead that the government increases the tax rate to t = 0.30. Calculate the full-employment budget surplus or deficit.

Question 2

Suppose that a balanced-budget amendment is passed and the government must balance the budget every year. What will happen to aggregate demand in a recession and in an expansion?

CHAPTER 21

Epilogue: Macroeconomic Policy in a Recession

INTRODUCTION AND REVIEW

KEYNES WROTE DURING the Great Depression, and the macroeconomic issues he analyzed pertained to such an economic environment. After the Second World War—which, by the way, some economists like Paul Krugman believe to be *the* "fiscal policy" to end the Great Depression—Western economies generally experienced full employment, with occasional short-lived recessions. You have seen the empirical evidence of this in Chapter 6. For this reason, economists mostly turned their attention to the analyses of why economies might deviate from the full-employment path, and how—and why—they return to it. Again, you have seen examples of such analyses in this book.

The economy can slip into a recession due to either a demand or a supply shock. A demand shock could be the result of a loss in consumer confidence, producer pessimism, or an unexpected reduction in money supply. A supply shock could be the result of an unexpected exogenous increase in oil prices. In either case, the real GDP decreases below the potential GDP, and unemployment increases. The real GDP, however, moves back to the potential level through the self-correcting mechanism. The idea behind the self-correcting mechanism is that in a recession, real resource prices (such as real wages) decline, leading to an increase in employment, ultimately ending the recession.

A question of considerable importance is whether or not the government should conduct any active demand management policy, such as an expansionary monetary or fiscal policy, during a recession. Economists have analyzed these questions at length and in depth, as you have witnessed in this book. You have also noticed that most of these analyses assumed normal conditions and the general equilibrium of the economy. For example, starting from a situation of full-employment equilibrium, an increase in the money supply ultimately only affects the nominal variables such as wages and prices, with no effect on real variables such as real GDP or employment. Money was said to be neutral. Similarly, fiscal policies ultimately crowded out private spending "dollar-for-dollar," with no effect on real GDP and employment. Moreover, the rational expectations and real business-cycle models suggested that most macroeconomic policies were either ineffective or unnecessary.

The problem is that most of these conclusions, such as monetary neutrality or crowding out, are derived from the models assuming normal conditions. Some of those results may not apply to conditions of recession or stagflation. In fact, one might argue that normal conditions call for different types of policies with different goals. For example, they should concentrate on long-run stable inflation and real GDP growth rates. This chapter provides a summary, with some occasional extensions, of the arguments regarding the appropriateness and effectiveness of a macro policy in a recessionary environment. You have seen most of these arguments in this book. The last part of the chapter will deal with a problem we have mentioned several times in the book, without much in-depth analysis: deflation.

SHOULD WE CONDUCT *ANY* POLICY IN A RECESSION?

Both monetary and fiscal policies affect the level of output through their effects on aggregate demand. That is why these policies are called *demand management policies*. The following diagram shows the intended effects of expansionary monetary and fiscal policies.

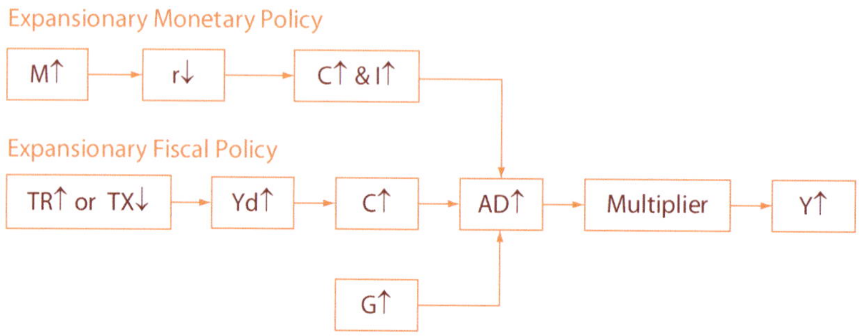

The opponents of conducting an expansionary demand management policy during a recession argue that the self-correcting mechanism inherent in a free market capitalist system will get the economy out of the recession. Low resource prices such as real wages would ultimately stimulate the hiring of workers and utilization of resources. Further, firms that are suffering from low demand will lay off workers and learn to be more efficient. As a result of this, the economy will come out of the recession stronger. Therefore, no policy is needed. And as we will see below, some polices could exacerbate the problem.

HYSTERESIS
The notion that cyclical unemployment could cause some workers to lose their skills, expertise, or work ethics—forever.

DEFLATION
A reduction in the general price level. Deflation results in negative inflation rates.

D
ISTRESS SALE
Selling assets at low prices to pay off debt. This usually happens during a deflationary period when firms are not able to raise enough revenue to service their debt. Distress sale of assets is one reason for ***deflation spiral****.*

Proponents of active policy point out that the self-correcting mechanism could take a long time, during which millions of people would be suffering, and unemployment would result in lost national output. In fact, part of the lost output could be permanent due to *hysteresis*, which is the notion that cyclical unemployment could cause some workers to lose their skills, expertise, or work ethics—forever. This permanent reduction in productivity could adversely affect the potential GDP for years to come. Additionally, the coordination failure due to sticky wages and prices could hamper the functioning of the self-correcting mechanism.

Then there is the issue of *deflation*, which many policy makers dread. Suppose prices start going down due to a lack of sufficient demand for goods and services. Besides having to lay off some workers, many firms may find it difficult to raise enough revenue to pay off their debts. The risk of bankruptcy would force these firms to sell some of their assets to raise cash for paying off their debts. This *distress sale* of assets would cause a further reduction in the general price level. A similar thing could happen to low-income households who have borrowed in the past to buy homes, cars, or appliances, and now find it difficult to pay back their loans due to a fall in their wages. They may have to sell some of their assets, such as their cars or even their homes, to service their debt. This puts further downward pressure on prices. Deflation begets deflation. This dreadful process is called a *deflation spiral*. This process may last for a long time. Japan experienced such a process during the 1990s, a period called *the lost decade*. The last part of this chapter analyzes this issue in more detail.

We now turn to more specific issues.

DEFLATION SPIRAL
A situation in which a deflation results in further deflation.

THE LOST DECADE
Refers to 1990s during which the Japanese economy was stagnant.

MONETARY POLICY

The Fed can increase the money supply in one of three ways:

a. Open market operations.
b. Changing the discount rate the it charges on its loans to member banks.
c. Changing the required reserve ratio.

All three affect the bank (excess) reserves, and the money supply increases through the bank lending process. Of the three, open market operations are the most widely used tool, because of their flexibility.

The United States House Financial Services Committee holding a hearing

Proponents of monetary policy argue that the money supply can increase quickly, and it is less intrusive. It can increase quickly, simply because the Fed does not need Congressional approval to conduct monetary policy. It is not intrusive, because all the Fed does is reduce the interest rate and let the private sector do the rest. It does not have any power to dictate to the private sector which firms should borrow and how much, and in what lines of business they should invest the borrowed funds. Similarly, monetary policy does not favor one industry over another. For this reason, politicians and special interests have no power to divert funds toward their own constituencies, or to achieve their own political objectives. So, monetary policy would preserve the efficiency of the private free market system.

Should we fear inflation? Inflation happens in the long run, as a result of a sustained increase in the money supply. The rate of inflation is, by and large, equal to the rate of growth of the money supply *in the long run*. However, in a recession, inflation is not generally a problem; it is *deflation* that worries policy makers. Moreover, we can temporarily increase the *level* of the money supply in a recession, without increasing the *rate of growth* of the money supply in the long run.

The opponents of monetary policy point out that, although the money supply could increase fairly quickly in a recession, it may take too long for it to take effect— and in fact, it may not even be effective. There are several reasons for this:

a. The interest rate will not fall if it is in the liquidity trap.
b. Banks may not be willing to lend due to uncertainty about the state of the economy.
c. Firms and households may not be willing to borrow. Firms may not have many profitable investment opportunities, and households could be uncertain about their future incomes.
d. As a result, consumption and investment may not be stimulated. Even if they do increase, the GDP may not increase much. This is because in a recession, marginal propensity to consume could be reduced, resulting in a reduction in the expenditure multiplier.

Note that it is not also true that monetary policy affects all industries evenly. Some industries are more strongly affected by interest rate changes than others. For instance, residential and commercial construction sectors are highly sensitive to changes in interest rates. Thus, monetary policy could drastically increase the demand for new construction, leaving the demand in some other industries totally intact.

FISCAL POLICY

Would you increase government spending or transfer payments, or reduce taxes to stimulate aggregate demand? Let's talk about these in turn.

Reduce Taxes (TX)

First off, for tax cuts to have their maximum effects, they should be permanent cuts in tax *rates*. In the real world, households and firms pay a fraction of their incomes to the government in taxes. That fraction is called the *tax rate*. Most economists believe that people plan their consumption expenditures ahead of time on the basis of their expected future disposable incomes (or permanent income). If a household's disposable income temporarily and unexpectedly increases, that household would choose to save the extra income in order to maintain its planned level of consumption. Similarly, if the household's disposable income temporarily and unexpectedly decreases, then it will draw on its past savings to prevent planned consumption from falling.

TAX RATE
The percentage of income taxed.

For these reasons, economists believe that a one-time reduction in taxes, such as a one-time tax rebate, would only affect a household's current disposable income. As such, it would not have much effect on a household's consumption. However, a permanent reduction in the tax rate will affect not only the current disposable income, but also the expected future levels of disposable income. Consequently, households will increase their planned consumption levels.

Some economists favor a tax reduction over an increase in government spending. Cutting taxes puts some extra money in the pocket of the private sector. This has several advantages. First, the decision makers in the private sector—firms and households—decide how to spend that extra money, and not the government. Since the private sector is generally more efficient, there will be less wastage in spending this money. Second, the government will not get big, and we won't need extra layers of bureaucracy to decide how to increase the government spending. Finally, politicians and special interests will not have too much say in the matter. If the government instead decided to increase spending, then California senators would want most of the money to be spent in California, and Arizona senators in Arizona. The airline industry would want a big chunk of the money to be apportioned to this industry as subsidies; and the teachers' unions would push for more high-tech equipment in classrooms.

A college computer lab

As counterarguments, realize that the above theories generally pertain to normal times, and may not carry to a recessionary environment. In a recession, even a permanent reduction in tax rates may not have much effect on aggregate demand. To begin with, the unemployed and other low-income households have very low disposable incomes, so that a lot of them are not taxable. Therefore, a reduction in tax rates will not affect their disposable income and consumption. Tax cuts will increase the disposable incomes of higher-income households. However, these households may have a small marginal propensity to consume, and hence save most of the resulting increase in their disposable incomes. Next, even those who are employed may not be sure if they will be able to keep their jobs in the future. Therefore, they may as well choose to save any additional disposable income brought about by a permanent cut in the tax rate for the future rainy days. Knowing that in the future you will pay a smaller fraction of your income in taxes may not be a consolation to you if you fear you may not have a job in the future—and therefore no income to speak of in the first place.

Finally, tax cuts could actually be quite politically charged. There are also a lot of distributional issues to consider. Whose taxes are you going to cut? Is this going to be a uniform 1% reduction across the board, or is it going to be a middle-income tax cut? Or, why don't you increase the tax rates on the rich and reduce them on the poor, in such a way as to keep the total tax revenue unchanged? What is the advantage of this? Well, if the rich have a small MPC and the poor a large MPC, then this policy could increase consumption and aggregate demand. As you can see, a lot of questions should be addressed. Besides that, the tax cuts should be approved by the Congress.

Increase Transfer Payments (TR)

Since an increase in transfer payments would increase disposable income, in the face of it the effect of this policy would be similar to that of a reduction in taxes. In the real world, though, there are differences between the two. On the positive side, an increase in transfer payments could be more expansionary than an equal reduction in taxes. This is because these payments are generally made to low-income households in the form of food stamps, unemployment, or welfare benefits. Since these households generally have a large marginal propensity to consume, such a policy could significantly affect the aggregate demand.

On the negative side, the opponents of such policies argue that such transfer payments during a recession would dull the incentives of these households to actively look for jobs. Moreover, in some cases, a household may find a job but reject it, because by accepting the job it may lose the food stamps or unemployment benefits it receives. If the unemployed person sees the combined benefit of receiving the food stamps and staying home greater than that of working and receiving wages in the new job, then that person would reject the job. Therefore, transfer payments may well prolong the unemployment problem.

Increase Spending (G)

The government can increase spending in three different ways:

a. Balanced budget increase: Finance the increase in spending by raising an equal amount of taxes. This will not increase the budget deficit.
b. Deficit spending: Borrow money from the private sector to finance the increase in spending. This will result in an increase in budget deficit.
c. Printing money: In the United States, this is done through *monetizing the debt.* This means the Treasury sells bonds (borrows) to raise money to finance government spending. Then the Fed conducts an open market purchase. buying those bonds and injecting money into the economy. In a sense. the government prints money to finance its spending.

Opponents of fiscal policy raise several issues. A balanced budget increase in spending could be quite ineffective, for the following reason. Suppose the government taxes you $100 and spends it on goods and services. Assume that your MPC is 0.80, like everyone else's in the economy, so that the expenditure multiplier is 5. When the government increases spending by $100, the GDP increases by $500. However, you have lost $100 of income, of which you would have consumed $80 and saved $20. Therefore, your consumption goes down by $80, resulting in a $400 reduction in GDP through the multiplier process. So the GDP increases by only $100, net (this is the good old unit multiplier story). Note that you also lose $20 of savings that you would have deposited in a bank, which someone else would have borrowed to invest in plants and equipment. So not only would consumption go down, but investment spending would also go down—so the actual multiplier could be even less than one!

As we have learned in previous chapters, deficit spending would reduce the amount of loanable funds for the private sector, and this would crowd out private spending. As a result, the private sector will shrink and the government sector will get bigger over time. This has two adverse effects on the economy. First, since the government is generally less efficient than the private sector, bigger governments would result in greater inefficiencies and lower national output over time. Second, the crowding out of the private investment means that less capital goods will be produced for future generations. Hence, they will suffer lower standards of living.

Finally, spending by printing money will ultimately cause inflation. This is mostly the way governments of third world countries conduct fiscal policy, because they don't have well functioning bond markets; they cannot borrow from the private sector. Further, they cannot collect sufficient taxes due to low incomes. So the only way to increase government spending is through printing money. Inflation acts like a tax on fixed income people. As the government spends more and prices increase, these households afford buying fewer and fewer goods over time, because of the erosion in the purchasing power of their incomes. So even printing money would crowd out private spending.

Therefore, according to the opponents of fiscal policy, no matter how you finance the increase in government spending, an expansionary fiscal policy would crowd out private spending, with adverse consequences for future generations. On top of this, we have the problem of long, variable, and unpredictable lags in the effects of fiscal policy on real GDP. First, there is a *recognition lag*: it takes time for the government to recognize and officially acknowledge that a recession has begun. Second, there is the *decision lag*: now that we are officially in a recession, what are we supposed to do? Do nothing, increase money supply, cut taxes, or increase spending? Suppose we decide to increase spending on roads and bridges. We then have the *legislative lag*: the time it takes the Congress to study our spending proposal, understand it, and approve it. We finally have the *implementation lag*: the time it takes to actually start the work on roads and bridges.

These lags are long, but also variable, and therefore unpredictable. In one recession, it may take only four months from the time we recognize that we are in a recession to the time we actually start work on roads and bridges; in another, it may take eight months. What is the impact of these lags on the effectiveness of fiscal policy? This is simple to understand. Suppose without any policy, the self-correcting mechanism would get us out of a recession in one year. Suppose also that the sum of all the lags is one year. So our fiscal policy will start to take effect exactly when the economy would turn around by itself. The two effects (lagged fiscal policy effect and self-correcting mechanism) would cause the real GDP to increase faster than without any policy, making real GDP more volatile and exacerbating business cycles.

The proponents of an active fiscal policy have several responses to these arguments. On the issue of crowding out, they argue that this is a problem pertinent to normal times. In other words, in a macroeconomic model. if we start from the point of general equilibrium with full employment and increase government spending, then in the long run the private spending will be crowded out. This is because the productive capacity of the economy is more or less constant. If the government buys more goods and services, the economy will not be able to increase production by the amount of the increase in the government spending. As such, less will be left for the private sector to buy. But this argument does not carry over to a recessionary environment, in which there is plenty of unemployment and excess productive capacity. In a recession, an increase in government spending can be accomplished by hiring those unemployed resources, without reducing the amount of goods and services purchased by firms and households. Moreover, in a recession there would not be much investment or consumption going on by business firms and households. So there would not be much private spending to be crowded out in the first place.

President Barack Obama, with Assembly Manager Teri Quigley, drives a new Chevy Volt, during his tour of the General Motors Auto Plant in Hamtramck, Michigan, July, 2010.

The effect of lags on fiscal policy may not be as bad as claimed. In particular, once the Congress approves the spending bill, households and firms become certain about the future increase in government spending. As a result, they expect higher disposable incomes and greater profits in the future. This results in an increase in current consumption and investment, as we know by now.

Finally, the government has the flexibility to spend the money on any industry, or in any region it deems most beneficial for the economy. For example, it may spend some of the money in areas that have been hardest hit by the recession. Another portion of the money may be spent on industries that are vital for the economy and are strongly suffering from the lack of demand. For instance, in the 2007–2008 recession, the government tried hard to keep General Motors Corporation from going bankrupt. That is because the collapse of GM would cause huge unemployment. Not only would workers at GM lose their jobs, but dealers selling the GM cars and factories making GM parts and components would go bankrupt, adding to the mass of the unemployed. This was a motivation for the Obama administration's "Cash for Clunkers" policy: provide up to $4,500 to anyone who trades his or her clunker for a new, fuel-efficient car.

Note finally that as is usual in such cases of discretionary targeted spending, politicians and special interests could divert the funds from socially desirable investments to wasteful activities. Every legislator would want to add pork to the bill benefiting his or her own constituencies.

DREADFUL DEFLATION

This section will discuss the problem of deflation. *Deflation* means a fall in the general price level resulting in negative inflation. To begin with, like inflation, an anticipated deflation is not that harmful, because people incorporate it into their contracts. It is generally the *un*anticipated deflation that becomes a problem. The effect of unanticipated deflation on lenders and borrowers is very similar to the effect of unanticipated inflation on these people. So I won't repeat that discussion here. An important aspect of deflation is what is called *debt deflation*. There are two views on this issue.

DEFLATION
A reduction in the general price level. Deflation results in negative inflation rates.

DEBT DEFLATION
The increase in the burden of debt for a borrower as the result of a reduction in the general price level.

Debt Deflation and Distressed Asset Sale

The American economist Irving Fisher advanced the first argument on this around 1930. When firms and households borrow money to buy fixed assets, they pay back the principal and interest of their loans through a series of fixed periodic payments. For example, a farmer borrows $500,000 from a bank for 10 years to buy the adjacent lot and some farming equipment. Every year for the next 10 years, he will pay back $80,000 to the bank. So in 10 years he will pay off the whole principal loan amount of $500,000, plus $800,000 in interest. Now when the prices of goods and services fall (including the price of wheat this farmer is producing), he won't be able to raise enough revenue to make the periodic payments. In that case, one of two scenarios will take place: In the first scenario, he will go bankrupt. The bank will take over the farm and the farming equipment and sell them to recover its money. If many such foreclosed farms and farming equipment come to the market by such banks, the prices of these assets will decline, creating more deflation. Deflation will beget deflation. This chain effect is called *deflation spiral*.

DEFLATION SPIRAL
A situation in which a deflation results in further deflation.

In the second scenario, to avoid bankruptcy, the farmer would sell some of the equipment he has and use the money to pay the bank. Moreover, he will lay off some of his workers to free some money to service his debt. This distress sale of the assets will depress their prices, creating more deflation. Furthermore, the resulting unemployment will reduce the demand for goods and services, pushing down the prices even further. So under this scenario, deflation again will lead to further deflation.

Note that if the farmer and the bank had anticipated this deflation when they were signing the loan contract, they would have made some arrangements to confront it. Perhaps the farmer would have asked for a lower interest rate, taken out a smaller loan, or would have avoided the loan altogether. So it is the unanticipated deflation that causes damage.

The counterargument to Fisher's argument is that deflation will also benefit some people in the society, such as lenders and fixed-income households. So the losses incurred by some may be netted out by the gains enjoyed by others—the society as a whole may come out even. For example, the purchasing power of fixed-income households will increase due to lower prices, and they will buy more goods and services. To produce the additional goods and services, business firms will hire more labor. So the overall employment may not be affected.

A similar thing happens in the mortgage markets. To make the story simple, suppose Brendan has borrowed $1 million from a bank to buy a house. The house is the collateral with the bank. After a few years, prices decline and Brendan's home is now worth only $0.5 million. What is he going to do? It is foolish to pay one million dollars plus interest for something that is worth only half of that. If he sells the house, he won't be able to pay back the bank. So he defaults on his loan and walks away from the house. Now that home prices are low, he tries to buy another lower-price house. The bank forecloses on the house and brings it to the market. These additional supplies of foreclosed homes further depress home prices. This is similar to the farmer's equipment sale. So deflation could cause further deflation.

Again, the rebuttal is that there are some other people in the society who can afford buying homes now that their prices are lower. So again, the housing market and the economy as a whole may come out even. Recently, though, economists have come up with a different line of argument, which implies that deflation may in fact impose a net cost on the society.

Debt Deflation and Agency Problem

Suppose a farmer borrows $1 million dollars from First Bank, and buys a farm and some equipment worth $1 million. After a few years, the value of the farm and the equipment (the assets) goes down to $0.50 million due to a recession-induced deflation. So the farmer owns assets worth only $0.50 million, but owes $1 million. He has an incentive to abandon the farm and walk away (perhaps in the hope of buying a cheaper farm). He would not be willing to pay one million dollars plus interest for something that is worth only a half million dollars. He has no stakes in the farm, the whole thing is owned by First Bank. In this case, other banks would not be willing to lend him any money, for two interrelated reasons.

In the first place, suppose Second Bank is foolish enough to lend our farmer some money. He works hard in good faith to produce wheat to maximize his profit and pay back the loans. But what if he does not succeed? Then Second Bank will take over the farm to sell it. But if it does sell the farm, it will make about $0.50 million from the sale and has to pay about $1 million to First Bank! So Second Bank will come out a total loser. For this reason, no bank would lend money to any firm whose liabilities exceed their assets.

Second, knowing that the farmer does not have anything to lose if he walks away, the farmer can get engaged in risky investments. Who cares that he might go bankrupt, he was about to abandon the farm anyway. Moreover, such firms are more likely to borrow money for risky investment. This is because they have nothing to lose if the investment goes sour. So during a deflationary period, the percentage of high-risk borrowers increases. Knowing this problem, lenders will not lend to our farmer. Even though he might have a bright future and some brilliant investment ideas, he will not be able to get funds for investment. Lenders will not be able to tell the high-risk investors from the low-risk ones. Since the percentage of high-risk investors has increased due to deflation, there is a higher probability that the borrower will be high-risk. To be cautious, therefore, lenders will reject most of the loan applications and/or increase their lending standards. Investment spending will go down in the economy, resulting in lower GDP and higher unemployment.

GLOSSARY

A

Absolute purchasing power parity (PPP) condition: The theory that the exchange rate between the currencies of two countries equals the ratio of the countries' price levels.

Adverse supply shock: Any event that results in higher prices and lower quantities supplied with the given demand conditions.

Aggregate demand: The sum of planned purchases by households, firms, the government, and foreigners.

Aggregate demand function: The combinations of the price and GDP levels that equilibrate (clear) the goods and money markets.

Aggregate expenditure function: The same as aggregate demand function.

Aggregate level of output: The sum total of all the goods and services produced in a country.

Allocative efficiency: Allocating the society's scarce resources to different economic activities in such a way as to produce the kinds and quantities of goods and services that result in maximum satisfaction for the members of the society. See also *economic efficiency* and *Pareto efficiency*.

Appreciation: The increase in the market price or value of any good or asset. See also currency appreciation.

Asset: Anything that has value because it will bring some benefits to its owner in the future.

Asymmetric information: A situation in which a party to a transaction knows more about the subject of the transaction than the other party

Automatic stabilizers: Factors that automatically cause the aggregate demand to increase (or at least not to decrease) in a recession, without any expansionary demand-management policy. Automatic stabilizers act in the opposite direction in an expansion.

Autonomous variable: A variable that does not depend on the real GDP.

Average labor productivity: The amount of output produced by a unit of labor.

B

Balanced-budget increase: An increase in government spending that is financed by an equal increase in taxes.

Barter system: An economic system without money.

Bonds: Also called IOUs. Financial instruments that are issued by an individual, a firm, or a government when borrowing money. They promise to pay predetermined and fixed amounts of money in the future.

Budget deficit: The amount by which a government's expenditures exceed its tax revenues during a certain period of time.

Budget surplus: The amount by which a government's tax revenues exceed its expenditures during a certain period of time.

Business cycles: Ups and downs in real GDP.

C

Cambridge k: The ratio of money supply to nominal GDP. Cambridge economists believed that this ratio is constant.
Capital account: A subaccount that records transactions in assets of the balance of payments of a country.
Capital account deficit: The amount by which capital outflows exceed capital inflows in a country's capital account of the balance of payments.
Capital account surplus: The amount by which capital inflows exceed capital outflows in a country's capital account of the balance of payments.
Capital gain: An asset owner makes a capital gain if the asset sells for a price higher than the purchase price.
Capital inflow: The amount of money that a country receives from foreigners—money flows in—from the sale of assets to them.
Capital loss: An asset owner makes a capital loss if the asset sells for a price lower than the purchase price.
Capital outflow: The amount of money that a country pays foreigners—money flows out—for buying their assets.
Ceteris paribus: A Latin phrase meaning all else the same.
Chain-weighted growth rates: Calculating the growth rates in the real GDP by moving the base year forward one year at a time and calculating the growth rates as the geometric average of the two adjacent growth rates.
Change in demand: A shift in the demand curve.
Change in quantity demanded: A movement along the demand curve resulting from a change in price.
Change in quantity supplied: A movement along the supply curve resulting from a change in price.
Change in supply: A shift in the supply curve.
Circular flow diagram: A diagram showing the flow of funds between the goods and factor markets.
Civilian noninstitutional population: Civilian population for short; includes persons 16 years of age and older who are not inmates of institutions such as penal and mental facilities or homes for the elderly, and are not members of the armed forces.
Classical aggregate supply function: The function that gives the combinations of price level and real GDP that clear the labor market.
Classical economists: The economists who wrote before John Maynard Keynes, and the present day economists who make similar assumptions and reach similar conclusions.
Classical model: A macroeconomic model, in which nominal wages and prices are fully flexible, so that we always have full employment; the velocity of circulation is constant so that the rate of price inflation equals the money supply growth rate; and the government spending crowds out private spending.
Closed economy: An economy that closes its doors to international trade
Commodity money: Objects like gold, silver, salt, or dried fish that some societies use as a medium of exchange. They have other uses besides being money, and therefore have some intrinsic value.
Complements: Goods consumers consume together, so when they consume more of one, they will also consume more of the other.
Consumer Price Index: A price index that is calculated by valuing a basket of goods purchased by an average household in 1984, using current prices.
Consumption: The aggregate amount of goods and services consumed by households.
Consumption function: A function relating aggregate consumption to its determinants such as disposable income.
Contractionary fiscal policy: A reduction in government spending and/or an increase in taxes aimed at reducing the level of aggregate demand for goods and services (in order to reduce inflationary pressures).
Contractionary monetary policy: A reduction in money supply aimed at increasing the interest rate and reducing the level of aggregate demand for goods and services (to reduce inflationary pressures).
Coordination failure: In reference to unemployment, it is the circular problem that the unemployed do not have enough income to buy sufficient amounts of goods and services; therefore, firms cannot hire them because they are not able to sell sufficient amounts.
Coordination problem: The notion that producers cannot coordinate their pricing policies. A producer is hesitant to raise its price, fearing that others will not follow suit and it will lose sales. The producer is also hesitant to reduce its price, thinking that others will follow suit and it will not gain any advantage from doing that.
Cost-of-living adjustment (COLA): Increases in wages by employers to adjust for increases in prices.
Countercyclical variables: Variables that move against the GDP.
Coupon bonds: Bonds that have maturities longer than one year and make periodic payments called coupon payments every year, or every six months.
Coupon payments: See ***coupon bonds***.

Credibility in monetary policy: The notion that people believe that the Fed will act on its promises.

Credit crunch: A dramatic reduction in the supply of loanable funds due to a substantial increase in credit risk.

Credit risk: The chance that a borrower may not be able to pay back (a part) of his or her loan to the lender.

Crowding out: A reduction in private spending (investment and consumption) resulting from an increase in government spending. See also financial crowding out.

Currency appreciation: The increase in the price of a foreign currency.

Currency depreciation: The decrease in the price of a foreign currency.

Current account: A subaccount of the balance of payments of a country that records transactions in goods and services (exports and imports), those that are consumed in the "current period."

Current account balance: The difference between the dollar values of the exports in goods and services and the imports in goods and services in a country's balance f payments.

Current account deficit: The amount by which imports exceeds exports in a country's current account of the balance of payments.

Cyclical unemployment: Unemployment due to business cycles.

Cyclically adjusted deficit: A measure of the government budget deficit that removes the effects of automatic stabilizers on the budget. The result is a budget deficit that is solely the result of an active fiscal policy. It is also known as the full-employment deficit.

D

Debt deflation: The increase in the burden of debt for a borrower as the result of a reduction in the general price level.

Decision lag: The amount of time it takes for the government to decide on the appropriate course of action after determining that the economy is in a recession.

Decision-making unit: An economic unit such as a consumer, producer, employer, laborer, lender, or borrower that makes a decision with the goal of furthering an economic objective.
Deficient aggregate demand: The level of aggregate demand that is not sufficient to bring about full employment.

Deficit spending (or deficit financing): An increase in government spending financed through borrowing from the public.

Deficit spending units: Households, firms, or governments that spend more than they earn.

Deflation: A reduction in the general price level. Deflation results in negative inflation rates.

Deflation spiral: A situation in which a deflation results in further deflation.

Demand for labor: The amount of labor that firms are willing and able to hire at different real wages. It is the marginal product of labor.

Demand management policies: Fiscal and monetary policies.

Demand for money: The portion of their total wealth that people wish to hold in the form of money. In other words, it is the amount of money people are willing and able (their wealth permitting) to hold at any point.

Dependent variable: Variables whose values depend on the values of some other, independent variables.

Depreciation: The decrease in the market price or value of any good or asset. See also *currency depreciation*.

Direct finance: Raising cash directly by selling stocks or bonds to investors, bypassing financial institutions such as banks. See also *indirect finance*.

Discount bond: A bond that promises just one payment in the future, called face value. They sell at a discount relative to their face value, so that the buyer can earn an interest out of the difference.

Discount loan: The money the Fed lends to banks when they are short of cash to satisfy their depositors.

Discount rate: The interest rate that the Fed charges on its discount loans.

Discretionary fiscal policy: Changes in the government spending or taxes that are the results of the deliberate actions of the governments, rather than due to automatic stabilizers.

Disinflation: A reduction in the inflation rate.

Distress sale: Selling assets at low prices to pay off debt. This usually happens during a deflationary period when firms are not able to raise enough revenue to service their debt. Distress sale of assets is one reason for deflation spiral.

Dividends: The profits distributed to shareholders by a corporation.

Double coincidence of wants: Finding someone in a barter system who wants to buy what you want to sell, and who wants to sell what you want to buy.

Double-entry bookkeeping: The conventional accounting system followed in developing balances of payments, resulting in an equal amount of a debit (negative) item for each credit (positive) item.

E

Economic efficiency: The same as allocative efficiency. See also *Pareto efficiency*.

Economic growth: Sustained increase in the real GDP over a long period of time.

Economic policy: An action taken by the government to alter certain economic outcomes.

Efficiency wages: Wages paid by a firm that are above-equilibrium wages in order to improve productivity and increase productive efficiency.

Efficient markets hypothesis: Financial markets are said to be efficient in Fama's sense if asset prices fully reflect all the available relevant information.

Endogenous growth theory: A theory that posits that economic growth takes place because entrepreneurs, trying to maximize their profits, spend substantial amounts of resources on research and development activities in order to develop new products, or to find better ways of producing existing products.

Endogenous variables: Variables whose values are determined inside the model on the basis of the values of the other variables.

Energy efficiency: Use of less energy to produce the same amount of goods and services.

Equilibrium: A state of rest. If a system is in equilibrium, there are no tendencies on the part of anyone to change anything. For example, if the goods market is in equilibrium, producers will have no incentives to increase or decrease production.

Equilibrium GDP: The level of GDP that is equal to aggregate demand.

Equilibrium interest rate: The interest rate at which demand for money equals supply of money (in the liquidity preference theory), or demand for loanable funds equals supply of loanable funds (in the loanable-funds theory).

Equilibrium price: The price at which the supply of a good equals demand.

Equilibrium quantity: The quantity at which the supply of a good equals demand.

Ex-ante real interest rate: Nominal interest rate minus the expected inflation rate.

Excess demand: A situation in which the quantity demanded exceeds the quantity supplied because actual price is below the equilibrium price. Also called shortage.

Excess reserves: Reserves held by banks in excess of what is required by law.

Excess supply: A situation in which the quantity supplied exceeds the quantity demanded, because actual price is above the equilibrium price. Also called surplus.

Exogenous variables: Variables whose values are determined outside the model by factors other than the endogenous variables, and are therefore known to the analyst.

Expansion: The phase of a business cycle in which the GDP is increasing.

Expansionary fiscal policy: An increase in government spending and/or a decrease in taxes, aimed at increasing the level of aggregate demand for goods and services (in order to reduce unemployment).

Expansionary monetary policy: An increase in the money supply aimed at reducing the interest rate and increasing the level of aggregate demand for goods and services (in order to reduce unemployment).

Expenditure multiplier: A factor by which GDP would increase as a result of an increase in aggregate expenditure.

Exports: Amount of goods and services sold to foreigners.

Ex-post real interest rate: Nominal interest rate minus the actual inflation rate.

F

Face value: The amount written on the face of a bond that the lender promises to pay in the future. It is also called final value.

Factor income: Income received by factors of production.

Factor market: The market, such as the labor market, in which firms demand production factors, and households supply these resources to the firms.

Factors of production: Resources that are used to produce goods and services: labor, land, and capital.

Fallacy of composition: The notion that what is true for one individual may not be true for the sum of all the individuals.

Federal funds market: The market in which banks borrow from each other overnight.

Federal funds rate: The interest rate banks charge on the loans borrowed in the federal funds market.

Federal Reserve System: The U.S. central bank in charge of conducting monetary policy, and seeing that the financial markets function smoothly.

Fiat money: Any object that has no intrinsic value, but is used as a means of payment by a government's order (fiat).

Final goods: Goods purchased by final consumers or users.

Final value: See *face value*.

Financial crowding out: Reduction in private spending as a result of an increase in the interest rate that itself is the result of an increase in the government budget deficit.

Financial institutions: Institutions that help channel funds from those who have to those who need.

Financial intermediaries: Same as financial institutions.

Financial markets: The market in which the deficit group (those who spend more than what they earn) would obtain the needed money from the surplus group directly.

Financial system: The combination of financial markets and financial institutions.

Fiscal policy: A change in government spending (G), taxes (TX), or transfer payments (TR) to change the state of the economy; especially, the real GDP or the unemployment rate.

Fisher Effect: The increase in the interest rate, as a result of an increase in the expected inflation.

Fixed exchange rate system: An exchange rate system in which governments of different countries keep exchange rates fixed, by standing ready to buy and sell foreign currencies at fixed, previously agreed upon prices.

Flexible exchange rate system: An exchange rate system in which exchange rates are determined by the free interplay of demands and supplies for currencies.

Flow variable: A variable that requires a time period to describe or measure its magnitude.

Foreign exchange market: A market in which foreign currencies are traded.

Foreign exchange rate: This is the amount of units of a domestic currency that the residents of a country must pay to buy one unit of a foreign currency.

Frictional unemployment: Unemployment that is due to frictions in the labor market. It is the result of the fact that it takes time to find jobs. In the case of frictional unemployment, there are enough jobs available for the unemployed.

Full employment: The situation in which the number of jobs available equals the labor force—those willing and able to work. Therefore, full employment means zero cyclical unemployment.

Full-employment budget deficit: See *cyclically adjusted budget deficit*.

Fully loaned out: A situation in which banks have loaned out all their excess reserves.

Future value: See *face value* and *final value*.

G

GDP deflator: An index of general price level calculated as Nominal GDP / Real GDP.

GDP gap: The amount by which the actual GDP falls short of the potential GDP.

GDP per capita: Real GDP divided by population.

General equilibrium: A situation in which all three markets—goods, money, and labor—are in equilibrium.

General price level: An index of the average of the prices of all the goods and services produced in the country. See also *GDP deflator*.

Goods market equilibrium: A situation in which demand for goods and services equals supply, so that there are no tendencies on the part of market participants to change their prices or quantities.

Goods and services market: A market in which business firms produce and supply goods and services to the market, and households buy them.

Government intervention: Generally, this refers to any government interference in a market. Specifically, it refers to a government's buying and selling of currencies in the foreign exchange market to smooth out the fluctuations in exchange rates.

Government spending: Purchase of goods and services by the government.

Great Depression: A prolonged recession in the 1930s in the United States.

Gross domestic product: The total market value of all the goods and services produced by the factors of production located in a country, except those produced by households for household consumption.

Growth rate: Percentage increase in the value of a variable. In economics, it usually refers to the rate of increase in the real GDP.

H

Historic costs: One-time costs that have occurred in the past and cannot be recovered. Also called sunk costs.

Human capital: All the knowledge, skills, and expertise acquired and possessed by an individual.

Hysteresis: The notion that cyclical unemployment could cause some workers to lose their skills, expertise, or work ethics—forever.

I

Implementation lag: All the delays in implementing a new policy.

Incentive: A desire to take an action by a decision maker to gain benefits or to avoid costs.

Income effect: In the case of a consumer: When the price of a good goes down, it is as if the consumer's income has increased. In the case of a worker: When the wage rate increases, the worker may decide to supply less labor, because now she can earn the same income as before by working fewer hours.

Independent variable: A variable whose values drive the values of another variable called the depended variable.

Indirect finance: This is when some people deposit their excess money in a financial institution such as a bank, a credit union, or a pension fund. Then, other people who need money borrow it from the financial institution. See also *direct finance*.

Industry: A collection of firms that produces the same or similar products.

Inferior good: A good that we buy less of if our income rises.

Inflation rate: The rate of increase in the overall price level.

Inflation targeting: A central bank policy aimed at keeping the inflation rate steady and close to a pre-announced target rate.

Inflation tax: A reduction in purchasing power as a result of inflation.

Inflationary expectations: Expectations about the future inflation rates.

Inside assets: Assets for which there are an equal amount of liabilities within the private sector of the economy. For example, bonds issued by private citizens of a country to borrow money are inside assets. See also *outside assets*.

Interest parity condition: The situation where the interest differential between two countries equals the expected depreciation of the exchange rate between the two currencies.

Interest rate: The rate of return on bonds.

Intermediate goods: Goods that a firm buys from other firms and uses up in production within a production period.

International economics: The branch of economics dealing with international transactions in goods and assets.

International finance: The subfield of international economics that deals with the financial aspects of international transactions.

International trade: The subfield of international economics studying the causes and consequences of trade in goods and services

Inventories: The amounts of finished goods, semi-finished goods, or raw materials that a firm holds to sell or use in the future.

Investment: A planned increase in plants and equipment, residential buildings, and inventories.

J

Joint products: Two products such that, if the production of one increases, the production of the other also increases.

K

Knowledge capital: The sum total of all knowledge in a society.

L

Labor force: Those who are willing and able to work.

Labor force participation rate: The fraction of the population that is willing to work, calculated as the ratio of the labor force over population.

Law of demand: Keeping all the other determinants of demand constant, as the price of a good increases, consumers will be willing to buy a smaller quantity of the good.

Law of diminishing marginal product of labor: The same as the law of diminishing returns.

Law of diminishing returns: The idea that, given a fixed amount of capital, the marginal product of labor declines as the firm hires additional labor.

Law of supply: Keeping all the other determinants of supply constant, as the price of a good increases, producers will supply a larger quantity to the market.

Leaning against the wind: Conducting an expansionary demand management policy in a recession and a contractionary policy in an expansion.

Legal tender: Anything the government mandates to be accepted in repayment of loans and payment of taxes.

Legislative lag: The amount of time—several months, or even years—it may take for both houses of Congress to pass a bill approving a proposed fiscal policy initiative.

Lender of last resort: Whenever the Fed realizes that a bank is temporarily out of cash and in risk of bankruptcy, it may rescue that bank by lending some money to it.

Liabilities: What you owe to other people.

Limit to growth: The idea that the real GDP cannot grow indefinitely due to the law of diminishing returns.

Linear function: A function whose slope is constant. The graph of such a function is a straight line.
Liquidity: Ease with which you can sell an asset.
Liquidity preference: The amount of money (liquidity) people want to hold.
Liquidity trap: The notion proposed by Keynes that, in a recession, the interest rate could go so low that the monetary policy could not reduce it any further.
Loanable funds market: The market in which borrowers borrow money from lenders.
Loanable funds theory: The theory that posits that the interest rate is determined by the demand for and supply of loans.
Long and variable lags: The idea that it would take a long time for the effects of fiscal and monetary policies to take effect and that these time lags vary from recession to recession so that they are generally unpredictable.
Long-run classical aggregate supply function: A vertical line that indicates that with wage and price flexibility an economy would produce the potential GDP regardless of the level of the prices. In other words, along this function the labor market would be in equilibrium.
Lost decade, the: Refers to 1990s during which the Japanese economy was stagnant.

M

Marginal analysis: The theory that posits that decisions are made at the margin. Decision makers are assumed to compare the marginal cost and the marginal benefit of taking an action to decide whether to take that action.
Marginal benefit: The benefit from any decision.
Marginal cost: The cost associated with any decision.
Marginal investors: Investors who are willing to pay the highest price for assets, and therefore are the ones who get to determine their prices.
Marginal private benefit: The benefit of a decision that accrues to the decision maker alone.
Marginal private cost: The cost of a decision that is born by the decision maker alone.
Marginal product of labor: The additional production amount made possible by the next unit of labor hired.
Marginal propensity to consume (MPC): The fraction of the additional real disposable income that households spend on goods and services.
Marginal propensity to save: The fraction of the additional real disposable income that households save, rather than spending on goods and services. It is one minus MPC.
Marginal social benefit: The benefit of a decision that accrues to the whole society.
Marginal social cost: The cost of a decision that is born by the whole society.
Market: An arrangement, institution, or mechanism that brings buyers and sellers of a good or service together.
Market power: The power to affect market prices. This happens when there are a small number of large sellers or buyers in the market, so that each has some control on the price of the good sold or bought.
Maturity date: The date at which a bond matures.
Maximum satisfaction: Maximum satisfaction is achieved when a decision maker undertakes an activity up to the point where its marginal cost just equals its marginal benefit.
Means of payments: See *medium of exchange*.
Medium of exchange: Means of payments. Any object people in a society use to buy goods and services.
Misperceptions theory: The idea that people and firms have a better idea about the prices of what they sell than the prices of all the other goods in the economy.
Monetary base: The sum of currency and reserves in the banking system.
Monetary policy: Changes in the money supply by the Fed to affect the interest rate in order to change the level of aggregate demand.
Monetizing the debt: The purchase of the bonds by the Fed that the Treasury has sold to the public to finance the government's budget deficit. It is effectively printing money to finance the deficit.
Money is neutral: The idea that changes in the level of money supply will not affect the real variables such as real GDP or employment.
Money multiplier: The ratio of money supply to monetary base. It shows by how much the money supply will change if the monetary base changes by one dollar.
Monopolistic competition: An industry structure in which a relatively large number of firms sell products that are slightly different from each other.
Monopoly: An industry structure in which a single firm produces a product for which there are no close substitutes.
Multinational corporation: A corporation with subsidiaries in different countries.

Multiplier process: A process through which an initial increase in aggregate demand leads to an increase in GDP that is several times larger than the initial increase in aggregate demand.

N

National debt: The accumulation of past borrowings to finance government spending. The amount of borrowing in each year equals the budget deficit for that year.

National income identity: The total output produced in a country over a certain period of time identically equals the total expenditure on those goods and services. The total expenditure consists of consumption, investment, and government spending, plus net exports.

Natural growth rate: The rate of growth of the population in the long run.

Natural resource: Resources, such as land, given to us by nature.

Natural unemployment rate: The sum of frictional and structural unemployment rates.

Negative externality: A situation in which an action taken by a decision making unit harms others, without any compensation.

Neoclassical growth model: The growth theory originally proposed by Robert Solow, which posits that the rate of growth of national output in the long run depends positively on the rate of growth of capital per labor. The latter can increase through additional savings.

Net domestic product: GDP minus depreciation of physical capital.

Net exports: The excess of exports over imports.

Net tax: The excess of taxes over transfer payments.

Net worth: What you own. Excess of your assets (what you have) over your liabilities (what you owe).

Neutrality of money: Money in the classical model is neutral: it only affects the nominal variables, not the real variables.

New classical economics: The two post–Keynesian models that make the classical assumptions of rational economic behavior and wage-price flexibility. These are the rational expectation models and the real business cycle models.

New growth theory: The theory advanced by Paul Romer, which argues that endogenous technological progress is the main engine of economic growth.

Nominal exchange rate: The amount of domestic currency you have to pay to buy one unit of a foreign currency.

Nominal GDP: The monetary value of all the goods and services produced in a country by the factors of production located in that country, except those produced by households for household consumption.

Nominal interest rate: This is the stated interest rate on loan documents or bank deposits. This is how much money you will earn if you lend one dollar. See also *real interest rate, ex-ante* and *ex-post.*

Nominal wage: Or money wage; the dollar amount workers receive from business firms per unit of time such as an hour or a year. See also *real wage.*

Nominal variable: A variable whose units are dollars, such as the money wage. See also the *real variable.*

Normal good: A good we buy more of if our income increases. See also *inferior good.*

Normative statements: Statements that involve norms or judgments. The person making the statement considers the present state of things or the outcome of a decision to be good or bad. See also *positive statement.*

O

Oligopoly: An industry structure in which a handful of companies produce and sell either an identical product or a differentiated product.

Open economy: An economy that is engaged in international trade.

Open economy macroeconomics: The subfield of international economics studying macroeconomic issues in an open economy.

Open market operations: Buying and selling of government bonds by the Fed to change the interest rate.

Open market purchase: Buying of government bonds by the Fed to change the interest rate.

Open market sale: Selling of government bonds by the Fed to change the interest rate.

Opportunity cost: The benefit forgone because of a decision.

Opportunity cost of waiting: By lending your money, you lose the opportunity to consume goods and services today.

Outside asset: Asset for which there is not an equal amount of liabilities in the private sector; example: money.

Overall employment: All the people who are willing to work, but who have no jobs. This consists of cyclical, frictional, and structural unemployment.

P

Pareto efficiency: A situation in which it is not possible to make someone better off without making someone else worse off; the same as allocative efficiency and economic efficiency.
Pareto improvement: when, as a result of government policy or a private transaction, some people become better off without anyone else becoming worse off.
Patent laws: Laws giving exclusive rights to the inventor of a new product to produce and sell it.
Peak: The point where an expansion phase of a business cycle ends.
Perfect competition: An industry structure in which there are a very large number of small, price-taking firms that produce an identical product. Entry into and exit from the industry are free. Market participants have perfect information about the market and technology conditions. This implies that new entrants into the industry are not in an information disadvantage relative to incumbents.
Periodic cycles: Cycles are said to be periodic if they are alike in shape and duration. Business cycles are not periodic.
Permanent income: The disposable income a household expects to earn in the future.
Permanent income hypothesis: The hypothesis advanced by Milton Friedman that posits that a household plans its consumption expenditures on the basis of its permanent income.
Phillips Curve: A negative relationship between inflation and unemployment rates.
Positive externality: An externality situation in which a decision made by a decision maker benefits other people.
Positive statements: Statements that do not make any value judgments about whether any particular state or outcome is good or bad.
Potential GDP: The total amount of goods and services that could potentially be produced, if all factors of production were fully employed.
Present value formula: The formula that calculates the present value of an asset on the basis of the cash flows the asset is expected to generate in the future.
Price maker: A firm that has some control on its price—has market power.
Price taker: A perfectly competitive firm that is too small relative to the size of the market so that it has no power to affect the market price, and so it must take the market price as given.
Principle of diminishing returns: Same as the law of diminishing returns.
Private capital: Capital goods owned by private citizens.
Private costs and benefits: Costs and benefits incurred or enjoyed by individuals.
Private goods: A private good is a good that is both rivalrous (two people cannot consume the same good), and excludable (the producer can refuse selling it to you—exclude you from buying it—if you do not pay.) See also *public goods*.
Private incentives: Incentives faced by individuals.
Private saving: Saving by the private sector.
Pro-cyclical variables: Variables that move with the GDP. See also *countercyclical variables*.
Production function: A relationship between inputs and outputs.
Production inputs: Resources we use to produce goods and services.
Production possibilities frontier (PPF): A graph showing the maximum amount of a good or service the society can produce given the production amounts of other goods and services.
Profit: The excess of what firms receive from the sale of their products to consumers, over their production costs.
Progressive income tax system: The income tax system where tax rates increase as incomes rise.
Promissory note: Same as a bond or an IOU.
Public goods: A public good is a good that is neither rivalrous (two people can consume the same good, at the same time, and by the same amount), nor excludable (the producer cannot refuse selling it to you—exclude you from buying it—if you do not pay.) The best example of a public good is national defense. See also private goods.
Public interest: Something that is in the interest of the whole society.

R

Rational economic behavior: Comparing the marginal cost and benefit of an activity and undertaking it if the benefit outweighs the cost. The marginal cost should exclude sunk and fixed costs, but should include explicit and implicit costs.
Rational expectations: The best possible forecasts of the future course of events, using all the relevant information currently available.
Rational expectations hypothesis: Proponents of this hypothesis believe that wages and prices are flexible, and that individuals and firms take all the relevant information into account in making decisions and predicting the future. Business cycles

happen because unanticipated events create misperceptions about relative prices. Anticipated events do not create misperceptions, and thus do not affect the GDP. See also misperceptions theory.

Rationing function of prices: The combined information and incentive functions of the prices that results in the goods and services being rationed among different consumers, in such a way that only those who are willing and able to pay the most get to buy them.

Real business cycle theory: The theory positing that business cycles are the effects of technological shocks that affect the demand for labor and potential output. In this theory, all unemployment is voluntary.

Real crowding out: Reduction in private spending, as a result of an increase in resource prices that is due to an increase in government budget deficit.

Real exchange rate: It measures how much of domestic goods we should "pay" to be able to buy one unit of foreign goods. See also *nominal exchange rate.*

Real expenditure: A measure of the quantities of all the goods and services purchased in a period of time.

Real GDP: A measure of the quantities of goods and services produced in a country by the factors of production located in that country, except those produced by households for household consumption. It is calculated as nominal GDP divided by GDP deflator.

Real interest rate: Equals nominal interest rate minus inflation rate. It shows by how much your real wealth or purchasing power will increase if you lend money.

Real variable: A real variable is a variable whose units are "real", i.e., non-monetary. Often the units are in terms of the quantities of goods and services. A real variable is obtained by dividing a nominal variable by the general price level.

Real wage: The purchasing power of nominal wage calculated by dividing the nominal wag by the price level.

Recession: A fall in the aggregate level of output or real GDP.

Recognition lag: The time it takes for government officials to recognize that there is a recession by studying the available data.

Recurrent cycles: Business cycles are recurrent in the sense that they keep happening. See also periodic cycles.

Relative purchasing power parity condition: The theory that says that the rate of depreciation of an exchange rate between the currencies of two countries equals the inflation different between the two countries.

Required rate of return: The rate of return investors require to earn from an asset.

Required reserve ratio: The fraction of the total deposits the Fed requires banks to keep on hand in the form of reserves.

Required reserves: The amount of the total reserves that banks are required to keep by law.

Ricardian equivalence: The idea that a deficit-financed increase in government spending would not be expansionary because people would expect the government to raise taxes in the future to pay off its debt. This would reduce the expected future disposable income, and hence current consumption.

Risk averse: Everything else the same, a risk-averse investor prefers less risk to more risk.

S

Sacrifice ratio: The ratio that indicates by how much unemployment rate will increase if the government reduces inflation rate by one percent.

Scarcity: The idea that human material wants are unlimited in relation to the available resources in the economy.

Self-correcting mechanism: The idea that a recession will end by itself without the help of the government. This is because, even though wages and prices may be rigid in the short run, they will adjust over time to clear the labor market.

Short run: The period of time too short for the wages and prices to adjust to market conditions. and for firms to be able to change the amount of their plants and equipment.

Shortage: See *excess demand.*

Slope: The change in a dependent variable for a unit change in an independent variable.

Social costs and benefits: Costs and benefits faced by the society as a whole.

Sources of funds: Sources of financing the purchase of an asset. An asset can be purchased by borrowed money (liabilities), or by the buyer's own money (net worth).

Specificity rule: The idea that the most efficient way to solve a problem is to interfere at a place closer to the source of the problem.

Stagflation: Inflation coupled with recession.

State of rest: See *equilibrium.*

Stock market: The market in which shares of corporations are traded.

Stock variables: Variables that we can measure at any point in time.

Stocks: Ownership rights in a corporation.

Structural unemployment: The situation in which there are jobs available, but not for workers with the kinds of skills workers possess.
Substitutes: Goods such that, if you consumed more of one, you would consume less of the other.
Substitution effect: In the case of consumer behavior: When the price of a good decreases, people substitute the now cheaper good for its substitutes. In the case of labor supply: When real wage decreases, workers substitute leisure for labor, so that the quantity of labor supplied decreases. The substitution effect results in a positive relationship between the real wage and the quantity of labor supplied. See also the *income effect*.
Supply of labor: The amount of labor households are willing and able to supply; the same as labor force.
Supply of money: The amount of money people actually hold at a point in time in their pockets, purses, and bank accounts.
Supply-side economics: The body of economic theories that argue that the government should adopt supply-side policies to encourage production and innovation, as well as improve productivity.
Supply-side policies: Policies intended to encourage production and investment. They are hoped to affect the supply side of the market, thereby increasing production and decreasing prices. Examples of such polices are tax breaks for research and development.
Surplus spending units: People, firms, or governments that earn more than they can spend. See also *deficit spending units*.
Surplus: See excess supply.

T

Tax rate: The percentage of income taxed.
Technological progress: Learning ways of producing new goods or better ways of producing the same goods.
Technology shocks: Events that affect the relationships between inputs and outputs and hence the productivity of inputs.
Technology: Knowledge of how to produce things.
The Fed: See the *Federal Reserve System*.
Transactions costs: The opportunity costs of conducting a transaction.
Transfer payments: Money the government hands over to some people without buying anything from them. Examples: food stamps and social security payments.
Treasury view: A view publicized by the staff of the Chancellor of the Exchequer in Britain in 1930s who argued that an expansionary fiscal policy would be ineffective, because it would merely shift financial resources from one industry to another.
Trough: The point where a recession ends and the expansion begins.
Twin deficits: The budget deficit and the current account deficit. During the Reagan years, some economists believed that the former was the cause of the latter, hence the name.

U

Unanticipated inflation: The actual rate of inflation in a period minus what people had anticipated in the past. It is nothing but error made in forecasting inflation.
Unemployment equilibrium: The situation in which the goods market is in equilibrium, but some people are still unemployed.
Unemployment rate: The percentage of people who want to work but don't have a job.
Unit multiplier: When the government increases spending and raises an equal amount of tax to finance it, the increase in GDP will equal the increase in spending.
Uses of funds: Values of assets held in a company or by a household.

V

Value added: The difference between the market value of output a firm sells and the money it pays for intermediate goods.
Value of marginal product (VMP): The market value of the output produced by the next (marginal) unit of labor. It is calculated as the price of output (P) times the marginal product of labor (MPL): VMP = P × MPL.
Velocity of circulation: The number of times a dollar changes hands in a period of time. It is the inverse of Cambridge k.
Volatility: Variability.
Volcker disinflation: Starting in 1979, the U.S. Federal Reserve System under Paul Volcker followed a tight money policy to fight inflation. This resulted in a recession and disinflation.
Voluntary unemployment: Unemployment that results when workers voluntarily decide not to work.

W

Wage rate: The income workers earn per unit of time, say per hour or per year, for their labor services.

X

X-intercept: The point where a function crosses the X-axis.

Y

Y-intercept: The point where a function crosses the Y-axis.

INDEX

D

E

F

G

H

I

K

L

M

N

O

P

R

S

T

U

V

W

Y

CPSIA information can be obtained at www.ICGtesting.com
Printed in the USA
LVIW01n1900070716
495522LV00003B/4